International business and

multinational enterprises

**The Irwin Series in Management
and The Behavioral Sciences**
L. L. Cummings and E. Kirby Warren   Consulting Editors
John F. Mee   Advisory Editor

International business and

multinational enterprises

STEFAN H. ROBOCK

Robert D. Calkins Professor of International Business
Graduate School of Business
Columbia University

KENNETH SIMMONDS

Professor of Marketing and International Business
London Graduate School of Business Studies

1983 • Third Edition

RICHARD D. IRWIN, INC.
Homewood, Illinois   60430

ISBN 0-256-02514-2

Library of Congress Catalog Card No. 82–83424

Printed in the United States of America

3 4 5 6 7 8 9 0 MP 0 9 8 7 6 5 4

Preface

One of the most dramatic and significant world trends of the last three decades has been the rapid, sustained growth of international business. In its traditional form of international trade as well as its newer form of multinational business operations, international business has become massive in scale and has come to exercise a major influence over political, economic, and social development throughout the world.

This growth in business activity across national boundaries has brought with it many changes. The rise of the multinational enterprise has confronted nation states with local business units that are closely linked with operations lying outside the nations' local jurisdiction. As a result nation-states have had to grapple with a wide range of new policy issues that are not satisfactorily covered by the traditional conceptual framework for thinking about the protection of national interests—a framework primarily focused on controlling transfers of goods and money as they cross national borders. The business executive has also been confronted with new management problems. Methods have had to be developed for operating simultaneously in many different and differently changing environments, for dealing with new elements of risk and conflict, and for assessing the impact of the firm on social and economic change. The management task has expanded and changed considerably from that faced within purely domestic operations.

It was not until the early 1960s that awareness of the problems that arise when business operations extend across national boundaries began to have any significant impact on business education. By this time there was a growing realization that existing theories, generalizations, and techniques of business management that had been built up largely from business experience within the United States were neither general nor universal. More explicit attention to the international dimension of business began to appear in business curricula.

Originally, the international business orientation frequently consisted only of selected tools and materials culled from the fields of international trade and international economics—a reflection of the newness of the field and the limited development of concepts and research. There tended to be a bias toward national issues and little direct attempt to develop the special skills demanded by the realities of multinational operations. Some courses simply joined together international aspects of conventional business courses, particularly finance and marketing, with little attempt to develop skills in assessing environmental differences.

With two decades of experimentation and research now behind it, however, international business has evolved into a field of study and research with its own identity. Its central focus is the set of management problems stemming from the movement of goods, human resources, technology, finance, or ownership across national boundaries. As befits a course for business managers, the field has a managerial orientation, and assessment of national issues is placed in this perspective. Furthermore, the field of international business has moved well beyond an applied international economics orientation to draw heavily upon other related fields such as politics, sociology, anthropology, and law, where materials from these disciplines are relevant to the tasks of the international manager. It is now widely accepted that international business courses can provide a basic frame of reference and develop the international dimension of business teaching in a way that other subject areas, with their own focus and conceptual approaches, are unlikely to achieve.

This book grew out of the authors' experience of teaching international business courses in graduate business schools and executive programs around the world since the early 1960s. It is a general introductory text designed for relatively advanced students, with a direct focus on the development of management skills in handling the problems of multinational business. Extensive footnotes have been included as an aid to more advanced study of areas in which students may have a special interest. While the book is primarily designed for readers with a business orientation, it has also proved useful for government decision makers who must take into account the present and future behavior patterns of international firms in designing national policies, and for students of political science.

The text is divided into six parts. Part One introduces the new field of international business and examines the forces underlying its expansion and the patterns that are emerging from this growth. Part Two presents the monetary, trade, and regulatory frameworks within which international business transactions take place. Part Three is concerned with the goals of nation-states with respect to international business, and the controls that nations adopt to achieve their goals. Part Four examines the construction of global business strategies including the assessment of demand and risks in the environment within which the international firm operates. It also presents and analyzes the alternative organizational structures available to firms for building and implementing global strategies. Part Five covers the operational management of the multinational firm, paying particular attention to the issues that are specific to international activity. Part Six looks ahead to the future of international business.

Experience in teaching has shown that a course covering topics in the order in which they are presented in this text produces a clear, interesting progression. It begins with an introduction to the concepts and terminology of international transactions, proceeds to the wider issues of the firm's relationship with different national interests, and then moves on to the strategic and operational decisions of individual multinationals. Whatever course design is adopted, however, students clearly appreciate a continual examination of the relevance of the material to the management task. Discussion exercises and questions designed with this in mind have been included at the end of each chapter. Also available at the end of the text is a series of problems and cases that can be drawn upon to support the course design adopted by the instructor. All of these materials are aimed at strengthening practical analysis and decision-making skills within international business situations.

Many professional colleagues and practitioners have given the authors invaluable assistance in the ongoing task of preparing the editions of the book. Particularly helpful in the preparation of this Third Edition have been Michel Amsalem, Warren J. Bilkey, Ian Giddy, Nathaniel Leff, David A. Ricks, Alan Rugman, William Stoever, J. Frederick Truitt, and Stephen Young.

In previous editions we acknowledged the support of the postal services on both sides of the Atlantic and wondered why they both made losses. Perhaps this time we should add a word of acknowledgment to the airlines that have made it possible for us to operate internationally, as international business professors should. We are sorry that the more we travel, the more they lose.

STEFAN H. ROBOCK
KENNETH SIMMONDS

Contents

transactions: *Hedging. Covered interest arbitrage. Swapping currencies. Outright speculation.* The actors. Forecasting foreign exchange rates: *The efficient market view. The forecasting services. Economic theories of exchange-rate determination.* The international money market: *The Eurocurrency market. International banking.*

PART THREE: THE NATION-STATE AND INTERNATIONAL BUSINESS

PART FOUR: GLOBAL BUSINESS STRATEGY

Country risk allowances. Incremental net present value, rationing, and re-alignment. Entry strategies. Ownership strategies. Strategy review and up-dating. A global habit of mind.

family. *Social structure.* Comprehensive cultural assessment. Understanding culture change: *Acceptance and resistance to change. Social dynamics of culture change.* Promoting culture change. International business as a change agent.

ment strategy. Reacting to economic exposure. Reacting to transactions and translation exposure. Foreign exchange forecasting. Implementation. Import and export financing. The tax variable: *National tax environments. The multinational tax environment.*

APPENDIX: A systems approach to financial optimization: An example.

PART SIX: EMERGING ISSUES

PART SEVEN: CASES AND PROBLEMS IN INTERNATIONAL BUSINESS

PART ONE

The nature and scope of international business

Chapter 1

The field of international business

A DEFINITION OF INTERNATIONAL BUSINESS

International business as a field of management training deals with business activities that cross national boundaries, whether they be movements of goods, services, capital, or personnel; transfers of technology, information, or data; or even the supervision of employees. International business has emerged as a separate branch of management training because the growing scale and complexity of business transactions across national boundaries gives rise to new and unique problems of management and governmental policy which have received inadequate attention in traditional areas of business and economics.

Business transactions between different sovereign political units are not new phenomena on the world economic scene. Some business firms

3

have had foreign direct investments and foreign operations for many years; predominantly in (but not limited to) companies in the fields of mining, petroleum, and agriculture.[1] Foreign trade, moreover, has a venerable history dating back to the emergence of the nation-state. But since the end of World War II a dramatic change has occurred in the patterns of international business activities. Thousands of business firms in many nations have developed into multinational enterprises with ownership control or other links that cross national boundaries. These firms take a global view of all aspects of business, from markets to resources, and they integrate markets and production on a world scale. Traditional international trade in the form of transactions between independent firms in different nations has continued to grow. But the *relative* importance of trade in the total picture has declined as other forms of cross-border business transactions have expanded more rapidly.

The international business field is concerned with the issues facing international companies and governments in dealing with all types of cross-border business transactions. The field encompasses international transactions in commodities, international transfers of intangibles such as technology, and the performance of international services such as transportation. It gives special attention to the multinational enterprise—an enterprise based in one country and operating in one or more other countries—and the full range of methods open to such enterprises for doing business internationally.[2]

International business, foreign operations, and comparative business

To clarify the scope of the authors' approach to international business, we should differentiate between international business, foreign business, and comparative business. The last two concepts are sometimes used as synonyms for international business. Foreign business refers to domestic operations within a foreign country. Comparative business focuses on similarities and differences among countries and business systems. The great merit of comparative studies in business, as well as in other fields such as politics, sociology, and economics, is the new perspective

[1] Mira Wilkins, *The Emergence of Multinational Enterprise: American Business Abroad from the Colonial Era to 1914* (Cambridge, Mass.: Harvard University Press, 1970). This study shows that U.S. direct foreign investment prior to 1914 was not limited to extractive industries and utilities but also included "a surprising number of . . . U.S. headquartered multinational manufacturing companies" (p. ix).

[2] David E. Lilienthal, "The Multinational Corporation," in *Management and Corporations 1985*, ed. M. H. Anshen and G. L. Bach (New York: McGraw-Hill, 1960). The term *multinational firm* was probably first used by David E. Lilienthal in a paper delivered at Carnegie Institute of Technology in April 1960.

and better understanding of home institutions and environments that is frequently secured.[3]

The three concepts—international business, foreign business, and comparative business—are interrelated and have large overlaps. The international manager may benefit greatly from many types of comparative business studies and from a knowledge of many aspects of foreign business operations. At the same time, foreign business operations and comparative business as fields of inquiry do not have as their major point of interest the special problems that arise when business activities cross national boundaries. For example, the vital question of potential conflicts between the nation-state and the multinational firm, which receives major attention in international business studies, is not likely to be central or even peripheral in foreign operations and comparative business studies.

An example from the field of accounting will illustrate the principal boundaries and focus of international business. A manager engaged in foreign business needs to know only the accounting practices in the host country. A comparative approach to accounting examines the systems and practices in many countries with the main objective of identifying similarities and differences among countries as well as universal patterns, if they exist. International business concentrates on the accounting needs for managing a multinational firm doing business across national boundaries. The accounting problems and techniques for international business operations are related to differences in national accounting systems. In some important respects, the accounting activities of the multinational firm will be influenced by tax and legal considerations of the specific countries in which the firm is operating. Within these constraints, however, accounting in international business is primarily concerned with fulfilling the needs of multinational operations through an effective and uniform accounting system that cuts across national boundaries.

THE SCOPE OF INTERNATIONAL BUSINESS ACTIVITIES

The scope of international business covers a wide range of significant business sectors. International transactions in physical goods involves products from mining, petroleum, agriculture, and manufacturing activities. Transactions in services are extensive in the construction, hotel, tourism, business consulting, and retailing and wholesaling sectors; in financial areas such as commercial and investment banking, securities,

---

[3] For example, see J. Boddewyn, *Comparative Management and Marketing* (Glenview, Ill.: Scott, Foresman, 1969).

and insurance; in air and ocean transportation; and in communications media such as radio, television, telegraph, telephone, magazines, books, newspapers, news services, and movies. Transactions in intangibles occur in fields such as technology, trademarks, and cross-border data transmission.

International business activities also include an extensive range of optional methods available to firms for doing business internationally that involve different degrees of foreign direct investment commitments. Even where it assumes an ownership position in foreign facilities, the firm has options ranging from the construction of sales offices, warehouses, and packaging and assembly operations to full-scale production facilities.

Foreign direct investments are defined as investments that give the investor effective control and are accompanied by managerial participation. In contrast, *portfolio investments* are undertaken for the sake of obtaining investment income or capital gains rather than entrepreneurial income. The dividing line between direct and portfolio investments is often difficult to determine.

Direct investment may be financed in a number of ways other than through capital movements abroad. Foreign investments may be financed by borrowing locally, by reinvesting foreign earnings, by the sale to the foreign affiliate of nonfinancial assets such as technology, or through funds generated by licensing fees and payments for management services to the parent company. More accurately, direct foreign investment is not so much international capital movements as capital formation abroad.

Without making foreign direct investment commitments, firms can engage in international business through exporting and importing, licensing of nonaffiliated foreign firms, sale of technology, foreign management contracts, and selling turnkey projects. In a turnkey project, the seller plans, constructs, and places in operation a foreign facility that is then transferred to a local owner. The seller receives a fee for its services but retains no ownership interest.

In addition to options as to scale and type of foreign operations, the direct investment approach offers a range of possibilities as to ownership patterns. Foreign facilities may be wholly owned or may be a joint venture with one or more partners. Generally, joint ventures involve partnerships with private firms or governments in the foreign area and reduce the investment required by the establishing company.

The multinational corporation

The multinational corporation has become well recognized as a key feature of the changing international business pattern. But general agreement on the definition of a multinational corporation does not yet exist.[4] Some definitions emphasize structural criteria such as the number of countries in which a firm is doing business, or ownership by persons from many nations, or the nationality composition of top management. Other definitions stress performance characteristics such as the absolute amount—or relative share—of earnings, sales, assets, or employees derived from or committed to foreign operations. Still other definitions are based on behavioral characteristics of top management such as "thinking internationally."

The definitional debate is not simply a matter of semantics. It reflects the reality that there are many types of so-called multinational enterprises. It is also a reminder that operational definitions will vary with the purposes at hand. Consequently, in dealing with the subject of multinational corporations, one must be alert to the specific definition being used.

In this book, the labels of multinational and international corporations will be used interchangeably. They refer to a cluster of corporations controlled by one headquarters but with operations spread over many countries. Also, multinational corporations can be of private, government, or mixed ownership.

With the growing international involvement of business firms, more and more companies—American, Canadian, European, Japanese, and others—are finding that a large share of their assets are deployed around the world, that many of their employees are foreign citizens, that a large amount of their earnings are in foreign currencies, and that they are operating to an important extent outside the legal jurisdiction of the country in which the parent company is incorporated. In these circumstances, the companies have become multinational corporations, and the nature of their operations has been significantly transformed. They come to be managed as world enterprises, with international considerations dominating their decisions. The world becomes the company's market and sphere of operation, and the home country becomes but one part.

The multinational corporation is not uniquely an American invention. In fact, if one were looking only a few decades ago for examples of multinational firms, the names of European rather than U.S.-based corporations would have come to mind: the British-Dutch companies— Unilever and the Royal Dutch Shell Group, Switzerland's Nestlé, Britain's Imperial Chemical Industries, the Netherlands' Philips Lamps, and Sweden's Ericsson Telephone.

---

[4] Yair Aharoni, "On the Definition of a Multinational Corporation," *Quarterly Review of Economics and Business,* Autumn 1971, pp. 27–37; see also "The Issue of Defining Transnational Corporations," in *Transnational Corporations in World Development: A Re-Examination* (New York: United Nations, 1978), pp. 158–61.

Not all international business is conducted by multinational corporations. Export and import activities, for example, do not require that a company establish and operate overseas branches, affiliates, or other units of the home corporation. The licensing of patents and technology in foreign countries can be accomplished without a predominantly domestic company becoming multinational.

The dividing line to mark the stage at which a company becomes multinational is difficult to determine. Many domestic companies go through a gradual evolution toward making direct investments, first establishing marketing, procurement offices, or warehouses in foreign countries. Even when a business firm crosses the imaginary and imprecise boundary between domestic and multinational, its degree of international commitment and internationalization may range over a wide spectrum.

In one sense, the emergence of the multinational corporation reflects a differential pace in the evolution of political institutions relative to business organizations. While business activities have become more and more internationalized, the development of international governmental organizations has not accompanied business and economic trends. Consequently, business corporations cannot be licensed by an international governmental agency as a world corporation. They still must be created and exist under the jurisdiction of a specific nation-state. Yet the multinational firm may have different patterns of ownership and control. In most cases, in the present stage of evolution, both ownership and control of the multinational corporation reside in the base country. In other significant cases, ownership and control are divided between two or more countries even though the enterprise is the legal creation of a single nation-state.

From the standpoint of business management, multinational operations raise many problems associated with the need to deal with a wide range of environmental factors in several different countries. They also raise new internal issues in organization and operations. From the standpoint of world-development aspirations, the multinational corporation offers a nongovernmental vehicle for transferring technology, financial resources, management techniques, and marketing experience among nations at various stages of development.

What is different about international business?

One can recognize the growing international involvement of business firms and the rapid trend toward multinational enterprises and yet question the need for international business as a separate field of study. The argument can be made that management principles are universal and that concepts being taught in the functional fields of marketing, finance, production, and control are as relevant to business management in one country as they are in another. The manager in the world economy, the argument goes, may need only supplementary training in the traditional fields of international economics and international trade.

Despite these arguments, a trend has emerged to give explicit attention to the international dimension of business and to recognize international business as a separate field in the business area. The trend is supported by the view that earlier theories, generalizations, principles, methods, and techniques, developed in response to norms in the United States where management training has had its greatest flowering, were neither general nor universal. In contrast to purely domestic operations, business activities across national boundaries require considerable familiarity with international means of payments and involve new elements of risk, conflict, environmental adjustments, and influence over social and economic change. At best, only some of these elements are covered in traditional international economics and trade courses and have been only briefly treated in traditional management courses.

There are four aspects of international business activity around which new types of thinking have developed. These four aspects overlap to some degree and do not exhaust the potential for new approaches that may evolve. Each stems from unique problems that develop when business crosses national boundaries, and each gives rise to a new area of study and body of concepts.

International risk.   The special risk elements confronted in international business activity include financial, political, regulatory, and tax risks. They arise from causes such as the existence of different currencies, monetary standards, and national goals, but they are all measurable through their effect on profitability or ownership.

The financial risk elements involve balance-of-payments considerations, varying exchange rates, differential inflation trends among countries, and divergent interest rates. In the political area, the risk of expropriation or lesser harassment directed toward the foreign firm must be considered for many years ahead when heavy capital investments are being contemplated. The regulatory risks arise from different legal systems, overlapping jurisdictions, and dissimilar policies that influence such conditions as the regulation of restrictive business practices and the application of antitrust laws. In the tax field, unforeseen changes in fiscal policies can affect significantly the profitability of the multinational corporation. Furthermore, uncertainty as to application of tax laws frequently creates a risk of double taxation.

The need has become recognized for a continuing business intelligence activity of considerable complexity to identify and predict international risks. Ideally, international risks should be analyzed for underlying causal forces, and projections into the future should be formulated in terms of probabilities and quantified in terms of potential costs.

Multinational conflicts.   Of major concern to international business are the conflicts that arise because of different national identities of owners, employees, customers, and suppliers and because of divergencies between the interests of sovereign national states and the business goals of multinational corporations. Some of the conflicts occur within the international firm, and others involve the firm's relationship to the external environment.

An extremely troublesome area of external conflict concerns profit-motivated decisions that result in the transfer of funds, production, and employment from one country to another. The results of these decisions may at times run contrary to the national economic policies of one or all of the countries involved. For example, extension of credit to foreign subsidiaries at times when the foreign nation is attempting to dampen purchasing power through monetary restrictions and exchange controls can undermine national objectives as well as place local firms at a competitive disadvantage. The list of areas in which conflicts occur also includes such matters as contribution to local exports or reduction of imports, national interests in strengthening local research and management, or the country's international competitive position.[5]

Within the international corporation, the mixture of national allegiances raises further issues. Home-country nationals tend to dominate top-management echelons of multinational firms, and there is a tendency to retain research and administration functions in the developed countries. Disparities in wage and salary rates have also led to widely practiced discrimination on the basis of nationality. A number of nations have already placed restrictions on the numbers of foreign expatriates they will allow in local operations.

The conflict aspect of international business requires thinking that will relate a multiplicity of interests, each with different objectives and different criteria for evaluating potential outcomes. No other business field covers this successfully. The international manager trained to identify each conflicting interest and to think through the possible actions and reactions from each viewpoint, will be better prepared to plot the best strategy in a complex situation. One of the functions of international business study should be to erase any tendency to make blindly nationalistic decisions or revert to pure economic arguments.

Multiple environments.   The most pervasive distinction between international and domestic business lies in the environmental framework. Aside from its relationship to the elements of risk and conflict discussed above, the multiplicity of environments in international business creates a wide range of operational problems that require new concepts, analyti-

---

[5] For example, see Raymond Vernon, "Saints and Sinners in Foreign Investment," *Harvard Business Review*, May–June 1963, p. 157.

cal methods, and information. The wider the scope of the firm's international activities, the greater become the environmental diversities and the more crucial becomes the task of identifying, evaluating, and predicting environmental variables. The environmental framework must be enlarged to include forces operating at a supranational level—such as the European Community—and forces involving relations between pairs of countries as well as variables associated with different national settings.

One important category of environmental variables relates to business activity open to the international business firm and to the form of business organization that must be used. Public utilities, including electric power, communications, and transportation, are not open to private enterprise in most countries. Business activity in natural resources such as petroleum and mining is restricted by many nations to domestic private or public enterprises. In some situations, the options open to international business firms require joint ventures with majority local ownership or joint ventures with government.

A second major category of environmental variables involves the diversity of the institutional settings. Labor unions, for example, are organized on different philosophical foundations and play different roles from country to country. Patterns of national, regional, and local economic planning vary greatly in scope and in their influence over business activity. Capital markets and financial institutions are in different stages of development and, in some cases, are evolving along different paths.

Another broad environmental variable involves cultural differences that affect business management. International managers need to know how cultural differences influence the behavior of customers, suppliers, and employees, and how these influences on behavior will change. This aspect of international business encompasses the full range of communication problems arising out of different languages, customs, and values.

International business has begun to develop its own body of cultural analysis following the functional division of business, with marketing questions receiving most attention. Considerable management literature has focused on the cultural adjustment of expatriate management and on the differences in foreign management and work force that might require adjustment of organizational structures or procedures. While concern for specific problems initially channeled cultural analysis along these functional lines, the common need throughout many business functions to understand cultural factors is for a more unified approach, which might be titled "Cultural Analysis for Business Decisions."

International business and development. International business is frequently a major change agent, a means of transferring technology, and a key force in the economic and social development of a nation. This is especially true for underdeveloped countries. Thus, international business requires new concepts that provide an understanding of what can and what cannot be achieved by the change agent and the potential contributions that international business can make to development.

The primary concern of underdeveloped countries is the contribution that a proposed international business activity can make to their economic, social, and political development. They recognize that the attractiveness of a project to the foreign firm in terms of business profits may diverge greatly from the attractiveness of the project to the country in terms of its development goals. It is a near certainty, therefore, that international firms will be required to justify their proposed activities in terms of costs and benefits to the country. To meet this requirement, international firms need considerable specialized knowledge on economic development.

To illustrate, consider the development issue of the positive and negative impact of international business on indigeneous entrepreneurship. On the positive side, the international firm may create new entrepreneurial opportunities external to the firm for local suppliers and merchants. On the negative side, by attracting much of the entrepreneurial potential in a country, the international firm may inhibit the possibilities for development of national enterprises.

The role of international business in development raises moral and ideological issues. It is frequently true that short-term profit motivation will keep a firm away from the less developed markets. Yet the opportunity for the greatest long-term good from the viewpoint of both the corporation's home country and the developing nations may strongly favor entering the developing country.[6]

Once a corporation has entered a developing country, a whole range of new issues arise. One such issue is the degree to which the firm should become involved in the community and undertake expenditures normally the function of the public sector.[7] As a number of studies have demonstrated, the paternalistic firm, which provides much of the normal functions of the public sector, can foster animosity among the local population.

INTERNATIONAL BUSINESS TRAINING

Some students will study international business as a field of concentration, intending to follow a career working in foreign countries or in the headquarters of a multinational firm that uses nationals for operating foreign subsidiaries. Others will study international business as a supplement to their concentration in the functional fields of accounting, mar-

---

[6] Nathaniel Leff, "Multinational Corporate Pricing Strategy in the Developing Countries," *Journal of International Business Studies*, Fall 1975, pp. 57–74.

[7] Clifton R. Wharton, "Aiding the Community: A New Philosophy for Foreign Operations," *Harvard Business Review*, March–April 1954, pp. 64–72.

keting, finance, and so on. Still others will be interested in international business as a preparation for working in government positions on the development and implementation of policies and programs for assisting and controlling business activities across national boundaries. For all these kinds of clientele, a minimum preparation for dealing effectively with the international dimension of business should include two goals: to develop familiarity with the body of knowledge on international business and to develop in the person special sensitivities, attitudes, flexibility, and tolerance.

The need for personal and emotional training to deal with international business matters deserves particular emphasis in this introduction because such training requires more than textbook reading. Ethnocentrism and personal parochialism can be diluted in a number of ways, some of which can be included within a broad framework of international business training. Student exchange programs can stimulate personal reconditioning through the experience of living and working in a foreign environment. When students from various countries and cultures are studying together, the students can be exposed to other cultures and values through class discussions and through team projects, if the teams are composed of different nationalities.

International managers need training experience that develops in them a special kind of personal and emotional radar to alert them to certain situations, where specific values and ways of action that they take for granted in their own environment are different in other cultures and nations. Successful international managers need enough flexibility to understand what underlies these differences and enough tolerance to recognize that types of behavior and sets of values different from their own may be valid for other people. In an operational sense, they must recognize that what are constants for domestic business may be variables in international business.

EXERCISES AND DISCUSSION QUESTIONS

1. "To deny that international business is a valid field for academic effort is to suggest by analogy that such subjects as international politics, international economics, and international law are equally not academically respectable. It is true that international business borrows very heavily from all three, as they borrow from each other, but the core problem in international business is quite different." Discuss.

2. Of the top 50 foreign companies in *Fortune*'s list of "500 Largest Industrial Corporations Outside the U.S.," which would you consider to be not multinational? Why?

3. There is no separate field of "international" chemistry or "international" physics. Why should there be a separate field of international business?

Chapter 2

Patterns of international business

The patterns of international business keep changing—and textbooks have to be revised. As long ago as 2800 B.C., international business in the form of trade existed between Egypt and the Phoenician city of Byblos, as revealed by recent excavations in Greece.[1] Over time, trade led to direct investment, primarily as a means of securing sources of supply for raw materials and natural resources. The British East India Company, founded in 1602 and not dissolved until almost three centuries later in 1874, was one of the world's first international corporations and an example of the direct investment, resource-seeking phase. The multinational

---

[1] See George Rawlinson, *Phoenicia*, (New York: G. P. Putnam & Sons, 1898); and Sabatino Moscati, *The World of Phoenicians* (trans.) (London: Weidenfeld & Nicholson, 1968).

enterprise as we know it today dates back to the mid-1800s when the Singer Company expanded internationally and began operating with a global horizon.[2]

Over the centuries, international business has expanded in both absolute terms and relative to the growth of nations. Current patterns are an extension of the quantum leap and radical change in the form of international business operations dating from the end of World War II. Although statistical data are not easily available on many dimensions of international business, the broad patterns and major changes in international business activity can be described with reasonable accuracy.

This chapter will present the available data on the size of international business, the industries and commodities that are highly internationalized, the nationalities of the participants, and the geographical patterns.

THE UNDERDEVELOPED DATA BASE

A reasonably complete statistical picture of international business patterns should have several components. It should show the types of internation transactions and their values—that is, transfers of goods, services, technology, foreign production, information and data, and so on. It should show the geographical patterns, that is, the nations involved in the cross-border movements. It should show the trends over time. It should show the relative importance of the international business sector within the total economic activity for specific nations and globally.

Unfortunately, the data base for presenting such a picture is underdeveloped. No international agency exists that has authority to request such information from business enterprises or from national governments. Thus the principal sources of data are the statistical programs of the individual nations, and these programs have been adjusting only slowly to the changing structure of international business. All nations collect detailed data on merchandise trade. But only a few nations have been collecting relevant data on international business activities other than trade. Even where relevant data are collected, the statistical definitions and coverage of the different programs can vary considerably.[3]

With the rise of global firms, companies can serve foreign markets or secure foreign products in many ways other than traditional importing and exporting. International firms can establish foreign production facilities that produce for local or third-country markets and thus substitute for home-country exports. Firms can also license foreign producers to

---

[2] Mira Wilkins, *The Emergence of Multinational Enterprise: American Business Abroad from the Colonial Era to 1914* (Cambridge, Mass.: Harvard University Press, 1970), pp. 37–47.

[3] The problems and limitations encountered in trying to develop a global picture of multinational business activity from national statistics are discussed at length in the United Nations report, *Transnational Corporations in World Development* (New York: United Nations, March 20, 1978).

manufacture goods that the licensing firm might otherwise export from its home country. These and other newer dimensions of international business activity are poorly covered by the existing data base. Although the data base has been improving, much more progress is needed to depict with greater precision what is really happening in the world today.

How much difference will it make if better information on international business is available? International agencies need such data in order to adjust the monetary system to the changed structure of the international economy. Nations need to know a great deal about the operations of multinational business firms to develop policies such as those relating to exports and foreign exchange earnings. The business firm interested in allocating its efforts over global markets also requires extensive information on international transactions and international business patterns.

THE BIG PICTURE

Let's start with the big picture based on available data and then examine the subsectors. The big picture has to be put together from different data sources, and the most recent year for which considerable data are available is 1978.

The size of the world economy, as measured by gross national product (GNP), was estimated at $8,800 billion for 1978. GNP, the value of total output, is the usual measure of the size of a country's economy. In the same year, international business activity had an estimated total volume of at least $2,600 billion, or the equivalent of about 30 percent of world economic activity. The expression *equivalent* is used because GNP is estimated on a value-added basis and cannot be compared directly with the total revenues from international business activity. This picture, of course, is only a snapshot at one point in time and needs to be supplemented with data on trends.

The estimate of $2,600 billion for international business activity includes both international trade and foreign production, with adjustment for the overlap. The overlap adjustment is necessary because a large share of so-called international trade consists of transfers between units of the same enterprise located in different countries. A number of foreign automobile assembly plants, for example, rely largely on imported components. A number of foreign pharmaceutical plants during an early state of development may receive bulk shipments from the home country and perform merely a repackaging and distribution function. The intrafirm transfers are recorded as international trade because they cross national boundaries. Double-counting occurs because these intrafirm transfers are also included in the value of production by the foreign affiliates.

In 1978, total world exports were at a level of $1,300 billion. Foreign production in the same year is estimated to have reached $2,000 billion.

The estimated overlap for exports also included in the value of foreign production is $700 billion. Thus, the global picture as of 1978 was an international business sector that measured a minimum of $2,600 billion ($1,300 billion plus $2,000 billion minus $700 billion). The size of the overlap is important because it indicates that about half of the so-called international trade was constituted of transfers among units of international enterprises.

Foreign production, as defined here, is the value of goods and services produced in a given country by a foreign enterprise. It normally involves moving management, personnel, technology, and capital, rather than final products, across national boundaries. The concept of foreign production has not yet been adopted by national statistical gathering agencies. But foreign production can be estimated from available foreign direct investment data.

Foreign direct investment statistics, however, are "stock" data. They present a static picture as of a given moment in time of the value of the accumulated investment flows over the years. Trade statistics are "flow" data. They measure movements during a given time period, usually a year. Consequently, to show total international business activity, the flow of goods and services from facilities established in foreign countries by international firms (foreign production) must be estimated and combined with trade flow data.

Foreign production as estimated from direct investment data, however, is necessarily incomplete because of data limitations. There are omissions from the usual foreign investment data. For example, aircraft used for international operations are mobile pieces of equipment and are not classified as foreign investment. Also, data are not available on the increased amount of cross-border arrangements that are not linked to foreign equity investments. Such activities include the licensing of trademarks and technology, franchising, management contracts, and the leasing of films and television reruns. Yet, in the absence of better alternative methods of measurement, the foreign direct investment method must serve.

MERCHANDISE TRADE

The merchandise trade component of international business is the easiest to examine in detail. The most comprehensive international business data collected by governments is on merchandise exports and imports. The value of world exports, as previously noted, was $1,300 billion in 1978 and reached a level of $2,000 billion in 1980 measured in current dollars.[4] The expansion of world trade, of course, reflects both increases in prices and in physical volume.

---

[4] General Agreement on Tariffs and Trade, *International Trade 1980/81* (Geneva, 1981).

Global trends.   In terms of physical volume, world trade has grown faster than world production of commodities. From 1963 to 1973, world commodity output increased at an annual rate of 6 percent but world exports increased by 8.5 percent annually, as shown in Table 2–1. After a

Table 2–1

Growth of world exports and production, 1963–1980 (annual average percentage rate of change in volume)

	1963–73	1973–80
World commodity output:		
All commodities	6	3
Agriculture	2½	2
Mining	5½	2
Manufacturing	7	3½
World exports:		
Total	8½	4
Agricultural products	4	4½
Minerals*	7	−½
Manufactures	11	5

* Including fuels and nonferrous metals.
Source: General Agreement on Tariffs and Trade, *International Trade 1980/81* (Geneva, 1981), p. 2.

quadrupling of international petroleum prices in 1973, both commodity output and trade volume expanded at slower rates. But the growth in trade continued to exceed that of commodity output—4 percent and 3 percent, respectively.

Manufactured goods had the most rapid growth rates in both output and trade volume over the decade from 1963 to 1973 and since 1973. The slowdown since 1973 in both output and volume of trade was sharpest in petroleum. In value terms, however, petroleum exports gained greatly in importance because of price increases.

Commodity patterns.   The commodity composition of world trade has been changing significantly. In terms of value, agricultural products and minerals other than fuels have been the slowest growth areas. Agricultural products as a share of the total value of world exports dropped sharply from 29 percent in 1963 to 16 percent in 1979, as shown in Table 2–2. The biggest gainer in value terms was petroleum, whose share of the total doubled to 20 percent after 1973. Manufactures have long been the largest component of world trade, maintaining their relative share of about 60 percent, more through increases in volume than in prices.

Agricultural exports consist of food products and agricultural raw materials. Food products have been accounting for 75 percent of the category and the principal food products in international trade have

Table 2–2

Commodity composition of world trade, 1963, 1973–1979 ($ billions and percentage shares)

	1963	1973	1974	1975	1976	1977	1978	1979
World exports ($ billions)*	155	574	836	873	991	1,125	1,300	1,625
of which:								
Agricultural products	29	21	18	17	17	17	16	16
Minerals (other than fuels)	6	6	6	5	4	4	4	4
Fuels	10	11	20	19	20	19	17	20
Manufactures	52	61	55	57	57	58	60	58

* Includes commodities not classified according to kind.
Source: General Agreement on Tariffs and Trade, *International Trade 1979/80* (Geneva, 1980), p. 4.

been cereals (wheat, corn, and rice), meat, fish, coffee, sugar, and fresh fruits (bananas and oranges). The principal agricultural raw materials have been oil seeds, pulp, rubber, hides and furs, cotton, and wool.

In the manufactures category, machinery and transportation equipment (motor vehicles and airplanes) account for half the trade. Consumer goods such as textiles, clothing, and household appliances account for only 20 percent of manufactured exports. The rest consists of nonferrous metals, iron and steel, chemicals, and other semimanufactures.[5]

An important category in international trade that frequently goes unmentioned in economic studies is arms and military goods. The international arms trade has been estimated to total over $20 billion.[6] The major exporters of arms in order of importance have been the United States, the Soviet Union, France, the United Kingdom, Germany, and, more recently, Brazil. For 1978, total U.S. arms sales to foreigners were estimated at over $13 billion,[7] or almost 10 percent of total U.S. merchandise exports.

Among the several major commodity categories, trade in agricultural products comes closest to the traditional trade pattern of transfers between independent importers and exporters in different countries. Although foreign private investment in such agricultural projects as tea, rubber, and banana plantations was characteristic of 19th-century patterns, it has moved almost entirely out of agricultural production in recent decades. In contrast, a large share of the trade in petroleum and in manufactures has been dominated by multinational enterprises and con-

---

[5] Ibid., Appendix Table 6.

[6] *Business Week*, February 9, 1981, p. 34; see also *World Military Expenditures and Arms Transfers 1968–1977*, U.S. Arms Control and Disarmament Agency, Publication 100, October 1979.

[7] Philip J. Farley, Stephen S. Kaplan, and William H. Lewis, *Arms Across the Sea* (Washington, D.C.: Brookings Institution, 1978).

sists of transfers between units of the same enterprise located in different countries.

The trade network.   The large bulk of world exports and imports have been flowing between the industrialized countries. As of 1980, the industrial areas accounted for 62 percent of world exports and 66 percent of world imports, as shown in Table 2–3. The principal change since

Table 2–3

Regional composition of world trade (percentage shares in world exports [X] and imports [M])

		1963	1973	1976	1978	1979	1980
Industrial areas	X	64	68	63	65	63	61½
	M	64½	69½	66½	65½	67	66
Traditional oil-exporting developing countries	X	6	7½	13½	11	13	15
	M	3	3½	6½	7½	6	6½
New oil-exporting developing countries	X	2	1½	2	1½	2	2½
	M	2½	1½	2	2	2	2
Other developing countries	X	13	10½	10½	10½	10½	10
	M	15½	13	12½	13½	14½	15
of which:							
Least developed countries	X	—	½	½	½	½	½
	M	—	½	½	1	1	1
Eastern trading area	X	12	10	9½	9½	9	9
	M	11½	10	9½	9½	9	8½

Source: General Agreement on Tariffs and Trade, *International Trace 1980/81* (Geneva, 1981), p. 5.

1973 in the geographical pattern has been the increased importance of the traditional oil-exporting developing countries, which have been accounting for two thirds of total world fuel exports. Since the 1973 escalation of international oil prices, this group of countries increased their share of exports from 6 to 15 percent and their share of imports from 3 to 6.5 percent.

As exporters, the regions that have lagged are the "other developing countries" and the Eastern trading area (the socialist countries). Since 1963, the share of total world exports from the "other developing countries" declined from 13 to 10 percent. The share from the Eastern trading area declined from 12 percent of the total in 1963 to 9 percent in 1980, but it has been rather steady at 9 percent since 1974.

The 10 leading exporting countries as of 1980 are shown in Table 2–4. Several observations can be made from this data. First, the European Community is the largest trading area, accounting for more than one third of total world exports. More than half of this trade, however, is intra-

Table 2–4

The leading exporting countries: 1980

Country	Exports (U.S. $ billions)	Exports as percent of Gross National Product
1. United States	217	10
2. West Germany	193	23
3. Japan	130	11
4. France	116	19
5. United Kingdom	115	26
6. Italy	78	21
7. USSR	77	6
8. The Netherlands	74	46
9. Saudi Arabia	103	102
10. Canada	64	26
European Community	660	—
of which: Intertrade	349	—

Source: General Agreement on Tariffs and Trade, *International Trade 1980/81* (Geneva, 1981); GNP data from *1981 World Bank Atlas* (Washington, D.C., 1982).

Community trade among the 10 member countries. Second, U.S. exports, although still greater than those of any other single country, are small in relation to the size of the U.S. economy. Part of the explanation is that U.S. firms have been more aggressive in undertaking foreign production than in exporting. Another part of the explanation is that the large size of the U.S. market permits many American companies to achieve economic levels of production efficiency without exporting. U.S. exports were only 10 percent of U.S. GNP, as contrasted to small countries like Ireland and Belgium-Luxembourg, where exports equaled about 50 percent of GNP. Third, Japan's exports, though large in absolute amounts, are a surprisingly small share of GNP—about 11 percent.

WHY TRADE PATTERNS ARE CHANGING

An understanding of the forces underlying changes in trade patterns can be helpful to the business enterprise interested in supplying world markets. Four principal factors have been the so-called Engel's Law, price trends, technological developments, and the expansion of multinational enterprises.

Engel's Law, named after the 19th-century German economist Ernst Engel, explains changes in consumer demands as incomes rise. The law states that as personal incomes rise, consumer expenditures for food grow at a lesser rate. In statistical jargon, the demand for food has an income elasticity of less than one. Engel's Law has been extended to predict that as incomes rise consumers will spend increasing *shares* of their income on luxury goods—generally manufactures—and decreasing *shares* on necessities including food. The logic of the law is that the capacity of individuals to enlarge their consumption of necessities is more limited than their capacity to enlarge their consumption of luxury goods.

Engel's Law has two related implications for trade patterns. One relates to consumer goods, the other to producer goods. After the end of World War II, the world experienced an unprecedented period of sustained economic growth. This growth trend was accompanied by changes in consumer demand and therefore in trade patterns. As might be expected from Engel's Law, trade in agricultural products expanded but at significantly lower rates than trade in manufactured goods.

The opposite side of the coin is that the development strategies of most nations have given priority to industrialization as the "fast track" for rapid economic growth. This has meant rapid rates of growth for international trade in manufactured producer goods to support industrialization programs.

The effect of price changes on trade patterns is illustrated by the case of petroleum. Since 1973, petroleum prices have risen but the physical volume of petroleum trade has not. The higher prices have discouraged petroleum consumption, encouraging fuel conservation and a shift to alternative cheaper sources of energy such as coal.

The third factor—technology—has affected world trade in a number of primary products through developing synthetic substitutes for natural raw materials. In the food category, synthetic products have been substituted for oils, fats, and sugar. Synthetic fibers have substituted for natural fibers, synthetic rubber for natural rubber, and plastics for metals. Synthetic substitutes can frequently be produced domestically with the result that international trade in certain natural raw materials has expanded only slowly.

A fourth factor explaining changes in trade patterns is the substitution by multinational enterprises of foreign production for exports. Many firms began their internationalization by developing demand in foreign markets through exports. As the level of demand grows to the point that it will support an economic-size production facility, the firm may substitute foreign production for exports. In other cases, as demand grows, the threat of protectionist measures against imports may be the motivation for shifting from exports to local production.

An example of this phenomenon is the case of Japanese television manufacturers such as Sony and Matsushita. Both firms secured large market shares in the United States through exports and subsequently established television manufacturing facilities in the States. Thus, even though Japanese exports declined, Japanese firms maintained and enlarged their share of a foreign market.

FOREIGN DIRECT INVESTMENT

Foreign direct investment data are the most widely used indicators of multinational enterprise activity. In concept, direct investment relates to financial flows accompanied by managerial involvement and effective control. Since "effective" control is sometimes difficult to determine, the various countries have adopted quantitative criteria from which control is inferred. The United States, for example, defines direct investment as an ownership interest in foreign enterprises of at least 10 percent. Individual country practices diverge, however, using minimum percentages of ownership ranging from 5 percent to 50 percent.[8]

On a global basis, the estimated book value of foreign direct investment was a minimum of U.S. $412 billion at the end of 1978. Book value estimates, however, substantially underestimate current values. They are cumulative totals of historical cost at the time the investment was made. They have not been adjusted for the effects of appreciation in values and inflation since the investment was made.

Also, the global estimate does not include a number of countries for which data are not available. The missing countries include the USSR and other East European nations. In 1976, according to one source, these socialist countries had an estimated 700 manufacturing and trading firms in foreign countries.[9] The oil-exporting developing countries have recently begun to make major direct investments in foreign countries but the governments have not made investment data available. In 1980 the government of Kuwait acquired a 10 percent interest in Volkswagen do Brasil. Kuwait also purchased a 14 percent interest in Daimler-Benz, the West German maker of Mercedes automobiles, and more than 25 percent of Korf-Stahl, a German steelmaker.[10]

A number of developing countries have been spawning their own multinationals and exporting investment capital, mainly to other developing countries.[11] Firms in Brazil, Hong Kong, India, Mexico, the Philippines, and Korea are among those that have gone multinational. Again, data are not available for including these direct investments in our global estimate.

The leading home-base country for the multinationals in 1978 was still the United States, with 41 percent of total foreign direct investment, as

---

[8] For a discussion of the definitional and statistical problems of using foreign direct investment data, see *Private Direct Foreign Investment in Developing Countries*, World Bank Staff Working Paper No. 348 (Washington, D.C.: World Bank, July 1979).

[9] *Vision*, February 1977, p. 46, as reported in United Nations, *Transnational Corporations in World Development*, p. 53.

[10] *The Wall Street Journal*, June 6, 1980.

[11] See D. Lecraw, "Direct Investments by Firms from Less-Developed Countries," *Oxford Economic Papers*, November 1977, pp. 442–57; Krishna Kumar and Maxwell G. McLeod, eds., *Multinationals from Developing Countries* (Lexington, Mass.: D.C. Heath, 1981).

Table 2–5

Foreign direct investment by country of ownership, GNP, and exports: 1978
(U.S. $ billions)

Countries	Total GNP		Exports		Foreign direct investment	
	Amount	Percent	Amount	Percent	Amount	Percent
United States	$2,135	24.3	$ 147	11.3	$168	40.6
United Kingdom	319	3.6	72	5.6	51	12.3
West Germany	632	7.2	142	10.9	40	9.7
Japan	885	10.0	98	7.5	27	6.5
Switzerland	82	0.9	24	1.9	25	6.0
The Netherlands	128	1.4	50	3.8	22	5.3
France	473	5.4	79	6.1	20	4.8
Canada	204	2.3	48	3.7	16	3.9
Belgium/Luxembourg	95	1.1	45	3.5	8	1.9
Sweden	87	1.0	22	1.7	8	1.9
Italy	261	3.0	56	4.3	7	1.7
Australia	115	1.3	14	1.1	2	0.5
Centrally planned countries	1,626	18.5	125	9.6	n.a.*	—
Other	1,751	20.0	378	29.0	20	4.9
Total	$8,793	100.0	$1,300	100.0	$414	100.0

* n.a. = Not available.

Source: Total GNP: *World Bank Atlas, 1980.* Exports: GATT, *International Trade 1978/79.* Foreign direct investment
data: Author's estimates generally based on data from national statistical programs.

shown in Table 2–5. The United Kingdom was next with about 12 percent. Other important home countries are West Germany, Japan, Switzerland, the Netherlands, Canada, the Benelux countries, and Sweden.
Switzerland is a special case because many firms from other countries
use Switzerland for tax and secrecy reasons as a conduit through which
investment outflows are channeled. Thus the data reflect much more
activity than that of truly Swiss firms.

How fast is multinational foreign investment increasing? The quality of
the data do not permit a precise answer. The U.S. data are probably the
most reliable, making adjustments for divestments overseas as well as
expansions.[12] In the case of the United States, the direct investment position abroad has expanded at an annual average growth rate of 10 percent
over the 30-year period from 1950 to 1980.[13] Over the last decade, with
greatly accelerated rates of direct investment by non-U.S. firms—particu-

---

[12] See Brent D. Wilson, *Disinvestment of Foreign Subsidiaries* (Ann Arbor: University of
Michigan Press, 1980); Jasbir Chopra, J. J. Boddewyn, and R. L. Torneden, "U.S. Foreign
Divestment: A 1972–1975 Updating," *Columbia Journal of World Business,* Spring 1978, pp.
14–18.

[13] Obie G. Whichard, "Trends in the U.S. Direct Investment Position Abroad, 1950–79,"
Survey of Current Business, February 1981, p. 40.

larly Japanese and German—the overall growth rate has probably approximated 15 percent annually.

FOREIGN PRODUCTION

The only country for which data are available on the value of goods and services produced in foreign countries through direct investment projects is the United States. The latest U.S. survey, for example, shows a total of $146 billion in U.S. direct investment and sales by foreign affiliates of $648 billion in 1977.[14] By using a factor similar to what the economists call a capital-output ratio, the U.S. data were used to develop an estimate for foreign production by all investor countries.

The U.S. data show investments and sales for each of the major industrial sectors. These varied from a sales-to-investment ratio of 1.6 for mining to 8.5 for petroleum. The specific industry ratios were applied to available data on the composition of direct investment for the major investing countries to secure the global estimate of foreign production.

The foreign production estimate includes some activities other than the production of physical goods. It includes foreign operations in retail and wholesale trade, finance, insurance, construction, transportation, communications, and services that are based on foreign direct investment. In this sense, the picture it presents of international business activity gets away from the myopic concentration on commodities as the main substance of international business activity.

The major omission is the international transfer to nonaffiliated foreigners of technology and industrial property rights, such as trademarks to nonaffiliated foreigners, that are not accompanied by direct investment. Such international trade in intangibles has become a significant component of international business activity. For example, the U.S. firms covered by the 1977 census of U.S. investment abroad reported trademark agreements with 11,000 unaffiliated foreigners; patent, and know-how agreements with 23,000 unaffiliated foreigners.[15] In that same year, payments to U.S. firms from unaffiliated foreigners for the use of rights or intangible property (copyrights, trademarks, patents, techniques, processes, formulas, designs, franchises, manufacturing rights, etc.) were about $1 billion.[16]

INVESTOR COUNTRY TRENDS

On a global basis, the expansion of foreign direct investment occurred in three rather distinct phases after World War II. The first phase began in

---

[14] U.S. Department of Commerce, *U.S. Direct Investment Abroad, 1977* (Washington, D.C.: U.S. Government Printing Office, 1981), pp. 47, 139.

[15] Ibid., p. 191.

[16] Meryl L. Kroner, "U.S. International Transactions in Royalties and Fees, 1967–78," *Survey of Current Business*, January 1980, pp. 29–35.

1946 and extended until the late 1950s. It was characterized by a dominance of business firms from the United States and the United Kingdom, with investments heavily concentrated in foreign petroleum and other raw materials projects. A second phase, beginning about 1958 and extending to about 1971, saw a resumption of activity by other Western European countries and Japan with a steady loss in dominance by the United States and the United Kingdom. Direct investments shifted from resource-seeking projects to manufacturing and trade activities and were heavily directed toward the European Common Market and European Free Trade Association countries. A third phase beginning about 1971 was characterized by accelerated activity by non-U.S. firms, considerable disinvestment in petroleum and mining projects, and a dramatic increase in the attraction of the United States as a host country for foreign investment.

It is not surprising that the countries that had not been devastated by World War II emerged as the dominant investor countries during the immediate postwar period. In Western Europe and Japan, most business firms were concentrating on domestic reconstruction.[17] Furthermore, these countries had serious shortages of foreign exchange and were restricting the outflow of capital through rigid controls. In addition, German and Japanese investors had lost their investments abroad through war-related expropriations and felt that the risks involved in foreign direct investment were high.

In contrast, American companies were in an especially advantageous position for expanding internationally. They had accumulated financial resources and developed new technologies during the war period. They were not constrained by government controls over dollar outflows. Furthermore, the official policy of the United States was to encourage foreign direct investment as an aid to European and Japanese reconstruction and as a form of assistance for the developing countries. In fact, it was common during this period to view the multinationalization of business through direct investment as an exclusive American phenomenon.

At the end of the 1950s, foreign direct investment from all investor countries probably totaled slightly less than $60 billion in current dollars. The United States accounted for an estimated 55 percent and the United Kingdom for another 20 percent of the total. The remaining 25 percent was accounted for mainly by the Netherlands, Switzerland, Canada, and France.

---

[17] See Vassilis Droucopolous, "Expanding the Frontiers of Capital: Evidence from West Germany," in *Recent Research on the Internationalization of Business,* ed. L. G. Mattsson and F. Wildersheim-Paul (Stockholm: Almqvist & Wiksell International, 1979), pp. 148–59; Sueo Sekiguchi, *Japanese Direct Foreign Investment* (Montclair, N.J.: Allenheld, Osmun, 1979).

The dominant event marking the second phase was the creation of the European Common Market in 1958 and the European Free Trade Association in 1960.[18] These major economic integration movements enlarged greatly the markets available to plants located in these areas and attracted large flows of direct investment for manufacturing projects. The investment activity of Western European and Japanese firms began to revive as government restraints on capital outflow were eased. The West German ban on direct investment abroad was completely revoked in 1961 and the Japanese restrictions began to be liberalized in 1969. Also, the "next door" location opportunities for European investors undoubtedly seemed to present low levels of political risk.

During the 1960s, the United States and the United Kingdom continued to be the dominant foreign investor countries. But their share of the total declined as direct investment by other countries began to expand. By 1970 the U.S. share declined to about 50 percent of the total and the U.K. share to about 16 percent. The investment patterns by industrial sectors of non-U.S. investors are not available for this period. In the case of the United States, the share of the total foreign direct investment in manufacturing rose from 32 percent in 1957 to 42 percent in 1971. The share accounted for by mining and petroleum declined from 45 to 33 percent of the total over the same period.

The third phase began in the early 1970s and has continued into the 1980s. Direct investment by non-U.S. investor countries accelerated and a large share of the increased investment flows was into the United States. During the 1960–70 decade, Japanese and European enterprises had achieved phenomenal growth in size, managerial capability, and access to resources, all of which supported international expansion. Also, the technology balance had shifted, with the successes of European and Japanese firms in closing the well-publicized post-World War II "technology gap." Still another factor was the devaluation of the dollar in the early 1970s, which for many industries made foreign direct investment a more economic way than exports for serving the U.S. market. The rise in the international value of European and Japanese currencies relative to the U.S. dollar also made the acquisition of U.S. firms "cheaper" in the revalued currencies, especially in periods when the U.S. stock market was depressed.

Many parts of the world other than the United States experienced large investment inflows. But foreign direct investments in petroleum and mining declined in importance. Many countries with petroleum and mineral resources had developed an indigenous capability to handle production domestically and were not receptive to further foreign investment in these industries.

---

[18] The economic integration movements are discussed in Chapter 7.

By the end of the 1970s, the U.S. share of global direct investment had declined to about 40 percent of the total and the U.K. share to about 12 percent. Whereas the stock of U.S. and U.K. overseas investment had doubled from 1971 to 1978, over the same period the stock of direct investment by Japanese firms had increased by more than fivefold and by West German firms almost fourfold. Increases by Switzerland, the Netherlands, and Sweden[19] were also at faster rates than those for the United States and the United Kingdom.

Most of the principal investor countries had about half of their overseas investments in manufacturing projects, with about 20 percent in extractive industries and the remainder in finance, trade, and service activities. West German firms, however, had three fourths of their investments in manufacturing and very little in extractive industries. Japanese investments were distributed about one third each in manufacturing, resource investments, and services. In the extractive industries, the United States, the United Kingdom, and the Netherlands were mainly in petroleum. Japanese resources industries investments included mining, forestry, fisheries, and agriculture as well as petroleum.

THE HOST COUNTRIES: WHERE DOES FOREIGN DIRECT INVESTMENT GO?

Which areas are the principal recipients of foreign direct investment? Globally speaking, the bulk of the investment flows have been "North-North," a shorthand expression for movements from one industrialized country to another. Of the total stock of overseas investment, three fourths has been placed in the economically advanced countries. The other one fourth, located in the less developed countries, is referred to as "North-South" flow. The "East-West" expansion of multinational business activity—to the socialist countries from the Western nations—is significant and has been expanding. But because special kinds of arrangements have been used in dealing with the socialist countries, this sector of international business activity is not reflected in the direct investment data.

The individual country that has long been host to the largest amount of foreign direct investment is Canada. Furthermore, because of its relatively small economy, Canada has the largest share of its total domestic output accounted for by foreign enterprises. The stock of foreign direct investment in Canada totaled $51 billion in 1977, the latest year for which data are available. Thus, with slightly more than 2 percent of total world GNP, Canada was host to about 14 percent of global foreign direct invest-

---

[19] See Sune Carlson, *Swedish Industry Goes Abroad* (Lund, Sweden: Studentlitteratur, 1979).

ment. Beginning in the 1970s, however, the Canadian government initiated a vigorous program of screening acquisitions by foreigners and of shifting petroleum investments to national ownership, all directed toward reducing the foreign dominance in the Canadian economy.

More recently, the United States has become the largest host as well as home country for foreign direct investment. In the late 1970s, inbound investment expanded at a rapid rate and reached a total of $65 billion in 1980. A decade earlier, U.S. firms had almost 6 times as much invested abroad as foreign firms had in the United States. By 1980, outbound U.S. investment was only 3.3 times inbound investment.

The United Kingdom and the other countries of Western Europe are also important host countries for foreign direct investment. Among the industrialized countries, Japan has the smallest share of inbound investment. Japan's policy has been to encourage the licensing of Japanese firms, and entry into Japan via direct investment was severely limited until quite recently.

Two clear geographical patterns have evolved in direct investment. One is geographical proximity. The other is a continuance of relationships between former colonial powers and their colonies. The proximity pattern is illustrated by the large two-way flow of direct investment between Canada and the United States. Likewise, a large share of the investments by European firms is in other European countries, and much of Japan's overseas investments is in nearby Asian countries.

The former colonial ties are illustrated by Britain and France. British overseas investments are heavily concentrated in Commonwealth countries that were former British colonies. If the United States is included as a former British colony, former colonial ties would be the overwhelming characteristic of U.K. overseas investment. French trade and investment relations are largely with former colonies, particularly in Africa, now referred to as the " franc area."

The surprising feature of host-country patterns is the minor share of foreign direct investment located in the developing countries. Furthermore, the share of direct investment flows from the industrialized countries to the developing countries has been declining. As noted earlier, multinational corporations have invested about one quarter of their overseas investments in developing countries. But this overall picture obscures several important sectoral and regional trends. The investments are concentrated in a few industries and in relatively few countries.

The oil-producing developing countries and the so-called tax havens (Bermuda, Cayman Islands, Panama, etc.) hold about one third of the total for the developing countries. The tax havens are countries that attract international business operations because of low taxes. Another 40 percent of the stock is concentrated in just 10 countries: Brazil, Mexico, Argentina, Peru, and Trinidad-Tobago in Latin America and India,

Malaysia, Singapore, Hong Kong, and the Philippines in Asia.[20] This leaves only a small amount of direct investment distributed among the 100 or so developing countries.

Comprehensive country information on foreign business relations with the socialist countries, other than trade, is not available. Under various forms of so-called East-West industrial cooperation agreements, the Western firm typically provides machinery, advanced technology, management assistance, and use of its marketing channels. The foreign firm is usually compensated by keeping part of the physical product or a portion of the foreign exchange earned through sales abroad. One source has estimated that the number of industrial cooperation agreements in force grew from about 600 in 1973 to over 1,800 at the end of 1976.[21]

U.S. firms have been participating actively in East-West industrial cooperation agreements. As of the mid-1970s, more than 200 large U.S. corporations had entered into more than 400 such agreements in the USSR and six associated Eastern European countries, excluding Yugoslavia.[22] By type of agreement, turnkey projects and technology licensing were most numerous. By business sector, the greatest number of projects were in manufacturing.

A few of the socialist countries permit joint ventures with investment participation by foreign firms. An estimated 150 joint venture agreements had been concluded between Yugoslavia and Western firms as of 1977. Hungary and Romania also have joint ventures with Western firms— some quite large.

Foreign direct investment in the People's Republic of China began in 1980 after the passage of a foreign investment regulation in that country. During 1980, an estimated $1 billion in foreign direct investment was arranged by China.[23]

SUMMARY

International business activity is large and growing rapidly. The premier role in international business still belongs to the United States, even though the growth rate of U.S. activity has been lagging behind that of most other industrialized countries. Its dominance, however, has been in foreign direct investment and foreign production rather than in exports. The 10 countries of the European Community play a leading role in both trade and direct investment; Switzerland, Sweden, and Japan are other major players in the international business field.

---

[20] United Nations, *Transnational Corporations*, p. 56.

[21] Ibid., pp. 69–70.

[22] Paul Marer and Joseph C. Miller, "U.S. Participation in East-West Industrial Cooperation Agreements," *Journal of International Business Studies*, Fall/Winter 1977, pp. 17–29.

[23] *IMF Survey*, April 6, 1981.

The relative importance of specific countries has been changing, with international business activity becoming more equally distributed among the advanced countries. The socialist countries have become active both as investor countries and as host countries to multinational business arrangements. In recent years, even the less developed countries have become the home country for multinationals.

The data and the estimates presented in this chapter provide a reasonably accurate overview of international business patterns. They are rough estimates in many cases, however, and do not have the precision to answer many specific policy questions of international agencies, national governments, or international business firms themselves. A determined effort to collect data that depict what is really happening in the world of today is urgently needed. A prerequisite for this effort would be a wider realization that today's world no longer fits the theoretically assumed image of how imports and exports occur. The need for a new theoretical framework is the subject of the next chapter.

EXERCISES AND DISCUSSION QUESTIONS

1. Write a report for government officials of a specified country suggesting a program for statistical collection with a view to monitoring and controlling multinational business operations as they affect the country. Explain the concepts you think are relevant and indicate the data requirements as precisely as you can.

2. For a selected minor country, assess the size and roles of multinational business within its economy. Indicate the sources of your information and how you have arrived at your particular estimates.

3. How would you explain the much greater concern about inbound foreign direct investment in Canada than in the United States?

4. How do you reconcile patterns of entering into joint ventures with Western capitalist firms by some socialist countries and the ideology of these countries that proscribes private ownership of property?

Chapter 3

International business theories

What general concepts explain international business patterns? For many centuries, international trade between independent buyers and sellers in different countries was the dominant form of inter-nation transactions. In such a world it was logical to look to international trade theory as a framework for understanding and predicting international business patterns. With the emergence of supranational business enterprises that conduct inter-nation transactions in many new forms other than traditional importing and exporting, trade theory has proved to be too limited for explaining the current realities of international business.

In response to the changing patterns, a growing number of theoretical contributions have been advanced. Each has added to our understanding and some of the contributions have been approaching a comprehensive explanation of recent patterns. This chapter examines trade theory and the various new theories of international business. It will emphasize both the explanatory power and limitations of the various contributions. It will also introduce a geobusiness model as a comprehensive theoretical framework.

INTERNATIONAL TRADE THEORY

With its long history and high refinement, the pure theory of international trade continues to shape much business thinking and, even more so, the actions of government. Thus, the international manager who is familiar with trade theory will be better able to understand, analyze, predict, and influence government policies in the international business field. Governments are constantly reshaping the environment within which the enterprise operates through changes in tariffs, import quotas, and nontariff barriers. Traditional trade theory is usually the underlying rationale for such policy changes.

The main questions on which classical and neoclassical theories focus are:

Why do countries import and export the sorts of products they do, and at what relative prices or terms of trade?

How are these trade flows related to the characteristics of a country and how do they affect domestic factor prices?

What are the effects of trade intervention such as tariffs?

What are the gains from trade and how are they divided among trading countries?

Within trade theory, the foundation stone for explaining patterns and gains from trade is the *doctrine of comparative advantage.* The doctrine demonstrates that if a country specializes in the products in which it has the greatest *comparative advantage* relative to other nations, and trades those products for goods in which it has the greatest *comparative disadvantage,* the country's total availability of goods secured from a given amount of resources will be enlarged. In other words, by emphasizing *comparative* rather than *absolute* advantages, the doctrine shows that every country has a basis for trade and that specialization and trade are more efficient than policies of national self-sufficiency.

The basis for trade

Absolute advantage. The easiest explanation for trade is the concept of absolute advantage. Mexico exports petroleum to Japan. Honduras exports bananas to the United States. The United States exports airplanes to Sweden. The examples illustrate the principle called absolute advantage wherein the exporting country holds a superiority in the availability and cost of certain goods.

Absolute advantage may come about because of such factors as climate, quality of land, and natural resource endowments or because of differences in labor, capital, technology, and entrepreneurship. Some nations have petroleum and most do not. This is a case of absolute advantage because of physical availability. A tropical country can produce bananas efficiently because of climate. The United States can import bananas at much less cost than if the United States tried to produce bananas in hothouses. The acquired advantages, as in the case of airplanes, can be the result of specialization and large-scale production.

The concept of absolute advantage can be illustrated by a simplified example of two countries and two products. Let us take Australia and Belgium as the countries and wheat and cloth as the products. To simplify the example even further, we will use units of resource input (land, labor, and capital) for comparison rather than introduce money and exchange rates at this stage. The following hypothetical example compares the production resulting from the use of 10 units of resources.

Production from 10 units of resources

	Bushels of wheat	Yards of cloth
Australia	100	40
Belgium	20	100

Clearly, Australia has an absolute advantage in the production of wheat. It produces 10 bushels of wheat per resource input as compared to 2 in Belgium. Belgium's absolute advantage is in the production of cloth at the rate of 10 to 4 over Australia. It appears sensible for each country to specialize in the product in which it has an absolute advantage and secure its needs of the products in which it has a disadvantage through trade.

The extent of the benefit from specialization and trade will depend, of course, on the prices at which trading takes place. Here we will introduce the concept of *opportunity cost,* meaning what a country will have to give up of one good in order to secure another. The opportunity cost for cloth in Australia is 1 unit of cloth for 2½ units of wheat, because one resource unit can produce *either* 4 yards of cloth *or* 10 bushels of wheat. If Australia can buy 1 yard of cloth from Belgium for less than its opportunity cost—say, 1 bushel of wheat—it will either save resources to be used for other purposes or end up with more cloth than by trying to be self-sufficient. Belgium will gain even more by trading cloth for wheat at the rate of 1 yard of cloth for 1 bushel of wheat, because Belgium would have to give up 5 yards of cloth to produce one bushel of wheat with its own resources.

Comparative advantage.   Trade based on absolute advantage is easy to understand. But what happens when one country can produce *all* products with an absolute advantage? Would trade occur? Should it occur? Can trade still be mutually advantageous to the trading partners?

Here we encounter the *doctrine of comparative advantage* first introduced by David Ricardo early in the 19th century. The doctrine emphasizes *relative* rather than *absolute* cost differences. As noted above, the doctrine demonstrates that mutually advantageous trade can occur even when one trading partner has an absolute advantage in producing *all* the products being traded. Although basically a simple concept, the doctrine of comparative advantage is sometimes elusive and is frequently misunderstood.

The details of the doctrine have been modified and further developed by other theorists since Ricardo, but the concept of comparative advantage is still widely accepted. The original Ricardo version assumed that costs are determined only by the amount of labor time required in production. The modern version takes all factors of production into account on the cost side and defines costs in terms of opportunity costs.

If international trade is based on differences in comparative costs, what explains these cost differences? The question is answered by the Heckscher-Ohlin theorem, which attributes differences in comparative costs to differences among countries in factor endowments.[1] Countries have a comparative disadvantage in and tend to import those goods whose production requires the factors in relative scarcest supply in that country.

Country A with large and fertile land resources and few people may produce wheat *relatively* cheaply compared to country B with little land and an educated urban population. Country B in turn may produce manufactured goods *relatively* cheaply. Country A would then export wheat and import manufactured goods, while country B would export manufactured goods and import foods.

In the simplest application of the doctrine of comparative advantage, factor endowments (or resources) would be classified as land, labor, or capital. For more advanced analysis, distinctions are drawn among different types of labor or management skills, the specific production and distribution facilities built up in the past, and the specific natural resources—minerals, rainfall, or agricultural land—that are abundant.

---

[1] See Bertil Ohlin, *Interregional and International Trade* (Cambridge, Mass.: Harvard University Press, 1933; rev. ed., 1967). For a more detailed examination of trade theory, see Peter H. Lindert and Charles P. Kindleberger, *International Economics*, 7th ed. (Homewood, Ill.: Richard D. Irwin, 1982) or Herbert G. Grubel, *International Economics*, rev. ed. (Homewood, Ill.: Richard D. Irwin, 1981).

A simple arithmetic example can illustrate how the principle of comparative advantage can lead to mutually beneficial trade *even where one of the trading parties has an absolute advantage in all of the products being traded.* Let us return to Australia and Belgium as the two countries and wheat and cloth as the two products. Assume that each country has a total of 100 productive units that can be used in the production of either wheat or cloth. The output of each product will vary with the number of productive units devoted to it. The production alternatives and outputs are shown in Table 3–1.

Table 3–1

Production alternatives for Australia and Belgium

Productive units devoted to		Production			
		Australia		Belgium	
Wheat	Cloth	Wheat (million bushels)	Cloth (million yards)	Wheat (million bushels)	Cloth (million yards)
100	0	100	0	40	0
75	25	75	20	30	15
50	50	50	40	20	30
25	75	25	60	10	45
0	100	0	80	0	60

If all the productive units in Australia were devoted to the production of wheat, the output would be 100 million bushels. If, instead, these same resources were directed to cloth production, the output would be 80 million yards. For combinations of the two products, Australia would have to forego 1.25 bushels of wheat for every yard of cloth produced. Thus, if Australia could not trade with the rest of the world and wanted 20 million yards of cloth, it would cost the Australians the alternative of 25 million bushels of wheat. This would be the *opportunity cost*, or price, for obtaining the cloth.

For Belgium, the extreme production alternatives are 40 million bushels of wheat or 60 million yards of cloth. In this case, only 0.67 bushels of wheat would be given up for each yard of cloth, and if the population wished to have 30 million yards of cloth it would cost them the alternative of 20 million bushels of wheat.

So long as the two countries remain isolated without trade, cloth will be exchanged internally for wheat at the rate of one yard for 1.25 bushels in Australia and one yard for 0.67 bushels in Belgium. These ratios are easily derived from Table 3–1, which is so constructed that the ratios remain constant for all production combinations of wheat and cloth. So prices in Australia and Belgium will differ, given our simplifying assumptions, and there will be opportunity and incentive for trade.

In this hypothetical example, Australia has an absolute advantage over Belgium in the production of both products. In the case of wheat, Australia can produce 100 million bushels as compared to 40 million for Belgium with the 100 productive units. In the case of cloth, Australia can produce 80 million yards of cloth as compared to 60 million for Belgium if all of the productive units are used. Thus, Australia's absolute advantage in wheat is 10 to 4 and in cloth it is 8 to 6. On a relative basis, Australia's comparative advantage is greatest in wheat (2½ to 1 versus 1⅓ to 1) and Belgium's comparative disadvantage is least in cloth (1 to 1⅓ versus 1 to 2½).

Trade under constant opportunity costs.   Continuing our example, what happens when trade takes place? Australia would specialize in wheat, which it then trades for cloth. Conversely, Belgium would specialize in cloth and trade the cloth for the wheat it needs. The opportunity for trade creates a single market for the two countries. If we overlook transport costs, a single price for cloth and wheat will emerge.

The new price will lie somewhere between the internal price ratios— that is, the national prices under isolated conditions. It has to be less than the Australian price of 1.25 bushels of wheat for a yard of cloth, otherwise Australia will not benefit from trade. It has to be higher than the Belgian price of 0.67 bushels of wheat for a yard of cloth or there would be no incentive for Belgium to forego its domestic production possibilities. At a price between these limits, the countries end up with greater production than if they tried to be self-sufficient. With trade, they no longer lose output by having to allocate resources to a product that another country could produce more cheaply.

The gains that result from trade can be seen by continuing the example. Let us suppose that Australians and Belgians each demand 30 million yards of cloth for consumption and that the trade price between Australia and Belgium is set at one bushel of wheat for one yard of cloth. This exchange rate lies between the rates at which wheat can be transformed into cloth. Through reallocating resources in either country, the introduction of trade enables total wheat production to increase from 82 to 100 while still maintaining the cloth requirements as shown in Table 3–2. Through trade, Belgium would concentrate on cloth and Australia on wheat, and they would exchange 30 wheat for 30 cloth. Both end up with a larger supply of wheat than before.

Each country does not have to limit itself to only one product. Had the total demand for cloth been 50 million yards and not 60 million, then Belgium would have produced some wheat as well. Nor does it necessarily follow that the gains from trade are shared equally by both countries.

Table 3–2

Gains from trade

	Australia		Belgium		Total	
	Wheat (million bushels)	Cloth (million yards)	Wheat (million bushels)	Cloth (million yards)	Wheat (million bushels)	Cloth (million yards)
Without trade:						
Production and consumption	62	30	20	30	82	60
With trade:						
Production	100	—	—	60	100	60
Exports (−)	−30	—	—	−30	−30	−30
Imports (+)	—	30	30	—	30	30
Consumption	70	30	30	30	100	60

For example, the trade price of one bushel of wheat for one yard of cloth gives the largest share of the gains from trade to Belgium. Belgium gets 30 million bushels of wheat through specializing in cloth and trading whereas it could produce only 20 million bushels of wheat by using the same resources to produce wheat domestically. This 50 percent gain for Belgium compares to a 25 percent gain for Australia. Through trade, Australia gives up 30 million bushels of wheat to get 30 million yards of cloth whereas it would have had to forego the equivalent of 37½ million bushels of wheat to produce the same amount of cloth domestically.

Trade with monetary costs. Up to this point the examples have used barter prices, measured by the opportunity cost of the alternative output possibilities. The example becomes more realistic if production is measured in monetary cost and exchange rates are introduced. Let us assume that each productive unit equals 1 million labor hours, that wage rates are $4 per hour in Australia and 100 francs per hour in Belgium, and that the rate of exchange is 25 Belgian francs for 1 Australian dollar.

Before trade, the costs and prices locally and in foreign exchange equivalents are as follows:

	Australian prices		Belgian prices	
	($)	(Fr.)	(Fr.)	($)
Wheat (cost per bushel)	4	100	250	10.00
Cloth (cost per yard)	5	125	167	6.67

Australia's absolute advantage shows clearly in that its costs, and therefore its prices, in dollars or francs, are below the Belgian prices for both wheat and cloth.

Let us again assume that the international price settles so that a bushel of wheat sells for the same price as a yard of cloth—say, a price of $5 (or 125 francs). It would then pay Australia to switch resources from cloth to wheat. In Australia, as shown in Table 3–1, one resource unit will produce either 1 yard of cloth or 1.25 bushels of wheat. The export of wheat will earn $6.25 as compared to the $5 worth of cloth given up by shifting resources. It would also pay Belgian firms to switch to cloth. In Belgium, the resources needed to produce 1 yard of cloth would produce only two thirds of a bushel of wheat. Belgium gains $5 for the cloth export and gives up the $3.35 that could be earned by using the same resources for producing wheat domestically.

Thus far we have been dealing with the case of constant opportunity costs at different levels of production. In the real world, situations of increasing or decreasing costs are more likely to be the rule. If Australia expands wheat production, less fertile land may have to be used and unit costs will increase. In capital-intensive manufacturing, increased output may reduce unit costs because of economies of scale. More elaborate versions of trade theory have been developed to deal with the cases of increasing and decreasing costs. They demonstrate that in the world of decreasing and increasing cost industries there are still gains from trade, and that countries will still find it profitable to follow their comparative advantage.[2]

The limitations of trade theory

It may be a disappointment for the international manager, after mastering the logic and examples of trade theory, to learn that international trade theory is in flux. Recent empirical tests have failed to support the theory convincingly and much additional theoretical work is under way to make the theory more realistic. "Unfortunately, however," as one writer notes, "through these modifications and extensions, international trade theory has also become much more complex, aesthetically less pleasing, and theoretically less powerful than the basic Heckscher-Ohlin-Samuelson model."[3]

The limitations of trade theory flow in part from the simplifying assumptions of the model. Some key assumptions are that the factors of production (land, labor, and capital) are immobile between countries, that perfect information exists as to international trade opportunities, and that trading firms in different countries are independent entities. Also, the model assumes perfect competition and does not allow for

---

[2] Lindert and Kindleberger, *International Economics*, p. 33.

[3] Grubel, *International Economics*, p. 85.

oligopoly or monopoly. Nor does it explicitly recognize technology, know-how, or management and marketing skills as significant factors of production which can be the basis for comparative advantage.[4]

Probably the most important limitation of trade theory is that it did not anticipate nor does it attempt to explain international business activity in forms other than the movement of goods. A direct reflection of this is the way that trade theory poses the key question it tries to answer. Trade theory asks the question, "Why do countries trade?" This is the wrong question.

The question should be, "Why are goods and services transferred between countries?" Then it becomes apparent that the decision-making unit is the business enterprise and not the country. To be sure, the enterprise may be state owned as well as private, and government actions and programs may heavily influence business decisions. Nevertheless, the initial focal point for explaining most international business transactions is the enterprise.

A shift in focus to the enterprise highlights the reality that the business firm has numerous ways besides traditional importing and exporting for supplying foreign markets or securing foreign goods. It can supply foreign demand through licensing or foreign production. It can secure foreign goods through direct-investment projects. Trade theory rules out these options through its limiting assumptions. It also misses the rationale behind the 20th-century development of marketing by assuming that commodities sold in the international marketplace are standard, basic, and transferable—wheat, cotton, and wine, for example. Today's firms, however, are continually adjusting many dimensions of their products against their assessments of customers' wants—against the market. There is no simple standard commodity.

The implications of the multinational enterprise for international trade theory have begun to receive serious attention by economic theorists and considerable reconstruction is under way, particularly to allow for some internationally mobile factors.[5] But the emphasis of the reconstruction efforts is more on ways to make traditional theory relevant than on developing a theoretical framework for explaining the multinational enterprise phenomenon.

---

[4] See Raymond Vernon, "The Location of Economic Activity," in *Economic Analysis and the Multinational Enterprise,* ed. John H. Dunning (New York: Praeger Publishers, 1974), p. 90.

[5] See W. M. Corden, "The Theory of International Trade," in *Economic Analysis and the Multinational Enterprise,* ed. Dunning, pp. 184–210; S. Hirsch, "An International Trade and Investment Theory of the Firm," *Oxford Economic Papers* 28 (1976), pp. 258–70; Asim Erdilak, "Can the Multinational Corporation Be Incorporated into the General Equilibrium Theory of Trade and Investment?", *Social and Economic Studies,* September 1976, pp. 280–90.

FOREIGN DIRECT INVESTMENT THEORIES

While trade theorists have been working to extend trade theory to include foreign direct investment, other theorists have been making important contributions under the rubric of theories of foreign direct investment or theories of the multinational enterprise.[6] Most of the new theoretical work, however, has been done outside the general equilibrium framework of international trade and investment theory. The various theories have added greatly to our understanding of modern international business patterns, but the process of developing a comprehensive theoretical framework is still under way.

As might be expected, the various theoretical contributions give special emphasis to the professional field of specialization of the contributors. Specialists in industrial organization have explained direct investment in terms of product differentiation, oligopoly, and imperfect product and factor markets. Specialists in international finance have focused on capital market imperfections. Management and decision theory experts have focused on the internal decision-making process of the firm.

The global horizons approach

An early contribution comes from the work of Aharoni on the forces that change the geographical horizon of the firm and stimulate it to "go international."[7] In classical economic theory, the issue of geographical horizons for the business enterprise does not arise. The firm is assumed to have perfect and costless knowledge of and be prepared to take advantage of attractive opportunities wherever they exist. The reality is that the business firm is usually born with a geographical horizon limited to a locality, a region, or a home country. Brilliant foreign opportunities may exist beyond the firm's geographical horizon of which the enterprise is not aware. But the horizon of the firm is not necessarily static or immutable.

As part of the growth process of the firm, geographical horizons change. The change may be a result of internal forces or exogenous stimuli stemming from the firm's environment. The internal forces may be the influence of a high executive, the development of new technology or products, dependence on foreign sources for raw materials, the desire to find a use for old machinery, the observed need for a larger market,

---

[6] See Neil Hood and Stephen Young, *The Economics of Multinational Enterprise* (New York: Longman Group, 1979); and A. L. Calvet, "A Synthesis of Foreign Direct Investment Theories and Theories of the Multinational Firm," *Journal of International Business Studies,* Spring/Summer 1981, pp. 43–59.

[7] Yair Aharoni, *The Foreign Investment Decision Process* (Boston: Harvard Business School, 1966).

and so on. External forces may be the influence of customers, the initiative of foreign governments, the foreign expansion of a competitor, or a dramatic event such as the formation of the European Economic Community. The role of horizon-widening factors, as part of the growth process of the firm, provides a necessary but incomplete explanation of modern international business patterns. These factors explain the awareness of opportunities. Other factors are needed to explain how the firm responds to the perceived opportunities.[8]

The market imperfections approach

Another major advance toward understanding international business patterns comes from the market imperfections approach. The core of this approach is a deceptively simple proposition. Assuming that the enterprise has a global horizon, the decision of the firm to invest is explained as a move to take advantage of certain capabilities not shared by local competitors.[9]

The foreign firm entering a specific country faces a number of additional costs or disadvantages as compared to a local firm. The local firm would have an intimate knowledge of the economic, social, legal, and governmental environment. The foreign firm can only acquire this knowledge at a cost. Furthermore, the foreign firm incurs foreign exchange risks, risks of possible errors and misunderstandings from cross-cultural operations, and additional costs of operating at a distance.

To operate successfully in foreign areas, therefore, the firm must have compensating advantages that more than offset the innate advantages of local firms. These advantages must be transferable within the enterprise and across distances. These advantages are referred to as *firm-specific* or *ownership-specific* factors.

The competitive advantage of firms is explained by imperfections in markets for goods or factors of production. In the theoretical world of perfect competition, firms produce homogeneous products and have equal access to all productive factors. In the more realistic world of imperfect competition, as explained by industrial organization theory, firms acquire competitive advantages through product differentiation, brand names, special marketing skills, and restrictions to entry. Other

---

[8] For related studies that emphasize the growth and evolution of the firm into multiproduct, multifunction, and eventually multinational stages, see L. Fouraker and J. Stopford, "Organizational Structure and the Multinational Strategy," *Administrative Science Quarterly*, June 1968, pp. 47–64; and Mira Wilkins, *The Maturing of Multinational Enterprises* (Cambridge, Mass.: Harvard University Press, 1974), p. 414.

[9] This theory was originally propounded in a thesis at the Massachusetts Institute of Technology by Stephen H. Hymer in 1960. The thesis was eventually published in 1976. See Stephen H. Hymer, *The International Operations of National Firms: A Study of Direct Investment* (Cambridge, Mass.: MIT Press, 1976).

sources of competitive advantage may be patented technology, internal or external economies of scale, or even differences in access to capital markets.

Technology advantages in a broad sense relate to special marketing skills, superior organization know-how and management techniques, as well as products and industrial processes. Basically, technology advantages are the possession of knowledge, and knowledge has been characterized as a "public good" to the firm—that is, the know-how, once developed, can be made available to foreign subsidiaries without any additional cost to the parent firm. In contrast, competitors would incur costs in obtaining the knowledge or skills.

A knowledge advantage, however, must be more easily transferable within the firm than between different firms. When the knowledge market is imperfect, the firm may be able to earn a higher return by using the knowledge within the firm than by selling it to a potential buyer.[10]

The market imperfections approach can explain both horizontal and vertical investments. Horizontal investments are to produce in foreign locations the same goods manufactured in the home market. Vertical investments are supply oriented, intended to produce abroad raw materials or other production inputs which are then supplied to the firm at home or to other subsidiaries. The foreign firm may have privileged access to raw materials or minerals because of firm-specific advantages such as an established marketing system, managerial capacity, control over transportation, or access to capital. The petroleum industry with a small number of international firms that dominated the world scene for a number of years is an example of supply-oriented direct investments. This industry is also an example of how the competitive advantage of firms can change and erode over time.

The oligopoly structure of certain industrial markets has been identified as a source of competitive advantage and a motivation for a "follow-the-leader" behavior in such industries.[11] An oligopolistic market is characterized by restricted entry and a small number of firms. Restricted entry may result from such factors as patented technology, unpatented secret know-how, large capital requirements, and economies of large-scale production. The market may be international rather than national, as in the case of aluminum and petroleum.

In the oligopoly model, each of the small number of firms is motivated to follow its competitors into foreign markets as a defensive strategy. By being in all markets occupied by its competitors, each firm has the potential of responding to price cuts or other competitive actions. Because of

[10] Richard E. Caves, "International Corporations: The Industrial Economics of Foreign Investment," *Economica* 38 (February 1971): 5–6.

[11] F. T. Knickerbocker, *Oligopolistic Reaction and Multinational Enterprise* (Boston: Harvard Business School, 1973).

this response potential, competition is reduced and the market situation becomes "stabilized." This pattern is also referred to as an "exchange of threat" motivation.[12]

The market imperfections model helps to identify the industries in which firms are likely to expand their direct operations either domestically or internationally. The model needs to be supplemented, however, by the global horizon contributions because it assumes that the firm is constantly aware of foreign opportunities. The model also leaves many important questions unanswered. Given the special advantage that permits the firm to invest abroad (i.e., the necessary condition), the model stops short of explaining why foreign production is the preferred means of exploiting the advantage (i.e., the sufficient condition). The firm's advantage can also be exploited through exporting or licensing. Furthermore, the theory needs a time dimension in the sense that the advantage may erode and require disinvestment.

Several other theoretical contributions that emphasize the financial aspects of international operations should be mentioned in a summary of market imperfections theories. One writer explains international business expansion as a response to imperfections in foreign exchange and capital markets.[13] Another contribution extends portfolio theory to explain international expansion as a means of diversifying risk and stabilizing earnings by being in a "basket of markets."[14]

The internalization approach

The internalization explanation extends the market imperfections approach by focusing on imperfections in intermediate-product markets rather than on final-product markets.[15] It assumes that the firm has a global horizon and it recognizes that the enterprise needs a competitive advantage or a unique asset to expand. But the emphasis of the internalization concept is on the motivations of the firm to extend its own direct operations rather than use external markets.

Many intermediate-product markets, particularly for types of knowledge and expertise embodied in patents and human capital, are difficult to organize and costly to use. In such cases, the firm has an incentive to

---

[12] Edward M. Graham, "Transatlantic Investment by Multinational Firms: A Rivalistic Phenomenon?", *Journal of Post-Keynesian Economics*, Fall 1978, pp. 82–99.

[13] Robert Z. Aliber, "A Theory of Direct Investment," in *The International Corporation*, ed. Charles P. Kindleberger (Cambridge, Mass.: MIT Press, 1970), pp. 17–34.

[14] Alan Rugman, *International Diversification and the Multinational Enterprise* (Lexington, Mass.: Lexington Books, 1979); see also Raj Aggarwal, "Investment Performance of U.S. Based Multinational Companies: Comments and a Perspective on International Diversification of Real Assets," *Journal of International Business Studies*, Spring/Summer 1980, pp. 98–104; V. R. Errunza and L. W. Senbet, "The Effects of International Operations on the Market Value of the Firm: Theory and Practice," *Journal of Finance*, May 1981, pp. 401–17.

[15] Peter J. Buckley and Mark Casson, *The Future of the Multinational Enterprise* (New York: Holmes & Meier, 1976), p. 33.

create internal markets whenever transactions can be carried out at a lower cost within the firm than through external markets. This internalization involves extending the direct operations of the firm and bringing under common ownership and control the activities linked by the market.

The creation of an internal market permits the firm to transform an intangible piece of research into a valuable property specific to the firm. The firm can exploit its advantage in all available markets and still keep the use of the information internal to the firm in order to recoup its initial expenditures on research and knowledge generation. In this respect, the internalization theory is similar to the "appropriability" approach. The appropriability approach emphasizes potential returns from technology creation and the ability of the multinational firm to ensure full appropriability of the returns.[16]

The internalization approach goes a long way toward synthesizing the various explanations of the motives for foreign direct investment.[17] The explanatory value of the internalization concept rests on an analysis of the costs and benefits to the firm. It suggests that the incentive to internalize depends upon the relationship of industry-specific factors (nature of product and industry structure), region-specific factors (geographical and social characteristics), nation-specific factors (political and fiscal relations), and firm-specific factors (management ability to organize an internal market). The main emphasis, however, is on industry-specific factors that include the knowledge factor.[18]

Internalization is a general theory that explains the expansion of multiplant firms both domestically and internationally. The expansion of the multinational enterprise is a special case of the general theory in which internalization of markets occurs across national boundaries. The theory focuses on the motives and decision process within the firm but gives only limited attention to the potential of national control policies and other external factors as they can affect the benefits and costs of internalization.

The product cycle model

The product cycle model relates trade and direct investment as sequential stages that follow the life cycle of a product.[19] The model sug-

---

[16] Stephen P. Magee, "Information and the Multinational Corporation: An Appropriability Theory of Direct Foreign Investment," in *International Financial Management*, ed. D. R. Lessard (Boston: Warren, Gorham, & Lamont, 1979), p. 57.

[17] Alan M. Rugman, "Internalization as a General Theory of Foreign Direct Investment: A Re-Appraisal of the Literature," *Weltwirtschaftliches Archiv* (Review of World Economics) June 1980, p. 370.

[18] Buckley and Casson, *Future of Multinational Enterprise*, pp. 33–34.

[19] Raymond Vernon, "International Investment and International Trade in the Product Cycle," *Quarterly Journal of Economics*, May 1966, pp. 190–207.

gests that firms innovate new products at home and in relation to the home market. In this *new product stage*, the product is manufactured in the home country and introduced into foreign markets through exports. In the *mature product stage*, the enterprise is induced to produce abroad, generally in other high-income countries. The product has become sufficiently standardized that price competition becomes important. As cost factors begin to dictate that foreign markets be serviced by local production, foreign manufacturing facilities are established.

In the third stage, the *standardized product stage*, price competitiveness becomes even more important. In this stage, production may shift to low-cost locations in low-income countries from which goods may be exported back to the home country or other markets. Or, only the labor-intensive phases of production may be separated and carried out in countries where labor is cheapest.[20]

The product cycle model provided a useful framework for explaining the early post-World War II expansion of U.S. manufacturing investment in other advanced countries. But its explanatory power has waned with changes in the international environment.[21] Many multinational enterprises have developed global networks of subsidiaries and a global scanning capability. With this capability, firms will develop innovations in response to the opportunity or threat in any of the markets to which it is exposed. Also, initial production does not necessarily occur in the market area that inspired the innovation. Production will be located wherever costs are advantageous and possibly at an appropriate facility already existing in the system. The model does not address the strategy issue of why multinational firms undertake investment abroad instead of, say, licensing.[22] Nor does it seem to explain supply-oriented raw materials foreign direct investments.

International production

The various foreign direct investment theories help to explain which firms tend to go international (those with a competitive advantage) and the motivation for engaging in foreign production (internalization). They do not explore to any extent the "where," or the pattern of location, for exploiting these advantages. The theory of international production addresses the issue of where foreign production takes place by integrating location theory into the theories of the multinational enterprise.

[20] R. W. Moxon, "Offshore Production in the Less Developed Countries," *The Bulletin*, Institute of Finance, New York University, July 1974, pp. 98–99.

[21] Raymond Vernon, "The Product Cycle Hypothesis in a New International Environment," *Oxford Bulletin of Economics and Statistics*, November 1979, pp. 255–67.

[22] Ian H. Giddy, "The Demise of the Product Cycle Model in International Business Theory," *Columbia Journal of World Business*, Spring 1978, p. 92.

The "eclectic theory of international production"[23] enlarges the theoretical framework by including both home- and host-country characteristics as additional explanatory factors. It argues that the propensity of a particular enterprise to engage in foreign production will also depend on the locational attractions of its home-country's endowments compared with those offered by other countries. Furthermore, the theory argues that many ownership-specific advantages are generated and sustained by characteristics of the home country—for example, large and efficient capital markets or government support for research and development.

International transmission of resources

A comprehensive framework for explaining international business patterns has been formulated around the role of the multinational firm in the transmission of economic resources among nations.[24] Extending the basic philosophy of resource transfers embodied in trade theory, Fayerweather enlarges the concept of resources to include technological, managerial, and entrepreneurial skills, as well as natural resources, capital, and labor. He then argues that differentials in the supply-demand relationship of resources among countries generate basic economic pressures for the inter-nation flow of resources and create opportunities open to the multinational firm. Governmental actions or policies distort or reshape these resource-differential relationships as basically determined by free economic forces into the actual patterns of opportunities open to the firm. In responding to these opportunities, the types of resources transmitted, the selection of countries, and the choice of transmission methods depend on the characteristics and strategy of specific multinational firms. In sum, three groups of factors—resource differentials, governmental actions, and characteristics of the business enterprise—determine the way in which the multinational firm plays a role in the international transmission of resources.

This conceptual framework broadly encompasses economic concepts related to international trade and investment as well as behavioral models of the business enterprise. It recognizes oligopoly elements as a stimulus to foreign investment by including oligopoly advantages within the broad category of skill resources. It assigns a major role to governments in influencing international business patterns through actions that affect resource-differential relationships and the entry conditions for foreign enterprise. It distinguishes the resource transmission role of the multinational firm from that of the strictly national firm in two ways.

---

[23] John H. Dunning, *International Production and the Multinational Enterprise* (London: George Allen & Unwin, 1981), pp. 72–108.

[24] John Fayerweather, "International Transmission of Resources," in *International Business Management: A Conceptual Framework* (New York: McGraw-Hill, 1969), pp. 15–50.

Having developed a global horizon, the multinational firm is concerned with resource differentials among countries. It is also critically concerned with the institutional constraints of nations that affect the flow of resources among nations.

The transmission of resources model is general enough so that it can incorporate most dimensions of international management. It does not, however, address itself to the process by which essentially domestic firms acquire their global horizons. Furthermore, it appears to be predominantly concerned with manufacturing activities and the role of markets in motivating international expansion.

The Marxist imperialism model

The Marxist imperialism model for explaining and predicting international business patterns has not attracted a wide following in business circles. But many political groups accept this explanation as a rationale for opposing multinational business, even though their philosophic position has been undermined by the pragmatic activities of the socialist countries. As mentioned previously, the USSR and other Eastern European countries have their own multinationals operating in nonsocialist countries. In the reverse direction, many special arrangements have been negotiated for permitting multinationals from the capitalist countries to operate in Eastern Europe. Even more significant has been the policy reversal of the People's Republic of China in the late 1970s, which resulted in an open invitation for foreign direct investment.

Box 3–1

Marxism versus pragmatism

Calcutta—The Marxist-led coalition government in the state of West Bengal said it is willing to put aside ideological differences and welcome foreign investment.

Chief Minister Jyoti Basu said West Bengal has slipped from its position as India's premier industrial state and needs the technology and jobs brought by multinational corporations. He added, "We want the latest in technology, whatever the company and whatever its complexion."

Mr. Basu made his remarks while inaugurating a $27.5 million investment by Hindustan Lever Ltd., the Indian subsidiary of the Anglo-Dutch Unilever group.

Source: *The Wall Street Journal*, October 15, 1979.

The Marxist view explains the international expansion of business and the multinational enterprise as a logical stage in the evolution of capitalist enterprise, "a stage during which innate tendencies of the capitalist firm come into full power."[25] The nature of capitalist enterprises impose on the individual firm the necessity to expand continuously. This expansion results in the accumulation of capital and a growing concentration of capital in fewer and fewer hands. These two factors—investment expansion and concentration of corporate power—along with the growth of world markets create a set of conditions that are uniquely fulfilled by the multinational corporation.

The Marxist view of multinational enterprises as a part of a historical process does not differ greatly from many of the non-Marxist explanations for the internationalization of business. The main difference relates to the social value of the international business phenomenon. The Marxist view is as follows:

> The multinational firm may indeed be a more efficient organism, but the issue is: efficient for what? Its superiority is in the realm of profit-making of oligopolistic organizations designed to exploit to the hilt the existing hierarchy of nations, in other words the imperialist world order.[26]
>
> The global corporations . . . have been built to obtain the maximum-profit advantage out of the artificial interdependence imposed by the long history of colonialism and imperialism.[27]

LIMITS OF INTERNATIONAL BUSINESS THEORIES

As a framework for explaining *overall* international business patterns, recent theoretical contributions have several limitations. Most explanations are partial in that they focus on only one method by which international business patterns change. They may throw light on either trade movements or direct investment but not on both as interrelated activities. Also, they generally have a limited view of the international strategies that may be adopted by the firm.

Some deal with the case of the market seeker but do not encompass the extensive activity of resource seekers. Another limitation is that existing theories are one way. They are not reversible. They offer explanations of investment and not of disinvestment.

These limitations are noted not as a criticism of the theories but as a recognition that the theorists had limited objectives. In general, their objective was to explain only certain aspects of the international business phenomenon. They touch the phenomenon at different points and provide partial explanations of it from different perspectives. In a nondis-

---

[25] Harry Magdoff, "The Multinational Corporation and Development—a Contradiction?", in *The Multinational Corporation and Social Change*, ed. David E. Apter and Louis W. Goodman (New York: Praeger Publishers, 1976), p. 200.

[26] Ibid., p. 211.

[27] Ibid., p. 212.

paraging sense, the situation can be likened to the fable of the blind men and the elephant.

> Four blind men feel an elephant's leg,
> tail, ear and body respectively, and
> conclude it is like a log, a rope, a fan,
> and something without beginning and end.[28]

For the wider objective of explaining *overall* international business patterns, the underlying model or framework must of necessity be appropriately broadened. As a guide for the business enterprise, the model should recognize the full range of internal and external variables that influence the firm's international operations. As a guide to governments interested in influencing international business patterns, the model should identify the ways in which country and inter-nation variables can shape international business patterns. Above all, governments should be aware that measures intended to control one form of business transaction may cause the foreign enterprise to shift to another method.

THE GEOBUSINESS MODEL

The geobusiness model attempts to provide a comprehensive framework for explaining and predicting overall international business patterns. The label "geobusiness" refers to the relationship between geography and international business in the same sense that "geopolitics" describes the relationship between geography and international politics.

The model encompasses the international business actions of *all* firms and not just those classified as multinationals. It incorporates a large number of key variables whose interaction changes the geographical source and destination of inter-nation business activity. It recognizes that the individual enterprise is the motive force and that international business patterns are shaped by the adjustments of specific enterprises, operating competitively over a range of national environments to survive and grow. The variables of the model can be grouped under three headings: (1) conditioning variables, (2) motivation variables, and (3) control variables, as illustrated in Figure 3–1.

The basic variables

The conditioning variables, or what the economist calls "necessary but not sufficient conditions," indicate whether an opportunity exists for business activity to cross national boundaries. They include characteristics of the product or service, characteristics of the home and host coun-

---

[28] Archer Taylor, *English Riddles from Oral Tradition* (Berkeley: University of California Press, 1951).

Figure 3–1

Basic variables of a geobusiness model

Conditioning variables:

Product-specific   Product and factor requirements, technology, and production characteristics.

Country-specific
- a. National market demands.
- b. Disparities in natural and human resource endowments.
- c. Disparities in technological, cultural, institutional, economic, and political environments.

Inter-nation   International financial, trade, transportation, and communication systems and agreements that affect the spatial movement of information, money, goods, people, etc.

Motivation variables:

Firm-specific   Geographical perception and resource availability.

Competitive   The relative competitive position of individual enterprises and competitor moves and threats.

Control variables:

Country-specific   Administrative actions, laws, and policies of home- and host-country governments that directly or indirectly influence international business through positive incentives and/or negative controls.

Inter-nation   International agreements, treaties, and codes of conduct directly affecting the pattern of international business.

try, and inter-nation variables. The interaction of these three sets of variables creates an incentive for business to cross national boundaries. They also determine the extent to which it is possible to carry the product or the services across national boundaries without the costs outweighing the gains.

The motivation variables indicate whether the enterprise perceives and has a motive to realize any such net gains. These variables include firm-specific factors such as the firm's geographical horizon and its access to necessary resources for crossing national boundaries. A firm's competitive position, as affected by moves and threats of direct and indirect competitors, will also motivate it to change its international business pattern in a specific direction. A rational firm is unlikely to make a move into competitive disadvantage—it must perceive some advantage to be gained.

Control variables indicate restricting or encouraging actions on the part of home and host countries to influence international business patterns. Even if the necessary conditions exist and specific firms are motivated to make a particular change in patterns, the change may be negated or redirected by the actions of an individual country or countries working in cooperation.

Conditioning variables

Product-specific. The necessity of foreign firms having a competitive advantage over local producers has been fully elaborated by existing theories. The types of competitive advantage are numerous. They can be in product development, product differentiation, production processes, managerial skills, marketing know-how, heavy capital requirements, economies of large-scale production, and other characteristics of the product, the firm, or the industry. These product and industry characteristics may operate as barriers to entry and result in oligopolistic markets.

Product-specific competitive advantages, of course, are not static. In mining and petroleum production, for example, access to technology, capital, and marketing networks has often been the basis for the competitive advantage of foreign firms. In many cases, however, these advantages have eroded over time and disinvestment has occurred. Conversely, industries specializing in energy conserving technologies and products, such as fuel-efficient automobiles, gained competitive advantages for foreign operations from "old" technologies as world scarcities in energy and natural resources developed in the late 1970s and fuel and raw materials prices escalated.

Country-specific. Specific home-country characteristics frequently generate and sustain the competitive advantages of enterprises.[29] The economic size and income levels of the home country, for example, both stimulated and inhibited U.S. firms in going international. For some firms, the large size of the U.S. market provided production advantages from large-scale production, extensive experience in managing multiplant companies that are distant from each other, and valuable marketing skills that have been built on as competitive advantages for international expansion. Other U.S. firms have been inhibited from developing international operations because the U.S. domestic market is sufficiently large for them to achieve scale economies and expansion aspirations. In contrast, the small size of the home market has spurred enterprises in countries like Switzerland to develop international horizons.

Home-country resource scarcities and resource availabilities can affect the motivations and capabilities of firms for expanding internationally. Japan's resource-poor situation, for example, has stimulated Japanese firms to engage heavily in foreign trade and direct investment to secure resources for their nation. The extensive international activity of U.S. firms in petroleum may be due to the fact that the modern petroleum industry began in the United States in 1859 when commercial quantities of oil were discovered in Pennsylvania. This and subsequent oil discoveries enabled U.S. firms to develop skills in this industry that gave them a competitive advantage for going overseas.

---

[29] See Dunning, *International Production and the Multinational Enterprise*, pp. 81–98.

Home-country environments can be a source of technology advantage where governments make heavy expenditures for research and large public investments in education and technical training. Home-country political systems have operated as both a pull and a push for international business. A number of European firms, for example, were motivated to diversify their operations internationally because of concern for the strong antibusiness political forces in their home country. A home-country infrastructure such as developed capital markets can provide a firm with an advantage in access to financial resources. Home-country social and cultural patterns can also play a role. Social mobility and a status hierarchy that gives prominence to business leaders are closely associated with the development of entrepreneurship and a dynamic business sector.

Host-country characteristics will condition whether an opportunity exists for business to cross national boundaries. Natural resource availability in the host country can be the attraction for a foreign resource-seeking enterprise. The size, growth trends, and income levels of the host-country market can be the attraction for market seekers. An underdeveloped capital market in the host country may be a source of competitive advantage for the foreign firm. Human resource availability may be important for production efficiency projects or research and development facilities. Cultural characteristics can condition local business opportunities as they affect consumer demands and the behavior patterns of potential employees. The host-country political environment may appear risky and act as a deterrent, or appear reasonably stable and act as an attraction.

Inter-nation variables.   The inter-nation variables have generally been neglected in the new theories. They include the operations of the international financial system, the international trade framework, international patent and trademark agreements, tax treaties, and so on. As they will be discussed in detail in the next five chapters, only a few examples will be cited here to illustrate their conditioning role.

The international financial system adopted at the end of World War II supported three decades of unprecedented international business expansion by reducing financial risks and achieving relative stability in the values of national currencies. Some have argued that the system overvalued the U.S. dollar for this long period and created unusually favorable conditions for the expansion of U.S. firms by direct investment. With the realignment of major world currencies during the middle 1970s, however, the reverse seemed to happen. The undervaluation of the U.S. dollar against other major currencies stimulated a wave of foreign direct investment in the United States.

In the trade area, many inter-nation agreements have affected international business activity. The creation of the European Common Market, international commodity agreements, the emergence of the producers' association in oil (OPEC), and agreements to reduce tariff and nontariff barriers have been some of the more important influences.

Motivation variables

Whenever conditioning variables favor a change in business patterns across national boundaries, only a proportion of firms will take action. The geobusiness model thus requires provision for variables that identify these firms and their motivations. Motivation variables are divided into those that are specific to the firm and those based on its competitive relationship to other firms.

Firms differ in their geographical horizons and these horizons change over time. The firms that are active in changing international business patterns must be aware of foreign opportunities. They must have a geographical perception capability.

The geographical perception of a specific firm at a point in time has both a spatial and a functional dimension. In a spatial sense, it will fall along a continuum from myopic to global. At a partial stage of horizon widening, for example, the firm may be alert to opportunities in Canada but not to those in Latin America or Asia. In a functional sense, the geographical perception may be global for exporting but not for direct investment. In Japan, for example, until the late 1960s a combination of historical, cultural, and public policy reasons limited the horizon for most Japanese firms to exporting.

The firm may have developed its radar so that potential foreign opportunities or threats are brought into view, but a companion capability is required to translate the data on the radar screen into effective business action. Unlike decision making for domestic expansion, the firm must be able to evaluate opportunities and threats that involve such variables as different currencies, foreign exchange risk, political risk, and so on. The firm must have access to sufficient expertise to give the international variables reasonably accurate values. Numerous examples exist of internationally inexperienced firms losing out on favorable opportunities because they were not capable of properly evaluating political or foreign exchange risk.

To take advantage of an identified foreign opportunity, the firm must have access to the necessary financial and managerial resources. Thus the German chemical industry was long aware of many foreign opportunities but did not have access to the capital needed to exploit these opportunities. During the 1970s, however, the industry was able to undertake major international investments because rapid domestic expansion had by then generated the large amounts of capital needed.[30] Access to personnel that could operate cross-culturally has limited the interna-

---

[30] *German-American Trade News*, July–August 1980, p. 19.

tional expansion of many Japanese companies. In a number of cases, however, the unique Japanese general trading companies have been able to supply this scarce resource.

The second group of motivation variables covers the firm's competitive position and the moves made by competitors. The requirement that the firm have a competitive advantage *specific to the target area of operations* has previously been noted. This requirement, however, is unnecessarily restrictive. The firm may act to remove a competitive disadvantage or to prevent the building of a competitor's advantage. The necessary conditions, perhaps, are that the firm will not expand into disadvantage and that it must perceive some ultimate gain from its action. Moreover, *this gain may be perceived in accounting terms as benefits captured in the enterprise system elsewhere than in the local project.*

The action alternatives for the firm, of course, may have a positive (expansion) or a negative (contraction) side. Emphasizing the positive side, most actions by the enterprise will be taken pursuant to one or more of the following strategies:

1. Market seeker.
2. Resource seeker.
3. Production-efficiency seeker.
4. Technology seeker.
5. Risk avoidance.
6. Defensive or "exchange of threat."

The market-seeker and the resource-seeker motivations are the basis for horizontal and vertical integration, respectively. The production-efficiency seeker changes the international pattern of its operations to take advantage of lower labor costs.

The technology seeker may take several types of international action. The enterprise may acquire foreign companies to secure access to some technology that the foreign firm controls. It may establish research facilities in a foreign area to take advantage of available trained personnel or to have access to unique materials such as tropical plants for medical research. It may undertake operations in an advanced product market to acquire product development and marketing experience used elsewhere in the multinational system.

The risk avoidance and diversification motives attempt to minimize the possibilities of production interruption, to achieve more stable demand through operating in a "basket of markets," or to reduce total political risk to the system. The exchange-of-threat strategy, as previously noted, occurs in oligopolistic industries.

Control variables

The potential match between a foreign enterprise and a local business opportunity may be present. One or more firms may be motivated to exploit this potential. Yet the potential may not be realized because of national control policies in either or both the home and host countries. National control variables consist of laws and administrative actions of both home and host governments intended to achieve national welfare goals. These control factors can act as incentives or constraints; they keep changing over time as national goals keep changing. The specific types of incentive and controls are myriad, and many of them represent great imagination and ingenuity. They are examined in detail in Part III of this text.

In the case of domestic expansions, firms may encounter both incentive and control factors. Many communities, states, and regions offer special tax and financial incentives to attract new business. At the same time, some domestic governments have constraints such as rezoning laws that limit industrial expansion in order to bring on slow "managed growth." But control/incentive factors are much more important in movements across national boundaries. The "foreignness" of firms raises many national policy issues that are not raised by domestic business expansion.

As a home country, the United States has export control laws restricting the export of goods and technology by U.S. firms that might "prove detrimental to the national security of the United States." For many years after World War II, Japan and most Western European countries adopted controls on capital outflows to improve a weak balance-of-payments situation. The effect of these controls was to allow national firms to use only the export option for engaging in international business. Home governments have also developed incentive programs to encourage international business expansion such as providing political risk insurance, loans, and allowing tax credit for tax payments to foreign governments.

Host-country control/incentive programs are more numerous and varied than home-country policies. They may proscribe certain business areas for foreign investors, restrict foreign exchange remittances, affect technology transfer agreements, require sharing of ownership with locals, and so on. They may even effectively ban foreign direct investment. Thus, Japan maintained controls over inbound investment until recently that left open only the licensing option for foreign firms in most business areas.

International controls are less extensive. The OECD (Organization for Economic Cooperation and Development), of which the industrialized countries are members, has adopted a voluntary code of conduct for multinationals. A related code is being developed by the United Nations.

A GEOBUSINESS THEORY OF INTERNATIONAL ADJUSTMENT OF THE FIRM

Against this specification of the underlying geobusiness model, it is possible to advance many theories of international business adjust-

ment. A highly simplified general theory might be that business transactions will cross national boundaries when such activity is profitable to the parties. This can be a valid explanation but of limited usefulness. A balance has to be struck between simplicity and explanatory
depth.

The theory advanced here is one based on the relatively simple rational global planning model for the firm. Its objective is to explain business actions by firms that have developed their geographical perception
into a global scanning capability and have access to the resources necessary for international operations.

The rational global planning model

On the basis of a world reconnaissance of opportunities and threats,
the firm selects the markets it wants to be in. Working back from its
market objectives and following location economics criteria, the firm will
develop logistic models on a world scale that represent rational patterns
for supplying the selected markets. The logistic models will include
sources of raw materials, production sites, service and marketing facilities, research activities, and even sources of labor, management, and
capital. By incorporating the marketing and logistic options into a general programming model, the firm develops its optimal business operations strategy.

The global planning approach is basically the same for either domestic
or international expansion, except that a new range of variables and risks
resulting from crossing national boundaries must be included in the
decision-making process. Thus the geobusiness theory recognizes that
many explanations for international business are not uniquely international. Necessary conditions such as a competitive advantage are also
necessary conditions for domestic expansion by a firm beyond its local
area. Some of the common factors differ only in degree. Other factors
such as currency risks are differences in kind rather than in degree, in
the sense that they are constants for domestic expansion and variables
for going international. This is particularly true for inter-nation and national control variables. Also, new variables such as tariffs, local content
requirements, etc. must be added to traditional location economics criteria in international decision making.

What methods of adjustment to the international pattern of a firm's
operations will the global planning approach lead to? The polar choices
are traditional trade, at one extreme, and complete internalization, at the
other. In between the poles are a range of methods involving varying
degrees of participation by the enterprise in foreign direct operations.
These include licensing, loan-purchase agreements for resource seekers,
establishing foreign procurement or subcontracting offices, or making
direct investments in foreign marketing and warehousing facilities, in
assembly and repackaging operations, or in full-scale foreign production.

Box 3—2

The rational model illustrated

Carbide Sells Plant Mounted on a Barge to Argentine Firm
Plant Will Be Built in Japan and Towed 14,000 Miles

New York—Union Carbide sold what it said was the world's first barge-mounted polyethylene plant to Ipako S.A. of Argentina.

(Argentine market) The 132,000-ton plant will make it Argentina's largest producer of low density polyethylene, a plastic material.

(U.S. technology) The plant will use Carbide's low-pressure Unipol process, which the company said reduces capital, energy, and space requirements. Carbide said the advantages of a barge-mounted plant include more controlled construc-

tion conditions, reduced costs, and shorter construction time.

(Production logistics) The plant will be built for Carbide in a shipyard by Ishikawajima-Harima Heavy Industries Co. of Tokyo and towed about 14,000 miles to a waterside site at Bahia Blanca, Argentina. The company said it can deliver a completed waterborne plant to a waterside site anywhere in the world 24 months after signing a contract, a year less than the lead time needed for construction of a conventional on-site polyethylene plant.

Source: Adapted from *The Wall Street Journal,* March 22, 1980.

In the case of direct investment, expansion through acquisition may be an alternative to initiating a completely new operation.

Where internalization advantages are not present, because intermediate product and factor markets are efficient, the firm will supply foreign markets through exports and secure inputs through imports. Where internalization produces net benefits because of imperfections in intermediate-product or factor markets, location factors will determine the location of production for either horizontal or vertical integration. The location factors are generally modified by government intervention. An internalization strategy, however, can lead to exporting at an early evolutionary stage and foreign production at a later stage.

Empirical testing

Empirical testing is needed to determine the validity and explanatory power of any theory. International business research, however, has only recently become accepted as a significant area of investigation and the amount of research presently available is still modest. Moreover, major data limitations exist. Most governments still do not collect data in a form that permits analysis of the interrelationships of various alternatives for transacting international business. There is also a vast data deficiency on the internal operations of international enterprises, such as motivations and decision-making criteria.

Broadly speaking, most of the relevant research available falls into three categories. A large amount of research has focused on trade patterns and determinants of trade. Unfortunately, few of these studies recognize and explore the interaction between trade and investment. A second group of studies focus exclusively on foreign direct investment and the internal operations of multinational enterprises. The direct investment studies attempt to explain the determinants of direct investment by examining the industrial composition of flows to specific host countries. The internal operations studies have been characterized as "neither comprehensive nor particularly satisfactory" and often "not designed to test the theory."[31]

A third category includes studies on the economic and political impact of the multinational enterprise on both host and home countries and the related issue of the incidence and effectiveness of national controls on multinational business operations. Most host-country impact studies relate to the less developed countries. The control studies are generally inconclusive as to how far individual countries have succeeded in improving their share of the benefits.

Among the more comprehensive studies available are studies of the international business patterns of Japanese firms[32] and a recent major study of foreign investment in the United States.[33] Both research programs have gone beyond statistical analysis to include field investigations and interviews. The results of these studies are broadly consistent with most aspects of the geobusiness model. They demonstrate that explanations and predictions of international business patterns hold good only for specified types of business activity flows between specific pairs of countries. Both research programs overlap to the extent that Japanese investment in the United States is examined both from the home- and host-country perspectives.

Japanese international business patterns reflect a dominant role played by home-country conditioning variables. Japan has extremely limited supplies of natural resources and depends heavily on foreign countries for almost all important raw materials and energy. To secure a stable supply of natural resources, a major share of Japanese overseas investment has been in agriculture, fishery, mining, and forest resource projects. Early investments in the resources area, particularly mining, were of the loan-purchase type, whereby the foreign capital supplied by Japa-

---

[31] Hood and Young, *Economics of Multinational Enterprise*, pp. 175–76. This publication presents an excellent survey of international business research.

[32] See Yoshi Tsurumi, *The Japanese Are Coming* (Cambridge, Mass.: Ballinger Publishing, 1976). The Ministry of International Trade and Industry (MITI) annually conducts a survey of the overseas activities of Japanese firms. A summary of the survey results are published in the ministry's yearly *Overseas Activities of Japanese Firms*.

[33] U.S. Department of Commerce, *Foreign Direct Investment in the United States*, vols. 1–9 (Washington, D.C., 1976).

nese firms was repaid by a share of the output from the project. At that time, Japanese firms preferred this strategy because of a shortage of experienced personnel for participating in the management of these projects. Over time, the necessary managerial resources were developed and the strategy shifted to equity investments with managerial participation.

Home-country labor market characteristics played a major role in another large category of overseas investments in labor-intensive industries. As wage levels in Japan continued to increase rapidly throughout the 1970s, the developing countries became increasingly attractive to Japanese manufacturers in such labor-intensive industries as textiles and home electronics. Inter-nation variables were also extremely important as a motivation for overseas production-efficiency seekers. Labor costs increased even more sharply as measured in foreign currencies because the Japanese yen had appreciated from ¥358 to U.S. $1 in 1970 to ¥210 to the U.S. $1 in 1978.

It is interesting to note that many Japanese firms had developed strong competitive advantages in a number of product areas such as steel, shipbuilding, home electronics, motorcycles, and automobiles that did not lead to overseas manufacturing investments. To a large extent, the firm-specific competitive advantage in these cases was dependent on home-country variables that dictated home-country production. The location pattern began to change somewhat in the early 1980s as some overseas production was initiated in several of these industries as a hedge against growing protectionism in many major market areas. Also, the pollution controls and scarcity of land in Japan forced some steel expansion to occur offshore, but in areas that fulfilled the input requirements rather than in the market areas.

Japanese firms have also been active as technology seekers. A major Japanese company, for example, made large investments in an American computer firm in return for access to the American technology in markets outside of the United States. Thus the Japanese patterns include resource seekers, production-efficiency seekers, technology seekers, market seekers, and defensive investments against the threat of protectionism.

Control variables have been of great importance in shaping Japanese patterns. Home-country controls that limited foreign investment in Japan gave Japanese firms a large and protected home market in which to develop technological competence and economies of large-scale production. The Japanese government also assisted Japanese firms in many other ways such as financial incentives and long-range planning to develop product-specific advantages for competing in foreign markets. Host-country control variables, as previously noted, have stimulated some Japanese firms to substitute foreign production for exports in response to growing protectionist sentiments in those market areas.

Another comprehensive research study is the study of foreign direct investment in the United States published in 1976. This project combined a complete statistical census of inbound foreign direct investment with extensive field investigation of the motives and behavior patterns of foreign firms. All of the enterprise strategies, except the production-efficiency strategy, which has been the basis for sourcing investments in low-wage countries, were identified as motivations for inbound U.S. investment.

Much of the recent foreign direct investment in the United States was by market seekers with a competitive advantage in the U.S. market. Some firms had extended their horizons through exporting to the United States and were substituting foreign production for exports because of the realignment of national currencies. The economic size, high income levels, and growth trends of the U.S. market were important attractions.

Other investments were by resource seekers, such as Japanese firms in the coal, forestry, and aluminum industries, representing an evolution from an importing strategy to direct investment and managerial participation. Foreign investors entered the United States as technology seekers by acquiring some U.S. firms with new technologies and by establishing research and development facilities in the United States.

Defensive investments were made in several oligopolistic industries such as petroleum and aluminum so that foreign firms could be in all of their competitors' major markets. The attraction of a politically safe U.S. environment produced another strategy for some firms with concern for political risk in their home country.

The U.S. study illustrates the dynamic nature of international business patterns as they relate to technology advantage. The technology gap that developed during World War II and that supported much international expansion by U.S. firms during the postwar period has been closing. With the revival of research and development in Western Europe and the emergence of dramatic technological progress in Japan, business enterprises in these countries had developed competitive advantages by the late 1960s and early 1970s that became a basis for extending their operations to the United States.

The recent U.S. experience as a host country for foreign investment also reflects the influence of home- and host-country control variables. As mentioned, the home-country controls that existed in most European countries and Japan after World War II had been removed by the 1970s. Thus the strategy options of European and Japanese firms had expanded and foreign direct investment had become a concrete possibility. On the side of host-country controls, the principal actions by the United States influencing the patterns were potential trade barriers that encouraged foreign firms to substitute local production in the United States for exports. The risk of possible restraints on imports was an important factor influencing a number of Japanese electronic firms such as Sony and Matsushita to establish production facilities in the United States.

SUMMARY

Practice has clearly run ahead of theory in the international business field. The new patterns of business transactions across national boundaries have become extremely complex. Traditional trade theory did not anticipate nor does it explain the internationalization of business in forms other than the international movement of goods.

A series of new approaches, evoked by the international business reality, are beginning to provide a theoretical framework for explaining and predicting international business patterns. Among these are growth theories of the firm and the emergence of the multinational enterprise as a mechanism for the international transmission of resources and as a means of exploiting oligopolistic advantages in foreign areas.

The geobusiness model is presented as a comprehensive framework against which a range of theories about international business changes can be advanced. It recognizes the enterprise as the active force in changing international business patterns. But the motivations and capabilities of the enterprise for changing international business patterns are not exclusively related to the characteristics of the firm. They also depend heavily on home and host country environmental factors, inter-nation variables, and national and international controls.

EXERCISES AND DISCUSSION QUESTIONS

1. Explain the difference between comparative advantage and absolute advantage.
2. What are the principal limitations of trade theory in explaining current international business patterns?
3. As an executive of a predominantly domestic firm that seems unaware of foreign opportunities, what would you do to expand the geographical perception of the firm and "go international"?
4. Why has the U.S. pharmaceutical industry been internationally minded while the iron and steel industry has not?
5. As an international manager, how could you use the geobusiness model to guide the international business activities of your firm?
6. As a government official, how could you use the geobusiness model to reduce (or increase) foreign direct investment in your country?

PART TWO

The framework for international transactions

A natural starting point for the study of international business is to examine the framework that has grown up over the centuries for dealing with business transactions across national boundaries. This overall framework is made up of three different though interrelated frameworks:

1. The *international financial framework* deals with the means (foreign exchange), the recording (balance of payments), and the control of international transfers of monetary claims (the international monetary system).
2. The *international trade framework* deals with the means, the recording, and the control of international transfers of goods and services.
3. The *international legal environment* deals with the nature, contents, and limits of arrangements nations have entered into for determining how to treat business rights, obligations, and opportunities that extend across national frontiers.

These three frameworks provide the basic vocabulary for international transactions, and as such introduce many of the terms and concepts necessary for describing international business. They also influence the language of government controls. Controls that governments place on international transactions are largely determined by information collection and reasoning that stems from the conventions of these frameworks. Knowledge of the traditional frameworks is thus important for understanding and predicting the environment within which international business operates.

None of these three frameworks, however, is focused uniquely on international business. They have been molded by the heritage of international trading between buyers and sellers residing in different countries and acting predominantly as merchants and at arm's length—quite different from the international transactions of large multinational businesses. This has produced a body of knowledge, theories, and controls that concentrates on aggregate flows of goods and finance across a country's boundaries and does not pay direct attention to the objectives and decisions of the businesses that arrange the transactions. The frameworks have limitations given the reality of today's world of multinational firms. Nevertheless, the international enterprise must still make international transactions, and these frameworks can provide managers with valuable knowledge and perspectives.

An essential similarity in the three frameworks is the absence of a world authority that overrides the jurisdiction of national governments. Each framework is, in effect, a system for relating a particular segment of the economic activities and regulations of different sovereign states. The financial framework is concerned with the way in which the currencies of individual countries are exchanged. With no legal international currency, international transactions must be measured, accounted for, and paid for by converting one currency into another. The trade framework is concerned with the relationship of the productive output of one country to that of another. What one country produces for another's markets is subject to a variety of natural and imposed conditions. Finally, the regulatory framework begins to provide a system whereby governments agree on how they will align their legal constraints and privileges for activities which carry into more than one jurisdiction.

Chapter 4

Foreign exchange and international money markets

In a world of many national currencies, participants in international business need a mechanism for exchanging one national currency for another. The institutional setting for this process, usually referred to as currency conversion, is the foreign exchange market, which also serves as a mechanism for reducing exposure to the risks of fluctuating exchange rates.

This chapter describes the foreign exchange market, the ways in which foreign exchange rates are quoted, the principal types of foreign exchange transactions, the participants in the market, and the relationship between foreign exchange and other financial markets. Foreign exchange rates fluctuate over time reflecting a country's economic conditions and external relations with other nations.

THE FUNCTIONS OF THE FOREIGN EXCHANGE MARKET

Foreign exchange is defined as the currency of another nation. To a Japanese firm the U.S. dollar is foreign exchange. To an American company the Japanese yen is foreign exchange. *Foreign exchange rates* are the rates at which currency conversion takes place. On July 20, 1982, for example, the exchange rate was 254.35 Japanese yen to U.S. $1.

The two main functions of the foreign exchange market—currency conversion and reduction of foreign exchange risk—can be illustrated by the case of a Japanese exporter selling steel products to Brazil. The Japanese seller might invoice the Brazil buyer in Japanese yen, Brazilian cruzeiros, or U.S. dollars, depending on which currency has been previously agreed upon by the parties. Whichever currency is used, one or both of the parties will need to transfer to or from its national currency. If cruzeiros are used, the Japanese seller will have to convert them into yen. If yen are used, the Brazilian buyer will have to transfer cruzeiros into yen. If dollars are used, the Brazilian buyer will have to change cruzeiros into U.S. dollars and the Japanese seller will need to convert the U.S. dollars into Japanese yen. The foreign exchange market provides the mechanism for these currency transactions.

Where time elapses between a transaction and payment, a risk exists that the exchange values of the national currencies may fluctuate. This risk is normally referred to as a *transactions exposure*. If the parties had agreed upon payment in U.S. dollars, both the Japanese seller and the Brazilian buyer are "exposed" in the sense that they are not certain as to how much local currency will be paid or received on the payment date. Exposure may result in either gains or losses to the party exposed.

Let us assume that payment is to be made in U.S. dollars and that the Japanese seller may prefer to make its normal profit on the sale rather than speculate on eventually receiving a greater or lesser profit as a result of changes in exchange-rate values. Through forward and futures contracts, the foreign exchange market provides a means of removing the foreign exchange risk. The Japanese seller may contract to sell U.S. dollars for future delivery at a fixed rate and thus be sure of the amount of Japanese yen that will be received when payment is made.

THE NATURE OF THE FOREIGN EXCHANGE MARKET

The foreign exchange market is a network of banks, brokers, and foreign exchange dealers in many locations connected by rapid means of communications. The more important exchange markets are in New York, London, Paris, Frankfurt, Amsterdam, Milan, Zurich, Toronto, Tokyo, and Hong Kong. These markets are so closely integrated that together they constitute a single world market despite the distances and the time differentials involved. This closeness exists even though the banks, brokers, and traders are not formally linked and do not share common facilities in various cities.

The foreign exchange markets are governed by an unwritten code of conduct for all participants. Most market transactions are handled in an informal manner by telephone or telex, rather than in written legal form. The apparently casual nature of the market transactions belies the strictness of the unwritten code and the swift punishment of anyone who reneges.

The major participants in the foreign exchange market are large commercial banks that operate at two levels—retail and interbank. At the retail level, they deal with bank customers who want to buy or sell foreign exchange. At the interbank level, they trade in foreign exchange with other domestic banks, usually in the same commercial center, and with foreign banks. In the United States, contacts among the banks are usually made through a broker who receives a small commission. When dealing with foreign banks the contact is normally direct.

Almost all foreign exchange trading takes place among a small number of currencies, the most important of which is the U.S. dollar. The nondollar segment of the market is dominated by the German mark, the British pound sterling, and the Swiss franc. Relatively few nations permit free convertibility of their currencies, and the currencies with restricted convertibility play virtually no role in the foreign exchange markets.[1] Full *convertibility* of a currency means that national governments permit both residents and nonresidents to purchase or to sell unlimited amounts of that nation's currency. An example of a nonconvertible currency is the Russian ruble, the import or export of which the USSR prohibits by law.

The size of the foreign exchange market is enormous and trading volume has grown phenomenally in recent years. Because the trading day normally begins in Europe, the largest trading volumes have traditionally occurred in London, Frankfurt, and Switzerland. The most active period in New York is from 7:00 to 9:00 in the morning when the business day is near closing in Europe. Nevertheless, trading volume in New York has expanded dramatically. In 1980, *daily* turnover in New York was estimated to have reached $23 billion, nearly a fivefold increase from 1977.[2] In 1982, trading volume in New York increased to an estimated $40 billion daily turnover, and the world foreign exchange market had reached a level of about $200 billion *daily*.

---

[1] The standard reference for exchange restrictions prevailing in specific countries is the *Annual Report on Exchange Arrangements and Exchange Restrictions*, published by the International Monetary Fund (Washington, D.C.).

[2] Patricia A. Revey, "Evolution and Growth of the United States Foreign Exchange Market," *Federal Reserve Bank of New York Quarterly Review*, Autumn 1981, p. 32; see also Ian H. Giddy, "Measuring the World Foreign Exchange Market," *Columbia Journal of World Business*, Winter 1979, pp. 36–48.

A specialized part of the foreign exchange market is the recently established institutions for trading in foreign exchange futures. The biggest of these is the International Monetary Market (IMM) in Chicago established in 1972. The newest is the New York Futures Exchange (NYFE) of the New York Stock Exchange established in 1980. These markets deal in commodities futures and one of the "commodities" is foreign exchange.

THE LANGUAGE OF FOREIGN EXCHANGE

Transactions in the foreign exchange market may be either *spot* or *forward*. In the spot market, currencies are traded for immediate delivery, although in practice delivery and payment are completed within two working days. In the forward market, trades are made for future dates, usually less than one year away. In the forward market payment is made upon delivery, but the rate of exchange is agreed upon when the contract is made. Forward markets, however, exist for only the major currencies.

The forward market and the futures market perform similar functions, but with a difference. In the forward market, foreign exchange dealers can enter into a contract to buy or sell *any amount* of a currency for delivery at *any date* in the future. Thus customers can tailor their needs as to amount and timing. In contrast, the IMM and the NYFE deal in contracts of a standard size (for example, 25,000 British pounds or 125,000 German marks) and the contract will be for a given month (March, June, September, or December), with the third Wednesday of the month as the delivery day.

Foreign exchange rates are usually quoted in the different national markets in terms of the local currency required to purchase a foreign monetary unit. Reading the vertical U.S. dollar column in Table 4–1, we see that on May 28, 1981, the spot rate for 1 British pound was U.S. $2.070. The reciprocal exchange rate, shown in the vertical British pound column, was £0.483 required to buy U.S. $1. The actual quotes would be on a buy and sell (or bid and offer) basis with a small margin, usually less than one tenth of 1 percent for large transactions, as a profit for the trader. Table 4–1 uses the "middle rate" between the actual bid and offer quotations.

The rates between each of the principal 10 currencies traded are shown in Table 4–1. Frequently, however, quotes are available only in terms of one currency such as the U.S. dollar as the unit of account. In such cases a *cross rate* for two currencies—say, the British pound and the German DM—can be calculated by relating them both to a third currency, the U.S. dollar. In Table 4–1, U.S. $1 = £0.483 or 2.327 DM. The price of the £ in terms of the DM, therefore, is

$$DM/£ = \frac{2.327}{0.483} = 4.8178 \ DM$$

Table 4–1

The value of major currencies

A. Exchange rates around the world

May 28, 1981, middle rate for:	U.S. dollar	Belgian franc	British pound	Canadian dollar	Dutch guilder	French franc	German mark	Italian lira	Japanese yen	Swiss franc
1 U.S. dollar	1	37.81	0.483	1.202	2.585	5.506	2.327	1160	224.3	2.074
100 Belgian francs	2.645	100	1.278	3.179	6.837	14.56	6.153	3068	593.3	5.486
1 British pound	2.070	76.25	1	2.488	5.350	11.395	4.815	2401	464.3	4.293
1 Canadian dollar	0.832	31.46	0.402	1	2.151	4.581	1.936	965.2	186.6	1.726
1 Dutch guilder	0.387	14.63	0.187	0.465	1	2.130	0.900	448.8	86.78	0.802
10 French francs	1.816	68.67	0.876	2.183	4.695	10	4.226	2107	407.4	3.767
1 German mark	0.438	16.25	0.206	0.517	1.111	2.367	1	498.7	96.42	0.891
1000 Italian lire	0.862	32.59	0.416	1.036	2.228	4.746	2.005	1000	193.4	1.788
1000 Japanese yen	4.458	168.6	2.154	5.358	11.52	24.54	10.37	5172	1000	9.246
1 Swiss franc	0.482	18.23	0.233	0.579	1.246	2.655	1.122	559.3	108.2	1

B. Other dollar rates

Currency	May 27, 1981	Week ago	4 weeks ago
Argentine peso*	3260.0	3237.0	3153.0
Australian dollars	0.88025	0.87525	0.8686
Brazilian cruzeiro	86.015	84.47	81.15
Finnish markka	4.3660	4.3060	4.2045
Greek drachma	57.05	55.70	53.60
Hong Kong dollars	5.4765	5.4425	5.3675
Iranian rial†	78.70	78.20	76.35
Kuwaiti dinar	0.2788	0.2780	0.2760
Luxembourg franc	38.28	37.42	35.98
Malaysian ringgit	2.3530	2.3335	2.3145
New Zealand dollars	1.1465	1.1360	1.1122
Saudi Arabian riyal	3.3920	3.3808	3.3590
Singapore dollars	2.1605	2.1450	2.1205
South African rand	0.8510	0.8425	0.81665

* Argentine rate is for free peso.
† Selling rate.
Source: *World Business Weekly*, June 8, 1981.

Likewise, the price of the DM in terms of the £ is

$$£/DM = \frac{0.483}{2.327} = £0.208$$

Spot rates are always "flat," that is, the exchange rate is written out with the proper number of decimal places. Forward rates are generally given either flat (also termed "outright") or in points "premium" or "discount" from the spot rate. Outright rates are given to retail customers. The quotes in terms of points of discount or premium are used by traders in the interbank market. The outright rate is the spot rate adjusted by the points of discount or premium.

Foreign exchange rates are published daily in financial papers such as *The Wall Street Journal* in the United States and the *Financial Times* in London. The spot and forward rates on July 20, 1982, for the British pound and the French franc published in *the Wall Street Journal* were as follows;

	U.S. $ equivalent	
	British (pound)	France (franc)
Spot	1.7395	.1466
30-day forward	1.7405	.1464
90-day forward	1.7473	.1458
180-day forward	1.7570	.1448

The 90-day futures of the pound were selling at a premium of 78 points (1.7473 − 1.7395). The French franc 90-day futures were selling at a discount of 8 points (.1466 − .1458).

A foreign currency is at a *forward discount* when the forward price is lower than the spot price. The opposite is true in the case of a *forward premium*. The forward discount reflects the judgment of the market that the spot rate in 90 days will be lower. The British pound premium reflects the market judgment that the spot rate will increase in 90 days.

Forward discounts and premiums are quoted in terms of percentage *per annum* as well as in points. The 90-day futures for the British pound are at a premium of 1.79 percent per annum. The formula for calculating the discount or premium is as follows:

$$\frac{\text{Forward rate} - \text{Spot rate}}{\text{Spot rate}} \times \frac{12}{\text{Number months forward}} = \begin{array}{l} \text{Premium or} \\ \text{discount as} \\ \text{percent p. a.} \end{array}$$

Applying the formula to the 90-day future quote for British pounds:

$$\frac{1.7473 - 1.7395}{1.7395} \times \frac{12}{3} = 0.0179 = 1.79\% \text{ p.a. premium}$$

FOREIGN EXCHANGE TRANSACTIONS

Transactions for immediate delivery are relatively simple. Travelers going abroad will exchange their national currency at a bank or foreign exchange dealer for the currency of the country they intend to visit at the spot rate on the date of the transaction. In a typical spot business transaction, an American firm arranging for an immediate payment of £1,000 to another firm in London would pay its U.S. bank about $1,739.50 (as of July 20, 1982) and the U.S. bank would cable its correspondent bank in London to credit the equivalent amount (£1,000) to the account of the London firm. Many if not most international business transactions, however, have a time dimension that may dictate the use of the forward markets.

Hedging

Hedging involves entering into a contract at the present time to buy or sell foreign exchange at a specified price on a given future date. Goods and services are usually paid for in the currency of the seller, but a different currency of payment can be agreed upon by the buyer and seller. If a U.S. importing firm (the buyer) knows that it must take delivery on goods valued at 200,000 German marks (DM) from West Germany in six months, the U.S. firm is certain that it will have to deliver 200,000 DM on that date. What the firm does not know is the "price" of DMs, that is, the exchange rate that will prevail at that future date and how many U.S. dollars will be required to make payment.

The U.S. importer can be sure of the cost by entering into a forward contract with a bank for delivery of those DMs in 180 days. As shown in Table 4–2, the 180-day futures rate for German marks was .4180 to the U.S. dollar on July 20, 1982, so the dollar price for DM 200,000 would be $83,600. There will be no transaction costs because the bank makes its profit through the margin between buying and selling rates. The importer has now *hedged* or *covered* its foreign exchange exposure. Whether the spot rate is higher or lower in six months, the importer knows what the U.S. price of the goods will be.

The commercial bank that agrees to supply the foreign exchange in the future will simultaneously make arrangements for an offsetting future purchase of foreign exchange from an exporter. By matching forward purchases with foreign sales, the bank eliminates its risk and avoids "taking a position" in foreign exchange. If the bank does not match its forward sales and purchase commitments of a specific currency, it is taking an uncovered position and speculating on the future of the currency.

The importer has several alternatives other than a forward market hedge. The firm can buy DMs immediately at the spot rate and hold them

Table 4–2

Foreign exchange rates (Tuesday, July 20, 1982)

Foreign Exchange

Tuesday, July 20, 1982
The New York foreign exchange selling rates below apply to trading among banks in amounts of $1 million and more, as quoted at 3 p.m. Eastern time by Bankers Trust Co. Retail transactions provide fewer units of foreign currency per dollar.

Country	U.S. $ equiv. Tues.	Mon.	Currency per U.S. $ Tues.	Mon.
Argentina (Peso)				
Financial	.00005	.00005	20000.00	20000.00
Australia (Dollar)	1.0116	1.0132	.9885	.9869
Austria (Schilling)	.0577	.0577	17.33	17.34
Belgium (Franc)				
Commercial rate	.02142	.0213	46.67	46.94
Financial rate	.0200	.0198	50.000	50.35
Brazil (Cruzeiro)	.00579	.00579	172.76	172.76
Britain (Pound)	1.7395	1.7410	.5749	.5744
30-Day Forward	1.7405	1.7427	.5745	.5738
90-Day Forward	1.7473	1.7492	.5723	.5717
180-Day Forward	1.7570	1.7583	.5692	.5687
Canada (Dollar)	.7965	.7952	1.2555	1.2576
30-Day Forward	.7944	.7933	1.2588	1.2606
90-Day Forward	.7921	.7910	1.2625	1.2642
180-Day Forward	.7885	.7875	1.2683	1.2698
China (Yuan)	.5208	.5208	1.9202	1.9202
Colombia (Peso)	.0157	.0157	63.84	63.84
Denmark (Krone)	.1175	.1175	8.5075	8.5125
Ecuador (Sucre)	.0303	.0303	33.00	33.00
Finland (Markka)	.2118	.2117	4.7210	4.7230
France (Franc)	.1466	.1452	6.8225	6.8875
30-Day Forward	.1464	.1451	6.8300	6.8920
90-Day Forward	.1458	.1446	6.8550	6.9125
180-Day Forward	.1448	.1437	6.9075	6.9575
Greece (Drachma)	.0144	.0144	69.40	69.30
Hong Kong (Dollar)	.1697	.1705	5.8935	5.8650
India (Rupee)	.1053	.1053	9.50	9.50
Indonesia (Rupiah)	.0015	.0015	657.00	657.00
Ireland (Pound)	1.4035	1.3935	.7125	.7176
Israel (Shekel)	.0402	.0402	24.88	24.88
Italy (Lira)	.000728	.000724	1374.00	1381.00
Japan (Yen)	.00393	.003926	254.35	254.70
30-Day Forward	.00395	.00395	252.98	253.15
90-Day Forward	.00399	.00399	250.33	250.35
180-Day Forward	.00406	.00406	246.10	246.20
Lebanon (Pound)	.1914	.1914	5.2250	5.2250
Malaysia (Ringgit)	.4256	.4263	2.3495	2.3460
Mexico (Peso)	.0206	.0206	48.64	48.59
Netherlands (Guilder)	.3674	.3667	2.7220	2.7270
New Zealand (Dollar)	.7421	.7432	1.3475	1.3455
Norway (Krone)	.1581	.1584	6.3260	6.3140
Pakistan (Rupee)	.0823	.0823	12.1476	12.1476
Peru (Sol)	.00147	.00147	681.37	681.37
Philippines (Peso)	.11806	.11806	8.47	8.47
Portugal (Escudo)	.01187	.01186	84.25	84.30
Saudi Arabia (Riyal)	.2908	.2908	3.4385	3.4385
Singapore (Dollar)	.4675	.4679	2.1390	2.1370
South Africa (Rand)	.8750	.8730	1.1428	1.1455
South Korea (Won)	.0013	.0013	740.80	740.80
Spain (Peseta)	.00896	.00897	111.58	111.45
Sweden (Krona)	.1640	.1637	6.0970	6.1070
Switzerland (Franc)	.4792	.4760	2.0870	2.1005
30-Day Forward	.4834	.4804	2.0686	2.0816
90-Day Forward	.4916	.4884	2.0342	2.0475
180-Day Forward	.5018	.4981	1.9925	2.0075
Taiwan (Dollar)	.0254	.0254	39.39	39.39
Thailand (Baht)	.0435	.0435	23.00	23.00
Uruguay (New Peso)				
Financial	.07997	.0799	12.505	12.505
Venezuela (Bolivar)	.2329	.2329	4.2938	4.2938
West German (Mark)	.4075	.4052	2.4540	2.4620
30-Day Forward	.4090	.4068	2.4451	2.4504
90-Day Forward	.4123	.4103	2.4250	2.4271
180-Day Forward	.4180	.4156	2.3922	2.3940
— — —				
SDR	1.09162	1.09235	.91606	.92105

Special Drawing Rights are based on exchange rates for the U.S., West German, British, French and Japanese currencies. Source: International Monetary Fund.

Source: *The Wall Street Journal*, July 21, 1982.

for six months until payment is due. At the spot rate of U.S. $.4075, the 200,000 DMs will cost $81,500, thus saving $2,100 as compared to the six-month forward rate. This gain of about 5.2 percent on an annual basis, however, must be balanced against the opportunity cost, or what might have been earned with the dollars, during the six-month period. The importer can use a money market hedge by depositing the DMs in Germany to earn interest during the six-month period. But as will be discussed below, interest rate differentials are generally the reverse of the discounts or premiums on foreign exchange futures, and the importer is likely to earn about 5.2 percent less on DMs deposited in Germany than on U.S. dollars deposited in the United States. In other words, the results of the forward market and the money market hedges are likely to be the same.

Another possibility is to do nothing at this time and wait six months to buy the DMs at whatever spot rate prevails at that time. This option makes the firm a speculator in foreign exchange and may result in a gain or a loss against using a futures contract. Using a futures contract means that the cost of the goods to the importer will be $2,100 more than today's price, but the cost is certain and can be passed along when the goods are distributed in the United States.

Unfortunately, managers do not always have the opportunity of arranging a hedge. Forward markets do not exist for many currencies, and even where they exist there may be difficulties. The supply of forward contracts may be inadequate or contracts may be unavailable for the precise period of time for which the cover is needed. Risk avoidance by borrowing the foreign currency may not be feasible, because of limitations on the use of local borrowing facilities or restrictions on the use of the foreign exchange market. Local bank credit is often scarce, particularly in developing countries and in situations where there is foreign exchange risk. Furthermore, local credit might be restricted for foreign exchange transactions.

Where hedging opportunities exist, the hedging mechanism to avoid a major loss due to exchange rate fluctuations may be applied to a variety of international business purposes such as protecting the value of foreign direct investments and portfolio investments. Other uses will be discussed in greater detail in the chapter on multinational financial management. In fact, virtually everyone who deals in or with foreign currencies may have a need for the hedging mechanism, although some scholars contend that habitual use of forward hedging may not be profitable.[3]

---

[3] Ian H. Giddy, "Why It Doesn't Pay to Make a Habit of Forward Hedging," *Euromoney*, December 1976, p. 23.

Covered interest arbitrage

Arbitrage is the simultaneous purchase and sale of an item in different markets to profit from unwarranted differences in prices. Arbitrage occurs in foreign exchange markets as well as in domestic securities and commodities markets. In a free market, a good such as money should have the same price wherever traded. Thus, interest rates should be the same around the world. Yet, as shown in Table 4–3, interest rates for

Table 4–3

Commercial bank lending rates to prime borrowers (at or near end of month)

	1978 Dec.	1979 Dec.	1980 Dec.	1981 Dec.	1982 June
United States	11.75	15.25	21.50	15.75	16.50
Canada	11.50	15.00	18.25	16.50	18.25
Japan	4.50	6.51	8.16	6.95	6.40
Australia	11.00	10.75	13.50	15.75	17.50
United Kingdom	13.50	18.00	15.00	14.50	12.50
Belgium	10.00	15.25	15.75	18.00	17.50
France	9.80	12.50	12.25	14.00	14.00
Germany	5.50	9.75	11.50	13.00	11.50
Italy	15.00	19.50	20.50	22.50	21.75
Netherlands	12.00	15.00	10.75	12.00	9.75
Austria	8.75	8.50	12.50	13.50	12.25
Denmark	10.00	13.75	13.75	15.00	15.00
Finland	7.87	9.06	9.83	9.84	9.06
Ireland	13.75	16.00	14.50	17.25	19.25
Norway	11.00	11.00	12.50	13.75	14.00
Spain	9.00	9.00	18.50	17.04	18.96
Sweden	8.50	10.75	11.75	13.50	12.50
Switzerland	5.00	5.00	5.75	8.00	7.00
Argentina	86.75	80.00	77.00	92.60	89.00
Brazil	64.34	59.60	96.45	138.09	141.04
Hong Kong	8.75	14.50	17.00	16.00	15.00
Korea	18.50	18.50	19.50	16.50	10.00
Mexico	17.50	19.00	24.25	31.81	54.01
New Zealand	9.75	11.75	13.00	13.00	13.00
Philippines	14.00	16.00	16.00	18.00	18.00
Singapore	7.65	9.50	13.60	11.83	10.98
South Africa	11.50	9.50	9.50	17.00	20.00
Venezuela	10.25	13.00	15.00	15.50	16.50

Source: Morgan Guaranty Trust Company, *World Financial Markets*, August 1982, p. 18.

loans or securities of similar risk and maturity vary among nations. According to the theory of interest rate parity, the differences in interest rates should be equal but opposite in sign to the forward exchange rate premium or discount between the currencies. Where there is an imparity in the various interest rates and forward exchange rate structures, interest rate arbitragers will be attracted to these situations and the process of arbitrage will bring these markets into parity. The arbitrager who seeks out the highest interest rates will always hedge in the forward market. Such capital flows are therefore "covered" or hedged arbitrage, rather than pure speculation.[4]

As an example of covered interest arbitrage, let us assume that U.K. Treasury bills with three-month maturity are selling to yield investors 12 percent per annum whereas comparable U.S. Treasury bills yield 14 percent. Under the interest parity theory and in normal markets, the forward premium rate of the pound would be 2 percent per annum. But let us assume that an imparity exists and that the three-month discount rate for the pound is 1 percent instead of 2 percent. An opportunity exists, therefore, for taking advantage of the higher U.S. interest rates without risk of losing the higher interest through foreign exchange fluctuations.

The arbitrager in London would sell British pounds for U.S. dollars at the spot rate and simultaneously cover the exchange exposure by entering into a three-month forward contract to purchase pounds in the amount of principal and interest. Then the arbitrager would purchase U.S. Treasury bills in the United States, wait 90 days for maturity, collect principal and interest, and exercise the forward contract in pounds. The transaction looks as follows:

Spot market	*Forward market*
Buy 200,000 U.S. dollars @ £.5740 per $ at a cost of £114,800	Sell U.S. $207,000—90-day futures ($200,000 principal + $7,000 90-day interest) @ £.5730 per $ to receive £118,611
Invest U.S. $200,000 in U.S. Treasury bills @ 14 percent	

90 days later:

Collect principal ($200,000) and interest ($7,000) on U.S. Treasury bills	Deliver U.S. $207,000 against forward contract	
	Receive	£118,611
	Original cost	£114,800
	Profit on transaction	£3,811

On an annual basis, these funds earned a return of 13.28 percent as compared to the 12 percent that could have been earned on U.K. Treasury bills.

Where foreign exchange and capital markets between two currency areas are open, a strong link exists between the short-term interest rates prevailing in the two areas and the foreign exchange discount or premium rates. At equilibrium, the currency of the lower-interest-rate coun-

---

[4] See Houston H. Stokes and Hugh Neuberger, "Interest Arbitrage, Forward Speculation and the Determination of the Forward Exchange Rate," *Columbia Journal of World Business*, Winter 1979, pp. 86–98.

try would be selling at a forward-rate premium in terms of the higher-interest-rate country's currency. The difference in interest rates between two countries should equal the spread between the forward and spot rates.

Swapping currencies

The currency swap is frequently used as a hedge where the use of forward or money markets is not feasible. Fundamentally, the swap is an alternative method by which a company can raise overseas finances without paying the currency premium. As an example, two companies, one in the United Kingdom and the other in the United States, each has a financing requirement in the other's country and each has surplus domestic cash. A swap is achieved by the parties selling their domestic cash to each other and simultaneously entering into an agreement to reverse the sales at some future date. In practice, a swap is entered into by the two parent companies who then lend the funds acquired to their respective overseas subsidiaries. For exchange control and tax reasons, underlying nominal interest rates are agreed upon at the outset. Either a floating rate basis can be adopted, or the interest rates can be fixed for the term of the swap.

The swap is a hedge in the sense that a foreign currency liability is matched by a similar foreign currency asset. Furthermore, neither loan requires the approval of any governmental agency regulating the use of credit for investment purposes. Another advantage of the swap is that the cost of funds can be cheaper than funds from alternative sources. Also, the swap may be one of the few sources open to nonresident companies for securing the use of foreign exchange over a period of time at a fixed rate.

A number of variations may occur on the basic swap transaction, including the use of foreign finance subsidiaries and triangular arrangements—say, between a U.K. firm and a French firm, each with subsidiaries in Brazil. Also, swap arrangements can include a maintenance of parity agreement in case the spot rates vary greatly. In such cases, the lenders may agree to bring the principal sums back to the new parity. In any event, the basic feature of repayment in the same currency as the loan will prevail.

A company wishing to use a swap arrangement will need, of course, to find another company with complementary financing needs. International banks or investment firms have become active in arranging such swaps because of their extensive worldwide connections.

A *credit swap* is more sophisticated than the currency swap and has become widely used, particularly where local credit is not available and where there is no forward exchange market. A credit swap is an exchange of currencies between a company and a bank (frequently a central bank) of a foreign country which is to be reversed by agreement at a later date. Such credit swaps have been common in Brazil. An American firm may deposit U.S. dollars with the Central Bank of Brazil and receive cruzeiros at the prevailing official rate. Although the cruzeiros may fall in value in relation to the U.S. dollar, the U.S. firm is only obligated to repay the cruzeiro amount it originally received. After repayment, the original deposit in U.S. dollars will be returned.

Why should the two parties engage in such a transaction? The motive of the Central Bank is that it receives use of the U.S. dollars interest-free. The U.S. firm has the advantage that it recovers the original dollar principal regardless of what happens to the value of the cruzeiro during the period of the arrangement. The basic attraction of the credit swap is the ability to minimize the risk and the cost of financing operations in a weak-currency country.

Outright speculation

Foreign exchange transactions by business firms are generally motivated by the desire to reduce risk. If risk is deliberately undertaken, the participant is a speculator, and foreign exchange markets—as is also true of commodity, interest futures, and other markets—provide a mechanism for outright speculation. Firms or individuals that have an established relationship with a commercial bank may be able to execute their speculative transactions through the foreign exchange department of a bank. For other speculators, the futures markets such as the IMM are more realistic options. Furthermore, the futures market allows participants to operate on *margin*, that is, without depositing the full value of the transaction.

Whichever market is used, if the foreign currency is expected to appreciate against the local currency (say, U.S. dollars), the speculator will want to buy the foreign currency, or go long. Conversely, if the expectation is that the foreign currency will depreciate, the speculator will want to sell the foreign currency, or go short.

The standard contract on the IMM for German marks is 125,000 DMs. On April 9, 1981, the June 1981 contract was quoted at $.46900. The speculator anticipated that the June 1981 price would depreciate and went short by selling a contract at that price. On April 23, 1981, the price for the June 1981 contract declined to $.46220 and the speculator bought a contract to close out the short position. The gain was $850 (125,000 × $.0068) minus a commission of $54. In other words, a change of U.S. $.01 in the price of the DM produces a gain or a loss of $1,250 per contract. In a later case, the speculator expected the DM to appreciate and on June 19, 1981, went long by buying a September 1981 contract at $.4279 for the

DM. But the DM depreciated and the speculator closed out the contract on June 25, 1981, by selling a future contract at $.4227, having a loss of $650 plus $54 in commissions.

THE ACTORS

Most of the principal actors or participants in the foreign exchange markets have already been mentioned. The importer or exporter uses the markets to convert currencies and to reduce the risk of foreign exchange fluctuations as they affect accounts receivable or payable. Firms engaged in multinational operations use the markets in connection with trading activities, as well as to hedge money flows such as expected repatriation of foreign currency profits or to reduce the risk of devaluation affecting assets held in foreign currencies. Business firms also engage in covered interest arbitrage to increase earnings on liquid funds. Still another set of actors are the arbitragers and the speculators.

Commercial banks actually make the foreign exchange market but usually claim that they participate in it only on behalf of business clients. The record shows that commercial banks have also participated on their own account, with only the extreme cases of losses becoming publicly known. Two well-publicized cases of bank failures attributed to foreign exchange speculation are that of the German Herstatt bank and that of the Franklin National Bank of New York, both in 1974.[5]

The other major participants are the central banks of countries. These government institutions frequently intervene in the foreign exchange markets for reasons of government policy. The central bank may want to keep the discount or premium on its currency within a certain range and may sell or buy currencies to achieve this goal. For example, in the three months ended April 30, 1980, the world's central banks intervened in foreign exchange markets with a near-record as of that time of purchases and sales totaling $37 billion. In that period, the U.S. dollar came under heavy selling pressure because of declining U.S. interest rates and political turmoil in Iran and other countries. To support the international value of the dollar, the Federal Reserve System of the United States participated heavily in the foreign exchange markets by buying dollars with German marks and Swiss and French francs. Also during the period and under an agreement among the central banks, the Federal Reserve System and central banks in Japan, West Germany, and Switzerland and foreign exchange brokers bought Japanese yen to avoid an excessive decline in its value.[6]

---

[5] Robert Z. Aliber, "International Banking: Growth and Regulation," *Columbia Journal of World Business*, Winter 1975, pp. 9–16.

[6] *The Wall Street Journal*, June 3, 1980.

Because of the floating rate system, to be discussed in the next chapter, central banks of the various industrialized countries have been intervening in cooperation with each other to smooth fluctuations in foreign exchange markets, and to strengthen and defend the international money system. Central banks on occasion offer large swap facilities to each other on a formal or ad hoc basis; that is, banks agree to lend their currencies to each other with the understanding that the original transactions will be later reversed. In this fashion, one central bank obtains large amounts of another country's currency.

FORECASTING FOREIGN EXCHANGE RATES

Are changes in exchange rates predictable on a relatively consistent basis? With fluctuating exchange rates a major cause of uncertainty in international business (see Figure 4–1), this question is extremely important for international business participants. On the one hand, many aca-

Figure 4—1

Effective exchange rates, 1977–1981 (weekly averages, ending June 1977 = 100)

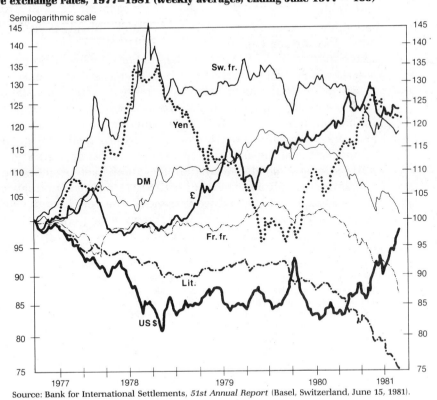

Source: Bank for International Settlements, *51st Annual Report* (Basel, Switzerland, June 15, 1981).

demic scholars claim to have demonstrated that the foreign exchange market is an "efficient" market where the forward markets are "unbiased" predictors of future spot exchange rates, and because anticipations of future exchange rate changes are reflected in spot and forward rates, there can be no gain from forecasting.[7] A directly opposing answer is implicit in the reality that numerous banks and specialized forecasting services have established foreign exchange forecasting services and that a sizable number of the services were beating the forward rate more than 50 percent of the time—far too often to be explained by chance alone.

The efficient market view

The efficient market view argues that prices (i.e., exchange rates) are determined by the expected rather than by the current demand and supply of a given currency. If competition exists and transaction costs are low, prices tend to respond rapidly to new information in such a way that profitable speculation opportunities are quickly bid away. According to this view, recent theory and empirical research demonstrates that the foreign exchange market fulfills the conditions of an efficient market. Exchange rate forecasting, therefore, cannot consistently beat the market forecast and "for those who do not have privileged access to new information, there is little value in trying to gain by buying or selling in the spot or forward markets."[8]

An opposing scholarly view challenges both the logic and the empirical tests of the efficient market position. It argues that because "market participants have diverse opinions about future events, speculative markets will approach full efficiency in the long run but can never reflect all information in the short run."[9] It questions the empirical results of efficient market research on grounds of statistical methodology and the reasonableness of the standard for testing forecasting accuracy.

The strongest challenge to the efficient market position, however, comes from recently available tests of the 1974 to 1979 performance of the leading foreign exchange advisory services. The Levich study calculates that anyone betting consistently with the numbers published by the top services could have earned as much as a 33 percent return on currency trading.[10]

---

[7] There is a vast literature on this subject. See Richard M. Levich, "The Efficiency of Markets for Foreign Exchange: A Review and Extension," in *International Financial Management,* ed. Donald R. Lessard (Boston: Warren, Gorham, & Lamont, 1979), pp. 243–76; Steven W. Kohlhagen, *The Behavior of Foreign Exchange Markets: A Critical Survey of the Empirical Literature* (New York: N.Y.U. Series in Finance and Economics, 1978).

[8] Ian H. Giddy, "Exchange Risk, Forecasting and Market Efficiency," Research Working Paper No. 266A, Columbia School of Business, July 1979, pp. 3–4.

[9] Levich, "Efficiency of Markets for Foreign Exchange," p. 251.

[10] Richard M. Levich, as quoted in *Business Week,* June 2, 1980. See also Richard M. Levich, "Are Forward Exchange Rates Unbiased Predictors of Future Spot Rates?" *Columbia Journal of World Business,* Winter 1979, pp. 49–61.

The forecasting services

The forecasting services use two types of forecasting techniques: judgmental and econometric models.[11] The judgmental forecasters make projections based on a detailed analysis of the economies of individual countries. They analyze economic indicators such as trade data and gross national product; political factors such as a forthcoming national election; technical factors such as potential intervention by the central bank, and psychological factors that might be called "a feel for the market."

The econometric modelers use equation-based forecasts with some judgment overlay. Specific models have been developed for individual countries that attempt to incorporate the fundamental forces on which exchange rates depend: inflation, industrial production, trade flows, and capital flows. The method is equation based, with judgment coming in when the results of the equations appear to be unreasonable.

Economic theories of exchange-rate determination

In considering the issue of foreign exchange forecasting, the international manager will find useful a familiarity with the basic economic theories that relate to exchange-rate determination. These include the purchasing power parity, the "Fisher effect," and interest rate parity theories.

The theory of purchasing power parity (PPP) holds that if the spot rates of two currencies are in equilibrium, differences between the two countries in rates of inflation tend to be offset by opposite changes in the spot rate.[12] In other words, the currency of the country with the higher rate of inflation will tend to depreciate as an offset to the loss in purchasing power. Thus, if Brazil is experiencing a rate of inflation of 50 percent over a year and the United States has a 10 percent inflation rate over the same period, the PPP theory predicts that the cruzeiro will decrease in value relative to the U.S. dollar by 40 percent over the period. The logic is that exchange rates will change to keep purchasing power equal in the two currencies, and on this premise all that is needed to forecast exchange rate changes is a forecast of comparative inflation rates.

The *Fisher effect*, based on a proposition advanced by Irving Fisher in his classic economic work *The Theory of Interest* (1930), holds that nominal interest rates in each country are equal to the required real return to the investor plus the expected rate of inflation. In foreign exchange mar-

---

[11] See *Euromoney,* August 1978, pp. 13–45, and *Euromoney,* August 1979, pp. 32–61, for a survey and evaluation of the foreign exchange advisory services as of those dates.

[12] The purchasing power theorem was first proposed and tested by Gustav Cassel in "The Present Situation of the Foreign Exchanges," *Economic Journal* 26 (1916); pp. 319–23, and in subsequent articles and books.

kets, therefore, spot exchange rates should change in an equal but opposite direction to the differences in interest rates between the countries. In other words, the effective rate of return from foreign investment after allowing for exchange risk is seen by investors as equal to the rate from local investment. If this were not so, the argument goes, then sums would flow to the more attractive market and away from the other until the changed supply of investment altered interest rates sufficiently to bring the effective rates into equilibrium.

The theory of interest-rate parity states that except for transaction costs a difference in national interest rates for securities of similar risk and maturity should be equal but opposite in sign to the forward exchange-rate discount or premium for the foreign currency. The rationale of this theory is that covered interest arbitrage will eliminate interest-rate differentials between equivalent interest-bearing securities denominated in different currencies.

All of the theories are interrelated.[13] Under conditions of a free market, the expected rate of change in the spot exchange rate, differential national inflation and interest rates, and the forward exchange discount or premium are all directly proportional to each other and mutually determined. A change in one of these variables tends to change all of them with a feedback on the variable that changes first.

Furthermore, a number of real world factors limit the ability of markets in equalizing prices among countries through exchange rates. Some of these factors are as follows:

1. Tariffs and trade controls isolate national markets, narrowing the scope for competitive forces to produce price equality. For example, agriculture imports are restricted by many countries to protect domestic farm incomes.

2. Many goods and a broad range of services do not enter international commerce—for example, bricks (high transport costs) and housing services.

3. Certain industries have monopoly power based on technological know-how, the introduction of new products, or the country's resource endowment.

4. Nonprice factors—product quality, delivery time, credit terms, and after-sales service—are more important than price competition in certain industries.

5. Existence of long-term contracts, imperfect knowledge, and sluggish responses ensure that exchange rate offsets to price movements occur only gradually.

---

[13] Ian H. Giddy, "An Integrated Theory of Exchange Rate Equilibrium," *Journal of Financial and Quantitative Analysis*, December 1976, pp. 883–92.

While there is much merit in the various economic theories, any simple formula is doomed to failure in an imperfect and changing world. This does not mean that PPP, for example, is not a useful long-term equilibrium model or that a more-complex model cannot be a useful forecasting tool. But the forecaster in international business cannot avoid the multiplicity of noneconomic as well as economic factors that might determine exchange-rate changes. While economic analysis can suggest what an exchange rate should be at any point in time, few governments allow their exchange rates to fluctuate freely. In most cases the decision to let exchange rates fluctuate without intervention will be influenced by a variety of local political, bureaucratic, and social pressures. Consequently, for short-term forecasting, the analyst must also become familiar with the views and behavior patterns of government decision makers. Forecasting involves timing of changes as well as amounts. And timing is extremely important because the cost of hedging against foreign exchange risk is high and increases with the time for which the cover is sought.

THE INTERNATIONAL MONEY MARKET

A firm may avoid foreign exchange risk by insisting that all of its transactions be denominated in its home-country currency. In this way, the firm can be sure that its money inflows and outflows will not fluctuate with changes in foreign exchange rates. When the firm's home-country currency is one of the major convertible currencies, parties dealing with the firm can secure the currency through the international money markets.

The international money market parallels the foreign exchange market. It is located in the same centers as its foreign exchange counterpart, but the market has few currencies in which to operate. Only those currencies for which forward exchange markets exist and that are easily convertible and available in sufficient quantity can be taken as deposits or placed as loans. In the currencies in which it is operative, the international money market channels money in and out of domestic markets. Regulations permitting, it also acts as a provider and user of funds for many parties that might not naturally be involved in foreign exchange. These include governments and corporations looking for long-term financing, and individual investors whose opportunities are severely constrained in the local national market.

The Eurocurrency market

The principal international money market is the Eurocurrency market. Eurocurrencies are monies traded outside the country of their origin.

Eurodollars are U.S. dollar deposits at either non-U.S. banks or branches of U.S. banks located outside the United States. Eurosterlings are sterling deposits outside the United Kingdom. Other Eurocurrencies are German marks, Swiss francs, Dutch guilders, Japanese yen, and French francs. They all share the Eurodollar's main characteristic. They are national currencies deposited outside their own borders.

The Eurodollar was the first of the Eurocurrencies and is still much the largest, accounting for over 75 percent of the whole market.[14] As its name implies, it was originally an American dollar held in Europe, and the Euro prefix has been subsequently attached to the other currencies even though the Euromarket no longer is exclusively in Europe. In 1969, an Asian version of the Eurodollar, called the Asian dollar, developed in Singapore when local officials permitted Singapore banks to have accounts not subject to exchange controls and exempt from a withholding tax on interest income to nonresidents.[15]

Why do these markets exist? The simple answer is government regulations. Eurocurrency markets have not been subject to regulatory restrictions, whereas national governments have imposed a host of restrictions on lenders and borrowers, including interest rate ceilings, reserve requirements, taxes, and the like. These national restrictions involve a cost and have caused lenders to seek out opportunities abroad where they could earn higher yields. Borrowers, in turn, have tapped the Euromarkets because monies in the local markets were either unavailable or could be obtained only on unattractive terms.

Paradoxically, it is the Soviet Union that gets credit for accidentally starting what is now characterized as the biggest and most efficient form of capitalist finance. After World War II, the Eastern European countries and the Soviet Union preferred to deposit the U.S. dollar balances they had earned through trade somewhere other than in the United States, for fear that these funds would be attached by U.S. residents with claims against the Communist governments. The dollar balances were deposited with Soviet banks in the West, such as the Narodny Bank in London, and in turn reloaned to other European banks.

These events demonstrated the feasibility of avoiding national controls by keeping a currency in a bank outside its country of origin, and the market expanded rapidly as other parties gradually discovered this method of securing higher yields and less restricted borrowing. In a relatively short time, the Eurocurrency market became a highly efficient form of financial intermediation that has attracted depositors and borrowers away from purely domestic financial institutions. In the 1970s, the OPEC (Oil Producing and Exporting Countries) members, in particular,

---

[14] Morgan Guaranty Trust Company, *World Financial Markets*, August 1981, p. 9.

[15] See A. Bhattacharya, *The Asian Dollar Market* (New York: Praeger Publishers, 1977).

added greatly to the size of the markets with their huge dollar surpluses received through the steep increases in oil prices.

The Eurocurrency market has expanded more than fortyfold from 1964 to 1980 and tenfold over the 1970–80 decade to an estimated $760 billion on a net basis—i.e., excluding interbank redeposits (see Table 4–4). The Asian dollar market has grown since 1968 to more than 100 licensed operators with total assets and liabilities of about $40 billion.[16]

Table 4—4

Growth of the Eurocurrency market (U.S. $ billions)*

End of period	Estimated market size	
	Gross†	Net‡
1965	24	17
1970	113	65
1975	485	255
1976	595	320
1977	740	390
1978	950	495
1979	1,220	615
1980	1,515	760
1981	1,800	890
1982 (March)	1,910	915

* Based on foreign currency liabilities and claims of banks in major European countries, the Bahamas, Bahrain, Cayman Islands, Netherland Antilles, Panama, Canada, Japan, Hong Kong, and Singapore.
† All foreign currency liabilities to residents and nonresidents, banks and nonbanks.
‡ Excludes interbank redeposits within the reporting area.
Source: Morgan Guaranty Trust Company, *World Financial Markets*, August 1982, p. 13.

The concept of an unregulated interbank deposit market in an international financial center is not new. What is historically unique is the extent to which the Euromarkets have become a critical structural element for hundreds of banks throughout the world, most of which did no business outside their borders until the late 1960s. The reason is that the modern Eurocurrency market "represents the highly efficient response of international banks to the desires of investors for high-yielding, safe

---

[16] *The Wall Street Journal*, March 26, 1980.

and liquid investments, and the needs of businesses (and governments) for low cost funds with a high degree of assured availability."[17]

The Euromarkets now provide a large pool of funds with about 70 percent of total lending as bank credits of generally short- and medium-term maturities and the rest as bonds of longer maturities such as 10 or 20 years.[18] Bank credits carry a variable rate of interest that is by convention tied to LIBOR, the London interbank offer rate. The actual rate is often a margin over LIBOR, the amount of the spread reflecting the credit rating of the borrower. The market is partly an interbank market and partly a market for commercial customers who need funds for financing trade or investment. The interbank transactions represent the difference between the gross and the net estimates of the market size in Table 4–4. Many of the developing countries have borrowed in the Eurocurrency markets rather than from the International Monetary Fund, because, as will be discussed in the next chapter, the IMF generally imposes stringent national economic policy conditions to be fulfilled by borrowers.

The rapid growth of the Eurocurrency market during the 1970s has made it the focus of controversy as to the wisdom of imposing some sort of controls. Its mammoth size, its rate of growth, and its freedom from national regulation have caused concern by several nations as to the influence of the market on worldwide inflation and exchange rate instability. The argument has been made that Eurocurrency markets can undermine or complicate national monetary policies in ways that tend to worsen inflation or contribute to worldwide inflationary pressures by increasing the flow of credit to deficit countries and by impeding the adjustment of balance-of-payments deficits. The views range from the position that the market is fundamentally out of control to the position, at the other extreme, that any attempt to tamper with the market would run the risk of seriously upsetting the recycling mechanism and driving Eurocurrency market business into other nonbank channels.

As of the early 1980s, the controversy over controls continues and several plans for control were being debated.[19]

International banking

Over the last two decades, international banking has expanded dramatically. In 1960, there were only 8 U.S. banks with branches abroad that numbered only 131. In 1978, 151 U.S. banks maintained more than 1,150 banking outlets in foreign countries. Conversely, foreigners operated

---

[17] Gunter Dufey and Ian H. Giddy, *Credit Creation and the Growth of the Eurodollar Market,* Research Paper no. 127 (New York: Columbia Graduate School of Business, 1976; see also Yoon S. Park, *The Euro-bond Market: Function and Structure* (New York: Praeger Publishers, 1974).

[18] *The Economist,* March 24, 1979, pp. 25–26.

[19] See *IMF Survey,* February 18, 1980, pp. 51–52.

about 410 subsidiaries, affiliates, and branches in the United States. In the same year, worldwide there were some 4,375 banking operations with direct or majority foreign ownership.[20]

Between 1970 and 1976, the top 10 U.S. commercial banks achieved a 30 percent annual rate of growth in overseas earnings. From just $167 million, or 17.5 percent of total profits, in 1970 their overseas contributions jumped to $825 million, over half of total profits. In 1977 and 1978, however, overseas earnings grew by only 10 percent.[21] The slowdown after 1976 of the U.S. banks reflects in part the competitive response of non-U.S. banks in the international field. There were four American banks in the world's top 10 of 1970 and only two in 1979; and the American banks' share of total deposits of the world's top 100 banks fell from 29 to 15 percent over the 1970 to 1979 period.[22]

As international business operations increased in size and number, bankers followed their domestic customers overseas to meet their needs better. In order to become truly "international," rather than just in the international loan business, many banks developed chains of foreign branches or acquired foreign banks.

Another major stimulant to international banking was the growth of the Eurocurrency market as a large and unregulated source of funds. This was particularly important to U.S. banks during the 1960s when various U.S. controls forced U.S. firms to seek assistance from their banks in securing loans overseas.

Still another growth factor has been the ever increasing demands for funds from the developing countries. If private banks' had not been available to supply credit, it is unclear how petroleum-dependent countries would have financed their foreign currency needs after the phenomenal escalation of international petroleum prices beginning in the early 1970s. As of 1982, non-OPEC developing countries had outstanding obligations of $400 billion, a large portion of which was to private foreign banks.[23]

The Edge Act Corporation is a feature of U.S. banking with special importance in international banking. Under Federal Reserve Board regulations, U.S. banks are not permitted to engage in activities abroad that are not permitted in the United States. However, the Edge Act passed in 1919 allows U.S. banks through an Edge Act Corporation to compete abroad more effectively against local banks by permitting them to engage in any activities allowed banks in the specific local market. In practice, the Federal Reserve has required that the activities must be closely related to banking. The issuance of general insurance, for example, has not been allowed. Nevertheless, the greater scope for both domestic and

---

[20] *The Wall Street Journal,* September 23, 1980.
[21] *The Economist,* March 31, 1979.
[22] *The Economist,* August 30, 1980.
[23] *New York Times,* August 10, 1982, p. A19.

international activities by U.S. banks through Edge Act corporations has resulted in a great expansion of such subsidiaries, particularly since 1978 when the scope of Edge Act corporations was liberalized by the International Banking Act of 1978.[24]

International banking patterns entered a new phase in the 1980s, characterized both by high exposure to loan defaults by foreign governments and by increased competition. During the late 1970s, the international banks had greatly increased their loans to the developing countries. With a subsequent slowing down of the world economy, this exposure became critical because many countries with large outstanding loan obligations were having severe difficulties in earning enough foreign exchange to service their debts. In 1982, for example, both Mexico and Poland had to reschedule massive foreign debts or go into default.

Increased competition among banks resulted from several new factors. The OPEC countries had been learning to handle their own money and were breaking away from their earlier dependence on Western international banks. Furthermore, their contributions to the growth of the Euromarket had declined because a weakening international market for petroleum sales had reduced the earnings of the OPEC countries. Also, other bank customers were shopping around and no longer assuming that their traditional banker would meet all their needs. Another factor was the growth of a wide range of "near-banking" activities—for example, leasing and advisory functions.

SUMMARY

The foreign exchange market is a worldwide network of traders, mainly working for commercial banks, linked by rapid means of communications. The market provides the mechanism for converting the currency of one country into the currency of another. It also provides a means of reducing foreign exchange risk.

International business firms are among the major users of foreign exchange markets. Other major participants are central banks, which frequently intervene in the markets for reasons of government policy.

Because exchange rates fluctuate, strong interest has developed in the feasibility of and techniques for forecasting them. Underlying this effort to forecast are various economic theories of exchange-rate determination.

The international money market parallels the foreign exchange market. The restrictions imposed by nations on domestic banks have stimulated the emergence of the unregulated Eurocurrency market. This mar-

---

[24] James V. Houpt, *Foreign Ownership and the Performance of U.S. Banks* (Washington, D.C.: Federal Reserve Board, July 1980).

ket, together with the expanding international networks of national banks, has come to play a major role in international business activity.

EXERCISES AND DISCUSSION QUESTIONS

1. What is meant precisely by *spot* exchange rates? How do they differ from forward rates?

2. Assume that the buying rate for deutsche marks spot in New York is $0.4297, what would you expect the price of the U.S. dollar to be in West Germany? If the dollar were quoted in Germany at DM 2.50, how is the market supposed to react?

3. Does an opportunity for covered interest arbitrage exist in the following situation?
   a. The 180-day interest rate in the United States is 17 percent per annum.
   b. The 180-day interest rate in the United Kingdom is 13 percent per annum.
   c. The spot quotation for the British pound in the United States is $1.842.
   d. The 180-day forward quotation for the British pound in New York is $1.869.

4. How can an investor take advantage of the above situation? Ignore transaction costs.

5. If the Swiss franc is quoted at U.S. $0.4792 spot and U.S. $0.5018 for a 180-day forward contract, how much is the forward premium in percent per annum?

6. Why has the Eurocurrency market developed and grown so rapidly?

Chapter 5

The international monetary system

The international monetary system provides the institutional setting, the instruments, and the rules and procedures within which the foreign exchange markets operate. An ideal international system might be a world central bank and an international currency, but nations have not been willing to transfer their sovereign right to issue currency and to control their monetary system to an international agency. They do, however, recognize the mutual need for maintaining a workable system of international payments and have entered into various cooperative arrangements. These arrangements are continually changing. At the present stage of evolution, the international monetary system is described as a managed float system. This chapter explains how the current system works. It also provides some essential historical background and identifies some major issues for the future.

SOME HISTORY

The gold standard

In the days when foreign trade was limited to a few luxury goods imported from abroad, payments were settled one by one in gold and silver, according to the market price of these precious metals at the time the settlement took place. But as international transactions expanded dramatically in the 19th century, a better means of international payments had to be found. The solution could not infringe on the jealously guarded sovereign right of each nation to issue currency. The system had to be both "neutral," so that it would not affect the "free interplay of market forces," and "automatic," in order to escape manipulation by any national government. The monetary arrangement that emerged in response to this demand and spread rapidly came to be called the gold standard. It was an arrangement that evolved naturally rather than a system established by formal agreements among nations.

Under the gold standard, national currencies were linked to gold at a fixed parity, that is, each nation defined its currency unit as equal to the value of a certain weight of pure gold. From the common gold denominator, the value of any currency in units of any other was easily determined. The U.S. dollar, for example, was defined as containing 23.22 grains of fine gold. As there are 480 grains in a troy ounce, the implied price of an ounce of gold was $20.67 (480 ÷ 23.22) at which price the U.S. government freely bought and sold gold. The British pound was defined as containing approximately 113 grains of fine gold. The exchange rate for pounds to dollars, therefore, was £1 = $4.8665 (113 ÷ 23.22). This dollar amount was termed the par value of the pound.

Rates of exchange were not supposed to undergo major variations. Governments were expected to maintain the value of their currency equivalent to the declared gold content by standing ready to buy and sell gold in unlimited quantities. In this way, deficits or surpluses in a nation's external accounts gave rise to gold movements that in turn were supposed to trigger an automatic adjustment process. A continuing surplus in one country would increase that country's gold stock and hence its money supply, thus provoking a general price rise. The price rise would result in falling exports and rising imports until the surplus disappeared. In the case of a persistent deficit, the money supply would diminish, causing the reverse phenomenon.

The gold standard worked acceptably for a period of more than 40 years up to World War I. The success of the system is explained in large part by the general economic tranquility of the period. The world economy was not subjected to shocks as severe as World Wars I and II, the Great Depression of the 1930s, and the OPEC oil price escalation of 1973–74. Also, virtually all of today's developing countries were then colonies and no one paid much attention to the balance of payments between a colony and its metropolitan power. The gold standard applied almost exclusively to the major European powers and the United States. The period is remembered with great nostalgia by many people, and some influential economists and politicians continue to recommend that it be reinstated.

The economic disruptions of World War I ended the stability of exchange rates for currencies of major industrial nations and the gold standard was temporarily abandoned. Most currencies were allowed to fluctuate freely as the war ended. All attempts to restore the gold standard in the early 1920s were short-lived. By the end of the decade the severest recession in modern history was beginning and great financial turmoil prevailed throughout the Great Depression of the 1930s. The outbreak of World War II in late 1939 prevented any new efforts to reestablish a more orderly international monetary system. Not surprisingly, during World War II, most of the major trading currencies except the U.S. dollar lost their convertibility.[1]

After World War II the United States stood virtually alone as a holder of wealth and producer of goods. Recognizing the need to restructure the international monetary system, free-world representatives met at Bretton Woods, New Hampshire, in 1944 and agreed to establish a new monetary order centered around the International Monetary Fund (IMF) and the International Bank for Reconstruction and Development (World Bank).

Gold exchange standard 1944–1973

The Bretton Woods agreement adopted a fixed exchange-rate system called the gold exchange standard. Member governments agreed to fix the value of their currencies in terms of gold but were not required to exchange their currencies for gold. The U.S. dollar was the exception. It remained convertible into gold at the fixed rate of $35 an ounce.

All participating countries agreed to try to maintain the value of their currencies within 1 percent above or below the official parity by selling foreign exchange or gold as necessary. If the currency became too weak to defend, the country could devalue up to 10 percent without formal approval by the IMF. Any larger devaluation required prior IMF approval. Because parities could be adjusted, the system was also called the "adjustable peg" system.

---

[1] See Mordecai E. Kreinen, *International Economics,* 3rd ed. (New York: Harcourt Brace Jovanovich, 1979), pp. 161–65.

The IMF was established as a permanent institution for consultation and collaboration on international monetary problems. Its main objective was to promote exchange stability by maintaining orderly exchange arrangements among members. Members were pledged to eliminate foreign exchange restrictions. The IMF could also provide temporary assistance to countries that would give them an opportunity to correct maladjustments in their external accounts without resorting to measures destructive of national and international prosperity.

It is important to note that the emphasis in the original IMF articles of agreement was on facilitating world trade. The phenomenal expansion of foreign direct investment and multinational enterprises, which later came to place severe strains on the IMF system, was not foreseen.

When the fund opened its doors in March 1946, 40 countries were members. By 1982, IMF membership had grown to 143 nations. The only Eastern European countries that are IMF members are Yugoslavia (a founding member), Romania (joined in 1972), and Hungary (joined in 1982). The USSR and the socialist countries of Czechoslovakia, Poland, and Yugoslavia participated in the Bretton Woods conference. The USSR chose not to join. Czechoslovakia and Poland joined but shortly withdrew. The reasons advanced for the abstention of the Eastern European countries relate to the system of weighted voting that gives the United States a veto power in respect to important decisions, the requirement that members report their gold and foreign exchange holdings and keep part of them in the United States where the IMF is located, and the terms on which members are allowed access to IMF resources.[2]

The IMF was funded by each member subscribing to a quota. The original quotas reflected the relative economic status of the members in the early postwar period but the quotas have been revised several times since the war. Originally, a member country's quota had to be paid 25 percent in gold (the gold tranche) and 75 percent in the member's own currency. Since 1978 the 25 percent of the quota previously required in gold (now called reserve tranche) is subscribed to either in currencies acceptable to the IMF or in special drawing rights (SDRs) that are described below. A country's quota determines its voting power in the Fund and the amount of foreign exchange that the country can draw. At any time a member can freely borrow or purchase from the IMF foreign exchange up to the amount of its gold or reserve currency subscription. Any borrowing in excess of the reserve tranche must have Fund approval and may be used only for remedying the country's balance-of-payments difficulties. The IMF's leverage over member countries comes from its ability to grant or deny access to the Fund's resources beyond the reserve

---

[2] "Background Notes on the International Monetary Fund," *Development Dialogue* 2 (1980), p. 96.

tranche and from the fact that Fund membership is a prerequisite for joining the World Bank.

The main concerns of the Bretton Woods negotiators were the avoidance of competitive rate manipulation and the maintenance of stable exchange rates among the main trading currencies. Currency devaluation was envisaged as a last resort, to be approved by the IMF only in the cases of fundamental equilibrium and to be avoided if possible by the use of IMF credits. Adjustments in parities were not excluded, but stability through the fixed relationships to gold was the prime objective of the system.

The special status of the U.S. dollar at the end of World War II gave the United States a unique position within the system. The U.S. dollar was universally accepted as an international reserve currency, and it was freely convertible into gold upon request from foreign official agencies. As the standard of value for other currencies, the dollar could be revalued or devalued under IMF rules only by changes in its parity with gold. This in effect meant changing the price of gold for the entire system, but the relationship of the U.S. dollar to other currencies would remain the same. The responsibility of member nations to maintain the value of their currency within 1 percent above or below official parity did not apply to the United States because it was formally required to meet all offers from foreign central banks to buy or sell gold for dollars at the official price of $35 per ounce. The resulting fixed exchange-rate system of foreign currencies pegged to the dollar and the dollar pegged to gold worked unusually well for more than 20 years.

Breakdown of the fixed exchange-rate system

The formal demise of the fixed exchange-rate system occurred in 1973, but the breakdown of the system began much earlier. During the 1960s, three major and interrelated problems began to emerge. The most basic of these problems was the dramatic economic revival of Western Europe and Japan, resulting in a sharply reduced relative position of the United States in the world economy. The other two problems reflected structural weaknesses in the Bretton Woods arrangement. The system did not provide a means for controlling international liquidity by international agreement nor for correcting imbalances resulting from persistent surpluses in the payments position of individual countries.

The Bretton Woods system, in practice, depended on the hegemony of the United States. At the time of Bretton Woods, the United States was the most powerful of the nation-states. With a highly self-sufficient domestic economy, the United States appeared to be relatively safe from the repercussions of economic breakdowns elsewhere. So long as there was confidence in the U.S. dollar's unchanging value and the United States remained committed to its convertibility into gold, the system worked well with the dollar as the international key currency.

As the world economy recovered from World War II, international transactions expanded at a rapid rate. To lubricate the growing world economy, the monetary system needed to provide for an increase in the supply of international reserves. Unlike a central bank that has power to regulate a nation's money supply, the IMF had no similar power to meet growing international needs. For various reasons, the supply of gold was not increasing significantly and greater liquidity was mainly dependent upon more dollars being injected into the system.

During the 1950s, the United States was supplying international liquidity through a steady net outflow of dollars for economic aid, military expenditures, and private foreign direct investment. At the time, the reconstructed nations of Western Europe welcomed the increased supply of dollars as a means of replenishing their depleted international reserves. They were willing to hold dollars rather than turn them in for gold because dollars could earn income and gold could not and because there was confidence in the dollar holding its value. Thus, without formal international agreement, the United States had taken on the role of world banker. A crucial element, however, was that international liquidity was being determined by U.S. policies rather than by the needs of the system.

Although the net outflow of dollars was supplying liquidity, there was still general concern in the early postwar period about a liquidity shortage. This concern resulted after extended negotiations in the creation of a new international reserve asset by the IMF in the form of special drawing rights (SDRs). But even as the SDR arrangement was being developed, concern about a liquidity shortage was being replaced by fears of a dollar surplus.

Continuing U.S. balance-of-payments deficits grew to massive proportions by the end of the 1960s, and the U.S. dollar was losing its status as a safe asset. The loss of confidence in the dollar reflected both political and economic developments. The Vietnam war, which accounted for large dollar outflows, was unpopular in many foreign countries and revealed certain weaknesses in U.S. military power. On the economic front, the United States was experiencing inflation, recession, and a loss of competitiveness in exports. As confidence in the dollar steadily eroded, holders of big dollar reserves increasingly switched to gold. The U.S. gold stock dropped from U.S. $24 billion in 1948 to U.S. $15 billion in 1964 and U.S. $11 billion in 1971. Under the fixed exchange-rate system, the United States was forced to bear large adjustment costs by losing its gold reserves or changing the rules. The United States opted to change the rules.

In the world economy of the late 1960s, the U.S. dollar had become greatly overvalued in relation to the major currencies of a revitalized Europe, and U.S. exports were losing their competitiveness. Under the fixed exchange-rate system, with the dollar as the reserve currency, there was no easy way to secure a realignment of the dollar with other major currencies. While the United States was running persistent payments deficits, other countries such as West Germany and Japan were having persistent payments surpluses. The Bretton Woods system gave the IMF leverage for adjusting imbalances by nations experiencing payments deficits because such nations were likely to come to them for assistance. Surplus nations do not need IMF resources. Consequently, the IMF had no means of inducing such countries to resolve surplus imbalances. This asymmetry in the adjustment role of the IMF contributed to the erosion of the fixed exchange-rate system.

The beginning step toward the managed float system occurred in 1968 when the United States suspended the sale of gold except to official parties, and on August 15, 1971, the United States closed the gold window completely. A series of additional measures forced the other industrialized countries to revalue their currencies against the U.S. dollar and by March 1973 the system of fixed rates was abandoned and virtually every major currency was floating without much formal discipline remaining.[3]

The result of the move from fixed exchange rates to the managed float on the international value of the major currencies is shown in Figure 5–1.

A short-lived effort to secure greater exchange-rate stability was attempted in 1972 by six members of the European Economic Community plus the United Kingdom and Denmark, which were about to join the EEC, through the creation of the European Monetary Union (EMU). Member countries agreed to limit fluctuations among their currencies within a small band, but the group as a whole could fluctuate against other currencies. The EMU had limited success, but the continued desire for monetary stability among the European currencies eventually resulted in formation of the European Monetary System (EMS) in 1979.

Special drawing rights

Special drawing rights continue to be a part of the system. The SDR is an international reserve asset, sometimes called paper gold, distributed by the IMF to member countries in quantities and at times agreed upon by IMF members. SDRs are used for official transactions among IMF member countries in a variety of ways—for example, to obtain a specific currency, for settlement of a financial obligation, or as security for a loan. They may also be used by member countries in transactions with the Fund. The SDR is the unit of account for all purposes of the Fund. Outside the Fund, it is widely used as a unit of account in private con-

---

[3] See Charles N. Henning, William Pigott, and Robert Hanley Scott, *International Financial Management* (New York: McGraw-Hill, 1978), pp. 129–39.

Figure 5–1

Effective exchange rates (index 1970 = 100)

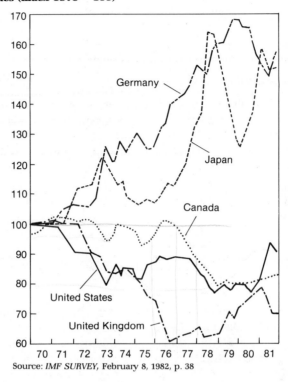

Source: *IMF SURVEY*, February 8, 1982, p. 38

tracts such as SDR-denominated deposits with commercial banks. A number of the Fund's member countries peg their currency to the SDR.

When first created, the SDR was linked to gold. But since 1974 its value is based on the daily market exchange rates of a basket of currencies. The basket in 1981 consisted of the currencies of the five members with the largest share in world exports—the U.S. dollar, deutsch mark, pound sterling, French franc, and Japanese yen.

The first allocation of SDRs, distributed to member countries in proportion to their quotas, totaled SDR 9.3 billion, or about U.S. $12 billion, based on the average rate in 1980 of SDR 1 = U.S. $1.30. The cumulative total allocations as of January 1, 1981, reached SDR 21.3 billion, or U.S. $27.7 billion. Although it is the declared intention of member countries that the SDR should eventually become the principal reserve asset in the international monetary system, the SDRs in existence as of 1981 still accounted for only 7 percent of total international reserves, excluding gold holdings.

THE MANAGED FLOAT SYSTEM

In April 1976, the IMF board of governors approved a number of amendments to the IMF Articles of Agreement that legitimized the changes that had occurred, and the international monetary system formally moved into the present managed float system.

Fixed versus flexible exchange rates

The relative merits of fixed exchange rates, flexible or floating exchange rates, or a compromise between them has long been a matter of policy debate in the international monetary arena.[4] Although a compromise solution evolved from the crisis of the early 1970s, the policy debate continues. The arguments pro and con are both theoretical and empirical. They focus heavily on the macroeconomic issue of how easy or hard it is for a country to stabilize its domestic economy under one or another foreign exchange regime. From the standpoint of international business, two key issues are how well the system facilitates the expansion of international trade and investment (the risk issue) and the relative ease or difficulty of managing international operations under the system.

From the macroeconomic standpoint, the argument that flexible rates weaken the pressure on countries to make necessary domestic adjustments appears to have some validity. The related argument that flexible rates breed destabilizing speculation, according to one authority, "is not persuasive on either theoretical or empirical grounds."[5] The argument that flexible exchange rates expose traders and investors to greater risks and uncertainties and thereby deter international business activity has not been supported by the empirical evidence of continued expansion in this activity after the demise of the fixed-rate system.

The managerial problem is somewhat different under the flexible as opposed to the fixed exchange-rate system but probably more manageable under flexible rates. Under both systems, changes in exchange values occurred. But under the fixed system, changes were generally abrupt and large. The fixed system often gave business firms a false sense of security and caused a neglect in exchange-rate surveillance and forecasting. Under the flexible system, business firms have become more alert to the existence of foreign exchange risk and better prepared to anticipate and adjust to changes in foreign exchange rates.

The managed float compromise

The compromise that emerged in the late 1970s as the international monetary regime was a mixture of fixed and floating rates called a man-

[4] See Herbert G. Grubel, *International Economics*, rev. ed. (Homewood, Ill.: Richard D. Irwin, 1981), pp. 499–511.

[5] Peter H. Lindert and Charles P. Kindleberger, *International Economics*, 7th ed. (Homewood, Ill.: Richard D. Irwin, 1982), p. 398.

aged float. In theory, floating means that the price of currency A in terms of currency B is determined by the daily market forces of supply and demand, not fixed by government fiat. In practice, however, most of the currencies of the smaller economies are fixed in the sense that they are tied to another currency, often that of their major trading partner. The currencies of the bigger economies are floating against each other, and most of the trade and investment flows are conducted across floating exchanges. Even among the smaller nations whose currencies are pegged, most of their transactions are with countries whose currencies are floating.

Among the pegged currencies, the largest number of small countries are tied to the U.S. dollar. Another large group tie their currencies to the SDR, and much of French West Africa remains linked to the French franc.[6] Some countries, mainly in Latin America, tie their currency to the U.S. dollar but adjust the exchange rate frequently according to a set of indicators. Brazil, for example, has a mini-devaluation policy of frequent small adjustments that are intended to compensate for the difference between Brazil and U.S. inflation rates.

Even among the so-called floaters, currency ties exist. Eight members of the European Community formed the European Monetary System in 1979 and fix their currency values in relation to each other, although they float en bloc against the rest of the world. This left, as of 1981, the U.S. dollar, Japanese yen, British pound, Swiss franc, and Canadian dollar as the principal untied currencies. But none of the floating rates are freely determined by supply and demand conditions in foreign exchange markets. As discussed in Chapter 4, central banks frequently intervene unilaterally to prevent their currency from moving up or down to a degree that is considered excessive or undesirable. They also intervene in cooperation with each other to smooth fluctuations in foreign exchange markets. At times the interventions can be massive, but there is no longer an official commitment to keep the fluctuations within fixed limits.

The compromise managed float differs from a free float system in two significant respects. First, under a free float the exchange rate of a specific currency is presumed to settle at or around its equilibrium value, that is, a value that reflects underlying economic factors and that would bring about a balance in that country's external accounts. In a managed float, no such presumption can be made. Intervention may have driven the exchange rate away from rather than to the equilibrium rate. Second, under a free float, a nation does not accumulate nor need international reserves because the exchange rate will always clear the market. By contrast, a country that is managing its currency needs reserves to sell for its own currency when moderating a decline in the exchange rate, and it

---

[6] The exchange-rate regime to which a specific country adheres is regularly reported by the IMF in the monthly *IMF Survey* and in its *Annual Report*.

accumulates reserves when selling its own currency to moderate an increase in the currency's value.

The currencies of the centrally planned or socialist countries remain inconvertible and outside the managed float system. International business transactions with these countries generally require barter arrangements so that money payments are not needed, or triangular deals. Under a triangular arrangement, the party scheduled to receive payment in a nonconvertible currency sells this asset, usually at a discount, to another party that needs the currency to buy goods or services from the particular country. In fact, a substantial banking business has developed in Vienna, Austria, for working out such triangular or multilateral deals.

Role of the IMF

In the managed float system, the role of the IMF has become greatly reduced. Member nations are required to notify the IMF of the exchange arrangements they are following and of any changes made in these arrangements. Also, as of 1978, the IMF is charged with surveillance of the floating system, but in practice, this surveillance of the major currencies has been weak. Members are supposed to refrain from "dirty floating," but dirty floating is ill defined. It does not mean just interference with the market but an attempt to steal some unfair advantage by doing so. Thus, a country floats "dirtily" if it attempts to hold down a strong currency in order to keep its exports competitive, when all objective analysis would suggest that the currency is undervalued.

The IMF is weak because it lacks sanctions to apply against strong economies. It has continued its role as a temporary supplier of resources to weak countries, and when a weak country ends up on its doorstep, the IMF can have considerable influence in getting the country to make policy changes. But strong countries do not need help from the IMF. Thus the IMF is stuck with the asymmetry of obligation that confirms the old rule of one law for the rich and another for the poor. The United States needs foreign currency only to support the dollar but not to finance its deficits because dollars are still a reserve asset. Thus the IMF's hold over its largest member is weak, even when the United States is in deficit.

The resources of the IMF for assisting members to meet their international needs have been greatly expanded since the Fund was established, but they are still relatively small. For short-term assistance, members can draw upon the reserve tranche previously mentioned and four additional credit tranches that require increasingly severe justifications. Under the fund's credit tranches, a member may draw up to the full amount of its quota. When a member country suffers from structural imbalances in production, trade, or prices, so that adjustment requires a longer period and larger resources than are normally permitted under basic credit policies, the member may make use of the extended facility. When a member receives assistance under the basic and extended facilities, it must adopt a program to overcome its payment imbalance. This aspect of the Fund policies is known as *conditionality*.

The Fund also makes resources available under two permanent special purpose arrangements—the compensatory and the buffer stock financing facilities—and under a temporary supplementary financing facility. Compensatory financing is available to members facing payments difficulties resulting from temporary shortfalls in their export earnings that are largely beyond their control, such as falling commodity prices and natural disasters, including bad weather. Buffer stock financing assists members having difficulties in financing their contributions to international buffer stocks that are maintained to stabilize world markets for commodities, such as those for tin, cocoa, and sugar. To meet special needs, temporary facilities have sometimes been established such as the temporary oil facility established in 1974 to assist members facing difficulties because of higher oil prices in 1974 and 1975. The financial facilities, their conditionality, and the possible cumulative purchases from the Fund are shown in Figure 5–2.

The European Monetary System

Europe's second scheme to lock intracontinental exchange rates came into existence early in 1979. The European Monetary System is the European Community's device for linking the currencies of West Germany, France, Italy, Ireland, Denmark, Belgium, Luxembourg, and the Netherlands within agreed limits in a joint float against the U.S. dollar and other major currencies. Britain, alone among the nine Community states, kept its currency out of the EMS. The fact that participating countries conduct almost half of their external trade with each other implies that stable rates among the EMS members would go far toward stabilizing their effective exchange rates.

Each member has a fixed "central rate" against a new international currency, the ECU (European Currency Unit). The ECU is a basket of the members' currencies weighted by the economic importance of each country. The system has intervention limits around the central rate that must be observed by both weak and strong currency countries. The system assumes that EMS members will work toward integrating their economies and harmonizing their economic policies.

As a future step, EMS members are committed to establish a European Monetary Cooperation Fund, which would comprise 20 percent of each country's official reserves of gold and foreign currencies. This step had not been achieved by the early 1980s because of difficulties in coordinating national monetary policies and a lingering reluctance to sacrifice policy making.

Figure 5—2

Financial facilities of the Fund and their conditionality

Tranche policies:
   Reserve tranche:
      Condition—balance-of-payments need.
   First credit tranche:
      Program representing reasonable efforts to overcome balance-of-payments difficulties;
      performance criteria and installments not used.
   Higher credit tranches:
      Program giving substantial justification of member's efforts to overcome balance-of-
      payments difficulties; resources normally provided in the form of standby arrange-
      ments which include performance criteria and drawings in installments.

Extended facility:
   Medium-term program for up to three years to overcome structural balance-of-payments
   maladjustments; detailed statement of policies and measures for first and subsequent 12-
   month periods; resources provided in the form of extended arrangements which include
   performance criteria and drawings in installments.

Compensatory financing facility:
   Existence of temporary export shortfall for reasons beyond the member's control; member cooperates with Fund in an effort to find appropriate solutions for any balance-of-
   payments difficulties.

Buffer stock financing facility:
   Existence of an international buffer stock accepted as suitable by Fund; member expected
   to cooperate with Fund as in the case of compensatory financing.

Supplementary financing facility:
   For use in support of programs under standby arrangements reaching into the upper
   credit tranche or beyond, or under extended arrangements, subject to relevant policies
   on conditionality, phasing, and performance criteria.

Possible cumulative purchases from the Fund (percent of quota)

	Tranche policy	*Extended facility*
Reserve tranche	25.0	25.0
Credit tranches		
4 × 25	100.0*	—
1 × 25	—	25.0
Extended facility	—	140.0
Supplementary financing†		
1 × 12.5 plus 3 × 30	102.5	—
With extended facility	—	140.0
Subtotal	227.5	330.0
Compensatory financing	100.0	100.0
Buffer stock financing	50.0	50.0
Cumulative total‡	377.5	480.0

* This limit may be waived by a decision of the Executive Board.
† The total amounts that a member could purchase under a standby or extended arrangement could
exceed these limits in special circumstances, i.e., when the magnitude and the nature of the member's need for financing from the Fund is such as to justify additional amounts. Any additional
amounts that may be made available in special circumstances would be met wholly with supplementary financing.
‡ In addition, some members have used oil facility drawings. The average use by those members was
equal to 75 percent of quota.
Data: IMF Treasurer's Department
Source: *IMF Survey,* September 1979.

SOME REFORM ISSUES FOR THE FUTURE

Although disagreement abounds as to the merits and demerits of the managed float system, a return to the old fixed-rate system is unlikely. But the new arrangement is still in process of evolution and forces for change and reform were strongly present as of the early 1980s. A continuing issue is the replacement of the U.S. dollar as the principal international reserve asset. A related subject is the monetary role of gold. Still another issue is the desire of the non-oil-producing developing countries for a basic restructuring of the system.

International monetary reserves

In periods when confidence in the U.S. dollar is weak, many nations have moved to diversify their international reserves by converting U.S. dollar holdings into the strong currencies of German marks and Swiss francs. Alongside this drift to a multi-reserve currency system, the IMF has increased its efforts to establish the SDR as the principal reserve asset in the international monetary system. In support of this goal, an IMF substitution account has been proposed but not accepted. Such an account, administered by the fund, would accept deposits of U.S. dollars from fund members in exchange for an equivalent amount of SDR-denominated claims. The objective of the plan is to reduce the uncontrolled liquidity arising from billions of U.S. dollars overseas, permit central banks to diversify their reserves without putting dollars on the market to buy other currencies, and augment the international reserve role of the SDR.

A more far-reaching proposal is to establish a world central bank and create a commodity-backed international currency. This is not a new idea. A world central bank and an international currency to be named "bancor" was proposed by Lord Keynes at the Bretton Woods Conference in 1944 and rejected.[7] The more recent version of the proposal would include the Eastern European countries as a member of the central bank in addition to the nonsocialist West.[8]

The monetary role of gold

Since the United States closed its gold window in 1971, various steps have been taken to reduce the monetary role of gold. The IMF abolished the official price of gold and its requirement that members make certain

---

[7] See John Maynard Keynes, *Proposals for an International Clearing Union*, April 1943, cited in *Development Dialogue* 2 (1980), p. 53.

[8] Justinian F. Rweyemamu, "Restructuring the International Monetary System," *Development Dialogue* 2 (1980), pp. 77–84.

payments to the Fund in gold. In addition, the IMF reduced its gold holdings by distributing one sixth of its reserves in 1975 to members of the Fund at the then official price of SDR 35 an ounce. Another one sixth was sold in a series of open auctions, and the profits from these sales were used for the benefit of the developing-country members.

Despite these partly symbolic actions and the strong intellectual and political forces that desire to end the role of gold as an international reserve, gold continues to retain its importance. It is strongly argued that it is a waste of resources to produce gold at great expense from the bowels of the earth, only to rebury it in the vaults of central banks. But rationality has not prevailed over the passion and emotion associated for centuries with gold as a storehouse of value. Even though gold has been symbolically demonetized, over the last decade private parties as well as central banks have added to their gold holdings and the value of gold in the free marketplace has soared to great heights. As of the end of 1981, the value of the gold reserves of all countries at market prices was U.S. $380 billion as compared to U.S. $396 billion for all other international reserves.[9]

Although the monetary role of gold has been reduced, the persistence of worldwide inflation during the early 1980s revived interest in a return to the gold standard. The crux of the argument for restoring the gold standard is that inflation and the troubles associated with it stem mainly from excess money in the domestic economy. The national monetary authorities, it is argued, are not willing or perhaps not able to tailor the money supply in a manner consistent with noninflationary economic growth. A return to the gold standard would take money-supply management out of the hands of central bankers who, pressured by domestic political forces, create excessive—and thus inflationary—supplies of money. An abbreviated explanation of how the gold standard is supposed to result in price stability is presented in Box 5–1.

Restructuring the international monetary system

A complete restructuring of the international monetary system has become a priority issue for the nonoil-producing developing countries.[10] These countries are adamantly convinced that the IMF has not adapted to the needs of the developing countries in terms of participation in decision making, adequacy of resources, and recognition of the Third World's need for long-term assistance that will permit structural reform. Voting power in the IMF is based on quotas and the five major "shareholders" are the United States, United Kingdom, Germany, France, and

---

[9] Bank for International Settlements, *Fifty-Second Annual Report*, Basle, Switzerland, 14 June 1982, p. 162.

[10] Rweyemamu, "Restructuring the International Monetary System," pp. 75–95.

Box 5–1

Gold at $10,000

At current rates of inflation, the dollar price of an ounce of gold will push into the $5,000 to $10,000 range within a generation, and consumer prices generally will double every 5 to 10 years in the United States.

In reacting to this disastrous inflation, the government will probably forget that inflation's origin lies in the breakdown of the gold standard and the lack of constraints on money creation by the Federal Reserve System.

The stability of prices under the gold standard rested upon control of the global quantity of money. Under a pure gold standard, a central bank would sell gold for old currency when its balance of payments was in deficit and its currency was weak on the exchanges, thus contracting the supply of currency. Similarly, when its balance of payments was in surplus and its currency was strong, it bought gold with new currency, thus expanding the supply of national currency and preventing undue appreciation on the exchanges.

When several countries were on the gold standard, the contractions and expansions balances out. There would be no significant change in global spending and therefore no systematic tendency for deflation or inflation in the world as a whole.

*   *   *   *   *

The internal gold standard has acted in the past as a catalyst for peace and order and can do so again.

Source: Adapted from an article by Professor Robert A. Mundell in the *New York Times* on October 19, 1980.

Japan. With 40 percent of the votes, these five Western industrialized countries—it is alleged—"are able to direct the management of the international monetary system in the way they wish."[11]

The restructuring movement has been a central item on the agenda for a New International Economic Order being debated in various United Nations' forums. In particular, the developing countries would like to shift decisions as to restructuring to a United Nations Conference on International Money and Finance. Each member nation would have an equal vote in such a conference as contrasted to the weighted voting system of the IMF. It is difficult to forecast the likely success of the movement for restructuring. But the realignment of political muscle in recent years suggests that these demands cannot be lightly dismissed.

THE WORLD BANK GROUP

The 1944 Bretton Woods Conference had two objectives: (1) to restructure the international monetary system and (2) to provide financial assis-

---

[11] Ibid., p. 49.

Box 5–2

The inadequacy and loss of legitimacy of the IMF

The IMF is an institution set up by international treaty which, besides denying its own principles, offers a rather poor performance, gives the persistent impression of being at best insensitive to the interests of the majority of its members, and does not include all nations while dealing with matters of interest to all of them. Such an institution is no longer legitimate, it has lived too long. The IMF has demolished its own foundations and has proved unable to set up a new system. Loss of legitimacy added to lack of efficiency make its survival an oddity. As a matter of fact, the public in the rich nations never hear or care about it. In the Third World, it is known because of the considerable number of people who suffer the consequences of policies it imposes.

*   *   *   *   *

A return to some concept of sound monetary management, together with the conviction that the world monetary system is the business of the entire international community, is necessary for the planning and construction of this centerpiece of a new international order. Good ideas already exist concerning the content of a new monetary system. Its foundation stones should be:

1. A universal and democratic world central bank, accommodating the needs of different development patterns and economic and social systems.
2. An international currency unit, based on real values and acceptable in international payments.

Source: Excerpts from Ismail-Sabri Abdalla, "The Inadequacy and Loss of Legitimacy of the International Monetary Fund," *Development Dialogue*, no. 2 (1980): 25–50.

---

tance for postwar reconstruction and development. The IMF was created in response to the former. The World Bank was established to achieve the latter. The World Bank, whose official name is the International Bank for Reconstruction and Development (IBRD), now has two affiliates—the International Finance Corporation (IFC) and the International Development Association (IDA). The three organizations, which form the World Bank Group, have become the major public international source of financing.

The World Bank proper is owned by the governments of member countries (139 in 1981). The Bank finances its lending operations primarily from borrowings in the world's capital markets and deals mainly in long-term loans to member countries for specific reconstruction or development projects. When governments endorse and guarantee loans, it can also lend for private projects.

After World War II, much of the lending was to European countries for reconstruction. More recently, lending has been exclusively to the developing countries. Traditionally, the bank concentrated on financing capital infrastructure such as roads and railways, telecommunications, and ports and power facilities. Increasingly, loans have been directed toward assisting the poorest segments of society in developing countries through projects for agricultural and rural development, urban water and sewage facilities, low-cost housing, and small industries projects. The World Bank is important to international business more as a general force for stimulating economic development than as a direct source for financing.

The IFC was established in 1956. Its function is to assist the economic development of less developed countries by promoting growth in the private sector of their economies and by helping to mobilize domestic and foreign capital for the business sector. The IFC can make both equity and loan investments, and such financing does not require government guarantees or endorsements. Thus the IFC is a source for financing international enterprises but it has not played a major role.

The IDA was created in 1960 for making soft loans—that is, loans with long maturity, low interest rates, and easy repayment terms—to the poorest of the developing countries. The terms of IDA credits, which are made to governments only, are 10-year grace periods, 50-year maturities, and no interest. An annual service fee of 0.75 percent is charged on the disbursed portion of each credit. IDA loans are made exclusively for development purposes and are concentrated in some 50 countries with an annual per capita gross national product of less than $625 (in 1978 dollars). As is true of the World Bank, the IDA's importance to international business is as a general force for stimulating development.

SUMMARY

Prior to World War II, the international monetary system was based on the gold standard. For 25 years following World War II, the free-world economies for the most part adhered to the tenets of the Bretton Woods agreement—namely, a system of fixed exchange rates that anticipated that individual countries would make adjustments to imbalances in their external accounts without resorting to exchange-rate depreciations or currency controls. On occasion, individual countries were unable to comply with the terms of the agreement. Yet the system remained intact until the late 1960s when the United States, the most important country for the viability of the international financial structure, concluded that the arbitrary discipline of the system was no longer tenable. With the subsequent devaluations of the U.S. dollar and unhinging of the dollar from gold, the free-world economies entered into an era of floating exchange rates. An arrangement has emerged (perhaps it too could be called a system) in which individual countries decide whether to permit their respective currencies to float or to remain pegged to the currency values of some other country. While disagreement abounds regarding the strengths and weaknesses of this new arrangement, most observers agree that a return to the old, fixed-rate system is unlikely during the foreseeable future.

If the only criterion were its impact on international business, the managed float system would have to be judged as reasonably satisfactory. Both trade and other forms of international business activity have continued to expand. From the standpoint of the developing countries and some of the industrialized countries, however, strong pressures for change and reform persist. The developing countries insist that a radically restructured system is required to meet their needs. Some of the advanced countries are vitally concerned about world inflation trends and feel that a system is needed that imposes greater discipline on national monetary authorities. These pressures, and structural changes that will continue to occur in the world economy, suggest that future reforms in the international monetary system are inevitable. Hopefully, the system will evolve smoothly and become even better adapted to the complex, and often conflicting, needs of an increasingly interdependent world economy.

EXERCISES AND DISCUSSION QUESTIONS

1. Which of the following opposing views would you accept? Why?

    An exchange rate is nothing but a price. Just as we do not fix the prices of manufactured products, so there is no need to fix the price of currencies in terms of each other.

    Exchange rates are not like any other price, for they involve monetary values. Just as it is essential to have a fixed ratio between the New York dollar and the California dollar, so it is useful to have fixed ratios between national currencies. Otherwise, commodity traders and investors cannot make advance estimates of costs and prices.

2. What are SDRs and what purpose do they serve?
3. Why was the Bretton Woods system able to last for 25 years?
4. What would be the advantages and disadvantages of a world central bank and an international currency?
5. What are the most likely next steps in the evolution of the international monetary system? Will there be a return to the gold standard as a way to reduce global inflationary trends?

Chapter 6

The balance of payments

In assessing a country's currency prospects, international firms must take numerous factors into account. Ranking highest among these factors is the nation's economic relations with other countries. A principal source of information on these external relations is the country's balance of payments. Just as the balance-of-payments accounts indicate the strength or weakness of a country's currency to its government officials, these accounts also permit the international firm to anticipate changes in the foreign exchange value of a currency. They also serve as a framework for analyzing and interpreting a wide range of problems dealing with a country's economic and business life.

This chapter describes the balance-of-payments accounting system and illustrates the methodology for interpreting the accounts. It also discusses the measures countries can adopt for adjusting their balance-of-payments situation. Fortunately for students who are not versed in business accounting, a business accounting background is not necessary for understanding and analyzing the balance-of-payments accounts.

THE BALANCE-OF-PAYMENTS ACCOUNTS

Each nation periodically publishes a set of statistics that summarize for a given period all economic transactions between its residents[1] and the outside world. This statistical statement is referred to as the balance-of-payments accounts. The accounts show how a nation has financed its international activities during the reporting period. They also show what *changes* have taken place in the nation's financial claims and obligations vis-à-vis the rest of the world. A focal point of the balance of payments is the nation's *external liquidity*, that is, the country's ability to meet claims and acquire goods and services from the outside world.

The standard presentation

The broad categories used for grouping international transactions are current account, unrequited transfers, capital account, and reserves. *Current account* items are concerned with the country's trading activities in real goods and services, including payments and receipts for the use of factors of production such as capital and technology. *Unrequited transfers* are items such as gifts, donations, and aid in the form of goods or money without expectation of payment. These transfers are also considered part of the current account. *Capital account* items are concerned with the country's transactions in monetary and ownership claims other than the transactions of the monetary authorities. The monetary authority items are grouped separately as the *reserve account*. Finally, an entry usually appears for *errors and omissions* or *statistical discrepancies*, which will be explained below.

The classifications, definitions, and statistical accuracy of items vary considerably from country to country. The IMF, however, has worked with significant success to standardize the system and the form of presentation.[2] An abbreviated version of the IMF's Standard Presentation is shown in Table 6–1. The official U.S. presentation differs somewhat from the IMF format, as we shall see. Nevertheless, it is important even for U.S.

---

[1] *Residents* are defined by the IMF as all persons and institutions who reside or have their "center of interest" in the country. Citizenship is not relevant except for government and military personnel stationed abroad who are treated as residents of their home country.

[2] See *Balance of Payments Manual*, 4th ed. (International Monetary Fund, 1977).

managers to be familiar with the IMF form of presentation because it is so widely followed.[3]

Double-entry system

The balance of payments is a double-entry system. Every transaction is recorded as if it consisted of an exchange of something for something else, that is, both as a debit and a credit. In the case of merchandise imports, for example, goods are normally acquired for money or debt. Imports are recorded as a debit and payment as a credit. Likewise, exports are recorded as a credit and payment as a debit. Where items are given rather than exchanged, special types of counterpart entries are made in order to furnish the required offsets.

The words *debits* and *credits* have no value-laden meaning—either good or bad. They are merely rules or conventions: they are not economic truths. Under the conventions of double-entry bookkeeping, an increase in assets of an entity is always recorded as a debit and an increase in liabilities as a credit. Thus a *debit* records (1) the import of goods and services, (2) increases in assets, or (3) reductions in liabilities. A *credit* records (1) the export of goods and services, (2) a decrease in assets, or (3) increases in liabilities.

For the reader who is unfamiliar with debit and credit concepts of double-entry accounting, it is probably easier to view the debit and credit classifications in terms of the net effect of transactions on a country's *external liquidity*, that is, its ability to meet foreign claims against it. Exports and capital inflows (*credits*) increase external liquidity. As shown on the *debit* side under the double-entry system, they result in increases in holdings of foreign assets or decreases in foreign liabilities. Imports and capital outflows (*debits*) decrease external liquidity as reflected in the counterpart *credit* entries as decreases in foreign assets or increases in foreign liabilities. For those who are familiar with accounting, a comparison of corporate accounts and balance-of-payments accounts is presented in the appendix to this chapter.

Referring to Table 6–1, we can begin analyzing the various transactions and identifying their debit and credit components.

The current account

The current account items are analogous to the revenues and expenses of a business. When combined, they provide important insights

---

[3] The annual *Balance of Payments Yearbook* of the IMF is a valuable source for comparing various countries because a comparable format is used for the balance-of-payments statistics of each nation.

Table 6-1

Balance of payments: IMF standard presentation

	Debits	Credits
I. Current account		
A. Goods, services, and income:		
1. Merchandise	Imports from foreign sources (acquisition of goods)	Exports to foreign destinations (provision of goods)
Trade balance		
2. Shipment and other transportation	Payments to foreigners for freight and insurance on international shipments; for ship repair; stores, and supplies; and international passenger fares.	Receipts by residents from foreigners for services provided.
3. Travel	Expenditures by residents (including internal transportation) when traveling in a foreign country.	Receipts by residents for goods and services (including internal transportation) sold to foreign travelers in reporting country.
4. Investment income	Profits of foreign direct investments in reporting country, including reinvested earnings; income paid to foreigners as interest, dividends, etc.	Profits of direct investments by residents in foreign countries, including reinvested earnings; income received by residents from abroad as interest, dividends, etc.
5. Other official	Foreign purchases by government not included elsewhere: personal expenditures of government civilian and military personnel stationed in foreign countries.	Expenditures of foreign governments for goods and services, not included elsewhere; personal expenditures of foreign civilian and military personnel stationed in reporting country.
6. Other private	Payments to foreigners for management fees, royalties, film rentals, construction, etc.	Receipts from foreigners for management fees, royalties, film rentals, construction, etc.
Goods, services, and income balance		
B. Unrequited transfers		
1. Private	Payments in cash and kind by residents to foreigners without a quid pro quo such as charitable gifts and gifts by migrants to their families.	Receipts in cash and kind by residents from foreign individuals or governments without a quid pro quo.
2. Official	Transfers by residents of reporting country for pensions, reparations, and grants for economic and military aid.	Transfers received by governments from foreigners in the form of goods, services, or cash as gifts or grants. Also tax receipts from nonresidents.
Current account balance		

II. Capital account

C. Capital, excluding reserves:

1. Direct investment	a. Increased investment in foreign enterprises controlled by residents including reinvestment of earnings.	a. Decreased investment in foreign enterprises controlled by residents.
	b. Decreases in investment in domestic enterprises controlled by foreigners.	b. Increases in investment in domestic enterprises by foreigners.
2. Portfolio investment	a. Increases in investment by residents in foreign securities.	a. Decreases in investments by residents in foreign securities.
	b. Decreases in investment by foreigners in domestic securities such as bonds and corporate equities.	b. Increases in investment by foreigners in domestic securities.
3. Other long term, official	a. Loans to foreigners.	a. Foreign loan reductions to governments.
	b. Redemption or purchase from foreigners of government securities.	b. Sales to foreigners of government securities.
4. Other long term, private	a. Long-term loans to foreigners by resident banks and private parties.	a. Long-term loans by foreigners to resident banks or private parties.
	b. Loan repayments by residents to foreign banks or private parties.	b. Loan repayments by foreigners to residents.
5. Other short term, official	a. S-T loans to foreigners by central government.	a. S-T loans to resident central government by foreigners.
	b. Purchase from foreigners of government securities, decrease in liabilities constituting reserves of foreign authorities.	b. Foreign sales of S-T resident government securities, increases in liabilities constituting reserves of foreign authorities.
6. Other short term private	a. Increases in S-T foreign assets held by residents.	a. Decreases in S-T foreign assets held by residents, increase in foreign liabilities of residents.
	b. Decreases in domestic assets held by foreigners, such as bank deposits, currencies, debts to banks, and commercial claims.	b. Increase in domestic S-T assets held by foreigners or decrease in S-T domestic liabilities to foreigners.

III. Reserves

D. Reserves:

1. Monetary gold **2. Special drawing rights** **3. IMF reserve position** **4. Foreign exchange assets**	Increases in holdings of gold, SDRs, foreign convertible currencies by monetary authorities; decrease in liabilities to IMF or increase in IMF assets position.	Decreases in holdings of gold, SDRs, or convertible currencies by monetary authorities; increase in liabilities to IMF or decrease in IMF assets position.

E. Net errors and omissions:

	Net understatement of recorded debts or overstatement of recorded credits	Net understatement of recorded credits or overstatement of recorded debits

Balances:

Balance on merchandise trade	A-1 credits minus A-1 debits
Balance on goods, services, and income	A-1 through A-6 credits minus A-1 through A-6 debits
Balance on current account	A and B credits minus A and B debits

into a country's international economic performance, just as a company's profit-and-loss statement conveys important information concerning its performance.

Merchandise trade.   For most countries, merchandise exports and imports are the largest single component of total international transactions. The sale of goods to foreigners (exports) is a source of funds and, as previously noted, is recorded as a credit. As payment for the exports, the exporting country acquires a claim against foreigners. This claim is recorded as a debit. Conversely, purchases of goods from foreigners (imports) are a use of funds and recorded as a debit. To pay for the imports, the importing country either reduces its claims on foreigners or increases its foreign liabilities. Either payment method is recorded as a credit.

A specific example, using Table 6–1, can illustrate the effects of a transaction on the U.S. balance of payments. Let us assume that Volkswagen in Germany sells $100,000 of engine parts to the Ford Motor Company in the United States. The imports would be recorded as a debit to the current account (A-1). If Ford pays for the imports by drawing on its dollar account with a New York bank, a credit is recorded to the "other short term" capital account (C-6b). The domestic bank deposits held by foreigners have increased. If Ford pays for the imports by drawing on its account with a German bank, a credit is recorded to the C-6a "other short-term" capital account. The short-term foreign assets held by U.S. residents have been reduced because VW now owns the offshore deposits previously owned by Ford.

In terms of U.S. external liquidity, what has been the effect of this transaction? Simply, the United States has reduced its external liquidity by either increasing its foreign liabilities or decreasing its foreign assets. The transfer by U.S. residents of U.S. dollar deposits to foreigners increased claims against the United States. The transfer of foreign currency deposits to foreigners reduced the ability of U.S. residents to meet claims against the United States.

Services.   The services category, sometimes called invisibles, includes freight and insurance on international shipments (A-2), travel and related tourist expenditures (A-3), personal expenditures of government, civilian, and military personnel stationed in foreign countries (A-5), payments for management fees, royalties, film rentals, and construction services (A-6). Purchases of services from foreigners are comparable to imports and recorded as debits. Conversely, sales of services to foreigners are similar to exports and recorded as credits.

As an illustration, continuing with the preceding example, Volkswagen's terms of sale are f.o.b. (free on board). Thus, Ford must pay international freight and insurance from a German seaport. Ford uses a German freighter at a cost of $1,000 and pays with a check drawn on its dollar account in its New York bank. The transaction is recorded as follows:

		Debit	*Credit*
A-2	Shipment	$1,000	
C-6*b*	Other short term		$1,000

Ford has in effect purchased a German shipping service—a debit to the current account. It has paid for this service by increasing the domestic short-term assets held by foreigners—a credit in the capital account.

Transactions for international services between residents of the same country do not enter into the balance of payments. Examples of such transactions might be a resident of France using a French airline for international travel or a French exporter insuring its international shipments with a French insurance company. Although such transactions save foreign exchange for France as compared to buying such services from a foreign firm, they are considered domestic transactions.

The investment income item (A–4) includes all interest payments, dividend remittances, and profits earned on investments in foreign enterprises effectively controlled by residents (direct investment). These financial transfers are included in the current account because they are considered as factor *income*, that is, payments for the use of capital. In contrast, factor *movements* such as capital flows are included in the capital accounts.

It is general practice to include all foreign earnings on direct investment in the balance-of-payments accounts even though some or all of the profits have not been transferred as dividend remittances. The rationale for including undistributed or reinvested earnings as a financial flow is that such earnings become the property of the foreign parent whether or not they are remitted. In order to follow the double-entry convention, therefore, profits accrued but not transferred that are included as investment income (a credit) must have an offsetting entry—reinvested earnings—in the capital accounts (a debit).

Assume that Volkswagen in the United States earned a profit of U.S. $1 million in a given year but remitted only U.S. $500,000 to Volkswagen in Germany by drawing on Volkswagen-U.S.'s New York bank account. The transaction is recorded as follows in the U.S. balance of payments:

		Debit	*Credit*
A-4	Investment income	$1,000,000	
C-1	Direct investment (reinvested earnings)		$500,000
C-6*b*	Other short-term		$500,000

Unrequited transfers.   Unrequited transfers are noncommercial international transactions without a quid pro quo made by either private parties or governments. An important type of private transfer for many countries is remittances from workers abroad to their families. Other private transfers may be philanthropic activities and relief organization shipments. Government transfers consist of money, goods, and services given as grants to other nations or foreign residents. Thus, the United States provides military pensions to many residents of the Philippines who served in the U.S. armed forces during World War II when that country was still an American colony. If the transfer is in the form of goods, the value of the goods is recorded as an export credit and a corresponding debit is recorded in the transfer account. If the transfer is in the form of money, the disbursing country would show a credit in the short-term capital account and an offsetting debit in the unrequited transfer account.

The American Red Cross, for example, sends $100,000 of food to Africa as part of a drought-relief program. The gift appears in the U.S. accounts as follows:

		Debit	*Credit*
B-1	Unrequited transfers, private	$100,000	
A-1	Merchandise exports		$100,000

The capital accounts

Capital account items are transactions in ownership claims. Financial assets and liabilities with a maturity of one year or less are regarded as short term. Those with longer maturities or no maturity (equity capital) are treated as long term.

Direct investment in a general sense involves managerial participation in a foreign enterprise and is also described as effective control. In a statistical sense, however, it has proved difficult to find an objective definition of direct investment. Consequently, the statistical criteria vary among countries. The United States classifies investments that give the investor more than 10 percent ownership as direct investments. *Portfolio investment* is defined by the IMF as "undertaken for the sake of obtaining investment income or capital gains" as contrasted to entrepreneurial income.[4]

If ITT, for instance, invests an additional $10 million in one of its

---

[4] John Alves, *The Balance of Payments: A Glossary of Terms* (Washington, D.C.: International Monetary Fund, 1979), p. 5.

foreign subsidiaries by supplying it with equipment, the balance-of-payments entries are as follows:

		Debit	Credit
C-1	Direct investment	$10 million	
A-1	Exports		$10 million

If the investment comes from ITT's undistributed foreign earnings, the credit entry would be:

A-4   Investment income $10 million credit

If the investment is made by drawing on ITT's bank account in the United States, the credit entry would be:

C-6*b*   Other short term $10 million credit

The "other long term" capital account differentiates between government and private transactions of the reporting country. The transactions may be either in the form of loans or securities with an original maturity of more than one year. They may involve foreign private parties or foreign governments, except for transactions exclusively between monetary authorities. A government loan to a private party might be a loan by the U.S. Export-Import Bank to a foreign airline to finance the sale of U.S. airplanes. A private loan to a foreign government could be a Chase Manhattan Bank loan to the government of Brazil.

The "other short term" capital accounts also separate government and private transactions. The principal government items are short-term loans and transactions in short-term securities of the reporting government. Private short-term items mainly cover short-term commercial obligations and deposits in or debts to banks. Commercial obligations and claims include trade bill acceptances and other short-term claims arising from the financing of trade. Open-book accounts and utilized lines of credit, except for intercompany accounts, are also included. Intercompany accounts are included as direct investment even though they may be short-term transfers.

As several of the examples illustrate, changes in the short-term capital accounts may be *compensatory* or *financing* shifts, in the sense that they result from current account transactions, transfers, or long-term investments. They can also be *autonomous* transactions undertaken for their own sake such as movements by short-term investors to take advantage of interest differentials among countries.

Reserves

Reserve assets are the actual (spot) holdings of SDRs, gold, and foreign convertible currencies, together with the country's IMF position. These are the assets available to the monetary authorities to meet balance-of-payments deficits. They are closely analogous to the cash and near-cash assets of a private company. Only purchases and sales by official monetary authorities such as the Federal Reserve System of the United States, the Bank of England, and the Bank of France are entered in this account. A country's own currency is not foreign exchange and, therefore, by definition is not included as reserve assets. On the other hand, because the U.S. dollar is a convertible currency, dollar holdings of the Bank of England and the Bank of France are reserve assets for Britain and France.

The Bank of France decides that it has accumulated too many dollar deposits and buys $2 million in gold from the Federal Reserve Bank of New York paying with a check on that bank. The U.S. balance-of-payments entries would be

		Debit	*Credit*
C-5b	Other short-term capital, official	$2 million	
D-1	Monetary gold		$2 million

The debit and credit treatment of reserve items may appear puzzling. How can a decrease in monetary gold stocks, for example, be a credit item? The reason is that, in the example noted above, the United States has reduced its liabilities to foreigners (dollar deposits owned by foreigners) in exchange for monetary gold. In a sense, the sale of gold is like an export of merchandise and thus a credit.

Net errors and omissions or statistical discrepancies

In theory, the balance of payments should balance since all debits are offset by credits and vice versa. In practice, they never balance. The sources on which the entries are based may be incomplete or inaccurate. Also, different sources that may not be consistent with one another are generally used for the credit and debit flows of the same transaction. The net errors and omissions is a balancing item that compensates for any excess of recorded credits over recorded debits or vice versa. The total can be large if the reporting system is weak or if clandestine transactions are important.

INTERPRETING THE ACCOUNTS

How does the international firm make use of the balance-of-payments statistics? The balance-of-payments data are a principal source for assessing a country's currency prospects. Furthermore, these currency prospects are a major consideration in shaping national control policies over international transfers of merchandise and funds. Another important reason for understanding the balance-of-payments accounts is that the international firm is frequently required to analyze the impact of its own operations on the balance of payments of both home and host countries. This aspect will be discussed in Chapter 11 on measuring benefits to the nation-state.

If the balance of payments always balances, in the sense that debits are equal to credits, why then do we hear of balance-of-payments "surpluses" or "deficits"? The reason for this apparent anomaly has to do with the methods used to interpret balance-of-payments results. A balance-of-payments *deficit* may be defined as a negative balance *of certain transactions* within the balance of payments as a whole. A *surplus* is a positive balance of the same types of transactions. Thus when reference is made to a deficit or a surplus, it is necessary to identify the transactions being referred to.

In order to analyze a firm's financial situation, various ratios are calculated from its balance sheet and income statement. Such items as the debt equity ratio and "number of times interest earned" provide clues as to a company's liquidity and ability to service debt. Similarly, analytical measures are derived from a country's balance of payments that focus on certain aspects of the country's financial situation.

Measures of deficits and surpluses

The conventional measures used to interpret a country's position are the merchandise trade balance, the current account balance, and the basic balance. Figure 6–1 shows the components of each and their interrelationships.

Figure 6–1

Measures of a country's balance-of-payments position

	Exports minus imports
=	Merchandise trade balance
±	Freight, net Military, net Investment income, net Other income, net Other services, net Transfers, net
=	Current account balance
±	Long-term net capital flows
=	Basic balance

Each of these measures attempts to detect future trends in national liquidity. And each measure pays particular attention to so-called autonomous transactions that have their own economic justification for taking place, independent of other entries in the balance-of-payments accounts. Autonomous transactions usually respond to business conditions at home and abroad. The financing or compensating transactions that balance the accounts, such as foreign exchange received in payment for commodity exports, are then disregarded. The sum of the autonomous transactions—also called "above the line" items—is a measure of balance-of-payments surplus or deficit. If autonomous payments exceed autonomous receipts, the resulting deficit indicates that a country's international purchasing power has decreased.

A country's deficit or surplus will change according to the definition of autonomous transactions. The merchandise trade balance designates only exports and imports as autonomous items. By this measure the surplus or deficit results exclusively from the country's performance as an international trader. The current account balance is wider. It includes invisibles and transfers, as well as merchandise trade, as autonomous items. This performance measure for a country is analogous to the net profit calculation for a business concern.

The basic balance considers long-term capital transactions together with current account items as autonomous. It is intended to measure longer-term tendencies in the balance of payments that are not distorted by fluctuating, easily reversible, or speculative short-term financial flows. A developing country may be expected (indeed encouraged) to incur current account deficits so long as long-term capital inflows offset the operating shortfalls. Under such circumstances, the basic balance may be the best indicator of overall country performance.

Of the various payments accounts balances, the simplest is the change in official reserves held by the government. Reserves are needed if the country wishes to intervene in the foreign exchange market or meet balance-of-payments deficits. But here, again, the significance of the measure varies from country to country. A small and shrinking reserve base may be dangerous for a purely trading country but simply efficient banking for a country whose currency serves as a medium for international trade and investment.

It should now be apparent that the determination of a surplus or deficit as a guidepost for policy action cannot be based on a single figure. Instead, an assessment of the external liquidity situation of a country requires an analysis of the balance of payments as a whole in the context of economic development at home and abroad. In recognition of this fact, the IMF publishes so-called analytic presentations that show several balances.

The United States has its own unique balance-of-payments characteristics, in particular the reserve currency role of the dollar. To fit its own special needs, the United States presently uses the modified form of presentation shown in Table 6–2. This presentation shows several types of balance (lines 76–79) but does not include the basic balance measure. The reason given for dropping the basic balance is that in many cases it is not possible to distinguish between short-term and long-term capital movements. For example, direct investment flows are classified as long-term capital movements. Yet this category includes short-term and easily reversible intercompany flows between parents and foreign affiliates.[5]

An analytical approach

Keeping in mind the different definitions of surpluses and deficits, the analyst can examine recent changes and trends in a country's external relations for valuable clues about the future. If the analyst determines that a serious balance-of-payments problem exists, some of the principal questions to be asked are the following:

1. What measures are most applicable to the country, given its present difficulties?
2. Is the payments deficit temporary or does it reflect more permanent, structural difficulties?

    A firm's loss for the year may either result from an extraordinary loss or be a trend. Likewise, a country's deficit may reflect an "extraordinary loss"—temporary rise-fall in imports/exports, natural disaster, labor disruption, and so on—or, alternatively, be evidence of a permanent condition.
3. Is the country heavily dependent on external debt and/or large capital inflows?

    If so, short-term liquidity questions are important even if the country has good medium- or long-term prospects. A crucial issue becomes the country's capacity to continue meeting its current obligations.
4. What are the composition and outlook for the nation's exports?

    Are exports diversified as to composition? As to markets? How "elastic" is the foreign demand for exports—that is, are foreign sales highly sensitive to changes in price and income?
5. Can imports be reduced without adverse consequences?

    Imports will be difficult to reduce if they are essential for producing export items, or if domestic demand is inelastic, that is, insensitive to price increases.
6. What are the country's medium and long-term prospects?

    Trading firms are most concerned with short-term prospects. Investors and creditors will be more affected by medium and long-

---

[5] Jack J. Bame, "Analyzing U.S. International Transactions," *Columbia Journal of World Business*, Fall 1976, pp. 74–76.

term prospects. The relevant issue for creditors is repayment prospects in the future. A key issue for investors is whether they will be able to repatriate profits or liquidate investments in the future.

7.   Are the country's reserves sufficient?
8.   What are the country's prospects for additional foreign borrowing from private, official, and international sources?
9.   Can the country depend upon inflows from private foreign investors and/or transfers of official aid?
10.   What is the government's commitment to remedying the deficit?

There are no ironclad rules to use in obtaining definitive answers to such questions. It is essential, therefore, to determine the most probable courses of action by government officials to remedy the imbalances. The strategy, or combinations of strategies, of governments will have different impacts on the domestic economy and on the foreign exchange markets. Any number of steps might be taken to remedy a trade deficit. Restrictions can be imposed on imports. Preferential exchange rates may be established to encourage certain categories of exports or discourage certain imports. Special tax incentives may be made available to promote exports or new industries with good potential for either export expansion or import substitution. Or the currency can be devalued.

A government's strategy mix to remedy payments imbalances will also have varying impacts on different types of international business operations. An international firm that uses domestic inputs for a manufacturing facility in the country may be indifferent to, or even benefited by, new restrictions on imports. Another firm that relies heavily on imported equipment or materials might find such an action to be disastrous. Hence we see the need to conduct balance-of-payments intelligence in devising a company's strategy for responding to environmental changes.

THE U.S. BALANCE OF PAYMENTS

It would be simpler to illustrate the methodology for analyzing a country's balance-of-payments situation by using the case of a relatively simple economy like Malawi in Africa, as is done in one of the IMF publications.[6] In contrast, the U.S. balance-of-payments accounts are highly complex. Yet, because the United States plays such a dominant role in the world economy, international managers generally find it essential to be informed on the U.S. situation.

From a balance-of-payments perspective, the decade of the 1970s was a traumatic period for the United States. From the end of World War II until the late 1960s, the United States was living in an idyllic balance-of-

---

[6] See Poul Høst-Madsen, *Macroeconomic Accounts: An Overview* (Washington, D.C.: International Monetary Fund, 1979), pp. 45–47.

payments world. The subject of balance of payments existed as the esoteric domain of a few academics and government officials. By the end of
the decade, however, the country had experienced a forced intensive
education in the subject, and business managers, labor leaders, politicians, and government officials had become conversant with the subject.

The events that led to the breakdown of the Bretton Woods agreement
and the fixed exchange-rate system were described in Chapter 5. By the
mid-1960s, the traditional U.S. trade surplus was rapidly eroding. The
continuing deficits caused by U.S. direct investment outflows, government grants for development and military assistance, and direct defense
expenditures had led to a massive buildup of dollar holdings by foreigners. With a resulting loss of confidence in the dollar, the United States
moved to abandon the fixed rate system in 1971 and the present managed float system evolved by 1973.

The results of the change in monetary regime and subsequent trade
patterns are shown in Table 6–2. In 1971, the United States experienced
its first trade deficit of the 20th century (line 76). Except for 1973 and 1975,
the merchandise trade deficit has persisted and enlarged throughout the
decade.

The forces that change a country's trade balance may be grouped
under two headings: The first is the relative growth of exports versus
imports, measured in physical volume terms. The second is a country's
terms of trade, which are expressed as a ratio, calculated by dividing its
export-price index by its index of import prices. A decrease in the ratio
means that the country must export more to pay for the same volume of
imports.

This two-headed method of analysis—using terms of trade and export-import volumes—shows why the U.S. trade balance moved as it did
in the 1970s (see Figure 6–2). In the first half of the decade the U.S. terms
of trade declined sharply, mainly because of a sharp rise in petroleum
prices and the dollar's depreciation. The successful actions of OPEC
caused the international price of petroleum to increase fourfold during
the winter of 1973–74. By 1975, the U.S. dollar had devalued by about 17
percent as compared to its fixed rate in 1970. Although the devaluation
made U.S. exports cheaper in foreign currencies and thereby stimulated
the physical volume of exports, the devaluation also meant that more
exports were required to finance imports. The 1974 decline in the terms
of trade was offset as the volume of U.S. exports grew faster than that of
imports, thanks to the dollar's depreciation.

In the second half of the 70s, growth in the volume of imports greatly
outpaced that of exports—reflecting a strong business upswing in the
United States and a more tentative recovery abroad. On top of this, the
terms of trade had a further mild decline. The result was that, in the late
1970s, the trade balance swung into deep deficit.

This brief overview of the recent past suggests several of the key factors
that must be considered in forecasting the future trade pattern of the

Table 6-2†

U.S. international transactions ($ millions)

(Credit +; debits −)[1]	Line	1971	1973	1975	1976	1977	1978	1979	1980	1981	Line
Exports of goods and services[2]	1	68,838	110,241	155,729	171,630	184,337	220,137	286,772	312,102	372,892	1
Merchandise, adjusted, excluding military[3]	2	43,319	71,410	107,088	114,745	120,816	142,054	184,473	224,237	236,254	2
Transfers under U.S. military agency sales contracts	3	1,926	2,559	4,049	5,454	7,351	7,973	6,549	8,306	9,747	3
Travel	4	2,534	3,412	4,697	5,742	6,150	7,183	8,441	10,058	12,168	4
Passenger fares	5	615	975	1,039	1,229	1,366	1,603	2,156	2,582	2,991	5
Other transportation	6	3,299	4,465	5,840	6,747	7,264	8,399	10,028	11,497	12,168	6
Fees and royalties from affiliated foreigners	7	1,927	2,513	3,543	3,531	3,883	4,705	4,980	5,780	5,867	7
Fees and royalties from unaffiliated foreigners	8	618	712	757	822	923	1,059	1,100	1,100	1,386	8
Other private services	9	1,546	1,985	2,920	3,584	3,848	4,296	4,396	5,412	5,940	9
U.S. Government miscellaneous services	10	347	401	446	489	557	620	320	362	426	10
Receipts of income on U.S. assets abroad:											
Direct investment	11	9,160	16,542	16,595	18,999	19,673	25,458	38,183	37,150	31,873	11
Interest, dividends, and earnings of unincorporated affiliates	12	5,983	8,384	8,547	11,303	13,277	14,115	19,219	20,133	18,894	12
Reinvested earnings of incorporated affiliates	13	3,177	8,158	8,048	7,696	6,396	11,343	18,965	17,017	12,978	13
Other private receipts	14	2,641	4,330	1,644	8,955	10,881	11,344	23,654	32,987	50,407	14
U.S. Government receipts	15	906	936	1,112	1,332	1,625	1,843	2,292	2,549	3,665	15
Transfers of goods and services under U.S. military grant programs, net	16	3,546	2,810	2,207	373	203	236	465	631	602	16
Imports of goods and services	17	−66,569	−99,219	−132,836	−162,248	−193,788	−229,880	−281,677	−333,800	−361,813	17
Merchandise, adjusted, excluding military[3]	18	−45,579	−70,499	−98,041	−124,051	−151,689	−175,813	−211,819	−249,575	−264,143	18
Direct defense expenditures	19	−4,819	−4,629	−4,795	−4,895	−5,823	−7,352	−8,584	−10,777	−11,288	19
Travel	20	−4,373	−5,526	−6,417	−6,856	−7,451	−8,475	−9,413	−10,397	−11,460	20
Passenger fares	21	−1,290	−1,790	−2,263	−2,568	−2,748	−2,896	−3,184	−3,607	−4,487	21
Other transportation	22	−3,130	−4,694	−5,888	−6,852	−7,874	−8,939	−10,457	−11,073	−11,611	22
Fees and royalties to affiliated foreigners	23	−118	−209	−287	−293	−243	−393	−523	−514	−429	23
Fees and royalties to unaffiliated foreigners	24	−123	−176	−186	−189	−196	−214	−241	−247	−264	24
Private payments for other services	25	−956	−1,180	−1,551	−2,006	−2,190	−2,573	−2,824	−3,065	−3,294	25
Payments of income on foreign assets in the United States	26	−746	−862	−1,044	−1,227	−1,358	−1,545	−1,718	−1,769	−1,930	26
Direct investment	27	−1,164	−1,610	−2,234	−3,110	−2,834	−4,211	−6,357	−9,470	−7,808	27
Interest, dividends, and earnings of unincorporated affiliates	28	−621	−699	−1,046	−1,451	−1,248	−1,628	−2,402	−3,303	−3,708	28
Reinvested earnings of incorporated affiliates	29	−542	−910	−1,189	−1,659	−1,586	−2,583	−3,955	−6,167	−4,099	29
Other private payments	30	−2,428	−4,209	−5,788	−5,681	−5,841	−8,795	−15,481	−20,794	−28,352	30
U.S. Government payments	31	−1,844	−3,836	−4,542	−4,520	−5,542	−8,674	−11,076	−12,512	−16,748	31
U.S. military grants of goods and services, net	32	−3,546	−2,810	−2,207	−373	−203	−236	−465	−631	−602	32
Unilateral transfers (excluding military grants of goods and services), net	33	−3,701	−3,881	−4,613	−4,998	−4,617	−5,030	−5,561	−6,783	−6,608	33
U.S. Government grants (excluding military grants of goods and services)	34	−2,043	−1,938	−2,894	−3,146	−2,787	−3,176	−3,550	−4,681	−4,504	34
U.S. Government pensions and other transfers	35	−542	−693	−813	−934	−971	−1,086	−1,180	−1,303	−1,459	35
Private remittances and other transfers	36	−1,117	−1,250	−906	−917	−859	−768	−832	−798	−645	36
U.S. assets abroad, net (increase/capital outflow (−))[4]	37	−12,475	−22,874	−39,703	−51,269	−34,785	−61,130	−64,344	−86,026	−109,294	37
U.S. official reserve assets, net[4]	38	2,349	158	−849	−2,558	−375	732	−1,133	−8,155	−5,175	38
Gold	39	866				−118	−65	−65		(*)	39
Special drawing rights	40	−249	9	−66	−78	−121	1,249	−1,136	−16	−1,824	40
Reserve position in the International Monetary Fund	41	1,350	−33	−466	−2,212	−294	4,231	−189	−1,667	−2,491	41
Foreign currencies	42	382	182	−317	−268	158	−4,683	257	−6,472	861	42

Line		C1	C2	C3	C4	C5	C6	C7	C8	C9
43	U.S. Government assets, other than official reserve assets, net	−1,884	−2,644	−3,474	−4,214	−3,693	−4,660	−3,743	−5,126	−5,137
44	U.S. loans and other long-term assets	−4,181	−4,638	−5,941	−6,943	−6,445	−7,470	−7,676	−9,854	−9,710
45	Repayments on U.S. loans [3]	2,115	2,596	2,475	2,596	2,719	2,941	3,908	4,459	4,370
46	U.S. foreign currency holdings and U.S. short-term assets, net	182	−602	−9	133		−131	25	269	204
47	U.S. private assets, net	−12,940	−20,388	−35,380	−44,498	−30,717	−57,202	−59,469	−72,746	−98,982
48	Direct investment	−7,618	−11,353	−14,244	−11,949	−11,890	−16,056	−25,222	−19,238	−8,691
49	Equity and intercompany accounts	−4,441	−3,195	−6,196	−4,253	−5,494	−4,713	−6,258	−2,221	−4,287
50	Reinvested earnings of incorporated affiliates	−3,177	−8,158	−8,048	−7,696	−6,396	−11,343	−18,965	−17,017	−12,978
51	Foreign securities	−1,113	−671	−6,247	−8,885	−5,460	−3,626	−4,726	−3,524	−5,429
	U.S. claims on unaffiliated foreigners reported by U.S. nonbanking concerns:									
52	Long-term	−168	−396	−366	−42	−99	−53	−3,307	−3,146	[14] −331
53	Short-term	−1,061	−1,987	−991	−2,254	−1,841	−3,800			
	U.S. claims reported by U.S. banks, not included elsewhere:									
54	Long-term	−612	−933	−2,357	−2,362	−751	[15] −33,667	[15] −26,213	−46,838	[15] −84,531
55	Short-term	−2,368	−5,047	−11,175	−19,006	−10,676				
56	Foreign assets in the United States, net (increase/capital inflow (+))	22,970	18,388	15,670	36,518	51,319	64,036	38,460	54,484	77,921
57	Foreign official assets in the United States, net	26,879	6,026	7,027	17,693	36,816	33,678	−13,697	15,442	4,785
58	U.S. Government securities [4]	26,570	641	5,563	9,892	32,538	24,221	−21,972	11,895	6,272
59	U.S. Treasury securities [4]	26,578	59	4,658	9,319	30,230	23,555	−22,435	9,708	4,983
60	Other [4]	−8	582	905	573	1,400	666	463	2,187	1,289
61	Other U.S. Government liabilities [5]	−510	936	1,517	4,627	773	2,476	−73	561	−69
62	U.S. liabilities reported by U.S. banks, not included elsewhere	819	4,126	−2,158	969	2,105	5,551	7,213	−159	−4,083
63	Other foreign official assets [6]		323	2,104	2,205		1,430	1,135	3,145	2,665
64	Other foreign assets in the United States, net	−3,909	12,362	8,643	18,826	14,503	30,358	52,157	39,042	73,136
65	Direct investment	367	2,800	2,603	4,347	3,728	7,897	11,877	13,666	21,301
66	Equity and intercompany accounts	−175	1,890	1,414	2,687	2,142	5,313	7,921	7,500	17,201
67	Reinvested earnings of incorporated affiliates	542	910	1,189	1,659	1,586	2,583	3,955	6,167	4,099
68	U.S. Treasury securities	−24	−216	2,590	2,783	534	[9] 2,178	[9] 4,960	[9] 2,645	[9] 2,932
69	U.S. securities other than U.S. Treasury securities	2,289	4,041	2,503	1,284	2,437	2,254	1,351	5,457	7,109
	U.S. liabilities to unaffiliated foreigners reported by U.S. nonbanking concerns:									
70	Long-term	384	298	406	−1,000	−347	−190	[14] 1,362	[14] 6,530	[14] 532
71	Short-term	−15	737	−87	422	1,433	2,079			
	U.S. liabilities reported by U.S. banks, not included elsewhere:									
72	Long-term [10]	−250	227	−280	231	373	16,141	32,607	10,743	41,262
73	Short-term [10]	−6,661	4,475	908	10,759	6,346		1,139	1,152	1,093
74	Allocations of special drawing rights	717								
75	Statistical discrepancy (sum of above items with sign reversed)	−9,779	−2,654	5,753	10,367	−2,465	11,866	25,212	28,870	25,809
	Memoranda:									
76	Balance on merchandise trade (lines 2 and 18)	−2,260	911	9,047	−9,306	−30,873	−33,759	−27,346	−25,338	−27,889
77	Balance on goods and services (lines 1 and 17)[11]	2,269	11,021	22,893	9,382	−9,451	−9,743	3,095	8,303	11,079
78	Balance on goods, services, and remittances (lines 77, 35, and 36)	610	9,078	21,175	7,531	−11,281	−11,597	3,083	6,202	8,975
79	Balance on current account (lines 77 and 33)[11]	−1,433	7,140	18,280	4,384	−14,068	−14,773	−466	1,520	4,471
	Transactions in U.S. official reserve assets and in foreign official assets in the United States:									
80	Increase (−) in U.S. official reserve assets, net (line 38)	2,349	158	−849	−2,558	−375	732	−1,133	−8,155	−5,175
81	Increase (+) in foreign official assets in the United States (line 57 less line 61)[11]	27,389	5,090	5,509	13,066	35,416	31,202	−13,624	14,881	4,854

Footnotes to Table 6–2

1. Credits, +: exports of goods and services; unilateral transfers to United States; capital inflows (increase in foreign assets (U.S. liabilities) or decrease in U.S. assets); decrease in U.S. official reserve assets.

Debits, −: imports of goods and services; unilateral transfers to foreigners; capital outflows (decrease in foreign assets [U.S. liabilities] or increase in U.S. assets); increase in U.S. official reserve assets.

2. Excludes transfers of goods and services under U.S. military grant programs (see line 16).

3. Excludes exports of goods under U.S. Military agency sales contracts identified in Census export documents, excludes imports of goods under direct defense expenditures identified in Census import documents, and reflects various other adjustments (for valuation, coverage, and timing) of Census statistics to balance of payments basis.

4. For all areas, amounts outstanding March 31, 1982, were as follows in millions of dollars: line 38, 29,944; line 39, 11,150; line 40, 4,306; line 41, 5,367; line 42, 9,121.

5. Includes sales of foreign obligations to foreigners.

6. Consists of bills, certificates, marketable bonds and notes, and nonmarketable convertible and nonconvertible bonds and notes.

7. Consists of U.S. Treasury and Export-Import Bank obligations, not included elsewhere, and of debts securities of U.S. Government corporations and agencies.

8. Includes, primarily, U.S. Government liabilities associated with military sales contracts and other transactions arranged with or through foreign official agencies.

9. Consists of investments in U.S. corporate stocks and in debt securities of private corporations and State and local governments.

10. Beginning with estimates for the second quarter of 1978, the distinction between short- and long-term liabilities is discontinued.

11. Conceptually, the sum of lines 79 and 74 is equal to "net foreign investment" in the National Income and Product Accounts (NIPA's). However, the foreign transactions account in the NIPA's (a) includes adjustments to the international transactions accounts for the treatment of gold, (b) excludes capital gains and losses of foreign affiliates of U.S. parent companies from the NIPA's measure of income receipts from direct investment abroad, and from the corresponding income payments, and (c) beginning with 1973-IV, excludes shipments and financing of military orders placed by Israel under Public Law 93-199 and subsequent similar legislation. Line 77 differs from "net exports of goods and services" in the NIPA's for the same reasons with the exception of the military financing, which is excluded, and the additional exclusion of U.S. Government interest payments to foreigners. The latter payments, for NIPA's purposes, are excluded from "net exports of goods and services" but included with transfers in "net foreign investment."

12. Includes return import into the United States, at a depreciated value of $21 million in 1972-IV and $22 million in 1973-II, of aircraft originally reported in 1970-III in line 3 as a longterm lease to Australia.

13. Includes extraordinary U.S. Government transactions with India. See "Special U.S. Government Transactions," June 1974 SURVEY, p. 27.

14. The maturity breakdown is available only on the limited basis.

15. The maturity breakdown is available only on the limited basis.

16. Includes foreign currency denominated notes sold to private residents abroad.

United States. The internal factors are the competitiveness of U.S. exports. This is affected by domestic productivity, domestic inflation rates, and the price elasticity of major export items. The import side depends on the relative competitiveness of foreign imports in the U.S. market and the price elasticity of these imports. Another major factor is the relative economic growth rates of the United States and its principal trading partners. Still another variable is the international value of the U.S. dollar,

Figure 6–2

Genesis of a trade deficit

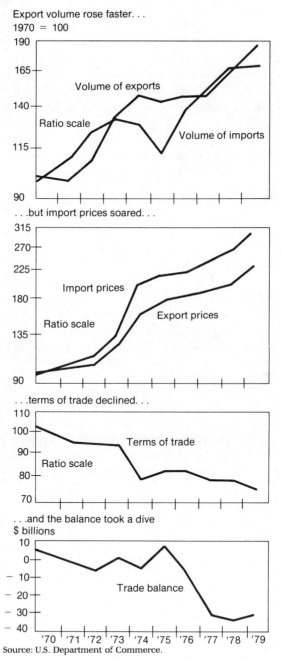

Export volume rose faster. . .

1970 = 100

Volume of exports

Ratio scale

Volume of imports

. . .but import prices soared. . .

Import prices

Export prices

Ratio scale

. . .terms of trade declined. . .

Terms of trade

Ratio scale

. . .and the balance took a dive

$ billions

Trade balance

'70 '71 '72 '73 '74 '75 '76 '77 '78 '79

Source: U.S. Department of Commerce.

which is influenced by many considerations other than the trade balance and is reflected along with domestic price trends in the terms of trade.

The U.S. balance on current account (line 79) has consistently been more favorable than the trade balance and frequently in surplus during the decade of the 1970s. This is a result of the large and steady increase in investment income on foreign direct investment (line 11). Throughout the 1970s, foreign direct investment by U.S. firms continued to grow significantly (line 65) and the return flows from these investments increased steadily in absolute terms and as a share of the total goods and services account.

Another notable feature of the current account is the small absolute increase in returns from fees and royalties (lines 7 and 8) and the relative decline as a share of the current account. This trend reflects the closing of the technology gap between the United States and other industrialized countries that existed at the end of World War II.

In the capital accounts, direct investment flows continued to be an extremely important item over the decade. The interesting pattern is that, although outbound U.S. direct investment continued to expand, inbound direct investment grew even more spectacularly. The annual flows of U.S. direct investment abroad increased from $7.6 billion in 1970 to $25 billion in 1979 (line 48), a more than threefold increase. Direct investment in the United States increased even more rapidly from $1.5 billion in 1970 to $11.9 billion in 1979 (line 65), an eightfold gain.

The reserve accounts (line 57)—foreign official assets in the United States—show that the U.S. balance-of-payments deficits have been financed largely by increased U.S. liabilities to foreign official institutions. The annual increase in foreign holdings of U.S. assets, mainly U.S. government securities, ran as high as $37 billion in 1977. The other principal balancing item has been the sizable increases in foreigners' bank deposits in U.S. banks (lines 72 and 73), which include petrodollar deposits in the United States by the oil-producing countries.

The statistical discrepancy, or errors and omissions account (line 75), deserves mention. This discrepancy reached a level of almost $30 billion in 1980. As a positive number, this meant that an unrecorded capital inflow of this amount had occurred. This large discrepancy has puzzled the experts and caused the U.S. government to consider changes in its reporting system.[7] One possible explanation is that unsettling political and military events in 1980 caused a number of foreigners to make unreported investments in the United States or open up U.S. bank accounts in the name of a U.S. intermediary such as a trust, U.S. lawyer, or U.S. relative. Another speculation was that some foreign countries may be deliberately understating the number of dollars that reside in their central bank coffers. The motivation for such an act may be to avoid pressure

---

[7] *Survey of Current Business*, March 1981, p. 43.

from the United States to ease up on its exports to the United States, or to reduce the possibility of speculation that would increase the value of the holder's currency if it were known that huge dollar surpluses were building up.[8]

THE INTERNATIONAL INVESTMENT POSITION

Although a country's balance-of-payments accounts are the principal guide to the strength of its currency, these accounts record only *flows* over a given time period. A separate statement referred to as a nation's net international investment position presents a static picture at a given point of time of a country's balance of indebtedness. The statement shows a nation's official reserve assets and its claims on and liabilities to nonresidents. It can also include valuation adjustments for changes in prices and exchange rates that are not included in the balance of payments. A nation's net position is the difference between that country's assets abroad and its liabilities to nonresidents. Although priority attention is generally given to the balance of payments, the two statements are often analyzed together.

Deficits do not all have the same effect on a country's international financial strength. A deficit caused by increased imports may have to be financed by a loss in reserves or an increase in liabilities to foreigners, permanently reducing the country's international liquidity. A deficit caused by capital outflows to purchase foreign securities or for direct investment, however, may reduce liquidity but build up foreign assets and increase the long-term strength of the country by generating return flows of investment income.

The international investment position of the United States is shown in Table 6–3. It reveals, as the balance-of-payments accounts do not, that the United States has a substantial net worth (line 1). At the same time, it also shows a striking difference in the composition of U.S. assets abroad and U.S. liabilities to foreigners.

U.S. assets abroad are predominantly privately held assets (line 5) such as direct investment, bank loans, and portfolio investment—in order of size. U.S. official reserve assets (line 3) are a remarkably small share of the total. In contrast, U.S. assets held by foreign official institutions, generally central banks (line 7), constitute almost 40 percent of U.S. liabilities and have consistently been large. Also, the liquidity of U.S. assets abroad, such as direct investment, is relatively low compared to foreign holdings of U.S. assets even though the United States has a net surplus position.

It should be noted, however, that the net asset position of the United States may well be understated. In particular, direct investment, the larg-

---

[8] *The Wall Street Journal,* July 29, 1980, p. 48.

Table 6–3

International investment position of the United States at yearend

Total (billions U.S. $)

Type of investment	1971	1973	1975	1976	1977	1978	1979	1980
1. Net international investment position (2 minus 6)	58.4	47.6	74.6	82.5	72.3	75.3	95.0	122.7
2. U.S. assets abroad (3 + 4 + 5)	179.5	222.4	295.1	347.2	383.0	450.9	513.2	603.6
3. U.S. official reserve assets:	12.2	14.4	16.2	18.7	19.3	18.7	18.9	26.8
Gold	10.2	11.7	11.6	11.6	11.7	11.7	11.2	11.2
SDRs	1.1	2.2	2.3	2.4	2.6	1.6	2.7	2.6
Reserve position in IMF	0.6	0.6	2.2	4.4	4.9	1.0	1.2	2.9
Foreign currencies	0.3	—	0.1	0.3	—	4.4	3.8	10.1
4. U.S. government assets other than official reserves:	34.2	38.8	41.8	46.0	49.6	54.2	58.5	63.6
U.S. loans	31.8	36.2	39.8	44.1	47.8	52.3	56.5	61.9
Foreign currency & S-T assets	2.4	2.6	2.0	1.9	1.8	1.9	1.9	1.7
5. U.S. private assets:	133.1	169.2	237.1	282.4	314.1	378.0	435.8	513.3
Direct investment abroad	83.0	101.3	124.1	136.8	149.8	167.8	192.6	213.5
Foreign securities	23.5	27.4	34.9	44.2	49.4	53.4	56.7	62.1
U.S. claims nonbanking	9.6	13.8	18.3	20.3	22.3	26.1	29.9	33.7
U.S. claims by U.S. banks	16.9	26.7	59.8	81.1	92.6	130.7	156.6	204.0
6. Foreign assets in United States: (7 + 8)	123.3	174.9	220.5	264.7	310.6	375.5	418.2	480.9
7. Foreign official assets:	52.5	69.6	86.9	105.6	141.9	174.8	160.3	175.7
U.S. government securities	44.4	53.8	63.6	74.0	106.8	130.9	108.3	118.2
Other U.S. liabilities	8.1	15.8	23.3	31.6	35.1	43.9	52.0	57.5
8. Other foreign assets in United States:	70.9	105.3	133.6	159.1	168.7	200.7	257.9	305.2
Direct investment	13.9	20.6	27.7	30.8	34.6	42.5	52.3	65.5
U.S. securities other than U.S. Treasury	30.1	46.1	45.3	54.8	52.9	55.4	61.9	74.0
U.S. liabilities, nonbanking	9.2	11.7	13.9	13.0	13.4	15.1	18.2	28.6
U.S. liabilities reported by banks	17.7	26.9	46.7	52.4	67.8	87.7	125.5	137.1

Source: *Survey of Current Business*, August 1981, p. 56.

est U.S. asset abroad, is reported at book value, not market value. Also, the value of gold reserves is reported on the basis of the official price of $42.22 per ounce as contrasted to the free market price of about $400 per ounce in late 1982.

ADJUSTMENT MEASURES FOR PAYMENTS IMBALANCES

With the advent of floating exchange rates, the significance of balance-of-payments deficits or surpluses has changed. Theoretically, if foreign exchange rates are freely floating, the market will automatically adjust for deficits through lower foreign exchange values and for surpluses through higher values. A lower exchange value, or a devaluation, should increase foreign exchange earnings through expanded exports and increased capital inflows. It should also reduce foreign exchange expenditures through decreased imports and smaller capital outflows. According to the theory, foreign exchange values will continue to change until equilibrium is restored. Under the floating rate regime, therefore, official reserves become unimportant or play no major role.

With the floating system in fact becoming a managed float for the major currencies and with most other countries still following a fixed exchange system, the issue of governmental measures that can be taken for payments imbalances still remains an important subject. As discussed previously, nations are still not ready to allow the value of their currencies to be freely determined by market forces because of numerous domestic and national policy considerations.

If deficits are temporary and recognized as such outside of a country, a country can use government reserves or borrowing from the IMF to meet the deficits. For more serious or persisting deficits, governments have the choice of several lines of action. If they need substantial IMF assistance, the IMF will require that certain actions be undertaken as a condition for such assistance. Adjustments can be attempted through changes in the exchange rate, through internal measures, or through controls.

With the devaluation approach, as previously noted, exports are stimulated because the price of a nation's goods in foreign currencies has been reduced. Imports are retarded because the domestic cost of imported goods has risen. The strength of these effects will depend upon the size of the devaluation and the price elasticities of demand. If consumers continue to purchase the same quantity of goods even if the price is measurably reduced or raised, demand is said to be highly price inelastic. But if buyers vary their purchases greatly with higher or lower prices, demand is considered to be highly price elastic. For imports or exports that are price elastic, devaluation can both increase foreign exchange export earnings and reduce foreign exchange expenditures on imports. A revaluation will have the reverse effect and contribute to equilibrium by reducing surpluses.

The capital accounts can also be influenced by a devaluation or revaluation. In the case of a devaluation, imports are likely to lose competitiveness in the domestic market and foreign firms will tend to make direct investments in the country to establish local production facilities. The opposite tendency is encouraged by revaluations, namely, a reduction in direct investment flows.

Adjustment measures through new or modified domestic policies are numerous and often difficult to accomplish. Domestic inflation, for example, may be responsible for increasing the prices of a nation's goods in foreign markets and reducing export earnings. In the early 1980s, however, solutions to the domestic inflation problem have not been easy to find. Furthermore, the traditional anti-inflation approach of controlling inflation by economic slowdowns and increased unemployment rarely wins domestic political support. The supply-side approach of the Reagan administration in the United States, adopted in 1981, of reducing inflation through productivity gains and increased supply rather than through reducing demand, is more acceptable politically. The effectiveness of this approach, however, had not been demonstrated as of this writing.

The imposition of exchange controls and import restrictions and/or export incentives may well be an easier political path than internal deflation for a country to take. The wide range of available control measures and the implications of protectionist policies are discussed at length in Chapter 9. Controls generally do not tackle the basic causes of the payments imbalance. At best, controls may provide some respite from further deterioration of a situation while other more basic remedies are being implemented. Yet, in many cases, restrictions and controls have remained as permanent fixtures.

SUMMARY

The balance-of-payments accounts reflect a country's economic and financial relations with the rest of the world. Using a double-entry bookkeeping system, various transactions involving a country's residents and their counterparts in other countries are collected and disseminated on a regular basis. To interpret the meaning of these data, one must make some judgments regarding which transactions are important—that is, induced by underlying economic and financial forces. Analysis of these autonomous transactions, in turn, permits one to assess whether a given country has balance-of-payments problems—difficulties in its external commercial relations. If there is a problem, the country in question must find a solution. By considering various options open to the country, the analyst can develop extremely useful insights into the likely strategies that the country will pursue. Foreknowledge of likely developments can be extremely crucial to the international business enterprise since steps may often be taken to reduce the corporation's vulnerability in advance of a full-blown crisis.

APPENDIX: CORPORATE ACCOUNTS AND BALANCE-OF-PAYMENTS ACCOUNTS

For the reader who is familiar with accounting, a short review of accounting concepts as applied to balance-of-payments accounting should clear up any difficulties in comprehending the classification of balance-of-payments items as debits or credits.

Under the conventions of double-entry accounting, the assets of an entity are always recorded as debits and the liabilities as credits. There are two sorts of liability, however, those to outside parties and those to owners of the entity. The liability to owners represents the basic net worth of the entity according to the rules adopted in keeping the accounts and may be expressed as the excess of assets over outside liabilities. Thus the fundamental equation in double-entry accounting is:

$$\text{Assets (debit)} = \text{Liabilities (credit)} + \text{Net worth (credit)}$$

It is a simple step from this equation to work out the debit and credit entries for any change in assets, liabilities, or net worth. For example, whenever an asset is added (debit), there must be an increase in liabilities (credit), an increase in net worth (credit), or a decrease in another asset (credit). Conversely, when an asset is reduced (credit), there must be a reduction in a liability (debit), a reduction in net worth (debit), or an increase in another asset (debit). For activities aimed at building net worth, the accounts classification is extended to introduce accounts for costs and revenue. Revenue represents an increase in net worth and hence is recorded as a credit, while costs, in effect, decrease net worth and are recorded as debits. Hence:

$$\text{Revenues (credit)} - \text{Costs (debit)} = \text{Net worth (credit)}$$

When costs are incurred (debit), there must be an offsetting credit— either an increased liability or a decreased asset. Likewise, when a revenue earning sale is made, revenue is credited and an asset or a liability account debited. The entry in an asset account might record the cash received or the customer debt for the sale. If the entry is in a liability account, it might record a reduction in the amount owing to a creditor.

Applying these double-entry concepts to balance-of-payments accounting, a country's international net worth can be viewed as the difference between the country's external claims against the rest of the world (debit) and the rest of the world's claims against the country's own wealth (credit). This net worth is not a measure of the country's entire wealth, only that portion of it that its residents have channeled through international transactions. When a country exports goods, international net worth is increased by the value of goods channeled into exports (credit), and there is an increase in claims against foreigners to whom the exports are made (debit). Or if a resident pays a foreign account with foreign currency that he obtains from his bank, the effect is to reduce the country's foreign liabilities by the amount paid (debit) and to reduce the country's foreign assets by the same amount (credit), that is, foreign currency held by the bank is reduced.

Corporate accounts and balance-of payments accounts are compared in Table 6A–1.

Table 6A–1

Corporate accounts and balance-of-payment accounts compared

Corporate accounts		Balance-of-payment accounts		
Debits	Credits	Debits	Credits	Relation to Table 6–1
Profit and loss items			*Current items*	
	Sales		Exports	A1 (cr)
	Other income		Other current account income	A2 − A6; B1 − B2 (dr)
Cost of goods sold		Imports		A1 (dr)
Other costs (except depreciation), taxes, and dividends		Other current account expenditures		A2 − A6; B1 − B2 (dr)
	Net retained profit before depreciation		Current account balance	A + B credits minus A + B debits
Balance sheet items			*Capital and reserve items*	
	Increase in current liabilities		Net increase in foreigners' short-term claims	C2b, C5b, C6b credits minus debits
	Increase in long-term liabilities and equity		Net increase in foreigners' long-term claims	C1b and C3b credits minus debits
Increase in current assets except cash		Increase in private short-term foreign assets		C2a, C5a, C6a debits minus credits
Increase in fixed assets		Increase in long-term foreign assets		C1a, C3a, C4a debits minus credits
Increase in cash		Increase in official holdings of gold and foreign exchange		D debits minus D credits

EXERCISES AND DISCUSSION QUESTIONS

1. What is meant by a balance-of-payment surplus or deficit?

2. How can a country have balance-of-payments deficits and still be strengthening its international economic position?

3. West Germany has revalued its DM several times. Why would a country revalue its currency?

4. Explain how the move to managed floating rates has changed the way the United States attempts to manage its balance-of-payments accounts.

5. As the manager of a U.S. manufacturing affiliate in Freelandia how would you measure the effects of your operations in Freelandia on the Freelandia balance of payments?

6. Show in double-entry format the entries that would be made in the U.S. balance-of-payments accounts. Use the account numbers of the U.S. presentation format as shown in Table 6–2. As an illustration:

   a. A Japanese company sells electronic equipment to RCA in the United States for $2 million. Freight ($3,000) and insurance ($2,000) are arranged in the United States and paid for by RCA. Payment to the Japanese company is made by check drawn on the Bank of America in New York.

Account no.	Debit	Credit
18. Merchandise imports	$2 million	
73. U.S. liabilities, short-term		$2 million

   b. A U.S. company decides to establish a new plant in Hong Kong to take advantage of cheap labor. The cost of setting up a plant during the year totaled $8.6 million. Half of this was paid out of an account held in Hong Kong, the rest from a U.S. account.

   c. A U.S. company exports $400,000 worth of agricultural equipment to New Zealand and accepts $200,000 worth of shares in the local distributor as part payment. The rest is paid in New Zealand dollars.

   d. Charles L. Hangover went on a trip to the Pacific islands. He paid for his airfare of $2,000 in the United States but half the travel was done on Quantas (Australian) and the rest on Pan American. The fare was divided between the airlines accordingly. He spent a further $1,500 in the islands.

   e. The U.S. government extends a loan to Israel to purchase military equipment. The loan is for $500 million. It is all spent on fighter aircraft bought from U.S. firms.

   f. An investment trust in the United States buys 30,000 Unilever, Ltd. shares in London Unilever for $40 each and pays for them from its U.S. account.

   g. Unilever directors declare a dividend of £1 and this is paid into the trust's U.S. account. The exchange rate is £1 = U.S. $2.

h.   The United States spends $1.5 million on military exercises in the Pacific. Of this, $.9 million is paid to foreign countries for the use of docking and airport facilities.

i.   Pedro Lopez migrated from Mexico to the United States and found satisfactory employment. After working for three months, he sent his mother in Mexico a check for $500 drawn on his new checking account with the Bank of America.

Chapter 7

The international trade framework

"No state shall, without the consent of the Congress, lay imposts or duties on imports or exports, . . ."
Section 10, Article 2, *Constitution of the United States,* signed September 17, 1787.

For more than two centuries, trade within the United States has been free of trade barriers, in accordance with the free trade principle adopted in the U.S. Constitution. In contrast, trade among nation-states has always been subject to trade barriers. During some eras of history, the barriers have been stringent and detailed. But since the end of World War II, many national barriers have been greatly reduced through international cooperation. Furthermore, an international trade framework of

137

permanent international and regional organizations has been established for negotiation and implementation of trade agreements.

This chapter will introduce the principal types of trade barriers and describe the international trade framework within which international business operates. The motivations of nation-states for imposing restrictions on trade are left for Chapter 9, which discusses national controls over all forms of international transfers.

TRADE BARRIERS

National governments use many devices to change or modify the prices, patterns, and volume of imports and exports. The two general categories of such devices are tariff and nontariff barriers.

Tariff barriers

A tariff is the most common form of trade restriction. A tariff is a tax, or duty, levied on a commodity when it crosses the boundary of a customs area. A customs area usually coincides with national political boundaries, although sometimes it includes colonies or territories of the country. A customs area that is extended beyond national boundaries to include two or more independent nations is called a *customs union* or *common market*.

Tariffs may be levied on commodities leaving an area (export duties) or on merchandise entering an area (import duties). Import duties are more common than export duties because most nations are anxious to expand exports and increase their foreign exchange earnings. Import duties may be either *specific, ad valorem,* or a combination of the two—*compound* duties. Specific duties are levied on the basis of some physical unit such as dollars per bushel, per kilo, or per meter. Ad valorem duties are calculated as a percent of the value of the goods. The term *drawback* refers to duties paid on imported goods that are refunded if the imported components are reexported.

A country's *tariff schedule* is a listing of all its import duties. The schedule may have one or more columns. In a *single-column* schedule, the tariff is the same for a specific good regardless of the country of origin. A *multicolumn* schedule discriminates among exporting countries, with lower rates applying to countries with which tariff treaties have been negotiated. The advantage of the multicolumn tariff is its flexibility for tariff bargaining.

Tariffs have the advantage that they can be selectively levied in terms of products and with differential rates. Thus a nation may achieve rather precise objectives with tariffs while at the same time increasing government revenues. The negative aspect of tariffs is that they increase the cost of imports to the customer. Also, they are difficult to reduce or eliminate because of political pressures from domestic groups benefited by the tariff. Such political pressures can limit a country's flexibility in bargaining with other nations, particularly where tariffs are established by law and a change of law is necessary to change a tariff.

An important feature of tariff agreements is the *most-favored nation (MFN) principle*. A nation entering into a tariff treaty that includes the MFN principle is required to extend to all signatories any tariff concessions granted to any participating country. The purpose of such a treaty provision is to simplify tariff bargaining and increase the likelihood of tariff reductions. All members of GATT, to be described below, are entitled to MFN treatment. As an illustration of the importance ascribed to the principle, a key issue in trade negotiations during the early 1980s between the United States and the USSR (not a member of GATT) was whether the United States was willing to grant MFN status to the USSR.

Nontariff barriers

Nontariff barriers (NTBs) are less visible than tariffs, but they are extremely effective restraints on trade. The principal categories of NTBs are as follows:

1. Government participation in trade.
   Discrimination in government procurement, state trading, subsidies, countervailing duties, and so on.
2. Customs and entry procedures.
   Regulations covering valuation methods, classification, documentation, health, and safety.
3. Standards.
   Standards for products, packaging, labeling, marking, and so on.
4. Specific limitations.
   Quotas, import restraints, licensing, exchange controls, and so on.
5. Import charges.
   Prior import deposits, credit restrictions for imports, special duties, variable levies, and so on.

Quotas or quantitative restrictions are the most common form of nontariff barrier. A quota limits the imports (or exports) of a specific commodity during a given time period. The limits may be in physical or value terms. Quotas may be on a country basis or global, without reference to countries of origin. They may be imposed unilaterally, as in the case of sugar imports into the United States. They can also be negotiated on a so-called voluntary basis, as in the case of Japanese automobile imports into the United States during the early 1980s. Obviously, exporting countries do not readily agree to limit their sales. Thus, the "voluntary" label generally means that the importing country has threatened to impose even worse restrictions if voluntary cooperation is not forthcoming.

Quotas are more certain and precise as trade restraints than are tariffs. An import duty that is not prohibitive will reduce imports, but it does not impose an absolute limit on imported goods. A quota system limits with certainty the extent of foreign competition in the domestic market. Quotas also provide greater flexibility in bargaining and administration. The greatest disadvantage of quotas is that they exert no pressure to keep domestic prices down.

In the importing country, quotas usually require a licensing system and an agency to distribute the quota shares to domestic importers. Where the total quota is small relative to the total domestic market, domestic prices are likely to be higher than the price of imports. Quota recipients, therefore, will gain windfall profits. Governments could capture the windfall profits by auctioning off the licenses to the higher bidder. The more general practice, however, is for the profits to go to private parties. Thus inequities and corruption may occur in the allocation of quotas.

In the exporting country, quotas also require a system for allocating shares of the export quota to individual exporting firms. Such allocations are frequently based on each firm's foreign market share before the quota limits go into effect. If a firm anticipates the future imposition of quotas, its strategy will be to gain as much market share as possible regardless of profitability. After the exporter is granted a sizable share of the quota, importers from the foreign country become dependent on the exporters with allocations as a source of supply. The exporting firm has then gained sufficient bargaining power to more than compensate for lost profits.

Many NTBs other than those specifically mentioned are used to restrict trade, and ingenious new barriers are constantly being developed. Some are legitimate regulatory functions, such as antipollution regulations that require automobiles to meet certain exhaust emission standards. Others may ostensibly be introduced for reasons of health, safety, or national security but are actually intended to restrict trade.

A BRIEF HISTORY OF COMMERCIAL POLICIES

A country's commercial policies are those designed to influence its trade relations with the rest of the world. Over many centuries, until David Ricardo published his theory of comparative advantage in 1817, mercantilist views shaped the trade policies of most nations. The mercantilists believed that the economic power of the state was enhanced by the accumulation of precious metals in the national treasuries. National policies, therefore, were directed toward achieving as large a trade surplus as possible by encouraging exports and restraining imports. The surplus of exports over imports was to be settled by payments in gold or other precious metals. Clearly, extensive government controls over trade and exchange were required to achieve the mercantilist goals.

As the theory of comparative advantage gained acceptance, mercantilism steadily gave way to a more liberal conception of international trade and economic relations. By the end of the 19th century, trade liberalization had become the dominant philosophy and nations were imposing relatively few restrictions on trade. The trend toward trade liberalization was interrupted by the Great Depression of the 1930s, when economic disintegration and fragmentation became widespread. Each nation geared its economic policies more and more toward autarky, that is, economic self-sufficiency. In the United States the height of protection was reached in 1930 with the passage of the Smoot-Hawley tariff.[1]

The return to the trade liberalization path was led by the United States with the passage of the Reciprocal Trade Agreements Act in 1934. Under this initiative, trade restrictions were significantly reduced through bilateral negotiations and agreements. But the liberalization move was again interrupted by World War II. It was resumed after the war, with the United States again providing leadership. The remarkable feature of the post-World War II period was the introduction of the multilateral negotiation principle and the creation of an international trade framework.

Until the postwar period, each nation fashioned its own trade policies unilaterally or through bilateral negotiations. Since World War II, international cooperation in the field of trade has become the general rule, and permanent international and regional organizations have been established for sponsoring multilateral negotiations and for overseeing the implementation of trade agreements.

The international trade framework that has evolved consists of a series of trading arrangements under various international organizations. These trading arrangements can be grouped into the following broad categories:

1. Global arrangements directed toward multilateral trade expansion on a nondiscriminatory basis.
2. Global arrangements directed toward international income redistribution through restructuring the "International Economic Order."
3. Regional arrangements that focus on the economic relations of a particular geographic or political area.
4. Commodity-product arrangements that focus on the international terms of trade of a specific product or commodity.

---

[1] For a history of U.S. commercial policies, see Delbert A. Snider, *Introduction to International Economics*, 7th ed. (Homewood, Ill.: Richard D. Irwin, 1979), pp. 202–25.

5.   Bilateral trading arrangements, although they normally do not involve international agencies, are also part of the international trade
framework.

THE GENERAL AGREEMENT ON TARIFFS AND TRADE (GATT)

The General Agreement on Tariffs and Trade, known as GATT, is the
principal global arrangement for trade liberalization. Although originally
designed as a temporary arrangement, GATT evolved into a permanent
and important institution. It became effective in 1948 with 19 countries as
members. Its membership has since expanded to include almost all of
the important noncommunist nations and several socialist countries of
Eastern Europe.

GATT's early accomplishments

The broad goal of GATT has been to reduce trade restrictions erected
by individual nations in pursuit of their narrow national interests. The
goal is to be achieved through multilateral negotiations, through rules of
conduct for GATT members, and through providing a forum for the settlement of trade disputes. Mutual tariff concessions are negotiated
among the so-called contracting parties and the parties commit themselves not to raise import tariffs above the negotiated rates. Nondiscrimination, a key rule of conduct, is achieved by generalizing the negotiated
rates to all contracting parties through the most-favored nation principle.

While aiming at "developing the full use of the resources of the world
and expanding the production and exchange of goods,"[2] GATT does not
envision full liberalization of all trade barriers. The emphasis is on "reciprocal" and "mutually advantageous" arrangements among contracting
parties. Thus GATT permits exceptions to its general rules that require
the eventual elimination of all import restrictions. But the exceptions are
subject to safeguards intended to protect the legitimate interests of other
trading nations.

The GATT exceptions recognize the special protection given to agriculture by most nations and allow many import restraints to protect
domestic farmers. The GATT rules make exceptions for countries that are
in balance-of-payments difficulties and allow the developing countries to
protect their infant industries. GATT also permits members to form customs unions, provided there is no overall increase in barriers to outsiders.

---

[2] GATT, *Basic Instruments and Selected Documents*, vol. 4, Text of the General Agreement
(Geneva, March 1969), p. 1 (Preamble).

From 1947 to 1967, GATT sponsored six rounds of multilateral trade negotiations. By the end of the so-called Kennedy Round in 1967, the weighted average tariff for the major trading nations had been reduced to the following low rates:[3]

7.7 percent on all industrial products.

9.8 percent on finished manufactured products.

8.0 percent on semifinished products.

2.0 percent on raw materials.

GATT's role in the settlement of trade disputes has also helped greatly to stimulate trade liberalization. Before GATT, there was no way to resolve trade disagreements between two countries. With GATT, a group of experts is convened when a complaint is received. The group establishes the facts, makes a judgment as to the merits of the complaint in light of the GATT rules, and recommends a solution to the dispute.

Thus, in spite of the remaining trade barriers, the situation after the Kennedy Round could be characterized as a liberal world trading system with a substantially free exchange of nonagricultural goods. This postwar movement toward trade liberalism, complemented by a stable monetary system, fostered an unprecedented, sixfold rise in the volume of international trade between 1948 and 1973.

The difficult 1970s

Early in the 1970s, major changes were occurring in the world economy. The fixed-exchange-rate financial system was moving toward an untried managed float system. International oil prices had quadrupled in 1973 and a sharp worldwide economic recession followed in 1974–75. A number of developing countries had diversified their export base and were challenging the industrialized countries in new sectors such as steel, shipbuilding, and electronics.

While GATT was preparing for the seventh round of multilateral trade negotiations to begin in 1975, the trade liberalization gains of the past were being threatened by rising protectionism.[4] The economic slowdown was provoking forceful demands by management and labor unions for protection against imports. Growing import competition in a number of sectors from the developing countries was creating strong pressures on the industrialized countries for structural adjustment.

The theoretical solution for the new import competition is for damaged nations to shift out of noncompetitive industries into new areas. But

---

[3] Bahram Nowzad, *The Rise of Protectionism* (Washington, D.C.: International Monetary Fund, 1978), p. 1.

[4] Ibid.

the hard fact is that governments do not like losing industries to foreign competitors. They may protect local steel production because it is essential to their sense of national security. Or they may protect non-competitive shoe factories because the workers have no place else to go.

Another characteristic of the negotiating environment was that tariffs were no longer major restraints on trade among the industrialized countries. But the steady decline in tariffs had revealed that many types of nontariff barriers were still in place. Thus nontariff barriers became a major agenda item.

After five years of negotiation, the Tokyo Round was completed in 1979. (The negotiations took place in Geneva but were labeled the Tokyo Round because they had been initiated in a Tokyo meeting in 1973.) Far more ambitious than the previous six negotiations, the Tokyo Round involved 99 countries and dealt with many aspects of international trade. The package of results is complex and contained in several thousand pages of documents.

The Tokyo Round was the first comprehensive attempt to control the use of nontariff barriers. In this area, codes were adopted covering methods of custom valuation, nondiscrimination in government procurement, simplification of import licensing procedures, subsidies and countervailing duties, and technical standards as barriers to trade. In the case of government procurement, countries signing the code agree to allow foreign firms to compete for large government orders. "Large" was defined as purchases of about $200,000 and above. Under this code, Japan agreed to open up Nippon Telephone equipment purchases of many billion dollars annually to U.S. and other foreign suppliers. The United States, in turn, agreed to waive the "buy American" restriction and permit Japanese companies to bid on U.S. government purchasing contracts.

Another result of the Tokyo Round was the agreement by the industrial countries to further reduce their tariffs by about one third over the next eight years. More significantly, the Tokyo Agreement changed many long-standing GATT rules. The nondiscrimination rule requiring equal treatment for imports does not apply to the new codes. Only signatory countries to each code enjoy the benefits of the code. Another major change is that preferential treatment for developing countries became recognized as a permanent feature of the world trading system. Previously, special preferences required a specific waiver of the nondiscrimination rules.

The uncertain future of GATT

As of the 1980s, GATT continued as the symbol of a broad international commitment to trade liberalization. But commitment to the ideal had weakened and the appropriateness of the GATT framework to the changing world economy was being questioned. The developing countries receive some benefits from GATT, but they are militantly convinced that GATT does not adequately represent their interests. As a result, they are expanding their negotiating activities outside the GATT system. Spurred on by domestic protectionist pressures, many of the industrialized countries are forsaking the open market commitment of GATT and organizing special arrangements, such as orderly market agreements, for specific industries.

In a structural sense, a fatal defect of GATT is that it does not encompass international direct investments as well as trade. GATT does not recognize that direct investment and trade are alternatives, and it still envisions trade in its traditional sense as transactions between independent parties. The reality of the 1980s is that a large and growing share of so-called international trade is the internal transfer of goods among units of multinational firms located in different countries. Such transfers show up in the international trade statistics but are not subject to normal market forces.

THE UNITED NATIONS CONFERENCE ON TRADE AND DEVELOPMENT (UNCTAD)

The developing countries constitute a majority of the GATT membership but most of them reject the free-trade approach and make extensive use of trade barriers. They may agree in principle that free trade maximizes world output *with a given international economic structure.* Their priority objective, however, is to change the international structure in order to accelerate their growth and narrow the economic gap between them and the industrialized nations. In their view, the path for achieving these goals is not through free trade. They are convinced that in the present world environment the terms of trade have been systematically turning against them.

Terms of trade

The terms of trade concept needs further elaboration, even though it was previously referred to in Chapter 6. There are several terms of trade concepts but the most commonly used is the *commodity terms of trade.* This measure is an index number showing how the price of exports has changed relative to the price of imports at some reference time. The commodity terms of trade, T_{nb}, is defined as

$$T_{nb} = \frac{P_{xt}/P_{xo}}{P_{mt}/P_{mo}},$$

where P represents an index of the prices of exports (x) or imports (m) and the subscripts t and o refer to the present and base-period times, respectively.[5]

The developing countries claim that the prices they receive for their exports, mainly primary commodities, are not rising as fast as the prices they pay for imports, mainly manufactured goods. The logical support for this belief is Engel's Law, discussed in Chapter 2, which suggests that the income elasticity for raw material exports is less than for manufactured imports. The developing countries also contend that, with the exception of petroleum, the world markets for their exports are highly competitive whereas the markets for their imports involve administered prices and oligopolistic structures. These views led the developing nations to press for global trade arrangements that would work for structural changes and international redistribution of income.

The birth of UNCTAD

When GATT was initiated in 1948, its principal concern was to liberalize trade among the industrialized countries. The postwar decolonization movement was only beginning, and the strong development aspirations of the Third World were yet to emerge. It is not surprising, therefore, that after observing the first decade and a half of GATT's operations, the developing countries became convinced that GATT was not the institution to represent adequately their trade interests.

In response to this sentiment, the United Nations Conference on Trade and Development (UNCTAD) was convened in 1964 and attended by representatives of 119 nations. The result of the conference was to establish UNCTAD as a permanent United Nations agency. Given its origin and structure, UNCTAD has come to represent the trade interests of the developing countries, and its prime objective has been the international redistribution of income through trade.

As the dominant force in UNCTAD, the developing countries have made major demands on the industrialized countries in each of the five UNCTAD conferences held from 1964 to 1979. At UNCTAD I, the developing countries asked for freer access to the markets of the industrialized countries for exports of manufactured goods. They wanted unilateral tariff reductions without reciprocal concessions by the developing countries as an aid in shifting their export base from primary commodities to manufactured goods.

After several years of continued pressure, the advanced countries agreed to this demand by establishing what is called a *generalized system of preferences* (GSP). Under GSP, the industrialized countries have

---

[5] See H. Peter Gray, *International Trade, Investment and Payments* (Boston: Houghton Mifflin, 1979), pp. 27–30.

reduced tariffs for fixed amounts of specific manufactured imports from the developing countries. GSP results, however, have not been substantial. The quotas have been restrictive as to products and amounts. Furthermore, only a few countries have been able to take advantage of the concessions, and these countries have not been the poorest of the developing countries. Probably more significant than GSP has been UNCTAD's success in pressuring the IMF to make easier credit available to countries suffering from a temporary shortfall in export prices.

The New International Economic Order

The developing countries escalated their demands in the early 1970s through having the United Nations endorse the need for a New International Economic Order (NIEO). The general thrust of NIEO is for a major restructuring of the international economy. Under the "old order," the developing countries feel that they bear an inequitable burden in times of economic recession and do not participate equitably in periods of world prosperity.

As of the 1980s, the details of the NIEO were still being spelled out. Some specifics of the NIEO emerged at the UNCTAD IV meetings in Nairobi in 1976. The developing countries pressed for an "integrated" program of commodity agreements with a common fund for buffer stock financing, a code governing international technology transfers, long-term financial assistance from the IMF, and measures for alleviating the debt problems of the developing countries. These issues were again on the agenda of UNCTAD V meetings held in Manila in 1979. The Manila meetings with 3,000 delegates from 159 nations participating were not a success. Many resolutions were processed, but without arousing specific pledges of support from industrialized nations.

As in the case of GATT, major changes in the world economy since the formation of UNCTAD have greatly modified the action potential of this global arrangement. The oil-producing countries have expanded the role of their own organization (OPEC) and have not been willing to include the energy issue in UNCTAD deliberations. Some of the rapidly developing middle-income countries are more and more identifying their interests with those of the advanced countries. Not only have the interests of the developing countries been diverging, but the UNCTAD procedures have become increasingly unwieldy. Sensitive negotiations are difficult to conduct in periodic public conferences with 3,000 delegates. As a result, some of the major NIEO issues have been shifted to other forums.

REGIONAL TRADE ARRANGEMENTS

Regional trade arrangements form another part of the international trade framework. The GATT agreement allowed for regional groupings—

with the proviso that such groupings should not result in increased discrimination against nonmembers. As subsequent events demonstrated, neighboring countries had strong desires to pool their political and economic strength despite the existence of global trade agreements. And the establishment of regional common markets and free trade areas, referred to as *regional economic integration*, began to occur.[6]

Regional economic integration can take various forms. The loosest and least intensive form is the *free-trade area.* In a free trade area all artificial restrictions on the movement of goods and services among the participating countries are removed, but each country may retain its own tariffs, quotas, or other restrictions on trade with nonparticipating countries. The *customs union* is one degree further along the scale. In addition to the complete elimination of tariffs and quotas on internal trade, a common external tariff is established on goods entering the union from outside. A *common market* represents the next higher degree of economic integration. Besides eliminating internal trade barriers and establishing a common external tariff, a common market also removes national restrictions on the movement of labor and capital among participating countries, and on the right of establishment for business firms.

The economic gains from the formation of a common market can be dramatic. With the elimination of internal tariffs, the market area can be greatly enlarged and no longer bounded by the borders of the individual countries. Gains from increased economic efficiency can arise from the reallocation of production within the area on the basis of national factor endowments and comparative advantage. These gains can be reinforced by economies of scale that individual firms may be able to achieve and by increased competition within the expanded market area. Even more important can be the impetus to economic growth induced by the reduction of internal barriers to trade.

The extent to which these gains are shared with or achieved at the expense of outside countries depends in large part on the balance between trade creation and trade diversion effects. *Trade creation* exists when the elimination of internal trade barriers increases the volume of trade by making lower cost goods and services available. *Trade diversion* occurs when less efficient producers inside the market area replace more efficient external producers because the outsider still faces external tariffs. The degree to which trade diversion occurs will depend, of course, on the height of the external tariffs.

The European Economic Community

The most successful case of economic integration has been the European Economic Community. It was established January 1, 1958, based on

---

[6] As a general reference on economic integration see Bela Balassa, *The Theory of Economic Integration* (Homewood, Ill.: Richard D. Irwin, 1961).

the Treaty of Rome, by Belgium, France, West Germany, Luxembourg, Italy, and the Netherlands. It was preceded by a Coal and Steel Community set up in 1952. Together with the European Atomic Energy Community (Euratom), also founded in 1958, the three groups are jointly referred to as the European Community (EC).

The original six nations were joined in 1973 by the United Kingdom, Denmark, and Ireland and in 1981 by Greece. The 10 members of the Community had a total population in 1980 of about 270 million, as compared to about 220 million for the United States. In terms of total gross national product in 1979, the EC and the United States were almost equal at about U.S. $2,400 billion. Although average per capita income in Germany, Luxembourg, and Belgium slightly exceeded the U.S. level of $10,820 in 1979, the average for the entire Community was somewhat lower at $8,418.[7] As a trading group, the Community has become the world's biggest exporter, accounting for 36 percent of world exports in 1979. Half of the exports, however, were intracommunity trade.

The European Community evolved out of a series of post-World War II moves toward economic and political union in Western Europe. The economic community was expected to reduce costly political and economic rivalries and evolve into a United States of Europe. The economic accomplishments have been phenomenal but the political results have been much less impressive. After 20 years, a European Parliament was established in 1979, but the new institution has limited authority.

Under the customs union agreed to in the Rome Treaty, all customs duties and restrictions on intra-Community trade were abolished by July 1, 1968. A common external tariff became fully operational at the same time. Through participation in the GATT multilateral negotiations, the external tariffs of the Community have been gradually reduced while retaining the principle of a common external tariff.

In the agricultural sector, the Community developed a protective common agricultural policy. The system adopted was one of domestic support prices for separate commodities and sliding tariffs. When domestic prices are low because of bountiful crops, the tariff protection is high, and vice versa. In the agricultural area, therefore, trade diversion is the result, with more efficient external producers being excluded.

The Rome Treaty has numerous provisions that could eventually lead to a full economic union. Some provisions, such as those concerned with a common antitrust policy, a common patent law, and the free movements of workers within the community have been implemented. Others related to a common transport policy and a communitywide company law are being worked on. The creation of the European Monetary System (EMS), mentioned in Chapter 5, is another move toward harmonization. But the goal of complete economic and monetary union is still distant. Such a degree of integration means additional sacrifices of national sov-

---

[7] These data are from the *1980 World Bank Atlas* (Washington, D.C.: World Bank, 1981).

ereignty, including centralized management of economic and monetary affairs.

Under the Rome Treaty, association with the community is open to all countries. The community has association and preferential agreements with a number of European countries, including the EFTA "free-trade agreements" discussed in the next section. The community also has a special relationship with 57 developing countries in Africa, the Caribbean, and the Pacific region, called the ACP countries. The Lome II convention, signed on October 31, 1979, represents an effort by the EC to assist the ACP developing countries and retain special commercial and financial relationships with their former colonies.

The Lome II convention expands and replaces an original 1975 agreement. In the field of trade, Lome gives the ACP countries free access to the Community for all but a tiny share of their exports, without the reciprocal obligation of giving free entry to EC products. It also continues and increases resources for the STABEX system, which provides financial assistance for stabilizing export earnings from agricultural exports. A major change in the new Lome agreement is a program to aid projects and programs in the mining sector of the ACP countries. Additional resources for financial and technical cooperation will continue to be available via the European Development Fund (EDF) and the European Investment Bank (EIB) of the Community.

European Free Trade Association

The European Free Trade Association (EFTA) was formed in 1960 by seven European nations that had a variety of reasons for not joining the EEC. These seven nations—Austria, Denmark, Norway, Portugal, Sweden, Switzerland, and the United Kingdom—were later joined by Finland and Iceland. As a free-trade area, EFTA has abolished internal tariffs and quantitative import restrictions on intra-association trade, but each member continues to impose its own external tariffs. EFTA, therefore, has adopted so-called *rules of origin*. Such rules ensure that only goods with a specified percent of their export value produced in the area can benefit from the tariff reductions.

Britain and Denmark resigned from EFTA at the end of 1972, on the eve of their accession to the EEC. Britain's great relative size had made it the dominant member of EFTA, and after the loss of Britain, EFTA became a more cohesive body. All of its members except tiny Iceland are roughly the same size and at a similar level of economic development. Also, Britain's and Denmark's entry into the EEC opened the way for the previously mentioned free-trade agreements between the individual EFTA countries and the EEC. The agreements provide for the progressive elimination of customs duties for industrial products, with minor concessions for certain agricultural products. They do not provide, however, for a customs union or for the obligation to harmonize legislation.

The formation of EFTA boosted trade among member countries. These gains, however, have become overshadowed by the large increase in trade with the EEC after the conclusion of the free-trade agreements. The EEC is EFTA's biggest trading partner, accounting in 1979 for more than 50 percent of EFTA's imports and exports (See Figure 7–1).

Figure 7–1

EFTA: The EEC's biggest trading partner

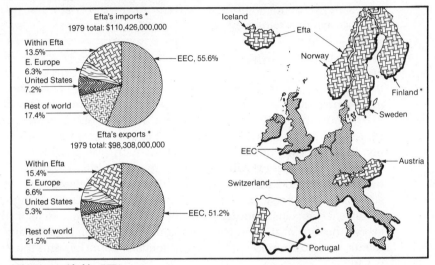

Efta's imports *
1979 total: $110,426,000,000

Within Efta 13.5%
E. Europe 6.3%
United States 7.2%
Rest of world 17.4%
EEC, 55.6%

Efta's exports *
1979 total: $98,308,000,000

Within Efta 15.4%
E. Europe 6.6%
United States 5.3%
Rest of world 21.5%
EEC, 51.2%

Iceland · Efta · Norway · Finland* · Sweden · EEC · Austria · Switzerland · Portugal

* Figures provided by EFTA.
† Associate member.
Source: *The Economist*, June 14, 1980, p. 58.

COMECON and East-West trade

The centrally planned economies of Eastern Europe formed the Council of Mutual Economic Cooperation (COMECON) in 1949 to coordinate their trade and other forms of economic relations. The council includes Bulgaria, Czechoslovakia, East Germany, Hungary, Poland, Romania, and the USSR. For a number of reasons unique to the centrally planned economies, COMECON has not become a vital component of the international trade framework.

In the COMECON countries, the government normally exercises complete control over exports and imports, and various state trading organizations have full responsibility for buying and selling a particular product. The state trading companies are separate from the state enterprises that produce or consume the product so that foreign traders do not deal directly with the user or vendor of goods and services.[8]

---

[8] See Franklyn D. Holzman, *International Trade under Communism* (New York: Basic Books, 1976), pp. 21–50.

With the exception of emergency situations, foreign trade is managed in accordance with national economic plans rather than market-determined commercial opportunities. Political as well as economic factors prevail. The yardstick is the requirement of the total plan rather than the benefits and costs to the individual state enterprise. Under such conditions, tariffs and subsidies for controlling or stimulating trade are unnecessary and not used. World prices are normally the guide for international transactions within or outside the bloc, and import and export prices may have no relationship to domestic prices. Nor are the planners necessarily constrained by cost-price relationships.

The absence of any necessary link between the cost and price of a product makes it difficult to apply the trading rules of market-oriented organizations such as GATT to trade between COMECON countries and the market economies. For example, it is practically impossible to determine whether exports from a COMECON country are subsidized.

The currencies of the socialist countries are not freely convertible. Consequently, trade is frequently arranged on a barter basis or with clearing systems whereby sales are balanced with purchases from another country.[9] This inconvertibility has encouraged bilateralism within the trade bloc. No socialist country is willing to run a surplus with another socialist nation because of the difficulties in spending the currency. As a result, each socialist country plans for a bilateral balance in its trade with every other socialist nation. For the same reasons, bilateral trading agreements are also common between the socialist countries and the Western world.

Regional integration among developing countries

Most developing countries favor regional integration as a promising strategy for accelerating their development aspirations. Yet few of the many regional integration attempts have succeeded. Most of the 14 regional arrangements shown in Figure 7–2 are in the talking stage, in process of being implemented, moribund, or defunct. After 20 years of extremely modest accomplishments, the Latin American Free Trade Area (LAFTA) was replaced in 1981 by the Latin American Integration Association (LAIA). Whereas LAFTA was based on the principle of negotiations by all member countries on a product-by-product basis, LAIA provides for negotiations between just two or a limited number of countries. LAIA envisions that such partial agreements will eventually lead to economic integration of the 11 nations of the region.

Among the few regional integration projects showing some momentum in the early 1980s are the Association of South East Asian Nations

---

[9] See Samuel Pisar, *Coexistence and Commerce: Guidelines for Transactions Between East and West* (New York: McGraw-Hill, 1980).

Figure 7–2

Regional and trade arrangements among developing countries

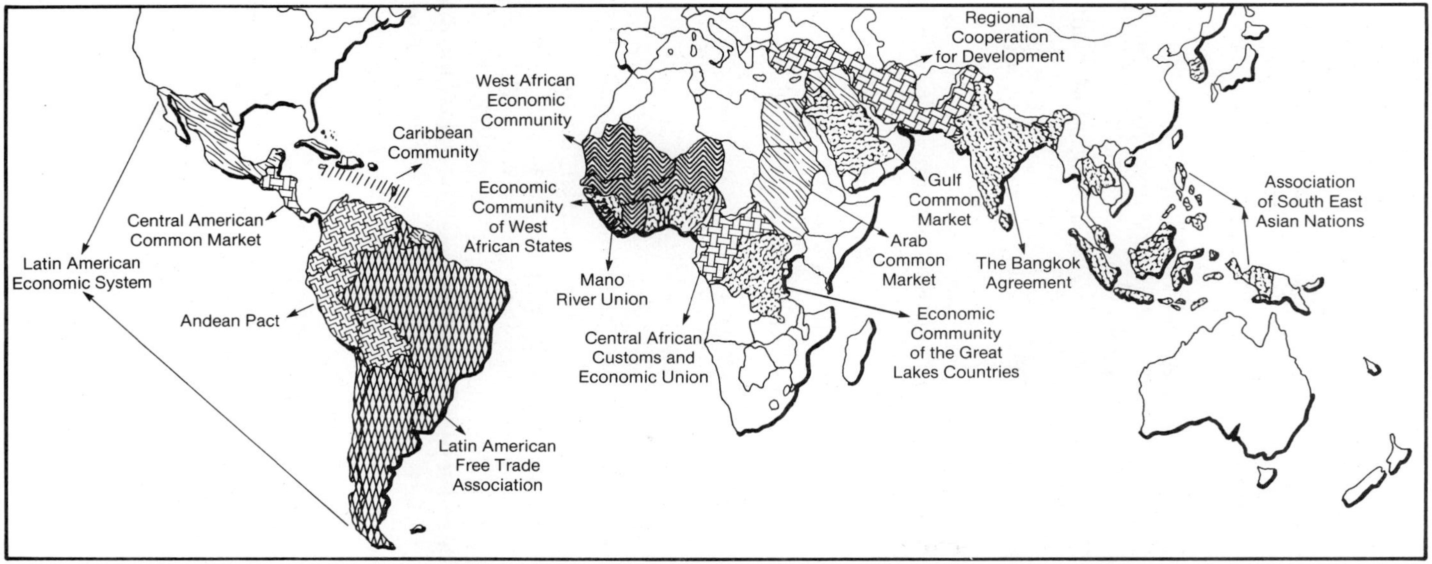

Source: *IMF Survey*, July 4, 1977.

(ASEAN) and the Andean Pact in South America. In the case of the Andean Pact, Chile withdrew in 1976 to follow its "open economy" experiment. Another member, Bolivia, had dropped its active participation in 1980 because the other pact members (Colombia, Ecuador, Peru, and Venezuela) had criticized a 1979 military coup that toppled Bolivia's civilian government. The Andean Pact, nevertheless, has achieved some significant results. Intraregional trade, for example, grew twelvefold over the 1969–79 decade with the gradual dismantling of intraregional tariffs.

Unlike the free-trade motivations of the EC and EFTA members, the developing countries look to regional integration mainly as an aid to their industrialization efforts. They need market enlargement to support modern industries and achieve a more efficient use of their resources. Thus, trade diversion through substituting regional production for imports takes precedence for them over trade creation. The countries are determined to industrialize, and regional integration can reduce the inefficiency of such efforts.

The developing countries have encountered severe political and economic difficulties in their attempts at regional integration. On the political side, a major barrier has been the different and frequently conflicting political orientation of the countries being embraced. On the economic side, critical difficulties have arisen because the production structures of neighboring counties tend to be competitive rather than complementary. Other problems are that custom revenues are often the major source of government finance, and that trade restrictions may be one of the few policy instruments available to the authorities.

Still another serious barrier has been the concern of the least-developed countries in the group—like Bolivia in the Andean Pact—that the more-advanced countries will capture most of the gains from the improved industrialization opportunities. One response to this concern is the Andean Pact commitment to region-wide industrial planning, which assigns various sectors of a planned industry to each of the member countries.

Significance to international business

Regional economic integration movements are certain to continue as a significant feature of the international business environment. And regional integration movements can have vital significance for international business operations. Some of the major effects are as follows:

1. Competitive conditions are changed as between internal and external producers. Firms previously exporting to the area may find it necessary to jump the trade barrier and establish local producing units. Firms located within the market can become more competitive through larger-scale producing units, if economies of scale are important to the industry.

2. The trade creation effects and more vigorous competition can stimulate growth rates and increase the attractiveness of markets in countries joining integration movements.
3. International firms established in common markets or free trade areas can become more competitive in third-country markets if the increased level of production secured within the home market permits reduced costs for exported goods.
4. Integration movements generally incorporate measures or policies that favor business enterprises from the area as against international enterprises of other nationalities. The EEC, for example, has promoted mergers of European firms as a defensive measure against the expansion of American and Japanese companies in the European area.
5. Changes in the rules of competition, such as adopting areawide antitrust policies, can cause problems for multinational firms that have previously given exclusive rights in specific member countries to subsidiaries or licensees.

For these and other business reasons, one of the challenging issues for the international manager is to be able to predict the establishment, probable success, and future development patterns of specific integration movements.

INTERNATIONAL COMMODITY ARRANGEMENTS

International commodity agreements and producer associations constitute another category of trading arrangements. Both types of arrangements attempt to control the terms of trade for specific commodities. They differ in that both producing and consuming countries participate in commodity agreements whereas only producer nations are members of a producers' association.

The initiative for such agreements has come mainly from the developing countries. From their perspective, commodity trade (excluding petroleum) has traditionally been burdened by two problems. One is the short-term instability of markets for primary products. The second is the previously mentioned conviction that long-term trends have been adverse, as reflected in deteriorating terms of trade and sluggish growth in export earnings.[10]

Short-term price instability in commodity markets has resulted from both changing supply conditions, due to the vagaries of climate, and fluctuating demand reflecting periodic recessions in the industrial nations. Such contingencies have caused sharp and damaging fluctuations in the export earnings of developing countries.

---

[10] See Isaiah Frank, "Toward a New Framework for International Commodity Policy," *Finance and Development*, June 1976, pp. 17–20, 37–38.

As one example, Zambia was hit hard by the copper price boom and bust of the early 1970s. The price of copper peaked in April 1974, then fell to less than half its peak level before the end of the same year. Zambia's ability to purchase imports fell by 45 percent between 1974 and 1975 and its gross domestic product decreased by 15 percent.[11]

Three basic approaches have been followed in dealing with the instability of primary commodity markets—compensatory financing, international commodity agreements, and increased processing by developing countries of their own primary commodities.[12] The IMF set up its compensatory financing facility in 1963 to extend credit to countries whose export earnings fall dramatically because of a commodity price slump. The STABEX scheme established by the European Community in 1975 is intended to perform a similar function for the community's associates in Africa, the Caribbean, and the Pacific. Both schemes are considered by the developing countries to be too restrictive as to conditions and available funds. Even if these schemes were liberalized, there would be limits to how far any of them could go toward easing the pressures on the most needy of the developing countries. Thus the continuing and growing emphasis on international commodity agreements.

International commodity agreements

The most common form of international commodity agreement is the buffer stock system. Under this arrangement, producing and importing countries establish a buffer stock fund and agree on fixed minimum and maximum prices. The fund manager buys the commodity when international prices are close to the minimum mark and sells when they rise toward the maximum. The purpose is price stability in an intermediate area, guaranteeing a minimum price for exporters while safeguarding the importers against price surges.

A buffer stock agreement on tin has existed since 1956 and a sixth renewal of the tin agreement came into effect on July 1, 1982. The United States, the USSR, and other Soviet-bloc countries, however, declined to join the tin pact. A cocoa agreement with export quotas and a buffer stock was launched in 1975 but collapsed in 1980. But neither these nor several other similar agreements, such as the International Sugar Agreement (1978), have been able to maintain prices even within their wide ranges. The arrangements encounter difficulties in agreeing on an appropriate price range, on sharing export quotas among the producers, and on the respective financial contributions of exporters and importers to

---

[11] *The Economist*, April 19, 1980.

[12] See F. Gerard Adams and Sonia A. Klein, *Stabilizing World Commodity Markets* (Lexington, Mass.: D. C. Heath, 1978).

the buffer stock fund. The fifth tin agreement ran out of buffer stock early in its life when tin prices soared to new high levels. The cocoa agreement amassed a large buffer stock fund from levies on international shipments. But a buffer stock was never acquired because world prices remained persistently above the intervention level agreed upon after the agreement went into effect.

Despite the largely unsuccessful record of commodity agreements, they still continue as a top priority item of the developing countries. The difficulties encountered in the agreements are looked upon as a challenge to improve the mechanism rather than as a deterrent. In the 1976 meeting of UNCTAD, the developing countries proposed an integrated commodity stabilization program that would include 18 commodities with buffer stocks financed by a common fund. The justification for the common fund is that it can be smaller than the sum of separate funds for each commodity because of different patterns and timing of fluctuations in the various commodity markets. The strategy of negotiating a series of pacts in unison is that participating nations can balance concessions on one commodity against an advantage on another.

By 1982, after six years of international bargaining, UNCTAD managed to persuade producers and consumers to enter into only one new commodity agreement—natural rubber. The member countries, however, had reached agreement on creating the "Common Fund," but with a modest financial base of $750 million as compared to the $2 billion initially envisaged.

Trade arrangements to moderate short-term fluctuations in commodity export earnings have considerable international support, but arrangements that attempt to shift the long-run terms of trade in favor of the producers do not. Changing the terms of trade is viewed as benefiting the producers at the expense of the consumers.

Buffer stocks of the stabilizing sort can be of practical benefit to consumers. Increasingly inflexible cost structures in the industrialized countries have meant that rises in commodity prices have a ratchet effect on inflation. Prices of final goods rise to reflect increases in raw material costs; they rarely fall in step once commodity prices start downward. On the producers' side, wildly fluctuating possibilities in future prices hamper investment. Sustained periods of falling prices lead to stagnant production facilities, and periods of sharply increased demand lead to destabilizing commodity price increases, because production cannot be quickly expanded. Stabilization, therefore, is perceived by both exporters and importers as in their mutual interest.

Thus, there are sound reasons for supporting some commodity stabilization schemes. But the mechanism that has been developed through international commodity agreements may not support the burden of good intentions. Nevertheless, international commodity agreements are certain to persist as a component of the international trade framework.

Producer associations

The Organization of Petroleum Exporting Countries is a leading example of producer associations. Since its creation in 1960, OPEC has worked to assert greater control over the petroleum resources of its members and to obtain greater benefits from petroleum production. Although well financed and expertly staffed, OPEC was slow to realize these goals. OPEC oil revenues hovered around $.75 to $1 a barrel from 1960 to 1970.[13]

In the early 1970s, two factors made it possible for OPEC to begin a spectacular escalation of oil prices. One factor was a tight supply situation in world markets as a result of rapidly expanding demand. A second factor was the erosion of the major oil companies' control over the international market. Smaller American and European oil companies were entering into petroleum exploration and production, thus weakening the position of the majors by enlarging the options of the oil-producing countries.

When the Israeli-Arab War of 1973 began, the effects of the shift in bargaining power toward OPEC became apparent. The oil ministers of the Arab nations decided to use the "oil weapon" to support the Arab cause and began an embargo against certain nations, principally the United States and the Netherlands.[14] OPEC revenues, which had reached $2.60 a barrel in 1973, skyrocketed to almost $10 in 1974. This new level remained relatively stable until 1979 when the Iranian revolution interrupted oil supplies. Anxious buyers scrambled for oil and bid up prices in the "spot market" to a level of $40 a barrel. The result was a new high level of oil prices.

The shift in bargaining power also permitted the OPEC countries to extend their control over their natural resources. Over the 1970s, such major producers as Saudi Arabia, Iran, and Venezuela nationalized the oil-producing operations in their countries.

OPEC is frequently referred to as a producer cartel. A true export cartel, however, goes beyond agreements on prices. It also controls production and allocates market shares. OPEC serves mainly as a meeting ground and information clearing house. Decisions are made at OPEC meetings, but the compliance of member countries is voluntary. There have been moves within OPEC toward controlling production, but such moves have not been effective. The latest attempt in this direction occurred in 1981 in response to a growing imbalance in the world oil markets.[15] If the challenge to control production is not met because of

---

[13] Suhayr Mikdashi, *The International Politics of Natural Resources* (Ithaca, N.Y.: Cornell University Press, 1976), p. 72; see also Faribosz Ghadar, *The Evolution of OPEC Strategy* (Lexington, Mass.: Lexington Books, 1977).

[14] Robert B. Stobaugh, "The Evolution of Iranian Oil Policy, 1925–75," in *Iran Under the Pahlavis,* ed. George Lenczowski (Stanford, Calif.: Hoover Institution Press, 1978), p. 244.

[15] *The Economist,* May 30, 1981, p. 57.

the different interests of the individual countries, the future power of OPEC to determine prices will be greatly eroded.

In a number of commodity areas other than oil, many producing countries have been trying to emulate the OPEC model. Producer associations have been initiated in copper, bauxite, phosphate, chromium, and rubber. As of the 1980s, the other producer association attempts have not had any marked success. To be effective, such an association must consist of a relatively small number of countries that control a large share of world production. Also, world demand for the commodity must be strong and growing.

BILATERAL TRADING ARRANGEMENTS

To complete the picture of the international trade framework, mention should be made of bilateral trading arrangements. Many such agreements exist, as previously mentioned, between the centrally planned and the market economies. Another example of bilateral arrangements is the U.S.-Canada Automotive Products agreement concluded in 1965. At the time the agreement was signed, it was considered to be a model that might be widely followed for obtaining the benefits of specialization and large-scale production by creating broader markets for a specific industry.

The agreement permits the integration of Canadian and U.S. production of automobile parts and vehicles. Thus production units in each country can produce at efficient levels, and most vehicles and parts can cross the border duty-free in each direction. The selection of products and plants in each country was intended to result in an equitable trade balance between the countries in the automotive field.

The agreement has not been a complete success. Since signing the auto pact, Canada has had a trade surplus in the automotive field for only three years: 1970–72. Subsequent Canadian deficits have led to pressure by Canada for changes. As of 1982, no agreement had been reached as to amendments.

SUMMARY

The large number of organizations and the complexity of the many trading arrangements suggest that a high degree of disarray exists in multinational trading. This is true in the sense that the multinational enterprise must keep informed about and even participate in numerous trade negotiations in many forums. In another sense, however, the picture is rather simple and clear-cut. There are "three worlds" involved and each has its own objectives. The industrialized world favors free trade and specialization and has resisted basic changes in the structure of the world economy. The developing countries are not in favor of free trade and want to use trade arrangements to achieve structural changes in their own economies and in their economic relations with the rest of the world. The centrally planned world would like to expand greatly its trading relations with the other two worlds but with a minimum of change in internal economic structures.

The multinational trade agreements "game" is one in which each of the participating groups, and each country within a group, is trying to move a few more steps toward its goals. The game cannot stop because of the growing interdependency of the three worlds. Also, there are usually enough mutual benefits involved to warrant the continuing search for new trade arrangements. The results of the negotiations depend, of course, on the respective bargaining power of the participants. The bargaining power keeps changing and involves geopolitical factors as well as economic considerations, such as growing world scarcities of certain natural resources.

Institutional arrangements frequently lag behind real needs and deal mainly with the problems of yesterday rather than those of today. This observation is relevant to the international trade framework on two dimensions. One is the relationship of the multinational enterprise and foreign direct investment to trade patterns. The second is the set of terms and conditions for international transfers of technology. Neither of these international dimensions has yet been given proper recognition by the institutional arrangements comprising the international trade framework, with one exception. UNCTAD has been the pioneer by including multinational enterprises and international technology transfers along with trade in its conference deliberations.

EXERCISES AND DISCUSSION QUESTIONS

1. Distinguish between a free-trade area, a customs union, and a common market.

2. What is the significance of the principle of "most-favored-nation" treatment? Why has it not weakened significantly the bargaining position of individual countries in their tariff negotiations with other countries?

3. "The time has come to create a GATT for investment. Trade negotiations must recognize that direct investment and foreign production are both alternatives and complements to traditional trade." Discuss.

4. Under what circumstances would you recommend that industrial consumer countries support moves by the developing producer countries for further commodity agreements?

5. "The basic problem underlying East-West trade is that the governments in the centrally planned countries make the trade decisions on the basis of national objectives. In the market economies, private enterprises make the trade decisions on the basis of private profit objectives with the government intervening only in a negative way to control trade that is not considered to be in the national interests." Comment.

Chapter 8

The international legal environment

The legal environment for international business consists principally of the laws and courts of the individual nation-states. Since no single international commercial legal system exists, the international firm is confronted with as many legal environments as there are countries. The national systems differ significantly in philosophy and practice, and each nation-state maintains its own set of courts in complete independence of every other nation. The closest approximation to an international legal framework is a patchwork system of treaties, codes, and agreements among certain nations that apply to selected areas of international business activity.

Both business enterprises and national governments are often frustrated by the legal environment. As the effective domain of the multinational enterprise exceeds the legal jurisdiction of individual nations, the enterprise constantly faces uncertainties and conflicts as to which laws apply. At the same time, national governments are seriously troubled because of their perception that multinational firms can and do escape from national regulations and laws.

This chapter provides the international manager with some background on the labyrinth that comprises the international legal environment. It also identifies some of the principal legal issues that are likely to concern the international business firm.

INTERNATIONAL LAW AND INTERNATIONAL BUSINESS

Although contrary to the facts, there is a widely held impression that a rather precise system of international law exists for guiding business transactions across national boundaries. This impression is particularly strong as it relates to the protection of foreign-owned private property. It is common to hear businessmen and government officials declare that the expropriation of foreign property without prompt and adequate compensation is a violation of international law. Such wistful views have long been popular in the economically advanced investor countries, but they are not generally accepted around the world. In order for rules and principles to become international law, nation-states must consider such rules and principles legally binding upon them.

What is normally called international law is more accurately described as *international public law* or the *law of nations*. It consists of a body of rules and principles that nation-states consider legally binding. It can be enforced through the International Court of Justice, international arbitration, or the internal courts of the nation-states, which lawyers refer to as municipal courts.[1] It is mainly concerned with the relationships between states, the delimitation of their jurisdictions, and control of war. In recent years, international law has also emphasized the protection of individual human rights, even against the individual's own state. Through the proliferation of treaty law and specialized international organizations, the substance of the law has expanded to include cross-frontier relationships of individuals and corporate bodies.

To be operationally meaningful for the multinational enterprise, international law must have a system for adjudicating legal disputes and enforcing legal decisions. Here is where the gap exists. The only international court is the International Court of Justice at The Hague. It is the principal organ of the United Nations, and all members of the United Nations are ipso facto parties to the statute establishing the court. The function of the court is to pass judgment upon disputes between states,

---

[1] See Noyes E. Leech, Covey T. Oliver, and Joseph M. Sweeney, *The International Legal System* (Mineola, N.Y.: Foundation Press, 1973).

and only states that have submitted to its jurisdiction are parties in cases before the court. Private persons or corporations do not have direct access to the International Court.

Private issues can only be adjudicated by the International Court when they are espoused by one of the member states. In some countries, business firms have had reasonable success in securing official government support. In most situations, however, this has not been easy because the political interests of governments must be the guiding rule. Furthermore, the governments representing both sides of a dispute must agree to accept the court's jurisdiction. Even if private issues reach the court and are decided, the problem still remains as to how the legal judgment will be enforced, given the relatively weak form of world government.

Box 8—1

Limits of the International Court of Justice

Los Angeles—Atlantic Richfield Co. said its subsidiary, Libyan American Oil Co., received an $80 million award ruling from an arbitrator appointed by the International Court of Justice.

The award was designated as compensation for the expropriation of Atlantic Richfield's assets and concessions in 1973 and 1974.

However, the award may be uncollectable. The Libyan government refused to participate in the arbitration procedure, and Atlantic Richfield said it must undertake "further proceedings."

Source: *The Wall Street Journal,* April 14, 1977.

In some cases, international law is applied by the municipal courts of a country. For example, the international law providing that foreign sovereigns and their diplomatic representatives enjoy certain immunities from municipal jurisdiction requires the cooperation of municipal courts for its realization. Interestingly enough, where governments trade through state companies incorporated in a foreign country, such as the USSR trading company Amtorg incorporated in New York, an important unsettled issue is whether the state corporation has diplomatic immunity.

From the standpoint of international business, the most important approximation to international law is the growing number of treaties and conventions covering commercial and economic matters. According to modern diplomatic usage, the more important international agreements are referred to as *treaties.* Those of lesser importance are called *conventions, agreements, protocols,* and *acts.* All of these forms are agreements between two or more nation-states which normally become legally enforceable through the municipal courts of the participating countries and an international court is not essential.

The weakness of the structure of international commitments through treaties, codes, and agreements is its inadequate coverage for many ingredients of business operations that have grown in importance with the internationalization of business. Furthermore, the number of countries participating in particular agreements may be limited in comparison with the global horizon of the multinational enterprise.

The right of establishment

Through bilateral commercial treaties, many governments seek to enlarge the opportunity for their nationals to transact business in foreign countries on a nondiscriminatory basis. The privilege of doing business in a foreign country and the conditions under which it is formally granted are the substance of a series of treaties known in the United States as Treaties of Friendship, Commerce, and Navigation. The objective of such commercial treaties is to secure for foreigners the right to trade, invest, or establish and operate a business in a country on a nondiscriminatory basis. The fundamental point underlying commercial treaties is that engaging in business transactions in a country other than one's own is a privilege and not a right. Usually, this privilege and the delineation of its conditions are worked out by negotiation between governments.[2]

Such treaties, of course, are not always observed. In the early 1960s, for example, the French government became greatly concerned because American firms were attempting to take over a number of French companies, including France's largest manufacturer of computers (Machines Bull). The French response was to restrict American direct investment through administrative delays and informal pressures. Although these restrictions violated France's Treaty of Establishment with the United States, the U.S. government never formally protested and apparently was not asked to do so by U.S. firms that were affected. However, the French ban on new direct investment did not last long because other Common Market countries were anxious and willing to receive the U.S. companies.[3]

The protection of industrial property rights

Most countries protect industrial property rights—a term that includes patents, know-how, and trademarks. Patents are granted and trademarks are registered by national governments and they are valid only within the territorial jurisdiction of the granting government. Conse-

---

[2] Henry Steiner and Detlev F. Vagts, *Transnational Legal Problems*, 2d ed. Mineola, N.Y.: Foundation Press, 1976), pp. 619–21.

[3] Christopher Layton, *Transatlantic Investments* (Boulogne-sur-Seine, France: Atlantic Institute, 1966), pp. 36–44.

quently, foreign exploitation of a patent or trademark requires a parallel grant by foreign governments. As might be expected, the requirements for trademark registration and the patent systems of the various countries differ significantly. To protect its industrial property rights, the international firm must file patent and trademark registration applications in every country in which these property rights are to be used. This requirement can be both burdensome and expensive. One large corporation estimated that the cost of obtaining foreign patents was running close to $2 million a year. As another example, 10 percent of the money spent on developing the British Hovercraft, a vehicle for rapid transportation over water, went for securing patents around the world.[4]

In many cases, companies have lost the foreign rights to trademarks and have had to pay royalties for their use or buy back these rights. An extreme example of trademark difficulties is the case of a U.S. citizen living in Mexico who registered in Mexico the brand names and trademarks of some 40 companies. These included such well-known names as "Carter's Little Liver Pills" and "Bromo Seltzer." Most of the companies succeeded in regaining control of their brand names, but lengthy litigation and official support of the U.S. government was required.[5]

Several international agreements have simplified the process of protecting industrial property rights in foreign countries. The Convention of Paris comprises a group of more than 50 nations, including the United States, that have agreed to provide national treatment for each other in regard to industrial property rights. This means that each country grants to nationals of other member countries the same rights it affords to its own nationals. The European Patent Convention that became operational in 1978 established a European patent office which can make one grant that is effective in 11 European signatory countries. A Patent Cooperation Treaty, approved by at least 35 countries at the diplomatic level, also became effective in 1978. The purpose of this treaty is to simplify and expedite the patent application process through providing centralized international search reports. Such reports can aid patent applicants in deciding whether patent protection should be sought in other countries.

Taxation treaties

In a world of separate taxing authorities, problems arise because the entity being taxed, or parts of it, may fall under the jurisdiction of more than one taxing authority. An enterprise may have its legal residence in one country, do business in another country, and have headquarters in still another country. How is the enterprise to be taxed and how can it

---

[4] *The Economist*, June 17, 1967.

[5] Philip R. Cateora and John M. Hess, *International Marketing*, 4th ed. (Homewood, Ill.: Richard D. Irwin, 1979), p. 197.

avoid paying taxes on the same base to more than one of the taxing jurisdictions? The solution to this problem must recognize both the right of the enterprise to be free from excessive taxation and the right of the different authorities to tax revenues.

The right to levy and collect taxes is one of the most sacred rights of national sovereignty, but there is no clear or universally accepted theory of tax jurisdiction. Nor is there an international law that specifies who has the right to tax and that sets limits to the reach of any country's tax jurisdiction. Business transactions across national boundaries, therefore, can be greatly influenced in both positive and negative ways by the problems or opportunities resulting from varying taxation policies of overlapping national tax jurisdictions.

The tax systems of different countries vary significantly in the treatment of who is taxed—that is, in concepts of residence of the firm or individual—and what sources of income are taxed.[6] As a result, two taxing jurisdictions may claim the right to tax the same property or income. This probability has caused governments to provide credits for taxes paid abroad and to negotiate bilateral tax treaties.[7] The United States has bilateral tax treaties with more than 25 countries, all of which are intended to provide relief from double taxation. No multilateral tax treaties have been realized as yet, but the Model Double Taxation Convention on Income and Capital approved by the Organization for Economic Cooperation and Development (OECD) in 1977 has been influential as a guide to countries in their bilateral negotiations.

The trend in tax treaties has been for host countries of international business firms to impose taxes up to the rates imposed by the home countries of the international business firm. Such a policy can maximize the share received by the host country without increasing the total tax burden on a company. Another trend is for nations to use tax exemptions or low taxes as an attraction for international business activities. But the effectiveness of such government policy depends upon the willingness of the home governments of the international business firms to grant "tax sparing," that is, to allow tax credits as if full taxes were paid. The United States, for example, does not grant tax credit for taxes spared abroad, and the advantage to U.S. firms of tax inducements in foreign countries may be offset by home-country taxation on the higher foreign profits resulting from the tax concessions.

Property protection in foreign jurisdictions

On December 12, 1974, the United Nations General Assembly adopted the Charter of Economic Rights and Duties of States. The charter states

---

[6] For example, see *Corporate Taxes: A Worldwide Summary* (New York: Price, Waterhouse, January 1982).

[7] See Walter H. and Dorothy B. Diamond, eds., *International Tax Treaties of All Nations* (Dobbs Ferry, N.Y.: Oceana Publications, 1980).

(Art. 2, sect. 1) that "Every state has and shall freely exercise full permanent sovereignty, including possession, use and disposal, over all its wealth, natural resources and economic activities." In effect, the charter asserts untrammeled discretion and the *absolute supremacy of national* law and jurisdiction in matters of nationalization, compensation, and the revision or termination of contracts. The UN vote was 120 to 6 with 10 abstentions. The dissenters included five Western European countries and the United States. The abstentions were Canada, Israel, Japan, and seven Western European nations. In effect, the vote was a case of the developing nations versus the industrialized countries.

Although not formally binding on member states, the UN resolution highlights the competing and conflicting positions of investor and host countries. The developing nations assert the principle of permanent sovereignty. The industrialized countries maintain that international law imposes certain limitations on the exercise of sovereignty and that its exercise can be further limited with binding effect by agreement.

As a general rule, foreign investors are not willing to rely solely on local courts for the protection of foreign property. As foreigners, they may have great difficulty in enforcing their rights. Under the principle of sovereign immunity, actions against the state in many countries are allowed only in exceptional cases. Furthermore, parliamentary sovereignty implies that one parliament cannot bind its successor so far as the legislative functions are concerned. Government policies, local laws, and even constitutional provisions may be altered unilaterally at some future date.

Also, in the crucial matter of compensation for the taking of property, the views of investor and host countries may differ sharply. The rule as usually asserted by investor nations—that compensation must be prompt, adequate, and effective—is not recognized by many developing and communist nations. Most developing countries take the philosophical position that "social" considerations may be paramount to the rights of the property owners. Furthermore, the requirement for full and immediate payment would deny to poor countries the right to pursue a broad program of economic and social reform. In the communist nations, expropriation without compensation has been justified as the means of implementing a philosophy opposed in principle to private property.

The international legal environment is clearly deficient in the important areas of protecting foreign property and the settlement of investment disputes between parties of different nationalities. Yet there has been a big gap between rhetoric and reality. At the same time that many nations were supporting the rhetoric of the UN Charter of Economic Rights, the same nations were entering into treaties that bound the contracting parties to specific substantive and procedural rules relating to foreign investments. Such rules deal with the conditions under which nationalization may take place, standards of compensation, settlement of disputes, and the like. The reality is that many nations are anxious to attract foreign investment, and they are convinced that assurances are needed to interest foreign investors.

The settlement of investment disputes

As of 1980, 83 governments were associated with the International Center for Settlement of Investment Disputes (ICSID) sponsored by the World Bank. As the name implies, ICSID is an international mechanism for settling disputes between states and foreign investors that came into being in 1967.

ICSID does not lay down rules defining the respective rights and obligations of investors and host states. Instead, it provides procedures for conciliation and/or arbitration of disputes if both parties agree to refer the dispute to the center. Proceedings are conducted by conciliators and arbitrators selected by the parties and administered by the secretariat of the center. Decisions by arbitrators are final and binding and must be recognized by all states that are parties to the ICSID convention. During the first 13 years of operations, nine arbitration cases were brought before the center.

All the industrialized countries are ICSID members, as are the Eastern European countries of Yugoslavia and Romania. Most developing nations in Africa and Asia are members, especially the small underdeveloped countries that hope to improve their attraction to foreign investors. But none of the Latin American countries are signatories because they view ICSID as an infringement on national sovereignty.

The Latin American position is represented by the so-called Calvo Doctrine, named after an Argentine jurist.[8] The doctrine asserts that a foreigner by entering a country implicitly consents to be treated as a national. In other words, the foreign firm does not have the right to invoke the protection of its own government in investment disputes. The Calvo clause appears in contracts, statutes, and even in some Latin American constitutions. But its importance has been diminished by new trends such as investment guarantee agreements.

Virtually all major investor nations have foreign investment guaranty programs, as discussed below in Chapter 15. These programs provide political risk insurance and other types of protection for national firms, but only for foreign investments in countries that have signed investment guarantee agreements. The agreements do not, as a rule, provide full and automatic protection against nationalization, but the host country usually agrees to provide fair compensation without undue delay. The agreements can be detailed agreements of substance, as in the case of the more than 40 treaties negotiated by Germany. Other agreements are limited to more procedural matters in the event that investments should be

---

[8] Steiner and Vagts, *Transnational Legal Problems*, pp. 522–30.

endangered, as in the case of the more than 100 agreements negotiated by the United States.[9]

Infrastructure treaties and conventions

The international legal environment includes many areas of intergovernmental cooperation as well as conflict. An important area of cooperation is that of infrastructure, where a series of UN specialized agencies perform valuable services that facilitate business transactions across national boundaries. The international agreements and activities in the fields of communications and transportation are of special importance.

The International Civil Aviation Organization (ICAO) fosters safe, regular, and efficient international civil aviation through developing international specifications for air traffic, airports, telecommunications, charts, operations, airworthiness, and personnel that are adopted and observed by member countries. The International Telecommunications Union (ITU) controls and allocates radio frequencies and facilitates international telegraph and telephone communications. The Universal Postal Union, initially based on a convention of 1874 and presently a specialized agency of the United Nations, has established compulsory provisions for member countries governing international postal service and operates as a clearinghouse in the settlement of certain accounts. The International Labor Organization (ILO) has adopted conventions on trade union rights and on the protection of the right of workers to organize and bargain collectively. The World Health Organization (WHO) works to improve health conditions and has various international duties relative to the standardization of drugs, epidemic control, and quarantine measures.

As new technologies are developed and new issues become of critical concern to nations, nations are stimulated to create new infrastructure agreements or institutions. Such has been the case with the development of the communications satellite, which led to the formation of the international consortium Intelsat. Intelsat facilitates and regulates the international transmission of television broadcasts and other newly feasible means of international communications. The same has been true in the field of environmental control.

In the area of access to deep seabed mineral resources, another international treaty may near completion. The ocean contains vast quantities of manganese, copper, cobalt, and nickel strewn over much of the deep seabed beyond the limits of national jurisdictions. How should access to these resources be regulated? The United Nations General Assembly unanimously declared in 1970 that the deep seabed resources are the "common heritage of mankind" and therefore must be under international control.

---

[9] Organization for Economic Cooperation and Development, *Investing in Developing Countries*, 3d rev. ed. (Paris, 1975), p. 16.

Box 8–2

Can the Third World rule the airwaves?

After 11 weeks of often bitter debate, the Third World has made it clear that the International Telecommunications Union (ITU), an arm of the U.N. that allocates the use of the entire radio-wave spectrum for everything from ham radios to microwave ovens and radar systems, is no longer a rubber-stamp organ for the industrial nations.

*   *   *   *   *

Since the last meeting in 1959 (World Administrative Radio Conferences are usually convened every other decade), the radio spectrum has become crowded by the explosion of data communications and other technologies that rely on radio waves. The industrial nations thus went to Switzerland seeking additional allocations or changes that would allow more efficient use of the radio spectrum. This time there were almost twice as many Third-World countries as were at the last WARC, and they were determined to stake out their own air-wave claims.

The less developed countries are alarmed by the prospect that, unless they curb the industrial nations' expanding use of radio frequencies, they will be frozen out of the telecommunications spectrum. They also want orbital "parking spaces" above the equator for geostationary satellites to be reserved on an equitable, country-by-country basis, as opposed to the current practice of assigning orbits on a first-come, first-served basis.

The United States and other industrial countries did manage to wring some compromises from the 130 nations that sent delegates to Geneva. But on two of the most politically sensitive issues, the concessions amount only to a deferral of a final decision. Voluntary conformity to ITU standards is crucial, because radio signals do not respect national boundaries. Without standards, one country's air-navigation signals could be distorted by a neighbor's television broadcasts.

Refusing to pledge compliance is an almost unprecedented action. It has happened only once before. But this time, the United States took that step on five issues, and several other major countries did the same at least once.

Source: Adapted from *Business Week*, December 17, 1979, pp. 37–38.

In 1980, after a decade of negotiations, the United Nations Law of the Sea Conference agreed upon a draft convention that was expected to be accepted by member nations. The treaty provides for the creation of an International Seabed Authority to administer a "parallel system." This will permit both private or state-owned mining companies and an international public enterprise to mine the deep seabed mineral resources. The enterprise, as proposed, would be the first completely internationally operated commercial institution.[10]

---

[10] The draft convention covers many other issues of interest to international business, such as the rights of coastal states to govern offshore fishing and petroleum exploration. See the special issue of *Columbia Journal of World Business*, Winter 1980, on the "Law of the Sea."

An emerging issue of great importance to international business is cross-border flows of computerized data and extraterritorial business data storage. Computer communications allow instant access to vast stores of information without regard to physical distance—or national borders. Not surprisingly, therefore, a number of nations have become concerned about transborder data flows and have enacted laws that control or restrict the collection and processing of data. Of particular concern has been the "privacy" protection of personal information stored in automated networks or files. But other issues, still vaguely perceived, are being debated.

In early 1981, the 21-nation Council of Europe completed an international treaty to protect persons against abusive use of computer data and to regulate the flow of computerized data across borders. Most of these nations have data-protection laws that safeguard personal privacy. A major objective of the treaty is to prevent the emergence of "data havens," akin to tax havens, by preventing sensitive personal data being shipped to countries without data-protection laws.

In a sense, this treaty is only the tip of the iceberg. The need for regulating cross-border data flows has been argued from many other standpoints. As stated by a high Canadian official, computer-communications technology "creates the potential of growing dependence, rather than interdependence, the loss of employment opportunities, an addition to the balance of payments problem, the danger of loss of legitimate access to vital information, and the danger that industrial and social development will largely be governed by the decision of interest groups residing in another country."[11]

Proposals have been made to require disclosure of cross-border data transmissions to facilitate law enforcement. This reflects a concern that computer service networks can facilitate tax evasion by billing a company in whichever country suits the customer's convenience. Other concerns are that electronic funds transfers may fuel inflation by accelerating the velocity of money, and that the greatly reduced cost of international transmissions of computer data by satellite is endangering the profitability of public telephone monopolies.[12] Several international organizations are studying the implications of transborder data flows, and important recommendations that may restrict international data flows are certain to result.

NATIONAL LEGAL SYSTEMS

The above review indicates that the regulatory framework for international business still rests predominantly on a multiplicity of national

---

[11] See Arthur T. Downey, "A Collision Ahead: Restriction on Transborder Data Flow," in *The International Essays for Business Decision Makers, Volume III*, ed. Mark B. Winchester (Dallas: Center for International Business, 1978), p. 128.

[12] *The Economist*, May 23, 1981, p. 93.

legal systems. Given the great diversity and complexity of national legal systems, the international firm will undoubtedly rely on specialized assistance for legal matters. The international manager, however, needs a general understanding of the national legal systems and the types of legal problems likely to arise.

Most national legal systems are based on either the common law or the civil law system. Civil law prevails in most continental European countries, in their former colonies, and in a number of Asian and African countries. Supplemented by Islamic law, civil law also predominates in Middle Eastern countries. The common law system, developed in England during the Middle Ages, has been adopted by most countries where the English settled or have governed.

Civil-law countries embody their main rules of law in a legislative code, and government officials are responsible for interpreting the codes and developing detailed working rules for implementing legislative acts. In common-law countries, the judiciary is the ultimate interpreter and decision maker in the legal system, and the judges are normally guided, not by a code, but by principles declared in previous decisions in similar or analogous cases.

In practice, the distinction between common and civil law is not clear-cut. Large parts of Anglo-American law are contained in statutes and codes. In civil law countries, large parts of the law have never been reduced to statutes or codes but have been developed by the courts. In general, however, civil-law countries place great reliance on the prestige of a career civil service as a counterpart to the judicial power in the Anglo-American system.

Differences in the formal structure of national legal systems are important. Equally crucial can be national differences in the legal process for resolving legal problems. The gap between the developed legal system and effective administration of justice will vary greatly among nations. In some countries, even the most advanced laws remain dead letters on the books because of a limited capacity to implement the laws or because an underdeveloped judicial system does not have the capability for an expeditious handling of litigation.

The American society probably goes further than any other in translating issues into legal questions and expecting the courts and lawyers to resolve them. By way of contrast, Chinese and Japanese societies go to the other extreme: abhorrence of lawyers, laws, and, above all, litigation. "It is better to be vexed to death than to bring a lawsuit," says a Chinese proverb. The Chinese and Japanese prefer conciliation and mediation to litigation. The aversion to litigation reflects a fear that legal rules are too impersonal and rigid to accommodate the realities of particular cases and a desire to avoid the disruptions of friendly relations attending a clear-cut victory and defeat in litigation.[13] In all of Japan, according to

---

[13] Steiner and Vagts, *Transnational Legal Problems*, p. 191.

official statistics, there are about 12,000 lawyers. This compares with 30,000 in Washington, D.C., 64,000 in New York State, and nearly 600,000 in the United States, with twice Japan's population.[14]

One important legal practice that may surprise American international managers is the prominent role of the notary public. In the United States notary publics perform only a minor function. In civil-law countries, the notary is a key figure. Trained as a lawyer, the notary gives conclusiveness in a legal sense to contractual instruments. The legal necessity to have virtually all legal instruments notarized requires time and may be considered excessive red tape by the American manager. But in Latin America, Western Europe, and other countries, it is absolutely essential that a transaction is adequately recorded, preserved, and made firm and certain by being recorded with a notary. The importance of the notary may be illustrated by the case of at least one Latin American country, where the privilege of being a notary is granted only by the president of the republic and is considered to be the most lucrative of all political grants.

SELECTED LEGAL PROBLEMS IN INTERNATIONAL BUSINESS

Jurisdiction in international trade

International trade is based chiefly on the use of standardized forms and practices. The standardized instruments contain most of the rules governing the parties. Sales memoranda, brokers' notes, bills of lading, charter parties, marine insurance policies, and letters of credit all embody familiar clauses which shipping clerks and bank tellers are trained to follow. Also, the import or export of goods can be, and usually is, arranged so as to involve the law of a single country. By including a "choice-of-law" clause in the contract, the parties can select the law that will govern their obligations on issues that lie within their contractual capacity—such as sufficiency of performance and excuse for nonperformance. But even with a choice-of-law clause, issues may arise that are outside the contractual capacity of the parties and on which the governing law is uncertain.

Another common legal issue in international trade is whether to include a clause in the contract prescribing the method of arbitration if future disputes arise. If arbitration is to take place in the United States, the normal clause provides that the rules of the American Arbitration Association will be followed.[15] If arbitration is to take place in Europe, the usual pattern is to follow rules developed by the International Chamber of Commerce. Where trade is with Eastern European countries, the

---

[14] *The Wall Street Journal*, February 9, 1981.

[15] See Clive Schmitthoff, *International Commercial Arbitration* (Dobbs Ferry, N.Y.: Oceana Publications, 1979).

agreement may be to submit disputes to the Moscow Foreign Trade Arbitration Commission.

Translation problems

A unique source of legal difficulties in the international business field is the problem of languages and translation. The problem is present in the drafting of contracts, in the preparation of corporate documents, in negotiation and settlement of disputes by arbitration or court proceedings, and in any reference to foreign laws or concepts. Legal instruments must be drafted with a view toward their meaning to a judge or arbitrator when foreign legal elements are involved. The translation problem expands the area of uncertainty not only because of the normal difficulties of translating the meanings of words from one language to another. The translation of legal language also involves a transfer of concepts rather than a mechanical matching of words. The vital issue for the international manager, according to one distinguished legal authority, is to make sure that the matter of translation is properly worked out during the period when the instrument is drafted.[16]

Whose law determines "Inc."?

In the present international legal environment, the business enterprise engaged in multinational operations cannot become an international corporation in a legal sense. No international agency has yet been created with the authority to grant international incorporation. Consequently, the multinational business enterprise must content itself with stringing together a series of corporations created by the laws of different nation-states. The legal complexities arising out of such a situation are immense. The presence of the same enterprise in many countries necessarily subjects it to different laws and legal climates, which in many situations may conflict.

In setting up multinational operations, one of the first considerations is to determine which country's laws will be applied to give life and motion to the component parts of the multinational enterprise. This issue has been posed by one legal authority as "Whose Law Determines 'Inc.'?"[17] The legal test of nationality varies among countries. Like an individual, a corporation can have dual nationality. It can also be "stateless," thereby exposing the members of the corporation to individual liability. The question of nationality may have significant tax conse-

---

[16] Henry P. de Vries, "The Language Barrier," *Columbia Journal of World Business*, July–August 1969, pp. 79–80.

[17] Henry P. de Vries, "The Problem of Identity: Whose Law Determines 'Inc'?", *Columbia Journal of World Business*, March–April 1969, pp. 76–78.

Conrad © 1975, Los Angeles Times. Reprinted with permission.

quences. It may also determine whether an enterprise can benefit from government subsidy programs or engage in certain strategic businesses.

The underlying U.S. view for all corporations is that a corporation secures its life and existence from a grant of the sovereign, and the nationality of the corporation is that of the sovereign power making the grant. In many other countries, particularly civil law countries, a corporation is considered to be created by the contractual intent of its members rather than by a grant from the sovereign. The nationality of such a corporation is not necessarily that of the country in which it is constituted. In determining the law applicable to a corporation's existence and internal relations, several countries look at the place of incorporation. Others look to the center of management or the place of the registered head office. As a result of these variations, multiple incorporation in various countries may be necessary to protect stockholders from personal liability.

The problems and risks arising from different concepts of nationality can be illustrated by a recent case brought before the German courts. A suit was filed against the U.S. stockholders of a corporation organized in the State of Washington to conduct mining operations in Mexico but with

the central management of the corporation meeting in Hamburg. Since
the corporation was administered in Germany but not constituted pursuant to German law, the court held that it was an unincorporated association in Germany and that the stockholders were personally liable for
corporate liabilities.

Choosing the form of business organization

What form of business organization should be used in different legal
jurisdictions? Tax considerations both at home and abroad may play a
key role in the choice of legal form. The principal objective, however,
normally will be that of insulating the parent organization or the investor
from direct liability for obligations incurred in local operations.

In the choice of legal form, a clear distinction exists between common-
law countries and civil-law countries. As noted previously, in common-
law countries a grant from the public authority gives life to the corporation. In civil-law countries, the corporation is created by a contract
between two or more persons, and the root concept is that of *société* or
Gesellschaft. Thus, the one-man corporation is a contradiction in terms,
and most civil-law countries tend to reject the one-man corporation and
the wholly owned subsidiary. In some countries, the acquisition by one
individual or legal entity of all the shares of a corporation may lead to its
automatic dissolution and to personal liability of the stockholder for the
corporation's liabilities.

In most countries, the choice of foreign business organization to operate as a subsidiary or affiliate will be between two forms, both similar to
the U.S. corporation. The two forms are a *société anonyme* (S.A.) or a
société á responsibilité limitée (S.A.R.L.). In German-speaking countries
the similar forms are the *Aktiengesellschaft* (A.G.) or the *Gesellschaft mit
beschrankter Haftung* (GmbH). The S.A. or A.G. is the most common form
of business organization for medium- and large-scale businesses outside
of the United States and British Commonwealth countries. However, the
S.A.R.L., often referred to as Limitada in Latin American practice, has
gained in favor as the form for foreign subsidiaries.[18]

The S.A.R.L. requires fewer formalities than the S.A. for formation and
operation. It can afford considerable flexibility through contractual details inserted into the charter, whereas the S.A. must conform to more
cumbersome mandatory legal provisions. The S.A.R.L. can have a simple
structure with management often centered in a single person and without a board of directors or other supervisory bodies required of an S.A.
This flexibility is of particular importance for controlled companies, as
well as for joint ventures with local interests.

---

[18] Henry P. de Vries, "Legal Aspects of World Business," in *World Business*, ed. Courtney
C. Brown (New York: Macmillan, 1970), pp. 289–93.

The establishment of a joint venture creates special legal problems because the stresses and strains of normal business operations may result in discord. In the choice of business form for a joint venture, the international enterprise should be alert to the problem of eventual liquidation and dissolution. The divorce may be far more complicated than the marriage, particularly where patents, trademarks, and the use of an internationally known firm name is involved.

Concession agreements

The right of a multinational enterprise to engage in certain activities in a host country may be based on so-called concession agreements, sometimes referred to as economic development agreements. In its most common form the concession agreement involves an extractive enterprise. The provisions of the agreements, which specify a series of rights and obligations for both the enterprise and the government, vary widely among countries and industries, generally reflecting the relative bargaining power of the government and the investor.[19]

The concession agreement is apt to be a unique instrument tailored to meet special needs. Furthermore, it may involve mineral rights or other interests controlled by the government and arrangements on matters, such as taxation, which are within a legislature's competence. These agreements often resemble special legislation governing relationships between the country and the international enterprise. For a variety of reasons, concession agreements are likely to generate disputes between the parties. The long-run trends in many concession contracts proceed through several identifiable stages.[20] The first stage begins when a country suspects that it has natural resource possibilities that might attract foreign investors. But the existence of such resources, as in the case of petroleum, or the economic feasibility of production, is not known. In this stage, the host government is negotiating from weakness because the risks as seen through the eyes of both parties are high.

A second stage begins when the investments have been made and the projects are successful. As judged by hindsight, the host government views the original concession agreement as excessively favorable to the foreign investor and begins to raise its sights regarding its share of the returns from the concession activities. With its bargaining power greatly strengthened, the host government tends to increase its demands in the form of taxation, requirements for foreign enterprise to provide educational and other public facilities, and a number of other ways.

[19] See David N. Smith and L. T. Wells, Jr., *Negotiating Third World Mineral Agreements* (Cambridge, Mass.: Ballinger Publishing, 1975).

[20] See Raymond Vernon, "Long-Run Trends in Concession Contracts," *Proceedings of the American Society of International Law at its Sixty-First Annual Meeting*, April 27–29, 1967 (Washington, D.C., 1967), pp. 81–89.

At a third stage, the government presses for greater linkage of the concessionaire's activities with the economic development aspirations for the local economy. For example, the foreign firm may be required to develop local sources of supplies for many types of equipment and services.

At a fourth stage, local governments become interested in sharing in the ownership of the foreign enterprise or in the process of decision making or both. As concession agreements move through these stages, it is the relative bargaining power of the parties, generally economic but sometimes political, that influences the patterns of conflict and resolution rather than conventional legal considerations.

Transnational reach of economic regulation: Antitrust

Transnational reach, or the extension of one country's laws or regulations to actions outside of that country, can create vexing problems for the international enterprise. The international enterprise can adjust most aspects of its operations to differences in national laws. But the effect of certain business policies or actions are not coterminus with the national boundaries of the country in which the decision or action is initiated. The policy or action may be legal in country A, where initiated, but illegal in country B, where the policy or action also has effects. As a result, country B may take legal action in its jurisdiction that affects activities in country A where the law of country B does not have jurisdiction. In this way, the international enterprise becomes the vehicle through which conflicts between nations arise.

Significant points of conflict between nations have occurred when American courts and government agencies have sought to extend the application of its antitrust laws to firms and activities outside of the United States.[21] Similar clashes periodically occur in the fields of securities regulation, antibribery and antiboycott enforcement, tax collection, and the regulation of shipping.[22] But none of these has the commercial scope or financial impact of antitrust actions.

Restrictive business practices have been illegal in the United States for many decades under various antitrust laws. Restrictive business practices are agreements among enterprises to fix prices, limit production, allocate markets, restrain the application of technology, or engage in

---

[21] For an assessment of the resentment by other countries to the extraterritorial application of U.S. antitrust laws, see Jack N. Behrman, *National Interests and the Multinational Enterprise* (Englewood Cliffs, N.J.: Prentice-Hall, 1970), pp. 114–27; and Joseph La Palombara and Stephen Blank, *Multinational Corporations and National Elites: A Study in Tensions* (New York: The Conference Board, 1976), pp. 89–93. For an analysis of the impact on U.S. firms abroad, see James B. Townsend, *Extraterritorial Antitrust: The Sherman Antitrust Act and U.S. Business Abroad* (Boulder, Colo.: Westview Press, 1980).

[22] See Jack Kaikati and Wayne A. Label, "The Foreign Antibribery Law," *Columbia Journal of World Business*, Spring 1980, pp. 46–51.

similar schemes likely to reduce competition. More recently, other nations have developed similar policies, notably the European Community[23] and some of its members. But no other nation assigns so central a role to prevention of anticompetitive business practices. Even more important, significant differences in national laws exist.

Although the jurisdiction of national laws is normally limited to the particular nation, the reality is that actions taken outside the national boundaries can affect competition within the national market. In recognition of this reality, the U.S. courts have extended the U.S. antitrust laws to actions abroad that "substantially affect" the commerce of the United States and competition in the U.S. market. This has produced jurisdictional overlap, since other governments never abdicate control over the activities of their own citizens in their own territory. Sovereignty itself becomes an issue.

Box 8–3

Antitrust suit by U.S. firm against Japanese company for actions in Indonesia

New Orleans—A ruling by the federal appeals court here has revived a $194.7 million antitrust suit brought four years ago against Mitsui & Company, a Tokyo-based trading concern, by Industrial Investment Development Corporation, a closely held Los Angeles company.

The suit alleges that Mitsui violated the Sherman Antitrust Act by inducing P. T. Telaga Mas Kalimantan Co., holder of an Indonesian government logging concession, to break a timber-cutting agreement with Industrial Investment and sign another with Mitsui.

Central to the admissibility of the suit is the act of state doctrine, usually called into play in cases involving nationalizations of property. The doctrine prohibits U.S. courts from ruling on the legality or illegality of actions by a foreign government.

The appeals court ruled that while it was the Indonesian government that eventually denied a logging license to Industrial Investment, acts alleged in the suit were alleged acts by Mitsui and Telaga Mas that preceded the government action and are subject to trial under U.S. laws.

Source: *The Wall Street Journal*, May 7, 1979.

The wide reach exercised by the U.S. law is illustrated by the landmark Swiss Watchmakers case. Two Swiss trade associations headquartered in Switzerland were held subject to U.S. jurisdiction because they had a liaison office in New York. The foreign associations were found guilty by U.S. courts of conspiracy to restrain the commerce of the United States through actions taken and policies developed in Switzerland. These

---

[23] The European Community assumed responsibility for regulating competition in its Common Market area based on articles 85 and 86 of the Rome Treaty (1958).

actions and policies had the active support and participation of the Swiss government. Furthermore, they were legal in the Swiss jurisdiction.

The U.S. courts attempted to break up the manufacturers' cartel by ordering sweeping changes in the bylaws of the Swiss Watch Federation and by imposing other prohibitions on actions and agreements outside the United States. After the Swiss government intervened directly with the U.S. government, important changes were made in the final court judgment. The changes included a provision that nothing in the judgment would limit or circumscribe the sovereign right and power of the Swiss government.

U.S. enforcement procedures have been another major conflict area. The legal procedures of one country can command a defendant in an antitrust case to deliver information to the state while laws of another country prohibit it. In an American antitrust case, many documents and records may be needed by the government to determine whether an infringement has taken place. U.S. courts and regulatory commissions have exerted pressures on foreign firms with offices in the United States to produce documents and records from abroad. The pursuit of foreign documents and records became a major issue in an antitrust action brought by Westinghouse against the international uranium cartel for price fixing. The cartel was legal in the home country of the foreign companies and its formation was encouraged by the foreign governments to stimulate the search for uranium.[24] The response has been a wave of legislation by other trading nations prohibiting release of domestic business records in response to foreign judicial orders.

Foreign mergers and acquisitions have been challenged under U.S. antitrust laws. The United States brought an action in 1968 against Gillette's purchase of Braun A.G. in Germany, the third largest manufacturer of electric razors in Europe. The legal complaint alleged that the acquisition would eliminate Braun as a potential competitor in the U.S. market.

America is not the only country to contend that its laws have extraterritorial reach. In antitrust matters, West Germany and the European Community have done the same. In a landmark case some years ago, the Common Market's Executive Commission held the local subsidiaries of big foreign dye manufacturers responsible for a price-fixing cartel operated by their parent companies outside the Community.

The problem of extraterritoriality of national laws, or of transnational reach, is being worked on in several international forums, including the Organization for Economic Cooperation and Development in Paris. Still, the possibility that an international firm will find itself in the middle of a conflict between sovereign nations is real.[25]

---

[24] See Thomas N. Gladwin and Ingo Walter, *Multinationals Under Fire* (New York: John Wiley & Sons, 1980), pp. 521–25.

[25] Detlev F. Vagts, "Extraterritoriality: The General Theory," *Journal of Contemporary Business*, Autumn 1977, pp. 133–45.

SUMMARY

The international legal environment is in a transitional stage of adaptation to new international business patterns. The conduct of multinational business has many ingredients in addition to the transfer of goods and money across national boundaries that ideally would be governed and facilitated by an effective world government and international legal system. In the absence of such a system, treaties, codes, and agreements negotiated by nations on a bilateral or multilateral basis have been the principal tool for building a substitute framework. Normally, treaties are obeyed and agreements adhered to. In any event, they serve as an important guide for predicting the behavior of national governments.

Although the paths are uncertain, the prospect is that a sizable number of countries will begin to evolve more comprehensive legal principles to govern the international corporation. There will also be forward movement by groups of countries—either by multilateral international treaties, the adoption of a uniform business law, or by some less formal and more unconventional approach—to evolve codes of legal principles for dealing better with the international business phenomenon. Progress will be uneven and novel approaches will have to be devised. But there are certain to be important changes in the regulatory environment. International business has become such an important component of the world economy that the international legal environment will have to adjust to this reality.

EXERCISES AND DISCUSSION QUESTIONS

1. "When a foreign firm does business in our country its local affiliate must legally become a national enterprise," explained the official of a host government. "As a national enterprise the affiliate is entitled to the full legal protection of our laws in case of expropriation, alleged breach of concession contract, and so on in the same way as any other national enterprise. Why should the investor countries and the international business firms be insisting on additional legal protection for foreign investment through international investment codes or international organizations to arbitrate what are essentially national legal issues? Such proposals violate our national sovereignty and discriminate against purely national companies." Discuss.

2. The legal doctrine, *rebus sic stantibus*, relates to the presumption in contracts that things will remain in the same condition as they were at the date of agreement. There is a difference of opinion among the authorities as to whether the principle of *rebus sic stantibus* is a recognized rule of international law. To what extent do you think that the principle should be clearly recognized in the settlement of disputes concerning concession contracts?

3. If national laws on antitrust and restrictive business practices were harmonized, as an international manager would you prefer the U.S. version that looks at the act or the European version that looks at the effects? Why?

4. If the United Nations were prepared to establish a new specialized agency with limited powers to improve the international legal environment for

multinational business operations, as a representative of the international business sector what specific activities 'would you recommend that this agency undertake? To what extent would you expect that your recommendations would be acceptable to host countries as well as to investor countries?

5. As the manager of a multinational enterprise, what strategies would you follow to improve the international framework for the transfer of industrial property rights and for expanding the network of tax treaties? Remember that your firm is operating in a number of countries and must appeal to the national interests of all governments.

PART THREE

The nation-state and international business

Business enterprises have become increasingly international, but the structure of world government has not moved along a similar path. Sovereign nation-states continue to be the dominant unit of government, and the number of states has increased phenomenally from about 65 at the end of World War II to more than 150 in 1982. Some observers argue that the nation-state is old-fashioned and not well adapted to serve the needs of the modern, complex world. Yet nation-states persist as the governmental unit with which international enterprises must coexist.

Each nation-state has its own nationalistic spirit and set of national goals. As a sovereign power, the nation-state sets the rules for governing business transactions within and across its national boundaries. In dealing with domestic business enterprises, governments normally feel competent to achieve their goals and do not consider their sovereignty threatened. In dealing with international business, and particularly with multinational enterprises, nation-states perceive special potentials for conflicts with national goals and threats to national sovereignty.

183

Such potential conflicts have little to do with good or bad intentions on the part of either international firms or nation-states. The potential exists because each has divergent goals that it is trying to maximize. It is the ineluctable result of the internationalization of business in a world of nation-states.

In the traditional fields of international business, nation-states have long recognized the need to control the transfer of goods and money flows across national boundaries in order to harmonize such economic activities with national objectives and to increase national benefits. The patterns of such traditional controls and the underlying national motivations are presented in Chapter 9. As nations have become more aware of the potential impact that multinational enterprises can have on national goals, they have responded by establishing control programs over the operations of multinational enterprises within their national boundaries. These responses and the objectives that nation-states are attempting to achieve with such controls are the subject of Chapter 10.

As a guide to the implementation of control programs, governments increasingly rely on techniques for measuring the benefits of international business projects to the nation. These techniques are presented in Chapter 11. The multinational enterprise is not without some means of protecting itself against controls that threaten its own objectives and existence. Its countervailing power is considered in Chapter 12.

Chapter 9

National controls over international transfers

Nation-states have developed a variety of ways to achieve national goals and protect national interests as far as international business transactions are concerned. Traditionally, their method was to control the international transfer of goods. They followed with controls covering transfers of money, personnel, technology, and legal rights across national boundaries. More recently, nations have developed ways of directly influencing the operations of multinational businesses within their boundaries. In this chapter, the focus is on understanding how and why nations attempt to control international transfers. The next chapter looks at controls over the operations of multinational businesses.

The concept of international transfers is broad and comprehensive. It includes the physical transfer of goods through importing and exporting.

It includes financial flows in the form of direct-investment capital, portfolio investments, profit repatriation, and other money flows induced by international business operations; the transfer of personnel either in support of business activities or directly as a form of international business, that is, tourism; the transfer of technology across national boundaries through licensing and technical assistance agreements; the transfer of legal rights such as patent protection or governmental concessions to exploit certain natural resources; and cross-border data flows.

NATIONAL MOTIVATIONS FOR CONTROLLING INTERNATIONAL TRANSFERS

In view of the widely espoused benefits of free trade, why do nations attempt to control international transfers? What national goals are they trying to achieve through particular controls?

Revenue goals.   Some nations rely on international transfers as a major source of government revenue. Many tariffs were originally imposed primarily to raise revenue. Tariffs are among the easiest taxes to collect because the import and export of goods are usually concentrated in a relatively small number of locations, such as ports. A tariff imposed entirely for revenue purposes, however, would be applied to different products and be at a lower rate than would a protective tariff. A tariff level that is too high may keep goods from entering or leaving a country or may encourage smuggling and evasion and yield no revenue.

Governments also use international transfers as a source of revenue through exchange controls. In Brazil, for example, the government appropriates part of the foreign exchange earned from coffee exports. The coffee exporter is required to turn foreign exchange over to the government and receives payment in local currency at a special rate below the free-market rate. Revenue goals also lie behind controls preventing the transfer of operations or profit outside a country into another tax domicile.

Job protection.   Strong domestic pressures for protection against foreign competition arise when established economic activities become threatened by foreign competitive forces. Protective controls are notable in the textile field in both the United States and the United Kingdom. The industry employs a large number of workers and is a major contributor to national output. As imports have threatened the position of the local industries in their home markets, both employers and labor have pressed for tariff increases and quota restrictions to protect domestic industry against "low-wage" foreign producers. The desire to protect domestic workers from foreign competition can also be a reason for restrictive immigration policies. The rationale is that the welfare of domestic workers will be undercut by influxes of foreign workers who might be willing to work for less money.

Development goals. Tariffs, quotas, and other nontariff barriers may be adopted to implement economic development goals and to encourage the establishment of new economic activities. Here we have the venerable "infant industry" argument that is directed toward changing the structure of a nation's economy and accelerating economic growth. The argument is that late-comer countries must provide a period of protection to infant industries for the time-consuming learning process and for expanding to an efficient scale of production. It assumes that new industries have a potential for becoming economically viable without protection after the learning period and after reaching a feasible scale of operations. To encourage such infant industries, nations ban or restrict imports through tariffs, foreign exchange controls, import quotas, and similar measures. It is interesting to note that in his Report on Manufactures submitted in 1791 to the U.S. House of Representatives, Alexander Hamilton elaborated most persuasively the infant industry argument as the central justification for U.S. policies to encourage manufacturing.[1]

Development goals may be the justification for creating special tax or foreign exchange incentives to encourage exports and foreign direct investment. In other situations, development goals may also be the reason for removing tariffs and moving toward free-trade policies that are expected to stimulate greater efficiency and higher levels of output from domestic industry.

Balance-of-payments goals. Nations are constantly under pressure to achieve equilibrium in their international transactions and to maintain relatively stable exchange rates. Controls over financial flows and international transfers of goods and services are frequently adopted on a temporary or indefinite basis to assist in the resolution of balance-of-payments problems, as discussed in Chapter 6.

Domestic economic adjustment. Even domestic economic adjustment may require controls over international transfers. For example, a government may feel it necessary to restrain financial inflows in order to implement its domestic anti-inflation policy.

Health and safety protection. Nations frequently restrict the import of certain commodities, generally agricultural or animal products, to protect the health of their citizens. Such restrictions, which attempt to

---

[1] See Alexander Hamilton, *Papers on Public Credit, Commerce and Finance,* ed. Samuel McKee, Jr. (New York: Columbia University Press, 1934), pp. 204–5.

keep out agricultural pests and diseases, may be temporary or permanent and generally are applied to commodities from specific infected areas. From time to time, beef products from Argentina could not be imported into the United States because of the danger of spreading hoof-and-mouth disease.

International political goals.   National policies over international transfers have long been used to reward political friends and to oppose political enemies. The Arab countries have imposed transfer constraints on foreign firms that do business with Israel. The United States created special trading preferences for the Philippines after that country emerged from 50 years of colonial status to become an independent nation. France maintained special relationships with its former colonies after the colonies secured independence. The United States imposes controls over East-West trade, that is, trade with the Soviet-bloc countries. Trade was completely forbidden with countries like Cuba, with whom the United States was not enjoying friendly relations, on the grounds that trade helps potential enemies to be stronger and eventually works to the political disadvantage of the United States.

National security goals.   The more traditional manifestations of national security goals have been in protecting high-cost domestic industries such as the U.S. steel industry, so that supplies of critical materials are more likely to be domestically available in the case of war. National policies have also emerged for controlling international transfers of nuclear raw materials and technology. The fact that a vast commercial industry in nuclear electric power plants has developed means that special national-security constraints and government participation in the sale of nuclear power equipment have become part of the civilian business scene.[2]

Special-interest groups in a country have used national-security arguments to limit competition rather than to achieve sound national-security goals. Often there is no general agreement in a country as to what are valid national-security considerations, and at times bitter controversies arise between different interest groups in a nation as to what kind of protection is justified on national-security grounds and as to the best way of achieving national security.

Opponents of controls over international transfers argue that the national-security policies on which these controls are based assume an obsolete type of warfare. In a nuclear war, they say, victories or defeats will be decided quickly, and the availability of materials after the initiation of such warfare will no longer be of critical importance. Further-

---

[2] See Lee C. Nehrt, *International Marketing of Nuclear Power Plants* (Bloomington: Indiana University Press, 1966).

more, by allowing more imports, domestic resources will be conserved for national defense emergencies rather than rapidly consumed.

CONTROLLING TRANSFERS OF GOODS

The pros and cons of protectionism

Protectionism is a mildly pejorative label attached to national policies that shelter certain domestic activities from foreign competition by preventing imports in these fields or by making them excessively expensive. The domestic producers and workers receiving protection generally attempt to identify their private gains as contributing to the national interests. Such national interests may be infant-industry protection, national security, the need to maintain domestic employment and income and reduce foreign exchange outflows, and the desirability of diversifying the domestic economy to improve economic stability and stimulate growth. Normally, domestic pressures for protection are resolved by political considerations and in favor of the domestic parties with the most political muscle. Yet, the political debate invariably revolves around economic arguments, some of which have qualified validity while others are highly questionable from the standpoint of national interests.

Protectionist measures generally favor one group in a country at the expense of other sectors of the economy. Therefore, nations have to evaluate the trade-offs involved in protectionist policies and determine the net benefits or costs to the country. If the American steel industry, for example, is given protection against foreign steel imports and domestic prices remain higher than they might otherwise be, the steel companies and the workers in the industry may directly benefit. The first-round effects may result in foreign exchange savings to the United States. On the cost side, other U.S. industries that use steel to produce machinery for export become less competitive in foreign markets. Their profits, their workers, and their foreign exchange earnings for the country are likely to suffer. Domestic consumers of steel products will have to pay higher prices and, in effect, subsidize the protected industry. Futhermore, foreign countries are likely to retaliate with their own protectionist measures, which could reduce exports, profits, and employment in other U.S. industries. Both the positive and negative effects will have different weights depending upon the economic situation of the country. Even where the net economic impact is negative, a nation may be willing to pay this price to satisfy long-run or noneconomic goals.

The infant-industry argument for protection can be a valid argument if the industry being protected has realistic possibilities of maturing into an adult that no longer requires protection. This justification has been used, however, for initiating types of business activities that are likely to remain infants and require what amounts to a permanent subsidy. National security can also be a valid justification for protection and worth the cost to a country if the national-security goals to be served are consistent with a sound, modern security strategy. Likewise, protectionist measures that encourage the diversification of the domestic economy may provide substantial long-term gains to a country that more than offset short-term costs.

Most of the other arguments for protection are questionable or invalid from an economic standpoint, even though they may have great emotional appeal that garners strong political support. Most common among these is the highly plausible but generally fallacious cheap-labor argument, which both industry and labor use to demand protection against "unfair" competition from low-wage workers in foreign countries. This argument has at least three fatal weaknesses.

First, the argument confuses wage rates and unit labor costs. Labor costs depend on labor productivity as well as wage rates. Productivity depends in turn on the other factors of production such as capital, management, and technology that are combined with labor in the process of producing goods and services. Assuming that all other factors are constant, low wages will mean lower labor costs. But in reality all other factors, including the skills of the workers themselves, are not constant, and high-wage industries in one country can, in fact, produce goods with lower labor costs per unit of output than competing industries in countries where wage costs are low.

Second, the low-wage argument for protection also assumes that the only important cost involved in the ability of businesses to be competitive is the cost of labor. Labor costs vary greatly from industry to industry as a share of total costs per unit of output. Therefore, even if labor costs (irrespective of wage rates) are lower in some countries, the competitive advantage may be minor compared with variations in other production or distribution costs. The cost of electric power, for example, is much more significant in the production of aluminum than labor costs.

Third, one nation may have comparative advantages in large supplies of low-cost labor. Other nations may have their comparative advantages in low costs of raw materials, transportation, capital, or electric power. The relative importance of the cost components depends on an industry's production function. Labor costs are neither the only, nor the most important, competitive consideration.

Some proponents of protection broaden the low-wage argument to a general plea for equalizing all production costs between foreign and domestic producers on the grounds of "fair competition." Such a policy would violate whatever validity there is in the argument that a country should specialize in those fields in which it has a comparative advantage due to differences in resource endowments and trade with others. It would be just as valid or invalid for Japanese steel manufacturers to ask for protection against the lower prices that U.S. firms are able to pay for coking coal because the United States happens to have favorable resource endowments in these fields. In fact, if the arguments for protection to equalize national differences in production costs were accepted, there would be no basis whatever for trade taking place.

The basic problem frequently underlying protectionism is that a country needs to make structural changes. It must move out of industries in which the nation is no longer competitive and into other activities where it has a comparative advantage. Such structural changes, however, are difficult to accomplish, particularly in periods of slow national growth.

Current levels of protection

In evaluating a country's degree of tariff protection, average tariff levels are not very informative. Tariff levels vary tremendously from product to product. Furthermore, nominal tariffs as they appear in government tariff schedules—that is, the rate of duty expressed as a percentage of the total value of the imported product—are not really a measure of the full effect of the tariff. If import protection on the raw material is zero, but 10 percent on a processed form of the product, the effective protection against imports of the product in processed form is much higher than the apparent, or nominal, rate of 10 percent.

The distinction between *nominal* and *effective* rates can be illustrated by the case of textiles. Fabric may enter at a duty of 20 percent and yarn at 10 percent. Suppose that $250 of yarn is required to produce $500 of fabric. The duty on $250 of yarn will be $25. The value added to the yarn by weaving would be $250. If the fabric were imported at 20 percent duty, the total duty on $500 worth of fabric would be $100. Thus, the difference in the duty between the yarn and the fabric, or the duty on the value added by weaving ($250), is $75. The net duty difference as a percentage of value added is the *effective*, as opposed to the *nominal*, tariff rate. This gives an effective rate of 30 percent, as compared with the nominal rate of 20 percent. Since tariffs normally escalate with each stage of manufacture, the effective rate on value added often exceeds the nominal rate by a substantial amount.

Generalizations about tariff patterns must necessarily be subject to many exceptions. Nevertheless, the general pattern seems to be as follows:

1. Low tariffs on raw materials that a country does not produce—to encourage domestic processing industries; high tariffs on semifinished products easily produced in many countries—to protect local producers.
2. High tariffs on agricultural products and minerals where local production is noncompetitive with imports and does not completely fill local demand.

Box 9—1

Protecting jobs at $81,000 per year

The U.S. public is paying over $3 billion a year to protect textiles and apparel

Textiles and apparel are the most heavily protected U.S. industries. The Council on Wage and Price Stability (COWPS), which is the government's inflation-monitoring agency, has studied the costs of this protection and finds that the 29.3 percent average tariff on apparel imports is costing American consumers $2.7 billion a year.

These inflated consumer costs break down this way:

$261 million goes to the government in customs duties.

$2.2 billion goes to U.S. apparel manufacturers who, because of tariff protection, can charge that much more for their own products.

$207 million is lost to the U.S. economy as a whole because tariff protection encourages domestic manufacturers to go on making uncompetitive products inefficiently and because U.S. consumers (forced to pay higher prices for both domestic and imported apparel) end up buying fewer garments. This is what economists call a "dead-weight loss" to the economy—lost production and lost consumption.

In addition to tariffs, textile and apparel imports are also subject to quotas which set rigid limits on the quantity of goods which 18 foreign countries are permitted to sell to the United States. According to COWPS, these quotas cost the American consumer $369.4 million a year, including $67.5 million in dead-weight loss.

COWPS calculates that it is costing the American public $81,000 per year *for each textile job protected* by these tariffs and quotas. This cost is unreasonable since the U.S. textile industry has been *expanding* employment since 1975. In fact, the United States has for a number of years *exported* more textiles than it imports. It is true, however, that jobs are declining in certain sectors of the domestic apparel industry—notably low-cost apparel, employing low-skill, low-wage labor.

Source: Council on Wage and Price Stability, *A Study of the Textile and Apparel Industries* (Washington, D.C., July 1978).

---

3. Low tariffs on products of advanced technology where producing nations have been successful in reciprocal bargaining and where local production may not be feasible. Average tariffs on manufactured and semimanufactured goods are now less than 10 percent for the major developed countries.

With tariff rates reduced to quite low levels, much attention has switched to nontariff barriers to the international transfer of goods, as outlined in Chapter 7. Some international firms believe these barriers have reached levels at which they are more burdensome than tariffs. Identifying that NTBs exist and that they do significantly distort trade, however, is a major problem. While most trade restrictions may eventually be detected and matched by other countries, the detection is slow and by no means certain. There is clearly a range of NTBs that can be adopted by individual countries with little chance of immediate retaliation. This being so, governments come under internal pressure to adopt them.

The GATT negotiations ending in 1979 (see Chapter 7) made a beginning on the removal of NTBs. The area most heavily strewn with NTBs, however, remains trade in agricultural products. The United States, for example, has restrictions on sugar imports. The European Community has its Common Agricultural Policy. Japan, also, protects its farmers with quotas on a range of agricultural items.

Export promotion

Nations adopt programs for promoting exports as well as for restricting imports. The less-developed countries in particular feel a great need to earn foreign exchange through expanding exports. And the United States itself, with persistent balance-of-trade deficits since 1970, has established programs for export promotion.

Governmental action to promote exports may even include assuming responsibility for normal business functions, such as sponsoring market research on foreign sales opportunities and establishing trade promotion offices in foreign countries. At the more traditional level, governments offer tax incentives such as exemption from certain domestic taxes if goods are exported, direct bonus payments or subsidies through administration of exchange controls, special credit for exporters, and insurance programs under which the government assumes varying degrees of political and commercial risk.

The United States has its Export-Import Bank, which promotes U.S. exports by providing medium- and long-term financing to foreign buyers. Under the Webb-Pomerene Act of 1918, American companies are exempted from the prohibitions of the Sherman Antitrust Act when they join with other companies, who might be competitors, in an export trade association.

Since 1962, export credit insurance has been offered to U.S. exporters by the private Foreign Credit Insurance Association, in partnership with the Export-Import Bank. As incentives for expanding exports, the association offers low-cost blanket insurance policies covering both commercial and political risks in selling abroad on credit. Most big exporting countries have a similar institution which provides exporters with cover against risk. Britain, for example, has its Export Credit Guarantee Department, which performs this function.

The issue of unfair competition frequently arises in connection with export incentive programs. Importing countries may interpret these incentives as encouraging *dumping* (i.e., selling at lower prices in foreign than in home markets) or unfair competition. From the standpoint of international business, such incentive programs may be significant, but they also create potentials for conflicts with importing countries.

Export restrictions

While restrictions on imports have traditionally been the main controls over transfers of goods, restrictions on exports have been increasing in recent years. More and more nations have been adopting such controls to achieve goals that vary from increasing world prices to restraining local prices, and from national defense to economic warfare.

The United States applies export controls as authorized in the Export Administration Act of 1969 and most recently amended in 1979. The law provides three grounds for denying export licenses—a potential for military use, foreign policy goals, and protection of the domestic economy from the excessive drain of scarce materials. The Department of Commerce administers the law with participation by the Department of State and the Defense Department. Licenses are required to export items on a "controlled commodities list" and for shipments of all goods to communist countries. Thus, licenses have been denied to export computers and computer equipment to the Soviet Union. As shown in Box 9–2, both the government agencies and the business community have frequently been bitterly divided as to whether specific products have significant military applications, or whether if the United States doesn't ship them, other countries will.

Box 9–2

White House approves Caterpillar's sale of pipeline-laying gear to Soviet Union

Washington—The Reagan administration has given the green light to Caterpillar Tractor Co.'s request to sell $40 million of pipe-laying equipment to the Soviet Union.

The decision ends a long-running dispute between the Pentagon, which opposed the sale, and the State Department. Pentagon officials argued that the equipment could be used on pipeline projects that would bolster Soviet defense production. State Department officials countered that Moscow already owns similar equipment and that if the U.S. doesn't sell the pipeline-laying equipment, Japan will.

*   *   *   *   *

The decision to sell the pipe-laying equipment to Moscow almost certainly will be cited by European leaders as justification for proceeding with a project to build a pipeline to bring natural gas from the Soviet Union to Western Europe. The United States has tried to discourage the pipeline project by encouraging Europe to seek alternative sources of energy.

Source: *The Wall Street Journal,* July 30, 1981.

Export controls are not unique to the United States. As another example, Japan in 1980 had a Foreign Trade Control Law under which 205 items were subject to license in order to control their export to specified socialist countries, or because of short supply in the domestic market (e.g., tungsten ore), or to forestall the imposition of import restrictions by other countries (e.g., on sewing machines and certain textiles).[3]

CONTROLLING TRANSFERS OF MONEY

Nations influence international transfers of money through foreign exchange controls, capital controls, policies of tied aid, supervision of the foreign operations of domestic banks and other financial institutions, and taxation. Many economists and some businessmen argue against any kind of national control over money transfers. They prefer freely fluctuating exchange rates determined by the market forces, which will provide automatic adjustments for balance-of-payments disequilibrium and allocate resources with market efficiency. But even for nations that have adopted fluctuating exchange rates, the normal policy has been to make frequent and extensive use of controls over financial transfers.

Foreign exchange controls

A major weapon used by nations for resolving payments imbalances is foreign exchange controls. With such controls a nation's currency becomes inconvertible; that is, it is not freely transferable into other currencies. There can be degrees of inconvertibility, depending on the nature and extent of the exchange controls. The government normally requires that all receipts of foreign exchange be turned over to the central bank or some other designated government agency. Exchange can be bought only for specified purposes and in amounts determined by the government. A license is therefore required for the purchase of foreign exchange. Exchange controls can be limited to import and export transactions, or they can also cover transfer payments such as profit remittances and capital flows.

Once exchange controls are established, the government determines the priorities and quotas for the allocation of foreign exchange, and the choice is often rather arbitrary. The system can vary from a simple allocation of available foreign exchange among domestic individuals or firms to a complex licensing system discriminating between many different categories of goods. Some exchange-control systems establish multiple exchange rates, which vary by category of goods and permit the import of

---

[3] International Monetary Fund, *Annual Report on Exchange Arrangements and Exchange Restrictions 1981* (Washington, D.C., 1981), pp. 240–41. This IMF report, published annually, describes current policies and practices of each member country of the IMF and is a valuable reference for international managers.

high-priority goods at the lower rates and nonessential or luxury goods at the higher rates. Some systems also require importers to make substantial deposits in order to obtain an import license. The deposit requirement ties up funds that might otherwise be earning a return and thereby increases the cost of importing.

Box 9–3

Honduras sets controls on foreign exchange to avoid devaluation

TEGUCIGALPA, Honduras (AP)—The Honduran government imposed foreign exchange controls to stave off devaluation of the lempira and shore up the country's sagging economy.

The new rules require that people buy and sell their foreign currency only to the central bank. The bank, in turn, will ration the sale of U.S. dollars and other currencies depending on the amount of reserves available.

A central bank decree said the controls affect mostly exporters, who must turn over their foreign currency receipts to the bank in exchange for lempiras, the Honduran money equivalent to about 50 U.S. cents, and importers who have to buy cur-

rency from the bank to finance purchases abroad.

Also, people traveling abroad must buy the dollars they need from the bank, which will set a limit on such purchases.

Central bank sources said Honduras' foreign currency reserves total between $160 million and $200 million after a massive flight of capital and a trade deficit with the other four Central American countries.

The sources said the trade deficit has slowly narrowed but the flight of capital has continued intensively, as wealthy citizens, alarmed by guerrilla activity in neighboring Guatemala and El Salvador, have transferred capital abroad.

Source: *The Wall Street Journal,* September 24, 1981.

Effective functioning of an exchange-control system requires that all foreign exchange purchases be regulated and that all foreign exchange receipts by individuals, businesses, and government agencies be captured and directed into a central pool. Consequently, an export licensing and policing system is needed to assure that foreign exchange receipts are turned over to the government in exchange for local currency at fixed rates. At times, a so-called free market is allowed to operate alongside exchange controls, but only limited types of transactions are legal in the free market. Exporters may be allowed to keep a share of their export earnings, which they can sell at the higher rates prevailing in the free market, and generally the free market is used by tourists for securing local currency.

A major problem constantly confronting exchange-control authorities is the black market, where exchange is bought and sold in disregard of official regulations. Depending upon the severity of the exchange controls and the administrative capacity of government agencies, black-market activities in foreign exchange and import licenses can be extensive. When the official rates are far below what would be a free rate, the opportunities for earning illicit profits are great, and extensive graft and corruption are almost certain to emerge.

Exchange controls may buy time while basic adjustments are undertaken to secure balance-of-payments equilibria or to implement development programs. However, the more serious the imbalance between supply and demand for local currency, the more difficult such a system is to administer effectively. Under all circumstances a government needs a high degree of knowledge concerning a nation's economy and its future prospects along with an honest and highly skilled administrative capacity. If exchange controls are substituted for policies to correct underlying imbalances and are maintained over long periods of time, illicit operations are inevitable, with their detrimental influence on business morality and the effectiveness of the controls. Yet while controls are at best a temporary measure, they frequently are retained as permanent fixtures.

From the standpoint of the international businessman, exchange controls complicate and burden international money transfers by adding to costs. They can be beneficial, however, to certain types of operations when used to encourage investment inflows or exports of particular goods. The financial management problem is increased in some ways but may be reduced in other ways if, for example, such controls avoid major devaluations.

Capital controls

Flows of short-term and long-term capital can be influenced by traditional exchange-control programs, but it is more common for nations to adopt special capital controls. Like foreign exchange controls, capital controls normally require licensing by governmental authorities for international transfers of funds. The motivation for capital controls has most frequently been to attain balance-of-payments equilibrium at desired exchange-rate levels. But they have also been used to implement national development priorities, to influence the patterns and size of international business operations in a country, and to support varied foreign policy objectives.

Normally the United States has had no controls over outward or inward flows of capital, except to selected enemy countries. Unlike the majority of countries, it offered a free capital market, and this was extended even to foreign governments. In the mid-1960s, however, the country became concerned about its persistent balance-of-payments deficit and initiated statutory and voluntary controls. An interest equalization tax was established in 1964 of up to 15 percent payable by American purchasers of foreign securities issued in the United States by most borrowers from developed countries in order to reduce the outflow of U.S. capital. Later, voluntary and then statutory restraints on outflows of direct private investment were adopted, and additional restrictions were placed on the foreign financial activities of U.S. banks. But there was considerable objection to the controls and they were dismantled in 1974.[4]

The importance of capital controls will vary from country to country, depending upon size of capital movements in relation to the country's balance of payments. Administration may be simpler than a full-fledged exchange-controls program, with fewer parties involved in either capital inflows or outflows. Furthermore, such controls generally allow governmental authorities a great deal of discretion to meet changing circumstances. The disadvantage of capital controls, however, may be that short-term benefits in improving the balance-of-payments situation are secured at the expense of even greater long-term gains. Profitable direct investment, for example, can generate a continuing stream of return flows in the form of repatriated profits.

Other controls

A number of new types of national controls over financial transfers are emerging in response to the growing importance of international commercial banking and the international securities industry. The home governments of multinational banking firms, particularly the United States, are showing increased interest in foreign banking activities as they affect domestic policies. An example is the expansion of loanable funds in the United States through Eurodollar borrowings abroad.

Taxation laws are used in many ways to influence international financial transfers. Taxation levied on remittances of profits, for example, encourages reinvestment and discourages remittance back into the tax jurisdiction. In both the United States and the United Kingdom the policy is moving away from taxation on remittances and toward taxation when the income arises, whether or not remitted. Taxation laws are also being created to discourage tax deferral through transfer of funds to corporations owned but registered in other tax jurisdictions.

Control over funds granted for foreign aid has at times been attempted through *tied aid* or *tied loans*. The granting country requires that funds be utilized in purchasing goods or services from the granting country, hoping to avoid balance-of-payments problems from the outflow of funds. However, the country receiving aid may be able simply to replace purchases it would otherwise have made; moreover, to force a country to

---

[4] For an example of the domestic debate over U.S. controls, see F. Michael Adler and G. C. Hufbauer, "Foreign Investment Controls: Objective-Removal," *Columbia Journal of World Business*, May–June 1969, pp. 29–37.

buy other than from the lowest cost source could defeat the objectives of the aid.

CONTROLLING TRANSFERS OF PERSONS

Nations have numerous policies affecting the movement of persons across national boundaries that are important to international business. The temporary movement of persons, as tourism, has itself become a major international business activity and a major source of foreign exchange earnings for many nations. International trade depends to a large extent on the ability of businessmen to move from nation to nation. The identification and exploitation of direct-investment business opportunities require even more that business executives be free to travel internationally. International business operations may be dependent upon the ability of management personnel or production workers to move across national boundaries.[5] The transfer of technology through the transfer of persons can be significantly influenced by national policies toward the international movement of persons.

National policies for controlling the entry and exit of persons from a country generally are not motivated primarily by international business considerations. Broader political, economic, and social considerations invariably underlie such policies, which generally distinguish between persons entering a country for a temporary stay such as tourists or, at the other end of the spectrum, persons who want to enter a country on a permanent basis. Between are persons who want to stay in a country for a reasonably long period without intending to seek employment in the country, such as students. Still another intermediate category would be foreigners who enter for a period of employment but do not intend to become permanent residents of the country.

Passports and visas are the basic means for controlling the international movement of persons. Passports are issued to persons by the country of which they are a citizen or permanent resident. The issuing country can restrict movements by not authorizing passport holders to enter specified countries, as the United States forbade its citizens to travel in Cuba. Visas are issued by the country into which persons desire to travel. Political considerations can be grounds either for refusing citizens a passport or for denying visas.

Generally speaking, restrictions on exit are regarded as morally less defensible than restrictions on entry. Apart from the communist bloc, only a few countries make it very difficult to depart. Few make any attempt to charge departing individuals with the cost of their education, but limitations on the right to export capital other than this human

---

[5] See John D. Daniels, "International Mobility of People," *South Carolina Essays in International Business*, no. 1, March 1980.

capital are common. Nationals of India, for example, are not normally granted any foreign exchange facilities for emigration purposes. In cases of exceptional hardship, up to 100,000 rupees (about U.S. $13,000) may be released at the time of emigration.

Most countries, anxious to expand their tourist industry, impose minimum restrictions on the entry of persons on temporary visits. The most restrictive policies are applied to persons who wish to seek employment in a foreign country or become permanent residents. During certain periods of history, such as the late 19th and early 20th centuries, countries like the United States encouraged immigration. Up until 1940, the United States received millions of immigrants from Europe. Australia and Canada aggressively encouraged and even promoted immigration during periods when they were trying to develop their vast countries. Argentina and Brazil have also had periods of relatively open immigration. But the general world pattern, except for internal movement in Western Europe and the Arab states, has become one of selective and limited immigration.

For most countries the basis for admitting immigrants has increasingly favored those professionally trained or highly skilled, with resources, and of a workable age so that they do not create a drain on social welfare systems. For the underprivileged of any country, the opportunity to gain admission to another country is steadily decreasing.

In Western Europe since about 1955, there has been a greatly increased movement of workers across national borders. A basic feature in the European Economic Community treaty was to permit the free movement of labor within the community. The major movements have been northward, especially to Switzerland, Belgium, France, and Germany, first by Italians and then by Greeks, Spaniards, Portuguese, and Turks. The mobility of workers in Europe has tended to limit wage-rate variations and has greatly improved the functioning of the European labor market.

The size of the international flows of migrant labor is impressive. In 1975, there were more than 6 million migrant workers in Western and Northern Europe making up about 7 percent of total employment.[6] In the same year, there were about 2 million immigrant laborers in the oil-exporting countries of the Middle East and North Africa. In Kuwait, for instance, immigrant labor constituted 71 percent of total employment.

From the standpoint of international business, national controls over the transfer of persons are likely to be more burdensome than prohibitive. Yet there are cases where countries have not granted work permits to foreign managers and technical staff of an international enterprise, as part of a policy of reserving such positions for nationals. To meet this

---

[6] Zafer Ecevit and K. C. Zachariah, "International Labor Migration," *Finance and Development,* December 1978, pp. 32–37.

kind of a situation, a firm must plan its recruitment and training policy so that the nationalities of its managerial strength will match the future global need for these nationalities.

CONTROLLING TRANSFERS OF TECHNOLOGY

The concept of technology encompasses technical and managerial know-how that is embodied in physical and human capital and in published documents and that is transmitted across national boundaries in various ways.[7] Traditional trade theory, by limiting its horizons to land, labor, and capital, did not direct the attention of economists and government officials to technology as a key production factor. But the situation has been changing rapidly, and governments have become keenly concerned about encouraging inflows of technology as a major means of achieving national development goals. At the same time, nations have become active in trying to minimize foreign exchange costs to a country and maximize national benefits through policies for influencing the amount, type, and conditions for transfer of technology.

In the industrially advanced countries, technological progress is encouraged through a patent system that gives the owner of new technology ownership rights during a fixed number of years—17 years in the case of the United States. In most cases, these countries have applied no controls over the international transfer of technology or even over the price received for transfers.[8] This is so even when the international sale of technology can produce major social costs in the shape of unemployment and redundant production facilities. Even taxation authorities have little say in transfer prices as long as they are determined at arm's length. One notable exception, however, is the U.S. restriction on "trading with the enemy," which places statutory prohibition on technology transfer, either directly as "naked technology" or embodied in products.

Attitudes in the less developed countries (LDCs) differ markedly. They are predominantly buyers rather than sellers of technology. To them, the question is whether the adoption of a patent system will help or hinder the country's access to foreign technology on acceptable terms. Consequently, national patent systems for production of rights over technology do not exist universally, and where they do exist, the right of foreigners to use the protection vary greatly. On the other hand, less developed countries are making more and more attempts to control the transfer of technology across their borders.

---

[7] Stefan H. Robock, *The International Technology Transfer Process* (Washington, D.C.: National Academy of Sciences, 1980).

[8] For a summary of U.S. policy, see *Foreign Direct Investment in the United States,* vol. 1 (Washington, D.C.: U.S. Government Printing Office, 1976).

The objectives of the LDCs are ambitious. They want to ensure that imported technology is appropriate to their needs, which generally means smaller-scale and labor-intensive technology, and that it will actually be transferred to local nationals. They particularly want to ensure that charges for technology, either explicit or concealed, are not excessive. And excessive is usually defined as any price above the lowest possible cost for obtaining the technology any other way. Another common objective is to minimize the restraints in technology transfer agreements, such as limiting the markets in which the licensee can sell or the quantity that can be produced. Such restrictions have been common in order to protect the licensor from competition from the licensee or to ensure that the licensed subsidiary fits into a global strategy. Finally, and inconsistently, many countries also want to retain for their own country all rights arising from local development of technology.

Attempts to achieve these objectives commonly take the form of a technology transfer law, requiring the registration of all documents and agreements to do with payments to foreigners for patent rights, trademark authorization, technical knowledge, engineering, technical assistance, and so on. Agreements that are not registered are by statute neither valid nor enforceable. Moreover, the act usually states grounds on which registration can be refused, such as those listed in the 1972 Mexican law, set out in Figure 9–1.

The prima facie evidence is that such controls are effective from the country's standpoint. Firms can be thrown into a negotiating position with government as their applications for registration are first rejected and then accepted after amendment. Reported royalty levels for Mexico registered in the first two years following the 1972 act were mainly below 3 percent, as against prior rates of 5–15 percent.[9] Such levels, however, can be deceptive. The really important indicators of success are much more difficult to assess. Does the law perhaps reduce the priority that firms place on the country as a site for more advanced development? Do restrictions on the multinationals' rights to locally developed technology discourage local research and development? Does the control of royalty rates lead to reduction in the quality of available technology or limit the terms of the agreement? With limited investment to meet worldwide demands, the answers to these questions are very likely in the affirmative.[10]

The developing countries have been attempting to improve the terms for international transfers of technology through pressures by UNCTAD, beginning in 1976, for a code of conduct. As a result of subsequent negotiations with the industrial countries, progress has been made toward a

---

[9] *Business Week,* July 14, 1975, p. 69.

[10] See *The Acquisition of Technology from Multinational Corporations by Developing Countries.* United Nations Publication No. E.74.II.A.7, p. 43.

Figure 9–1

Grounds for refusing to register contracts in the Mexican national register of technology transfer

I. When their purpose is the transfer of technology available in the country free of charge or under more advantageous conditions than those governing its acquisition abroad, provided the same technology is concerned.

II. When the price or the compensation is not related to the technology acquired, or it constitutes an unfair or excessive levy on the national economy.

III. When clauses are included whereby the supplier is permitted to control or intervene, directly or indirectly, in the administration of the party acquiring the technology.

IV. When the obligation is established to transfer, onerously or gratuitously, to the party providing the technology, the patents, trademarks, innovations, or improvements which may be obtained in the country.

V. When limitations are imposed on the research or technological development of the party acquiring the technology.

VI. When the obligations are established to acquire equipment, tools, parts, or raw materials of an exclusively determined origin.

VII. When the total prohibition is established on exportation or the possibilities of the party acquiring the technology are limited with regard to exporting, in a manner contrary to the interests of the country.

VIII. When the use of supplementary technologies is prohibited.

IX. When the obligations are established to sell on an exclusive basis to the supplier of the technology the goods produced by the party acquiring the technology.

X. When the party acquiring the technology is obliged to permanently utilize the personnel indicated by the supplier of the technology.

XI. When production volumes are limited or sales or resale prices are imposed for domestic production or for the exports of the party acquiring the technology.

XII. When the party acquiring the technology is obliged to enter into selling contracts or exclusive representation agreements with the supplier in Mexico.

XIII. When excessive validity periods are established. In no case can said periods exceed ten years and be obligatory for the party acquiring the technology.

XIV. When presentation is made to foreign courts-of-law of the facts or resolution of the judgments which may derive from the interpretation or compliance with the aforementioned memoranda, contracts, or agreements.

Source: Government of Mexico, *Diario Oficial*, December 30, 1972, Article 7.

possible convention. The industrial countries, however, have resisted having the code apply to intrafirm transactions.[11]

Many countries will continue to negotiate individually the terms and quantity of international investment with multinational firms, and firms will tend to favor the more attractive opportunities. While identifiable payments for technology may be decreased, firms may be rewarded in other ways.

---

[11] See Miquel S. Wionczek, "The Major Unresolved Issues in the Negotiations on the UNCTAD Code of Conduct for the Transfer of Technology," *CEPAL Review*, April 1980, pp. 94–102; Howard V. Perlmutter and Tagi Sagafi-nejad, *International Technology Transfer: Codes, Guidelines, and a Muffled Quadrilogue* (New York: Pergamon Press, 1981); see also Edward M. Graham, "The Terms of Transfer of Technology to the Developing Nations: A Survey of the Major Issues" in *North-South Technology Transfer: The Adjustments Ahead*, ed. J. H. Dunning et al. (Paris: Organization for Economic Cooperation and Development, 1982) pp. 55–87.

CONTROLLING TRANSFERS OF RIGHTS

Governments can also regulate the international transfer of rights. Rights of nonnationals to own, hold concessions, or operate a business, for example, may be restricted either absolutely or for certain areas of the economy. Such restrictions are common for natural resources and land. A few countries expressly prohibit all foreign ownership of land, others extend the prohibition to only agricultural land or forestry rights. Concessions for mining radioactive materials, such as uranium or thorium, are restricted in some cases to domestic enterprises. Other areas in which restrictions apply are those with a strong national cultural and political impact, such as newspapers, magazines, and broadcasting; those that form an integral part of any national security network, such as telecommunications operation or military manufacturing; and those that are essentially part of the economic regulatory mechanism, such as major banks.[12]

The motivations behind limitation of foreigners' access to local rights are partly xenophobic and partly reasoned economic, political, or security precautions. Where foreigners' rights are removed, the method used is quite likely to be public nationalization of the activity in question. Local private rights are removed at the same time so the action appears less like expropriation of foreign property. In fact, the underlying motivation may have little to do with a belief in state ownership of the particular field.

SUMMARY

The transformation of the world economy from a dominance of trade to a flourishing of international business will gradually move governmental and business thinking out of the traditional framework of national controls over trade and international payments. International business depends upon a much wider range of international transfer than those of goods and money. Even within the field of money and goods transfers, the concern of nations for influencing these flows has broadened considerably from the traditional patterns designed for a world of trade.

In principle, international business firms prefer a minimum of national interference over transfers of goods, money, persons, technology, and rights across national boundaries. They support their position by traditional free-trade theory, which argues that economic output for the world as a whole can be maximized under conditions of free international flows. In practice, international enterprises can be benefited as well as hindered by restrictive national policies.

---

[12] Policies and regulations of the United States and major industrial nations are summarized in *Foreign Direct Investment in The United States* (Washington, D.C.: U.S. Government Printing Office, 1976), chaps. 8, 10.

The nation-states give lip service to the venerable concepts of the virtues of free trade, but in practice they have chosen not to let free-market forces prevail. One of the most basic reasons, generally more implicit than explicit, motivating nations to influence international transfers is the fact that maximizing output for the world as a whole does not necessarily mean that each country will share these benefits in a satisfactory proportion. Thus, many controls and incentives to influence transfers have been designed by nations to attempt to increase their shares of the benefits.

EXERCISES AND DISCUSSION QUESTIONS

1. What policies do you think the United States should follow with regard to East-West trade? To what extent should the United States use pressure to influence policies of other Western nations in regard to trade with the socialist countries?

2. "Export promotion activities can produce just as much distortion to free trade as do tariffs, therefore no nation should actively stimulate exports." If you disagree with this statement, compile a list of export promotion activities the United States should undertake and suggest how the limit should be determined for each activity.

3. "The Ford Motor Co. finally joined forces with the United Auto Workers Union to formally request restrictions of shipments of Japanese-built cars and trucks to the United States. It filed a petition with the International Trade Commission for a temporary remedy to restrain Japanese imports, which it charged are causing serious injury to auto employment and investment in the United States." (*The Wall Street Journal*, August 5, 1980.) As a member of the ITC, how would you decide on this petition and why?

4. What are the principal objectives of exchange-control systems and how do exchange controls serve these objectives?

5. "To prevent the outflow of direct private investment is to kill the goose that lays the golden eggs." Discuss.

6. "There is no cost in making technology available that has already been developed for other purposes, therefore an acquiring nation will maximize its benefits by strictly limiting the amount that can be charged for existing technology. The return permitted on investment associated with any technology transfer, however, should be set in a much different way." Comment on these statements and draw up a set of practical rules for a developing nation to use in controlling the returns going to foreigners for technology and investment.

Chapter 10

National and international controls over multinational operations

As long as international business consisted mainly of arm's-length transactions between independent parties in different countries, nation-states were able to rely on traditional controls over international transfers to protect and advance their national interests. But the rise of the multinational enterprise created a new set of challenges and opportunities for the nation-states that are not met through transfer controls. With a growing conviction that something more is needed, most nations have adopted additional measures specifically directed toward multinational business. Slowly but inevitably, both investor and host countries have been moving toward a general and coordinated national policy in this area.

The responses of host and home countries have not been uniform, either in timing or in substance. Significant differences in national-control programs exist that reflect variations in country characteristics, in national goals, and in levels of sensitivity to multinational enterprises. Furthermore, the control policies for a specific country are likely to change over time.

Because of these variations, this chapter will not attempt to provide a comprehensive survey of the many national control programs. As the need arises, the international manager will want to make use of the standard references available in order to be currently informed on the details of a specific country's controls.[1]

Instead, this chapter will focus on the rationale underlying the various control measures. Even though national programs differ in detail, the underlying rationale is frequently similar. The chapter will also review the status of efforts to establish regional and international controls over multinational enterprises. The techniques used for measuring the costs and benefits of specific multinational projects are being increasingly relied upon as a guide for control activities and are the subject of the next chapter.

WHY NATIONS ADOPT CONTROLS

Why do nation-states feel the need for special controls over the activities of multinational enterprises? The basic issue is simple. Each nation-state has its set of national goals. Each multinational enterprise has its set of supranational goals toward which it directs the corporate family of diverse nationalities under its control. Some, if not most, of the goals of the enterprise may be in harmony with the goals of a specific nation within which the firm is operating. And some of the enterprise goals may potentially conflict with the goals of one or more nation-states. The situation of divergent goals that may be in harmony or in conflict pertains to both home and host countries for multinational enterprises.

Most discussions of control policies emphasize almost exclusively the conflict potentials and the negative curbs and constraints imposed by nations to protect their national interests. The reality is that nation-states are also aware of the potential of multinational enterprises for advancing national goals and have exercised their sovereign power to encourage through incentives and other policies those activities of multinational enterprises considered to be in harmony with national goals.

The potentials for both common interests and potential conflicts can

---

[1] A standard reference source is *Investment Laws of the World* (Dobbs Ferry, N.Y.: Oceana), a loose-leaf service prepared by the International Centre for Settlement of Investment Disputes. Other sources are the information guides for individual countries published periodically by accounting firms such as Price Waterhouse & Co. and Arthur Andersen & Co.

be illustrated by the example of employment impact. As firms expand internationally, they create employment opportunities in host countries. Host countries are generally anxious to have more local jobs available and frequently offer inducements to attract foreign industries. At the same time, labor unions in the home country may feel that overseas expansions result in a loss of jobs in the home country and press for negative curbs by the home country.

Although anxious to secure more jobs, the host country is also interested in having as many as possible of these jobs filled by its nationals. It may therefore also use constraints, along with inducements, requiring that a specified share of the labor force, or technical personnel, be reserved for nationals.

INVESTOR OR HOME-BASE COUNTRIES: INCENTIVES

Historically, the United States and several other major investor countries have adhered to a basic economic philosophy favoring the free flow of investment and technology among countries. These nations have liberal policies that encourage direct investment abroad by multinationals with home bases in these countries, and they have erected few if any constraints on inbound direct investment by foreigners. The other major investor countries also have liberal policies to encourage outbound direct investment but, at the same time, impose screening or constraints on inbound investment.

The rationale for the liberal policies is the assumption that investment abroad increases trade and expands exports, jobs, markets, and government revenues for the investor country. These policies implicitly assume that the interests of the multinational enterprise and its home country are largely in harmony. To state the belief in a provocative way, the assumption is that "what's good for U.S. International, Inc., is good for the United States."

In recent years, there has been growing skepticism concerning the domestic costs and benefits of the liberal policies, and some modifications in the policies of investor nations have resulted. These developments will be discussed below in the section on investor country restraining controls.

The prevailing situation is that many investor countries, including the United States, Canada, and West Germany, impose no restrictions whatever on outward direct investment. Some of the other investor countries have only formal regulations requiring that the government be notified of such investments.[2] In support of their liberal policies, the major investor

---

[2] See *International Direct Investment: Policies, Procedures and Practices in OECD Member Countries* (Paris: OECD, 1979).

nations have incentive programs that generally include risk insurance, capital assistance, tax incentives, and, at times, political representation.

Foreign risk insurance. All major investor nations now have insurance programs to cover major types of foreign investment risks. The key features of each country's investment guaranty programs are presented in Table 10–1. The geographic coverage varies from worldwide to invest-

Table 10–1

Investment guaranty schemes (generally covering expropriation, war, and transfer risks)

Country	Date established	Geographic coverage	Investment coverage	Premium rate per year (percent)	Amount out-standing end of 1974 (millions)
Australia	1966	Worldwide	All types	0.75	$ 24.1
Belgium	1971	Worldwide	Equity and loan	0.75	4.0
Canada	1969	Less developed countries	All types	0.3–0.9	44.6
Denmark	1966	Less developed countries	All types	0.5	14.1*
France	1971	Selected less developed countries and countries with bilateral agreements	Mainly loans	0.8	17.3
Germany	1960	Countries having signed bilateral agreements (44)	All types	0.5	406.0*
Japan	1956/57	Worldwide	All types	0.55–0.70	1,075.5
Netherlands	1969	Less developed countries	All types	0.8	21.4
Norway	1964	Worldwide	Equity plus loans, if equity present	0.5	24.7
Sweden	1968	11 selected countries	Equity and loans, if controlling interest	0.7	n.a.
Switzerland	1970	Less developed countries	All types	†	42.7
United Kingdom	1972	Worldwide	All types	1.0	30.1
United States	1948	Countries having signed bilateral agreements (114)	All types	0.3–1.50	2,985.8

n.a. = Not available.
* As of end of 1973.
† Normal rates: principal—1.25 percent, profits—4 percent of expected profits.
Source: *Investing in Developing Countries*, 3d ed. (Paris: OECD, 1975), pp. 12–14.

ments in 11 selected countries in the case of Sweden. The types of risks generally insurable are those of expropriation, war losses, and inability to transfer profits. Some countries extend the insurance to exports of home-country goods, and Japan also insures investments in non-Japanese companies engaged in developing mineral resources for import into Japan.

The U.S. program warrants special attention as the earliest, the largest, and in some ways a model that others have followed. The program got started as part of the Marshall Plan to provide an incentive for U.S. firms to invest in Europe. Later, it became attached to the Agency for International Development (AID). Beginning in 1969, the program was established as the Overseas Private Investment Corporation (OPIC), an autonomous government corporation "under the policy guidance of the Secretary of State."

Since its establishment, OPIC has been the focus of considerable controversy that has resulted in major program modifications. Such issues have been raised as the claim that OPIC insurance could involve the U.S. government in political conflicts with other governments that are not in the U.S. national interest. OPIC has also been charged with helping to export U.S. jobs by insuring "runaway" textile plants in low-wage countries that led to the closing of plants in the United States.[3]

One of the major modifications has been to require OPIC to give priority to investments in truly low-income countries. Another change has been to give special emphasis in OPIC's loan program to foreign investments by U.S. small businesses. As a result of the various changes, one observer reached the pessimistic conclusion that OPIC "is not now, nor is it likely to be, a major policy instrument in protecting United States overseas investors against the risk of expropriation."[4]

Associated with the insurance of investment risks, a number of countries have negotiated bilateral investment agreements with the governments of host countries. By the end of 1974 the German government had concluded bilateral agreements with 44 developing countries for the protection and promotion of German direct investment, and the United States had signed investment-guarantee agreements with 114 countries. The German experience has been that the developing countries have been careful to avoid even minor breaches of the agreements. The German agreements provide for an arbitration procedure. If a country is condemned under the arbitration procedure, it may lose international standing, which may lead to a loss of creditworthiness. Thus, in a not so subtle sense, insured investments carry with them an implicit hint that

---

[3] Paul E. Sigmund, *Multinationals in Latin America: The Politics of Nationalization* (Madison: University of Wisconsin Press, 1980), pp. 314–20.

[4] Ibid., p. 319.

investor countries will be concerned about the imposition of controls and the adoption of policies that will require insurance payments.

Capital assistance. Many investor nations have special funds or banks that make government loans to firms wishing to invest in developing countries.[5] Moreover, several countries have official export credit programs that help to finance equipment exports. The U.S. Export-Import Bank, for example, promotes investment overseas by making it easier and cheaper to buy the capital goods and machinery in the United States necessary to establish overseas subsidiaries.

Tax incentives. Steps to eliminate double taxation of foreign income, mainly through bilateral tax treaties, have been motivated to maintain a degree of equity rather than to encourage foreign operations. Some nations, however, do maintain lower tax rates, exemptions, or special deductions for income earned abroad. Two common provisions that may act as incentives to foreign investment are the tax deferral and tax credit provisions. Deferral provides that taxes will not be levied by the home country until profits are repatriated. Tax credit provides that direct taxes paid to a foreign government will be credited against the tax liability to the home country. These two provisions have been part of U.S. legislation for over 50 years but have come under considerable recent criticism for their purported subsidy of foreign investment. Deferral has been circumscribed by minor regulatory changes in recent tax acts, such as removal of the provision for profits left in tax havens and requirements for full allocation of common overheads between chargeable and deferred income.

Political representation. Investor countries have used their political influence to persuade host countries to relax their restrictions over inbound foreign business investment. For example, in recent years the United States has pressured Japan directly and through the OECD to liberalize its stringent limitations on foreign investment. Also, the U.S. Congress has given official government support to U.S. investors overseas by legislating quasi-automatic sanctions against governments that nationalize American holdings without full compensation. These sanctions may be in the form of terminating U.S. foreign aid, denying eligibility for import privileges under the Generalized System of Preferences (GSP), or opposition to loans from international agencies.

---

[5] For further detail on capital assistance programs, see *Investing in Developing Countries,* 3d ed. (Paris: OECD, 1975).

INVESTOR COUNTRIES: RESTRAINING CONTROLS

Most investor countries have some controls over direct investment outflows. But, with the exception of Japan and Sweden, such restraining controls have been motivated by considerations other than a national policy to influence international business activity.

Virtually all investor countries, including the United States, have at times controlled capital exports for balance-of-payments reasons. Several nations use such controls on a regular basis in response to immediate balance-of-payments difficulties. But the objective is simply to limit balance-of-payments deficits rather than to promote certain national goals through foreign direct investment.

Some countries, particularly the United States, have used controls to support foreign policy goals such as boycotts on dealing with certain communist countries. As of 1981, the United States had restrictions on certain transactions with, or involving, Cuba, Democratic Kampuchea, the Democratic People's Republic of Korea, and Vietnam.

In contrast to the laissez-faire policies of other investor nations, Japan has a long history of controlling overseas investment by Japanese firms so as to achieve specific national goals. During an early period, Japan's control program encouraged foreign investments in natural resources projects, even though most other types of investments were restricted because of foreign exchange shortages. In a later period, Japan gave priority to exporting low-productivity and polluting industries.

Before 1971, each overseas investment had to be approved by Japan's Ministry of International Trade and Industry (MITI). Since 1971, MITI does not review overseas investments on a case-by-case basis. Nevertheless, the government maintains an industrial strategy policy that firms are expected to observe.

Sweden's control program governing outbound foreign direct investment became effective in 1974. It requires prospective investors to include in their applications to the government an analysis of the effects of their overseas project on domestic employment and industrial policies. Applicants are also required to include the views of the labor unions representing their workers. When necessary "to achieve the objectives of national economic policy," the government is authorized to block a foreign direct investment. In 1978, out of 1,145 applications for outward investment, 29 were refused.[6]

In the United States, the belief that uncontrolled overseas direct investment is in the national interest began to be challenged by labor unions and others in the 1970s. The Burke-Hartke bill, introduced in the U.S. Congress in 1971 but never passed, would have established extensive

---

[6] OECD, *International Direct Investment*, p. 71.

controls over the foreign operations of U.S. firms.[7] Both economic and political impact issues have been raised in support of the demands to establish controls.

The economic arguments for controls stressed the economic costs to the investor country. According to this view, overseas investments have a negative impact on the home country through the loss of jobs, reduced foreign exchange earnings, and a steady erosion of the competitiveness of the United States in the world economy because of the export of technology to foreign subsidiaries.

The challenges to the conventional wisdom provoked a flood of studies by business advocacy groups, labor unions, and government agencies that attempted to provide definitive answers to the economic questions being raised. Thus a considerable controversial literature exists on most of the economic questions but there are no clear and compelling answers.[8] The controversies as to the economic costs and benefits to the investor country continue into the 1980s. But the challengers to established U.S. policies have not yet succeeded in persuading the Congress to establish controls over outbound direct investments.

The political impact argument is that a distinction must be made between the foreign policy interests of the home country and the specific interests of the multinational corporation. It follows, therefore, that the impact of U.S. investments in foreign countries can have a negative as well as a positive impact on U.S. foreign policy.

In the past, the U.S. government often assumed responsibility for protecting the interests of international business firms with U.S. nationality, but this practice began to change in the early 1970s. In 1969 the government of Peru expropriated the assets and operations of the International Petroleum Company, a Canadian company whose shares were almost completely owned by Standard Oil of New Jersey (now EXXON).[9] In 1971 a new Marxist government in Chile expropriated the local subsidiaries of major U.S. copper companies.[10] In both cases, for reasons of foreign policy and political relations with Latin America, the United States backed

[7] See Robert G. Hawkins and Bertram Finn, "Regulation of Multinational Firms' Foreign Activities: Home Country Policies and Concerns," *Journal of Contemporary Business* 6, no. 4 (Autumn 1977), pp. 7–30; Kent H. Hughes, *Trade, Taxes, and Transnationals: International Economic Decision Making in Congress* (New York: Praeger Publishers, 1979), on the Burke-Hartke controversy.

[8] Some of the issues and studies will be discussed in the next chapter on benefit-cost measurement; see also Edward M. Graham, "Technological Innovation, the Technology Gap, and U. S. Welfare," *Public Policy*, Spring 1979, pp. 185–202.

[9] See Adalberto J. Pinelo, *The Multinational Corporations as a Force in Latin American Politics: A Case Study of International Petroleum Company in Peru* (New York: Praeger Publishers, 1973).

[10] See Theodore Moran, *Multinational Corporations and the Politics of Dependence: Copper in Chile* (Princeton, N.J.: Princeton University Press, 1974).

away from a hard-line position and did not impose the retaliatory actions called for by law.

These cases raise the issue of the need for screening programs by investor nations that assume responsibility for protecting the nation's foreign policy interests in foreign areas. The political problem was bluntly raised as far back as 1962 by Secretary of State Dean Rusk, in testimony before the Foreign Relations Committee on the hearings of the Foreign Assistance Act of 1962:

> I don't believe that the U.S. can afford to stake its interests in other countries on a particular private investment in a particular situation, because someone has to live with the results anyhow . . . . If we are to tie American policy by law to the private investor overseas, then I think that we, of necessity, must reassure ourselves as to the operations, the conduct, the financial structure, and other aspects of those private investors.[11]

As the absolute and relative importance of international business increases, the potential for conflicts with the foreign policy of the major investor countries seems to increase almost geometrically. One alternative for investor countries is a comprehensive screening program as was used by Japan. In the early 1970s, when Japan became concerned about rising resentment toward its business expansion, which was being viewed as neocolonialism in some Southeast Asian countries, it added a review of political impact to its examination of proposed outbound investments.

Another alternative is to screen only those projects that apply for government risk insurance. Still another alternative is for the home country to be neutral and require international business firms of its nationality to assume all of the risks of dealing with foreign governments. The latter alternative may be feasible if the foreign interests of national firms are small. But for countries like the United States, international firms are powerful domestic political forces. Many of them expect their government to give them protection. Furthermore, the activities of international firms may have significant repercussions for an investor country, even though such a nation is not anxious to assume responsibility for its international firms. Disputes may cause difficulties for the home country whether it likes it or not.

Will investor countries increase their controls over outbound investment in the future? Two underlying trends suggest that increased controls are likely. First, the long-prevailing view in investor countries that outbound investment always brings positive benefits has been successfully challenged. As a result, the policy debates are revolving more and more around technical studies and specific evidence rather than ideolo-

---

[11] *Foreign Assistance Act of 1962. Hearings Before the Committee on Foreign Relations,* U.S. Senate, 87th Congress, 2d sess. (Washington, D.C.: U.S. Government Printing Office, 1962), p. 31.

gies and beliefs. A second element is the burgeoning controls of host countries. These host-country controls are likely to create the need for investor countries to protect themselves against their own enterprises as these firms react to meet the demands of other nations.

Box 10–1

British debate exchange curb

London, Oct. 22—Two years after Prime Minister Margaret Thatcher dropped foreign exchange controls, a flood of money out of the country has provoked a spate of calls for renewed strictures. Demands for controls have come from politicians and agencies representing a variety of persuasions.

Supporters of exchange controls argue that, in view of the nation's troubles, Britain would be justified in taking what are essentially protectionist actions to develop jobs for the 3 million people out of work. Even many normally unsympathetic economists accept this view.

But other economists note that if Britain's investors are forced to keep their money at home, interest rates would tend to be lower. That in turn would discourage non-British investors from bringing money here, even temporarily. The exchange rate would also probably be higher, which would exacerbate the problems British companies already have in competing in the export market.

Mrs. Thatcher has remained adamantly opposed to controls. Her cabinet ministers do not share the "siege economic view that if money flows overseas, it will deprive people of jobs." "It makes economic sense in government policy," a Treasury official said, "to build up this level of overseas dividend flow."

Source: Adapted from story by Steven Rattner in the *New York Times*, October 23, 1981.

HOST COUNTRIES: INCENTIVE CONTROLS

For obvious reasons, the less developed countries and the less developed regions within an economically advanced country are most likely to be offering incentives to attract industry. But a country may offer attractive incentives at an early stage of development, and later reduce its incentives and even impose restraints. Or it may have a mixture of inducements for some fields and restraints in others. Normally, the incentives are available to either domestic or foreign firms—such as Italy's long-standing effort to accelerate development of its poorer southern region. But in the case of the newly industrializing nations, where indigenous enterprise is weak or nonexistent, incentive programs are intended primarily to attract foreign business firms.

Incentives offered reflect a nation's stage of economic development, its specific development priorities, and its need to compensate for such business limitations as small local markets. Many small, newly independent countries with little local industry may offer a broad range of incentives that are not selective as to type of business activity. On the other hand, the semi-industrialized or even industrialized countries may direct their incentives to specific types of new activities. For example, Brazil decided in the middle 1950s to develop a domestic automobile industry and established a series of attractive incentives specially designed to persuade new investors to enter this field.[12]

Great ingenuity has been shown in developing incentives to fit the particular goals of individual countries, or individual states or provinces as in the cases of the United States and Canada. Flexibility is increased, moreover, by a common practice of wording the enabling laws so as to leave considerable bargaining discretion for government administrators. As a result, incentives within one particular country might vary according to the location of the investment, the size of the investment, the industry, the employment created, or even, as in the case of India, according to the number of shifts worked. In some cases, usually through administrative discretion rather than published regulations, countries try to encourage a mix of nationalities for inbound investment so as to reduce the appearance or reality of foreign economic domination by one country.

Incentives offered generally fall into the following categories:

Tariff protection.   Potential import competition is reduced or eliminated by special high tariffs or import controls.

Duty-free imports.   Equipment and sometimes future supplies of raw materials or components are allowed to enter the country duty-free or on special concessionary terms.

Financial assistance.   Short- and long-term loans, generally from government agencies, may be available at special low-interest rates.

Tax concessions.   Tax reductions, deferrals, and even 10-year tax holidays are being offered in certain countries.

Foreign exchange guarantees.   Specific governmental guarantees that foreign exchange will be granted for profit remittances and capital repatriation.

Other governmental assistance.   The government may assist in assembling parcels of land or agree to build roads or other public facilities needed to complement a project, or even provide subsidies for training personnel.

An important force in shaping incentive programs has been the competition among host countries, states, or provinces as potential locations for the international enterprise. This has been particularly important in relation to regional integration movements. With the elimination of internal tariff walls within the European Economic Community, a foreign firm locating in any of the member countries gained free access to the markets of the others. Consequently, competition developed among the countries in attracting foreign investment. Some of the smaller member countries,

---

[12] Lincoln Gordon and Englebert Grommers, *United States Manufacturing Investment in Brazil* (Boston: Harvard Business School, 1962), pp. 46–64.

in particular, have offered strong inducements to foreign industry interested in the Community.[13] A similar pattern has developed within the United States in recent years. Competition among the states has resulted in extremely attractive inducements being offered to foreign investors.

The establishment of a free port, foreign trade zone, or border industry program can attract foreign investment by using a combination of incentives. In the case of free ports and foreign trade zones, goods may be imported, processed, or stored indefinitely duty-free, with payment of appropriate duties only when goods are shipped from the port or zone into the customs territory. In the case of the border industry program, industries are permitted to import materials and components duty-free, employ local labor to assemble them, and export the products paying a duty on only value added.

In the United States, there were some 40 active free trade zones as of 1980 and over 1,000 business firms were shipping in excess of $2 billion annually through the zones.[14] Mexico's National Frontier Program, adopted in 1966, attracted within six years 280 U.S. plants employing an estimated 40,000 Mexican workers in a 12-mile zone along Mexico's border with the United States.[15] The sites are generally leased in order to circumvent Mexico's prohibition against foreign ownership of land along the border.

Investment promotion efforts are not limited to the nonsocialist countries. Several Eastern European socialist countries have taken special steps to permit and encourage foreign private companies to make direct investments in their countries.[16] The investment promotion measures being used illustrate the reciprocal nature of inducements and restrictions because reductions in restrictions have operated as incentives. In 1967, for example, Yugoslavia passed new foreign investment legislation that reinterpreted its concept of *social ownership* to permit joint industrial ventures with foreign capitalist companies under a *pooling-of-funds contract.*[17]

The effectiveness of incentives in implementing host-country policies and aspirations varies greatly. In countries where the ingredients neces-

---

[13] J. J. Boddewyn, *Western European Policies toward U.S. Investors.* The Bulletin, nos. 93–95 (New York: Graduate School of Business Administration, Institute of Finance, New York University, March 1974) p. 52.

[14] Edgar W. Kossack and William R. McDaniel, "Predicting Financial Benefits of U.S. Foreign Trade Zone Use," Florida Atlantic University, Boca Raton, Fla., October 17, 1981 (mimeograph).

[15] See Donald W. Baerresen, *The Border Industrialization Program of Mexico* (Lexington, Mass.: D. C. Heath, 1971).

[16] See Martin Schnitzer, *U.S. Business Involvement in Eastern Europe* (New York: Praeger Publishers, 1980).

[17] Miodrag Sukijasovic, "Foreign Investment in Yugoslavia," in *Foreign Investment: The Experience of Host Countries,* ed. Isaiah A. Litvak and Christopher J. Maule (New York: Praeger Publishers, 1970), pp. 385–406.

sary for making an international business project viable and profitable are not present, even the most attractive incentives will not yield the desired results. On the other hand, in a case such as Brazil's effort to develop quickly a major automobile industry, the special incentives almost certainly were a major factor in the decisions of the foreign firms to establish automobile assembly and components plants. The size of the market was large, and many other conditions appeared to be favorable. The incentives provided a significant reduction in risk.

HOST COUNTRIES: RESTRAINING CONTROLS

Host countries are at many different stages in devising policies and programs for restraining multinational business. A growing number of nations, having addressed themselves directly to the issue, have formulated a comprehensive set of policies and devised a coordinated set of control instruments.[18] Many other countries follow an evolutionary case-by-case approach in negotiating investment agreements.

Given the variations in national goals, national control programs differ in the aspects of multinational business on which they focus and the tools used. Tax measures, foreign exchange controls, and legal restrictions are used in varying proportions. A growing tendency has been to supplement restrictive measures over multinational firms with affirmative policies to strengthen domestic industries—through mergers, financial assistance for research and development, and other means. Where these incentives discriminate against foreign-owned firms, those firms are in effect penalized to the extent of the advantage accorded their competition.

From the standpoint of the international enterprise, it is important to note that control activities generally focus on new enterprises and new projects. The operations of established foreign enterprises, which may have an even greater impact on host-country goals, are frequently neglected.

Entry and takeover controls

In most countries foreign investors must request approval for a new investment project or for takeovers of existing local firms. In France, foreign firms must apply to the Ministry of Finance for permission. In India, a Foreign Investment Board coordinates the review of foreign direct investment applications, but decision-making authority on separate features of a project is decentralized. The United States is almost unique in that no permission whatever is required. As one foreign firm entering

---

[18] See Centre on Transnational Corporations, *National Legislation and Regulations Relating to Transnational Corporations* (New York: United Nations, 1978).

the United States observed, "We were confused when we invested in the States. Every other country has a door that says 'Enter here to request permission.' We couldn't find any such door in the States."

The majority of developing countries and two advanced nations, Canada and Australia, have established procedures for systematic screening of foreign investment. The investment laws in these countries generally specify broad criteria to be used in the evaluation of foreign investment requests. The criteria may be extremely general as in the case of Kenya— "projects furthering economic development or of benefit to Kenya, as determined by the Minister of Finance." In the case of Mexico, the criteria are "the importance of the activity to development, including export production, the use of domestic inputs, the effect on employment, wages, prices, and the balance of payments, the transfer of technology and the training of technical and managerial cadres, the diversification of investment, regional development, the respect of national and social values and a general identification with the national interest."[19]

By requiring a potential investor to gain approval, the host country throws onto the would-be investor a responsibility to describe operational, financial, and expansion plans in some detail and to justify the anticipated contributions to national goals. The reviewing authority is automatically placed in a position of power to open negotiations on adjustment of particular aspects of the proposal.

Where government authority is widely dispersed, where guidelines are vague, and where strict ethical standards do not prevail, the process of controlling the entry of foreign projects may involve crude or highly sophisticated forms of bribery and corruption.

If the host nation has signed a treaty of friendship, commerce, and navigation with the home country of the investor (see Chapter 8), it might technically be a breach of the treaty for the reviewing authority to withhold approval. The would-be investor should be accorded "national treatment" identical to the treatment of local firms. Delay in approval, however, is not a breach, and most investors would think it very dangerous to establish a business against a host government's wishes.

Prohibition of foreign ownership

In numerous countries, foreigners are excluded from specific business fields. They are excluded from the tobacco and mining industries in Sweden; from development of certain natural resources in Brazil, Finland, and Morocco; from retail trade in the Philippines; from Norway's textile and shipping industries; and from holding mining rights in Italy. Mexican exclusions are particularly sweeping. Mexico prohibits foreign ownership of land within 31 miles of the coastlines or 62 miles of the

---

[19] Ibid. p. 212.

borders with other countries, and Mexican companies permitting foreign shareholders are not allowed to own land in the restricted zones. In accordance with the constitution, the petroleum industry, the generation and distribution of electric power, railroads, and telegraphic communications are legally reserved for the government. Private enterprise, whether domestic or foreign, is therefore restricted from these fields. Foreigners, except as minority investors, are not permitted to invest in Mexican banks or other credit institutions, or in insurance companies. Recent administrations have also required, but not retroactively, either 100 percent ownership or a majority of Mexican ownership in a wide range of industries, including radio and television broadcasting; production, distribution, and exhibition of motion pictures; all phases of the soft-drink industry; advertising and publishing; and fishing and packing of marine products.

Public-utility fields are widely restricted, either because of ideological preferences for public enterprise or because the activities are considered indispensable for national development. Governments generally restrict the communication fields such as television, radio, and news publications to domestic firms or the government for protection of vital national interests. As a Canadian government report explains, "Communications media lie at the heart of the technostructure of modern societies. Canadian ownership and control facilitate the expression of Canadian points of view."[20] Protecting national interests is also the rationale for prohibiting foreign ownership in the banking, insurance, and other financial fields. To quote the Canadian report again, "Financial institutions, because of their pervasiveness and their potential as bases for influence and control, constitute the commanding heights of the economy. Canadian ownership and control facilitate the exercise of Canadian economic policies."[21]

Controls over natural resource extraction

Host-country policies controlling international business activity in natural resource fields have a special ideological and even emotional flavor. In most countries of the world, subsurface mineral rights and often forestry resources are reserved by law as the *property of the Crown*, or of the nation as a whole. This legal pattern results from the belief that resources provided by nature should be used for public benefit rather than private profit. Thus, the international business firm operating in the natural resource field is frequently dealing directly with government officials rather than with private owners of property, and with an issue that is of public rather than private concern. The situation is further complicated when the natural resource being exploited is exhaustible, and the

---

[20] "Foreign Ownership and Structure of Canadian Industry," *Report of the Task Force on the Structure of Canadian Industry* (Ottawa: Queen's Printer, 1968), p. 389.

[21] Ibid., p. 389.

nation cannot expect the project to continue indefinitely making its contribution to the national economy and public welfare.

The issue of controls over foreign firms does not arise, obviously, where countries restrict the exploitation of certain natural resources to government or domestic enterprises. But where foreign firms are allowed to operate, special controls or policies are generally imposed. The standard arrangement has been for a foreign company to purchase a concession giving it exclusive rights to explore in a particular area and to develop and produce the minerals or the petroleum found in that area for a stated number of years. The host government receives royalties on the materials extracted and income taxes on the net earnings of the concessionaire. The production of petroleum and minerals is generally for export, frequently to other foreign affiliates of the producing companies. The bulk of international business activity in resource exploitation is located in the less developed countries, and in these countries the resource industries are likely to be major sources of foreign exchange earnings, domestic employment, and economic growth. Consequently, host countries are especially anxious to secure a maximum share of the benefits by extending national controls over production, pricing, and marketing.

Specially negotiated concession agreements are intended to spell out the conditions under which foreign enterprises can operate. But in many of the countries, governments have changed with great frequency, and the new government may endeavor to alter or renegotiate the agreements.[22] In fact, the renegotiation of concession agreements is almost certain when foreign enterprises have secured unusually favorable arrangements and when the respective bargaining power of the two parties changes.

Over time, the degree of ownership and control by foreign firms is likely to decline because the unique contributions that the foreign firm makes to the domestic resource industries are also likely to decline. The bargaining power of the foreign firm is ultimately based on the degree to which its capital, technical skills, managerial ability, and marketing knowledge are needed by a foreign country. As the foreign enterprise earns profits for the country and trains local technical and operating personnel, it undercuts its own bargaining power by making less scarce the unique contributions that it had to offer initially.

Expropriation

Strictly used, the term *expropriation* refers to governmental action to dispossess someone of property, but with compensation. Government

---

[22] See. R. F. Mikesell, ed., *Foreign Investment in the Petroleum and Mineral Industries: Case Studies on Investor-Host Relations* (Baltimore: Johns Hopkins University Press, 1971); William A. Stoever, *Renegotiations in International Business Transactions* (Lexington, Mass.: D.C. Heath, 1981).

takeover without compensation is referred to as *confiscation,* as occurred with the takeover of foreign investment in Cuba in 1960. Distinction should also be made between expropriation and nationalization. Expropriation normally refers to the taking of a single property or business activity by the state. Nationalization usually means the taking of all activities or properties in a certain field—such as the nationalization of the steel industry in Great Britain, of the banks in Tanzania, and of petroleum distribution in Ceylon. Nationalization may involve a number of expropriations. Nationalization and expropriation are, however, frequently used interchangeably or even replaced with such terms as *indigenization* or *domestication.*[23]

Expropriation is in many ways the ultimate host-country control over foreign enterprises. The firm is forced to give up assets and profitable operations for which it risked capital. The compensation following expropriation has usually been less than the "going concern" value of the subsidiary to the parent firm. On some occasions, the loss of a subsidiary may mean the creation of a competitor.

The number of expropriations and nationalizations since World War II has been significant. A study by the United Nations identified 875 takeovers of foreign enterprises in 62 countries over the period from 1960 to mid-1974.[24] These takeovers, however, were highly concentrated in terms of both countries and types of business activity. Two thirds of the recorded takeovers were accounted for by just 10 nations, including such high-incidence countries as Argentina, Chile, Cuba, Peru, Algeria, Libya, and Iraq. By business sector, natural resources activities together with banking and insurance accounted for the bulk of the cases.

The United Nations study and another similar study that examined takeovers of U.S. foreign affiliates[25] both conclude that the frequency of takeovers had increased in the early 1970s from the rate in the 1960s. It appears, however, that the mid-1970s was a peak period for expropriations and that the trend has turned toward more limited use of this control strategy. One reason for the trend reversal is that past expropriations of foreign investment in petroleum, mining, public utilities, insurance, and so on have discouraged new investments in these sectors and left relatively little to expropriate. Another reason is that many developing countries have moved from ideological motivations to pragmatism and discovered that there can be a heavy cost side to expropriations and that

[23] J. Frederick Truitt, *Expropriation of Private Foreign Investment* (Bloomington: Graduate School of Business, Indiana University, 1974), pp. 9–11.

[24] United Nations Economic and Social Council, *Permanent Sovereignty over Natural Resources (A/9716)* (New York: United Nations, 1974).

[25] Robert G. Hawkins, Norman Mintz, and Michael Provissiero, "Government Takeovers of U.S. Foreign Affiliates," *Journal of International Business Studies,* Spring 1976, pp. 3–16.

alternative approaches exist that can achieve the goals of nationalization without its costs.[26]

Nationalization risk has generally been considered to be limited to the developing and socialist countries. But patterns keep changing. As of the late 1970s and early 1980s, the advanced capitalistic countries of Canada and France were the most active areas for nationalization. Under Canada's federal system, provincial governments possess broad powers over local mineral resources. In 1978, Saskatchewan invoked these powers to nationalize much of its potash industry and reduce foreign ownership in this area. Quebec has also moved to expropriate foreign investment in asbestos mining. The nationalization program of the Mitterand government in France has been directed toward specific business areas and is not exclusively focused on foreign investors. Nevertheless, the areas that were nationalized involve foreign as well as domestic investors.

Limitation of foreign control

Policies to minimize the effects of foreign ownership are two-pronged. They can be designed to strengthen domestic enterprise or weaken the power of foreign firms. Sometimes, both objectives are accomplished in single actions. The Japanese government has long had a policy of encouraging licensing rather than direct foreign investment. Such a policy can be effective if a country is extremely attractive to international business firms, and if the domestic industry sector is strong and has potential and resources for fully utilizing the technology part of the foreign business package without the accompanying investment and management resources.

Governments also attempt to minimize foreign domination by opposing or prohibiting the acquisition of domestic firms by international enterprises. Canada, for example, created its Foreign Investment Review Agency (FIRA) in 1973 to screen all foreign takeovers of existing Canadian firms. The yardstick used by FIRA for approval is that foreign ownership must provide "significant benefit to Canada."[27] With the same objective of restricting foreign investment, France has followed the strategy of promoting and encouraging mergers on the assumption that larger and presumably more competitive domestic firms will reduce the competitive advantage of foreign firms.

---

[26] Sigmund, *Multinationals in Latin America*, pp. 256–302 on "Nationalization and Its Alternatives"; see also James K. Weekly, "Expropriation of U.S. Multinational Investments," *MSU Business Topics* 25 (Winter 1977).

[27] Charles J. McMillan, "The Regulation of Foreign Investment in Canada: Experience and Prospects," *Journal of Contemporary Business*, Autumn 1977, pp. 31–51; Alan M. Rugman, "The Regulaton of Foreign Investment in Canada," *Journal of World Trade Law*, July/August 1977, pp. 322–33.

Policies requiring that ownership and control of foreign business projects be shared with local firms are another means of reducing foreign control. India, for example, has imposed a 40 percent foreign ownership ceiling on foreign business projects since 1973. Exceptions may be made to this limitation for specific types of investments such as predominantly export industries, defined as companies exporting at least 60 percent of production. The reactions of IBM and Coca-Cola to this policy are shown in Box 10–2.

Box 10–2

IBM and Coca-Cola Leave India

New Delhi, June 1 (AP)—The International Business Machines Corporation closed down its manufacturing and maintenance operations in India today after refusing a government demand to cut IBM's share of ownership to 40 percent. Earlier, the Coca-Cola Export Corporation shut down its operations in India rather than consent to sell 60 percent ownership of its local branch, which the company felt threatened the secrecy of the Coke formula.

Throughout its history, IBM has been adamant about running the whole show, saying it had to if it was to operate efficiently. India, in a drive to strengthen its domestically owned business base, had ordered IBM to sell 60 percent of its equity, saying its operation was "low technology," selling mainly obsolete computers.

"The activities of the Coca-Cola Company in India during the last 20 years," said India's Minister of Industry, "furnish a classic example of how a multinational corporation operating in a low-priority, high-profit area in a developing country attains runaway growth and, in the absence of alertness on the part of the government concerned, can trifle with the weaker indigenous industry in the process. The manufacture of beverages should by 'Indianized' and the outflows of foreign exchange from the industry should be halted."

Source: *New York Times*, June 2, 1978, and August 9, 1977.

Mexico has also taken a hard line on having Mexicans share in the ownership of Mexican affiliates or subsidiaries of international business firms. Its Mexicanization policy is promoted through bargaining when permission is granted for foreign firms to establish business in the country and through policies that limit certain tax exemptions or export permits to companies at least 51 percent owned by Mexican nationals.

Controls over local content, employment, and production

Some governments have developed what are called *local-content* policies. Prospective investors are asked to commit themselves to a schedule of increasing the locally produced content of the final product over a stated period of time. Such local-content policies have been widely applied to automobile manufacturers who have expanded in Latin America, with the hope that the development impetus of new types of activity will continue over time and be extended into other related areas of activity. But countries may have to pay a high price for having local content when local markets are not large enough to permit economic scale production for many parts and components.

Another way of increasing local benefits is through employment policies imposed on international enterprises. The labor law of Mexico provides that at least 90 percent of a foreign company's employees must be Mexican citizens. Executives are generally excluded in calculating this percentage. The immigration of foreigners for managerial and other positions is permitted only if qualified Mexicans are not available. Some countries also establish limits in relation to the total payroll.

Exports strategies of multinational enterprises have become the focus of another set of controls. Countries have realized that the global strategies of multinational firms may not allow or encourage subsidiaries and affiliates to compete freely for export markets. Some countries thus make it a requirement for approval of all new operations that the units are completely free to export and earn foreign exchange. Some nations will even force divestiture if a specified proportion of output is not exported. And there are many pressures exerted for foreign processing of local materials before export.

Financial and fiscal controls

Balance-of-payments objectives are increasingly obvious in the development of controls over financing. Many host countries require external financing for new foreign investments and some limit the access of foreign firms to local sources of capital. Other common policies are to set limits or establish continuing control over remission of profits, repatriation of capital, and royalty payments to the home office of the foreign enterprise. To back these controls, however, more and more countries are realizing that they need additional controls to regulate transfer pricing for goods and services moving among units of the international enterprise.

REGIONAL AND INTERNATIONAL CONTROLS

The principal controls that confront multinational firms are those of the individual nation-states. There have also been related control efforts at the regional and international levels. The regional moves have been to reduce competition among host countries by agreeing on standard controls. The international moves have been to establish a code of conduct for multinational enterprises.

The principal example of a common regional approach to foreign direct investment is the Andean Pact. Negotiated in 1971 by Bolivia, Chile, Colombia, Ecuador, and Peru and joined later by Venezuela, the Pact took a hard line toward foreign investors. Under Decision 24 of the Pact, new foreign investment was excluded from the areas of public utilities, the mass media, advertising, and banking. Existing firms in these areas were given three years to sell 80 percent of their stock to local nationals. The profit rate on invested foreign capital was limited to 14 percent for re-patriation purposes and 5 percent for reinvestment. New foreign enter-prises wishing to take advantage of tariff reductions were required to sell 51 percent ownership to national investors or governments over a period of 15 to 20 years.

The success of such a hard-line approach depends in large part on the attractiveness of the host countries to foreign investors and the relative bargaining strength of the countries and the foreign investors. While the common policy certainly reduced competition among the Andean coun-tries, the net result has been to discourage foreign investment.[28] Although some of the restrictions have been relaxed, Chile withdrew from the Pact in 1976 because it still considered the regulations to be too rigid.

At the international level, the international business community and some investor nations have long been pressing for a multilateral conven-tion establishing a code for fair treatment and protection of foreign in-vestment. Not too surprisingly, the codes proposed by the investors and investor countries focused heavily on the responsibilities and obligations of the host countries.

Most national governments were slow to join the movement for inter-national codes of conduct. By the mid-1970s, however, the governments of the industrialized countries (through the OECD) and the developing countries (through the UN Commission on Transnational Corporations) began to demonstrate considerable enthusiasm for an international code. But the difference between the concerns of multinational firms and those of governments became sharply apparent. To the international business community, international regulation means restraints on gov-ernments. To the governments, international regulation means restraints on multinational enterprises. Somewhat ironically, the movement for a code of fair treatment and protection of investors had become trans-formed into a movement for the fair treatment and protection of coun-tries.

The first product of this new-found concern of governments was a Declaration on International Investment and Multinational Enterprises approved by OECD countries in 1976. The declaration includes rather detailed Guidelines for Multinational Enterprises that "aim at improving

---

[28] Robert E. Grosse, *Foreign Investment Codes and the Location of Direct Investment* (New York: Praeger Publishers, 1980).

the international investment climate," at strengthening "confidence between multinational enterprises and states," and "at encouraging the positive contributions of multinational enterprises to economic and social progress and minimizing or resolving difficulties that may result from their activities."[29] Although an intergovernmental consultation procedure has been established, the guidelines are voluntary and the parties to the declaration do not include any of the developing countries.

What are the prospects for global agreement on standard controls? The issues to be resolved are not simple. If many countries benefit significantly, other are likely to perceive costs. As the vast majority of United Nations members are host countries only, their majority pressure for controls has been against the interests of the investor countries. The investor countries agree that multinational corporations should adhere to codes of good conduct, but they insist that governments as well as enterprises must respect obligations undertaken by them.

The changing ambience for multinationals and the growing assertion by governments of their regulatory powers are realities. As the U.S. representative on the UN Commission on Transnational Corporations has observed, "Whatever may have been the governmental restraints in the past, that period, in comparison with what is likely the future, may seem to have been a veritable Eden of freedom. Surveillance and restriction are in the air. The multinational finds itself under steady assault from host and home government alike." But he also concludes, "It does not seem likely, however, that the multinational has much to fear from a broad international agreement."[30] As is suggested by another study, the apparent enthusiasm by both governments and some international managers for international codes "masks different conceptions of who is going to be controlled, who is going to do the controlling, and what the purposes of the control will be."[31]

Some internationally agreed upon measures are likely to emerge. But the forecasts are for only modest accomplishments at the international level. In 1980, after 10 years of discussion by members of the United Nations Conference on Trade and Development, the industrialized, developing, and communist nations adopted a set of guidelines for controlling restrictive business practices in international trade. The guidelines, however, will not affect national laws because they are voluntary. In 1982, the UN Commission on Transnational Corporations was still bogged down, with key issues unresolved, in its six-year effort to draft a code of conduct for multinational corporations. Consequently, the prevailing

---

[29] OECD, *International Investment and Multinational Operations* (Paris, 1976).

[30] Seymour J. Rubin, "Developments in the Law and Institutions of International Economic Relations," *American Journal of International Law* July 1974, p. 487.

[31] C. Fred Bergsten, Thomas Horst, and Theodore H. Moran, *American Multinationals and American Interests* (Washington, D.C.: Brookings Institution, 1978), p. 398.

view is that "control" will continue to be exercised nationally rather than internationally.

SUMMARY

International business operates across and within the boundaries of many discrete sovereign nation-states. The business firm has its private goals that it pursues within a geographical area of its own choosing, which includes the sovereign domains of several or many national governments. Governments have their public purposes, some of which are in harmony with and others that may run counter to the private global goals of the international corporations. As sovereign nations, governments will exercise their power to influence the operating patterns of the enterprises. Through incentives, they encourage those activities considered to be in harmony with national goals. Through negative curbs, they try to constrain those activities likely to conflict with national goals. The multinational enterprise will try to thread its way through the multiple and often conflicting claims of many governments with the minimum of sacrifice to its goals.

The stimulus for national control programs does not come primarily from bad experience with multinationals, although many examples exist of what nations consider to be "negative behavior." National governments have long used controls over international transfers of goods, money flow, and persons to increase their share of national benefits from such international transactions. Similar controls have now been adopted by nations to increase a nation's share of the global benefits generated by multinational enterprises and to reduce the negative effects, such as a threat of economic domination and challenges to economic and political autonomy.

EXERCISES AND DISCUSSION QUESTIONS

1. "Investment-guaranty insurance merely encourages both investing companies and host governments to behave more irresponsibly, knowing that the investing company's government would bail the company out. Safeguards should be written into such schemes that would prevent a company claiming on the guarantee scheme if it had somehow provoked the host government into nationalization, for instance by bad labor practices or disguised political activity locally." Discuss.

2. The United States has a vital national-security interest in acquiring dependable foreign sources of critical minerals at a reasonable cost. Therefore, it should give maximum support and protection to the foreign direct investments of U.S. international resource industries in such fields as petroleum and copper, where U.S. domestic production is insufficient for U.S. needs. Discuss.

3. You have been retained by an industrialized country, such as France, to recommend strategy and policies for regulating the entry and continuing operations of foreign multinational companies in that country. What are the two or three most important issues that you would have to resolve? What information would you need to complete your assignment? In what ways would the key problems and the nature of your recommendations be different if you were working for a less developed counry, namely, a small, newly independent country in Africa?

4. Host-country policies that require multinational companies to share ownership with nationals are frequently used to minimize the economic power of foreign interests. But such policies will also reduce the amount of foreign capital transfers to the host country and reduce the supply of local capital for domestic entrepreneurs. Why do you think so many host countries are insisting that foreign firms share ownership with locals?

5. Under what circumstances would you as a host country prohibit foreign companies from acquiring domestic companies?

6. In formulating an investment promotion program to attract foreign direct investment to a less developed country, which incentives do you think would be most effective and why?

Chapter 11

Measuring benefits to the nation-state

Who benefits from the expansion of multinational enterprises? As the multinationals have expanded, so has the ideological controversy over the benefits of foreign investment. The international business community holds the view that the multinationals benefit both home and host countries. An opposing view argues that the multinationals are the agents of the capitalist-imperialist countries, producing and maintaining a pattern of inequality and dependency among the developing countries. Still another view, the global-reach position, argues that the effects of the multinationals are negative on home and host countries alike.

But while the ideological debate has waxed and waned, most host countries have been moving to a less ideological and more social cost-benefit approach to foreign direct investment. This approach recognizes that foreign investment has costs as well as benefits to the nation. Consequently, governments must evaluate each case in an effort to distinguish between the positive and negative effects, both actual and prospective.

This chapter will discuss the major areas of controversy in the ideological debates, the concepts underlying social cost-benefit techniques, and illustrate the approaches being used for measuring benefits to the nation-state.

THE IDEOLOGICAL DEBATES

The ideological debates on the vices and virtues of multinational enterprises have generated a vast academic and popular literature. Although the negative views have great overlaps, they can be broadly classified into the neoimperialist view, the *"dependencia"* school, and the global-reach interpretation.[1]

The neoimperialist view would recommend that host countries should not permit the entry of foreign direct investment because the multinationals are a tool for exploiting host countries to the exclusive benefit of their capitalist-imperialist home countries. As was discussed in the chapter on international business theories, the position of the neoimperialists has been sabotaged by the pragmatic behavior of the Marxist-socialist countries. The People's Republic of China and the countries of Eastern Europe in cooperating with the multinationals implicitly accept several propositions that negate the neoimperialist view. These nations apparently recognize that the multinational enterprise and its home country are not an identity, that host countries also have power, and that the host countries can secure benefits from collaboration with multinational enterprises.

The *dependencia* school, which has flourished in Latin American intellectual and government circles, has roots in the Marxist tools of analysis but a somewhat different emphasis and prescription.[2] It pictures the world economy as consisting of the major capitalistic countries as the "center" and the underdeveloped countries as the "periphery." It attributes the development problems of the periphery to an unbalanced relationship with the center. The result of this unbalanced relationship is that economic growth in the less developed countries has been distorted and limited by being subordinated to the economies of the major capitalist countries. Foreign investment may stimulate growth in the periphery countries but it is likely to be growth of the wrong products and indus-

---

[1] For an in-depth discussion of these ideologies, see C. Fred Bergsten, Thomas Horst, and Theodore H. Moran, *American Multinationals and American Interests* (Washington, D.C., Brookings Institution, 1978) pp. 309–53.

[2] See, for example, Andre Gunder Frank, *Capitalism and Underdevelopment in Latin America* (New York: Monthly Review Press, 1967); Osvaldo Sunkel, "Big Business and Dependencia, A Latin View," *Foreign Affairs*, April 1972.

tries. There may be growth of income, but for the elite who are allied with the multinationals and not for the needy.

The *dependencia* view has supported demands at the international level for the redistribution of economic power to reduce the dependency of the developing countries. At the national level, the policies called for would promote industrialization by government enterprises and local private efforts. But the dependency view has lost force in recent years. One factor has been considerable negative experience with nationalized enterprises.[3] Another factor has been the growing realization that host countries have a great deal of power for shaping the participation of foreign enterprises in their economies.

The ideological debates have given way to pragmatism in many countries. Yet a number of the issues raised by the debates are included in the evaluation process of social cost-benefit analysis. Some of the major areas where the costs and benefits of international business are open to debate are examined below.

THE IMPACT ON NATIONAL SOVEREIGNTY

Ideally speaking, the nation-state has both internal supremacy and external independence. External independence or freedom from outside control, however, is never absolute. In practice, the nation-state must be guided by the impact of its decisions on other sovereign nation-states. The multinational enterprise is subject to the sovereign power of a nation-state over its business activities within that state's territory. But, unlike purely domestic firms, the multinational also responds to outside commands emanating from the parent, other family members, or even indirectly from other sovereign states. Furthermore, the local subsidiary can rely for support on the economic power of the entire system and at times on the political power of other sovereigns. The presence within a nation of an appendage of a powerful multinational system may thus generate local tensions and appear to be a threat to national sovereignty.[4]

Nations' general attitudes toward international business are built from their evaluations of individual business activities. Yet, the threats to sovereignty reflect considerations over and above the sum of the net benefits or costs of individual international business activities. As a result, any

---

[3] Paul E. Sigmund, *Multinationals in Latin America* (Madison: University of Wisconsin Press, 1980), pp. 256–301; Raymond Vernon, "Multinational Enterprises in Developing Countries: Issues in Dependency and Interdependence," in *The Multinational Corporation and Social Change*, ed. David E. Apter and Louis W. Goodman (New York: Praeger Publishers, 1976), pp. 40–62.

[4] The "threat to sovereignty," however, can also be an "extension of sovereignty" with the host country able to extend its sovereignty into the home country. See Joseph S. Nye, Jr., "Multinational Corporations in World Politics," *Foreign Affairs*, October 1974, p. 158.

specific international business project may become subordinated to the broader issues and may not be evaluated as an independent event. International firms, therefore, should not ignore the more general nationalistic concerns in the cost-benefit analyses.

THE POLITICAL CHALLENGE

The history of foreign investment during the 19th and early 20th centuries contains many examples of foreign firms, particularly in the extractive industries, exercising their power to influence political events in host countries. Probably the best known cases of political intervention are the activities of United Fruit in Central America and ITT in Chile (see Box 11–1). However, direct attempts at political influence by multinational firms have steadily declined. The multinational now tends to face more

Box 11–1

Dollar diplomacy, 1972 style

I helped make Mexico safe for American oil interests in 1914. I helped make Haiti and Cuba a decent place (sic) for the National City Bank boys to collect revenue in. I helped purify Nicaragua for the international banking house of Brown Brothers. . . . I brought light to the Dominican Republic for American sugar interests in 1916. I helped make Honduras "right" for American fruit companies in 1903. Looking back on it, I might have given Al Capone a few hints.

Maj. Gen. Smedley D. Butler
USMC, 1931

By the time Smedley Butler pridefully described his role in Latin America, economic colonialism by the world's prosperous nations had come to be regarded almost as a matter of course. For nearly two and a half centuries, Britain's East India Co. had provided stunning evidence of just how far the practice could go by ruling one fifth of the world's population, maintaining its own standing army, and producing revenues that actually exceeded its homeland's. But if America was a latecomer, it quickly made up for lost time. Washington spent the first three decades of the 20th century wielding its big stick on behalf of U.S. business interests, intervening in Latin America alone an astounding 60 times.

*   *   *   *   *

Against this background, the recent charges that officials of International Telephone and Telegraph Corp. had conspired with the CIA to block the election of Chile's Marxist president, Salvador Allende Gossens, seemed . . . evidence that, for all their low profile and talk of corporate good citizenship, some multinational corporations of 1972 may operate just as cynically as the United Fruit of 1928.

Source: *Newsweek*, April 10, 1972.

subtle political problems in which it is unintentionally caught between opposing political interests of different nation-states.[5]

To the host country, the local subsidiary of a multinational enterprise can be perceived as a political arm of the home-country government. Through its control over the parent company, home governments can and have interfered in the political affairs of another, or host country. Over certain periods, for example, the U.S. government has placed partial or complete embargoes on exports of goods and transfers of technology to certain countries such as mainland China, Cuba, and the Soviet-bloc countries. American subsidiaries in England and in Europe have been coerced into turning away business from Cuba and Soviet-bloc countries, even though the nations in which the subsidiaries are located have different policies.[6]

Other conflicts with host countries have occurred in the area of extraterritorial jurisdiction. As discussed in Chapter 8, the best known example is the enforcement of U.S. antitrust laws, which has had the effect of banning activities in another country that are not against the laws of that country.

Still another type of political challenge to a host country occurs when the home country of the multinational parent assumes political responsibility for protecting the foreign interests of its citizens. Although foreign subsidiaries are normally incorporated within the countries in which they are operating and subject to national laws as a national corporation, home-country governments are not always willing to accept the results of expropriation under local law. The interests of the multinational enterprise and those of the home country, however, are not identical, and the use of home-country political power to intervene in the relations between foreign subsidiaries and host governments often becomes a controversial political issue in the home country. Such intervention can be at the expense of other political interests of the home country.

The multinational enterprise faces a complex and ambiguous situation in the political conflict area. It has little, if any, capability for reducing the political challenge it represents to host countries when it is used as a political arm of the home government and in cases involving extraterritoriality. It does not relish its role as a carrier of controls. At best, it can urge the conflicting nation-states to undertake bilateral negotiations or participate in intergovernmental programs to harmonize laws or mediate disputes.

In their relations with home countries, multinational companies have mixed and, at times, ambivalent views. Some companies would like to be independent of the political interests of a home country. Some have even expressed the desire to have an island somewhere in international wa-

---

[5] Ibid., p. 160.

[6] See Jack N. Behrman, "Export and Technology Controls," in *National Interests and the Multinational Enterprise* (Englewood Cliffs, N.J.: Prentice-Hall, 1970), pp. 101–13.

ters as their home base. Other firms place a high value on having a home-country government that will protect their operations in a foreign country and represent their interests in intergovernmental negotiations on such matters as tariffs and trade policies. In still other cases, multinational enterprises would like to be politically free from their home country on some issues and yet be able to call for its political muscle on other issues.

REDUCTION IN ECONOMIC INDEPENDENCE

In any individual case, a multinational firm may offer sizable net benefits to a nation in which it is operating. But when a dominant share of the domestic economy comes under foreign ownership and control, the merits of the individual case become subordinated to a nation's broader concern for maintaining its economic independence. Over many decades, the new jobs and other benefits generated by foreign investment in Canada were sufficiently appealing to quiet national fears of foreign economic domination. But when 60 percent of Canada's manufacturing industry, 75 percent of her petroleum and natural gas industry, and 60 percent of her mining industry came under control of foreign corporations by the mid-1960s, national sovereignty tolerance levels were breached. As one Canadian scholar expressed this concern: "Once the most dynamic sectors of our economy have been lost, once most of the savings and investment is taking place in the hands of foreign capitalists, then the best prediction is a steady drift toward foreign control of the Canadian economy with the only certain upper limit being 100 percent."[7]

The Canadian example illustrates a nation's concern because of the total share of the national economy that is foreign owned. Nations also become agitated when foreign enterprises dominate a number of key growth industries. Writing in 1901, a British author observed, "The most serious aspect of the American industrial invasion lies in the fact that these incomers have acquired control of almost every new industry created during the past fifteen years."[8] Referring to the British, he concludes, "We are becoming the hewers of wood and the drawers of water, while the most skilled, most profitable, and the easiest trades are becoming American."[9]

Somewhat ironically, the necessary conditions for successful international business expansion can also be responsible for creating national tensions. Foreign firms must have something to offer over and above what is available from domestic enterprise. Multinational enterprises have little to offer in the production of low technology and standardized

---

[7] Mel Watkins, in the preface to Kari Levitt, *Silent Surrender: The American Economic Empire in Canada* (New York: Liveright, 1971), p. xi.

[8] Fred A. McKenzie, *The American Invaders* (New York: Street and Smith, 1901), p. 31.

[9] Ibid., p. 157.

products for local markets. Bricks are an example of such products. But in sophisticated technology and rapid growth areas such as computers, international firms have a competitive-advantage basis for entering foreign areas. Thus arises the national fear of becoming technologically dependent upon foreigners.

The multinational threat to national economic autonomy is perceived in many dimensions. As host nations may complain, the decision centers that control many of their key economic sectors are outside of the country and less subject to national controls. The multinational enterprise can shift resources within the system and thus reduce the effectiveness of national programs to control inflation, improve the balance of payments, or expand employment. The research centers for multinational enterprises are likely to remain in the home country, with the result that a host country becomes technologically dependent on outsiders. Foreign enterprises that command mammoth resources and have a head start in key growth areas are viewed as slowing the emergence of local entrepreneurship in these fields.

The less developed countries, which can benefit most from the transfers of resources, management skills, and technology of the multinational enterprise, are especially sensitive to the economic domination issue. Some of them characterize the issue as economic neocolonialism, particularly at intermediate stages of development. Foreign investment, as they see it, can change over time from a development stimulant to a retardant. As Hirschman has articulated the case, "Foreign investment can be at its creative best by bringing in 'missing' factors of production, complementary to those available locally, in the early stages of development of a poor country. The possibility that it will play a stunting role arises later on, when the poor country has begun to generate . . . its own entrepreneurs, technicians, and savers and could do even more along these lines." The increased domestic capacity for supplying missing factors may in large part be the contribution of multinational enterprise. But, as Hirschman argues, institutional inertia makes for continued importing of so-called scarce factors even when they become locally available. This line of thinking has resulted in proposals that foreign enterprises should be forced to withdraw, or disinvest, at the stage when the factors brought in by the multinational enterprise are no longer complementary to local factors but become competitive with them and prevent their growth.[10]

NET NATIONAL BENEFITS: UNDERLYING CONCEPTS

Most nations might agree in principle that the free movement of multinational enterprises across national boundaries can improve overall

---

[10] Albert O. Hirschman, *How to Divest in Latin America, and Why,* Princeton Essays in International Finance, no. 76 (Princeton N.J.: International Finance Section, Department of Economics, Princeton University, November 1969).

economic efficiency on a world basis. Yet this acceptance does not remove an active concern for how the global gains are distributed among individual nations. Thus the multinational enterprise must focus on individual national benefits rather than on world benefits.

In evaluating national benefits and costs, national authorities may consider political, social, or spiritual effects as well as economic effects. And they may value each effect explicitly or implicitly through the decisions they take. The mix of effects included in any evaluation, however, will vary from nation to nation and reflect differences in national priorities. The same effect will almost certainly be weighted differently by different nations, and the effects considered will change over time as national priorities change.

While these points may be readily grasped at the conceptual level, in practice, the quantification of costs and benefits remains a highly ambiguous subject, even in the economic area. How does a nation measure the value of a transfer of technological and managerial know-how to nationals of that country? What is the value of a foreign enterprise's contribution to national goals of economic and social modernization, or what are the costs of having prized cultural values changed? How much is it worth to have more competition injected into an economy or for indigenous entrepreneurship to be stimulated (or stunted) by the entry into a country of foreign firms? For the home as well as the host country, the quantification problem is equally formidable.[11] Yet, implicitly more often than explicitly, each nation-state makes such calculations, or intuitive leaps, in establishing and exercising controls over international business.

With each nation aiming for a surplus of benefits over costs from the operations of multinational enterprise, it might appear that the international firm is in the middle of an impossible situation. In order for one nation to have net gains, does another nation have to have net losses? Fortunately, two characteristics of the situation help to reduce the stress placed on the multinational enterprise in a world of nation-states. One saving feature is that the cost and benefit items have different values for different nations. A loss of jobs to a full-employment Swiss economy because of the establishment of overseas production facilities by a Swiss multinational enterprise will be valued as a small cost to Switzerland. The same employment will be valued as a great benefit by a host country with a high degree of unemployment that receives a new subsidiary. The second saving feature is that international business activity is not necessarily a zero-sum game in which one nation has to lose in order for another nation to gain. If international business results in a more efficient use of world resources, all parties can secure increased benefits. Because the pie to be divided is larger, each nation can have a larger slice.

---

[11] A major attempt at overall assessment of benefits accruing to the United States from its own multinationals is presented by: C. Fred Bergsten, Thomas Horst, and Theodore H. Moran, *American Multinationals and American Interests: The Economic and Political Effects and Proposals for a New Policy* (Washington, D.C.: Brookings Institution, 1978).

Conceptually, the final or "bottom line" calculation in measuring national benefits involves three steps that must be understood by the foreign firm. First, it is not benefits from business expansion per se that are being measured. Instead, the focus is on contributions by the foreign firm that would not otherwise be available to the nation. Only the net contributions over what might have been available from domestically controlled business activities really count. Second, costs as well as benefits are calculated and the foreign enterprise must provide a surplus of benefits over costs. Third, it is not enough for the benefits to be positive. The surplus must be greater than that for other alternatives available to the nation in order for significant common interests to exist between the enterprise and specific nation-state.

RESOURCE TRANSFER EFFECTS

A very important component in the calculation of net national benefits is the extent to which the multinational enterprise increases the availability of resources and the supply of productive facilities in the countries where it establishes operations.

In industrialized countries, the important resource transfers may be in the fields of technology, management, and skilled technical manpower. In the less developed countries, the range of resource transfers has generally been much broader. Outside capital has often been a major contribution. Where foreign exchange is a major constraint on growth, foreign capital can help to break this bottleneck. The transfer of technology and the import of management, marketing, and production skills may be valued even more highly than in the more advanced countries. To the extent that the inflow of resources consists of "missing factors," they may complement and effectively "increase" the supply of local factors heretofore idle or less productively used. Thus, the resource transfer effect may be both the net addition from the outside as well as the net increase in the effective value of domestic resources.

Resource transfers have a cost as well as a benefit side. The multinational enterprise may use local resources that are scarce rather than in excess supply. Although local management skills may be in short supply, the foreign enterprise is frequently under pressure to hire nationals. It is then likely to be charged with the opportunity cost of preempting managers who otherwise would be available to initiate and direct indigenous enterprises. Or enterprises may be required by national policies to form joint ventures by enlisting local capital and may be charged on the cost side with preempting scarce local capital that should be available for local enterprises.

Whether such opportunity costs are valid costs in calculating net national benefits is a complex question. For example, by using local capital foreign enterprises may enlarge rather than reduce the total supply of that resource. In countries that are attempting to strengthen local capital markets, the selling of stock locally by a well-known and presumably financially secure and profitable international firm can provide the confidence essential for developing such institutions and thereby help in attracting more savings to capital markets for equity investment.

The profits earned by foreign enterprises can be considered an offsetting cost by a nation. To the extent that a multinational firm transfers profits out of the country, there is a foreign exchange cost. The foreign exchange question will be considered separately below. If the firm reinvests profits within the country, the cost to the nation may be that a larger amount of the national patrimony comes under foreign ownership. What is frequently overlooked by antagonists to foreign investment is that such profits come out of newly created increments to domestic GNP generated by the multinational enterprise, and that the profits are generally a small share of the total increment. The firm gains profits; the nation gains an even greater increment in GNP and employment.

Turning to a question posed earlier, if the host countries are gaining resources, aren't the home countries losing? This possibility exists, of course. The normal situation seems to be, however, that resources are being transferred from countries in which they are relatively abundant to areas where such factors are in relatively short supply, and that the opportunity cost of such resource outflows may be low. Offsetting these home-country costs are a flow of benefits such as repatriated profits, payments to the parent company for royalties and management services, increased exports to overseas subsidiaries, increased exports as an indirect result of expanding world output, and even return flows of technology.

It should be noted that the resource transfer capability of the multinational enterprise extends far beyond that of bilateral transfers between home and host country. Operating with a global strategy, the firm can transfer resources among any of the nations in which it is operating.

Under most circumstances, in order to welcome international firms a nation must feel that the net value of resource transfers from such operations is positive. There may be some cases where a net cost, rather than a net benefit, is acceptable because of large indirect or linkage benefits. The establishment of an agricultural processing plant by a foreign firm may not in itself result in a net inflow of resources, but the stimulus of this plant to agricultural employment and farm output may be a more than offsetting benefit.

Resource transfers, of course, have a time dimension. When a direct-investment project is initiated, benefits are greatest and certainly most spectacular. In the initial stages, capital flows in, plants are built, local workers are hired and trained, and local supply contracts are let. After a new project has been started, or a new product or process introduced, a steady decline in benefits is likely to set in. The benefits may never phase out completely. Yet, over time they may lose much of their value to a nation.

The longer the enterprise operates on its original technological, organizational, and other resource transfer base, the smaller is the value placed on the original benefits by the host country. In many, if not most, cases stimulated by opportunity or pushed by local pressures, enterprises have responded by continually adding to or upgrading their initial technological, organization, or product contribution. Where firms do not continue adding, the question is likely to be raised by the host country as to whether payments to the foreign investor should continue indefinitely since the net contribution to the nation has declined and may even cease over time.[12]

BALANCE-OF-PAYMENTS EFFECTS

The impact of multinational business operations on a nation's balance of payments has long been a controversial issue. A number of scholarly studies have attempted to resolve the controversy in this area. Still, considerable uncertainty prevails as to the total impact on either investor or host countries. The conflicting conclusions emerging from the studies are explained mainly by different assumptions as to what would have happened if the foreign investment had not been made and by the completeness of the effects that have been measured.

A simple calculation frequently used by host countries is to compare the initial capital inflow—usually a once-and-for-all effect—with the continuing outflows of dividends, interest, royalties, and administrative charges to the parent company. For example, over the 10-year period from 1960 to 1969, the net capital inflow to the less developed countries from U.S. multinationals averaged about $650 million per year. Over the same period, U.S. firms returned to the United States as repatriated earnings an average of $2,500 million per year, plus additional amounts as royalties and fees. From these data, the conclusion can be drawn that the host countries suffered a substantial net loss in foreign exchange from the operations of multinational enterprises and that the investor countries had a substantial net gain.

This type of calculation is misleading because it does not take into account the full range of effects, particularly the effects on trade. In a quantitative sense, the effects on the trade accounts—exports and imports—generally overshadow the effects on capital inflows and repatriation outflows. The foreign firm can generate foreign exchange benefits for a country through expanding exports or substituting for goods and services previously imported. The net result will be a surplus of export

---

[12] Peter P. Gabriel, "The Investment in the LDC: Asset with a Fixed Maturity," *Columbia Journal of World Business*, Summer 1966, pp. 109–19.

earnings and import savings over the foreign exchange expenditures for raw materials or intermediate inputs that the multinational enterprise must import.

A more comprehensive evaluation of foreign exchange effects can be illustrated by a study of 132 projects financed by the Overseas Private Investment Corporation.[13] In fiscal 1976 these projects had a positive balance-of-payments effect for the host countries of $722 million annually. As benefits, the projects generated $837 million in import substitution savings plus $434 million in exports. As costs, the projects required $279 million for importing production inputs and $270 million for profit repatriation and other payments to the parent company. This study assumed that the same business activity would not have occurred without the foreign investment.

The importance of the assumption as to available alternatives is underlined by another study of 159 companies in six developing countries over a five- to seven-year period in the late 1960s.[14] This study concluded that the balance-of-payments impact of the multinational firms was negative for all countries except Kenya. The net negative effect, however, derived mainly from the assumption in this study that someone else would undertake the production in the absence of the foreign investor.

An important and often emotional issue relating to balance-of-payments effects is transfer pricing. The transfer price is the price at which a transfer or sale of goods takes place *within* a firm, regardless of whether the firm spans several countries. Intracompany transfer prices have tax and other implications, as discussed in Chapter 22 on multinational financial management. Insofar as transfer prices operate against the interests of any host country, such as the parent company charging high prices to its foreign subsidiary, the balance-of-payments gains from foreign investment are less, or losses more, than they would otherwise have been.

The role of the multinational enterprise in expanding export earnings may be either positive or negative, depending on the particular case. The multinational enterprise following a global strategy will assign its world markets to the various subsidiaries and attempt to supply its export demand from areas of lowest cost, or where excess capacity exists, or where national pressures or incentives for exporting are most effective. Thus, the subsidiary in any specific country may have a better or a worse chance, but not a free chance, of competing for all export markets. As an independent local company, the same operation would have a free, but

---

[13] See "U.S. and Development Effects Data Output Sheet for Groups of OPIC Assisted Investors," Report no. 18 (Overseas Private Investment Corporation, Washington, D.C., September 8, 1976; processed).

[14] S. Lall and P. Streeten, *Foreign Investment, Transnationals and Developing Countries* (London: Macmillan, 1977); see also Neil Hood and Stephen Young, *The Economics of Multinational Enterprise* (New York: Longman, 1979), pp. 212–15.

probably worse, chance of expanding exports. With its ties to other affiliates in the multinational enterprise system, a local subsidiary may bring to a country special export advantages because the system provides an easy conduit to sales in other countries. But many different possibilities exist and the conclusion will depend upon the specific case being considered. On the whole, the various studies available suggest that the multinational enterprise has been a means of expanding, rather than constraining, exports.[15]

Most certainly, foreign investments in raw materials industries are a major source of increased exports. But, here again, the evaluation of net foreign exchange benefits depends on whether these products would be produced and exported in the absence of foreign investment and at what price. Until recent years, it was realistic to assume that no local alternative to foreign enterprise was available in many developing countries. But as a result of technology transfers and the opportunity to accumulate capital that followed from multinational business operations, a more reasonable assumption for many of these countries is that local production and export can take place without foreign investment. Some countries have hired foreign technology and management on service contracts that limit the foreign exchange costs in amount and over time. Direct investment requires a continuing outflow of repatriated profits.

How about the home countries of the multinationals and the impact of outbound foreign direct investment on their balance of payments? The controversy over this issue has stimulated a plethora of sophisticated studies.[16] As in the case of the host-country studies, the conclusions of the investor-country studies depend on the assumptions as to the alternatives available to the multinational enterprises.

If an enterprise can be competitive in foreign markets through exports from the home country, the establishment of a foreign production facility will result in a net foreign exchange loss to the home country. The home country will earn some foreign exchange through the repatriation of profits and the export of components and services to the foreign subsidiary. But the size of these foreign exchange earnings will be much less than what could have been earned through the export of the final products. If, however, the foreign market is likely to be lost to local producers or other foreign competitors, the net balance-of-payments effect will be positive because there will be no loss from export substitution. Foreign

---

[15] *Foreign Ownership and the Structure of Canadian Industry,* Report of the Task Force on the Structure of Canadian Industry (Ottawa: Queen's Printer, 1968), pp. 203–7.

[16] See W. B. Reddaway et al., *Effects of U.K. Direct Investment Overseas: Final Report* (London: Cambridge University Press, 1968); G. C. Hufbauer and F. M. Adler, *Overseas Manufacturing and the Balance of Payments* (Washington, D.C.: U.S. Treasury Department, 1968); *Implications of Multinational Firms for World Trade and Investment and for U.S. Trade and Labor,* Report to the Committee on Finance of the United States Senate, 93d Congress, 1st sess. (Washington, D.C.: U.S. Government Printing Office, 1973); M. D. Steuer et al., *The Impact of Foreign Direct Investment on the United Kingdom.* (London: HMSO, 1973).

production may also be the only feasible alternative where a country has established formidable quota or tariff barriers to force the establishment of local import-substituting industries.

If foreign production is for export back to the home country and substitutes for goods previously manufactured in the home country, there is a foreign exchange cost. If domestic producers have been losing the local market to foreign producers anyway, foreign production by a home-country enterprise may result in a net benefit because there is no loss on the trade account, and the repatriated profits are likely to more than compensate for the initial investment outflow on the capital account. Furthermore, in many cases the multinational enterprise raises some or all of its capital for foreign investment outside of the home country.

In the case of balance-of-payments effects and the employment issue to be discussed below, the interests of the multinational firm and its home country may be in conflict. In some situations, the multinational company may be able to compete profitably in both home and foreign markets through home-country production. But the firm can make even greater profits through foreign production. In such cases, it is logical for the firm to maximize its profits. But the additional private gains to the enterprise mean a loss in national benefits to the home country.

EMPLOYMENT EFFECTS

The employment effects of multinational business expansion are a major social cost-benefit issue in both home and host countries. In the home countries, labor unions are concerned about the export of jobs when firms expand overseas (see Box 11–2). In the host countries, the principal concern is that foreign firms do not create enough jobs because the technology being transferred is not "appropriate" to the factor endowments of the host countries.

In the United States, labor unions did not become sensitive to the employment implications of multinational business expansion by U.S. firms until the late 1960s. But in 1971, during a year of economic stagnation and increasing unemployment in the United States, the U.S. labor movement launched an attack on multinational enterprises for harming the national interest through exporting jobs.[17] In response to labor union pressures, the U.S. government commissioned several studies to determine whether the spread of multinational business had reduced U.S. employment.

The studies did not resolve the controversy. A broad study by the U.S. Tariff Commission concluded that the question could not be answered

---

[17] Industrial Union Department, AFL–CIO, "New Breed of International Cat," *Viewpoint*, Summer 1971, pp. 10–15.

Box 11–2

GM union leaders in Europe demand data on firm's plans

New jobs in some countries could lead to cutbacks in others, workers assert

GENEVA—Union leaders for General Motors Corp. workers in Europe demanded that the company provide details of how GM's European expansion plans will affect employment.

New workers in some countries could mean "disemployment" for workers elsewhere, the union leaders contended.

The union representatives, at a conference organized by the International Metalworkers Federation, discussed company plans for five new European plants and the expansion of existing facilities involving an investment of $2.4 billion.

"While the company press relations department proudly produces a few figures promising new jobs in a few countries, it is as silent as a tomb on its present and projected disemployment plans," the federation's general secretary, Herman Rebhan, told the meeting.

The company will hire substantial numbers of workers in Portugal, Spain, Austria, Northern Ireland, and France, said Mr. Rebhan, a former official of the United Auto Workers in the United States. "But what are its intents regarding employment in the Federal Republic of Germany, in the Netherlands, Luxembourg, and in the United Kingdom?"

He also asked: "How will the import of more than 600,000 engines from Australia, Brazil, and perhaps Japan affect our members? What are the consequences of the U.S.-European integrated product lines, involving increasing numbers of robots, on terms of employment on both sides of the Atlantic?"

Mr. Rebhan said "all the important decisions are made in Detroit, in the office of the president." Workers can't "accept this Kafkaesque situation" in which a distant person "pulls the strings."

In Detroit, a GM spokesman declined comment.

The European meeting is to be followed up late this year or early next year with a "General Motors world council" at which unions representing all the company's 839,000 workers will participate. GM employs 130,000 workers in Europe.

Source: *The Wall Street Journal*, May 21, 1980.

---

definitively.[18] Not surprisingly, the reason given was that "both the analysis and the answer must depend on crucial assumptions" about the extent to which foreign markets would have been lost if foreign production facilities had not been established. Another study commissioned by the U.S. Department of Commerce concluded that foreign investments did not result in an export of jobs from the United States.[19] This study examined in depth nine selected cases of foreign investment. The con-

---

[18] *Implications of Multinational Firms for World Trade*, pp. 6–7.

[19] Robert B. Stobaugh et al., *U.S. Multinational Enterprises and the U.S. Economy* (Boston: Harvard Business School, January 1972).

clusion necessarily followed from the fact that in each case, according to the researchers, the companies were forced to invest overseas to preserve their markets. The Commerce study, however, was challenged on the grounds that the nine cases were not a "representative sample" from which a general conclusion could be drawn.

A number of business organizations have also sponsored studies that purport to show that foreign investment does not export jobs. As an example, a Business International study concludes that "the job-export theory is totally unfounded" by showing that a sample of 104 highly foreign-investment-oriented U.S. companies increased U.S. employment faster than other U.S. manufacturing firms over the 1970–79 period. "If foreign corporate investment does export jobs," the study argues, "then the highly foreign-investment-oriented set of companies in the BI sample should have ever-falling numbers of employees in the U.S."[20]

The validity of this analysis, however, can be seriously questioned. The international companies are generally in high-technology and rapid-growth industries. Consequently, even though a multinational computer or telecommunications firm is expanding abroad, the same company should also be expected to be expanding at home more rapidly than traditional industries.

The limitations of the "job export" studies seem to suggest that the issue is best examined on a case-by-case basis. Also, because the crucial element is whether home-country production is a feasible alternative to foreign production for the firm, the same issue as that mentioned in the balance-of-payments discussion must be critically examined. If the foreign investment is *desirable* to increase profits, rather than *necessary* for avoiding losses, the national interest of the home country might be better served by a trade-off of more local employment as against greater business profits.

In host countries, and particularly in the less developed nations, unemployment and underemployment is likely to be a major economic problem. As a result, host countries are anxious to secure as many new jobs as possible from every foreign investment project. If capital-intensive technology is imported into these countries by multinational firms, severe limits may be placed on the degree of labor absorption possible.

This problem raises the "appropriate technology" issue. The technology of the multinationals, in most cases, has been developed in the industrialized countries where labor has been relatively scarce and expensive and capital relatively abundant and cheap. Against this environment, new technology is normally capital intensive and labor saving. In contrast, labor is usually abundant and relatively cheap and capital is scarce and relatively expensive in the developing countries. Conse-

---

[20] Business International, *The Effects of U.S. Corporate Foreign Investment: 1970–79* (New York, June 1981), p. 21.

quently, many host countries would like to have the foreign firms use a technology more appropriate to the factor endowments of their country—namely, more labor-intensive technology.

The appropriate technology question, also called the "factor-proportions" problem, is enormously important to the less developed countries. But the issue of choice of technologies is not easy to resolve.[21] Labor-intensive technologies appropriate for the developing countries may not be available. Host countries may be offering incentives such as low interest rates on capital that bias expansion decisions toward capital-intensive technology. Nevertheless, the multinational firm must be aware of the appropriate technology concern. To the extent that a more labor-intensive technology can be used, without endangering the profitability of a project, the national benefits to the host country can be enlarged.[22]

SOCIAL COST-BENEFIT CALCULATIONS

The measurement of national social value is not a standardized procedure. In fact, it would be risky to use the same evaluation procedure for all assessments. Important effects could be left out or effects could be evaluated in a way inappropriate to the particular use for which the assessment is required. Each case in practice shapes its own format.

Common to all cases will be four stages in the evaluation procedure. The first stage is the identification by the country of the individual effects of a foreign investment project that are most crucial for achieving national goals. The second stage is to measure these individual effects after adjusting for distortions in market prices that typically exist because competition is weak or because of government intervention in the marketplace through tariffs, minimum wage laws, and so on. The third stage is to combine the individual effects into an overall quantitative assessment of the social value of the investment. The fourth stage is to supplement the quantitative results with qualitative evaluations of significant effects that do not lend themselves to quantification.

An insight into how such an overall assessment is commonly put together should help the international manager to marshal the data needed for a positive evaluation, or to adjust the proposal to match national goals more closely. As an example, an appraisal of a proposal from a multinational firm requesting permission to construct a new plant in a developing nation is presented in some detail below. The expertise in

---

[21] There is a wide range of literature on appropriate technology. See Richard S. Eckhaus, *Appropriate Technologies for Developing Countries* (Washington, D.C.: National Academy of Sciences, 1977); Thomas N. Gladwin and Ingo Walter, *Multinationals under Fire* (New York: John Wiley & Sons, 1980), pp. 480-84.

[22] For cases where more might rationally have been done, see L. T. Wells, Jr., "Economic Man and Engineering Man: Choice of Technology in a Low Wage Country," *Public Policy*, Summer 1973, pp. 319-42.

placing quantitative assessments on social value and social cost that is illustrated here falls within the field of project analysis. A considerable literature is available in this field.[23]

Nitrogene: A worked example

A European-based multinational firm has requested permission to construct a new plant in Asiatica for the production of Nitrogene, a chemical fertilizer based on a patented process. Although there are other foreign licensors, none shows any interest in submitting competitive proposals. The currency unit in Asiatica is the lira and the proposed investment comprises an equity sum from foreign currency sources of 500,000 lira supported by local long-term financing within Asiatica of a further 500,000 lira at an interest rate of 12 percent per annum.

Annual costs and revenues from operating the proposed plant are estimated as shown in the first column of Table 11–1. The second column records adjustments to the operating estimates to register the social value of the proposal to Asiatica. In this case, there are five major types of adjustment as follows:

1. Gross social benefits. Adjust the value of gross social benefits to eliminate the price distortion due to tariffs. The social value to Asiatica of the project (social opportunity cost) is the cost of securing the same output from the lowest cost alternative source if the project were not undertaken. In this case, the alternative would be imports and the gross social benefit would be the cost of the imports.

To attract the new industry, Asiatica has agreed to establish a tariff on imports to protect the new plant from foreign competition. As a result of the tariff, world market prices are 20 percent *below* the projected price of local production. Because local prices are certain to reflect the cost of imports plus the tariff, *the value of output, therefore, should be reduced by 20 percent* (2,000 × 20% = 400).

As a related point, it should be noted that without the tariff protection the sales revenue of the project would be reduced by 400,000 lira and the project would not be profitable to the enterprise.

2. Social opportunity costs. Two kinds of adjustments are made to show the "real" costs to the country. First, where market prices are

[23] See Louis T. Wells, Jr., "Social Cost-Benefit Analysis for MNCs," *Harvard Business Review*, March–April 1975, p. 40ff.; Ian M. D. Little and James A. Mirrlees, *Guidelines on Project Evaluation* (Vienna: UNIDO, 1970); A. K. Sen, *Methods of Evaluating the Economic Effects of Private Foreign Investment*, Report for 5th session of UNCTAD Committee on Invisibles and Financing Related to Trade, United Nations, publication no. TD.B.C.3. 94.add. 1; Anandarup Ray and Herman G. van der Tak, "A New Approach to the Economic Analysis of Projects," *Finance and Development*, March 1979, pp. 28–32.

Table 11—1

Calculation of national social value for proposed Nitrogene investment in Asiatica (in thousands of lira)

	Annual Operating Estimates	Adjustments (numbers refer to written description)	National Social Value (+ = value, − = cost)
Sales (local)	2,000	−400 (1) +320 (5)	+1,920
Costs:			
Labor (including services)			
Local	500	−250 (2a)	− 250
Foreign	100	+ 20 (5)	− 120
Materials			
Local	200	—	− 200
Imported	700	−140 (2b) +112 (5)	− 672
Taxes			
Local	100	−100 (2c)	—
Capital charges			
Local interest	60	+ 90 (2d)	− 150
Depreciation	100	−100 (2e)	—
Total costs	1,760		
Net profit	240		
Taxation on profits	120	−120 (2c)	—
Profit after tax (remitted as dividends)	120	record as cost(3) + 24 (5)	− 144
Social externalities		+ 20 (4)	+ 20
Net social value			404

distorted, "shadow prices" or "social opportunity costs" are substituted. *Shadow prices* are the values that goods and services would yield in an alternative use under free market conditions. Second, costs to the firm that are not costs to the country are eliminated. Such costs might be characterized as transfers from one pocket to another but in the same pair of pants.

a.   *Labor.*   Union and statutory hiring rules require that labor be paid going rates although heavy unemployment among unskilled labor means that there is no social cost to Asiatica in providing unskilled labor input. The shadow price of unskilled labor is zero. For the Nitrogene production, unskilled labor represents 50 percent of labor costs. *Reduce local labor cost by 50 percent.*

b.   *Materials.*   Imported costs include import duties levied at a tariff of 25 percent. Duties collected by the government are not a cost to the country. *Reduce imported material cost by 20 percent.*

c.   *Taxes.*   Local tax payments do not reflect an additional cost to the country. *Eliminate local taxation payments.*

d. Interest. The annual local interest cost of 12 percent to the firm understates the social value of using the local capital for alternative investments. The shadow price for alternative use of capital is calculated at 30 percent. *Increase interest cost to 30 percent.*

e. Depreciation. If remitted outside the country, depreciation would be a social cost. In this case, depreciation is planned to be retained for plant improvements. There is, therefore, no social cost. *Eliminate depreciation charges.*

3. Exported benefits. Adjust the social value to record dividend remittance as a social cost. After-tax profits will be remitted from Asiatica annually as dividends and thus should appear as a social cost to the country. *Include profit after tax as a social cost.*

4. Externalities. Adjust the social value to record the value or cost of "externalities" not recorded in operating figures. The new operation will train managerial and technical labor and generally extend Asiatica's industrial capability in the chemical processing field. The social value of this training and development is assessed at a national figure of alternative cost of 20,000 lira per annum. *Add external social value of 20,000 lira.*

5. Foreign exchange adjustments. Adjust the social value to record the "real" lira value of entries involving foreign currency. For economic and political purposes, the official exchange rate has been maintained at a level that overvalues the Asiatican lira by about 20 percent. On a free market, it is estimated that instead of the official rate of 5 Asiatican lira = U.S. $1, the market would clear at 6 Asiatican lira = U.S. $1. *Increase the lira value of all foreign currency items by 20 percent.*

Social profitability

After the adjustments have been made, the social profitability of the project can be summarized in several ways. For most purposes, the end result is the same no matter which method is used.

1. Net national benefit. The net national benefit is the social benefits *minus* the social costs for all inputs. The Nitrogene project shows a positive annual net benefit or social value of 404,000 lira (1,940,000 − 1,536,000).

2. Benefit–cost ratio. The benefit–cost ratio is the social benefits *divided* by the social costs for all inputs. The Nitrogene project shows a benefit–cost ratio of 1.26 (1,940/1,536). The benefits are positive, of course, as long as the ratio is greater than 1.

3. Social return. This method measures the social profit derived from the local capital utilized. The test is whether the return from this scarce local resource is greater than might be secured through alternative uses. Social return is the social benefits *minus* social costs other than capital, *divided* by the amount of local capital used.

The local capital in this case is 500,000 lira, with an opportunity cost of 30 percent, or 150,000 lira. By omitting this cost, the social benefits from this project become 554,000 lira instead of the 404,000 shown in Table 11–1. The social return from the local capital utilized is then 111 percent (554,000/500,000). By this measure, the project appears attractive to Asiatica because the social return greatly exceeds the opportunity cost of 30 percent for alternative uses of local capital.

4. Return on domestic resources. This method compares the value of *all* domestic resources used in the project with the net foreign value of the production. The net foreign value is the foreign market value of the output less the cost of foreign inputs measured in foreign currency—say, U.S. dollars. The domestic resources used are valued in local currency, or lira. These two figures produce an implicit exchange rate, so many lira per dollar. The more lira of domestic resources it takes to produce what could be purchased abroad for a dollar, the less attractive is the project. If the implicit rate is below the actual exchange rate, presumably the local resources could be used to more account elsewhere.

The return-on-domestic-resources method appears to have growing appeal for host countries. It is useful, therefore, to follow through the calculation for the Nitrogene project. Net foreign value is $164,000 per annum, calculated as follows:

Sales (at world market price—1,600 lira @ 5 lira/U.S. $1)....		$320,000
Less foreign costs translated at offical rate		
Labor..	$ 20,000	
Materials, before import duties	112,000	
Dividends	24,000	156,000
Net foreign value...................................		$164,000

Domestic resource costs at their social cost levels are 580,000 lira:

Labor......................	250,000 lira
Materials....................	200,000
Capital charge..............	150,000
Externalities.................	−20,000
Total	580,000 lira

The implicit exchange rate that translates the foreign value into domestic resource costs is 3.54 lira = U.S. $1. This compares to the estimated "real" or free market rate of 6 lira = U.S. $1. By this measure, the project also is worthwhile. Through local production, Asiatica secures $1 of foreign value by using only 3.54 lira of local resources, whereas Asiatica would otherwise have to spend 6 lira of local resources to get $1 of foreign value.

Some limitations

Social cost-benefit measures are extremely useful for host countries, but they have their limitations. They are useful because they are quantitative, relatively simple in concept, easy to calculate and to explain. Furthermore, they provide a consistent basis for comparing multiple projects. In such comparisons, the test is not simply whether the social benefits are positive, but which project produces the largest surplus of social benefits.

The limitations are that the analysis is static, important factors that are nonquantifiable may be omitted, and the tests may not be sufficiently related to the country's development strategy. Nevertheless, the measurements may be extended to include a longer time horizon. The flow of costs and benefits may be analyzed for a longer period than one year. The method may also be adapted to take into account the time value of money through estimating the internal rate of return, payoff period, or discounted present value. The time horizon of the country's decision makers is often a crucial element. The political cost of slow achievement can be very high.

SUMMARY

The international business community has long embraced the view that multinational enterprises are engines of development that provided the developing countries with needed capital, technology, and know-how essential for the modernization of their economies. Thus, it came as a violent shock during the late 1960s to discover that many government officials, political leaders, and academic scholars were expressing serious misgivings about the economic, political, and cultural impact of the multinationals on the developing countries. Equally disturbing was the emergence of antagonistic views by groups in the home countries toward outbound foreign direct investment.

These misgivings were reflected in the spread of ideologies that espoused a negative view on the benefits of multinationals. But over time, the ideologies have lost influence as policy makers began to recognize that neither the automatic harmony of interests assumed by the advocates of free enterprise nor the inevitable conflict of interest espoused by the Marxists is an accurate description of the relation of multinational enterprises to the host and home countries. The result has been that the use of social cost-benefit has spread and in many countries has replaced the "Multinational, Go Home" attitude.

The international manager will continue to encounter the various negative ideologies among certain groups in both home and host countries. Some familiarity with the ideologies and their limitations, therefore, is important. Also essential is an understanding of social cost-benefit analysis so as to be aware of how specific multinational operations impact on the national interests of home and host countries.

The matrix of common interests and potential conflicts in goals makes for a love-hate relationship between international corporations and nation-states. The countries love the benefits but hate the costs and the national tensions that accompany the benefits. Furthermore, the benefits may be greatest at the time of the wedding and steadily decline thereafter. On balance, the trade-off to both host and home countries appears to have been generally in favor of the benefits, as evidenced by the continued rapid expansion of international business activities.

The need to identify its common interests and potential areas of conflict with many different nation-states is a continuing and never-ending operating requirement for international enterprises. The diversity and dynamic nature of these relations do not permit easy generalizations; nor is a general understanding adequate background for the international manager. He must deal with specific business situations in relation to specific national environments. A specific type of business activity may face one kind of response in country A and a completely different type of response in country B and country C. The only certainties are that the situation will constantly be changing and that, in order to maintain its tenure, the international enterprise must be ever ready to justify to a nation-state not only its entry but its continued presence.

EXERCISES AND DISCUSSION QUESTIONS

1. "It is characteristic of direct-investment projects that their first-order benefits are greatest, certainly most spectacular, in the initial stages of the undertaking. On the other hand, the explicit costs of the foreign investment to the host economy generally behave in an opposite fashion." Explain what the writer meant by this statement and evaluate its validity.

2. Under what circumstances can an acquisition of an existing domestic business operation by a foreign multinational enterprise be justified as contributing national benefits to a country? Under what circumstances would it be difficult to justify an acquisition?

3. As a government official evaluating a proposal for investment by a foreign corporation that could have a 20-year life span, suggest how the streams of national benefits and national costs should be treated in reaching a decision.

4. "To control the export of American technology, much of which was financed by public funds and the export of American jobs, the government should regulate, supervise, and curb the export of technology and the substantial outflows of American capital for the investments of U.S. companies in foreign operations." Would you agree or disagree with this statement?

Chapter 12

The countervailing power of international business

International business is not without its own power for countering the impact of national controls. There is a landmark English legal case in which Lord Justice Tomlin ruled that every man is entitled to order his affairs so as to minimize the tax for which he would be liable (*Inland Revenue Commissioners* v. *Duke of Westminster*—1936). A similar concept applies to the international enterprise. It is entitled to use legal means to avoid controls that may hinder attainment of its legitimate global business objectives.

The experienced international enterprise goes even further. It will plan to avoid *future* controls. It will examine the existing strategies of relevant countries toward multinational business and international transfers, project the likely pattern of change, and adapt its own strategy

253

accordingly. The firm is not an unprotected, misused pawn of omnipotent nations; it is a powerful player in the international business game.

This chapter introduces some of the means at the command of international firms for adjusting to controls and for exerting countervailing power. The focus is on the ways in which the business enterprise can act to mitigate the effects of national controls. The decision-making procedures by which businessmen choose an appropriate mix of these adjustments are the subject of Parts IV and V of the book.

REFUSAL TO PARTICIPATE

The simplest and most direct form of countervailing power available to the international enterprise is refusal to participate. Where national controls make the business environment unattractive, the international firm can refuse to make new investments. And it can even divest and discontinue existing operations, as occurred in the cases of IBM and Coca-Cola in India noted in Chapter 10.

A nation's optimum strategy is to set its controls at a level that maximizes net national benefits. Above this control optimum, the nation will lose benefits from investments not made and business activities discontinued. With nationalistic enthusiasm, nations have frequently exceeded the control optimum and been forced to relax or abandon controls when they became aware of what they were losing in potential new investments and expansions, or in terminated operations.

In both developed and less developed countries, the loss of future foreign investments has operated as a constraint on national control policies. In the case of France, for example, during the period between 1963 and 1968 when strong de Gaullist policies restricted foreign investment inflows, U.S. investment increased much more rapidly in Holland, West Germany, and Belgium, than in France. The trend did not coincide with Present Pompidou's view of France's national interests. Shortly after he was elected in mid-1969, national control policies were sharply altered. In contrast to France's previous refusal to allow General Motors to build a major plant in the Strasbourg area, French officials in 1970 began aggressively to solicit another major American automobile manufacturer, the Ford Motor Company, to invest in France.[1]

Argentina offers a similar example. In 1973 the Peronist-controlled congress approved a highly restrictive foreign investment law and foreign investment came to a virtual halt. Within three years, the regime that overthrew President Isabel Peron drafted a new law, eliminating among other restrictions a 12.5 percent limit on profit remittances and reducing from five to three years the period before capital repatriation may begin.[2]

---

[1] *The Economist*, February 28, 1970.

[2] *The Wall Street Journal*, February 8, 1977.

A change in national controls may alter the optimum locational pattern for the operations of an international firm and the ranking of its alternatives on its investment schedule, as will be discussed in Chapter 15. In some cases, the firm will choose an alternative country in which to expand. In other situations, a prospective expansion may be deferred or abandoned because expected profits no longer fall within the investment limits of the firm.

HOME-COUNTRY SUPPORT

Investor countries vary in their willingness to lend official support to their international enterprises. But where support for private companies can be wrapped in the mantle of national interests, investor countries may be enticed to support the private interests of its citizens in foreign situations.

In 1971, for example, the United States used economic pressure on Chile after Chile's expropriation of U.S. copper companies. The U.S. Export-Import Bank announced that credit guarantees for purchase of American jet aircraft by the Chilean airline were being "postponed" pending resolution of the copper compensation question.[3] The U.S. government has also used its influence with the World Bank and the Inter-American Bank to deny financing to countries that had taken undesirable action against U.S. companies.

But the United States is not alone in lending its official support to counter host-country measures against multinational enterprises. In a countermove following Algeria's seizure in 1971 of 51 percent of French oil interests, the French government officially requested the U.S. Export-Import Bank to deny a $150 million loan that Algeria was seeking for a natural gas plant. France also threatened to discontinue the sizable financial and technical assistance it was giving to Algeria in order to negotiate a better settlement on the oil expropriations. When Libya expropriated the oil assets of British Petroleum in 1971, the British foreign office is reported to have approached other oil-importing nations, "expressing concern for BP's rights."[4]

In some situations, home-country support can be more direct. The United States and other countries have pressured the Japanese to reduce their restrictions on the entry of foreign investment. The United States in particular has mentioned the possibility of retaliation through increased restrictions on Japanese business access to the U.S. market.

Still another way in which the home country can give support to its multinational enterprises is through legal actions in the World Court, as

---

[3] Paul E. Sigmund, *Multinationals in Latin America* (Madison: University of Wisconsin Press, 1980), p. 153.

[4] *The Wall Street Journal*, December 31, 1971.

discussed in Chapter 8. But such support through World Court litigation has not been an effective source of countervailing power.

When foreign projects are covered by home-country investment-guarantee schemes, the international enterprise may secure home-country support as well as risk insurance. Such programs, however, do not explicitly guarantee that the home country will intervene on behalf of the international enterprise.

MEASURES TO DETER HOST-COUNTRY CONTROLS OVER FOREIGN INVESTMENT

Stimulating local enterprise

If the international firm accepts the hypothesis that a host country's receptivity varies inversely with the share of the total economy or of key sectors controlled by foreign interests, it can take steps to increase receptivity and deter controls by stimulating the growth of indigenous enterprise. It can, for example, plan and implement aggressive programs for encouraging independent local firms to become suppliers, processors, further manufacturers, and sellers of the product of the foreign-financed venture. The linkage benefits are much heralded by proponents of foreign investment but, too frequently, the linkage opportunities are left to slow natural forces or are realized not by domestic business but by other foreign investors.

More by necessity than by design, Sears Roebuck de Mexico demonstrated three decades ago the effectiveness of policies to stimulate local enterprise in increasing host-country receptivity without prohibitive costs. In establishing its first large, modern department store in Mexico, Sears had assumed that it would import about 70 percent of its merchandise from the United States. But in late 1947, less than a year after opening its first store, the company had to face a drastic change in the Mexican economic situation. Due to foreign exchange difficulties, Mexico placed an embargo on a wide range of consumer imports. To meet this unexpected challenge, Sears responded by a mammoth program of encouraging new local enterprises as sources of supply. Within six years, and through cooperation with 1,300 local firms, Sears was able to buy in Mexico 80 percent of the merchandise it sold there.[5]

Developing local allies

Another interesting example of measures to deter national controls is the case of Firestone's rubber-growing operations in Liberia. As a

---

[5] Richardson Wood and Virginia Keyser, *Sears Roebuck de Mexico, S.A.* (Washington, D.C.: National Planning Association, 1953).

planned strategy, Firestone initiated a rubber-growers assistance program designed to help Liberians grow rubber on their own farms. As
reported in another NPA study,

> Firestone provides not only free trees but also free technical services. It will
> survey the planter's farm and draw up a planting program for him. When
> the trees reach tapping age, the Company will prepare a complete manage-
> ment plan, which includes a detailed map of the tree stands, their division
> into tasks and the marking of each tree with its task designation, and a
> tapping schedule best suited to the needs and capabilities of the farm. At
> the farmer's request, the Company will periodically inspect his rubber
> trees and advise him on improved care, cultivation, and tapping. It will set
> up his bookkeeping and records systems and teach him how to keep them
> current. It will provide free biological services in the event of tree disease,
> storm damage, or other difficulties. Firestone will sell him at cost and on
> interest-free credit terms all of the plantation equipment and supplies he
> needs both initially and subsequently.
>
> Finally, the Company will market his production and will transport it to
> the Harbel and Cavalla plantations if the farmer has no suitable vehicle of
> his own.[6]

Through assisting local enterprises, a number of which happen to be
owned by political leaders and government officials, Firestone increased
its supply of rubber while reducing its relative share of the local rubber-
growing industry. It was also protecting itself against adverse governmental controls by helping many nationals secure a vested interest in favorable governmental actions toward rubber growing.

Sharing ownership through joint ventures

Probably the best-known deterrent to host-country controls is the
sharing of ownership in local subsidiaries with nationals. Although the
decision to engage in joint ventures involves many considerations other
than a defensive move against national controls, this strategy can have
the multiple effect of reducing the apparent threat of foreign domination,
securing local allies, and enlarging the role of indigenous enterprise in
the local economy.[7] Complete ownership of local subsidiaries gives the
multinational enterprise greatest flexibility in such areas as organization,
intercompany pricing, and dividend policy. Yet, many firms find that
divestment of some equity can provide more than offsetting benefits
through protection against controls. The greater the proportion of own-

---

[6] Wayne Chatfield Taylor, *The Firestone Operations in Liberia* (Washington, D.C.: National Planning Association, 1956), p. 94.

[7] For example, see Lawrence G. Franko, "Joint Venture Divorce in the Multinational
Company," *Columbia Journal of World Business*, May–June 1971, pp. 13–22; Richard W.
Wright, "Joint Venture Problems in Japan," *Columbia Journal of World Business*, Spring
1979, pp. 25–31.

ership that is divested, the greater the gain in protection and the greater the loss of parent-company control.

The distribution as well as the share of the local ownership can be important. The advantage of having local ownership in the hands of a small number of local partners is that such partners are likely to take an active interest in protecting the profitability of their investment from erosion by government controls. The advantage of a wide dispersion of local ownership is that the international firm may be able to retain a degree of control greatly in excess of its ownership share.

Under the pressure of necessity, the negative attitudes of multinational enterprises toward local sharing of ownership have been changing. A common objection by many companies has been that host-country security markets are not sufficiently developed to absorb any significant amounts of stocks. This argument has limited validity. In 1968, for example, when General Electric made a public offering of 10 percent of the total stock in its Mexican subsidiary, the issue was quickly oversubscribed.[8] In the mid-1960s a joint venture of the Cummins Engine Company in India offered 24½ percent of its shares to the public through the Bombay stock exchange and the purchase orders received totaled more than 50 times the number of shares being offered.[9]

At one time partnership with national governments was almost completely avoided by international corporations. It was regarded by many American executives as next door to communism. Realization of some of the advantages, however, has made this sort of arrangement more common. With the local government as a partner, there is a negative incentive for controls or harassment—and in some cases an incentive for positive advantages. Moreover, a government usually has ample funds for desirable expansion, is less interested in profit distribution than in growth, and is generally uninterested in taking over the business itself or undertaking day-to-day management. Private partners frequently produce problems on each of these counts.

Selective ownership divestment

Another ownership strategy is selective divestment. The various parts of the business operation can be separated. The commercial or technical side can remain in the hands of the international enterprise and heavy local ownership may be arranged for the capital-intensive parts requiring physical assets. With a large share of the total investment in local hands, the risk of expropriation is greatly reduced. Also, local investors may prefer to retain the pattern rather than become involved in a wider range of activities with which they are not familiar. United Fruit, a favorite leftist target in Latin America for many years, finally divested itself of its land-

---

[8] *The Wall Street Journal,* July 5, 1968.

[9] Personal interview with Cummins' officials, 1965.

holdings and banana growing. It then continued its activities in the banana business by concentrating on its marketing and transportation operations.[10]

Conversely, some international firms may find that retention of marketing activity by local entrepreneurs is advantageous. In many countries, the importer-distributor is a powerful political force. Working through such an outlet may ensure continued access to the market, even though the international company would be able to carry out much more effective distribution on its own account.

Multiple nationality for international business projects

The domination of the foreign business sector by firms of a single nationality may be an important stimulus for stronger national controls. One response to the fear of economic domination is for multinational enterprises to acquire multiple nationality. Both Royal Dutch Shell and Unilever have carefully nurtured the dual Dutch-British nationality of the parents because they have found the ambiguity to be useful. When Indonesia's Sukarno was unfriendly to the Dutch, these enterprises emphasized their British identity. Where antagonism emerges against the British, it is the Dutch identity that comes to the fore.

Another response is for firms from several nations to join in undertaking a project. Consortia of international firms of different nationalities have been common in the field of mining. Some examples are the Fria bauxite project in Guinea, the Freeport nickel project in Indonesia, and iron ore mining projects in Australia.

Some have argued that ownership should be spread to include multinational institutions like the World Bank and sale of securities in international financial centers such as Zurich or London, as well as business partners from many nations. The theory is that the host country would act more circumspectly if tempted to repudiate the terms of an agreement when faced with the multinational "establishment."[11] A somewhat similar strategy practiced by firms in natural resource fields is to sell output forward to buyers in a number of countries in order to increase the problems that the host country would face if it attempted to expropriate.[12] Kennecott Copper worked out such a defense prior to Chilean nationalization in order to protect its compensation position.[13]

---

[10] *Business Week,* November 22, 1969.

[11] Joseph S. Nye, Jr., "Multinational Corporations in World Politics," *Foreign Affairs,* October 1974, p. 157.

[12] Theodore H. Moran, "Transnational Strategies of Protection and Defense by Multinational Corporations: Spreading the Risk and Raising the Cost for Nationalization in Natural Resources," *International Organization* 27, no. 2 (Spring 1973).

[13] Charles T. Goodsell, *American Corporations and Peruvian Politics* (Cambridge, Mass.: Harvard University Press, 1974).

Changing nationality

A multinational enterprise may find that its greatest countervailing power lies in its ability to change its nationality, either to avoid home-country controls or to be better received by host countries. A number of firms have switched domicile in recent years from the United Kingdom to Australia, Canada, and elsewhere. Several have left Canada. Even Massey-Ferguson, one of Canada's largest, threatened to leave Canada following a change in the law that would have led to taxation of nonremitted foreign profits not earned from its primary business.[14] With the threat of the Burke-Hartke legislation in the early 1970s, many U.S. firms had laid plans to establish binational structures in order to place their foreign activities with a non-U.S. corporate entity. Corporate emigration is not, however, a procedure that receives automatic blessing from the home country.

ENTRY AND OPERATING STRATEGIES

A wide range of defensive measures for avoiding national controls can be grouped under the rubric of entry and operating strategies. These defenses make use of the inherent flexibility and total enterprise capability of the multinational firm. They permit a company to adjust or rearrange its patterns of location, its logistics, and its operating policies to have activities take place where the costly effects of national controls are minimized.[15] Some of the options, as discussed below, are the choice of business activity, selection of products, location of production sites, location of intangible assets, sourcing and movement of funds and profits, ownership divestment of certain assets, and control of distribution and markets.

The choice of business activity

One of the most obvious ways for a firm to avoid controls is to change its type of activity. Gone are the days when a maker of buggy whips limited his activity to making and trading in nothing but buggy whips. Confronted with restrictions concerning one area of business, the firm can quickly move to others. For many international corporations this is particularly easy. Most have many facets to their business and can develop those in which controls do not hamper achievement of the firm's objectives. When ITT's telephone company was bought out by the government of Peru in the late 1960s, the company shifted its Peruvian activities into more acceptable company lines, such as the construction of a Sheraton hotel (ITT subsidiary) and the manufacturing of electrical

---

[14] "Canada: A Tax Law May Go Too Far," *Business Week*, March 17, 1973.

[15] See Yves L. Doz, *Government Control and Multinational Strategic Management* (New York: Praeger Publishers, 1979).

equipment. Where the compensation terms for the sale or expropriation of a company's assets require reinvestment for a period of time in the same country, such as in the case of ITT, the choice of new business activity will be influenced by the locational restriction. In other situations, the company can scan the global environment for opportunities, thus placing all interested nations that might receive the investment in competition with each other.

The prime criteria in the selection of expansion opportunities will almost certainly be growth, risk, and return on capital. These criteria will favor expansion where capital and profits look least vulnerable to erosion by government controls or by political risk. Variations in the vulnerability of different types of business activities will be discussed in Chapter 15 on political risk. A few decades ago, foreign investments in public utilities were politically and economically popular with both host countries and investors. But styles have changed and public utilities presently have the highest degree of vulnerability to expropriation and national controls and are generally avoided for new investments. The extractive industries, particularly petroleum and mining, also have a high degree of risk. By using a high-risk factor in evaluating such investments, international firms weigh them less favorably as attractive choices for business activity.

Lower vulnerability is likely to occur in intermediate production that buys from and sells to local entrepreneurs. Both supplier and customer can act as buffers against imposition of controls. In many cases the intermediate type of production is likely to be essential to the customer's output, and to require technological expertise that neither supplier nor customer could or would want to provide for itself.

Location of operations

Some national controls attempt to increase the production level of local subsidiaries by requiring the subsidiaries to export and make greater use of higher cost local raw materials or components. Such external pressure to maximize production at any one location may cause the firm to become less competitive in export markets, and may vitiate the firm's potential to minimize production costs through a systemwide locational strategy that seeks economies of scale, reduced transportation costs, and minimum tariff burdens.

To the extent that the firm has flexibility in the location of its facilities, such flexibility can be a countervailing power to restrain countries in imposing such controls. As soon as a nation's controls are raised above those of alternative locations, the country becomes a less likely location for new investments or expansions of existing facilities by international firms. Conversely, when it reduces its control level, as in the case of Jamaica as shown in Box 12–1, a country is more likely to be a recipient of future investment.

Box 12–1

Jamaica: Exceeding the control optimum

The government of Jamaica, abandoning its policy of seeking ever higher prices for its bauxite, signed an agreement in October 1979 with North American aluminum producers that reduces the levy on the basic ore from which aluminum is made. In return for the lowered levy, the producers will begin restarting the bauxite mining and refining operations they had halted on the island following Jamaica's previous bauxite-pricing policies.

In 1974, Jamaica led six other bauxite-producing countries in boosting the levy on bauxite 600 percent. The new levy increased total government revenues by over 60 percent in that year. The trouble was that it also made Jamaica unattractive. Three other Caribbean bauxite producers followed Jamaica's lead, but the two biggest producers (Australia and Guinea) did not. The five multinationals in Jamaica predictably scaled down their operations, and the cutbacks cost Jamaica, the world's largest bauxite exporter, substantial income in recent years.

Jamaica's bargaining position was weakened by the moves taken by aluminum companies to expand their bauxite mining and refining operations in Surinam, Brazil, and Australia to make up for reduced Jamaican output. As of July 1979, Jamaican exports of alumina, an intermediate product in the aluminum-making process that is refined from bauxite, were valued at $170 a ton compared with $137 a ton for alumina from Australia, which doesn't charge a levy.

Since Jamaica reduced its levy, the industry has perked up considerably. Two bauxite refineries are being expanded and a new one built. The existing plants are now operating much nearer to full capacity than they have been for five years. Although bauxite exports are expected to fall by about 5 percent in 1980, alumina exports should increase by about 18 percent.

Source: Adapted from *The Wall Street Journal*, October 15, 1979, and *The Economist*, June 21, 1980.

An interesting case of using location to avoid what the company considered unacceptable pollution controls was the decision of Hoechst AG to locate a new steel plant in Dortmund, West Germany, when Dutch authorities raised antipollution objections to a planned Hoechst plant near Rotterdam. The Rotterdam plant was to be a joint project with the Hoogovens of Holland.[16]

In some industries, firms have been known to maintain reserve production potential in several countries as a deterrent to individual nations imposing added controls. In the 1950s, for example, United Fruit kept large amounts of improved land prepared for banana planting but unplanted. The stated company objective was to have land reserves in case

---

[16] *The Wall Street Journal*, July 6, 1971.

its plantations were exposed to diseases or other natural hazards. Another obvious advantage was the possibility of shifting the location of production as a defense against national controls.

Strength can be built against both home and host countries by setting up directly competing units within the same organization but located in different countries. Such an arrangement can be particularly effective in limiting national controls if the subsidiaries directly compete with each other for the same export markets. Any restraining controls applied locally might give the competing subsidiary an export advantage.

Yet another defense available to the multinational enterprise lies in adoption of a truly international production network in which each plant specializes in some part of the total process. This means that most subsidiaries will contribute export income to the country of residence. Any insistence by the local government on further local production could be demonstrated by the international corporation as likely to jeopardize exports to units elsewhere in the network.

The location of management can be changed as well as the location of production. The U.S. business community in Britain made strong representations to the British government in 1974 that the proposed imposition of high U.K. taxes on the unremitted foreign income of U.S. nationals in Britain would force them to leave. Some relaxation of the proposals was gained, but there was subsequently a significant transfer of multinationals' offices to Paris and other locations.[17]

Location of intangible assets

A powerful source of strength for international firms in combating national controls is their ability to control the location of intangible business assets. These include research and development ability, technical, marketing, and management know-how. When the firm controls essential technical know-how, the extent to which any host country can move against it is severely circumscribed. If the activity requires continual injections of updated research output, expropriation of purely production facilities could be self-defeating. More gradual attempts at creeping controls, such as limitation of profit remittances or permission to expand, could be offset by the firm through withholding new developments as a bargaining gambit. The same situation prevails when the international firm retains the production, marketing, and management expertise through the use of expatriate personnel rather than training nationals. This suggests, unfortunately, that countries perceived to be high-risk control areas are less likely to maximize the technology-transfer benefits from multinational enterprises.

---

[17] *Business Week,* March 10, 1975.

Control of distribution and markets

When production or extraction is located in one country and the consumer in another, the international firm can build a strong position through control of access to the market. If the firm owns the channels of distribution or has built an unassailable market position, controls imposed over production must not take the costs beyond those the marketing organization could obtain elsewhere. So long as no supplying country is in a monopoly position and supplying countries do not act in unison, any action by one will be checked by the failure of the others to act likewise. In some cases, international corporations have built themselves into virtually single-buyer positions from competing suppliers.

But just as a nation's bargaining position can be undercut by the availability of other sources of supply, so can the bargaining strength of an international enterprise be sapped when other companies are willing to do the marketing. In 1971 Guyana nationalized its bauxite mines owned by Alcan. Given a world oversupply of bauxite, Alcan was unlikely to have trouble finding other sources of supply. In the closely knit world of a small number of aluminum producers, it appeared that Guyana was going to have serious difficulty in selling its bauxite.

To Alcan's dismay, Guyana demonstrated its own marketing capability by securing independent Swiss and British marketing agents and by actively searching out new markets in the USSR, China, and Yugoslavia.[18] With its market control eroded, Alcan agreed to a settlement that it considered much below the true value of its assets.

Even within one country, an international business firm likely to be hampered by creeping controls may build a stronger position by retaining dominance of the market. Some of the U.S. manufacturers of branded consumer goods in Japan, for example, seem to have adopted a policy of purchasing supplies from a range of local suppliers while retaining all the marketing in their own hands. This limits the amount of investment required, and at the same time builds added protection against controls. Small producers without experience in marketing branded consumer products should act as a buffer against Japanese government interference, being in a position to make growing production profits and not at all keen to take over the marketing themselves. There would be no incentive to expropriate foreign owned operations and a great deal of difficulty in expropriating marketing know-how.

Sourcing and movement of funds and profits

When governments restrict remittances and the use of local funds in order to improve their balance of payments, implement domestic eco-

---

[18] J. Frederick Truitt, *Expropriation of Alcan's Bauxite Mining Subsidiary* (Boston: Intercollegiate Case Clearing House, 1974), Part D.

nomic policies, or avoid excessive profit taking, the multinational firm is in a strong position to avoid much of the intent behind these controls. Using a variety of legal forms of incorporation, it can generally arrange to allocate the ownership control of its assets and activities to a preferred pattern of jurisdictions. It can use assets in one nation to support borrowing in another, obtain funds from outside a nation for inward remittances at a time when local firms would find great difficulty obtaining further capital, or adopt a range of other financial management policies discussed in Chapter 22. This strength has been used frequently in both home and host countries in times of inflation and tight monetary controls to build up a larger market share at a lower cost than would be the case were local competitors on the same footing.

The international movement of funds can also be carried out through a range of internal transactions that are difficult to police. Charges for royalties, interest, travel, training, research and development, corporate overheads, machinery, advice, use of overseas facilities, and so on endlessly, can be arranged in such a way that few governments could prevent significant transfers of funds without stopping all business transactions. Then there are the more controllable, but still quite effective, possibilities of altering the transfer prices for components, raw materials, part assemblies, or finished goods.

All these actions affect the location of profit. They may thus equally be used for arranging the place at which profit is taken so that taxation is minimized. In some cases, however, the arrangement that would minimize taxation is not that which would locate the funds in the way the business would find optimal. In such cases, the avoidance of taxation may dominate the other motives.

TRADE-OFF DEALS

The use of trade-offs and bargaining as a countervailing power to national control policies can be illustrated by the case of Merck Sharp & Dohme in India. During the 1950s, Merck had developed a solid market in India for drugs through exporting and some local packaging. In 1955 and 1956, the Indian government made it clear that it was moving in the direction of producing more antibiotics in its fully owned company, Hindustan Antibiotics (Private) Limited. In support of this plan, India received technical assistance from the USSR in developing a master plan for expanding government production in the pharmaceutical field and an offer of a large loan at extremely low rates of interest.

At the time these plans became known, representatives of MSD International were in India negotiating to establish a plant on quite different terms. Because of the preeminence of MSD's technological know-how, the Indian government suggested a partnership with a government corporation. It also suggested as an alternative that MSD provide technical assistance and train personnel to help Hindustan Antibiotics establish a plant for manufacturing streptomycin. After a period of bargaining, agreement was reached on a compromise plan. MSD was permitted to join forces with a privately owned Indian firm to manufacture a wide range of products in return for providing technical assistance to the state-owned company for the production of streptomycin. MSD agreed to prepare the plans for the government plant, train Indian personnel, and make its know-how in this field available for a modest fee.

As a key official of MSD explained, "We ended up not on our initial terms but not on theirs either. it was a period of often tough bargaining, but never chiseling. A basic understanding was reached by the willingness to appreciate each other's philosophy, motivation, objectives, and problems. Should we have adopted the attitude that she would do business with us on our terms or not at all? Should we have surrendered the field to Russia by default? I hardly think anyone would seriously advocate that course."[19]

The key source of MSD's bargaining power was its superior technical know-how. With this as a starting point and a willingness to bargain and consider trade-offs, it was able to bend a government policy that was rapidly moving in the direction of precluding private and foreign enterprise from an important business field.

LEGAL AND OTHER DEFENSES

The local subsidiaries of multinational firms generally have the option of contesting national control actions in the local courts. Two American copper companies, whose properties were nationalized by Chile in 1971, appealed the terms of settlement offered by the government to a special tribunal created by the constitutional reform that permitted the nationalization of these properties. Although such appeals may take a long time to be decided and although the international companies are uncertain about success, in the judgment of the companies such resort to legal defense in local courts appears to warrant the effort.

Another related strategy has been to undertake legal action in the courts of nations other than the host country. One of the American copper companies expropriated in Chile brought suit in a U.S. federal court in New York to block Chile's use of assets in the United States pending resolution of the copper company's claim for compensation. Subsequently, Chile agreed to pay the copper company for a loan it made to its Chilean subsidiary for developing a copper mine in Chile. As reported by an American newspaper, "There was some speculation that

---

[19] Dr. Antonie Knoppers in a speech to the Pharmaceutical Manufacturers Association, New York, December 8, 1958.

President Allende cleared payment to unfreeze the government's assets in the U.S."[20]

Where the output of multinational firms is exported from the host countries, international firms have used boycotts as an effective means of countervailing power. When Libya nationalized the local assets of British Petroleum in 1971, BP advertised in more than 100 newspapers around the world advising potential purchasers that the company reserved its rights with regard to Libyan oil. Although both BP and the British government denied that they had organized a formal boycott of Libyan oil, other petroleum companies and oil-importing nations began to shun the purchase of crude oil from the expropriated properties.

DIRECT INFLUENCE OVER GOVERNMENTS

A review of the countervailing power of international companies must include the possibility of influencing governmental authorities through direct action and lobbying.[21] In a political world it would be unusual if the business firm could not find some basis for exerting influence. For an international enterprise there may always be some local interest that would identify with it and be prepared to lobby accordingly. The larger the involvement, the stronger the incentive for those interests locally identifying with it, and in some countries particular interest groups exercise influence disproportionate to the importance of their claims. In fact, on many occasions international firms have decided, not to use direct influence simply because the arrangement they would be able to make would be so inequitable in their favor that a later backlash would be very likely.

COMPETITION BETWEEN COUNTRIES

The encouragement of competition between different countries is also an option open to the international firm if the nature of its business permits a number of alternative locations. Auction markets for internationally traded commodities ensure this competition, for example. For the international investor, it is just as feasible to move from requesting permission to carry on business in a particular country to a solicitation of what amounts to bids from competing countries. In some cases, the weakest countries will be adding taxation holidays, dividend-remittance guarantees, and many other incentives in order to attract investment away from countries in which location is initially more attractive to the international investor.

---

[20] *The Wall Street Journal*, February 28, 1972.

[21] See Jack N. Behrman, J. J. Boddewyn, and Ashok Kapoor, *International Business-Government Communications* (Lexington, Mass.: D. C. Heath, 1975), chap. 4.

Whenever a business has something of value that can be offered to several nations, the power to control can be eroded by competition between countries. And the limits on the exercise of this power are set by the weakest of the nations concerned. No other nation can impose on a firm a higher cost in terms of controls unless that cost is offset in some other way by higher profitability. In the same way, competition among firms can set limits on the countervailing power of the enterprise.

SUMMARY

This chapter has shown that indeed the international enterprise is not without protection against the nation-state. In fact, its countervailing power is much greater than suggested by the picture of sovereign nations and their control programs. The enterprise has a range of protective measures available that vary in effectiveness with its type of business operations and with the alternatives available to the host countries. Some of the measures, such as sharing ownership with local government or private interests, may imply an opportunity cost and reduced profitability. Yet the cost may be a reasonable price to pay for protection against future controls.

EXERCISES AND DISCUSSION QUESTIONS

1. "The management of a multinational firm should in no way take it upon itself to decide what different contributions the firm will make to the various societies in which it operates. Within the external pressures and constraints surrounding the firm, management's first task is to ensure the firm's survival, and beyond that to pursue the balanced interests of its owners, employees, and customers." If you do not agree with this statement, what guidelines would you give to the management of multinational firms?

2. Discuss the following proposals: The chief executive of a multinational corporation *should not:*
   a. Accept any politically motivated direction from the government of the corporation's home country that would limit the performance of a foreign subsidiary.
   b. Seek partnership with a foreign government in order to gain privilege or protection for its operations.
   c. Use power stemming from its domestic operation to lobby the home government to intercede on the firm's behalf with foreign governments under whose jurisdiction the firm's subsidiaries operate.
   d. Select expatriates for the top management of foreign subsidiaries because they can be trusted to place the firm's interests ahead of the local environment.

3. "In order to protect their traditional international business operations some multinational firms monopolize distribution channels and effectively deny small producers in developing countries reasonable access to international

markets. Such action is against the principles underlying U.S. commercial law and should not be permitted under U.S. law simply because those harmed fall outside its jurisdiction." Comment on this statement. Can you identify any firms to which you think this statement might apply?

4. It has been argued that one way a multinational firm should use its strength is to ensure that countries know they are really in direct competition for its new investment. If you agree, how would you suggest the firm go about ensuring this awareness and what risks do you see?

5. What are the distinguishing characteristics of product areas that will in general have low vulnerability to government controls in less developed countries and what reasons do you have for your expectations?

PART FOUR

Global business strategy

Two prime tasks of top management in a multinational corporation are to determine the firm's overall global strategy and to shape the organization to achieve that strategy. This section of the book is concerned with how such a global strategy is built and how the organization structure of a multinational is likely to affect its success in achieving its strategy.

A global strategy encompasses the planning, timing, and location of a firm's activities and resources as well as its strategies for how it will enter new markets, what it will own, and how it will manage the global operation. The construction of a global strategy on a rational basis requires a careful assessment of the global alternatives and the risks involved for each. A prototype approach for building a strategy in this way is set out in Chapter 13.

Assessments of the economic and demand environments of the different countries in which a multinational may locate its activities are basic inputs into its global strategy. These assessments are examined in Chapter 14. Environments are dynamic and constantly changing and future conditions are far more important to the strategy than the past situation described by historical data. Macroeconomic and market forecasting skills are, therefore, required in projecting the assessments that are needed.

The political environment will also change and increase the risk of national actions that may conflict with any strategy based purely on economic assessments. Chapter 15 examines how the prudent multinational may form a view on the likelihood of political risks and national controls and take these into account in deciding its strategy.

The range of organizational structures that are used in multinationals is very wide. Chapter 16 classifies the structures by their predominant line of responsibility and examines their strengths and weaknesses. No structure is perfect. Each has its blind spots and the performance of each is determined as much by the management processes with which it is supported as by the structure itself. Nevertheless, at different stages of international growth and facing different environmental and competitive stresses, different structures will have a major impact on performance.

Chapter 13

Building a global strategy

Most business firms become international by a process of creeping "incrementalism" rather than by strategy choice. Some firms are first attracted to foreign markets by unsolicited export orders and, after discovering new opportunities, move through a series of stages to the establishment of foreign production facilities. Other firms initiate international activities in response to threats to an oligopoly position. Still others respond to specific opportunities for developing supplies of resources, acquiring foreign technology, or achieving greater production efficiency through foreign operations. And in some stage of becoming a global enterprise, many firms could be best characterized as a portfolio of diverse and separate country companies tied together by a network of ad hoc relationships.

Rarely are these early moves part of a comprehensive global strategy. But as pressures arise from competition on an international scale and from country control programs, and as firms become increasingly aware of synergistic benefits, more and more are building global strategies and adopting global planning procedures. A global strategy is a plan expressing an enterprise's strategy for maximizing its chosen objectives through geographical allocation of its limited resources, taking into account competition from whatever geographical source and the geographical opportunities and constraints. To build a global strategy, the decision maker must be free of any national blinders and consider world markets and world resource locations and not simply the markets or resources of a particular country in isolation. A global strategy aims to maximize results on a multinational basis rather than treat international activities as a portfolio of separate country businesses.

WHY A GLOBAL STRATEGY?

The basic reasons for having a global strategy are that most product and factor markets extend beyond the boundaries of a single country and that the competition that ultimately determines performance is not constrained to individual locations and country markets. To remain competitive, or to become competitive, the strategy horizon for most firms must, therefore, encompass threats and opportunities of both domestic and foreign origin. If its domestic competitors extend their horizons to include a broader sales base, the firm could find itself unable to maintain the same pace of research or product development given its smaller sales base. Even where domestic competition is not moving rapidly to other markets, foreign firms may be developing strategies that pose a threat. European and U.S. firms that disregarded the higher growth rates of Japanese firms in a number of industries were largely unprepared for the competitive challenge when the Japanese firms broke into their traditional markets on a significant scale. Automotive firms that had failed to build global coverage in the price segments the Japanese attacked were at an immediate cost disadvantage. In the motorcycle industry the effects of leaving rapidly growing markets to Japanese competitors were even more dramatic. Many well-known firms disappeared completely.[1]

Many U.S. firms did not need in the past to think globally in the early stages of a product's life because leadership coincided with achievement in the U.S. market. With its large population, high-wage rates, high discretionary spending power, and high propensity to innovate, the U.S. market was for many years the leader in adoption and growth rates for many products. Conversely, firms outside the United States had more need to

---

[1] Boston Consulting Group, *Strategy Alternatives for the British Motorcycle Industry* (London: HMSO, 1975).

plan globally from the beginning of any product development. A U.K. firm introducing a technological advance was likely to find that U.S. demand grew more rapidly than U.K. demand. If U.S. demand was left to U.S. competitors, the sales and experience of U.S. competitors soon outpaced that of the U.K. firm.[2] Now that U.S. wage rates and per capita GNP no longer have such a lead over Europe, perhaps U.S. firms in their turn should be designing products against European markets that might lead the United States in adoption of those products.

Absence of global thinking also shows up where firms have been left behind in the competitive race because they failed to tap the cheapest sources of supply. In still other cases, firms may have achieved global market share and cheapest supplies, but at the expense of their financial strength or flexibility relative to foreign competitors. Assisted by a fluctuation in demand or technological change, smaller competitors have been able to overtake them.

THE MULTINATIONAL'S BUSINESS MISSION

At the core of its corporate strategy, no firm limits its business possibilities to its existing products or services. Instead, it seeks to identify demand areas where its capability for performance against competitors is greatest, even though the specific customer needs that are to be met differ from those the firm has been meeting in the past.[3]

Since there are so many countries in the world, the multinational firm must establish priorities for selecting those markets against which it will make this strategic evaluation and choice of its business mission. It must decide whether strategic evaluation is carried out against one major single market, many single markets, or some segments of many markets. It must also decide how it is going to organize the responsibility for carrying through this strategic assessment. Will it be done by central headquarters, by multinational committees, or by national units?

In the major single market, or central market, approach, the firm selects its mission based on one national market, establishes a marketing mix, and later expands to other national markets. This approach reduces decision problems and can bring high profits because of the low marginal cost of geographic extensions. But which central market should the firm choose? Normally, the firm begins with its home market, but this may not be the best choice. Some Japanese and European firms have selected the high-income, sophisticated U.S. market for selected product lines. The size of the U.S. market has both advantages and disadvantages.

---

[2] For a discussion of European strategic planning, see Renato Mazzolini, "European Corporate Strategies," *Columbia Journal of World Business*, Spring 1975, pp. 98–107.

[3] Kenneth Simmonds, "Removing the Chains from Product Strategy," *Journal of Management Studies*, February 1968.

Many Europeans see the cost of communications and coordination efforts in such a large market as a deterrent to producing products first in the United States as part of their world product strategy.[4]

The multiple market approach implies a high degree of decentralization. It may be the best strategy in situations where special local conditions require particular products, such as fertilizers and pesticides, where economies of large-scale production are not important, and where the firm's competitive advantage depends upon capabilities other than advanced product design. In the case of an industrial product such as aluminum ingots, for example, the market characteristics such as product usage patterns, customer attitudes, and target consumer groups may be quite similar for many countries, and the best strategy may be to focus on developing a more economical production process to bring a competitive cost advantage.

In the market segment approach, the firm identifies segments of national markets that could profitably be given separate treatment across national boundaries. Small market segments in individual countries may be insufficient for any one country unit to justify development of an appropriate product or to make the necessary investment in market development. Worldwide or for a number of countries, however, such a segment may readily justify the expense.

GLOBAL STANDARDIZATION VERSUS DIFFERENTIATION

Having made its choice as to general market focus, the multinational firm must still be concerned with identifying which segments of the global market should be treated differently. The advantages of product differentiation to meet the special needs of smaller segments of the market conflict with the advantages of reducing unit costs through standardization.[5] Standardization can bring great savings from production economies and from spreading such expenditures as research and development, advertising, promotion, and general management over a greatly expanded sales base. Consequently, an international firm's best strategy, if the local environment is not excessively unreceptive, could be to avoid detailed adjustment of its product to local markets and to act as a change agent transplanting its culture around the world.

The pressures toward differentiation, however, are great. The international firm usually considers individual countries as the basic building blocks for its organization and it prefers to identify with each country. One way to achieve this identification is to adjust products to fit country

---

[4] Business International, *European Business Strategies in the United States* (Geneva, Switzerland, 1971), p. 24.

[5] See Robert D. Buzzell. "Can You Standardize Multinational Marketing?", *Harvard Business Review*, November–December 1968, pp. 102–13.

markets. In fact, the orthodox emphasis in marketing is to adjust the marketing mix against an assessment of each market's characteristics. The difficulty confronting the firm is to decide when market differences are sufficient to justify the loss of standardization.

The case for standardization or differentiation of products rests on the impact of the alternatives on revenues and costs. Differentiation is easiest when the adjustments to individual markets are not costly and when the initial design of a product has taken important market differences into account.

The most costly elements to adjust in a product already designed are its physical characteristics. If agricultural equipment, for example, is designed to be marketed in many countries, it must be tested to withstand extremes in temperature and not simply for performance in one particular climate. Also, the design should recognize variations in attitudes regarding repair and maintenance of machinery and variations in the availability of technicians and repair facilities, or else a design for the market of a developed country might produce equipment that is unusable in less developed areas.

Designing products for international performance is not an easy task. A large number of different cultural settings need to be examined for ways in which a product is purchased and used to develop a list of important design criteria. Even better guidance can be obtained if test samples can be made available to those concerned with selling in different countries and shown to outlets and users.

Despite the potential costs of failing to consider the global suitability of different product features at the design stage, the product design strategy of even globally oriented firms has generally been to focus heavily on establishing a product in just one market. This practice may result in major impediments to later expansion in other country markets. A marketing success in the initial market can unwisely reinforce the practice of not considering international performance criteria in the initial design work.

Although expenditures by U.S. firms for research and development carried out abroad reached $1.5 billion by 1977,[6] the vast majority of U.S. firms do not conduct any R&D abroad. Moreover, a recent study of major U.S. multinationals who do have foreign R&D disclosed that under 30 percent of the foreign research laboratories had new product research missions.[7] Only 5 percent had "world" market orientation to develop

[6] Industry Studies Group, Division of Science Studies, U.S. National Science Foundation, "U.S. Industrial R&D Spending Abroad," *Reviews of Data on Science Resources*, NSF no. 33 (April 1979), p. 1.

[7] Jack N. Behrman and William A. Fischer, "Transnational Corporations: Market Orientations and R&D Abroad," *Columbia Journal of World Business* 15, (Fall 1980), pp. 55–60. See also Robert C. Ronstadt, "International R&D: The Establishment and Evolution of Research and Development Abroad by Seven U.S. Multinationals," *Journal of International Business Studies* 10 (Spring–Summer 1978), pp. 7–24.

products for a range of markets and not just the market in which the laboratory was located. Significantly, these few "world" market firms were more attracted to the concentration of knowledge and talent in the foreign country when setting up their R&D, than to the market size of the foreign country. Several of these foreign establishments were characterized as having "achieved a level of competence in a technical area which far surpassed the capabilities of other research groups in the corporation."

As compared with changes in physical attributes, changes in product title are more easily made. But a name change can be costly if the spillover from advertising into other areas is lost and brand loyalty must be established anew. Coca-Cola stands out as an example here. While the flavor can be easily adjusted to local palates, a change of name in any market would mean a great loss in an established market value. It becomes important, therefore, that the product title initially selected does not have any unfortunate meaning in any of the major languages. The Chevrolet Nova, for example, was rather unfortunately named, given that "*no va*" means "does not go" in Spanish.

A PROTOTYPE APPROACH TO GLOBAL STRATEGY

This section presents a prototype approach to building a global strategy. While it is adaptable for use in a wide range of businesses, it is presented here as though developed for an existing product already marketed multinationally and for which the firm carries out its own production and marketing globally. The reader should bear in mind, however, that this prototype is just one possible approach out of many. Furthermore, no single approach will *guarantee* a viable strategy. The very nature of competition within a changing and complex environment demands creativity and thought in arriving at a strategy. No procedure could ever replace the need for these two ingredients. The approach does, however, allow for consideration of the essential elements of a strategy in a step-by-step framework. The reader may feel that any step should be amended or discarded, but at least to start with the approach provides a consistent and rational basis for building a global strategy. The better the underlying structure against which decisions are made, the better the decisions might be.

The prototype approach includes 14 steps. These steps are enumerated in Figure 13–1 and elaborated below.

The horizon for global strategy

How far into the future should the firm plot its strategy? This will depend on the time horizon of the decision maker. Given the inflexibility of investment once it has been committed, an early horizon may produce a supply pattern that is far from optimum for the subsequent market pattern.

Figure 13-1

A prototype approach to global strategy

1. Select a horizon year.
2. Predict country demands for the product or service annually up to the horizon year.
3. Assess the firm's competitive strength overall and in each country.
4. Decide emphasis to be placed on developing competitive market position in each country, and the general approach to be used.
5. Set annual target sales for each country to horizon year.
6. List countries where production or other operations *must* be located to meet sales targets in horizon year.
7. List countries where production in horizon year is not required but probably economic.
8. Estimate costs of investment and operation for the set of alternative production sites, and the transport and tariff costs from these into alternative markets.
9. Calculate an optimum location and logistics pattern for horizon year.
10. Assess country risks.
11. Prepare schedules of annual additions to investment that meet the annual targets and the horizon patterns.
12. Calculate the expected cash flow and net present value.
13. Calculate limits to available investment.
14. Align investment plans and sales targets.

On the other hand, if the horizon is set far in the future, intermediate profits will be more likely to suffer, the market pattern more likely to vary from the prediction, and current management less likely to see the full fruits of its decision. In practice, a four- or five-year horizon is common.[8]

Market assessment

The prototype approach is market based. It starts by formulating targets for individual markets and works backward to decide the location of activity and investment to achieve those targets. Although the prime objective may be to obtain the greatest return on invested capital, it is not reached by taking country after country and calculating the return from expansion in that country.

The selection of market targets in turn requires prediction of demand and competition in the different markets. With different rates and patterns of growth in each market, any simple extrapolation of the current situation would be inappropriate. A more refined prediction of market growth is needed. In making such predictions, a whole range of forecasting methods can be used, as will be discussed in Chapter 14.

Whatever the methodology, the basic data required will involve past measurements of actual demand, indicators or determinants of demand,

---

[8] George A. Steiner and Warren M. Cannon, *Multinational Corporate Planning* (New York: Macmillan, 1966), and James M. Hulbert, William K. Brandt, and Raimar Richers, "Multinational Planning in the Multinational Subsidiary: Practices and Problems," *Journal of Marketing* 44 (Summer 1980), pp. 7–15.

and then estimates of how indicators or determinants will behave in the future. As the firm develops an international planning system, it can begin to rely on its foreign subsidiaries for much of this information. But in the initial stages, decentralized inputs are likely to be extremely slow because of the time required to receive information from around the world. Furthermore, consistent forecasts are probably more important than accurate forecasts when they are to be used for allocating emphasis among markets. To call for estimates from a wide range of sources is to invite major inconsistencies. Different individuals will have different biases in assessing future market growth for their areas. Initially, then, the firm may rely on market data sources centrally available, such as from international agencies.

Competitive assessment

The essence of strategy is that it is competitive. There are opponents. Whatever objectives a firm adopts, their achievement will be relative to the achievement of other firms. In most cases the competition will be direct and immediate. For some lucky firms it may be indirect and with delayed impact, but it is always there. At its best, a global strategy will be devised so as to gain a significant and continued advantage over competitors. The strategist will be looking to identify the performance and strategic emphasis by country of the leading global competitors and to plan accordingly. The plan may give priority to areas where competition is absent, it may directly oppose competition in one place and encourage it in another. Whatever form strategy takes, however, it will certainly not be the straightforward application of a formula, but a creative plan based on competitive assessments.

Assessment of competition has received renewed emphasis in recent years as marketing and strategy literature have developed an industry perspective to explain why profitability differs among firms.[9] The concept of the experience curve lies at the heart of much of the writing.[10] The price experience curve plots the change in real price as industry experience in producing and marketing a product accumulates. Many empirical measurements have shown that, as accumulated experience doubles, the unit price reduces in real terms by between 20 percent and 30 percent.[11] Of course, as experience builds up and demand stabilizes, the period it takes for accumulated experience to double gets longer, hence price reduction in real terms slows down.

---

[9] Charles W. Hofer and Dan Schendel, *Strategy Formulation: Analytical Concepts* (St. Paul, Minn.: West Publishing, 1978); Michael E. Porter, *Competitive Strategy: Techniques for Analyzing Industries and Competitors* (New York: Free Press, Macmillan, 1980).

[10] Winfred B. Hirschmann, "Profit from the Learning Curve," *Harvard Business Review*, January–February 1964, pp. 125–39.

[11] Patrick Conley, "Experience Curves as a Planning Tool," *IEEE Spectrum*, June 1970, pp. 63–68.

Such a downward sloping price experience curve over time does not imply a move from industry profits to industry losses. Real cost reduction by individual firms in the industry underlies the price reduction. This cost reduction can come about in many ways, from productivity in manufacture, through redesign with consequent material savings, to economies of scale and increased efficiency in advertising and marketing. Moreover, a cross-section of an industry's experience on price and cost at a point in time is likely to show individual firms in different competitive positions because of their varying accumulated experience and varying success in cost reduction. It is these varying competitive positions that the firm preparing a global strategy will wish to monitor on an international basis. A competitor of the same nationality may be gaining greater volume and more accumulated experience through international expansion or be reducing costs through relocation of production or supply. Foreign competitors, too, may be building cost advantages outside the geographical limits of the firm's operations. The task may not be easy. The global strategist may have to estimate the costs of a competitor in a foreign location and perhaps attempt to decompose the cost structure of a complex multinational. It may also be necessary to forecast exchange fluctuations in order to predict how competitor costs will differ for delivery into a particular market.

Figure 13–2 shows graphically such a cross-section of industry cost and experience. Firm A has the highest accumulated experience and the

Figure 13–2

Accumulated experience, market share, unit cost, and unit profit for three competitors (log-log scale)

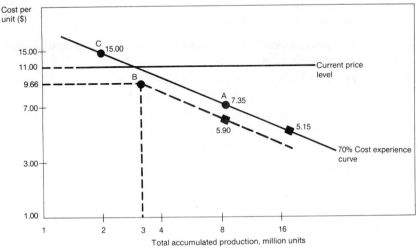

Current market shares:
A = 50 percent
B = 30 percent
C = 20 percent

greatest current market share. At the current price level of $11, A is also making the highest profit per unit of $3.65. Firm C has only 20 percent of the market and is taking a loss. It is likely to go out of business. Firm B, on the other hand, has managed to reduce costs to $9.66 per unit even though, with 30 percent of the market, its accumulated experience amounts to only 3 million units. Perhaps firm B has entered the market recently with a more efficient new plant and an effective promotion scheme to build market share quickly. If both firm A and firm B now maintain their relative market shares and both manage to reduce costs with experience on 70 percent cost experience curves, then B poses a significant threat to A. By the time A's experience doubles to 16 million units, B would have added another 4.8 million units, that is, $^{30}\!/_{50}$ of A's. At this point, A's costs would be $5.15 per unit and B's would be $5.90 per unit. A needs to watch B very closely. At the current time, A has a major cost advantage and can control the market. Later, A's lead will not be so sure. Perhaps now is the time to reduce price in order to gain higher market share and with the increased volume build a more efficient plant.

Market emphasis

Once market demand and competitive assessments have been made, the next and most important step in the prototype approach is to select a set of decision rules against which the firm will allocate its efforts to different markets. These rules reflect the essence of the firm's territorial attack on its competitors.

Such rules are best expressed as criteria for classifying markets according to the emphasis to be placed on sales achievement. Examples of decision rules expressed in this way are as follows:

Enter all markets with demand above $5 million and in which direct competitor retaliation can be avoided.

Enter new markets only if necessary to match competitors X or Y who would otherwise build a strong position unchallenged.

Expand as fast as possible without actually incurring losses to buy market share, in all markets above $10 million with growth rates above 10 percent per annum over the next five years.

Expand through margin reductions in all markets in which competitor X has a market share of over 35 percent, our share is below 5 percent, and margins are above 30 percent.

Develop export agents in all markets estimated at between $2 million and $5 million per annum.

Withdraw from direct participation in all markets below $5 million demand and $100,000 actual sales and in which five-year growth rates are under 5 percent per annum.

Pay no marketing attention to country markets below a country size of $2 million per annum.

These rules should enable all country markets to be classified one way or another. Once classified, each market can then be allocated a sales target appropriate to the rule under which it falls. Such sales targets and the manner in which they are to be achieved, however, will be conditioned by the characteristics of the individual markets and the firm's existing position in those markets. For example, a decision by a capital goods firm to expand at a maximum rate in a particular market might require only a local agent to obtain inquiries for bids and maintain a local base for customer service. Yet for a firm manufacturing a branded consumer good, fastest possible expansion may require full local production, warehousing, and direct merchandising. Even then, the expansion rate possible may be limited if the firm has not earlier established a brand recognition among customers. Entry considerations and appropriate strategies are discussed in more detail later in this chapter.

It cannot be emphasized too much that the classification of markets according to the different emphases to be accorded them should express a strategy effective against competition. It may be helpful in achieving this if the decision rules for market emphasis are actually expressed in terms of how they will each affect competitive positioning. Alternatively, an overall strategic focus may be established first and then the emphasis rules developed from that concept. An approach that produces emphasis rules in this way has been suggested by Ayal and Zif.[12] Shown in Figure 13–3, they propose 10 feasible strategies based on three strategic considerations as follows:

Competitive posture.   The posture may be either:

1.   Defensive—to retain market share
2.   Offensive—to build market share.

Location of competitive action.   The market emphasis may be focused in one of three ways, on:

1.   Home markets—where the firm has the advantage of being already well established.
2.   Neutral territories—where the competitors are on roughly equal footing.
3.   Competitor's home markets—where the competitor has prior-establishment advantages.

---

[12] Igal Ayal and Jehiel Zif, "Competitive Market Choice Strategies in Multinational Marketing," *Columbia Journal of World Business*, 13 (Fall 1978), pp. 72–81; and "Market Expansion Strategies in Multinational Marketing," *Journal of Marketing* 43 (Spring 1979) pp. 84–94.

Figure 13–3

Alternative international strategies

	Location of competitive action		
	Home market(s)	Neutral territory	Competitor's home market(s)
		Offensive strategies	
Concentration (few markets)	"Munitions factory": Recommended for moving rapidly down experience curve for later international expansion, when home markets are large, developed, and with weaker competition than outside.	"Advance base" Recommended for firms with insignificant product or cost advantages over competition and when home market is already dominated, small, or competitive and, therefore, less attractive.	"Frontal assault" Recommended for a strong firm trying to preempt an emerging competitor or weaken a failing one, and when competitor's home market barriers are not high.
Diversification (many markets)	Not applicable	"Pincers movement" Recommended for firms as under "Advance base" but with high resource availability and favorable product/market factors—e.g., low threshold at which neutral markets respond to marketing and low requirement for product adaptation.	"Broad sweep" Includes neutral markets, too. Recommended for very strong firms with weak, fragmented opposition and when product/market factors overwhelmingly favorable.

Defensive strategies

	"Walled city":	"Perimeter defense"	"Counter strike"
Concentration (few markets)	Recommended for small firms without international competitive advantages when barriers exist or can be erected around small home market.	Recommended for weak firms at competitive disadvantage where pre-emption of neutral markets may avoid further competitor gains, hence protecting home market.	Recommended when a strong competitor has overstretched in attack and counteraction in competitor's home market will either weaken the attack or else yield cheap gains to offset losses to the competitor.
		"Rear-guard action"	"Guerrilla warfare"
Diversification (many markets)	Not applicable	Recommended when stronger competition has launched a pincers movement and product/market factors do not overwhelmingly favor concentration. May be desirable even at a loss to hold competition from building strength with more costly later attacks.	Includes neutral markets, too. Recommended as for "Rear-guard action" but also as harassing action by strong firms facing strong competitors to force real fighting onto neutral territory.

Source: Adapted from Igal Ayal and Jehiel Zif, "Competitive Market Choice Strategies in Multinational Marketing," *Columbia Journal of World Business,* Fall 1978, pp. 72–81.

Expansion mode.   Efforts to expand performance may be allocated through either:

1.   Concentration—where the resources are concentrated on a few markets, or
2.   Diversification—where resources are spread over many markets.

Each of the 10 feasible strategies has been given a title appropriate to the mix of competitive posture, the markets on which the strategy focuses, and the degree of market concentration involved. Two alternatives are not classified as it is not possible to focus on the firm's home market while at the same time following a diversified market strategy of expanding in many markets.

The conditions under which each of the 10 strategies should be adopted are summarized briefly in Figure 13–3. Size of the different markets, height of the entry barriers, and the strength within markets relative to competition are important. In addition, 10 product-market factors, as listed in Figure 13–4, are put forward as the basis for choice between

Figure 13–4

Major product/market factors affecting choice between diversification and concentration

Product/market factor	Diversification preferred if:	Concentration preferred if:
1. Threshold of response to marketing effort	Low	High
2. Growth rate of each market	Low	High
3. Sales stability in each market	Low	High
4. Competitive lead time	Short	Long
5. "Goodwill" spillover effects	High	Low
6. Need for product adaptation	Low	High
7. Need for communications adaptation	Low	High
8. Economies of scale in distribution	Low	High
9. Program control requirements	Low	High
10. Extent of constraints	Low	High

Source: Igal Ayal and Jehiel Zif, "Competitive Market Choice Strategies in Multinational Marketing," *Columbia Journal of World Business* 13 (Fall 1978), p. 73.

concentration or diversification. It is possible that one of these factors alone might be strong enough to swing the decision between concentrating on one or two markets or diversifying effort across many markets. For example, if a very high advertising expenditure were necessary to gain a significant response from a market, it might pay to allocate all resources to that market. Normally, however, it will be a grouping of factors that reinforce each other in suggesting diversification or concentration. Working backwards from an overall strategy chosen in this way, individual markets will still have to be allocated specific sales targets. These might be set directly, bearing in mind how a market might contribute to the overall concept; or, alternatively, they can be set after markets have been classified into groups as already outlined. For example, from the role a market is given within the strategy its target might be set to:

1. Maximize sales growth.
2. Maintain sales.
3. Run down sales.
4. Withdraw completely.
5. Receive no marketing attention.

Location of supply, production, and investment

While alternative sources of supply may have been loosely considered in setting the market sales targets, detailed planning of the sources of supply must wait until after targets have been set. It will then be possible to design a supply system from raw material to final delivery to the customer that would minimize costs of achieving the targets. Few firms can determine supply independently for each market without throwing away significant economies from coordinating supply.

While it is theoretically possible to calculate a profit-maximizing pattern of supply and the consequent investment needed to meet market targets up to the horizon year, such calculations would invariably be too complicated for practical application. The number of alternative supply patterns is infinite. The ownership options are many and will influence the investment required. And the introduction of a sequence of changing targets for each market further complicates the issue. Here, again, the calculation may be simplified by adopting a set of rules that limit the alternatives considered without moving the result too far away from a best solution. Decision rules that might be used are:

1. Retention of existing locations as against new locations when sunk costs are high and an experienced labor force is a valuable asset.
2. Consideration of new sites when the local market is above a certain size, resource costs are below a certain figure, or tariffs exceed a certain level.

In some cases, too, the adoption of targets for particular markets will require local production or licensing because of the local regulations concerning access to the market.

With the reduced number of required and potential siting alternatives determined, the next step is to estimate the costs of investment and operation at alternative sites and from each the transport and tariff costs into alternative markets. For each possible alternative, the lowest cost of supplying the market targets in the horizon year might then be calculated.

The methodology used for calculating the costs of alternative sourcing patterns can become very advanced. It may, however, be possible to reduce the alternatives to a linear cost format and use a linear-programming model.[13]

Country risk allowances

Up to this point no direct allowance has been made for risks of losses that may arise because of the country locations of assets or activities. Losses can occur through expropriation or restrictions placed on capital assets, as well as through restrictions that reduce or remove the earning power from a market or increase costs in a country. An assessment of these risks is needed for each country likely to be incorporated in the global strategy.

This assessment may require the forecasting of government controls that affect transfers across the country's borders as well as controls aimed specifically at the operations of multinationals. Also needed may be an assessment of general political and economic conditions and the exchange rate for the country's currency. Chapter 15 deals specifically with control and political risk forecasts. Some methods of risk forecasting are designed to produce indices of country risk. The disadvantage of indices, however, is that they are difficult to integrate into decision approaches based on discounted cash flow or internal rate of return calculations. Imagine alternative investments in Egypt, Pakistan, or India each with a calculated internal rate of return of 25 percent before allowing for country risk. How meaningful would it be to have a risk index of 120 for Egypt, 118 for Pakistan, or 110 for India? Furthermore, the organization or ownership structure of a particular investment may be such that the risk of loss is higher in a less risky country overall.

It is preferable to compile country risk assessments in a way that fits into the firm's approach to investment decisions. The global strategy prototype requires country risk assessments expressed in terms of their likely impact on specific costs or revenues and the probability of the impact occurring. From such assessments expected costs can be calculated, and the cash flows from any strategy alternative reduced accordingly.

An example of risk assessments presented in this way is shown in Figure 13–5. The cost and revenue projections for investment of $20 million in a new operation in Oceania are shown, along with the costs and probabilities of government actions that would affect these operating figures. Note that the probabilities have been assessed to indicate the probability of the government action in any year, provided that the action

---

[13] Robert E. McGarrah, "Logistics for the International Manufacturer," *Harvard Business Review,* March–April 1966; David P. Rutenberg, *Stochastic Programming with Recourse for Planning Optimal Flexibility in Multinational Corporations* (Ph.D. dissertation, University of California, Berkeley, 1967); Ronald H. Ballou, "Dynamic Warehouse Location Analysis," *Journal of Marketing Research,* August 1968, pp. 271–76.

Figure 13–5

Proposed $20 million investment in Oceania

	Year				
	1	*2*	*3*	*4*	*5*
Operating projections ($ millions):					
Revenue	20	40	80	80	100
Costs (excluding depreciation)					
Imported materials	10	20	40	40	50
Local labor	8	12	20	20	25
Local expenses	4	6	8	8	8
	22	38	68	68	83
Profit	(2)	2	12	12	17
Local tax 30 percent	—	—	4	4	5
Net profit	(2)	2	8	8	12
Country risk projections:*					
Government price controls reducing revenue by 10 percent; probability	.1	.1	.1	.1	.1
Tariff imposition of 40 percent ad valorem; 90 percent can be passed on to customers; probability	—	—	.2	.3	.4
Profits tax levy on foreign-owned firms 10 percent; probability	—	.05	.05	.1	.2
Expropriation of foreign-owned plants with resulting total loss of net earnings. Compensation or insurance repayment $10 million; probability	—	—	—	.2	.2

* Probabilities assume actions from beginning of year.

has not been taken before. For example, we estimate that there is no probability of a tariff increase until year 3, when there is a 20 percent or 1 out of 5 chance of a loss of 4 percent that cannot be passed on to customers. In year 4, there is a .2 chance of the loss having arisen the previous year plus a .3 chance of it arising this year if it had not already arisen. This may seem a little complex, but it is simply .2 plus .3 times the .8 chance the tariff had not been imposed by the beginning of the year. In some situations, it might be easier to forecast directly the cumulative probability that an action will have been taken by that year. Note also that the various actions and their probabilities are independent of each other.

Based on these projections, Figure 13–6 presents a calculation of expected losses from government actions and a risk-adjusted cash flow. Note how the cash flow from the projected operations over the five years is both reduced by the risk and changed in pattern to show a peak of expected profit in year 3 instead of year 5. But for the certainty of compensation following expropriation, the cash flow would have been even more seriously reduced. For a more extended period than five years, however, the return would drop dramatically, given this high expectation of expropriation.

Figure 13—6

Oceania: cash-flow projection adjusted for country risk ($ millions)

	Year				
	1	2	3	4	5
Revenue	20	40	80	80	100
Less price controls 10 percent	2	4	8	8	10
Cumulative probability	.1	.19	.27	.34	.41
Expected cost	.20	.76	1.96	2.72	4.10
Reduced revenue	19.80	39.24	78.04	77.28	95.90
Costs	22.00	38.00	68.00	68.00	83.00
Plus tariff increase:					
4 percent of materials (10 percent of 40 percent)	—	—	1.6	1.6	2.0
Cumulative probability	—	—	.2	.44	.66
Expected cost	—	—	.32	.70	1.32
Increased costs	22.00	38.00	68.32	68.70	84.32
Profit	(2.20)	1.24	9.72	8.58	9.58
Local tax:					
At 30 percent (losses c/fd.)*	—	—	2.62	2.57	2.87
Plus 10 percent increase	—	—	.88	.86	.96
Cumulative probability	—	.05	.1	.19	.35
Expected cost	—	—	.09	.16	.34
Increased tax	—	—	2.71	2.73	3.21
Profit after tax	(2.20)	1.24	7.01	5.85	6.37
Expropriation allowance					
Compensation repayment $10 million:					
Probability occurs in this year	—	—	—	.2	.16
Expected recovery	—	—	—	2.00	1.60
Loss of profits:					
Cumulative probability	—	—	—	.2	.36
Expected cost	—	—	—	1.17	2.29
Expropriation cost	—	—	—	(.83) cr.	.69
Cash flow adjusted for country risk	(2.20)	1.24	7.01	6.68	5.68

* Losses carried forward.

Incremental net present value, rationing, and realignment

At this point the strategist following the prototype approach to global strategy will be able to compare cash flows adjusted for country risk of several possible sourcing and investment strategies, chosen initially on the basis of their costs in meeting the sales targets of the horizon year. The alternative with the highest present value of its cash flow up to the horizon year could be selected.

Most firms would require, however, that these strategic alternatives be related to the customary investment allocation procedures of a firm. How can this be done? First, the horizon investment requirement must be translated into annual investment requirements over the period up to the horizon year. The final investment may not all be needed in the first year. One practical decision rule would be to invest for each year in that portion of the additions ultimately needed to achieve the sales targets for the horizon year, which would minimize the cost of meeting the earlier year's targets.

Once the annual investment requirements have been established, it would be usual to calculate the net present value of the stream of earnings from each investment unit. The cash flow attributed to each unit is not so much what it produces directly as the incremental cash flow from the global system as a whole. This might be calculated on a marginal or opportunity cost basis and estimated further into the future than the horizon year if that is normally expected for net present value calculation. Expectations of changes in controls and other risks already prepared for the global strategy will also be available for this assessment.

Calculations of net present values will require a further discounting rate. Country risks have already been taken into account, so it may be argued that the use of the firm's normal cost of capital for discounting would take them into account twice. The cost of capital, however, is normally determined predominantly by risks inherent in the business operations themselves so we suggest its use here. Readers wishing to pursue this point should consult international finance texts, but anyway the refinement is unlikely to change the global strategy selected.[14]

Finally, each year's investment may be subject to a cut-off limit determined by the firm's capacity to expand. Firms frequently operate with expansion capacity limited by management's ability to cope with expansion. This capacity might be expressed as a maximum investment sum for any year that, together with reinvestment funds, is available to meet the schedule of investment opportunities. The firm then accepts these opportunities in decreasing order of net present value per unit of capital invested until the investment sum is fully committed. It is assumed that this sum is committed to projects for which the least attractive would show a high net present value using the cost of capital as the discount rate. Furthermore, the multinational firm's capacity to handle expansion is taken to limit investment in the short term and not the cost of capital. If the available investment is not used up, then the firm will raise its market targets and repeat the entire global planning process. Conversely, targets that cannot be met will have to be lowered.

The simplified global planning example presented in Figure 13–7 illustrates the choice of a logistics pattern for extending capacity and then shows how the extension might be assessed for incremental cash flow.

---

[14] See David K. Eiteman and Arthur I. Stonehill, *Multinational Business Finance*, 2d ed. (Reading, Mass.: Addison-Wesley Publishing, 1979), chap. 10.

Figure 13–7

A simplified application of the prescriptive model for global planning (given: demand, sales, and cost data)

				Seven country markets				
	A	B	C	D	E	F	G	Total
Market projection and sales targets in 00s units:								
Year 1 Market	260	400	320	800	250	470	510	3,010
(Target)	(60)	(90)	(80)	(160)	(100)	(80)	(110)	680
Year 2 Market	280	420	350	840	260	480	510	3,140
(Target)	(65)	(95)	(90)	(165)	(100)	(80)	(105)	700
Year 3 Market	310	420	390	880	270	490	480	3,240
(Target)	(70)	(100)	(110)	(175)	(100)	(90)	(105)	750
Year 4 Market	360	420	430	930	280	510	460	3,390
(Target)	(90)	(105)	(130)	(185)	(100)	(100)	(100)	810
Year 5 Market	410	440	470	930	290	560	460	3,560
(Target)	(110)	(105)	(150)	(195)	(100)	(110)	(100)	870
Market price per unit	$85	$100	$100	$90	$90	$95	$85	
Current annual production in 00s units	—	90	—	300	200	—	140	730
Production cost per unit with existing plant	—	$70	—	$65	$60	—	$60	
Cost of standard plant extension of 5,000 units annual capacity $250,000								
Production cost per unit from a new extension	—	$65	$75	$65	$55	$70	$55	
Transfer cost per unit (including transport and duty, in dollars)								
From A to:								
B	15	—	20	10	15	15	20	
C	20	25	—	10	15	15	5	
D	25	25	10	—	15	10	5	
E	20	25	15	20	—	10	5	
F	20	25	15	20	15	—	5	
G	25	25	15	15	15	15	—	

Simplifying Assumptions

1. Five-year horizon with plant extensions possible for year 3.
2. No change expected in sales prices.
3. Production cost per unit excludes plant cost and is taken as directly variable.
4. All transfer costs directly variable and no possibility of customs duty saving through manipulation of transfer prices.
5. Production strategy to be determined independently of corporation tax considerations.

Decision Analysis

Inspection of the following table shows that all expansion should be located at E to supply A's requirements and the balance of F. (Where one alternative is not so dominant a linear-program calculation would be needed to establish profits of the alternatives.) Extensions should be completed to increase capacity by a further 5,000 units in each of years 3, 4, and 5.

Incremental return can be based on the profit that would be foregone if the extension were not available. If this meant simply the elimination of sales to the least profitable market given the reduced supply system, it would be solely sales to A in years 3 and 4, but in year 5 production would be reallocated and 1,500 sales foregone in B, 1,000 in C, and 500 in F for a total lost revenue of $262,500.

Profits per unit from alternative location of plant extensions (in dollars)

		Destination					
Source	A	B	C	D	E	F	G
A	—	—	—	—	—	—	—
B	5	35	15	15	10	15	—
C	-5	5	25	10	5	10	10
D	-5	20	25	25	10	20	15
E	10	20	30	15	35	30	25
F	-5	5	15	—	5	25	10
G	5	20	30	25	10	25	30

ENTRY STRATEGIES

The strategies or approaches adopted by a firm for entering and penetrating individual markets are often an important consideration in building global strategy and warrant more attention at this point. The firm has a choice of alternative approaches for penetrating new markets and for establishing new sources of supply. These alternatives imply different levels of commitment for the resources of the firm. They also have a time dimension and can operate as a building block or an obstacle to the achievement of long-term goals.

Moving from a minimum to a maximum commitment of company resources, entry strategies can be grouped into the following five categories:[15] (1) licensing, (2) exporting, (3) local warehousing with direct sales staff, (4) local packaging and/or assembling operations, or (5) full-scale local production and marketing.

Within these categories, several options exist.[16] Direct export and sales through a local company sales organization, for example, can be done by setting up regional distribution centers or warehouses. Or the firm can create a regional sales branch office and/or subsidiary. Or it can organize an overseas franchise system with independent, or a combination of company and independent, franchises.

A similar set of entry strategies is available for initiating projects that are primarily a source of supply for the multinational enterprise. A minimum commitment of resources would be involved in establishing only a buying office in a foreign location. A maximum commitment of resources would be needed to invest in company-operated production facilities and in supporting infrastructure such as transportation, electric power, or housing, health, and educational facilities for employees. Many alternatives are available between these two extremes.

Given these many alternative entry strategies, what are the variables that determine the best choice for a company? For a market seeker, the decision variables will be both external and internal to the firm. Most of the decision variables apply also to the entry decision for supply projects.

External factors:
  Host-country policies and controls
  Size and attractiveness of markets
  Competitive conditions in the foreign market
  Availability of local supply sources in the country
Internal factors:
  Characteristics of technology and products
  Enterprise-wide availability of productive capacity

---

[15] Business International Corporation, "Alternative Ways to Penetrate a Foreign Market," *100 Checklists: Decision Making in International Operations*, Reprint Report, 1970, pp. 6–8.
  [16] Ibid.

Minimum economic size for producing units

Locational characteristics of production

Availability of capital and managerial resources

Company's willingness to assume risk

Long-term corporate goals

In many cases, one or a few of the decision variables will dominate the decision on entry strategy and, in effect, sharply reduce the available options. Until recently, Japan followed severely restrictive policies regarding foreign investment. In many cases, the only practical options available to an international company for entering the Japanese market were licensing, exporting, and holding a minority position in a joint venture. In some instances, quota or tariff restrictions further reduce the options to only licensing. Or a less developed country attempting to encourage foreign direct investment may have such prohibitive import restrictions that the only realistic option for entering its market is to establish a foreign production subsidiary. Or the size of the market may be so small in relation to the minimum economic size required for efficient production that exporting is the only sensible initial entry strategy.

Japanese firms have in the past made extensive use of loan-purchase agreements whereby they assisted in the establishment of foreign supply sources by making loans and by agreeing to buy a given share of the output from the new project. In this way, Japanese companies expanded the availability of needed resources without taking an equity position and without assuming any managerial responsibility for new projects. Another interesting strategy used by some textile companies operating in Southeast Asia has been to establish local warehouses for raw materials and finished goods but to subcontract the manufacturing function to independent local companies. The international firm does the purchasing of supplies, the design and fashion work, and the international marketing, but not the actual manufacturing. Other strategies are to establish producing facilities in free port or border industry areas, primarily to make use of lower labor costs in a foreign country.

For each project, the feasible alternatives will have to be sorted out and compared as to profitability and consequences for achieving the firm's long-term goals. In all cases, the firm should make sure that its initial entry strategy will not create future obstacles for achieving long-run objectives. Interim moves should be designed to achieve long-term goals. Licensing is a relatively low-risk and low-cost entry strategy, available to both large and small firms that have something to sell. It is an option that allows a company to spread out the cost of its research and development and has the potential benefit of technology feedback. Furthermore, it enables a firm to move into markets where there are strict import or investment laws. Frequently, however, licensing is not an optimum way to maximize the gains from a company's competitive advantage.[17] The conditions under which licensing may be a preferred strategy are discussed below in Chapter 19 under "Managing International Technology Transfers."

OWNERSHIP STRATEGIES

Ownership strategies are another important component of overall global strategy. Should foreign subsidiaries be wholly owned by the multinational enterprise, or joint-ventures in which ownership is shared with local interests, either private or government? If the joint-venture approach is adopted, should the international firm seek a majority or minority participation? Ownership policies change investment requirements and other resource commitments for new projects. They also affect the extent to which individual subsidiaries participate in an enterprise-wide global strategy.[18]

In many countries, ownership policies for foreign firms are prescribed by national-control policies or laws. Mexico and India are examples of countries that require joint ventures, generally on a minority participation basis. In such countries, a few firms that control a product or technology keenly desired by the host country have been able to establish a wholly or majority owned subsidiary. But in general the ownership strategy alternatives are limited in these countries. For other countries, however, the multinational firm has considerable choice.

The benefits to be gained by joint ventures fall into three areas: technical resources, financial advantage, and political considerations.[19] A joint venture with an established local enterprise may be the means of acquiring local marketing know-how or other managerial skills at substantial savings in time and expense as compared to the alternative of creating an entirely new organization. Moreover, by participating with a strong local firm that has access to or controls supplies and resources necessary to the company's operations, such as one of the large trading companies in Japan, the company will insure a supply of such items, perhaps even on a more favorable basis. Frequently, the small firm trying to expand internationally at a rapid pace to keep up with its larger competitors may have little choice because of its limited resources. But actual benefits will depend upon whether the local partner in fact has the complementary abilities needed for the kind of local operations desired by the international enterprise.

---

[17] See David B. Zenoff, "Licensing as a Means of Penetrating Foreign Markets," *IDEA*, Summer 1970, pp. 292–308.

[18] See Richard D. Robinson, *International Business Management*, 2d ed. (Hinsdale, Ill.: Dryden Press, 1978), pp. 357–411.

[19] Michael Z. Brooke and H. Lee Remmers, *The Strategy of Multinational Enterprise*, 2d ed. (London: Pitman, 1978), pp. 205–22.

The joint venture that Xerox Corporation entered into with the Rank Organization of the United Kingdom to produce and market its copying machines outside the United States has been explained by the rapid growth in the U.S. market for Xerox machines. Domestic business expanded at such a rate that all available managerial resources of Xerox were being absorbed at home. Rather than lose out on the vast potential that foreign markets promised, Xerox opted for a partner and a joint venture.

The financial advantages of joint ventures may permit an international enterprise to enter into more foreign projects when its financial resources are limited or its home country is imposing restrictions on the export of capital. In some cases, local partners will accept the technological know-how, patent rights, or even the trade name of the international enterprise as a substitute for capital in payment for a share of the subsidiary's equity. Joint ventures also lessen the risk of foreign exchange losses by reducing the amount of investment at stake.

Political considerations have probably been the most important motivation for joint ventures in many countries. Sharing ownership with nationals can encourage national identification and reduce the appearance of foreignness and thus the risk of expropriation. Furthermore, local partners may in some cases be able to contribute political influence and protection against the possibility of increasingly severe national controls. The maximum local protection could be achieved by a joint venture with the national government, although where governments change with frequency, even this strategy cannot be a complete defense. In terms of public-relations benefits, a wide distribution of shares among the investing public may be the best strategy.

Studies of the joint-venture experience of the principal U.S. multinational firms suggest that a company's long-run tolerance for joint ventures is closely related to its product strategy.[20] Firms following a strategy of foreign product diversification aimed at continually enlarging their range of products and services and their coverage of foreign markets have found joint ventures positively useful in both the short and long run. In such firms, marketing and production decisions are largely taken at the subsidiary level, and marketing policies are relatively unstandardized across a number of countries. Joint ventures also appeal to companies involved solely in raw material extraction. These firms rely on a foreign partner to provide a market for their "products." They are not concerned with controlling the market just as long as they can supply it.[21]

---

[20] Franko, "Joint-Venture Divorce in the Multinational Company, *Columbia Journal of World Business*, May–June 1971, pp. 20–21; John M. Stopford and Louis T. Wells, Jr., *Managing the Multinational Enterprise* (New York: Basic Books, 1972), pp. 99–168.

[21] See Louis T. Wells, Jr., "Joint Ventures—Successful Handshake or Painful Headache?", *European Business*, Summer 1973.

Conversely, product-concentrating firms, specializing in providing few products or services to their customers, find it most difficult to succeed with joint ventures.[22] In such firms, marketing and production-output decisions need to be relatively centralized on a supranational or regional level. Marketing policies tend to be standardized across borders and expenditures on product differentiation tend to be high. A coordinated export strategy is required so that the firm avoids meeting itself in many export markets. Under these circumstances, a high potential exists for conflicts between the parent company and the local partners over market decision making. As an example, the Coca-Cola Co. uses a marketing approach that relies heavily on advertising. This has worked well in the United States and they want to use the same strategy worldwide. Often, however, their local subsidiaries protest the large advertising budget. So, when the Coca-Cola Co. does enter a joint venture it tries to control the marketing operations.[23]

The disadvantages of joint ventures revolve largely around the desire and need of the multinational enterprise to retain control over the decisions of foreign subsidiaries. This control issue can be the source of many conflicts between the international firm and its local partners. Where the special advantages of the multinational enterprise lie in a unification of markets and the rationalization of production, finance, and other functions on a regional or global basis, the interests of any subunit and the local partners owning shares in that subunit are likely to conflict with global objectives and opportunities. As one example, in order to build volume the firm might prefer to adopt a transfer-pricing policy that would leave all profits in the marketing subsidiary, but might be discouraged from doing so if the subsidiary is only part owned. Or local partners may prefer dividends rather than retaining earnings as a source of financing expansion.

In the past, many international enterprises have followed strongly fixed attitudes that insisted on having 100 percent ownership at all times and under all circumstances.[24] Such policies have been justified in terms of the need for complete control or by the attitude expressed by one executive, who said, "We do all the work and take all the risk; if it's a success why should we let the locals in on it? If it's a flop, they won't be interested. Either way, I can't see the point."[25] Other strong opponents of sharing ownership locally have argued that nationals can share in the operations of a subsidiary by purchasing shares in the parent company, either in the home-base country or when listed on local exchanges.

---

[22] Franko, *Joint-Venture Survival Multinational Corporations* (New York: Praeger Publishers, 1971), pp. 15–16.

[23] Wells, "Joint Ventures—Successful Handshake or Painful Headache?"

[24] See Richard D. Robinson, *International Business Policy* (New York: Holt, Rinehart & Winston, 1964), pp. 147–74, for results of a 1956–59 study of 172 American firms.

[25] Brooke and Remmers, *Strategy for Multinational Enterprise*, p. 221.

But with a growing body of experience and greatly increased pressures for control by host countries in the developed as well as in the less developed countries, multinational enterprises have moved toward more flexible and pragmatic views on joint ventures. Indeed, with increased government regulation and control, the joint venture is sometimes the only available entry strategy.

As in the case of entry strategies, the decision criteria that should influence ownership strategies will be a mixture of factors internal and external to the firm. The internal factors will be the product strategy of the firm, the availability of adequate financial and other managerial resources, the degree of operating experience it can command for new and different situations, and the speed with which it desires to initiate new projects for competitive or other reasons. The external factors will be the control policies of the host countries,[26] the availability of local partners or of adequate financial markets where widely shared local ownership is desired, and the local competitive situation, which may require that entry be made through acquiring a local firm that desires to retain an ownership interest.

Home-country policies may be another important external factor. U.S. tax policies, for example, limit foreign tax credits for the parent company to situations where a specified minimum of ownership is held. Or antitrust liability may arise where agreements exist between the parent company and jointly owned subsidiaries, whereas the same arrangements with a wholly owned subsidiary would not be challenged. Or home-country investment-guarantee programs may be unavailable for foreign projects with less than a certain minimum ownership.

STRATEGY REVIEW AND UPDATING

As the planning process dictates, it is also important for the firm to make regular reviews of the particular business techniques being used in its different product and factor markets. Factors such as inter-regional shifts, urbanization and suburbanization, technology, transportation, competition, social pressures, local expertise, changing buying patterns and selling outlets, and government policies and regulation make periodic examinations essential if the company is to stay abreast of changing conditions.[27] A firm that does not modify its style of operation according to changes in local conditions and laws, e.g., "choosing to invest in a market only as a majority owner or selling only through its own sales force, may be passing up opportunities for great profits. None of the

---

[26] The United Nations in 1971 published a *Manual on the Establishment of Industrial Joint-Venture Agreements in Developing Countries* (New York: United Nations, 1971) in response to the desire of LDCs to secure joint ventures.

[27] Business International Corporation, "Alternative Ways to Penetrate Foreign Market," p. 6.

many possible routes to market penetration should be overlooked in a company's periodic review of its approaches."[28] Likewise, possible new routes to reduce production costs and acquire new technology should not be overlooked.

The issue of ownership strategy has a time dimension. The point has been made that the stream of benefits of the foreign investment to the host country may decrease over time. Such a maturing of benefits and an increase in the alternatives open to a country can reduce the bargaining power of the foreign enterprise for maintaining 100 percent or even majority ownership.[29] And in a number of countries, the international firm may encounter national policies that require gradual divestment of foreign ownership over time, or what has been called a fade-out policy.[30] Or the enterprise itself may want to change ownership patterns over time. A joint venture may have served the purpose of helping a firm acquire local experience in the initial entry stage but no longer serves this need at a later stage. The reverse can also be true; firms may develop preferences for joint ventures during mature stages of foreign market penetration. For example, certain international banks with extensive overseas branch networks have begun to form joint-venture banks in the same countries where they currently operate branches. The reason for the tactical shift is to provide protection against possible policy moves by local governments to evict or substantially curtail foreign banks. The point is simple. Conditions change and firms must routinely review and adjust their plans, operating strategies, and ownership arrangements to compete most successfully in international markets.

A GLOBAL HABIT OF MIND

In the last analysis, developing a global strategy depends upon the way executives think about doing business around the world. The design and implementation of a global strategy require that managers in both headquarters and subsidiaries follow a worldwide approach which considers subsidiaries as neither satellites nor independent city-states but as parts of a whole, the focus of which is on worldwide as well as local objectives. And each part of the system makes its unique contribution with its unique competence. This approach, which Perlmutter has popularized as "geocentrism," involves collaboration between subsidiaries and headquarters to establish universal standards and permissible local variations on the basis of which key decisions are made.[31] However,

---

[28] Ibid.

[29] Peter Gabriel, "The Investment in the LDC: Assets with a Fixed Maturity," *Columbia Journal of World Business,* Summer 1966, pp. 109–19.

[30] Albert O. Hirschman, *How to Divest in Latin America, and Why* (Princeton, N.J.: International Finance Section, Princeton University, November 1969).

[31] Howard V. Perlmutter, "The Tortuous Evolution of the Multinational Corporation," *Columbia Journal of World Business,* January–February 1969, pp. 9–18.

geocentrism requires a reward system for subsidiary managers that motivates them to work for worldwide goals and not just to defend country objectives.

Three general types of headquarters orientation toward subsidiaries in international enterprise have been described by Perlmutter. While they never appear in pure form, and there is some degree of each philosophy in most firms, they are clearly distinguishable as ethnocentric (home-country oriented), polycentric (or host-country oriented), and geocentric (world oriented).[32]

The ethnocentric attitude can be characterized as: "We, the home-country nationals, are superior to, more trustworthy than, and more reliable than any foreigners in headquarters or the subsidiaries." In such firms, performance criteria and decision rules are generally based on home-country standards. Ethnocentrism works against a global strategy because of a lack of good feedback and because the experience and views of managers familiar with local conditions in the areas of operation do not carry appropriate weight in decision making.

Polycentric firms go to the other extreme by assuming that local people always know what is best for them and that the unit of the multinational enterprise located in a host country should be as local in identity and behavior as possible. A polycentric firm is more akin to a confederation of quasi-independent subsidiaries. A polycentric management philosophy is likely to sacrifice most of the unification and synergistic benefits of multinational operation. The costs of polycentrism are the waste due to duplication of effort and inefficient use of home-country experience. The approach has the advantage of making intensive use of local resources and personnel but at the cost of global growth and efficiency.

Geocentrism also has costs, largely- related to communication and travel expense, time spent in decision making because of the desire to educate personnel about global objectives and to secure consensus, and the expense of a relatively large headquarters bureaucracy. But the pay-offs are a more objective total enterprise performance, worldwide utilization of resources, improvement of local company management, a greater sense of commitment to worldwide goals, and, last but not least, more profit. A globally oriented enterprise, of course, depends on having an adequate supply of managers who are globally oriented.

SUMMARY

Few, if any, companies are born with a global philosophy or a worldwide view. They normally become international by a process of creeping incrementalism, adding a series of international units to the parent com-

---

[32] For the interested reader, the relevance of this framework to international marketing strategies and decisions is discussed in Yoram Wind, Susan P. Douglas, and Howard V. Perlmutter, "Guidelines for Developing International Marketing Strategies," *Journal of Marketing* 37 (April 1973), pp. 14–23.

pany as isolated reactions to perceived opportunities or competitive threats. But at some stage of internationalization, either as a result of growing experience of competitive pressures, the firm becomes aware of the need for a global strategy and a global decision model in order to benefit from the synergy potential of multinational operations and to maximize results on a worldwide basis. At this stage, if not before, the truly multinational enterprise engages in a system of international strategic and long-range planning.

The formulation of global strategy starts from the examination of global markets and identification of competitive position and works back to determine the location of supply and production activities and investments to achieve optimum performance in these markets. It requires decisions as to the best entry strategies for securing access to markets and foreign locations of resources or production. Another component of a global strategy is a company's decisions concerning ownership. Above all, the formulation and implementation of a global strategy requires managers with a global, or geocentric, state of mind.

EXERCISES AND DISCUSSION QUESTIONS

1. If a global strategy is required to maximize the special advantages and synergistic benefits of multinational operations, why have so many firms been successful in their international operations by responding to perceived opportunities and competitive threats without international strategic planning and global decision models?

2. How can an enterprise simplify the complexities of international possibilities and reduce to management proportions the variables it includes in its decision making?

3. Under what circumstances would global planning be desirable, even if the firm's international involvement is minor?

4. What decision rules other than those mentioned in the chapter might be used for choosing among alternative sources of supply?

5. "Global planning based on a sales horizon of four or five years and annual return on investment from those sales is in direct conflict with the normal return-on-investment calculations of financial management. But the top executive of the multinational firm will be measured on his five-year profit achievement before anything else." Comment.

6. "Entering a new market through licensing is generally the best strategy because market potentials can be tested with little or no investment." Comment.

7. "A multinational firm needs to have complete control over its subsidiaries in order to make optimum use of its resources and compete most effectively. This generally means 100 percent ownership." Comment.

Chapter 14

National economic and demand assessment

For the business firm newly venturing into international activities, the task of analyzing the economic and demand environment in many nations of widely varying characteristics will appear formidable. Nevertheless, even at its early stage of internationalization, the firm can reduce the task to manageable proportions. First, it must be selective and focus on those aspects of the environment that are of special importance to its field of business activity and its specific interest in a country as a market seeker, resource seeker, or production-efficiency seeker. Second, the firm can obtain much of the needed information from data and reports published by national and international agencies. And third, short-cut techniques are available for a preliminary scanning of the economic and demand environment in many countries to reduce the number of situations where in-depth analysis is required.

As the enterprise becomes multinational, the task of assessing and forecasting the economic and demand environment will be decentralized and shared among the various units of the system. The foreign subsidiaries will assume primary responsibilities for economic and market studies in their areas of operations. Headquarters staff can then limit its responsibilities to making cross-national comparisons, integrating national forecasts into an enterprise-wide forecast against which global policy decisions can be made, and assessing the international financial framework and trends in inter-nation relationships.

Much of the environmental-forecasting activity of the subsidiaries will be to guide local operating decisions. But as part of a multinational system, the subsidiary will have to fulfill two additional requirements. First, it will have to follow a sufficiently standardized approach so that headquarters can make cross-country comparisons and combine individual country results into a broader mosaic. Second, each subsidiary will have to include sufficient information in its assessment so that the links can be made between the economic environment of the subsidiary and the rest of the multinational system.

At the headquarters level, the assessments of national economic and demand environments are needed for guiding strategy and operating decisions, for formulating systemwide policies, and for exercising a review function. When the firm expands into new countries where there is no subsidiary, headquarters will also have to assume full responsibility for the local environmental analysis.

The technical responsibility for assessing and forecasting will usually be handled by specialists. But in order to use such forecasts, the international manager will need to have considerable familiarity with techniques and limitations. He or she must be aware of statistical perils, inaccurate perceptions, and the risks inherent in making cross-national comparisons or in integrating information based on different data bases into broader mosaics.

A manager should be generally familiar with the process of appraising overall growth prospects of different countries and should comprehend the need for and the limitations of balance-of-payments forecasting. In dealing with the less-developed countries, the manager should have an understanding of the development process, international development-assistance programs and the importance of national development priorities. International managers may also have to adjust to new and unfamiliar patterns in economic institutions and policies. Faced with government enterprises as major features of a foreign nation's economy, for example, some managers will have to discover how such enterprises operate and how they are controlled.

ECONOMIC SCANNING

Economic scanning makes use of standard economic measurements to provide a general comparison of the potentials of different countries from the viewpoint of an international business. The indicators are primarily macroeconomic measures of economic size, income level, and growth trends, but they can also extend to indicators of sectoral growth and economic dependence.

Economic size

The economic size of a nation is measured by its total gross national product (GNP) or by a similar measurement, gross domestic product (GDP). GDP measures the value of goods and services produced in a country without taking account of the nationality of those supplying the labor or the capital. When factor income received from abroad is added and factor income paid abroad is deducted, the resultant figure is GNP. Recent estimates by the World Bank of the GNP for countries are shown in Table 14–1.

Table 14–1

Comparative estimates of gross national product and population for 1980 (for countries with GNP over $500 million)

Country	Gross national product at market prices (U.S. $ millions)	Population (millions)
United States	2,582,460	227.3
USSR	1,212,030	266.7
Japan	1,152,910	116.6
Germany, Federal Republic of	827,790	60.9
France	627,700	53.5
United Kingdom	442,820	55.9
Italy	368,860	56.9
China, People's Republic of	283,250	976.8
Brazil	243,240	118.7
Canada	242,530	23.9
Spain	199,780	37.4
Netherlands	161,440	14.1
India	159,430	673.2
Mexico	144,000	67.5
Australia	142,240	14.5
Poland	139,780	35.8
German Democratic Republic	120,940	16.9
Belgium	119,770	9.8
Sweden	111,900	8.3
Switzerland	106,300	6.5
Saudi Arabia	100,930	9.0
Czechoslovakia	89,260	15.3

Table 14–1 (*continued*)

Country	Gross national product at market prices (U.S. $ millions)	Population (millions)
Nigeria	85,510	84.7
Austria	76,530	7.5
South Africa	66,960	29.3
Argentina	66,430	27.7
Denmark	66,350	5.1
Turkey	66,080	45.4
Indonesia	61,770	146.2
Korea, Republic of	58,580	38.5
Yugoslavia	58,570	22.3
Venezuela	54,220	14.9
Romania	52,010	22.3
Norway	51,610	4.1
Finland	47,280	4.9
Hungary	44,990	10.8
Greece	42,190	9.3
Iraq	39,500	13.1
Bulgaria	37,390	9.0
Algeria	36,410	18.9
Philippines	34,350	47.9
Colombia	31,570	26.7
Thailand	31,140	46.5
Kuwait	30,900	1.4
United Arab Emirates	26,850	.9
Libya	25,730	3.0
Pakistan	24,870	82.2
Chile	23,980	11.1
Egypt	23,140	39.8
Portugal	23,140	9.8
Malaysia	22,410	13.4
Hong Kong	21,500	5.1
New Zealand	20,680	3.3
Israel	17,440	3.9
Morocco	17,440	20.2
Peru	16,470	17.6
Ireland	16,130	3.3
Syrian Arab Republic	12,030	9.0
Bangladesh	11,170	90.2
Puerto Rico	11,070	3.7
Singapore	10,700	2.4
Ecuador	10,230	8.4
Ivory Coast	9,920	8.6
Sudan	8,640	18.4
Tunisia	8,340	6.4
Uruguay	8,240	2.9
Guatemala	7,790	7.0
Kenya	6,630	15.9
Zaire	6,340	28.3
Dominican Republic	6,200	5.4
Qatar	6,020	.2
Burma	5,910	33.3

Table 14–1 (*continued*)

Country	Gross national product at market prices (U.S. $ millions)	Population (millions)
Cameroon	5,660	8.4
Luxembourg	5,200	.4
Trinidad and Tobago	5,110	1.2
Ghana	4,920	11.7
Tanzania	4,780	18.1
Zimbabwe	4,640	7.4
Ethiopa	4,320	31.5
Paraguay	4,110	3.1
Sri Lanka	3,990	14.8
Oman	3,900	.9
Costa Rica	3,820	2.2
Uganda	3,750	13.2
Angola	3,320	7.1
Jordan	3,270	3.2
Zambia	3,220	5.8
Bolivia	3,190	5.6
Panama	3,170	1.8
Madagascar	3,030	8.7
Mozambique	2,810	10.5
El Salvador	2,690	4.5
Yemen Arab Rep.	2,680	5.8
Brunei	2,620	.2
Iceland	2,620	.2
Senegal	2,560	5.7
Gabon	2,420	.6
Papua New Guinea	2,360	3.0
Bahrain	2,350	.4
Jamaica	2,250	2.2
Cyprus	2,210	.6
Honduras	2,070	3.7
Reunion	2,010	.5
Nepal	1,980	14.3
Nicaragua	1,930	2.7
Niger	1,760	5.3
Guinea	1,590	5.4
Martinique	1,510	.3
Namibia	1,420	1.0
Malawi	1,390	6.0
Haiti	1,340	5.0
Mali	1,340	6.9
Guadeloupe	1,270	.3
Malta	1,190	.3
Fiji	1,160	.6
Congo	1,120	1.5
Upper Volta	1,110	5.7
Netherlands Antilles	1,100	.3
New Caledonia	1,100	.1
Benin	1,080	3.5
Rwanda	1,040	5.1
Mauritius	1,020	1.0

Table 14—1 (*concluded*)

Country	Gross national product at market prices (U.S. $ millions)	Population (millions)
Togo	1,020	2.5
French Polynesia	1,004	.2
Suriname	1,000	.4
Liberia	980	1.9
Sierra Leone	950	3.5
Channel Islands	900	.1
Burundi	830	4.1
Yemen, People's Democratic Republic	810	1.9
Bahamas	800	.2
Barbados	760	.2
Guam	740	.1
Botswana	730	.8
Central African Republic	680	2.3
Bermuda	660	.1
Macao	640	.3
Virgin Islands (US)	630	.1
Guyana	550	.8
Chad	530	4.5
Mauritania	530	1.6
Lesotho	520	1.3
GNP not available for:		
Viet Nam		54.2
Iran		38.1
Korea, Democratic People's Republic of		17.9
Taiwan		17.6
Afganistan		15.9
Cuba		9.9
Somalia		3.9
Lao People's Democratic Republic		3.4
Albania		2.7
Lebanon		2.7
Mongolia		1.7

Source: *1981 World Bank Atlas* (1982).

In terms of total size, the United States is at the top of the economic ladder with a GNP of $2,582 billion (expressed in 1980 dollars). At the bottom of the scale are small countries with total GNPs of less than $600 million, such as Chad and Lesotho.

The attraction of the developed countries on the basis of economic size is highlighted by several comparisons. France's GNP is over twice that of mainland China, even though China has nearly 20 times France's population. Netherlands has about the same GNP as India, although India has 48 times as many people. Denmark's total GNP is greater than that of Indonesia, even though Indonesia's population is 29 times as large.

Income levels

GNP per capita—total GNP divided by total population—can be used as a rough guide to the purchasing power of a country. It does have many limitations, however, including its failure to allow for different patterns of income distribution.[1] From Table 14–2, it can be seen that of the countries with over 1 million population the top-ranking GNP per capita is recorded for Kuwait with $20,250 per person. There is then a drop to Switzerland with $15,360 and Sweden and West Germany with around $12,200. The United States registers only $10,610. At the bottom come countries with GNP per capita of around $100, such as Ethiopia, Bangladesh, and Bhutan.

Countries are often classified as developed or developing countries based on average per capita GNP. Developing countries are also referred to as LDCs (less developed countries). Although there is no general agreement as to where the dividing line should be, one representation of the gap between the LDCs and the economically advanced countries of the world is shown in Table 14–3. From this table, it can be quickly calculated that 75 percent of world population receives less than 20 percent of world GNP.

The development gap is both a cause and an effect of the more rapid expansion of international enterprise in the advanced countries of North America, Western Europe, and Japan. It explains the aspirations of the less-developed countries for a greatly accelerated rate of economic progress, toward which international enterprise can make valuable contributions. At the same time, though, the development gap nourishes nationalistic feelings and defensive controls, which often make the LDCs unattractive to the international enterprise. Yet much of the world's population is in LDCs and many are making remarkable economic progress, so they should receive careful consideration in the economic scanning of the globally oriented business enterprise.

Growth trends

Data on economic size and income levels must be supplemented by recent trend data in order to secure a more dynamic picture of a country's economic attractiveness. Country A may have high income levels but be relatively stagnant. Country B may have lower levels of income but

---

[1] See Hollis B. Chenery, "Poverty and Progress—Choices for the Developing World," *Finance and Development*, June 1, 1980, pp. 12–16.

Table 14—2

Gross national product per capita for 1979, GNP real growth 1970—1979 and population growth 1970—1979 (for countries with over 1 million population)

Country	GNP per capita		Population growth rate percent 1970-79
	Amount 1979 (U.S. $)	Real growth rate percent 1970-79	
Kuwait	20,250	1.4	6.2
Switzerland	15,360	0.2	0.3
Sweden	12,250	1.1	0.3
Germany, Federal Republic of	12,200	2.6	0.0
Denmark	12,030	2.1	0.4
Norway	11,230	3.7	0.5
Belgium	11,020	2.9	0.2
France	10,650	3.0	0.6
United States	10,610	2.2	0.9
Netherlands	10,490	2.2	0.8
Saudi Arabia	9,960	9.6	4.6
Canada	9,410	2.9	1.1
Austria	9,130	3.5	0.1
Australia	8,870	1.4	1.5
Japan	8,730	3.9	1.2
Finland	8,520	2.2	0.6
Libya	8,480	−1.6	4.2
United Kingdom	7,390	1.9	0.1
New Zealand	6,400	0.5	1.6
German Democratic Republic	6,310	4.7	−0.2
Italy	5,730	2.2	0.7
Czechoslovakia	5,190	4.1	0.7
Spain	4,920	3.0	1.1
Ireland	4,480	2.3	1.2
Israel	4,230	1.6	2.7
Greece	4,140	4.1	0.6
USSR	4,040	4.1	0.9
Trinidad and Tobago	3,910	4.5	1.2
Hungary	3,780	4.8	0.4
Poland	3,770	5.2	0.9
Singapore	3,770	6.7	1.4
Hong Kong	3,640	6.5	2.6
Bulgaria	3,630	5.6	0.6
Venezuela	3,440	2.7	3.4
Puerto Rico	2,840	−0.3	3.0
Iraq	2,710	9.3	3.4
Uruguay	2,500	2.9	0.3
Yugoslavia	2,370	5.4	0.9
Argentina	2,210	1.0	1.6
Romania	2,100	9.2	0.9
Portugal	2,060	1.1	1.4
South Africa	2,000	0.6	2.7
Chile	1,890	0.8	1.7
Mexico	1,880	1.9	3.0
Algeria	1,770	2.8	3.4

Table 14–2 (*continued*)

| Country | GNP per capita | | Population growth rate percent 1970–79 |
	Amount 1979 (U.S. $)	Real growth rate percent 1970–79	
Brazil	1,770	6.1	2.3
Costa Rica	1,630	3.2	2.5
Panama	1,550	1.3	2.3
Korea, Republic of	1,510	8.1	1.9
Malaysia	1,450	5.4	2.3
Turkey	1,380	3.5	2.5
Jordan	1,200	6.0	3.5
Syrian Arab Republic	1,170	4.6	3.6
Tunisia	1,160	5.7	2.1
Paraguay	1,140	5.3	2.9
Ecuador	1,110	5.4	3.3
Jamaica	1,110	−3.7	1.6
Ivory Coast	1,070	1.3	5.7
Colombia	1,060	3.7	2.3
Dominican Republic	1,030	3.7	3.0
Guatemala	1,010	3.1	2.9
Nigeria	910	5.3	2.5
Peru	850	0.2	2.7
Morocco	780	3.5	3.0
Papua New Guinea	760	0.3	2.3
Congo, People's Republic of the	670	−0.2	2.5
El Salvador	640	1.4	2.9
Philippines	640	3.9	2.7
Nicaragua	610	−1.6	3.3
Thailand	600	4.4	2.5
Cameroon	590	3.1	2.2
Bolivia	550	2.3	2.6
Zimbabwe	550	−1.7	3.3
Zambia	540	−1.9	3.1
Honduras	520	0.5	3.4
Liberia	520	0.5	3.4
Egypt, Arab Republic of	500	5.3	2.0
Senegal	450	0.1	2.6
Sudan	450	1.5	2.7
Angola	430	−9.6	2.4
Yemen Arab Republic	420	n.a.*	1.8
Ghana	400	−3.0	3.1
Togo	400	1.2	2.4
Kenya	390	2.6	3.5
Indonesia	370	4.6	2.3
Lesotho	370	9.5	2.4
Yemen, People's Democratic Republic of	370	n.a.	2.4
Madagascar	330	−2.5	2.5
Mauritania	300	−0.7	2.7
Niger	300	−1.2	2.8
Uganda	290	−3.5	3.0
Central African Republic	280	0.9	2.3
Benin	270	0.6	2.9

Table 14–2 (concluded)

Country	GNP per capita		Population growth rate percent 1970–79
	Amount 1979 (U.S. $)	Real growth rate percent 1970–79	
Guinea	270	0.6	2.9
Pakistan	270	1.5	3.1
China	260	3.8	1.9
Mozambique	250	−5.3	2.5
Sierra Leone	250	−1.2	2.6
Tanzania	250	0.8	3.4
Haiti	230	1.8	1.7
Sri Lanka	230	2.5	1.7
Malawi	220	3.0	2.9
India	210	1.6	2.1
Zaire	210	−2.6	2.7
Burundi	190	1.5	2.2
Rwanda	190	1.6	2.8
Mali	180	2.5	2.6
Upper Volta	180	−1.2	1.6
Burma	150	2.0	2.2
Nepal	130	0.3	2.4
Chad	120	−2.4	2.0
Ethiopia	120	0.3	2.2
Bangladesh	110	0.8	3.0
Bhutan	80	−0.1	2.2
Afghanistan	n.a.	n.a.	2.6
Albania	n.a.	n.a.	2.5
Cuba	n.a.	n.a.	1.4
Iran	n.a.	n.a.	3.0
Korea, Democratic People's Republic of	n.a.	n.a.	2.6
Lao People's Democratic Republic	n.a.	n.a.	1.3
Lebanon	n.a.	n.a.	−1.0
Mongolia	n.a.	n.a.	3.0
Somalia	n.a.	n.a.	2.3
Viet Nam	n.a.	n.a.	2.9

* n.a. = not available.
Source: *World Bank Atlas*, (1982).

have more attraction to the international enterprise because the country is growing rapidly. Such trend data for population and GNP per capita are also shown in Table 14–2.

Low rates of population growth are associated with higher GNP per capita with the exception of the oil counries of Kuwait, Libya, Saudi Arabia, and Venezuela, which have a very unequal income distribution, and the countries with a substantial immigrant increment over the 1970–78 period such as Australia, New Zealand, Israel, and Hong Kong. It

Table 14–3

Countries grouped by 1979 GNP per capita

Income group	Population mid-1979 (millions)	GNP 1979 (U.S. $000 millions)	Average GNP per capita 1979 (U.S. $)
Less than $330	2,037	464	230
$330 to $759	388	185	477
$760 to $3,249	642	1,047	1,590
$3,250 to $7,589	547	2,568	4,690
$7,590 and over	567	5,892	10,392

Source: *World Bank Atlas*, 1982.

is particularly noticeable, too, that communist countries generally record significantly lower population growth rates than noncommunist countries with roughly similar GNP per capita. A few countries, such as Saudi Arabia, Iraq, Brazil, Jordan, Syria, and Ecuador have managed to maintain a high rate of growth in GNP per capita while population also expanded at high rates. The predominant relationship, however, is the opposite. At the bottom end of the scale are numerous poorer African countries with high population growth and actual decreases in real GNP per capita.

Historically, as a nation's income levels rise and urbanization increases, the rate of population increase slows down. Population control as an affirmative development measure is being adopted to some degree in the less-developed countries, but whether rapid increases in population are a burden on economic development efforts is still a controversial question in many countries. Yet the arithmetic is clear. The faster population expands, the larger is the overall rate of growth required to achieve per capita increases. Countries with rapid population growth normally have a large share of their population in the lower age groups. As a result, the potential labor force will be a relatively small share of total population. Expenditures required for education will be disproportionately large, and the heavy educational costs have to borne by the relatively small share of the population that is productively employed.

Sectoral trends

The multinational enterprise may need to extend its scanning of the economic environment into individual sectors of an economy. A firm whose markets lie in the agriculture sector, for example, may need to compare the size and trends of that sector in different countries. Sectoral data can also provide indications as to the overall potential for growth of individual countries.

Growth potentials are generally less for countries where agriculture comprises a large share of national output. More than in other sectors, growth in agriculture is constrained by low income elasticities in the demand for foodstuffs and by the rate at which new production techniques can be adopted. As industry approaches agriculture in size, countries become capable of more rapid growth, particularly during the period in which domestic manufacturing is substituting for imported goods.

Empirical studies have shown a regular pattern of change in economic structure associated with rising levels of income. As income increases, the shares spent by consumers for necessities decrease, while the shares for luxury goods, services, recreation, and other goods produced by the manufacturing (secondary) sector and the trade and services (tertiary) sectors increase. As a rough average, primary production, including agriculture, fishing, and forestry, falls continuously from around 60 percent of GNP in the least-developed countries to under 10 percent in the most developed.[2] Meanwhile, industry, including mining, grows from under 10 percent to 40 percent of GNP. The remainder is accounted for by services and utilities, which grow from 30 percent to 50 percent.

Structural changes within sectors generally accompany the changes in the relative importance of the sectors and again follow a regular pattern. For example, the manufacturing sector of low-income countries is likely to have a predominance of textile and food processing industries, whereas high-income countries have a heavy concentration in the manufacture of machinery and other technologically sophisticated products. The development pattern of a specific country will deviate in varying degrees from the normal pattern deduced from the growing number of empirical studies. Yet the normal patterns are still extremely useful in forecasting the growth prospects for industries or products closely related to the sectoral structure of a country.

External dependence and economic integration

The degree to which a country's economy is dependent upon external forces can be another important indicator of the economic environment. The ratio of foreign trade to GNP indicates a national economy's vulnerability to fluctuations in international trade. Thus the Netherlands, with foreign trade representing the equivalent of around 50 percent of GNP, depends to a high degree on economic expansion trends in the countries

---

[2] Hollis Chenery and Moises Syrquin, *Patterns of Development 1950–1970* (London: Oxford University Press, 1975). pp. 20–21. See also Hollis Chenery, *Structural Change and Development Policy* (London: Oxford University Press, 1979).

to which it is exporting. At the other extreme, a nation that has a closed or relatively self-sufficient economy has maximum control over its economic future, and the forces influencing such trends will be predominantly domestic. The United States, with exports representing only 10 percent of GNP, is less affected by fluctuations in other countries. Both the USSR and the People's Republic of China also have very low external dependence.

Another form of external dependence is a country's obligations to service and repay foreign loans. External debt and interest obligations can be compared to foreign exchange earnings as a measure of the capacity to repay. For many less-developed countries, annual public debt service and investment-income payments have risen to a level of more than 10 percent, and, in a few cases, more than 25 percent of foreign

Box 14—1

Debt indicators

Simple ratios that relate a country's external debts to its ability to repay those debts (gnp or exports) are always misleading. However, do not throw them all out of the window. Use some simple precautions such as:

Relate debt to GNP rather than GDP. The latter omits remittances from nationals working abroad, which are sizable for many heavily indebted countries.

Remember that most measures of debt include only loans with an original maturity of more than one year. The true burden of servicing debts is often grossly understated.

Look at the composition of exports. A heavy concentration on a few commodities makes foreign currency earnings vulnerable to violent lurches.

Look at imports to see how much they can be squeezed without suffocating economic growth.

Do not ignore the level of official reserves. Three month's import bill is generally considered a minimum safety margin.

Remember that debt service ratios usually relate to actual rather than scheduled payments of debt. A debt service ratio may be low (good) only because a country has fallen behind on its payments (bad).

Do not be fooled by rising debt ratios over a number of years. It may be because of more comprehensive reporting or from turning (excluded) short-term debt into (included) long-term debt.

Distinguish between interest and principal. A creditworthy country can roll over its principal. Its ability to pay interest is a more appropriate indicator of its ability to remain creditworthy.

Look at the proportion of debt which is on floating rather than fixed interest rate terms. That shows the vulnerability of a country to rises in interest rates.

Source: Extracted from *The Economist*, International Banking Survey, March 20, 1982, p. 99.

exchange earnings (see Box 14–1).[3] But a high ratio of debt service to foreign exchange earnings is not necessarily an indication of crisis. The capital inflow may have been invested so as to increase future capacity to repay through increased exports or import substitution.

External dependence is not good or bad per se, but high external dependency means that a careful analysis of external forces must be included in assessing and forecasting a country's future prospects. A high degree of external dependence may mean a high foreign exchange earning capacity and an ability to secure a great deal of external stimulation to internal growth.

Sources of economic data

National economic statistics are published regularly by international agencies such as the United Nations, the World Bank, the International Monetary Fund, and the Organization for Economic Cooperation and Development (OECD). Of particular significance for economic scanning is the monthly OECD publication *Main Economic Indicators*, which is designed to provide a picture of recent changes in the economies of member countries. Every two years, the monthly statistics over the last decade are published as a companion volume. These sources also include data on the performance within individual sectors of economies.[4]

NATIONAL ECONOMIC COMPARISON

Pitfalls in translation rates

Special problems arise in making comparisons between countries. Financial data expressed in national currencies must be converted to a common unit. Most commonly, current exchange rates are used to translate measures in local currencies to a common currency unit such as the U.S. dollar or the currency of the enterprise's home country.

Ideally, translations to a common currency should be derived from national currency figures on the basis of purchasing power parities or through direct real-product comparisons. However, such comparative data are available for only a limited number of countries and generally relate to different periods.

Those concerned with economic development have long recognized the deficiencies inherent in the exchange-rate approach to comparative income analysis and have been searching for better ways to compare

---

[3] Bahram Nowzad et al., *External Indebtedness of Developing Countries* (Washington, D.C.: International Monetary Fund, May 1981), p. 19.

[4] For example, see the table for each country in "Gross Domestic Product by Kind of Economic Activity," in *United Nations Yearbook of National Account Statistics 1979* (New York, 1980); also *National Accounts of OECD Countries 1962–1979* (Paris: OECD, 1981).

countries' economic progress. The most ambitious effort undertaken in this area is the UN International Comparison Project (ICP),[5] a study begun in 1968 jointly by the United Nations Statistical Office and the University of Pennsylvania with the support of the World Bank and a number of other international, national, and private institutions. The ICP has developed a highly sophisticated method for measuring total expenditure, which can be used to derive more reliable and directly comparable estimates of per capita income than previously possible. The published ICP findings represent detailed comparisons for 50 countries and will be extended to cover 75 countries.

The figures produced by this study illustrate how economic differences between countries can be overstated using current exchange rates, especially as between countries in the highest and lowest income categories. When the comparison was based on exchange rates, for example, the U.S. GNP per capita in 1975 exceeded that in India by a ration of 50 : 1. But based on a purchasing power parity calculation, this ratio was reduced to 14 : 1.[6]

The reason for such different results lies primarily in the divergent price and product structures of different countries. Exchange rates, even when they approximate balance-of-payments equilibrium rates, equate at best the prices of only internationally traded goods and services. They may bear little relationship to the prices of goods and services not internationally traded, which in most countries form the large bulk of the total national product. Specifically, the prices of farm products and of services in less developed countries are in most cases considerably lower relative to industrial prices than in the more developed countries. Moreover, agricultural output generally accounts for the major part of overall national output in the LDCs, whereas the opposite is true in developed countries. As a result, the internal purchasing power of the currency of a low-income country will generally be greater than indicated by the exchange rate.

The use of exchange rates for converting national currency data into a common currency is further complicated by the fact that official or par value rates do not always constitute equilibrium rates. Economic history provides countless instances where a given exchange rate has been maintained for a lengthy period of time, even though the internal price level has long since fallen out of line with prices in other parts of the world. A straight conversion on the basis of the overvalued rates would

---

[5] The results of the ICP have been published in three volumes: Irving B. Kravis, Zoltan Kenessey, Alan Heston, and Robert Summers, *A System of International Comparisons of Gross Product and Purchasing Power*, 1975; Irving B. Kravis, Alan Heston, and Robert Summers, *International Comparisons of Real Product and Purchasing Power*, 1978; Irving B. Kravis, Alan Heston, and Robert Summers, *World Product and Income: International Comparisons of Real GDP*, 1981 (Baltimore and London, Johns Hopkins University Press.)

[6] See "Technical Note" in *World Bank Atlas* (Washington, D.C.: International Bank for Reconstruction and Development, 1977).

overstate both absolute levels and changes over time. An additional problem arises when no single or unique rate of exchange exists. The international enterprise wishing to express national data in a selected currency is given the choice of free rates, controlled rates, preferential, basic, auction, nonpreferential rates, and so forth, depending on prevailing national policies.

To the extent that nations follow flexible exchange-rate policies, the problems of multiple and nonequilibrium rates are reduced. But no easy solution exists for the problem of inter-country comparisons.

Pitfalls in comparability of statistics

The likelihood of inaccurate perceptions of economic environments is always high because of variation in the concepts, coverage, and quality of national statistics. Also, a country's stage of development can result in statistical biases.

Biases frequently exist in GNP per capita. Although most nations use the same general concept,[7] the extent to which statistical estimates reflect the actual situation in different countries can vary significantly.[8] In less developed countries, levels of economic activity are generally understated. Statistical coverage becomes increasingly comprehensive as economic levels rise and the availability and quality of data improves as a country becomes more affluent and develops more complex institutions and improved record keeping. Moreover, as an economy develops, an increasing share of economic activity passes through the marketplace and is counted as national output. For example, housewives purchase bread instead of baking it themselves.

But not all economic activity is recorded, even in developed countries. High progressive tax rates and other limitations on the accumulation of personal wealth have contributed to the buildup of substantial "underground economies" of unrecorded or underrecorded cash, barter, and offshore transactions. Such transactions can account for a significant proportion of an economy's growth and leave a poor reported performance for what is much stronger basically.[9] Italy revised 1975–78 figures upward by about 10 percent. France, Germany, Japan, and Sweden have

---

[7] This is not true for centrally planned economies. See M. A. Jansen, "Problems of International Comparisons of National Accounting Aggregates between Countries with Different Economic Systems," *Review of Income and Wealth*, March 1973, pp. 69–77.

[8] See T. P. Hill, *The Measurement of Real Product* (Paris: OECD, February 1971). This study examines growth rates of gross domestic product for all OECD member countries and for many individual industries from the standpoint of the different types of measurement used and the margin of error attached to each.

[9] Vito Tanzi, "Underground Economy Built on Illicit Pursuits Is Growing Concern of Economic Policymakers," *IMF Survey*, February 4, 1980, pp. 34–37; Konstantin Simis, "Russia's Underground Millionaires," *Fortune*, June 29, 1981, pp. 36–50; Adrian Smith, "The Informal Economy," *Lloyd's Bank Review*, July 1981, pp. 45–61.

also made upward revisions recently. In the United Kingdom, the figure has been acknowledged as being as high as 7.5 percent but the adjustment made has been under 3 percent.

Another statistical peril involves country variations in official definitions. The label "manufacturing activity" is an example. French statistics, unlike those of most other nations, include fishing and the quarrying of building materials as manufacturing, whereas wine production is classified as agriculture.

Even where definitions and statistical coverage are similar, statistics can vary greatly in quality or in margins of error. Statistical quality varies among nations, among different items in the same country, and among different statistical observations for the same item in a country. Statistics of LDCs are likely to have large gaps and wide margins of error.

Variations in statistical quality among economic sectors result in large part from the greater difficulty of collecting data in one area as against another. For example, data on imports and exports are usually the best, while data on agricultural production are the weakest. The high quality of foreign trade statistics results from the fact that imports and exports generally flow through a limited number of ports of entry and involve some government surveillance for tax or control purposes. Contrast this situation with the problem of collecting agricultural data from hundreds of thousands (or millions) of reporting units widely separated geographically and from an agrarian social group that frequently has low levels of education and record-keeping experience.

For the international manager, the degree of error that can be tolerated depends upon the decision being made. In many situations, a wide margin of error would not seriously affect a decision. For example, national product estimates for a country may understate the economic reality. Yet, if the statistical bias is rather consistent from year to year, the business firm can draw a reasonable conclusion as to whether a country is expanding and even as to the rate of expansion. Likewise, cost-of-living data for a given country may be based on observations in only one or two principal cities but they may provide a reasonable indicator over time of general trends in price levels.

MACROECONOMIC FORECASTING

For many reasons, the international enterprise may require a deeper assessment of a country's economic prospects than is involved in economic scanning.

Basic economic forecasts

Comprehensive long-range planning studies and economic forecasts are available for most countries. Such planning studies vary immensely in quality and in validity. Still, many are highly useful and reasonable guides to future prospects and future growth patterns. Such planning studies may be for the nation as a whole, for regions, and for sectors of the economy.[10] For the less developed countries, extensive planning studies are frequently available from national agencies and from international organizations. The World Bank, in particular, has sent economic survey missions to most of the less-developed countries, and many of the mission reports are publicly available. For the industrialized countries, future outlook studies may be available from the OECD and from government and nongovernment sources within the country.

When acceptable economic forecasts are not available for a country, the international firm will have to build its own. There is a comprehensive literature and advanced expertise in macroeconomic forecasting; for a detailed treatment the reader should refer to one of the standard texts.[11] Seldom, though, will the international firm require a comprehensive forecast of an entire economy. Beyond the general trends of economic growth, the usual need will be for specific forecasts of price-level changes (i.e., inflation), changes in the country's external accounts with the rest of the world, and changes in the international exchange rate for its currency. The following sections provide a brief introduction to practical forecasting of these three aspects. It must be remembered, however, that macroeconomic variables are not independent of each other. The price level, the balance of payments, and the exchange rate are closely interrelated. While it is possible to forecast each separately, forecasts obtained by examining a complete economic system are more soundly based.

Price-level forecasts

Inflationary pressures are of particular significance to the international enterprise because inflation may be the prelude to devaluation of the country's currency in the foreign exchange market. Furthermore, an inflationary environment requires special business strategies.

A standard source for data on past price levels is the monthly *International Financial Statistics* of the International Monetary Fund. For forecasts of future price-level changes, the analyst should also look to changes in monetary and fiscal policy, probable rates of change in labor costs and productivity, as well as any inflationary pressure particular to the country under consideration. Countries dependent on export earnings from raw materials or primary products can experience major inflationary pressures following increases in world prices for their exports.

---

[10] See, for example, George Cyriax, ed., *World Index of Economic Forecasts*, 2d ed. (Aldershot, Hants., England: Gower Publishing, 1981).

[11] See Charles R. Blitzer, Peter B. Clark, and Lance Taylor, eds., *Economy-Wide Models and Development Planning* (London: Oxford University Press, 1975).

The forecasting of monetary and fiscal policies is an art in itself. For short-term forecast of price levels, however, it is possible to gain an indication of whether the quantity of money that the authorities have permitted will have further inflationary impact. Wage increases that outstrip productivity increases can also have a major impact. In developed countries particularly, the processes of wage adjustment have gained a momentum that can carry wages upward even with no increase in productivity either before or after the increased wages. The situation of "stagflation" that can result has become a major problem for industrialized countries.[12]

Finally, it is necessary in price-level forecasting to examine the measures used to minimize or neutralize the effects of inflation. Loans, savings accounts, pensions, or other fixed obligations, as well as wages and salaries, can include provisions for cost-of-living adjustments. Brazil has probably the most comprehensive policies where fiscal correction is applied to virtually all incomes, long-term debt obligations—both private and government—and even delinquent taxes. With such a policy, Brazil was able to achieve real growth from 1970–80, averaging 7 percent annually, despite the persistence of a high rate of inflation—climbing from 40 percent in 1976 to 100 percent in 1980.

Balance-of-payments forecasts

The most practical way to proceed in balance-of-payments forecasting is to analyze each item in the balance-of-payments accounts.

Foreign exchange earnings prospects.   Future supplies of foreign exchange will depend upon exports of goods, sale of services (including tourism), unilateral transfers, and both short- and long-term capital inflows. Forecasting future export prospects involves conventional supply and demand analysis of a country's principal export products and prospective new exports. In the case of traditional exports, an examination of recent trends in both quantity and price of specific exports and growth trends in the principal buyer countries can provide considerable insight into future prospects. Additional considerations will be a country's capacity for increasing the supply of export goods, possible variations in supply conditions due to weather and related conditions, the price and income elasticity of demand for specific products, the competitive position of countries that are alternative sources of supply, and the possibilities for changes in tariff and quota regulations imposed by buyer countries.

Unilateral transfers can be either from foreign governments or from individuals. Foreign exchange inflows from development-assistance

---

[12] International Monetary Fund, *World Economic Outlook* (Washington, D.C.: International Monetary Fund, June 1981), pp. 7–10.

grants can be sizable, though the prospects of future flows will depend heavily on political and security policies of donor governments and the availability of resources from international development agencies. Private unilateral transfers are significant for some countries such as Israel, which has received sizable foreign donations; or countries such as Egypt, Turkey, and Greece where nationals have migrated to work in other countries and are sending regular remittances to families remaining at home, representing as much as 50 percent of exports.[13]

Capital inflows will depend on the interest of foreign firms in making direct investments and on the policies of the country toward encouraging or controlling foreign investment. Future prospects for inflows of portfolio investment, loan funds, and short-term deposits attracted by high-interest rates must also be analyzed.

Foreign exchange needs.   Set off against the forecast of future foreign exchange availability will be an estimate of foreign exchange needs for imports, for purchases of foreign services, and for servicing foreign debt and the capital accounts. The forecast of import requirements can begin with an analysis and a projection of recent trends in both quantities and prices of principal import items. The projections should then be modified to reflect significant future changes likely to occur. Such a change might be the discovery of new resources that will substitute for imports (for example, petroleum), or a one-time need for large imports of capital goods to initiate a major industrialization project, or a high demand for kinds of goods not being produced within the country stimulated by rapidly rising consumer incomes.

Exchange-rate forecasts

Foreign exchange forecasting has already been introduced in Chapter 4. Most textbook treatments of exchange-rate forecasting, however, deal at greater length with various theoretical relationships between national differences in interest rates, forecast rates of inflation, and the forward exchange rate.[14] There are four common relationships.[15]

Purchasing Power Parity Theory.   Exchange rates adjust to maintain purchasing power parity between currencies.

---

[13] Anand G. Chandavarkar, "Use of Migrants' Remittances in Labor-Exporting Countries," *Finance & Development* 17 (June 1980), pp. 36–39.

[14] See David K. Eiteman and Arthur I. Stonehill, *Multinational Business Finance*, 2d ed., (Reading, Mass.: Addison-Wesley Publishing, 1979).

[15] Richard M. Levich, "On the Efficiency of Markets for Foreign Exchange," in *International Economic Policy: Theory and Evidence*, ed. Rudiger Dornbusch and Jacob A. Frenkel (Baltimore: Johns Hopkins University Press, 1979), pp. 246–67.

The Fisher Effect.   Exchange rates adjust to maintain real interest rate parity between countries.

The International Fisher Effect.   Exchange rates adjust to maintain actual interest rate parity between countries.

The Theory of Interest-Rate Parity.   The formal exchange rate discount or premium for a foreign currency adjusts to offset the difference in interest rates between the two countries (subject to transaction costs).

While this literature provides a theoretical base for initial projections of exchange-rate changes. The forecaster must also take into account the motivations and pressures that affect the actions and timing of governments and other parties that may be able to affect exchange rates in the short term.

FORECASTING NATIONAL INSTITUTIONAL ENVIRONMENTS

The international firm may want to extend its investigation into aspects of the institutional environment that are of special importance for the activity being considered. The firm may need to know about local banking and other financial institutions, as well as the extent to which local capital markets operate effectively. Other significant factors may be the role of labor unions and patterns of labor-management relations, the importance of government enterprises and the business fields in which they are operating, the influence of economic planning agencies, the types of business regulation that will be encountered, and patterns of social-welfare programs.

In some situations, an assessment of the institutional environment may heavily influence the firm's decision to invest or initiate operations. For example, the prospective business opportunity may be in a field where future expansion possibilities for a private foreign company may be restricted because government enterprises are likely to extend their activities in this area. In other situations, assessing the institutional environment may not be critical for the investment decision but of primary importance in shaping the business project and in providing guidance for future operations.

Where rapidly changing dimensions of the institutional environment have to be projected into the future, the forecasting task can be difficult. Techniques for forecasting the institutional environment are not well developed. Furthermore, unlike the situation in economic forecasting, the international firm cannot yet look to international and national governmental and research organizations for a large flow of institutional forecasting studies.

Yet good forecasts are possible. In some cases, countries appear to be moving toward a harmonization of substantive laws,[16] and forecasts for specific nations will emerge from the broader forecast of the legal environment. In other cases, forecasting can be done by an analogy technique whereby patterns in one country can be projected on the basis of patterns in another country at a higher stage of development.

Where institutional patterns clearly follow different evolutionary paths in different countries, forecasting will require more speculative techniques. For example, the role played by labor unions and patterns of labor-management relations appears to be following quite different patterns in Italy, Japan, and the United States. Consequently, it is unlikely that the role of labor unions in Italy will eventually become similar to present U.S. patterns. In such situations, the forecasting approach will have to identify in each country the particular factors that have been shaping institutional patterns and then attempt to forecast trends in the underlying factors. Italian labor unions generally have a political affiliation and play an important, direct political role in the country. Furthermore, many of the issues that are normally resolved in the United States through collective bargaining, such as vacations and pensions, are resolved in Italy through governmental legislation. Consequently, a forecast of labor union patterns in Italy would require that considerable attention be given to the political situation and political trends.

FORECASTING THE DEVELOPMENT PROCESS

Some business firms have long been active in the less developed countries (LDCs) as resource seekers for supplies of petroleum, minerals, and tropical agricultural products such as tea, cane sugar, and bananas. More recently, some production-efficiency seekers have established feeder plants in the LDCs to produce textiles, apparel, and electronic components for export to the advanced countries.

As market seekers, international enterprises have been showing only modest interest in the LDCs because of their small markets, low income levels, and perceived political risk. Yet, the LDCs have most of the world's population, and many of the LDCs are achieving relatively high growth rates. As incomes rise, effective demand rises even faster for the kinds of advanced products that can be supplied by international firms. It is a reasonably safe forecast that the LDCs will have a much greater business attraction for the multinational enterprise in the future than they have had in the recent past.

Since most international managers have acquired their international experience in dealing with economic environment issues in the ad-

---

[16] Seymour J. Rubin, "The International Firm and the National Jurisdiction," in *The International Corporation*, ed. Charles P. Kindelberger (Cambridge, Mass.: MIT Press, 1970), p. 193.

vanced countries, it is quite likely that the reservoir of experience and knowledge may be inadequate for assessing and forecasting the significantly different economic environments of the LDCs. A few brief comments should suffice to demonstrate the complexity of the development process and the need for considerable expertise on the part of the international enterprise in forecasting the economic conditions.

The LDCs almost universally give top priority to the achievement of rapid economic and social development. The challenge of trying to raise economic levels for such a large share of the world's population has stimulated considerable research on the development process. Theories have been advanced to account for low levels of economic activity, ranging from climate and natural resources endowment to cultural and social factors.[17] The various theories, however, are more complementary than contradictory and are gradually evolving toward a complex explanation that recognizes the need to move on many fronts in order to accelerate economic growth.

In terms of general strategy, the early approach of most nations was to emphasize capital as the prime mover. Increasing savings and stimulating capital formation through domestic or foreign means were seen as the principal needs for accelerating economic growth. As experience and understanding increased, development strategies became broader and more complex. Capital continues to be recognized as a crucial bottleneck, but not necessarily the only one. Other issues are emphasized, such as increasing the absorptive capacity of a country for capital flows, the elimination of institutional blocks, investment in human resources, and international technology transfers. Foreign exchange as a constraint has also received considerable attention, leading to an emphasis in many nations on expanding exports and attracting more public and private transfers of capital. In virtually all cases, heavy reliance has been placed on national economic planning and on government enterprise as a source of entrepreneurship.

The development process requires much more than preparing economic blueprints or injecting more capital into a system. Many preconditions for investment must be established in order to secure significant results. Such preconditions may be a mixture of increasing the skills of people, improving the administrative capacity of private and public institutions, creating new technologies, and securing greater efficiency in the operations of political institutions and political decision making in a country. The detailed requirements for a specific country will vary, de-

---

[17] The theoretical literature on economic development is vast. For a survey and synthesis, see Gerald M. Meier, *Leading Issues in Economic Development*, 3d ed. (New York: Oxford University Press, 1976); Everett E. Hagen. *The Economics of Development*, 3d ed. (Homewood, Ill.: Richard D. Irwin, 1980). For a different view pertinent to multinational enterprises, see Fernando Henrique Cardoso and Enzo Faletto, *Dependency and Development in Latin America* (Berkeley: University of California Press, 1979).

pending upon resources, the present state of the economic infrastructure such as transportation and communications facilities, soundness of economic policies, and so forth.

In most cases, development-minded countries give great emphasis to industrialization as a means of expanding national productivity and creating new employment. Industrialization strategies vary greatly. In many countries, industrialization policies are first directed toward opportunities for further processing of raw materials normally exported from the country. Import substitution industries will also be encouraged as an easy means of stimulating the industrialization process, because a domestic market will already be available, and because such industries hold the promise of saving foreign exchange. But the growth possibilities for import substitution industries appear to decline after an initial period.[18]

The agricultural sector traditionally receives a great deal of attention because it is generally the largest sector in the LDCs and because productivity is generally low. Land-reform proposals to increase output often face major opposition in this sector.

Conflict among economic, political, and social goals is a general phenomenon. Most countries have less developed regions such as the south of Italy or the northeast of Brazil where, for political reasons, development will have to receive special incentives. Geographic distribution to satisfy political goals may conflict with achieving rapid growth rates. From the social-welfare viewpoint, the issue invariably arises as to how increased economic gains should be distributed between increased consumption and increased investment. On the one hand, there is widespread desire for economic growth to be reflected quickly in improved living conditions. On the other hand, increased consumption generally means the reduced availability of savings for new investment in further growth.

Conflicts also arise concerning the use of capital-intensive rather than labor-intensive technologies. Most of the less-developed countries have serious problems of unemployment and underemployment. Thus the preference is for adopting new technologies that will create maximum employment.[19] But in many situations, the only technology options available are capital-intensive ones developed in the advanced countries to fit the needs in such countries. In other cases, where the labor-intensive technology option is available, its adoption may make the enterprise less competitive than if capital-intensive technology is used.[20]

---

[18] See Albert O. Hirschman, "The Political Economy of Import-Substituting Industrialization in Latin America," *Quarterly Journal of Economics*, February 1968, pp. 1–12.

[19] Guy Pfeffermann, "Men and Machines in Africa," *Finance and Development*, March 1974, pp. 16–19.

[20] R. Hal Mason, "Some Observations on the Choice of Technology by Multinational Firms in Developing Countries," *Review of Economics and Statistics*, August 1973, pp. 349–55; Austin Robinson, ed., *Appropriate Technologies for Third World Development* (London: Macmillan Press Ltd., 1979).

The advanced countries and the international agencies recognize the development gap between the LDCs and the advanced countries as a critical world problem and have established a wide range of governmental programs to transfer financial and technological resources to the LDCs. The United Nations concentrates a major share of its activities on development assistance. The World Bank has become a major multilateral source of development assistance. Many regional development banks such as the Asian Development Bank and the Inter-American Development Bank have also been created as multilateral agencies to support the development efforts of the poor countries.

The specific content and the size of bilateral and multilateral development-assistance programs change as a result of political forces and experience. Yet their importance to the international enterprise should continue. Development-assistance programs can play a key role in determining future economic trends in specific countries and can also be a source of financial resources and other types of support for a wide range of international business projects. The development role that can be played by international enterprise has been well recognized. Thus many development-assistance programs have included specific incentives to encourage the expansion of international business activities, and considerable attention has been devoted to finding ways to expand the flow of foreign private investment that are acceptable to the host countries.

MARKET DEMAND FORECASTING

Collecting the basic demand data

After screening the global horizon and making a preliminary identification of countries that appear to have attractive economic situations, the globally oriented firm will want to examine the market-demand prospects for its products in countries that appear promising. In large part, market-demand forecasting requires the same skills and techniques whether it is directed to domestic markets or foreign markets.[21] But there are differences.

Variations among countries in the availability and quality of the needed data may require less-familiar and less-sophisticated techniques than are customary for domestic market research. The multinational enterprise with a global strategy will want the market-demand studies for different countries to be sufficiently standardized so that cross-country comparisons can be made. From the standpoint of cost, relatively inexpensive techniques may be needed so that a large number of potentially

---

[21] For a standard reference on market forecasting, see Spyros Makridakis and Steven C. Wheelwright, *Forecasting: Methods and Applications* (Santa Barbara Calif.: John Wiley & Sons, 1978).

interesting market opportunities can be appraised. Another difference may be in the time period used for international as against domestic market-demand forecasts. Longer-range forecasts may be needed where foreign opportunities involve initiating new operations and require a large commitment of resources, and where a high degree of risk is perceived because of limited familiarity with operations in a new country.

The American firm "going international" may have to make an especially large adjustment in its market-demand forecasting activity. Not only is the United States outstanding in the availability of data from government, trade associations, and other sources, but it has also accumulated an impressive stock of market research studies, market research organizations, and skilled personnel. Furthermore, the flowering of market research in the United States has been aided by a cultural variable that favors considerable openness concerning economic and business information as contrasted to the attitudes of secrecy prevailing in many other countries.

The first place to look for international demand data, therefore, is within the United States. Commercial sources may already have data available. Business International, Frost and Sullivan, and Predicasts are organizations with an extensive library of international market surveys. The U.S. Department of Commerce also makes available a wide range of market surveys prepared on a contract basis by private research organizations or by Commerce Department market research officers abroad.[22]

The market demand for many products and services results directly or indirectly from governmental programs to expand infrastructure facilities and services such as transportation, electricity, education, housing, and health. In such areas a considerable amount of national government planning work is likely to be available. From these data, the business firm can obtain excellent guidelines to future market demand. Where the less-developed countries are soliciting international financing from agencies like the World Bank, market studies must normally be prepared as a component of the project proposal submitted for financing.

The types of planning studies usually undertaken for planning future infrastructure needs vary greatly among the particular fields. In the case of electric power, future needs are derived from growth targets for the total economy and the planned expansion of specific types of industrial and other productive activity. Such planning studies have a high probability of being implemented. Electric-power projects are revenue producing, and thus can provide some of their financing. Electric power must also be available in order that other growth targets can be reached. In the case of housing, education, and health, the implementation of official plans is likely to be more uncertain because social-welfare plans are

---

[22] U.S. Department of Commerce, *Publications for American Business* (Washington, D.C.: U.S. Government Printing Office, 1975).

generally limited by the future availability of government revenues. For political and welfare reasons, governments frequently establish ambitious targets in these fields that may not be realistic.

In many countries, particularly the less-developed nations, data problems, however, will arise. First, actual sales data may not be available. Second, data may not be available on some of the important variables that influence future demand, with the consequence that forecasts will have to be based on fewer variables than would be desired. Third, some or all of the bare minimum of data required are not available for the country being studied, so data and relationships used for forecasting will have to be based on the experience in other countries.

Where actual sales are not available for a country, trade and production data may be used as a proxy for market-demand patterns. These data are relatively easy to secure from national and international publications. Through the adoption of a uniform tariff classification by many countries, the comparability of trade data among countries has been improved. The United Nations now publishes import-export data in great detail for most countries.[23] Market demand, also called *apparent consumption*, is estimated by combining local production and imports, and then making adjustments for exports and fluctuations in inventory levels.

A major problem in relying on published statistics is the time lag before publication. Another complication is that inventory data generally are not available in countries with underdeveloped statistical systems. One way to compensate for short-term inventory and other fluctuations is to use longer time periods and calculate an annual average or a moving average. The disadvantage of this adjustment is that the estimate may not indicate current sales rates.

Extrapolating past demand patterns

Forecasts of future market demand can be made by extrapolating historical patterns of actual or apparent consumption. Where imports supply a large share of local market demand, an extrapolation of historical apparent consumption may, however, understate future demand if imports have been controlled. Furthermore, when local production replaces imports, domestic demand may increase faster than suggested by import trends, merely because local facilities can provide quicker and more flexible service to customers.

The appropriate projection pattern must also be decided. A straight extrapolation is most valid for a short time period and for a relatively mature economy. But it assumes that future trends will follow the patterns of the historical past. This assumption is precarious for a low-

---

[23] United Nations, *Yearbook of International Trade Statistics.*

income country that is expanding rapidly and undergoing structural changes.

One basis for modifying extrapolations may be the industrial growth patterns already experienced by other countries of the world. The typical patterns of growth in manufacturing industries based on trends in 7 to 10 countries are shown in Figure 14–1. Within the manufacturing sector, the

Figure 14–1

Typical patterns of growth in manufacturing industries*

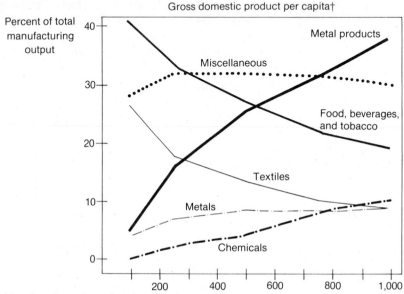

* Based on time-series analysis for selected years, 1899–1957.

† Dollars at 1955 prices.

Source: Alfred Maizels, *Industrial Growth and World Trade* (Cambridge, England: Cambridge University Press, 1963), p. 55.

chart relates the percentage of total manufacturing production accounted for by major industrial groups to gross domestic product per capita. The typical patterns do not necessarily describe the actual pattern that any given country will follow. Yet they suggest that the share of income spent on textiles, as one example, should be extrapolated at a declining rather than a constant rate, whereas the demand for metal products can be expected to increase at a rate faster than gains in per capita GDP.

Forecasting with income elasticities

In many situations, market-demand forecasting can be partially or wholly based on income elasticities. The concept of income elasticity measures the relationship between the change in demand for a product and changes in income.

Symbolically, the formula below measures the income elasticity for commodity A where Q represents the quantity demanded, Y is the income, and Δ refers to quantity changes.

$$\frac{\dfrac{\Delta Q_A}{Q_A}}{\dfrac{\Delta Y}{Y}}$$

If demand increases at the same rate as income, a product would have an income elasticity of one. If demand increases only half as fast as income, the income elasticity of a product would be 0.5. Goods with values of more than one are income elastic. Goods with values of less than one are income inelastic. Income elasticities have been calculated for individual or family incomes and separately for various levels of income. Where detailed data on family and personal income distribution are not available, as in many LDCs, income elasticities have been calculated for a country as a whole in relation to average per capita income for the country. In the absence of better market information, the latter form of income elasticities can be a reasonably satisfactory approach to market-demand forecasting.

Market-demand forecasting by the income-elasticities method requires four steps. First, current levels of demand are determined. Second, average per capita income is forecast for the selected future period. Third, income elasticities are determined either from a country's own historical experience or from the experience of other countries. Finally, future market demand is estimated as current demand times a factor derived by multiplying the projected increase in per capita income and the income elasticity for the commodity. If per capita income is expected to increase by 50 percent in the forecast period and the income elasticity of the product is 1.5, total demand should increase by 75 percent.

Income elasticities are widely used by economic planners for establishing development targets for a country. Consequently, a considerable amount of information has been developed on income elasticities.[24] In general, the empirical information follows the patterns suggested by Engel's law. The income elasticities for food and other necessities are generally less than one and for luxury goods more than one. The results of several income-elasticity studies that cover both consumer and industrial products and some services are shown in Table 14–4. The data are averages and may not apply equally to all income groups. Also note the differences that can result by calculating the elasticities through cross-

---

[24] See United Nations, *Industrialization and Productivity*, Bulletin 9, "Analysis and Projections of Consumption Demand: Methodological Notes" (New York, 1965), pp. 49–81.

Table 14–4

Income-elasticity measurements

Commodity	Cross-section	Time series
Food and beverage, excluding alcoholic beverages	0.54,† 0.53‡	0.8*
Alcoholic beverages	0.77†	—
Tobacco	0.88†	—
Clothing	0.8,* 0.9,*	0.7,* 0.8*
	0.84,† 0.89*	
Textiles	0.5*	0.8*
Household and personal services	1.19†	—
Communication services	2.03†	—
Recreation	1.15†	—
Health	1.80†	—
Durable consumer goods	—	2.7*
Furniture	1.61‡	—
Appliances	1.40‡	—
Metals	1.52‡	—
Chemicals	—	2.1*
Machinery and transportation equipment, except passenger cars	—	1.5–2.0*

* Source is Meritt L. Kastens, "Organizing, Planning, and Staffing Market Research Activities in an International Corporation," *Market Research in International Operations*, Management Report no. 53 (New York: American Management Association, 1960), p. 42.

† Source is Milton Gilbert and Associates. *Comparative National Products and Price Levels* (Paris: OECD, 1958), p. 66.

‡ From author's calculations.

Source: Reed Moyer, "International Market Analysis," *Journal of Marketing Research*, November 1968, table 2.5, p. 356.

sectional analysis—comparing a number of countries at different levels of income for the same time period, and through times series—comparing patterns over time for the same country.

Several cautions in the use of income elasticities should be noted. High-income elasticity for a product does not necessarily mean a high-volume market. It merely indicates that demand will increase rapidly as incomes rise. In terms of volume, the large markets in most countries will be in necessities, even though the growth in these markets may be relatively slow. Furthermore, income elasticities indicate a constant relationship between demand changes and income changes. For specific products, such as consumer durables, the demand is likely to increase at an increasing rate after income reaches a certain level.

Prices also affect the elasticities in several ways. If prices in a country for the products of a new industry are relatively high, and if such prices fall as the industries become more mature, demand for such products will increase from a combination of price and income factors. As between countries, prices can vary greatly because of taxes, subsidies, and other factors. Such differences must be taken into account in using income elasticities. Thus, income elasticities are useful guides but no perfect substitutes for specific market research.

Estimating by analogy

Patterns of demand in more-advanced countries can be used to estimate future market demand in later-developing economies. This approach assumes that product usage moves along a standard path as a
country's stage of development advances. The use of cross-sectional income elasticities to forecast demand is an example of estimation by
analogy in this way.

Careful grouping of countries by similar characteristics can provide a
basis for more refined comparison than simply grading countries by
stage of development as indicated by their GNP per capita. Groupings can
be arrived at easily by classifying countries that are reasonably similar
over a range of specific characteristics—for example, dependence on
agriculture, degree of urbanization, or level of education. Alternatively,
the groupings could be arrived at more formally using cluster analysis.[25]

Blind reliance on analogy, however, can result in erroneous estimates.
Differences in culture, tastes, and habits that dictate consumption patterns may limit the validity of analogies. Technical advances such as new
inventions or substitute products may cause future patterns of consumption in late-developing countries to change sharply from the patterns of
presently advanced countries. Price differences among countries—because of import tariffs, for example—can also cause errors. Nevertheless,
used with caution, the method can be extremely useful where data are
limited.

Regression analysis

Regression analysis can be a powerful tool in forecasting market demand, especially for countries where data on current demand are scarce.
Also, where estimates are made by income elasticities or by analogy,
regression analysis provides a basis for checking the reasonableness of
estimates.

Regression analysis is simply a statistical technique for determining
the relationship between two or more variables. A regression equation
can express the quantitative relationship between the demand for a specific product and a gross economic indicator. This relationship can be
determined for *country B*, or a number of countries, and then applied to
country A in which the firm is interested, even though information on
current market demand for the product is not available in *country A*. In
such a case, the market-demand estimate is based on both regression

---

[25] See, for example, S. Prakash Sethi, "Comparative Cluster Analysis for World Markets,"
Journal of Marketing Research, August 1971, pp. 348–54; S. Prakash Sethi and Richard H.
Holton, "Country Typologies for the Multinational Corporation: A New Basic Approach,"
California Management Review, Spring 1973, pp. 105–18; and A. Coskun Samli, "An Approach
for Estimating Market Potential in East Europe," *Journal of International Business Studies* 8
(Fall–Winter 1977); pp. 49–53.

analysis and analogy, as the relationship discovered for other countries is assumed to be applicable for the country in which the business firm is interested. Regression analysis can also be used when data on current consumption are available for *country A* to compare market-demand patterns in *country A* with the experience in other countries so that future forecasts can be verified or modified.

Some regression results that relate the consumption of various commodities to a gross economic indicator are summarized in Table 14–5. A

Table 14–5

Regression of consumption on gross national product (various products)

Product	Number of observations	Regression equation	Unadjusted R^2
Autos	37	$-21.071 + 0.101x$	0.759
Radio sets	42	$8.325 + 0.275x$	0.784
TV sets	31	$-16.501 + 0.074x$	0.503
Refrigerators	24	$-21.330 + 0.102x$	0.743
Washing machines	22	$-15.623 + 0.094x$	0.736

Source: Reed Moyer, "International Market Analysis," *Journal of Marketing Research* 4, no. 5 (November 1968); based on United Nations, *Statistical Yearbook*, 1962; Alfred Maizels, *Industrial Growth and World Trade* (Cambridge, Eng.: Cambridge University Press, 1963), pp. 308–9.

linear regression model ($y = a + bx$) was used with y as the amount of a product in use per thousand of population and x as per capita GNP. The equations explain from 50 to 78 percent of the variation in the dependent variable as shown by R^2. Actually these regression results are an example of using a proxy for demand data, because they are based on the amount of each product in use per capita rather than on sales.

The regression results in Table 14–5 show that an increase of $100 in per capita GNP will result, on the average, in an increase of 10 automobiles, 10 refrigerators, 9 washing machines, 7 television sets, and 27 radio sets per 1,000 population. This, however, is a very simple way of predicting demand for consumer durables. More-advanced predictions that allow for saturation of the market, life of the product, and replacement rates are common.

More-complex multiple regression models use more variables as the basis of prediction. Such a model for forecasting world sales of cameras has been built, using variables that include total population, proportion between ages 15 and 64, literacy rates, nonagricultural employment, living standards, adults per household, and rainfall.[26]

The data-collection task for developing and for using more-complex regression models is substantial. The selection of the minimum number

[26] J. Scott Armstrong, "An Application of Econometric Methods to International Marketing," *Journal of Marketing Research* 7 (May 1970), pp. 190–98.

of variables to include in the model requires considerable testing and judgment. For many firms, however, the cost of a solidly developed quantitative estimate of the potential in each market is justified by the need for long-range commitments to expensive production facilities. Detailed forecasts can have the additional benefit of producing information that can be used for guiding marketing and other operations once a project is established in the country being studied.

Input-output forecasting

Input-output tables can also be used for market-demand forecasting, particularly for industrial products where much of the demand will be derived from the growth of other industries.[27] Input-output tables have been published for many of the developed countries, such as the United States, Japan, and the Netherlands, and for a large number of underdeveloped countries. An interindustry model used for Japanese sectoral planning divided the total economy into 60 productive sectors, resulting in what is called a 60 by 60 matrix. However, many of the tables break down the entire economy into only a small number of broad industry groups and cannot provide much detail on specific products.

Conceptually, input-output tables recognize the interrelationships of each sector in an economy to all others (see Table 14–6). The total output of one sector reading across the rows in the transaction table—for example, agriculture—becomes the input of all sectors (including the agricultural sector itself). At the same time, reading down each column, each sector receives its inputs from the other sectors. The input and output relationships of each sector, including households and foreign trade, to all the others are quantitatively expressed by coefficients.

Where input-output tables are sufficiently detailed, one can trace the direct and indirect impact on the demand for one product of changes in demand for the products of other industries. The tables can show the extent to which sales are made to final users or consumed as intermediate goods. Also, input-output tables can provide information on the number of sectors that are users of the products from another sector.

Input-output analysis has its limitations. A tremendous amount of data and analysis is required to construct tables that can provide detailed industry or product information. Data limitations and the lack of resources have often resulted in tables that are too general or too incomplete to be of great value for specific market-demand forecasting. Also, input-output tables normally use fixed technical coefficients. This means that the effects of changes in production processes or in production

---

[27] Jack G. Faucett, "Input-Output Analysis as a Tool of International Market Research," *Market Research in International Operations,* Management Report no. 53 (New York: American Management Association, 1960), pp. 41–59: Roger K. Chisholm and Gilbert R. Whitaker, Jr., *Forecasting Methods* (Homewood, Ill.: Richard D. Irwin, 1971), pp. 62–95.

Table 14–6

Input-output tables: A simplified illustration

Country A—transactions, 1960

	Agriculture	Food processing	Coal	Electric energy	Plastic products	Apparel	Consumer expenditures	Government operations	Exports	Investment	Total final demand	Total output
Agriculture	25	50	—	—	—	—	100	—	50	—	150	200
Food processing	—	10	—	50	40	5	150	—	25	—	175	200
Coal	—	30	5	—	25	5	15	5	—	5	25	100
Electric energy	10	10	—	5	—	5	35	10	—	30	75	150
Plastic products	—	10	—	5	—	—	10	—	220	—	230	250
Apparel	—	—	—	—	—	—	50	—	150	—	200	200
Wages and salaries	80	50	40	30	100	70	—	20	—	100	120	490
Imports (total)	35	20	15	25	40	75	150	10	—	175	335	545
Agricultural chemicals	20	—	—	—	—	—	5	—	—	15	—	—
Paint and varnishes	5	—	—	5	10	—	15	—	—	—	—	—
Textiles	5	—	5	5	—	60	—	—	—	10	—	—
Iron castings	—	—	10	5	—	—	—	—	—	150	—	—
Other	—	20	10	15	30	15	130	10	—	50	—	—
Profits, interest, depreciation, taxes	50	30	40	40	75	40	—	—	—	50	50	325
Total output	200	200	100	150	250	200	510	45	445	360	1,360	2,460

Country A—Production coefficients, 1960

	Agriculture	Food processing	Coal	Electric energy	Plastic products	Apparel
Agriculture	—	0.250	—	—	—	—
Food processing	0.125	0.050	—	0.333	0.250	0.025
Coal	—	—	0.050	—	—	0.025
Electric energy	0.050	0.050	—	0.033	0.050	0.025
Plastic products	—	0.050	—	—	—	—
Apparel	—	—	—	—	—	—
Wages and salaries	0.400	0.250	0.400	0.200	0.400	0.350
Imports (total)	0.175	0.100	0.150	0.167	0.160	0.375
Agricultural chemicals	0.100	—	—	—	—	—
Paints and varnishes	0.025	—	—	0.033	0.040	—
Textiles	0.025	—	—	—	—	0.300
Iron castings	0.025	—	—	—	—	—
Other	0.025	0.100	0.100	0.100	0.120	0.075
Profits, interest, depreciation taxes	0.250	0.150	0.400	0.267	0.300	0.200
Total output	1.000	1.000	1.000	1.000	1.000	1.000

Source: Reprinted by permission of the publishers from AMA Management Report no. 53, Market Research in International Operations, © 1960 by the American Management Association, Inc.

levels are not taken into account by forecasts based on the tables. There could be a variety of other dynamic changes, too.

SUMMARY

International firms require assessments and forecasts of individual economies and their market demands for a variety of reasons and with varying requirements for precision and comparability. All the conventional limitations of forecasting the future that exist in domestic economic forecasting carry over to the task of forecasting the economic dimensions of the international business environment. In addition, the great variations in national patterns plus the influence of the inter-nation economic framework make the task more complex and difficult.

The forecasting of structural changes can be of major significance for a specific type of international business activity. This may require the forecasting of differential growth sales for different sectors of the economy. As the economic structure of national economies is certain to change with economic growth, an extrapolation of past trends would be almost certain to give misleading forecasts for the future. Analogies with other countries at a higher stage of development are one basis for such structural forecasting.

To the extent that national economies and markets are dependent upon external economic considerations—foreign markets or inflows of private investment or external development assistance—the economic forecasts will have to examine carefully such external forces and external future prospects.

In a growing number of countries, government planning reports or available market research studies can supply the international firm with sufficient information on which it can decide whether or not it will undertake a detailed business opportunity analysis for the country. In other situations, particularly in the less-developed countries, the firm will need to make its own market-demand studies, using techniques that are not too costly and that can produce reasonable results where the availability of data is limited.

A number of such techniques have been suggested. In general, they make use of analogies and methods that relate the market demand for a product to one or more general economic or demographic indicators. As a subsequent step, in-depth field surveys will be required to examine the competitive and operating environment that the international firm will encounter in the promising markets.

EXERCISES AND DISCUSSION QUESTIONS

1. As an exercise in macroeconomic scanning, rank the first five African nations with a population of 1 million or more in terms of the total size of their

economy. In terms of growth rates in per capita GNP, what are the five fastest growing Asian economies with a population of 1 million or more?

2. According to the normal pattern, what would you expect industry's contribution to total GNP to be in France, Malaysia, and Brazil? How do these expected patterns compare with the actual structure?

3. Would you have considered establishing operations in a country like Brazil, experiencing annual rates of inflation over 40 percent from 1976 to 1980? Why or why not? (Note that real GNP expanded at an average rate of 7 percent over this period.) If inflation were dramatically reduced along with growth and employment, would this make Brazil more attractive?

4. "A country may have a trade surplus, but still have an increasingly serious balance-of-payments deficit because of capital outflows or rising remittances. Careful assessment must be made of short-term versus long-term outflows." Discuss.

5. "Whatever the causes, rapid increases in prices mean a currency is depreciating internally—and an external depreciation may become necessary." Discuss. Under what circumstances would domestic inflation *not* lead to devaluation?

6. Compile a list of sources of economic and market data for a specified African nation other than South Africa.

7. Country A's GNP rose from $6 billion by a further $550 million during 1980 and its steel consumption, all imported, rose by 400,000 tons to 3.8 million tons. Population also increased from 10 million to 10.4 million. What is the income elasticity of demand for steel? Do you think this would provide a very accurate indicator for predicting steel usage over the ensuing five years?

8. Select a less-developed country and for either textiles or metal manufactures determine the forecasting methods you think would have been most appropriate for forecasting demand at each of two dates within the last 20 years, separated by at least five years.

9. "It may be true that all European countries are travelling the same road towards what has been called 'salvation through industrialization' and it may be possible, therefore, to forecast some of the probable changes in living habits as the process continues. Even so, there are still great differences between one place and another, between one nation and another, and in the rates at which they change. These differences reveal themselves in a great diversity of what people will buy. Economic development is certainly affecting culture and customs, habits and attitudes, traditions and mentality; but these, in turn, are reacting on what is going on in the economy—in production, consumption, and distribution. You may detect the general trend; but look around Western Europe and you will discover all sorts of subtle variations in the speed and character of the change. Here the emancipation of women may be moving more slowly. There peasant and aristocratic attitudes may persist."

In the light of this extract, what types of products would you expect to follow dissimilar demand patterns over time in European countries? Of these, would you expect a country's past demand to provide a better basis for predicting demand than analogies with other countries at a more advanced stage?

10. Give your own definition of the market saturation point for a consumer durable, such as washing machines, and explain why the level may vary from country to country.

11. "Comparison of either total demand or per capita demand for different countries may be misleading for the purposes of formulating a global strategy, particularly if major variations occur within countries." Elaborate on this statement and suggest how the problem might be overcome.

12. You would expect to find some relationship between a country's demand for medical drugs and the numbers of doctors and hospital beds in the country. What other indicators might be used for forecasting the level of drug purchases? As the basis for a global marketing plan how would you go about predicting a country's spending on drugs five years hence?

13. Explain how demand for the ouput of a primary industry might be forecast using an input-output table. What are the limitations in the input-output method?

Chapter 15

Assessing political risk and national controls

As firms expand internationally, they must deal with the fragmenting influence of a large number of different political environments. The most cataclysmic political events affecting business operations have become referred to as political risks. But these are only the tip of the iceberg. Beneath the surface, less dramatic changes take place in day-to-day political and administrative policies and practices that even more frequently affect the viability of multinational operations and the achievement of corporate objectives. The dividing line between discontinuities and continuous change is difficult to mark precisely, yet there is enough difference in the political forces at play and the business response to warrant examining the two phenomena separately. The potential cost of both types of event must be assessed for each country incorporated in a firm's global strategy.

Political risk has long been a familiar term in the lexicon of international business, but political-risk assessment has only recently emerged as an established managerial function in international firms. A survey of U.S. firms made in the mid-1960s found no evidence of a systematic approach to political-risk assessment.[1] In contrast, a 1980 survey revealed that over half of the companies contacted had taken some steps toward formal assignment for the function and over one third had established political assessment units.[2] Numerous consulting firms have also sprung up to provide both general political risk summaries and studies of specific projects. The recent surge of interest began with the unexpected fall of the Shah's regime in Iran (1979–80) and was reinforced by the overthrow of apparently secure regimes in Nicaragua and South Korea during the same period.

POLITICAL-RISK ASSESSMENT

Some general observations

A pervasive factor. The mention of political risk is most likely to bring to mind the notion of unstable, less-developed countries, bearded revolutionary leaders, and threats of expropriation. But political risk is a more pervasive influence, both geographically and in the ways it affects international enterprises. Political risk arises in host countries that are industrialized, such as France and Canada, as well as in the LDCs. It can also arise in the home countries of investors like Sweden and the United States.

The 1980 election of Mitterand in France brought a radical change in the French business environment with the adoption of a policy to nationalize a number of major industries, including ones involving foreign investors. In the same year, Canada sharply reversed its traditional welcome for foreign investment in the area of petroleum by adopting a new energy policy intended to reduce foreign participation in this field from 75 to 50 percent.

Home-country political risks have emerged in the form of political boycotts in the United States against national firms doing business in South Africa and with Soviet-bloc countries. In Sweden, domestic political forces were responsible for legislation prohibiting Swedish firms from

---

[1] Franklin Root, "U.S. Business Abroad and Political Risks," *MSU Business Topics*, Winter 1968, pp. 73–80.

[2] Stephen Blank et al., *Assessing the Political Environment: An Emerging Function in International Companies* (New York: The Conference Board, 1980); see also Stephen J. Kobrin, *Environmental Assessment in the International Firm: Politics as a Problem of Managerial Process* (Berkeley: University of California Press, 1982).

investing in South Africa and Namibia (South-West Africa) and requiring them to cut back existing operations there.[3]

Gains as well as losses.   Political risk usually connotes the possibility of losses. Yet, as in the case of other types of risk, political risk can result in gains as well as losses. For example, dramatic political changes that improved the business environment for foreign firms occurred in the 1970s in the People's Republic of China. And the overthrow of the Allende government in Chile (1973) resulted in a return of expropriated foreign investments.

The need for continuing assessments.   Political assessments should serve management in two phases of decision making. Political assessments are needed in preinvestment decisions where political-risk assessments are integrated with parallel studies of marketing, production, logistics, and finance. They are also needed on a continuing basis to guide, protect, and nurture already established operations.

Country or sovereign risk.   Country or sovereign risk should be differentiated from political risk although the two are clearly related. Sovereign risk is a principal concern of financial institutions making loans in foreign countries.[4] It refers to the risk that countries will have the capacity to meet foreign debt obligations and has to do with a country's external liquidity. In contrast, political risk is a much broader concept and extends to changes in a country's environment that affect the operations of a foreign firm within the country.

Defining political risk

Political-risk assessment for international business operations must start with a precise and operational definition. Although there is no general agreement on how to define political risk,[5] the following definition has become widely accepted. *Political risk is the likelihood that political forces will cause drastic changes in a country's business environment that affect the profit and other goals of a particular business enterprise.* Thus, political risk includes four necessary elements:

1.   Discontinuities—drastic changes in the business environment.
2.   Uncertainty—changes that are difficult to anticipate.

---

[3] *Business Week*, June 20, 1977, p. 44.

[4] For further information on country risk, see Ingo Walter, *International Capital Allocations: Country Risk, Portfolio Decisions and Regulations in International Banking* (New York: Graduate School of Business, New York University, 1980); and David Gisselquist, *The Political Economics of International Bank Lending* (New York: Praeger Publishers, 1981).

[5] For a summary of different political risk definitions see Stephen J. Kobrin, "Political Risk: A Review and Reconsideration," *Journal of International Business Studies,* Spring/Summer 1979, pp. 67–70.

3. Political forces—defined as power and authority relationships in the context of society at large.[6]
4. Business impact—potential for affecting significantly the profit or other goals of a particular business enterprise.

Political risk, therefore, focuses on discontinuities in the business environment. National-control forecasting, to be discussed below, focuses on changes in the business environment that reflect continuity in government policies and political forces and that can be anticipated with greater certainty. Tax laws, for example, are constantly changing. But most of the changes do not represent a radical departure from past trends and are not too difficult to anticipate.

Political risk and political instability are separate though related phenomena. Instability is a property of the environment. Risk is a measure of how that instability might affect the business enterprise. It follows that political fluctuations that do not affect the operating conditions for the firm do not represent political risk for international business. Furthermore, political risk is firm-specific. What is political risk for one firm may not be political risk for another.

Political scientists have done considerable research on the subject of political instability, and a number of empirical studies have attempted to analyze the relationship between selected indicators of political instability and foreign direct investment.[7] Although methodological problems cloud the results, it is clear from the studies that political instability is neither a necessary nor a sufficient condition for policy changes relevant to foreign enterprise. Discontinuities that affect international business can occur with or without major changes in political leadership. Conversely, major changes in political leadership can occur without greatly affecting the business environment.

Political and economic risk should be differentiated wherever possible because they have different sources and may require different managerial responses. Government decisions are always political—by definition. Yet the forces dictating the decisions may be purely economic. For example, political-risk insurance offered by the U.S. government for foreign investments includes currency inconvertibility as a political risk. Yet currency inconvertibility can occur for predominantly economic reasons in politically stable nations and at times when political systems and political leadership are not changing.

In the case of currency inconvertibility, however, political rather than economic forces may be the dominant factors, or there may be an intermingling of political and economic motivations. Political uncertainties in

---

[6] See David Easton, *The Political System* (New York: Alfred A. Knopf, 1968).

[7] See David A. Jodice, "Sources of Change in Third World Regimes for Foreign Direct Investment, 1968–76," *International Organization* 34 (Spring 1980), pp. 193–98; Stephen J. Kobrin, "The Environmental Determinants of Foreign Direct Manufacturing Investment: An Ex Post Empirical Analysis," *Journal of International Business Studies*, Fall–Winter 1976.

some nations have stimulated large outflows of flight capital, which in turn caused a balance-of-payments crisis. Or internal political forces in opposition to foreign enterprise have compelled governments to limit the repatriation of profits and other financial transfers by foreign firms. An example of the intermingling of forces is the general strike that occurred in Tunis during 1978 that began as an economic event—a protest against wage restraint—and ended as a full challenge to the Bourguiba government. But even where considerable intermingling exists, the international firm may get useful results by trying to separate the political factors from the others.

Macro political risk.   The international business enterprise may encounter both macro and micro types of political risk. Macro risk occurs when *all* foreign enterprises are affected in much the same way by politically motivated discontinuities in the business environment. Micro risk occurs when the changes affect only selected industries, firms, or even projects.

Macro risk can be indirect and spasmodic. At times of political turmoil, foreign companies and foreign management personnel are tempting targets for political factions opposed to the regime in power. An example of the indirect type of macro political risk was the wave of kidnappings of foreign executives by terrorist groups that occurred in the 1970s (see Box 15–1).

Box 15–1

The political risk of executive-napping

In Argentina, bodyguards are an accepted part of the business scene, thanks to the urban guerrillas and nonideological gangsters who have seized on executive-napping to make a political point or to turn a peso. Over the last year, guerrillas have seized at least six executives of foreign firms and extracted ransoms ranging from $750,000 (paid by the First National Bank of Boston for the release of a branch manager) to $1.8 million (the amount paid by the British-American Tobacco Co. for the release of its Argentine board chairman).

Experts estimate that the ransom total so far in 1973 is more than $5 million and adds up to $20 million for the past two years. Ford Motor Co., which was forced last month to hand over $1 million in cash, ambulances, food, and books to the People's Revolutionary Army (ERP) in order to spare its local chief executive, claims that it was the 26th American firm to meet either ransom or extortion demands in Argentina.

Executive kidnapping is not confined to Argentina. Mexico, Venezuela, and Colombia, among other countries, have been the scenes of similar incidents, and snatching businessmen for profit has been thriving in Sicily, Sardinia, and southern Italy for centuries.

Source: Adapted from *Newsweek*, June 11, 1973, p. 9.3

Direct and relatively permanent macro risk can be illustrated by the takeover of private enterprise in 1959–60 by the Castro government in Cuba. Foreign enterprises were seized along with domestic firms. In part, the broad-sweep confiscation of foreign investment was explained by a basic change in political philosophy brought about by the Cuban revolution—a shift from a market to a socialist economy. Also, the large size of the foreign-owned sector of the economy and the domination by foreign firms of several strategic fields[8] of business activity supported pressures to end the "economic colonial" status of the country.

The Cuban case is not an isolated example of macro risk. In recent years, international enterprises have felt the impact of broadside actions—frequently along with domestic private enterprises—in Algeria, Burma, Chile, Egypt, Ghana, Indonesia, Uganda, and Libya. These are in addition to the communist expropriations in Eastern Europe and China following World War II. More recently, however, the incidence of macro-risk situations appears to be declining. A study of expropriations in 76 LDCs over the years 1960–76 concluded that ideologically motivated mass expropriation actually occurred in less than 10 of the countries.[9]

Macro-risk situations can also result from broad action taken against foreign enterprise as a political boycott. In the Middle East, various Arab countries began in 1955 to boycott companies that had branches in Israel or allowed use of their trade name there. Direct trade with Israel was ignored. But any permanent investment in that country, or any long-term agreements such as licensing arrangements or technical assistance, earned the company a place on the blacklist. The implementation of such policies, however, has been sporadic.

Micro risk.   Macro political risk is dramatic. Micro political risk is more prevalent. With considerable frequency, the international manager is likely to encounter abrupt and politically motivated changes in the business environment that are selectively directed toward specific industries, firms, or projects. In technical jargon, micro risk is industry, firm, or project specific. The types of business operations with a high vulnerability to micro risk will vary from nation to nation and over time in the same nation. And vulnerability may vary with the product or service, level of technology, ownership structure, or management style.

At a particular point in time and for a specific country, it should be possible to rank types of business activities according to their degree of political risk vulnerability. Such rankings, however, keep changing. A few decades ago, public utility investments were popular with both host

---

[8] See Leland L. Johnson, *U.S. Private Investment in Latin America: Some Questions of National Policy*, Memorandum RM-4092 ISA (Santa Monica, Calif.: Rand Corporation, July 1964).

[9] Stephen J. Kobrin, "Foreign Enterprise and Forced Divestment in LDCs," *International Organization*, Winter 1980.

countries and investors. More recently, worldwide trends have been toward domestic—usually government—ownership of electricity, transportation, and communications enterprises because of national security
and developmental goals. As a result, most of such enterprises owned by
foreigners have been nationalized and international firms have not been
active in these fields.

In a current ranking of industry vulnerability, technologically dynamic
industries dependent upon a continuing import of new technology from
abroad would have a low degree of political risk. In contrast, natural
resources projects and financial institutions have a high degree of political-risk vulnerability. Petroleum and mining projects in particular are
frequently endangered by growing nationalistic feelings and a conviction
that natural resource endowments should be developed for the welfare
of all people in a nation rather than for private profit. Financial institutions are vulnerable because of "their pervasiveness and their potential as
bases for influence and control."[10]

Two factors can change the political-risk vulnerability of an industry
over time. One is the dominance of foreign enterprise in a major industry
sector. The second is the capacity of nationals to operate a business
successfully. Vulnerability from industry dominance is illustrated by the
previously mentioned case of Canada's 1980 policy reversal intended to
reduce foreign ownership in its petroleum industry from 75 to 50 percent.

The second factor—local operating capability—has a somewhat
ironic aspect. At an early stage in a nation's development, foreign enterprises may be welcomed because they provide scarce capital, management know-how, and technical skills not available locally. Over time,
countries manage to accumulate capital and local managerial and technical skills as a result of the successful operations of the foreign enterprise. To the extent that local personnel have been trained for copper
mining, running a tea plantation, or managing other types of businesses
initiated by foreign firms, the political pressures for curtailing foreign
enterprises are likely to increase.

Sources of political risk

What are the sources of political risk? The conceptual framework presented in Figure 15–1 suggests the major underlying political forces that
can cause abrupt policy changes. The framework also indicates the
groups or political actors through which political risk can be generated,
and the political-risk effects on international business operations. It
should be noted that some of the specific effects shown in the far right

---

[10] *Foreign Ownership and the Structure of Canadian Industry: Report of the Task Force on
the Structure of Canadian Industry* (Ottawa, Canada: Information Canada, 1970), p. 389.

Figure 15–1

Political risk: A conceptual framework

Sources of political risk	Groups through which political risk can be generated	Political-risk effects: Types of influence on international business operations
Competing political philosophies (nationalism, socialism, communism)	Government in power and its operating agencies	Confiscation: loss of assets without compensation
Social unrest and disorder	Parliamentary opposition groups	Expropriation with compensation: loss of freedom to operate
Vested interests of local business groups	Nonparliamentary opposition groups (e.g., anarchist or terrorist movements working from within or outside of country)	Operational restrictions: market shares, product characteristics, employment policies, locally shared ownership, and so forth
Recent and impending political independence	Nonorganized common interest groups: students, workers, peasants, minorities, and so forth	Loss of transfer freedom: financial (for example, dividends, interest payments), goods, personnel, or ownership rights
Armed conflicts, internal rebellions for political power, and terrorism	Foreign governments or intergovernmental agencies such as the EEC	Breaches or unilateral revisions in contracts and agreements
New international alliances	Foreign governments willing to enter into armed conflict or to support internal rebellion	Discrimination such as taxes, compulsory subcontracting
		Damage to property or personnel (kidnapping) from riots, insurrections, revolutions, wars, and terrorism

column are not exclusively associated with political discontinuities. For example, pressure for local sharing of ownership can òccur in relatively stable political situations. Also, the loss of financial transfer freedom may result from economic rather than political forces.

The six general sources of political risk shown in Figure 15–1 are of particular importance to international business. The most frequently encountered risk arises from political forces hostile toward foreign enterprise for philosophical reasons that diverge sharply from prevailing government policies. Others are social unrest and disorder, the private vested interests of local business groups, recent or impending independence, new international alliances, and armed conflicts or terrorism. Less predictable, and political only in the sense that it is a tool of politicians, is the exposure of corruption or scandal. It is often linked to a government official who might well have provided influence for a foreign firm.

Latent hostility. Some latent hostility to foreign enterprises is present in most nations, including the United States. The potential strength of such hostile forces affects the degree of political risk. The avenues available for making such political strength effective in changing government policies are numerous. The basic form of government can be changed, as happened in Cuba. The leadership of government can change but the political system remains the same, as happened when Mitterrand succeeded Giscard d'Estaing in France. Or concessions can be exacted from the political parties and leaders in power without changes in the form or leadership of the existing government.

A drastic change in policy without a change in political leadership can be illustrated by events in Zambia and in Trinidad. The Zambian case was described by *The Economist* in its August 30, 1969, issue: "For some time internal strife in Unip, the ruling party, has threatened to bring down the whole government. It was partly to prevent this happening that President Kaunda announced at the Unip national council meeting earlier this month the 51 percent nationalization of the copper mines." The Trinidad case followed a similar pattern. According to *The Economist* in its August 29, 1970, issue: "Trinidad's Dr. Eric Williams has pulled off a major coup to regain the confidence of his electorate and to disprove his critics who maintain that he is a mere puppet of foreign capitalists. At the beginning of this month he announced that the government will buy 51 percent of the island's largest sugar producer, Caroni, a subsidiary of the British Tate & Lyle group."

The hostility of strong internal factions of a country to foreign enterprise may arise out of adherence to socialist or nationalist philosophies. They may also spring from attempts to achieve specific national goals, whether of security, welfare, or development.

Socialism commonly means government rather than private ownership of the means of production. Yet political labels can be misleading.

"Socialism" as a label has been extremely popular in many parts of the world in recent decades. But the specific goals of political forces banded together under the socialism label vary greatly. For example, government leaders in India have declared that India's guiding political philosophy is socialism. Although the public-enterprise sector is large in India, a substantial share of the business activity has been reserved for private enterprise, much of which is foreign. Likewise, Yugoslavia calls itself a communist or socialist country, yet numerous joint ventures with foreign private enterprise have been negotiated in recent years. Thus, the international enterprise must look behind labels for the specific goals of political groups in different countries.

The nationalistic philosophy generally asserts that control over a nation's economic destiny should be in the hands of nationals and that nationals should have preference over foreigners in benefiting from economic and business opportunities in the country. Both of these views can generate political risk for international business enterprises.

An example of national-welfare goals that can create political risk is the persistent pressure in many countries of the world for land reform. If land-reform measures are suddenly accelerated, as occurred in El Salvador and Nicaragua in the early 1980s with drastic changes in government, foreign as well as domestic business firms with landholdings are likely to be expropriated.

National aspirations for economic development can create political risk for international business when the nation believes that the ultimate goal of development is to enlarge the domestic capacity for *self-generating* growth. This view implies that a country does not want to increase its dependence on outside forces any more than is necessary.[11]

Other sources of risk.   Social unrest and disorder may create political risk, not because of specific hostility to foreign enterprise, but because of general disruption of business activities. The causes of social unrest may range from the existence of extreme economic hardships, to racial disorders, religious disputes such as have occurred in India, and even student riots. Ineffective law enforcement can also be included in this category. It can result in risk to property and to persons and can greatly influence the costs of doing business and the efficiency of production, transportation, and communications.

The risk that can result from the political influence of local business interests that consider themselves threatened by foreign enterprises should never be underestimated. In Japan, local business interests have been extremely successful in influencing government policies or decisions that restrict the activities of foreign enterprise.

---

[11] See Fernando H. Cardoso and Enzo Faletto, *Dependency and Development in Latin America* (Berkeley: University of California Press, 1979).

Nations recently attaining independence, or about to do so, are likely to face great political uncertainty. In many cases, a nation secures widespread political cohesion on the issue of gaining independence but not on what policies should be followed after independence. In addition, new nations frequently lack experienced political leadership and undergo considerable turmoil while experience is gained and the policies and political power of various groups are tested. The role to be played by private enterprise and the attitudes toward foreign investment are not always clarified in the early stages of organizing a new nation. Mr. Mugabe's policies in Zimbabwe, for example, are still not clear.

Internal rebellion may be an extreme stage of social unrest and disorder. The situation in Central America during the early 1980s illustrates the kind of political risk that can occur. The effects on foreign business may be similar to those on domestic business or they may be accentuated because of the leverage that the opposing groups think they have in gaining support by putting pressure on foreign firms.

Armed conflicts between nations such as the ones that have occurred between Britain and Argentina and Israel and the Arab states can greatly affect the feasibility and profitability of foreign business operations.

New international alliances would include the case where a country joins a common market or free-trade area and in the process agrees to give preference in certain ways to business activities of common market nationality. Or, as in the case of the Andean Common Market in Latin America, the member countries agreed to harmonize their policies toward foreign private investment. When such intergovernmental agreements are concluded, some national policies under which international enterprises are operating may drastically change.

Political-risk effects

Political-risk effects on international business operations fall into two categories. They can affect ownership of assets through expropriation or partial divestment. They can restrict operations and ultimately reduce cash flows or returns. Both types of effects have been discussed in the chapters on controls and the legal environment.

Concession agreements are especially vulnerable to political risk. The prevailing philosophy in many countries, particularly newly independent nations, is that agreements can be revoked or revised at the discretion of the host country if the national interests are no longer being adequately served. Such revisions are likely to occur when the goals of national governments change, when a new political regime feels that contract revisions will strengthen its domestic political support, and when key circumstances surrounding an agreement change.[12]

---

[12] See William A. Stoever, *Renegotiations In International Business Transactions* (Lexington, Mass.: D. C. Heath, 1981), for a detailed analysis of copper renegotiations in Zambia and petroleum renegotiations in Indonesia during the 1970s.

In September 1969, for example, a group of young military officers seized control of Libya, sweeping aside the monarchy of King Idris I, and established a "socialist republic." The announced goal of the new Qaddafi regime was to reduce foreign influences in the country. Shortly after the 1969 change in government, Libya began to revise its agreements with the international oil companies.[13] One of the reported motivations was the need felt by the new regime to prove its toughness to the people by standing up to the oil companies, and the oil companies were blamed for corrupting the previous government with bribes.

To the sophisticated international enterprise, political risk, including expropriation risk, is not a bar to investment but an element to be weighed against prospective gains. And the time dimension is crucial. The firm may foresee high expropriation risk sometime in the future. Yet the profit possibilities up to the time when expropriation risk is high may be sufficiently attractive to make a project of interest. Such an approach has been characteristic of the petroleum industry.

Political-risk perceptions and realities

To what extent are perceptions of "political instability" a reliable guide to political risk? The question deserves special attention because political instability is so frequently cited as an obstacle to flows of private foreign investment.

In a broad study of investors from the 12 major capital-exporting countries—Belgium, Canada, Denmark, France, Germany, Italy, Japan, the Netherlands, Sweden, Switzerland, United Kingdom, and United States—many investors reported that they had eliminated countries and even whole geographical regions from their investment considerations for political reasons. By far the most frequently cited political obstacle was political uncertainty or political instability.[14]

With such a high sensitivity to political instability, it is quite possible that inexperienced international enterprises have missed business opportunities because they perceived more political risk than actually existed. When international managers with limited background perceive political risk, it often means that they are not familiar with the political patterns and styles of a foreign country and would feel insecure trying to operate in a strange environment. In such cases, the problem is to come to terms with an unfamiliar rather than a hostile situation.

Another possibility is that international managers are applying ethnocentric standards, based on political systems with which they are familiar, which are not appropriate to the country being considered. And

---

[13] Riad A Ajami, *Arab Response to the Multinationals* (New York: Praeger Publishers, 1979), pp. 110–11.

[14] National Industrial Conference Board. *Obstacles and Incentives to Private Foreign Investment, 1967–1968* 1 (New York, 1969).

because the criteria for political stability are different for each political system, the perception does not fit the reality.

Most American managers have not been exposed to formal political training and are not familiar with politics as a process in the sense that they understand marketing, finance, or economics. Furthermore, as nationals of a large country where a single political system spans a continent, they have not had the advantage of close contact with a wide range of governments in a limited geographical area that European managers have had.

To interpret frequent changes in the leadership of governments as political risk can be highly misleading. (see Box 15–2). The more funda-

Box 15–2

Political instability doesn't necessarily mean political risk
El Salvador: U.S. plants hum along despite turmoil

U.S.-owned companies in El Salvador are operating relatively smoothly despite the political violence and economic sabotage there. Although a number of U.S. companies have left, those that still operate Salvadoran facilities—including Texas Instruments, Dataram, Chevron Oil, Phelps Dodge, and Kimberly Clark—report that disruptions have been minimal and that their employees are coming to work regularly. Notes the president of a U.S. electronics company with a factory there, "We missed less production in El Salvador because of that country's problems than we did in our plant in South Carolina be-cause of snow."

U.S. executives cite several reasons why their factories in El Salvador continue to run smoothly. The most important is the work ethic of the Salvadorans—known as "the Japanese of Central America."

Most U.S.-owned factories in the country, like Dataram's, are assembly operations for export, with no local sales outlets and little need for local credit. Most are managed and staffed almost entirely by Salvadorans; fewer than 15 U.S. managers still work and live in the country full time. Many factories are in out-of-the-way locations and keep a low profile.

Source: Adapted from *Business Week*, April 13, 1981, p. 60.

---

mental question is whether strong factions are present with divergent views from those of the government on policies toward foreign business. Furthermore, the potential for political risk in countries with centralized political control, sometimes headed by a military dictator, can also be great. One-man governments often behave erratically and generate underlying tensions. Considerable uncertainty may exist as to how an orderly transition to a successor will be possible.

Forecasting political risk

Corporate practices vary greatly among the international firms that have formalized the political risk assessment function. Political assessment "units" range from the part-time involvement of an assistant international treasurer to full-time staffs of political scientists, ex-foreign service officers, or other country specialists. The political assessment approach may involve no more than a checklist or an outline for a country study, or it may entail a relatively sophisticated system designed to gather and process expert-generated opinion.[15]

While considerable progress has been made in developing methodologies, the state of the art for political risk forecasting is still greatly underdeveloped compared with most economic and business forecasting functions.[16] The underdeveloped state of the art can be illustrated by a study of the pre-1978 published predictions for Iran based on the principal political risk models. Only two of the 10 models offered reasonably accurate forecasts of the impending 1978 Iranian revolution and the resulting massive expropriation of foreign direct investment.[17]

The task of political-risk forecasting involves four basic steps. First, a profound understanding is required of the type of government presently in power, its patterns of political behavior, and its norms for stability. Second, the characteristics of the multinational's own product and operations must be analyzed to determine the kinds of political risks likely to be encountered in particular areas. Third, the potential sources for these risks should be identified and evaluated. The fourth step is to project into the future the possibility of political risks in terms of probabilities and time horizons.[18]

Throughout the process, the emphasis must be on political forces that can cause abrupt change in the environment for the business firm. What companies ultimately must know is not how stable a country will be, but how what happens in that country will affect its interests there.

Understanding the political system.   The necessary background information on a country's political system goes far beyond a knowledge of the present administration's policies toward foreign private enterprise. The need is to understand within a nation's historical context its type of government, its political parties and forces, and their philosophies.[19] The real challenge is to perceive the path along which policies and attitudes have been traveling, particularly those of political forces that are not shaping the policies of the present administration but are likely to do so.

---

[15] Blank et al., *Assessing the Political Environment*, pp. 22–42.

[16] Stephen J. Kobrin, "Political Assessment by International Firms: Models or Methodologies?" *Journal of Policy Modeling* 3, no. 2 (1981), pp. 251–70.

[17] Charles R. Kennedy, Jr., "Multinational Corporations, Political Risk Models and the Iranian Revolution," Working Paper no. 81-10 (Austin: College of Business, University of Texas, April 1981).

[18] Stefan H. Robock, "Political Risk: Identification and Assessment," *Columbia Journal of World Business*, July/August 1971, pp. 6–20.

[19] See Lee C. Nehrt, *The Political Climate for Foreign Private Investment* (New York: Praeger Publishers, 1970), for an excellent analysis of political risk in North Africa. Nehrt suggests a model for political analysis and applies it to Tunisia, Algeria, and Morocco.

Both internal and external sources can be used to develop this understanding. One of the most important internal sources is the managers of overseas subsidiaries. In addition, many companies secure the assistance of government and academic experts on the political systems of specific countries. Still another source of information and analysis is the growing number of political risk services.

An example of the political risk services is the Business Environment Risk Index (BERI), which has been available to business firms for some years. In common with other services, BERI makes use of a large panel of country experts.[20] On a quarterly basis, the panel rates 15 factors that affect the business climate on a scale of 0 (unacceptable) to 4 (superior). The factors are weighted and an overall index is computed for the 45 countries being evaluated. Given some consistency in the panel, changes in country scores over time should be useful indicators of the need for more extensive analysis. An important limitation of such services is that they do not take industry- and firm-specific factors into account.

Analyzing specific risk vulnerability.   The identification of the specific types of political risk that might be encountered requires an analysis of the enterprise's products and patterns of operation. Is the problem one of macro or micro risk? Is the project vulnerable to expropriation and loss of assets? Or are operational restrictions the principal risk? The answers to such questions as the following will be invaluable in this analysis:

Do nationals have the capability to operate the business successfully?

Are the foreign firm and its foreign managers highly visible in the local setting?

Are periodic external inputs of new technology required?

Will the project be competing strongly with local nationals who are in, or trying to enter, the same field?

Is the operation dependent on natural resources, particularly minerals or oil?

Does the investment put pressure on balance of payments?

Does the enterprise have a strong monopoly position in the local market?

Is the product socially essential and acceptable?

Does a social cost-benefit analysis of the project show attractive and continuing benefits to the country?

In general, projects or products that contribute strongly to national goals are likely to receive favorable political attention when first initiated.

---

[20] F. T. Haner, "Rating Investment Risks Abroad," *Business Horizons*, April 1979, pp. 18–23.

But as the projects become taken for granted over time and a local capacity is developed to operate such projects, political favoritism may shift to new fields.

Sources of risk.   Once the types of company-specific risks have been identified, the assessment procedure should examine the sources—factions and circumstances that influence the occurrence of the political risk event. The specific risk might be expropriation and the sources of this risk might be ideological shifts or the vested interest of local groups. The easiest situation in which to evaluate risk is that of a parliamentary democracy where the opposition views can be determined from parliamentary debates or political platforms. Such was the case in the early 1980s with the political shifts in France and Canada. At the other extreme is the difficult task of determining views and weighing the political strength of antagonistic opposition forces in a dictatorship where considerable censorship occurs. In such cases, political forecasting should include an examination of the views of political exiles.

This step of identifying the sources of risk may result in a considerable amount of error and uncertainty. But over time, skill can be developed to accomplish this task within reasonable limits of probability.

NATIONAL-CONTROL FORECASTING

The most frequent changes in the business environment come not from political-risk discontinuities but from the ever present desire of nations to increase national benefits from foreign investments. To predict changes in national controls emanating from this "natural" desire requires an underlying theory. This section attempts to develop a predictive theory of controls based on the interplay of the objectives and decision rules of representative firms and representative countries.

International business as a game

The imposition of controls over international business can be depicted as a vast international game. There are players, moves, strategies, and payoffs. The players are firms and countries. The moves of the firms can be changes in the location of business investments and operations. The moves of the countries can be changes in the nature and level of controls. The moves of the players interact to determine the payoff to each. For purposes of this theory, the players are depicted as representative firms acting to achieve payoffs of return on investment and representative countries acting to increase national benefits.

A simplifying assumption of rationality provides an efficient basis for prediction when applied to an aggregation of countries and firms over time. Yet for any individual firm, its investment pattern may not approximate a profit-maximizing one. And for any individual country, its policies at a specific point in time may not maximize national benefits.

The international business game proposed here is a non-zero-sum game. A gain by one player does not necessarily result in a loss by the same amount to the opposing player. Nevertheless, some of the objectives of the players are in definite conflict. Where this is the case, controls that increase the benefits to one country are likely to reduce the payoff to firms in some way. The same controls may also decrease the benefits to some other country.

The players are thus not arranged simply with countries on one side and firms on the other. Countries also compete with countries, and firms compete with firms. It is the competition among countries for shares of global business activity and among firms for foreign business opportunities that plays the major role in determining the pattern of controls. This formulation contrasts with the common view that controls may be explained by a narrow examination of conflict potentials between specific countries, independent of other countries, and individual firms.[21] This formulation has also been recognized by the United Nations, which reported as follows:

> Unilateral measures relating to transnational corporations adopted by one developing country can no longer be assumed to have little effect on others. In some instances, the demands of a developing country for greater production may lead transnational corporations to divert some of their production from other developing countries rather than from industrialized home countries.[22]

The game is sequential and dynamic with continually evolving action and reaction. Players do not all disclose their hands at the same time before knowing their opponents' moves. With a large number of players competing under these conditions, it is not feasible to extend the formal presentation of the game to the point of proving optimum strategies. The prediction of strategies is based instead on the following simplified sequence of play:

1. International firms locate business activity for a "practical maximization" of expected net cash flow subject to allowances for the risk of potential controls.
2. Countries alter controls to maximize national benefits, bearing in mind the likely reactions of firms and ultimate reactions of other countries.

---

[21] See Charles P. Kindleberger, *American Business Abroad* (New Haven: Yale University Press, 1969), p. 150ff.; Raymond Vernon, "Conflict and Resolution between Foreign Direct Investors and Less Developed Countries," *Public Policy*, Fall 1968, pp. 333–51.

[22] United Nations, *Transnational Corporations in World Development: A Re-Examination* (New York: United Nations, 1978), pp. 133–34.

3.   Firms realign existing operations and redirect new investment in the light of the changed controls.
4.   Other countries feel indirect effects of the changed controls and move to alter their own controls.

The prime focus of the theory is the prediction of step 2 in the sequence—the strategies of countries. Step 4, of course, will be covered by the same prediction. This prediction is itself made against the backdrop prediction of where firms locate their activity with an existing set of controls and how they react to changes in controls. Firms' objectives are therefore the starting point for the analysis.

Objectives and decision rules of the representative firm

The representative international firm is defined as motivated toward a "practical maximization" of the present value of expected cash flows from its activities. It identifies market targets and location alternatives for supplying these markets through the global strategy approach developed in chapters 13 and 14. And it relies on national-control and political-risk forecasts for incorporating risk allowances in the firm's decision process.

A change in any control can alter the optimum location pattern for a firm's existing operations and possibly the ranking of its investment alternatives. As a general rule, at the margin, foreign business activity and investment will be discouraged when controls that decrease profitability are extended, and encouraged when such controls are reduced.

When an adverse change in controls appears likely, the representative firm may take protective steps to reduce the probability that controls will be changed. It may use some of the countervailing measures for reducing risk discussed in Chapter 12. An example would be to seek local associates who could act as a local buffer against pressures to increase controls. There is an incentive to arrange for protection when the estimated loss of profits that would result from the control change, multiplied by the probability that the change will occur, is greater than the cost of protection.

Objectives and decision rules of representative countries

A representative country for this theory is motivated toward maximization of net national benefits. As elaborated in Chapter 11, the costs to the country must be balanced against the gains to calculate net benefits. Moreover, only the incremental benefits over domestic or international alternatives open to the country should be included. It is assumed here that controls are independent and their individual benefits additive. Country control strategies can then be expressed in terms of a collection of separate controls.

The representative country acting rationally to maximize national benefits will set each individual control at its *control optimum*. This is defined as the level at which the control brings maximum net national benefit over some future time period. The national benefit from adjusting any control is the incremental benefit accruing as a result of the adjustment. A control change, for example, may increase national benefits from foreign business activity already established in the country. But the control change may also result in an opportunity loss of benefits by discouraging the entry of new foreign investments and future expansions of existing firms. A country's control optimum is exceeded when the opportunity loss of national benefits from discouraged international investment or business activity outweighs the gain from imposing the control.

Implicit in this definition of the control optimum for any control is an allowance for reactions by other countries, and reaction may be expected when alteration in controls will alter the control optimum of another country. The greater and the more immediate the effects on another country's business activity, the more likely the other country is to take matching action. With a fixed supply of international business investment, the lowering of controls by a less developed nation might siphon off a large proportion of the investment that another marginal recipient of such investment would have received. This second country might then move very quickly to offer the same or greater incentives.

In many cases, countries will be unable to predict what reactions their actions will produce from individual competitor countries. There are too many countries, too many investors, and too many controls for individual effects to be assessed accurately. The reaction of many other countries to change by one country is, moreover, likely to be a gradual process over time and best predicted as a decay in the benefit gained from a control as a function of time. Where it is clearly apparent that competition among countries can weaken each country's bargaining position and the number of such competing countries is relatively small, as in the case of the oil-producing countries, a possible strategy is to form a cartel and bargain as a group. This possibility, however, is limited to countries in an oligopoly situation as suppliers of raw materials.

General features of country strategies

Some general features of country control strategies can be derived from the juxtaposition of country objectives and decision rules against prediction of strategies for representative firms. The control optima are likely to be high for those controls that produce a given gain in national benefits with the smallest reduction in expected profits of investors, or, what amounts to the same thing, where a given reduction in expected profits is accompanied by large gains in national benefits. This may occur when a control:

1. Results in a crucial contribution to the country's development.
2. Was anticipated by firms and, therefore, does not alter the expected cash flow to firms.
3. Takes effect a considerable time in the future.
4. Is not reflected in discounted cash-flow calculations.
5. Restricts access to the local market to gain power over location of production.

A requirement that foreign firms use nationals as local managers is an example of control that could contribute greatly to national development with a small cost to foreign firms. Such controls may impose some immediate costs on foreign firms, but they can bring future offsetting benefits.[23] Local management reduces the foreign image, adds personnel attuned to local culture, secures local allies, and may cost less than expatriates. For the country, the control contributes to development by increasing the supply of nationals with management experiences.[24]

Certain controls may be anticipated by firms through effective forecasting or through messages that countries have relayed about future controls. In such cases, investment decisions will have already allowed for the risk and countries will have nothing to lose by imposing the anticipated controls. Also, the further in the future that increased controls begin to take effect, the less the discouragement to firms. Any control affecting an investor's cash flow after the first 10 years is likely to carry little weight in the investment decision. Its discounted cost would be infinitesimal, given the discounting rates commonly used for assessing international opportunities.

Controls that do not affect investors' discounted cash-flow calculations may also increase national benefits without having a strong negative effect on international business decisions. For example, by limiting the right of a foreign firm to expand into further business areas, a country can retain opportunities for national firms. Yet such a control is unlikely to be weighted heavily in a discounted cash-flow calculation for any investment that by itself is worth undertaking. Controls that limit the share of foreign ownership reduce foreign participation in a country's market but may not reduce the return to investing firms. Controls on transferring funds out of a country are also likely to create minimal discouragement to further initial investments if returns remain high and profitable local opportunities exist for local reinvestment.

---

[23] John C. Shearer, *High-Level Manpower in Overseas Subsidiaries* (Princeton, N.J.: Industrial Relations Section, Princeton University, 1960), chap. 3.

[24] Peter P. Gabriel, *The International Transfer of Corporate Skills* (Boston: Graduate School of Business Administration, Harvard University, 1967); Harry G. Johnson, "The Multinational Corporation as a Development Agent," *Columbia Journal of World Business*, May–June 1970, pp. 25–30; Frederick Harbison and Charles A. Myers, *Industrialism and Industrial Man: The Problems of Labor and Management in Industrial Growth* (Cambridge, Mass.: Harvard University Press, 1960).

Controls that restrict access to the local market to gain power over the location of production are also likely to have high control optima. Production for the home markets of many countries will not be located locally in the absence of controls, and production that has been located locally will tend for some to move to lower cost locations. Controls such as tariffs, import licensing, or local component requirements that would change firms' location decisions are thus likely to bring high national benefits, particularly for countries with large, advanced markets. While many economic studies have investigated the conditions under which reactions by other countries will eliminate any gains, the imperfections of the multilateral international business game are likely to mean that for individual countries the national benefits are not always eliminated.[25] And on the firms' side of the game, it may well be that investment required to supply the market from within the restricted areas remains profitable, further supporting the argument that the optimum level for these controls will be high for some countries.

What types of controls have low optimum control levels? Controls that threaten assets are likely to produce much greater negative reactions than other equally effective controls aimed at operations. The removal of the right to capital that is clearly recorded in the firm's books is more menacing than an equivalent reduction of potential earning capacity.[26]

Controls that can be avoided through an international firm's foreign ramifications will also have low control optima. Attempts by the United States to prevent foreign subsidiaries of U.S. firms from trading with the communist bloc countries were not very successful. French attempts to prevent the expansion of U.S. ownership in some industries have similarly been thwarted by the ease with which the same firms can locate in other European Community countries and then export to France.

Another dimension of country control strategies is that they will vary with the type of attraction the country has for foreign direct investment. Where potential foreign investors are market seekers, control patterns will emphasize increasing national benefits through encouraging as much production activity as is feasible to be undertaken locally. Where the principal potential investors are resource seekers, control patterns will try to increase the amount of processing of natural resources that is performed locally. Where the attraction of the country is mainly for production-efficiency seekers, controls are likely to facilitate such operations by measures such as permitting duty-free imports of raw materials and components.

---

[25] Harry G. Johnson, "Optimum Tariffs and Retaliation," *Review of Economic Studies* 21, no. 55 (1953–54), pp. 142–53.

[26] National Industrial Conference Board, *Obstacles and Incentives to Private Foreign Investment 1967–1968.* (New York: Conference Board, 1969), p. 9: "An act of expropriation lingers long in the minds of potential foreign investors, swaying investment decisions for many years after the event."

Country strategies over time

Optimum control levels—and hence controls—can change over time. It can be argued, for example, that the following trends could permit optimum control levels to rise:

1. When a country's level of development increases significantly, its potential gains from foreign investment are reduced because the country is likely to have better local alternatives, whereas the potential returns to foreign firms increase with the growth in the country's market.
2. When low-technology types of foreign investment mature, such as mining, countries will have developed local skills and the necessary capital to do more with their own resources.
3. When the supply of prospective foreign investors increases, as occurred with the accelerated overseas expansion of German and Japanese firms after the mid-1960s, the bargaining power of host countries is correspondingly greater.

The control policies of Brazil in the case of the telecommunications industry can illustrate how control optima can change over time. Brazil is a large market that has experienced high growth rates in the last two decades. With this growth the market for telecommunications equipment, sold mainly to the government-owned telecommunications companies, expanded greatly. In the late 1970s, the government announced that it would purchase its telecommunications equipment only from companies that had majority national ownership. The market had become so important that companies like Ericsson of Sweden and ITT of the U.S. with great agony divested themselves of 51 percent ownership to nationals in order to retain access to it.

With optimum control levels changing over time, in part because countries do not have adequate information about firms' other investment opportunities, countries will be reduced to experimentation and adjustment as results are fed back. Over time, countries' control strategies should come nearer to their control optima—by definition, their best strategies.

This process of adjustment over time raises the question as to whether initial strategies will undervalue or overvalue the optimum control levels. One likely hypothesis is that the greater the gap between a given country and the most advanced country, the higher are its unfilled aspirations and the greater is the likelihood it will increase controls beyond the control optima. Since national benefits from additional business investment are high for relatively backward countries, there will be a tendency to add controls to achieve the maximum from international firms—only to produce the opposite effect. Conversely, more highly developed countries are likely to underestimate their control optima in the absence of a major lag in their development, particularly when their own international firms dominate the market.

It seems generally clear that the stronger hand in the international business game lies with the more developed country. The weaker a country's attraction to firms, the less it will find it worthwhile to impose controls to increase national benefits. While countries' strategic positions with respect to international business will vary markedly with such factors as population, business capabilities, agreements with other countries, ownership of international business, and level of gross national product, the strategies of countries in similar positions should have major similarities. Drawing on the elements of our outline theory, the strategies of four broad classes of country can be projected in sketch form.

Less-developed countries.   This group covers the great number of countries for which foreign investment is deemed to be of outstanding national benefit. Not only are the national benefits and hence the opportunity cost of foreign investment high for these countries, but elasticity of investment in response to controls is likely to be high. Except for investments in extractive resources, there will be many other countries almost as attractive to international investors and ready to replace those countries in which profitability is impaired in any way.

Countries in this situation are likely to avoid high controls because there will always be some other country not invoking equivalent restrictions which would gain the investment. A good initial strategy for the least-developed countries would be to present an environment as attractive as possible to international business with no hints of national animosity. On the other hand, nationalistic pressures against foreign ownership will frequently build up to produce controls in excess of these very low control levels. When this happens, the inflow of investment will slacken, and if the controls are high enough, or the nationalistic pressures seem likely to produce such controls, the inflow may dry up altogether. Interests from within the country that realize that investment is being forgone are then likely to begin advocating policies that will bring the country back toward its control optima, pointing out the national benefits from doing so.

As a country develops, it can gradually raise its controls. Mexico, for example, has been able to increase controls and yet successfully maintain capital inflow. Rapid and sustained growth, political and monetary stability, greater infrastructure to support local production activity, and less open hostility to foreign investment have all contributed to higher control optima. Moreover, the high controls on foreign ownership, foreign personnel, and local content that Mexico imposed may have discouraged less investment than would controls over capital and profit repatriation.

Countries with their own foreign investments. For countries with significant foreign investment, their dual capacity as investors as well as recipients of foreign investments will influence their control strategies. Such countries as the United States, United Kingdom, Germany, France, and Switzerland are likely to avoid controls on inbound investment for which the national benefits might be offset by retaliatory controls over their own foreign investments.[27] The potential cost of retaliation can be high if other countries are prepared to escalate their response. Even a small amount of investment in another country gives that country scope for escalation.

To avoid retaliation, controls in this grouping of countries are more likely to be shaped as positive encouragement of desired patterns rather than negative restrictions. Such encouragement might be lower tax rates for foreign subsidiaries that have a high degree of local ownership. There is also likely to be more informal administration of controls than formal published regulations.

Positive steps may also be taken to strengthen a country's own international business operations, through such measures as subsidized political-risk insurance and loan programs for overseas investments. If indigenous international companies are not strong enough to compete in research and scale of operations with foreign multinationals, governments increasingly give their national firms a hand, perhaps through forced merger, government aid, or protected home markets. Such ideas are not new. The United Kingdom successfully created the Imperial Tobacco Company in 1902 to oppose the American Tobacco Company and in the interwar period created ICI to meet German and U.S. competition.

Control policies that support the foreign operations of locally based firms are not likely to continue along a straight progression. As previously discussed, the possibilities for divergence between the objectives of firms and what is seen as maximizing national benefits are many indeed. As countries perceive a growing divergence of interests, the support policies are likely to change.

Investor countries can become greatly preoccupied with the need to retain their own international position. Retention of central head office functions, maintenance of financial centers, and preserving technical leadership through high spending in research and development will be advocated. Controls will be steadily oriented toward these "leadership" ends, quietly, positively, and not competitively—yet definitely using the

---

[27] "Insofar as multinational companies played a part in the formulation of taxation policy, the Treasury's objective was to encourage inward investment and prevent the most blatant forms of tax evasion, without taking stern measures which might provoke retaliation against the overseas subsidiaries of British companies." Michael Hodges, *Multinational Corporations and National Government* (Lexington, Mass.: D.C. Heath, 1974), p. 97.

multinational enterprise as an intermediary in the competition to stay ahead.[28]

The strategy for this class of countries, then, might be summarized as cautious discouragement of others' international activities, coupled with positive encouragement of desirable locally owned activities.

Minority partner countries.   These are small countries that are partners to economic integration agreements and that may be less preferred for major investments than their larger partners. The outstanding examples are the smaller European Community partners, Belgium, Holland, and Ireland. When a large number of such countries compete among themselves, or when the advantages of their larger partners appear large to foreign investors, competition to deescalate controls is likely, even to the extent of positive encouragement. Such a strategy has emerged in Belgium, somewhat to the detriment of France. Low-cost sites, capital, and interest subsidies, and various types of taxation remission have been offered.

If the partners to such trade agreements can also agree to eliminate competition in foreign investment controls, the optimum control level for the group as a whole will increase. But with divergent country interests, such agreements are difficult to achieve, as demonstrated by the Andean Common Market experience. A similar tendency to weaken controls also occurs within countries where states, provinces, regions, or cities have significant power to offer incentives.

Centrally controlled countries.   Another type of strategy is appropriate for the communist-bloc countries and Japan. These countries have strong central control and strong approaches to foreign investment. They have evolved policies of securing foreign technology while excluding foreign direct investment or limiting it to minority participation. Such policies may have delayed the inflow of the most advanced technology, because multinational firms are likely to protect their technological supremacy by withholding the latest advances. On the other hand, when multinational corporations accept that they cannot gain majority ownership, they have often shown that they will settle for whatever participation they can get on the principle that something is better than nothing.

A corollary to this sort of strategy is that these countries develop their own local operations able to move into international attack. Initially, this attack aims at building export markets, and outgoing investment is largely to acquire outlets and market position. As their international at-

---

[28] Both the United Kingdom and the United States have carried through government-financed studies that evidence major concern for technical leadership. For example, see chapter 3 in M. D. Steuer et al., *The Impact of Foreign Direct Investment on the United Kingdom* (London: Department of Trade and Industry, 1973).

tack meets with success, their strategy is likely to change to something like the global planning of our representative multinational firm.

Pressure to relax the restrictions on foreign investments in the home markets of these countries is unlikely to be effective until the reverse investments and exports of this group can be used as a lever. Yielding to repeated pressure, Japan reduced controls on inward investment beginning in the late 1960s.[29] Nevertheless, entry by foreign multinationals has since been slow. The Japanese industries have built up to international strength and are not easy to beat on their home ground. Furthermore, obstacles are still placed in the way by government authorities.[30] In comparison to Japan, the communist countries are behind in their international expansion. But they have recorded notable successes in obtaining technology at the lowest competitive rates by pitting Western suppliers against one another.

In summary, the strategy pattern of this class of countries is predicted as limitation of foreign ownership with maximum acquisition of technological know-how, followed by international expansion that shapes them as investing countries.

RISK FORECASTING PROCEDURES

Projecting into the future

As there is no way of forecasting the future with certainty, the assessment of risk is basically a process of developing a model and arriving at subjective probabilities for the variables, or events, in the model. Expert opinions are secured on the likelihood of the specific events occurring and the degree of confidence the experts hold concerning their predictions. Alternative scenarios can also be developed and evaluated. The probability assessments associated with each element or each scenario can then be combined into a consensus of opinions or a composite view for use by the decision maker. Such a composite view is referred to as an aggregate probability estimate.[31]

In actual practice, as the 1980 Conference Board study concluded, "Quantification remains a distant—and debatable—goal, and even the achievement of such rigor as would be entailed in the development of structured formats for qualitative assessment still represents, for most

---

[29] Herbert Glazer, "Japan Unbars a Door," *Columbia Journal of World Business,* July–August 1967.

[30] See Charles Smith, "Foreigners' Stake," *Financial Times,* November 12, 1975, also *Foreign Direct Investment in the United States,* vol. 1, Report of the Secretary of Commerce to the Congress (Washington, D.C.: U.S. Government Printing Office, April 1976), p. 240.

[31] For more detail on the formal procedures available for combining expert opinions, see Alan R. Fusfeld and Richard N. Foster, "The Delphi Technique: Survey and Comment," *Business Horizons,* June 1971, pp. 63–74; D. W. Bunn and M. M. Mustafaoglu, "Forecasting Political Risk," *Management Science,* November 1978, pp. 1557–67.

firms, an aspiration rather than a reality. . . . Some of the most effective corporate analysts operate at a relatively low level of *technical* sophistication—which is not to say that they are unsophisticated—and several of the more technically sophisticated approaches to environmental assessment that have been offered to companies or tested by them are considered to be utterly nonsensical in the real business world."[32]

How one company forecasts

The ASPRO/SPAIR system was developed by Shell Oil Company and has been extended to a broader range of industries.[33] ASPRO is an acronym for Assessment of Probabilities. SPAIR is an acronym for Subjective Probabilities Assigned to Investment Risks.

The approach is structured because it involves developing an explicit model of the potential impact of the political environment on a specific project. As originally developed, the model defined risk in the context of an oil exploration/production contract and then constructed a causal model composed of independent events that could produce the specified risks.

Risk is defined as the probability of not maintaining a concession contract that is considered to be equitable by both company and host country over a 10-year period. Risks are assumed to fall into two categories: those that result in a unilateral change in the initial contract so that the return is inadequate, and those that restrict the free flow of funds or oil entitlements out of the host country.

These two general contingencies are then decomposed into nine events that would increase the probability of risk to the project if they occurred. These events include civil disorders, sudden expropriation, taxation restrictions, restrictions on remittances, and oil export restrictions. In turn, a complete set of factors are specified for each political event that could increase the probability of the event occurring. For example, factors considered in evaluating the probability of sudden expropriation include ideological shift, strength of the economy, and the economic role of foreigners.

Expert panelists are recruited from a variety of backgrounds to review each factor for each event. Through interviews, the experts present their judgments as to the likelihood that the event will occur and indicate their degree of confidence in the judgment. A computer program then combines systematically the probability assessments for each factor into an

---

[32] Blank et al., *Assessing the Political Environment*, pp. 61–62. A survey of French firms concluded that "numerical risk evaluation" was not widely used. See Bernard Marois, "Assessment and Management of Political Risk: Practice of French Firms," Research Paper, Centre D'Enseignement Supérieur des Affaires, Jouy-en-Josas, France, 1980.

[33] C. A. Gebelien, C. E. Pearson, and M. Silbergh, "Assessing Political Risk of Oil Investment Ventures," *Journal of Petroleum Technology*, May 1978, pp. 725–30.

aggregate probability estimate. The program uses the judgment and degree of confidence to generate a density function for the probability of the event occurring given the factor in question. Using Bayes' Theorem, the density functions are combined across factors to generate a panel assessment of the probability of the event occurring.

The ASPRO/SPAIR technique presents a number of problems. It involves a major and costly effort that restricts frequency of application. Its greatest value is for the specific project being assessed and much of its value is lost if more general assessments for a number of industries or projects are attempted. In addition, there is concern about the applicability of Bayes' theorem to combine the probabilities, including the actual degree of independence of the factors.

Minimizing political and control risk

It is obvious that risk forecasting can be crucial to the international enterprise in reaching a "go" or "no go" decision on a particular project. It may be less obvious that risk identification and evaluation can guide the firm in reshaping a project so that a "no go" can become a modified "go." The international enterprise is not helpless in the face of political and control risk. To the contrary, it has a significant range of options for minimizing the magnitude and effects of such risks.[34] Some of the possibilities have been discussed in Chapter 12.

SUMMARY

International firms must face the risk that political forces in both host and home countries will cause significant changes in the business environment. These forces affect the operations of multinational enterprises through abrupt changes, generally referred to as political risk, and through gradual changes in national-control policies intended to maximize a country's benefits from the participation of international firms in its local economy.

International firms have always been concerned about the impact of politics on their operations. Until recently, however, few companies had established formal systems to assess political factors in their multicountry business environments. The lack of a process for systematically evaluating political risks and evolving national controls increases the probability that the multinational enterprise will invest in countries when it should not or refrain from investing when it should.

Considerable recent progress has been made in developing methodologies for political risk forecasting. Nevertheless, the state of the

---

[34] See Jean Boddewyn and Etienne F. Cracco, "The Political Game in World Business," *Columbia Journal of World Business*, January–February 1972, pp. 45–56; and W. R. Hoskins, "How to Counter Expropriation," *Harvard Business Review*, September–October 1970.

art for political risk forecasting is still greatly underdeveloped compared with most other business forecasting functions. The major advance has been to make more objective the political risk elements included in decision making and to increase awareness of available means for minimizing political risk.

The risks that result from changes in national-control strategies should be easier to forecast than political risk discontinuities. Given the concept of the international business game and an embryo terminology for analysis, the international manager should be able to anticipate, with a reasonable degree of accuracy, the pattern of controls that specific countries are likely to adopt to increase their national benefits. With such forecasts, the manager can develop cost and benefit calculations as a basis for business decisions. Such calculations will be limited by the assumptions made about the various interacting strategies, but control risk will be quantifiable. For any investment the cash flow can be reduced by the cost of controls multiplied by the expectation (probability) that they will occur.

EXERCISES AND DISCUSSION QUESTIONS

1. How would you define political risk? Would you consider a political risk the "inability to convert into dollars foreign currency representing earnings on, or return of, the investment or compensation for sale or disposition of the investment," one of the items included as political risk in the U.S. risk-guaranty program?

2. "Political stability is equated with democracy, with elections, with modernization, with a broad income distribution, with consensus, with participation, and so forth. This conception is derived from an ideologized model of what the American type of democracy is supposed to be like, projected on to other societies." Evaluate and discuss.

3. How would you rank types of business activities as to their political risk vulnerability? What is the basis for your ranking?

4. What is the relationship between political instability and political risk for international business? What criteria would you use to identify political instability?

5. How can a business project be modified to reduce political risk?

6. Numerous writers have observed an "inevitable tension" between multinational companies and nation-states and proposed ways for governments to control the operations of these firms. Is the conflict really between firms and countries, or simply between countries just as it has always been? What are the implications of this distinction for the sort of controls that might be recommended?

7. In recent years the Canadian government has been introducing more and more controls over the Canadian operations for foreign firms. What would you expect will be the characteristics of further controls to be imposed in the forseeable future, and why?

8. Select one country and, as a consultant to its current government, prepare an overall strategy for control of international business activities that fall within its jurisdiction.

9. What types of controls will be most likely to affect the performance of international firms as against simply being passed on by the firm to its customers? Does it make any difference?

10. Criticize the assumptions of the model that has been proposed in this chapter for forecasting controls.

Chapter 16

Organization of the multinational

The organization structure of a firm doing business internationally is a vital determinant of success. In particular, the organization structure must provide an effective decision-making process and a smooth flow of communications between various parts of the enterprise. And because of the many special elements in international operations an organizational structure designed for purely domestic business is usually unsuitable for multinational operations.

The different organization structures used by international firms are as diverse as the strategies they have been following in achieving growth abroad.[1] Few, if any, are identical and no simple criteria exist for selecting the best organizational form. Despite the diversity within the broad organizational categories, a number of useful guidelines exist for resolving the organization problems as a firm develops from a domestic to a multinational enterprise.

STATUTORY AND MANAGERIAL ORGANIZATIONS

The international enterprise encompasses two distinct but interwoven component structures: the statutory, or legal, organization, and the managerial organization.[2] The statutory organization exists on paper only. It is designed to conform to legal requirements while best meeting the objectives of the firm, for example, minimization of commercial restrictions or taxation. The managerial organization may cut right across the statutory structure and is concerned with the authority and responsibility of each executive and their lines of communication. It is also concerned with the information that flows along these lines of communication and the procedures for channeling and processing the information.

The statutory organization defines the legal and ownership structure that links the parent company with its various units. Each unit may have a different statutory status—branch, subsidiary, holding company, and so forth—depending in part on the legal requirements of the jurisdiction in which it is established. Holding companies in low-tax areas have often been used for the statutory organization, with the statutory center rarely serving as the operating center. In fact, some statutory centers may consist of only a part-time local lawyer and a mail clerk. Thus, the statutory and managerial structures must be considered as separate entities. The lawyers and tax experts will be primarily responsible for designing the statutory structure. The international manager will be involved mainly in the design and function of the managerial structure—the subject of the rest of this chapter.

EVOLUTIONARY STAGES
OF MULTINATIONAL ORGANIZATION

The evolution of the organizational structure of an enterprise can be viewed as a series of stages, with each stage a modification or adaptation of the structure in the previous stage. A description of the detailed orga-

---

[1] See, for example, Michael G. Duerr and John M. Roach, *Organization and Control of International Operations* (New York: The Conference Board, 1973); Business International, *New Directions in Multinational Corporate Organization* (New York, 1981); John M. Stopford and Louis T. Wells, Jr., *Managing the Multinational Enterprise* (New York: Basic Books, 1972); and Stanley M. Davis, *Managing and Organizing Multinational Corporations* (New York: Pergamon Press, 1979).

[2] John G. McDonald, "New Organizational Concept of the World Enterprise," *Management International* 1, no. 5/6 (1961).

nization structure at any specific stage is something like a snapshot, or still picture from a film, that shows isolated but typical moments in a continuing process of organizational change. The speed of the process varies from company to company. Some tread cautiously and take one step at a time, whereas others rush through certain stages and bypass others.[3]

In the early stages of entering foreign markets through exports, a company may assign the export responsibility to an independent trading company. As foreign sales increase, the enterprise may establish an export department with some medium-level company official as export manager. Still concentrating on exports, the firm may go further and set up its own sales, service, and warehousing facilities abroad.[4] In the early stages, the basic organizational structure of the firm is left undisturbed.

The Japanese firm typically follows a different pattern in entering foreign markets through exports because they have been able to rely on the services available from the giant Japanese trading companies (sogo shosha) instead of forming their own export departments.[5] The Japanese general trading firms have few comparable counterparts in other countries. Their basic business is foreign trade and they can handle many of the international business functions that U.S. and European companies normally perform for themselves. While there are several thousand trading companies, the nine largest handled 48 percent of Japan's exports and 55 percent of its imports in 1979.[6] Some Japanese firms, such as the major automobile and consumer electronics companies, have followed an evolutionary pattern similar to that of U.S. companies. Their products required consumer service facilities and other specialized attention that the giant trading companies could not provide.

As international operations change from exporting to a mix of exporting, licensing, and foreign production, and as international sales become of more than incidental importance to the firm, conflicts of interest arise between internal units of the firm that are not easily handled by an export department type of organization. Where a need has emerged to establish production facilities in areas served by exports, the export department may fail to recognize the need. Or it may prefer to continue with exports because foreign production may mean a loss of export sales attributed to the department. The usual organizational response by U.S. companies to such conflicting interests has been to create a full international division, which includes the previously independent export unit.

Some companies pass through an intermediate stage where the firm

---

[3] Stopford and Wells, *Managing the Multinational Enterprise*, p. 11.

[4] See James Greene, *Organizing for Exporting* (New York: National Industrial Conference Board, 1968).

[5] See Alexander Young, *The Sogo Shosha* (Denver: Westview Press, 1979).

[6] *The Wall Street Journal*, December 17, 1980, p. 56.

acts only as a holding company for largely autonomous foreign subsidiaries. This pattern can be adopted without making any significant changes in the organizational structure of the remainder of the company. It occurs where foreign ventures are first established, not as a result of planning but in response to a specific threat or opportunity. Because such first ventures are small and not critical to the success of the organization, and because the parent firm has insufficient international experience to make much of a contribution to the new foreign ventures, foreign managers are allowed virtually unlimited powers of decision and action. As one study explains, "The need for learning exceeds the desire for control."[7] The subsidiary will have rather loose financial ties to the senior financial officer of the parent company, but its operating freedom will be great so long as the financial results of the venture are satisfactory.

For U.S. companies, the autonomous subsidiary phase may have a short life, particularly if the foreign units grow rapidly and accumulate significant resources. The success of foreign ventures increases their significance to the total enterprise. The international experience that ownership of the subsidiary has brought to the parent firm enables it to approach the design and implementation of controls with more assurance. Furthermore, the prospects of economic gain from coordinating the foreign subsidiaries will generate pressures for organizational changes that permit a greater degree of central control over the subsidiaries' decision making.

The establishment of an international division, generally of equal status to other major divisions, normally results from four factors. First is the matter of size. The international commitment of the firm has reached an absolute size and a relative importance within the enterprise to justify an organizational unit headed by a senior manager. Second, the complexity of international operations requires a single organization unit that can resolve within it such conflicts as the best means for entering foreign areas on the basis of a broad view of the firm's international opportunities. Third, the firm has recognized the need for an internal group of specialists to deal with the special features of international operations. And finally, the enterprise wants to develop an affirmative capability for scanning the global horizon for opportunities or competitive threats rather than simply responding to situations that are presented to the company.

By the early 1960s, the international division approach was the most common type of structure in large U.S. enterprises with foreign operations. However, the continued growth of these divisions sowed the seeds of their destruction by enlarging the interest of top management in the international opportunities. By the mid-1960s, a growing number of firms had abandoned their international divisions in favor of a global organiza-

---

[7] Stopford and Wells, *Managing the Multinational Enterprise*, p. 20.

tional structure.[8] As Clee and Sachtjen have observed, "The really decisive point in the transition to world enterprise is top management recognition that, to function effectively, the ultimate control of strategic planning and policy decisions must shift from decentralized subsidiaries or division locations to corporate headquarters, where a worldwide perspective can be brought to bear on the interests of the total enterprise."[9] Unless all components of the enterprise are judged on their performance worldwide, they will not be motivated to act in accordance with the worldwide interests of the enterprise.

At the global stage, responsibility for both foreign and domestic business is moved to the top echelons and new subdivisions are specified on either a functional, regional, or product basis. The choice among the functional, regional, or product division structures depends primarily on the business strategy of the enterprise.

A simple global structure, however, is not the final stage in the development of organizational structures capable of providing effective administration for a multinational enterprise. Simple global structures are based on the management principle of unity of command: one man having sole responsibility for a specified part of the business, either subdivided by function, product, or geographic areas, and accountable to a single superior officer. But the conflicting need for coordinating function, product, and geographic areas can still remain a serious problem. Some firms have adopted more complex structures in which managers have dual or multiple reporting relationships and where area, function, and product responsibilities overlap.

THE NATIONAL SUBSIDIARY STRUCTURE

In a national subsidiary structure, each foreign subsidiary reports directly to the president or main board of the parent, without intermediate layers of management either at regional headquarters or international division headquarters. In some cases, subsidiary management reports only to its local board of directors, although the parent company is usually represented on that board and the parent company president may also be the subsidiary president.[10] The pattern is illustrated in Figure 16–1.

This pattern gives the subsidiary a considerable degree of autonomy. While there may be legal autonomy, however, in managerial terms there will usually be an adherence to some common reporting and conferral

---

[8] Ibid., p. 25.

[9] Gilbert H. Clee and Wilbur M. Sachtjen, "Organizing a Worldwide Enterprise," *Harvard Business Review*, November–December 1964, p. 67.

[10] Jacques Picard, "Organizational Structures and Integrative Devices in European Multinational Corporations," *Columbia Journal of World Business* 15 (Spring 1980), pp. 30–35.

Figure 16–1

A national subsidiary structure

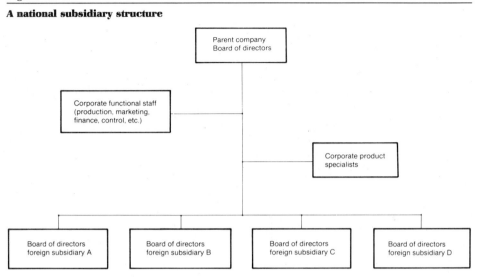

requirements.[11] But headquarters' units will not have direct responsibility for the subsidiary, its functions, or its product sections.

The national subsidiary structure has been more common for European multinationals than for United States multinationals, which have tended to adopt it only as a passing phase. The structure of some of the European multinationals evolved before modern communications made a closely integrated organization possible. Others built from a small home-country market and from an early stage treated the foreign operations as of equal importance with the home unit.[12]

Strengths

Individual country affiliates can work as independent, responsible enterprises within their individual environments. They can make many decisions at the national level and adjust rapidly and with utmost sensitivity to the needs of local markets and governments. Local ownership is most easily accommodated with this structure and it also permits a more complete career structure for local nationals within their own coun-

---

[11] G. Garnier, T. N. Osborn, F. Galicia, and R. Lecon, "Autonomy of the Mexican Affiliates of U.S. Multinational Corporations," *Columbia Journal of World Business* 14 (Spring 1979), pp. 78–90.

[12] See Hans Schollhammer, "Organizational Structures of Multinational Corporations," *Academy of Management Journal*, September 1971, pp. 345–65; Andrew J. Lombard, Jr., "How European Companies Organize Their International Operations," *European Business*, July 1969, p. 37; and Lawrence G. Franko, *The European Multinationals* (London: Harper & Row, 1976), chap. 7.

try. Local ownership and the use of nationals as managers were perceived in a recent survey as the most important moves for reducing local tension against multinationals.[13]

The individual affiliate's problems are directly visible at the highest levels of the multinational. There is less chance of important issues for the particular country being subordinated to the concerns of an intermediate regional, product, or functional layer. The advantages for top management of direct involvement at a country level are also marked. If parent company board members each hold responsibility for particular affiliates, they can bring multiple international perspectives built from direct experience into the highest decision-making levels. Direct top management involvement both elevates the importance of the local management and adds weight when a top manager becomes involved in contacts and negotiations with senior government officials of the affiliate's country.

Weaknesses

Direct access to top management can, on the other hand, be a disadvantage. Top management's time can be used inefficiently, or in the case of smaller affiliates, important questions can get completely overlooked. When an affiliate's top management interacts with numerous functional and product specialists at headquarters on a whole range of issues, there is also a danger of completely diffusing responsibility for international issues. The introduction of a regional level into the international organization can avoid most of these problems.

One potential weakness often claimed for the subsidiary structure is that decisions will tend to be taken in the light of the subsidiaries' particular horizons and individual interests. Instead of maximizing the worldwide performance of the overall system, the units will suboptimize. There are likely to be benefits to the multinational enterprise as a whole that are not perceived by the individual units. There are ways, however, for central staff to arrange for these benefits to be translated into rewards to the subsidiary for taking the preferred action. So long as corporate staff can see the benefits clearly, there is an internal price mechanism for expressing them.

THE INTERNATIONAL DIVISION STRUCTURE

A representative organization diagram for a firm using an international division structure is shown in Figure 16–2. The international division is usually headed by a vice president who reports directly to the president

---

[13] William H. Newman, "Adapting Transnational Corporate Management to National Interests," *Columbia Journal of World Business* 14 (Summer 1979), p. 85.

Figure 16–2

An international division structure

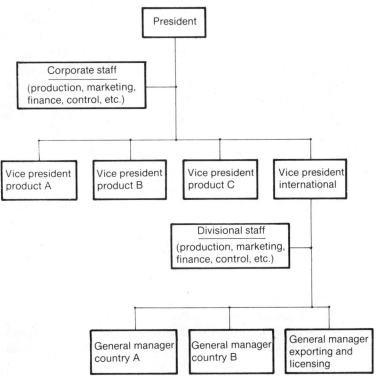

or chief executive of the company. Some enterprises form a separate international company headed by a president, which plays essentially the same role as an international division. In most cases, the international division is responsible for policy and global strategic planning for international operations. There is considerable variation, however, in administrative practices for maintaining links between the international activities and the domestic side of the enterprise.

The international division usually has direct responsibility for all export and licensing activities of the parent company and is accountable, directly or indirectly, for the operations of overseas manufacturing and sales units. Its task is to coordinate all the international activities so as to raise the level of performance above that likely where subsidiaries are autonomous and other international functions, such as exporting and licensing, are dispersed within the firm. The division may be able to reduce the cost of capital for a subsidiary by borrowing in some other area or in international capital markets. It can be the channel for the transfer of experience among subsidiaries. It may be able to reduce tax liability through transfer-pricing policies. In brief, it has responsibility for improving total performance through the unification or synergy potentials of multinational operations.

At an early stage, the corporate staff groups, except for finance and control, are likely to continue to be domestically oriented. The international division will rely mainly on its own divisional staff. As policy and strategic planning shifts to the corporate level, the marketing, manufacturing, research, personnel, and other staff will become internationally oriented. Both patterns can occur while maintaining the international division or international company structure.

Strengths

For the firm extending its activities internationally from a large domestic market like the United States that has dominated the company's attention, the international division provides an organizational umbrella for all the foreign activities of the enterprise and a focus for learning about the management of international operations. It permits centralized direction of a company's foreign operations, particularly during the developmental and expansion stages of the international program. It concentrates international know-how and skills in a separate unit detached from domestic responsibilities and makes possible a concentrated drive on market expansion and investment overseas.

The cadre of internationally experienced executives developed in an international division can be a positive strength to a company needing to make a rapid international impact. The team specializes in international issues and develops a multinational way of thinking and coordinating that would be difficult to create without this specialization. The skills built up in this way are also valuable additions to domestic divisions when international staff is transferred to a domestic division.

An international division also adds a champion of foreign activities to the top-management echelons and a strong voice for allocating the necessary resources. Where the division has been built alongside an existing product organization, moreover, the international voice is also created as an impartial arbiter between product divisions.

From a competitive strategy viewpoint, perhaps the major advantage of creating an international division is that it can overcome product divisions erecting a mental fence around the domestic market and failing to plan their strategy globally. Not all international divisions develop a strategic approach, but the need to decide which markets should be developed, and when, usually pulls through at least a cursory comparison with global competitors.

Weaknesses

Where the products manufactured or sold abroad are the products developed at home, as is normally the case, the international division is heavily dependent on the domestic product divisions. In this respect, the international division has less autonomy than the product divisions and depends upon their assistance more than they depend on each other. The international division normally does not have its own product development, engineering, and research and development staff, and the domestic divisions controlling these important components of the overseas operations are frequently reluctant to give priority to foreign needs because they are measured solely by their domestic performance. Thus the international division depends heavily on the communication and cooperation procedures that are worked out with the domestic product divisions for making the specialized skills of the domestic units available to the international operations. As product divisions become more familiar with international needs, the effectiveness of the communication and cooperation devices can improve. But the inherent conflict between the goals of the domestic and international divisions is never completely eliminated.

There is always some conflict between international and domestic divisions on transfer pricing; this would not occur if domestic divisions were able to operate globally and receive directly the benefit of sales in foreign markets. This conflict may exist even if the transfer pricing rules adopted do in fact benefit the multinational system. This conflict, along with the specialization in domestic or foreign environments, further add to creating a rift between the international and the domestic staff, each regarding the other as a competitor rather than identifying with its successes or setbacks.

Specialization and separate accountability often lead to a failure to use managerial know-how and potential to the utmost. Underutilized skills may rest in domestic divisions and never be turned to international problems they have already coped with domestically.

There is also the problem of product divisions forming a coalition against the international division. Not infrequently, the international division may be growing more rapidly than domestic divisions—on the back of their earlier experience. International may even have become much larger than several of the domestic divisions combined. It is not unknown in such a situation for product division heads to form a coalition to obtain more resources for their own growth. In some cases, product divisions go even further and instigate a move to break up the international division so as to allocate its growth and power across the product divisions.

The international division also has constraints on its ability to assist the foreign subsidiaries. As a division, it normally does not have the resources to develop detailed knowledge about the environments and characteristics of large numbers of local areas and must heavily delegate direct operating responsibilities to the foreign subsidiaries. It cannot centralize many decisions because the competitive position of the subsidiary may be reduced by the time lag involved in securing decisions

from the international division. In general, the amount of decentralization will vary with the particular functions involved, product characteristics, the degree of expertise accumulated at the divisional level, and the
time taken to refer matters to the division. Firms engaged in the production and sale of a narrow line of mature goods with relatively stable
technologies and markets, for example, tend to move farther in the direction of centralization than firms expanding into many different markets
with diversified lines of new products involving rapidly changing technologies.

The fact that the international division structure remains dominant in
many U.S. multinational companies, despite a strong move toward global
structures and matrix arrangements, suggests that many firms have been
able to work out informal arrangements or formal devices for resolving
the problems inherent in dividing the international unit from the rest of
the company. One outstanding example is the International Business Machines Corporation, which continues to handle its extensive international operations through its separate IBM World Trade Corporation
while integrating basic research, product development, and manufacturing activities on a worldwide basis.

THE FUNCTIONAL STRUCTURE

The functional organization structure for international operations was
the traditional form used by European countries. The division of responsibility at headquarters is organized by functions such as marketing,
manufacturing, and finance; and the heads of these divisions have worldwide responsibilities as line executives (see Figure 16–3). The marketing
or sales division, for example, has worldwide marketing responsibility,
with direct control over all sales companies and distributors, wherever
located. In addition, the division normally has staff responsibility for

Figure 16–3

A functional organization structure

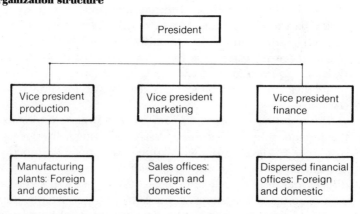

coordinating the marketing of manufacturing subsidiaries, which usually control sales of the goods they produce, except for exports that are handled directly by the marketing division. The manufacturing division usually has line control over domestic plants, staff responsibility for worldwide product standardization, product development, quality control, and research and development, and a mixture of staff responsibility over the foreign manufacturing subsidiaries.

Strengths

The functional structure has the advantage of concentrating management attention on the internal functions. If these are carried through well on a global scale, they may provide the key to advantage over competitors and, hence, strategic success. The structure is most appropriate for a company with a fairly narrow product line that has reached a rather stable plateau of global coverage and demand and does not face major changes in competitive attack. Mintzberg refers to this class of organization as a "machine bureaucracy," arguing, "Bureaucracy has become a dirty word. Yet this is the configuration that gets the products out cheaply and efficiently."[14] Knowledge and experience in the functional fields is concentrated and applied to the firm's activities and operations in all regions and product lines.

This structure also enables a relatively small group of officers to maintain line control over an organization without much duplication. There is, moreover, no conflict between profit centers. The functional specialists at any level can devote their full attention to overall profitability of the organization as related to their specialist function.

Weaknesses

There is a general feeling that the disadvantages of a functional organization quickly outweigh the advantages for a multinational. The structure breaks down for multiple product lines. The functional specialists would either need to have expertise in the details of each product line or they would have to specialize by product line within functions. This latter alternative would be unwieldy unless the organization moved to a product structure and grouped the functions by product line.

Another basic weakness is that sales and production tend to become separated in their objectives. Disputes that arise between production in one country and sales in several others, for example, would have to go to the highest levels for adjudication. If general managers of foreign subsidiaries are superimposed on the functional structure, they may find them-

---

[14] Henry Mintzberg, "Organization Design: Fashion or Fit," *Harvard Business Review* 59 (January–February 1981), p. 109.

selves reporting to more than one person. Some European firms that have grown rapidly, however, have experienced difficulties with the somewhat hazy responsibility assignments of this organizational form and with breakdowns in the informal lines of communication and reporting.[15]

Finally, the structure results in tremendous duplication with regard to environmental inputs. Each of the functional divisions may need its own regional specialists and could be making different assumptions about future trends in the various areas of operations.

THE REGIONAL STRUCTURE

Under a regional structure, the primary operational responsibility is assigned to area managers, each being responsible for a specific region of the world, as shown in Figure 16–4. Corporate headquarters retains re-

Figure 16–4

A regional structure

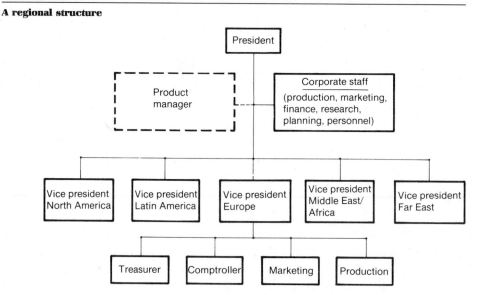

sponsibility for worldwide strategic planning and control. Where the regional form of organization has replaced the international division in U.S. companies, the United States becomes simply one of a number of world markets. Each regional division has responsibility for all functions within its area and is able to coordinate marketing, production, finance, and so forth, within its region.

---

[15] Lombard, "How European Companies Organize International Operations," p. 38.

Strengths

The regional structure tends to give greater emphasis to the country subsidiary as an important profit center and as a unit for which product attributes and other elements of the marketing mix must be adapted. The structure is particularly appropriate to situations in which marketing adaptations require modest levels of technological skill. It is also a good structure for situations where economies of scale in production call for a region-sized unit for basic production with minor feature, packaging, and communication adaptation for individual country markets. Food, pharmaceutical, and oil companies are examples of firms with these product characteristics.

A regional structure also offers an improvement over functional or national subsidiary structures in simplifying top management's task in running the worldwide business. Regional matters of less-than-strategic importance can be dealt with more quickly and knowledgeably. There is also an argument that regional expertise can be built up, with appropriate regional strategies. Others, however, feel that regional cohesion is more a mirage than a reality.

Weaknesses

The principal difficulties of the regional organization arise when the firm has a diverse product range. The structure does not easily handle the tasks of coordinating product variations, transferring new product ideas and production techniques from one country to another, and optimizing the flow of product from source to worldwide markets. One organizational response has been to create a global product manager at the corporate level who is assigned worldwide responsibilities for particular products or product lines. This requires molding a global product strategy and facilitating the transfer of experience from one area to another. But the operating relationships between the global product manager and the area managers who have line responsibility are likely to be ambiguous.

A regional structure usually requires a large number of internationally experienced executives to staff the various regional headquarters. It may result in too much information being screened from corporate headquarters and undue focus placed on the performance of the specific regions as opposed to the company's worldwide interest. It may also require considerable duplication of functional and product specialists within the enterprise. This can be very costly.

The very idea of regional identification, though, is perhaps the biggest handicap. A business that is large enough to have regions is in global competition. For this it needs a global strategy and does not want to have to fight to impose such a strategy on regional executives who are busy molding a regional character. All manner of barriers are likely to build between strong regions. When it comes to building one worldwide plant for some item, regional differences in standards, transfer pricing, and other internal bureaucracy may be difficult to surmount.

THE PRODUCT DIVISION STRUCTURE

The product division structure assigns worldwide product responsibility to product division executives as the primary line managers (see Figure 16–5). Overall goals and strategies for the company are set at

Figure 16–5

A product division

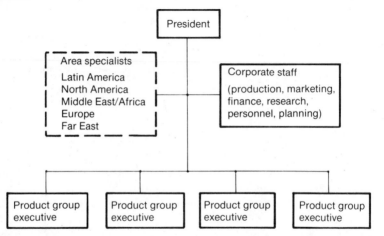

corporate headquarters and, within these corporate guidelines, the plans of each product group are reviewed and approved by top management. Each product group, however, has primary responsibility for planning and controlling all activities for its products on a worldwide basis. It is usual to have a top layer of functional staff management but less common to have a layer of regional specialists as indicated in the diagram. When this layer is added, their function is to provide area expertise and coordinate activity for all products in their area.

Strengths

The product structure works best when a company's product line is widely diversified, when products go into a variety of end-use markets, and when a relatively high technological capability is required. It is also advantageous when high shipping costs, tariffs, or other considerations dictate local manufacture of the product. The structure puts a prime emphasis on product market and production know-how, aiming at its exploitation worldwide. There is no conflict between domestic and foreign operation as with the international division structure, and those with skills are in a worldwide unit for exploiting those skills.[16]

The concept of global market performance comes through almost automatically with this structure. Certainly, if competition is attacking on a product front globally and picking individual country markets in which to do so—the product division executive is in a position to see it and to react. There is perhaps more tendency, too, to look for international segments, and to design new products against markets other than the home market.

Weaknesses

The most important problem with the product structure is that worldwide responsibility is frequently assigned to managers with great product expertise whose experience has been largely domestic. Similar problems can arise at all levels when the personnel assigned are selected because of their product expertise and may have little experience and capability for dealing with the new kinds of problems that arise out of international operations.

Another problem inherent in the product structure is the difficulty of coordinating the activity of different product divisions in any given area. Suppose, for example, that product division A wanted to license a European company to manufacture product A, while product B's European plant was operating below capacity and could avoid a loss only by taking on an additional product. Without someone on the local scene responsible for the success of the enterprise as a whole, the two divisions might be unaware of each other's needs. Product division A would incur the unnecessary expense of licensing the European plant. Product division B would take a loss. The company as a whole would suffer.

The local coordination problem and the problem of weak local knowledge is partially overcome with the addition of some sort of country management. These managers do not have profit responsibility under this structure, however. They report to the appropriate product divisions for their shares of the local activity and perhaps to an area staff specialist for their "janitorial" role in maintaining the local presence.

Multidivisional plants are a classic problem under the product division structure. Allocation of costs and capacity can be a particular headache if there are major fluctuations in the demand for different products. One way out is to base any plant firmly within one division and have it

---

[16] See James R. Basche, Jr., *Shifting Patterns in International Organizations: U.S. Experiences in the 1970s* (New York: The Conference Board, September 1978), p. 10.

operate on an arm's-length basis in contracting for the supply requirements of other divisions.

MATRIX STRUCTURES

A matrix organization is structured as a grid with intersecting responsibilities. There is a dual rather than a single chain of command and some managers report to two bosses rather than to one boss. It requires a move away from the traditional hierarchy of power and unity of command of the single-dimension structures to a balance of power and sharing of responsibility.

There are three roles in a matrix organization that differ from those in single-dimension structures. First, there are the managers who report to two different matrix bosses; then there are the matrix managers who share subordinates; and, finally, there is the top manager who must head the dual structure and balance and adjudicate disagreement. For each of these roles there are special requirements.

Matrix management is not new. It has been with organizations for 50 years since the matrix concept of brand managers and product managers first began developing in American consumer goods firms.[17] There is, therefore, a great deal of expertise in managing matrices and developing their strengths. What is more recent, however, is the movement to incorporate matrices at a much higher level in multinational firms. The scale of the matrix is immediately enlarged many times.

Most multinational firms that have adopted a matrix structure have organized with dual reporting along product and regional lines, where the region can be a national subsidiary, a world region, or international versus domestic. There is not just one matrix structure, however; combinations of two or even the three dominant dimensions of function, product, and region can be arranged at a variety of levels.

The structure adopted by General Electric Company is a good example of a product-regional matrix, as illustrated by this comment on how its strategic business units (SBU) plan product and country strategies:

> General Electric Company effectively joins product-related and geographic concerns. The firm is working toward a product SBU organization in which each SBU has worldwide strategic planning responsibility. GE has identified a number of priority countries. Each product SBU head sets forth what he plans to accomplish in each country within a certain time frame. The country executive develops a comprehensive country opportunity plan to cover all products and strategies. This is a difficult task, because the country manager lacks the expertise to decide authoritatively what is optimal for each product and strategy—but it is important that he contribute to the planning effort. The country plan is then compared with the individual

---

[17] See, for example, Gordon H. Evans, *The Product Manager's Job* (New York: American Management Association, 1964).

product SBU plans for that country. The outcome is a merging of informational and strategic input from both sources. Conflicts are identified and proposals made for their solution. Some conflicts may be resolved at the country level, others at the area or even the sector level. Each party may push issues up its relevant hierarchy for higher-level review.[18]

Strengths

Each matrix pattern will have its own strengths and weaknesses according to the combination of dimensions adopted. There are, however, general strengths and weaknesses of the matrix approach.

The case for adoption of a matrix is strongest when there are strong pressures along more than one dimension simultaneously; and failure to take a dimensional pressure into account could be disastrous for the firm's performance. This is precisely the situation for multinationals facing aggressive competitive attack through product or process technology and at the same time strong pressures from individual countries to adapt to national objectives. The firm is torn between its product strategy and its global location strategy. If the firm under these pressures organizes on a single geographical dimension, the sum of the geographical units may not add up to maintaining its competitive performance. Alternatively, if the firm organizes on a product division basis, the growing country pressures may not be seen as they develop and the firm may find its global strategy crimped by loss of a market to a competitor or even expropriation of assets.

Under a matrix structure, the two viewpoints can be continually monitored and compared. Doz et al. describe the process well:

> Some managers, attuned to local needs and sensitive to the power of host governments and national interest groups, favor, on almost any issue, more subsidiary autonomy and greater freedom in responding to national demands. Other managers, more concerned with worldwide competitive strategies, strive to increase coordination and integration across geographic boundaries. In trying to gain power and in defending their own areas of responsibility, these managers unearth different facts, analyze them differently, and propose different strategic decisions. By confronting conflicting views constructively the organization can learn.[19]

The aim of a matrix structure is not, however, to seek out the actions on which opposing dimensions of the matrix can agree or readily compromise. The aim is to show up the conflicting viewpoints as clearly as possible and then to analyze objectively which, in the long run, is most justified. There is thus a greater emphasis on market, competition, and

---

[18] Business International, *New Directions in Multinational Corporate Organization,* p. 132.

[19] Yves L. Doz, Christopher A. Bartlett, and C. K. Prahalad, "Global Competitive Pressures and Host Country Demands," *California Management Review* 23 (Spring 1981), p. 66.

environmental facts and in their analysis than there is in unidimensional structures where the data and recommendations come up a single hierarchy and are unlikely to be inconsistent.

The matrix shape makes it possible for the organization not only to diagnose the need for action along more than one dimension, but also to adjust between these dimensions. It is a highly adaptable organization structure well suited to stress and change.[20]

Weaknesses

The main weakness of matrix organizations is that the pattern can be negated by managers who do not operate according to its requirements. Managers who have a strong drive for organizational power, for example, are likely to try to dominate the matrix organization at their level. They will generally fail to acknowledge the power of the analytical approach in justifying the best path for the overall organization. If they succeed, they destroy the matrix.[21] Others who are less tolerant of conflict but less dominating may continually seek for compromise and create the worst of all worlds—a nonstrategy.

If at any level of a matrix organization, proper attention is not given to the detailed analysis of conflicts, it is very likely that the organization will be left with the structure and not the output. Managers reporting to dual superiors will quickly realize when careful analysis is not being carried through and may then proceed to operate in an anarchistic way with only perfunctory reporting of the real issues.

Matrices are intrinsically complex. Every effort, therefore, should be made to specify quite explicitly the detailed interrelationships and responsibilities. Matrix design, on the other hand, can run away with itself. When a multinational blossoms into matrices with conflicting specializations at different levels, the resolution of basic problems can be hampered. In one large multinational, the international personnel department developed its own matrix of training, personnel, industrial relations, and social relations, overlaid with regional specialists and functional specialists. The Western European marketing training manager certainly had an advanced specialization—but his interests did not make it easy for him to discuss the general training needs of the consumer appliances manager of the consumer division of the French national subsidiary.

Excessive internal meetings and discussions without decision and action are also a danger within matrices. The complexity of the relation-

---

[20] Stanley M. Davis and Paul R. Lawrence, *Matrix* (Reading, Mass: Addison-Wesley Publishing, 1977), p. 46.

[21] Stanley M. Davis and Paul R. Lawrence, "Problems of Matrix Organizations," *Harvard Business Review* 56 (May–June 1978), pp. 131–42.

ships may lead to executives checking with base after base before acting only to find that a global competitor with a single line of command has beaten them to it.

COMBINATION STRUCTURES

For very large multinational businesses it is possible, and in many cases desirable, to combine two or more of the standard organization designs. Different businesses with different patterns of global demand, supply, and competition—and for which different variables have been chosen as important to strategic success—demand different management structures. If the size of a business sector (or activity) is large enough, the multinational should consider setting up the activity as a separate global entity reporting to its top management more or less as a holding company. A multinational adopting this approach would quickly end up with a patchwork global organization composed of different designs for each business. Superimposed over this patchwork would very likely be an international regional organization for liaison with governments at the highest level, and for servicing in combination those business units not large enough to justify their own global organization.

CHOOSING AMONG ALTERNATIVE ORGANIZATIONAL STRUCTURES

The basic organization problem common to all firms operating internationally can be summed up in three questions:

1. Should the corporation be divided into domestic and international divisions?
2. Should line responsibility be subdivided for management purposes according to major functions, major product lines, or major geographic areas?
3. What is the best way to provide for needed specialization and coordination according to the other two variables, or how should the three necessary inputs—functional, product, and geographic—be meshed?

Clearly, there is no one right way to organize, no perfect organizational structure, and no organization form that can remain static when once adopted. Successful companies are using various organizational patterns to manage their international business operations effectively.

Although there are no standard requirements, the choice of organizational pattern has generally been determined by a relatively small number of variables. The variables that help to choose an organizational form that best fits the needs of a given firm in a given set of circumstances are the following:

1. The relative importance in the present and future of foreign and domestic markets as perceived by top management.
2. The historical background of a firm and its evolutionary stage in international operations.
3. The nature of a firm's business and its product strategy.
4. The management traits and management philosophy of the firm.
5. The availability of and willingness to invest in internationally experienced management personnel.
6. The capacity of an enterprise to adjust to major organizational changes.

The absolute size of international sales will determine the desirability of moving from an export-manager form of organization to an international division for most U.S. companies. The choice between an international division and a global structure will be influenced by the relative importance of international and domestic markets as perceived by top management. The benefits of having all senior managers experienced in the diversities of international business may be great. But when a company's future is likely to be dominated by a large domestic market like the United States, the investment needed to man a global organization with internationally experienced personnel may not be warranted. Also, so long as domestic activities promise to continue to be much larger than international operations, separate attention may continue to be required for international activities so that they do not become subordinated to domestic considerations.

The choice of organizational structure is inevitably influenced by a company's history and past experience. A company that has operated internationally for decades and possesses a top management experienced in dealing with worldwide problems will approach organizational change differently from a company that is a comparative neophyte on the international scene. During a firm's early stages of growth abroad, its organizational decisions are likely to be influenced by the need to encourage a concentrated drive on international opportunity by separating foreign from domestic activities. At a more advanced stage, organizational decisions will be increasingly motivated by the potential gains to be realized from coordinating all components of the enterprise on a worldwide scale.

As a firm's international activities become large relative to domestic business, the choice of organizational structure is closely related to the nature of the company's business and its product strategy. Where there is little product diversity, and where the success of the firm is not heavily dependent on diverse trends in different geographic markets, a functional structure can be effective. Where there is a limited product line and great similarity in end-user markets and in marketing techniques and distribution channels, but where area expertise plays a major role, a regional or geographic structure operates well. In such cases, it is less costly to duplicate product and functional expertise than area expertise. Where product lines are diverse, have a high-technology component, serve different end-user markets, and where production and sourcing can be advantageously rationalized on a worldwide basis, the product division structure has major advantages. The product structure facilitates the transfer of technology and sales support from producing divisions to international operations and can accelerate growth by forcing domestic divisions to become more aware of the markets and potentials of foreign areas.

Management traits and philosophies can be other key variables determining the organizational structure of a firm. Some managements are bold and willing to make frequent organizational changes. Others are cautious and make changes only when absolutely necessary. The management philosophies and heritage of executive experience of European-based multinational companies favor structures that facilitate a potentially more centralized control over the totality of corporate operations by a few key executives, thus giving preference to functionally oriented organization structures. The management philosophy of U.S. firms is more likely to favor structures that provide greater opportunities for decentralized decision making, but with formal control devices like the profit center concept that allow for more strict supervision, control, and coordination within the product-oriented or regionally oriented divisional activities.[22]

Another dimension of a firm's management philosophy is its orientation toward foreign people, ideas, and resources in headquarters and subsidiaries, and in host and home environments. These attitudes have been described as ethnocentric (home-country oriented), polycentric (host-country oriented), regiocentric (region oriented), and geocentric (world oriented).[23] A polycentric firm would have something akin to a holding company structure with loose connections to quasi-independent subsidiaries. A geocentric philosophy leads to a global structure that permits a worldwide approach in both headquarters and subsidiaries.

But, even if a firm can determine the merits of one organizational form over another, the question arises of finding qualified managers. All global structures require an increase in the number of internationally experienced managers, and a shortage of such managers can be a serious barrier to adopting a global structure. As noted previously, the investment required to expand the international experience of the numerous managers needed for a global structure would have to be justified in

[22] Schollhammer, "Organizational Structures of Multinational Corporations," pp. 352–53.

[23] David A. Heenan and Howard V. Perlmutter, *Multinational Organization Development* (Reading, Mass.: Addison-Wesley Publishing, 1979), pp. 17–21.

terms of the future relative importance of international activities as compared to domestic business.

A final variable, related in part to management traits, is the capacity
and willingness of an enterprise to adjust to organizational changes.
Major organization realignments are likely to disrupt delicate working
relationships. Executives of domestic divisions may be unwilling to accept new managerial roles until there is overwhelming evidence of the
need for change. Or a forceful manager of a successful international
division is likely to use his record of success to resist reorganization
pressures that would dilute his responsibility and authority over international activities. Where the capacity and willingness of an enterprise to
adjust to organizational change are limited, informal arrangements and
devices other than a major organizational change may have to be
adopted to secure some of the prospective benefits of a major change.

Organizational structures normally cannot be changed and operated
effectively when they are imposed unilaterally by top management. The
choice of structure must emerge out of a political process of group bargaining in which decisions are frequently reached by coalitions of
groups. As one study of the process of structural change in multinational
corporations emphasizes, "Although the choice of structure is ultimately
the responsibility of top managers, they have the role of identifying a
workable solution, persuading each group of its logic, and implementing
the reorganization."[24]

ORGANIZATION PROCESS WITHIN THE GLOBAL STRUCTURE

The formal organization structure of a multinational establishes the
main lines of authority but is not on its own enough to guarantee viable
operation in a complex and changing environment. Three other important organizational facets must be established and managed over time.
First, there will need to be a set of conventions and instructions as to
where decisions of different types are to be taken within the organization.
Second, the type of data that is recorded and reported and the way it is
used as the basis for decisions will significantly influence the organization's performance. Third, rules for temporary organization to cope with
problems that cut across the organization's lines of authority will substantially influence flexibility.

Location of decisions

The ideal relationship for implementing a global strategy is for corporate management to determine overall corporate objectives, to specify

---

[24] Stopford and Wells, *Managing the Multinational Enterprise*, p. 75.

organization-wide strategies and policy guidelines, to decide on the allocation of corporate resources to the various operating divisions, and to institute effective systems of communications, coordination, and control. Within this framework, managers of individual units are supposed to be free to determine a specific course of action for achieving the expected contribution to corporate objectives.

But whatever the stated ideology and intentions of the company, complicated and contradictory pressures cause relationships to oscillate between varying levels of centralization. Among factors that determine the degree of centralization or decentralization are the age, size, and profitability of a specific subsidiary. Large, long-established, and profitable subsidiaries are likely to have a maximum degree of autonomy.[25] Another important factor is the amount of confidence placed in subsidiary management. Still another force that can press for local autonomy is an environment with strong national governmental controls that requires frequent and unique local decisions. Factors that work toward centralization are an increasing integration of multinational operations, an increasing speed of technological change, and the rapid development of global techniques, strategies, and communications. Brooke and Remmers, after studying in depth the organization of subsidiaries and the power and control systems operating between the head office and foreign subsidiaries of a large number of multinational companies of nine different nationalities, concluded "that a decentralizing ideology masks a centralizing reality."[26]

In virtually all cases, however, the relationship will vary by function. Corporate control will be strongest in those functional areas in which the suboptimization problem is likely to arise and where important economies of scale can be achieved by the joint utilization of high-cost specialized personnel.[27] Depending, of course, on a firm's product strategy, the opportunities to optimize for the entire system may be in a regional or worldwide rationalization of production,[28] in the field of purchasing, or in research and development activities. Such functions tend to be centralized, whereas the marketing function tends to be most decentralized.

Of all the functions, it is finance over which the closest headquarters supervision is usually exercised. Partly, this continues the bias toward controlling businesses through their use of finance that is common in domestic firms. But also accounting standards are widely adhered to

---

[25] For extended discussion and case studies of the "Relationships With Foreign Subsidiaries and Affiliates," see Enid Baird Lovell, *The Changing Role of the International Executive* (New York: National Industrial Conference Board, 1966), pp. 140–48.

[26] Michael Z. Brooke and H. Lee Remmers, *The Strategy of Multinational Enterprise*, 2d ed. (London: Pitman, 1978), p. 68.

[27] Richard D. Robinson, *International Business Management*, 2d ed. (Hinsdale, Ill.: Dryden Press, 1978), pp. 648–49.

[28] Yves L. Doz, "Managing Manufacturing Rationalization within Multinational Companies," *Columbia Journal of World Business* 13 (Fall 1978), pp. 82–94.

around the world and it is much easier to impose standard reporting requirements in finance than in, say, marketing where measurement practices vary widely. Tight central control is usually exercised over capital spending, and often the levels that a subsidiary manager can commit on his own authority are very low indeed. Most companies also centralize the search and analysis of potential acquisitions, but some are beginning to involve subsidiaries in the process.

The Conference Board survey made in the early 1970s reported from a study of North American multinationals that many corporate headquarters are expanding their financial role.[29] Four reasons were given:

1. Trends toward foreign fund raising by multinationals.
2. Performance pressure to improve consolidated results.
3. Trends away from international or regional divisions.
4. Need to build stronger financial controls as operating control is delegated to national units.

Apart from centralized control motivations, however, there are also pressures to centralize finance to gain economies. Central cash and capital management can often open up economies by reducing transfers and their associated costs and by reducing the money stocks that are required. Central expertise can also add a supranational protection of the value of assets and revenues against loss through exchange and other risks that national units could not engage in themselves.

The very design of matrix organization requires frequent adjudication at a level above that at which proposals are prepared in the matrix units. In fact, the "planned-conflict" design can produce so many directly opposed proposals from the opposing matrix units that a decision overload can be built up at top management level.[30] This is one reason why regional offices are advocated. The adjudication can be moved down a level and the less crucial conflicts sorted out before they reach the top of the organization.

Specification of data and its decision use

In all firms, the data that is required to be reported and the ways in which it is expected to be analyzed shape the organization's performance. Information and the release of its energy is the blood flow that gives life to the organization structure.

Careful specification of information requirements is of particular importance in multinationals in which global economies are large, and where injudicious emphasis on the wrong countries can place the firm at

---

[29] Duerr and Roach, *Organization and Control of International Operations*, pp. 18–25.

[30] Doz, Bartlett, and Prahalad, "Global Competitive Pressures and Host Country Demands," p. 68.

a major competitive disadvantage. Information requirements are also important in matrix organizations where the rationale for the structure is to allocate responsibility for collecting, analyzing, and presenting the case for action along the dimensions on which the matrix is structured. Management must design reporting requirements so that conflicting views are effectively represented at the appropriate higher level for adjudication.

Because the conflict structure of a matrix involves adjudication rather than compromise, there will inevitably be managers whose case is not adopted. To avoid the sense of failure in these cases, many organizations have adopted procedures for review of conflicting plans and proposals in open meeting. With a consistent emphasis by top management on analysis to show the best decision for performance of the overall system, a climate can be created in which clear analysis of facts is the mark of the good executive. Management of the multinational becomes more analytical and turns away from political protagonists encouraged to bias data and presentations to produce the most attractive case from their subunit viewpoint. Equally, with less-nonparticipative adjudications from on high, decisions are seen less as "wins" and "losses" and the problem of alienated managers who are not committed to the decision is much reduced.

In shaping the way in which a multinational organization operates, the planning and budget instructions that specify the content, format, and review procedure are perhaps even more important than the formal organization structure. By changing the planning process, a top executive can change the entire shape of the decisions that emerge. Thus, in many multinationals, the basic outcome of conflicts is often established at the planning stage. If plans for a national subsidiary, for example, are approved independently of product divisions' plans, inherent conflicts might never be resolved as the subsidiary adheres steadfastly to the "contract" established by its plan.

Throughout the review process of a multinational, a very strong influence will be the personal values of top management in their approach to information and search for problem solutions. The values exhibited will color the ways in which decisions are implemented and future plans are presented. The process of review thus offers a formal platform to educate a multinational to the style of management that the top team is seeking.

Temporary initiatives

From time to time top management will find that any combination of organizational structure and processes, however appropriate to the bulk of decisions, will fail completely to face a decision or to change as soon as it should or in the direction it should. To overcome the difficulty, management must introduce temporary procedures that cut across the established patterns.[31] Suppose, for example, that an organization based on a matrix of geographical and product divisions is in an oversupply situation requiring a dramatic cost-cutting exercise. Neither national units nor product divisions want to initiate the scheme, all hoping for a future demand increase. To rely on functional control specialists to work through the organization against the wishes of the matrix managers to whom they report would be to invite only partial success. In this case, an alternative would be to establish a temporary task force to recommend and monitor cost reduction, reporting directly to top management and dominated by financial control executives.

Task forces and committees, as in this case, may have to be designed with a clear bias in their composition simply to offset the power of established groups. Even then, there may be little support for views that conflict with the dominant organization dimension, if members can see only personal career disadvantage in espousing recommendations that go against the organizational wishes and are not likely to be adopted.

Another type of temporary initiative is to build a cadre of trusted executives who can be transferred for short assignments within the organizational structure to bring about changes that go against the structure. Home-base or third-country nationals, for example, may be less inclined to take a suboptimizing national viewpoint to the detriment of the total firm.

Reliance on temporary initiatives, however, has its drawbacks. First, the need for action is likely to be recognized too late, after early diagnosis has been suppressed by the existing organization. Solutions are likely to be needed more to overcome the resulting weaknesses than to build on strengths. Ad hoc committees, moreover, may not be in a position to implement recommendations, nor want to do so. Temporary initiatives are also very expensive in their demands on top management time. Designing and composing groups takes time and much personal interaction. So does monitoring effectiveness, particularly if intervention is required in sensitive situations or to keep the initiative moving.

SUMMARY

An international commitment by a business enterprise normally requires significant changes in a firm's organizational structure. There is no one organizational structure that is ideal for multinational operations, and any structure once adopted must be continually reviewed and revised as internal and external factors keep changing. At the senior management level, the broad types of organization options for assigning responsibility and authority are relatively limited. But within the broad patterns, considerable diversity is possible.

[31] Christopher A. Bartlett, "Multinational Structural Change: Evolution versus Reorganization," in *The Management of Headquarters—Subsidiary Relationships in Multinational Corporations*, ed. Lars Otterbeck (Aldershot, Eng.: Gower, 1981), p. 135.

The organizational structure of most international enterprises evolves over time in a series of stages. American companies have typically moved from an export unit structure to a separate international division or international company as operations are extended to foreign areas. As top management becomes increasingly interested in international opportunities, a global organization structure may be adopted. International companies based in Europe and Canada tend to skip the international division stage and move directly to a global structure because domestic markets are smaller and less important to their overall success. Global structures can be organized with primary emphasis on function, product, or geography. Some firms have attempted to build complex grid structures where managers have multiple reporting relationships, and function, product, and area responsibilities overlap.

The choice among alternative structures depends on a small number of variables. The key problem is the inherent conflict between three dimensions of a firm's activities—functional, product, and geographic. A functional structure has the benefits of integrating marketing, finance, and production, but at the cost of area coordination and difficulties in transferring product and technological expertise from the parent company to the subsidiaries and among foreign operations. The product structure reduces problems of transferring technology and new products among locations, but it incurs the costs of duplication in functional tasks and of coordinating all the interests of an enterprise in a foreign area. The area structure gives good coordination geographically, but at the cost of product coordination among areas and duplication in functional expertise. In the final analysis, the choice of organization structure will reflect management's choice between sets of problems.

The relationships between corporate headquarters and the foreign subsidiaries present another difficult organizational problem—namely, centralization versus decentralization. In general, the preference is for headquarters to be responsible for strategy and the final decisions on long-range goals, and for the subsidiaries to have maximum responsibility and authority for operations. Here again, a firm's product strategy becomes a key determinant. Where the product strategy may result in suboptimization by not taking advantage of enterprise-wide unification possibilities, such functions as manufacturing, research and development, and financial management are likely to be closely controlled or coordinated at the center. At the other extreme, where great diversity in products and in end-use markets exists, marketing is particularly likely to be decentralized.

EXERCISES AND DISCUSSION QUESTIONS

1. What are the principal considerations that make organizational structures that work well for domestic operations less suitable for multinational operations?

2. "There is no single best structure for all international companies. Each company's operations are different, and each company has an almost unique set of needs to be served by its organizational structure." Discuss.

3. Select a multinational corporation and from its latest published annual report construct its international organization pattern. What do you think will be the chief weaknesses of this organization pattern in the current business situation?

4. Under what conditions would you recommend a functional structure at the topmost level as against a regional or international division structure?

5. Why do you think one of the major U.S. automobile companies retains an international division structure whereas a company like General Electric has a structure that emphasizes global business units?

6. "The key to successful matrix organization in a multinational is the set of rules that are developed for compromise between the demands of national interests and the imperatives of worldwide competition in the firm's businesses." Discuss.

7. "Within a tendency toward greater centralization of decision making, there is yet a discernible trend to greater individual independence for managers in multinational enterprises. Increased independence can accompany a reduction in the area of decision making by subsidiary managers." Discuss.

PART FIVE

Multinational operations management

Whatever a multinational firm's global strategy, it still requires sound operating management to achieve its objectives. This section of the book deals with basic issues that arise in the operations management of a multinational, paying particular attention to those aspects that are uniquely international.

Multinational management is, first and foremost, multicultural management. The first chapter in the section is accordingly devoted to the assessment of cultural differences and culture changes that will have an impact on the way in which a multinational is managed. Chapter 18 moves on to marketing management in a multinational setting, examining the ways in which marketing practices are standardized or differentiated across country boundaries. Similarly, Chapter 19 pays special attention to the considerations that arise in transferring technological expertise from country to country.

The next three chapters are devoted to the accounting and financial reporting and control of multinationals. Financial reporting, as examined in Chapter 20, has become a complex field, given the multiple purposes

for which accounts are required, differences in national accounting practices, and fluctuating exchange rates. The design of internal information
and control systems in multinationals is the subject of Chapter 21. Control measurements can have a major effect on the decisions taken by
managers throughout a multinational. Badly designed control measures,
for example, can lead managers of individual units within a multinational
to take actions clearly opposed to those that would be best for the
multinational as a whole.

With the added risk and opportunities introduced when operating
within multiple currencies and capital markets, multinational financial
management also requires a great deal of special attention within the
multinational firm. Chapter 22 surveys the management of the finance
function within the multinational.

The final chapter (Chapter 23) is concerned with multinational human
resource management. Policies on nationality of executives, cross-
national transfers, and differences in national compensation are among
the thorniest of issues in many multinationals.

Chapter 17

Cross-cultural management

Crossing national boundaries involves a step into different social and cultural environments. The enterprise that does business in one language and one culture will encounter many new problems when dealing with two, three, four, or perhaps fifty, languages and cultures. Groups of people, or societies, differ in their values and beliefs, in their aspirations and motivations, and in the ways they satisfy their desires. Such cultural differences pervasively influence all dimensions of international business activity.

THE MEANING OF CULTURE

By culture we mean the whole set of social norms and responses that condition a population's behavior. It is these that make one social envi-

401

ronment different from another and give each a shape of its own. The basic discipline that is most relevant here is cultural anthropology. Cultural anthropologists have devoted a great deal of time and effort to definitions of culture, arguing what should or should not be included.[1]

Culture is acquired and inculcated. It is the set of rules and behavior patterns that an individual learns but does not inherit at birth. For every society these norms and behavioral responses develop into a different cultural pattern that gets passed down through the generations with continual embellishment and adaptation; but with its own focus on aspects that are most highly developed.

For much cultural conditioning, the individual is unaware of the learning. The subtle process of inculcating culture through example and reward or punishment is generally much more powerful than direct instruction, and the individual unwittingly adopts the cultural norm. This process of learning a cultural pattern, called *enculturation*, conditions individuals so that a large proportion of their behavior fits the requirements of their culture and yet is determined below the level of conscious thought.[2] To individuals, cultural conditioning is like an iceberg—they are unaware of nine tenths of it.

The concept of culture is so broad that it gives little guidance to anyone wishing to study or compare cultures. Some classification scheme is needed as a basic framework for grasping the cultural pattern. One such approach is Murdock's elaborate list of more than 70 cultural universals that occur in all cultures. Arranged in alphabetical order to emphasize their variety, these are listed in Figure 17–1. While this one-dimensional checklist has major limitations, it can nevertheless be of considerable value. The international firm selling razors and razor blades, for example, must be aware that it is dealing with the puberty customs of different cultures. Moreover, as most razors are given as gifts the seller is also dealing with gift giving, courtship, and family patterns. An examination of cultural patterns under each of these headings will certainly suggest differences in marketing strategy from country to country.

A sensitivity to differences in the elements of culture brings with it an ability to analyze any happening from its cultural perspective. What on the surface appears as a similar happening in different cultures may be composed of many different cultural elements. The apparently simple phenomenon of a family meal, for instance, could be viewed as an extensive set of different rules concerning the time the meal is eaten, the seating arrangements, the roles played by each in initiating or ending

---

[1] See A. L. Kroeber and Clyde Kluckhohn, "Culture: A Critical Review of Concepts and Definitions," (Papers of the Peabody Museum of American Archaeology and Ethnology, Harvard University, Cambridge, Mass., 47. no. 1, 1952), pp. 1–223.

[2] Melville J. Herskovits, *Cultural Anthropology* (New York: Alfred A. Knopf, 1963), p. 326.

Figure 17–1

Cultural universals

Age grading	Food taboos	Music
Athletic sports	Funeral rites	Mythology
Bodily adornment	Games	Numerals
Calendar	Gestures	Obstetrics
Cleanliness training	Gift giving	Penal sanctions
Community organization	Government	Personal names
Cooking	Greetings	Population policy
Cooperative labor	Hairstyles	Postnatal care
Cosmology	Hospitality	Pregnancy usages
Courtship	Housing hygiene	Property rights
Dancing	Incest taboos	Propitiation of
Decorative art	Inheritance rules	supernatural beings
Divination	Joking	Puberty customs
Division of labor	Kingroups	Religious rituals
Dream interpretation	Kinship nomenclature	Residence rules
Education	Language	Sexual restrictions
Eschatology	Law	Soul concepts
Ethics	Luck superstitions	Status differentiation
Ethnobotany	Magic	Surgery
Etiquette	Marriage	Tool making
Faith healing	Mealtimes	Trade
Family	Medicine	Visiting
Feasting	Modesty concerning	Weaning
Fire making	natural functions	Weather control
Folklore	Mourning	

Source: George P. Murdock, "The Common Denominator of Cultures," in *The Science of Man in the World Crises,* ed. Ralph Linton (New York: Columbia University Press, 1945), pp. 123–42.

conversation and in interrupting or changing the subject, the comments regarded as humorous, the facial expressions used, the values placed on different foods, the attitudes toward age, and so on. Moreover, the shape and size of the table will differ, as will the utensils, the way they are used, and how the people eat.

CULTURE AND COMMUNICATION

A language is inextricably linked with all aspects of a culture, and each culture reflects in its language what is of value to the people. Culture is largely inculcated through language—spoken or written. Language, then, becomes the embodiment of culture. It may even condition what we look for and therefore see. One anthropologist comparing the structure of languages pointed out that Eskimo languages have several different words for types of snow, while the English language has one, and Aztec uses the same basic word stem for snow, ice, and cold.[3]

---

[3] Paul Henle, *Language, Thought, and Culture* (Ann Arbor: University of Michigan Press, 1958).

When communication involves translation from one language into another, the problems of ascertaining meaning that arise within one culture are multiplied many times. Translation is not simply a matching of words with identical meanings. It involves interpretation of the cultural patterns and concepts of one country in terms of the patterns and concepts of another. Awareness of translation difficulties is particularly important for legal agreements. As a distinguished international lawyer has noted, "When contracts cross national borders, they may alter in character as well as language."[4]

Communication does not always take the form of language. All behavior communicates and each culture may differ in the way it experiences and uses time, space, relationships, and a variety of other aspects of culture (see Box 17–1).[5] The use of time may convey quite different mean-

Box 17–1

Breaking through the cultural barrier

Companies report much difficulty in training so-called primitive peoples, such as Eskimos and Australian aborigines, to accept basic working techniques or to stick to regular work routines. Professor Allen Ivey of the University of Massachusetts claims, however, that the problem is not idleness or stupidity as managers tend to assume but rather an entirely different cultural approach to problem solving.

"A Western manager faced with a problem attempts to come up with a solution as quickly as possible," said Ivey. "I found that managers in Australia kept complaining that their aboriginal workers were too slow in getting things done. What they didn't understand is that the aborigines are actually much more complex thinkers than we normally assume. Before they do anything, they like to think about all the implications of it. This may take a long time.

"Managers also get angry when an aborigine doesn't respond to questions promptly. What they interpret as stupidity or obstructiveness is most likely simply that the employee is still thinking about it."

One of the fundamental differences in communicating behavior turned out to be the way aborigines pay attention. Said Ivey: "I asked them, 'Show me how you attend.' They sat side-by-side instead of face-to-face and looked down. They then looked up and gazed slowly down the body of the person beside them. This would make a Westerner feel very uncomfortable."

The discomfort and embarrassment of the trainer was obvious to the aborigines, who became embarrassed themselves. The more embarrassed they became, the more difficult it was to teach them anything.

Source: Extracted from a report by David Clutterbuck, senior editor, *International Management*, December 1980, p. 41.

---

[4] Henry P. deVries, "The Language Barriers," *Columbia Journal of World Business*, July–August 1969, p. 79.

[5] Edward T. Hall, *The Silent Language* (New York: Doubleday, 1959); *The Hidden Dimension* (New York: Doubleday, 1966); *Beyond Culture* (New York: Anchor Press/Doubleday, 1976).

ings in different cultures. To be 30 minutes late for an appointment with a business associate may be the height of rudeness in culture A but in culture B it may be early and unexpectedly reliable. Different messages may be conveyed by the amount of notice given for a meeting, the time of departure, invitations to future commitments, or the way in which a party agrees to the order of discussion at the meeting.

Operating difficulties can arise when workers from an agrarian peasant society are required to accept the kind of scheduling of time and routine essential for efficient industrial operations. In most agrarian societies, work is not equated with time and is not regularly and precisely scheduled. Instead, work is geared to seasonal emergencies, climatic threats, or sporadic exhaustion of supplies or resources.[6] Thus, setting time schedules or deadlines will evoke a positive response in certain cultures and a negative response in others.

In a similar way, the use of space conveys different meanings. The distance one person stands away from another indicates the degree of relationship or interest and can dramatically influence what is said. Different cultures have different norms for the appropriate distance for a given type of interaction. Middle Easterners and Latin Americans, for example, stand much closer than Western Europeans. The size of an office in relation to other offices conveys a great deal about the status of an American executive. In the Arab world, the size and location of an office are poor indicators of the importance of the person who occupies it.

ADJUSTING TO CULTURAL DIFFERENCES

The international firm has a special need for cultural sensitivity and adjustment. It has an existence outside each local culture in which it operates and many of its actions, such as cross-national transfers of old products or standard company practices, may represent a local innovation. And in many cases, the international firm may encounter unexpected problems because it is an unwitting agent for transplanting aspects of one culture into another.

The experienced international enterprise will try to accept the values of local culture patterns and seek to work within the accepted behavior patterns and customary goals that underlie these beliefs, in preference to substituting those of another culture pattern. As a general rule, national sensitivities tolerate less deviation from local standards by foreign firms than by native companies.

Lee suggests that three general classes of business adaptation are important—product, individual, and institutional—and that the degree of necessary adjustment ranges from none, or token, to comprehen-

---

[6] Conrad M. Arensberg and Arthur M. Niehoff, *Introducing Social Change: A Manual for Americans Overseas* (Chicago: Aldine Publishing, 1964), p. 164.

sive.[7] Adaptation is defined as the achievement of business goals with a minimum of problems and setbacks due to the various manifestations of cultural conflict.

Adaptation in product policies, which includes marketing strategies, can be illustrated by the experience of the Singer Sewing Machine Company in meeting different requirements of cultural patterns in the various markets it sells. In Moslem countries, the women's position had been a secluded and protected one, particularly with strangers. The practice of purdah, or wearing a veil so as to be screened from the sight of strangers, reflected this cultural pattern. Successful selling of sewing machines had been through sewing classes which Moslem women would not ordinarily be permitted to attend. In fact, at least one sewing machine salesman was sent to jail in Sudan for trying to encourage the wives to attend sewing classes. Singer overcame this problem by first selling the husbands, through demonstration classes, on how much additional work the women could do with sewing machines after taking sewing lessons. The men became convinced of the advantages and then ordered the wives to attend.

Individual adjustment is required of managers, and in the case of overseas personnel, of their spouses and families. An expatriate manager who wishes to motivate natives in a host nation, not merely order them around, must first make some personal changes. The manager should learn the local language, make adjustments in the manner of dealing with people, and adapt to local behavior norms such as time patterns.

Institutional adaptation relates to changes in organizational structure and organizational policies to fit cultural differences. Hiring practices developed by a U.S. parent company, for example, may purposely overlook class distinctions and assume that people from different areas and factions will work well together. When, operating in Lebanon, though, the same company might encounter serious difficulties in hiring Palestinian Moslem refugees to work side by side with native Christian Lebanese.

Adjustment of the multinational enterprise is needed at two levels—the national and the multinational. The issues at the national level might be characterized as bicultural. The situation is largely of a "we and they" type. The manager of a subsidiary must be aware of possible conflicts between local conditions and the cultural assumptions underlying the business practices being imported. Essentially these problems are two-sided, and management personnel of subsidiaries must be the bridge between the local situation and the international enterprise.

At the multinational level, or more specifically at global or regional headquarters, the international enterprise must coordinate and integrate business activities that are operating in many different cultural environ-

---

[7] James A. Lee, "Cultural Analysis in Overseas Operations," *Harvard Business Review*, March–April 1966, pp. 106–14.

ments. Managers must deal with many languages and across many cultures. The problems are both horizontal—across many cultures—and vertical—between each subsidiary and headquarters. And the organizational structure and policies of the global enterprise must facilitate communications and the implementation of policies across many cultures in order to achieve global goals.

METHODOLOGY FOR CULTURAL ASSESSMENT

The impact of cultural differences on international business makes quite clear the need for skills in cultural assessment on the part of the international manager. The manager may never become an expert cultural anthropologist in addition to being a management specialist, but should at least develop skills in assessing the key cultural elements that will have a direct bearing on effectiveness as a manager.

There is no one method to adopt in making cultural assessment as a basis for specific business decisions. Business problems cover such a wide range that the methods used may extend from a narrow depth study of receptivity to a new management practice, through to broad assessment of a society's attitudes to spending. In this section the characteristics of various approaches that the business manager might adopt are outlined. The remainder of the chapter then concentrates on the basic content of cultural assessment.

Approaches for assessing cultural differences

The most common approach to cultural assessment is a partial approach confined to studying particular aspects of a culture. Partial approaches are less powerful than comprehensive approaches that endeavor to identify and classify an entire range of cultural differences. The immense number of elements that can vary between cultures, however, makes overall approaches extremely unwieldy and costly to use. A compromise, often used by social anthropologists, is to compose a word picture of some constrained slice of behavior in the culture being examined, emphasizing, as would an artist, the more significant elements in the subject. Examples of such word pictures would be a description of a day in the life of a typical consumer,[8] or the motivation and thinking leading an employee to instigate a major confrontation with another worker.

In examining cultural patterns the manager should be aware of similarities as well as differences. Cross-cultural analysis for international business tends to emphasize differences because they are likely to create

---

[8] Oscar Lewis, *Five Families: Mexican Case Studies in the Culture of Poverty* (New York: Basic Books, 1959).

business problems. But to err by perceiving more differences than actually exist can also cause serious difficulties. Take the matter of managerial
preferences for risk taking. The American executive may see the Japanese
as different, whereas some cross-cultural studies suggest that they are
alike.[9] An American might needlessly overexplain a particular position,
trying to convince the Japanese to be more adventuresome.[10]

Another general caveat is that observed cultural patterns may be representative of a national group yet not applicable to everyone in the
group. What is usually being discussed is a modal pattern, and considerable variation from the mode will exist within a group or a subset of the
group. In fact, for some cultural characteristics there may be a wider
range within a given society than between societies. The manager should
be careful always to define the limits of the group that is of interest and
still be prepared to allow for individual differences.

Approaches for assessing culture change

A cultural assessment may be either static or dynamic. A static assessment serves only to identify the differences in variables between cultures.
A dynamic assessment seeks to indicate which variables will change and
perhaps in what order and with what speed. For the international manager, the identification of what changes will be readily accepted and what
will be rejected can mean the difference between success and failure.

Two approaches may be helpful in mapping culture change as a basis
for business decisions. The first is a mapping of the way any change is
expected to diffuse through the culture. The second is a mapping of the
decision-making and influence process for the key individuals to be affected by the change at each stage. Such mappings make quite explicit
the assumptions that are held about the change process and frequently
provide a necessary framework against which to specify actual research
questions. Without some mapping of these two processes, any quantification on which to base a decision to introduce the change could hardly
be soundly based.

Research into the pattern and speed of adoption, diffusion, or negative
diffusion (i.e., elimination) of products or practices within cultures has
received a great deal of attention in recent years.[11] An increasing tendency is to examine the process of change quantitatively over time.[12] The

[9] Bernard M. Bass, *The American Adviser Abroad*, Technical Report 27, Management
Research Center of the College of Business Administration (Rochester, N.Y.: University of
Rochester, August 1969), p. 12.

[10] For a summary of the literature on Japanese cultural differences, see Lane Kelly and
Reginald Worthley, "The Role of Culture in Comparative Management," *Academy of Management Journal* 24 (1981), pp. 164–73.

[11] See Everett M. Rogers and F. Floyd Shoemaker, *Communication of Innovations*, 2d ed.
(New York: Free Press/Macmillan, 1971).

[12] Robert Y. Hamblin, R. Brooke Jacobsen, and Jerry L. L. Miller, *A Mathematical Theory of
Social Change* (New York: John Wiley & Sons, 1973).

accumulated curve for numbers adopting a particular change has been widely shown to be S shaped. This basic shape holds for social changes in, for example, education, divorce, and career patterns, as well as for technological advances and changes in business practices. Moreover, a general logistic equation fits these diffusion curves almost as well whether the adopting units of the social system are individuals, families, firms, or governments.

The generality of these accumulated findings on diffusion suggests that quantitative analysis of change will be a valuable line of approach for the international manager. To date, most attention has been confined to demand forecasting of the direct adoption of products, but forecasting of social changes that influence the demand for a product should prove equally useful. Attempts to project ahead the rate of adoption of a new product, based on the rate of adoption at very early stages, have so far proved of only limited value, but accuracy increases as the degree of penetration expands.[13]

Avoiding cultural bias

In all cases requiring cross-cultural assessment the problem of cultural bias will be present. Everyone tends unwittingly to bias their view of other cultures by unconscious acceptance of their own cultural conditioning. It takes a great deal of discipline to force the mind to see things that one's own culture ignores or places in low value.

Cultural bias can be reduced by using researchers from the culture to be studied and through the development of culturally sensitive management. Specific attempts to eliminate what Lee has called the "self-reference criterion" (SRC), however, can be built into the research approach.[14] The problems are first defined in terms of the cultural traits, habits, or norms of the home society, and then redefined, without value judgments, in terms of the foreign cultural traits, habits, and norms. The difference between these two specifications indicates the likely cultural bias, or SRC effect, which can then be isolated and carefully examined to see how it influences the concept of the problem. Following this examination, the problem is redefined with the bias removed. Such an approach can be used for a wide variety of business problems. Its value lies in forcing researchers or managers posing the problem to make very specific the assumptions held about the cultural elements affecting the problem and to question whether they hold for another culture.

Green and White[15] have outlined the need in cross-cultural research to

---

[13] Frank M. Bass and Charles W. King, "The Theory of First Purchase of New Products," in *A New Measure of Responsibility for Marketing*, ed. Keith Cox and Ben M. Enis (Chicago: American Marketing Association, 1968).

[14] Lee, "Cultural Analysis in Overseas Operations."

[15] Robert T. Green and Philip D. White, "Methodological Considerations in Cross-National Consumer Research," *Journal of International Business Studies*, Fall–Winter 1976, pp. 81–87.

make appropriate adjustments to the results if any of three types of equivalence do not exist:

Functional equivalence.   The phenomena on which the research focuses may not fulfill the same function in each society. Bicycles, for example, provide basic transportation in some countries but are essentially for recreation and for children's use in others.

Conceptual equivalence.   The concepts employed in describing or measuring behavior may not apply to all societies.[16] Some of the more esoteric constructs of consumer and organizational behavior, for example, are definitely culture-bound.

Instrument equivalence.   The research instrument used to measure the phenomena in different societies may not provide an equally valid indication for each. Questionnaires aimed at identifying attitudes toward motherhood, for example, might have to ask quite different questions even if basic attitudes are the same because the cultures express these attitudes differently. Instruments may be classed as either "emic" or "etic".[17] Emic instruments are tests constructed to study a phenomenon within one culture only. Etic instruments are "culture-independent" and the identical instrument, properly translated, can be employed in any number of societies. There are few etic tests in existence,[18] however, and most research instruments require to be altered to some extent for each society.

PARTIAL CULTURAL ASSESSMENT: SOME KEY ASPECTS

This section briefly introduces some key cultural aspects that are fundamental to the way in which business is managed and yet vary greatly among cultures.

Attitudes toward work and achievement

The dominant view in a society toward wealth and material gain can have significant bearing on the types, qualities, and numbers of individuals who pursue entrepreneurial and management careers as well as on the way workers respond to material incentives.[19] In most countries,

---

[16] R. Sears, "Transcultural Variables and Conceptual Equivalence," in *Studying Personality Cross-Culturally*, ed, Bert Kaplan, (Evanston, Ill.: Row Peterson, 1961), pp. 445–55.

[17] R. Brislin, W. Lonner, and R. Thorndike, *Cross-Cultural Research Methods* (New York: John Wiley & Sons, 1973).

[18] See, for example, Y. Tanaka, T. Oyama, and C. Osgood, "A Cross-Cultural and Cross Concept Study of the Generality of Semantic Space," *Journal of Verbal Learning and Verbal Behavior* 2 (December 1963), pp. 392–405.

[19] Richard N. Farmer and Barry M. Richman, *Comparative Management and Economic Progress* (Homewood, Ill.: Richard D. Irwin, 1965), pp. 177–89.

wealth tends to be considered desirable and the prospect of material gain operates as a significant motivation. But there are societies where a worker will be on the job until he earns a certain amount of money and then be absent until these earnings are exhausted.

Variations among cultures in the dominant views toward achievement and work, which can be a vital determinant of management performance and productive efficiency, have been the subject of considerable research under the rubric of "achievement motivation."[20] The achievement motivation of an individual refers to a basic attitude toward life, namely, the willingness to commit oneself to the accomplishment of tasks considered by the person to be worthwhile and difficult. An achievement-motivated person makes accomplishment an end it itself. Tangible rewards are not rejected but they are not essential.

Measures of achievement motivation have been devised, and desires for achievement within different countries compared. Also, experiments have been undertaken in various countries on the effectiveness of techniques in changing achievement motivations. McClelland maintains that achievement motivation is the prime factor in managerial success.

Attitudes toward the future

Some of the principal differences among cultures lie in assumptions and attitudes relating to man's ability to influence the future. For example, an assumption that people can substantially influence the future underlies much of U.S. management philosophy. Long-range planning becomes a worthwhile investment because of confidence that planning can influence what is to happen. In cultures where other attitudes prevail, management practices based on such assumptions are not likely to be effective. On the other hand, care must be taken not to overgeneralize. Despite a general view that Moslem cultures are fatalistic, Muna found Arab executives most amenable to planning, quoting a saying in the Moslem *Hadith* that admonishes man first to think and plan ahead then put his trust in God.[21] Some Moslem peasant groups may indeed be fatalistic, but this is probably not an irrational attitude on their part. For peasants operating at base subsistence level it may be a just estimation of the enormous, and discouraging, weight of the chancy factors that condition the success of their efforts."[22]

Whatever the explanation for varying attitudes, the critical issue for business operations is whether individuals believe that events will occur regardless of what they do and whether they can help shape future

---

[20] David C. McClelland, *The Achieving Society* (Princeton, N.J.: D. Van Nostrand, 1961).

[21] Farid A. Muna, *The Arab Executive* (London: Macmillan Press Ltd., 1980), p. 95.

[22] Maxime Rodinson, *Islam and Capitalism*, Eng. ed. (Harmondsworth, Middlesex: Penguin Books, 1974), p. 113.

outcomes significantly. The self-determination or "master of destiny" attitude is generally qualified by the accompanying view that future aspirations must be realistic and that hard work is necessary to achieve future goals.

Patterns of decision making

Reliance on objective analysis in decision making varies greatly among cultures. In U.S. business, decisions are supposed to be based on objective analyses of facts, and all persons who can contribute relevant information are expected to do so. Such a norm leads to large collections of data and the development of impersonal decison-making techniques.

In other societies, the personal judgment of a senior executive may be the accepted basis for a decision. A request that the executive explain or give the rationale for his decision would be interpreted as a lack of confidence in the executive's judgment. Furthermore, it may be considered inappropriate for a senior executive to seek facts and consult others—especially juniors—on matters on which the senior is already presumed to be wise. In such cultures, hierarchical, emotional, and mystical considerations, rather than objective analyses, may dominate.

Attitudes toward authority

The dominant view of authority in a society may range from an autocratic system at one extreme to a democratic-participative system at the other extreme. In autocratic systems, managerial decisions would typically be highly centralized with little delegation of authority. At the other extreme, managerial authority would be shared with subordinates and workers, and considerable decentralization in decison making would be typical of business enterprises.

It is not possible to say which forms of managerial authority along the continuum are best in terms of efficiency or in achieving other business goals. The forms vary greatly from Japan to West Germany and from the United States to Yugoslavia. Yet each of these countries has had impressive records of business performance and economic growth. Whatever authority system prevails in a given country, the international enterprise will have to relate its management patterns to the expectations and traditions of local employees.

Authority systems are also highly relevant to marketing. It is important to know whether purchasing decisions within buying units are typically decentralized or reserved for the top-echelon executives. In negotiating with governments, the international manager will have to know whether decision authority resides with low-level bureaucrats or must be handled at the highest levels of government bureaucracy.

Expression of disagreement

Differences among societies in frankness of expression and tolerance for personal differences affect interpersonal relations. In Far Eastern cultures it is traditional to value politeness over blunt truth. The Japanese business executive finds it inappropriate to say no in many situations. In dealing with an American, the Japanese may make all kinds of barely favorable noises and then maybe say, "I'll think about the matter." The Japanese has actually told the American no, but it is entirely possible that the American thinks that the answer was yes, and later imagines that the Japanese was being deceptive.

In many Latin American countries, frankly expressed differences in views do not easily fit the culture. If a person expresses criticisms of a policy in order to improve the quality of decision making, such statements are likely to be interpreted as personal attacks. If a subordinate disagrees with the boss, the boss will most certainly feel insulted. Persons in subordinate positions are expected either to present information or judgments that support the ideas of senior officials or be silent.

Responsibility to family

In some countries, businessmen operate as individuals independent of family.[23] In others, some version of the extended family prevails. Under this pattern large numbers of near as well as quite distant relatives are encompassed in a system of shared rights and obligations. All members of this group are interdependent, and it is the responsibility of the leaders to see that the economic resources are available to satisfy the needs of each member of the group. Writing about the Arab executive, Muna claims:

> The use of personal (family and friendship) ties and connections is not only widespread, but is also an important and necessary means of doing business. This approach is in direct contrast with the reliance upon official, institutional, or formal business channels for conducting business affairs. In the Arab world the use of such personal ties and connections is evident in a wide range of activities. Typical examples that were provided by the executives include: (a) expediting and getting a work-permit, a passport or a visa, and generally bypassing or expediting most governmental formalities and paperwork: (b) obtaining referrals or employment; and (c) knowing about, negotiating, and eventually securing a multi-million dollar business contract. . . .
>
> For the Arab executive, there is a powerful incentive to use personal (family and friendship) ties instead of institutional or formal channels in

---

[23] Peter Marris and Anthony Somerset, *African Businessmen* (London: Routledge and Kegan Paul, 1971), chap. 6.

getting things done. This is partly due to the inefficiency, and sometimes the absence, of institutional systems and procedures; and partly due to the importance of family and friendship ties which are usually more powerful than institutional rules and procedures.[24]

Strong and extended family ties can result in what has been characterized as patrimonial management.[25] Ownership and key positions in a business enterprise are held by family members. Nepotism is generally dominant in the full range of employment decisions, and business goals are oriented toward family interests and aspirations. Such patrimonial management has the advantages of encouraging teamwork, loyalty, and mutual interest. Family codes can enforce morality in financial and other matters, and family loyalty attracts and holds managers in situations where the supply of qualified managers is limited.

The extended family situation also has drawbacks. It emphasizes nepotism rather than competence. It can vitiate the will to work by limiting personal incentives. Family business may be run like an authoritarian household with little concern for considerations other than family goals. And family enterprises may suffer from a lack of invigorating ideas and innovations that can come from outsiders. Even where the family is not dominant within an organization, top executives in countries in which the extended family is important may expect and be expected to behave as head of a family.[26]

Family patterns can be extremely important from the standpoint of marketing as well as general management. (see Box 17–2). In Western societies, the husband and wife typically share decision making on family purchases, with children and other members of the family having a secondary vote. In the extended family, the family patriarch holds the key decison-making position, although this is declining with the monetization of the economy, the demise of family enterprises, and an increase in geographic and social mobility.

Social structure

A final category of cultural elements can be grouped under the general heading of social structure. It includes such variables as interclass mobility, determinants of status, and patterns of education.

Few societies in the world assume that all men are equal. Instead, societies have traditional systems of ranking individuals and groups. Relative positions in the social hierarchy are based on ethnic, cultural, edu-

---

[24] Muna, *The Arab Executive*, pp. 74–75.

[25] Frederick Harbison and Charles A. Myers, *Management in the Industrial World* (New York: McGraw-Hill, 1959), pp. 69–73.

[26] Muna, *The Arab Executive*, pp. 40–41, see also Dennis Anastos, Alexis Bedos, and Bryant Seaman, "The Development of Modern Management Practices in Saudi Arabia," *Columbia Journal of World Business* 15 (Summer 1980), p. 83.

Box 17–2

The foreign family as buyer

The family is the focal point of Japanese life. The woman predominates in family decisions. She holds, plans, and administers the family budget. She would condone intrusion of work associates to her family, but in general the private life is intentionally kept out of her husband's work sphere. Seldom is a Japanese executive invited to homes of his colleagues with his wife. If ever invited, the work group alone would be there. The executive would be spending so much time outside of office hours with his work associates that there can hardly be a point of extending the contact beyond into the privately guarded family life of each other.

The family, in turn, keeps in touch with others through routinized and ritualized social functions such as biannual gift giving and gift exchange on special commemorative occasions and family festivities. So ritualized is this routine of gift giving, for instance, that only a token contact might be established between the work group superior and subordinate. Department stores may be delivering the biannual gifts on behalf of many customers who prefer not to visit the other's home, when giving the gift. A budget-minder may venture into delivering a bottle of expensive Scotch received from someone else. Thus personal contacts would be held to the minimum. Likewise, no significant sentimental values are attached to the gifts. Department stores offer an exchange service where not-wanted gifts could be brought in for refund or for outright exchange with something else.

Source: Extracted from Hiro Matsusaki, "Conflicts in Cross-Cultural Management: The Asymmetric Contrasts of Business Practices in Japan and North America," in *Recent Research on the Internationalization of Business*, ed. L. G. Mattson and F. Wiedersheim-Paul (Stockholm: Almqvist & Wiksell International, 1979).

---

cational, and linguistic differences, as well as on economic position. Sometimes traditional social structures are fairly rigid, such as the caste system of India. Sometimes the distinctions are more fluid and considerable interclass mobility is the rule. In most countries of the world there is a distinction between the elite, who have political and economic control of the country, and the relatively underprivileged peasant groups.[27]

Two aspects of social structure are a special concern to the international enterprise—interclass mobility and the status assigned by a society to individuals who engage in business occupations. If a rigid social structure prevents a substantial number of individuals from moving into the ranks of management or other responsible business positions, managerial effectiveness is likely to be constrained in many, if not most, business activities. If the status assigned to business pursuits is low in the social structure, it will be difficult to attract adequate numbers of competent persons to business positions.

---

[27] Arensberg and Niehoff, *Introducing Social Change*, p. 41.

COMPREHENSIVE CULTURAL ASSESSMENT

The international manager may have neither the time nor the need to build a comprehensive picture of a particular culture. Yet familiarity with ways to conceptualize the overall culture can provide the manager with a checklist of elements that are important for particular business problems but likely to be overlooked. Two such approaches, both two-dimensional, will be briefly outlined here.

Edward Hall presents his map of culture as a two-dimensional matrix composed of 10 aspects of human activity, which he calls Primary Message Systems.[28] These are shown in Figure 17–2. While each aspect can

Figure 17–2

Primary message systems of Edward Hall's *The Silent Language*

Primary message system	Depicts attitudes and cultural rules for:
1. Interaction	The ordering of man's interaction with those around him, through language, touch, noise, gesture, and so forth.
2. Association	The organization (grouping) and structuring of society and its components.
3. Subsistence	The ordering of man's activities in feeding, working, and making a living.
4. Bisexuality	The differentiation of roles, activities, and function along sex lines.
5. Territoriality	The possession, use, and defense of space and territory.
6. Temporality	The use, allocation, and division of time.
7. Learning	The adaptive process of learning and instruction.
8. Play	Relaxation, humor, recreation, and enjoyment.
9. Defense	Protection against man's environment, including medicine, warfare, and law.
10. Exploitation	Turning the environment to man's use through technology, construction, and extraction of materials.

Source: Adapted from Edward T. Hall, *The Silent Language* (Garden City, N.Y.: Doubleday, 1959). pp. 61–81.

be examined alone, Hall shows how a grasp of the complex interrelationships of a culture can be obtained by commencing with any of the 10 aspects and studying its intersection with each of the others. In a matrix there will be two intersections of each pair of aspects.

For a direct application of Hall's matrix to international business, take the example of a large manufacturer of toys and games assessing opportunities in a new country. The firm will be directly engaged in the play aspect of the new culture, and it is certain that the cultural patterns with respect to play will differ from those the firm is currently dealing with.

---

[28] Hall, *Silent Language,* especially chap. 3.

Use of Hall's matrix would raise 18 categories of questions about play patterns in the new culture. Stemming from the intersection of play with the remaining primary message systems, the first two categories would ask about interaction in play and about play in interaction, the second two would ask about the associations—that is, organizations involved in play and games involving associations, and so on. Questions raised within the 18 categories are illustrated in Figure 17–3, but it must

Figure 17–3

A business application of Edward Hall's map of culture

Intersections of play and other primary message systems	Sample questions concerning cultural patterns significant for marketing toys and games
1. Interaction/play	How do people interact during play as regards competitiveness, instigation, or leadership?
2. Play/interaction	What games are played involving acting, role playing, or other aspects of real-world interaction?
3. Association/play	Who organizes play and how do the organization patterns differ?
4. Play/association	What games are played about organization; for example, team competitions and games involving kings, judges, or leader-developed rules and penalties?
5. Subsistence/play	What are the significant factors regarding people such as distributors, teachers, coaches, or publishers who make their livelihood from games?
6. Play/subsistence	What games are played about work roles in society such as doctors, nurses, firemen?
7. Bisexuality/play	What are the significant differences between the sexes in the sports, games, and toys enjoyed?
8. Play/bisexuality	What games and toys involve bisexuality; for example, dolls, dressing up, dancing?
9. Territoriality/play	Where are games played and what are the limits observed in houses, parks, streets, schools, and so forth?
10. Play/territoriality	What games are played about space and ownership; for example, Monopoly?
11. Temporality/play	At what ages and what times of the day and year are different games played?
12. Play/temporality	What games are played about and involving time; for example, clocks, speed tests?
13. Learning/play	What patterns of coaching, tuition, and training exist for learning games?
14. Play/learning	What games are played about and involving learning and knowledge; for examples, quizzes?
15. Defense/play	What are the safety rules for games, equipment, and toys?
16. Play/defense	What war and defense games and toys are utilized?
17. Exploitation/play	What resources and technology are permitted or utilized for games and sport; for example, hunting and fishing rules, use of parks, cameras, vehicles, and so forth?
18. Play/exploitation	What games and toys about technology or exploitation are used; for example, scouting, chemical sets, microscopes?

be clear that the map does not magically produce the right answers or even the right questions. This is simply one structured approach to investigating how a new culture may differ. The reader who rejects a structured approach, however, should be sure that an ad hoc alternative does develop an adequate sensitivity to the important cultural differences.

Farmer and Richman also use a matrix approach.[29] They propose a list of critical environmental constraints, or cultural elements, against which they set another list of 77 critical elements in the managerial process. The general categories for the critical elements are planning and innovation, control, organization, staffing, direction, leadership and motivation, marketing policies, production and procurement, research and development, finance, and public and external relations.

Managerial effectiveness, Farmer and Richman contend, is largely determined by the pattern of external constraints. As the environment changes, so too must the pattern of management. By examining the managerial alternatives against the background of external constraints, managers will move toward a pattern of business practice most appropriate to the situation and away from absolute rules imposed without regard for the situation. In a simple application, for example, the internal procedures and organization structure should change radically where the bulk of the workers do not accept the idea of cause and effect, that is, the scientific method. Fewer rational requests and guiding principles will be called for and more direct rules and internal checking procedures will be required.

This type of matrix approach can be readily adapted to any business situation. On the vertical axis would appear relevant cultural variables and along the horizontal axis the dependent variables of interest to management. The body of the matrix would show the nature of the relationship between cultural variables and each management variable.

UNDERSTANDING CULTURE CHANGE

Acceptance and resistance to change

A characteristic of human culture is that change does occur, although it may not be rapid or without resistance. The manager operating cross-culturally therefore needs an understanding of what aspects of a culture will resist change and how those will differ among cultures, how the process of change takes place in different cultures, and what the speed of change will be.

There are two seemingly contradictory forces within cultures. On the one hand, people attempt to protect and preserve their culture with an elaborate set of sanctions and laws invoked against those who deviate

---

[29] Farmer and Richman, *Comparative Management and Economic Progress.*

from their norms. On the other hand, the environment within which a culture exists is continually changing, and a culture must change in order to ensure its own continuity.[30] Where a culture comes into contact with other cultures, this same dichotomy exists. There is, on the one hand, an ingrained belief, called *ethnocentrism*, that the ways of one's own culture are superior to those of other cultures, and on the other hand, a realization that a culture must be competitive if it is to retain its own identity.

These conflicting forces make some elements of culture highly resistant to change. Others immediately fall to innovations, even though some of them may give an impression that they are immutable. How can these elements be differentiated?

Edward Hall classifies cultural aspects into formal, informal, and technical, based primarily on differences in the way the cultural norm is learned, the culture's level of awareness of the norm, and the response to a deviation from the norm.

Formal rules are at the core of the culture and really determine its essence. They are taught through example and admonition as rules for which there is either right or wrong, with clear indication of when a mistake has been made. There is a formal awareness of the norm and a great deal of emotion if the norm is violated. Most societies, for example, have a formal rule that there should be no enjoyment from hurting others physically or from seeing them hurt. The rule is made clear from early childhood and penalties are imposed for breaking it.

Informal rules are not taught so directly. Usually the learner picks them up by imitation and is unaware of learning them. The society is generally unconscious of the rules, and if one is violated, there would be only an expression of anxiety or some informally learned reaction. The average child does not receive direct instruction in how to play but is left to observe others and to do likewise. If the child attempts to dominate playmates, for example, the playmates will very likely develop ways of excluding the child. Thus, by experience rather than direct instruction, the child learns how to behave in groups.

Technical rules are usually taught by instruction in a logical and coherent manner. These are at the highest level of awareness as they are verbalized, reasoned, and explicit. Few emotions are attached to the violation of a technical rule. Breaking a rule by adopting a different training approach for an athletic sport, for example, would occasion intellectual interest but little emotion.

The aspects falling into each category differ from culture to culture. If we continue with a sporting example, for instance, we might find that the English regard acceptance of the referee's rulings as a fundamental principle of sportsmanship—a formal rule that would produce an emotional

---

[30] Arensberg and Niehoff, *Introducing Social Change*, p. 99.

response from most of the population if they were confronted with a direct violation. On the other hand, the Germans may have a clear set of technical rules for when and how to object to rulings, while Americans adopt an informal approach that objections should be made as and when justified. Any aspect of culture could be compared between cultures in this way.

Attitudes toward change clearly differ for each of the three classes. Formal rules would be held with great tenacity, change very slowly, and be particularly resistant to any attempt to force change from outside. Informal rules can change more easily. There is room for more deviation by individuals and imitation can be selective in one direction or another. Change comes most easily with technical rules, because they are readily observed, talked about, transmitted, and accepted at a more or less rational level. The key to culture change seems to lie in the informal system. In a complex and changing environment, imitation of others will not be perfect. When some of the variants that emerge seem to work better than others, they are copied and eventually develop as technical rules.

Technical changes are most likely to deal with details of an activity— for example, the use of a new fertilizer or the introduction of a new type of motor. But a series of changes in technical rules, initially consonant with the existing formal systems can cause more fundamental changes in the formal and informal systems. Technical and informal rules seem to surround each part of the formal system, and when these supports are removed, formal rules may eventually give way. This may explain why some parts of a culture reject change persistently only to collapse later on. Hall illustrates this sort of phenomena with the change in attitude toward premarital chastity in the United States.[31] Changes in women's social life, education, career patterns, and dress habits, and the widespread use of the private car removed many technical supports to the formal rule. After resisting change for many years, the rule eventually changed very rapidly.

Not all the new elements that evolve from within a culture, or are introduced from outside, are adopted by the culture. They have to fall on fertile ground in the sense that there is a perception of the need for the change and a broad acceptance of it. The social structure of the society and those who introduce the change or are aware of it will thus be important factors in its acceptance, as examined in the next section. Cultures also tend to develop a particular interest in some parts of their system—called a *cultural focus*. A culture is more likely to develop and adopt changes in those areas on which it places this emphasis. Conversely, less important areas will change less and there will be lower tolerance for change in them. The Arabs, for example, have regarded the "fellahin" engaged in agriculture as of very low status and have adopted

---

[31] Hall, *Silent Language*, p. 113.

few agricultural innovations in comparison with the Israelis who accord agriculture high status and reward successful agricultural innovation with almost national fame.

Social dynamics of culture change

It is as important for the international manager to identify the roles different people will play in the change process as it is to identify what cultural aspects will resist change. Cultural change implies change in the pattern of behavior of the individuals adhering to that culture. The order in which persons with different characteristics adopt an innovation and the influences that affect their decision are thus of particular importance. The field of diffusion studies has a great deal to say about these.

Adopters of any innovation are conventionally classified into five groups, according to the order in which they adopt the innovation, as follows:[32]

Adopter category	
Innovators	First 2.5%
Early adopters	Next 13.5%
Early majority	Next 34%
Late majority	Next 34%
Laggards	Remaining 16%

The idea behind this classification is that common characteristics may be identified for the adopters of each stage.

"Innovators" are regarded by themselves and by others as deviants from the norms of their culture or subculture. They tend to have a characteristic venturesomeness and to have seen more of other cultures than later adopters. One study of firms commencing export activity showed almost all the innovators to have international backgrounds.[33] "Early adopters" tend to have a higher position in the social hierarchy than innovators and to rate high as opinion leaders. They may have a considerable influence on later adopters. The "early majority" seems to be characterized by their capacity for deliberation. They do not adopt until other respected persons have done so, seldom emerging as leaders. Contrasted with this, the dominant value of the people who make up the "late majority" is skepticism. They tend to wait until the weight of public opinion strongly favors the innovation before they proceed. "Laggards" tend to be older, to be suspicious of innovations, and to take the past and tradition as their point of reference.

---

[32] Rogers and Shoemaker, *Communication of Innovations.* Chapter 5 provides the references for most of the research generalizations that follow in this section.

[33] Kenneth Simmonds and Helen Smith, "The First Export Order: A Marketing Innovation," *British Journal of Marketing,* Summer 1968.

Associated with the study of diffusion, and particularly relevant for cultural change, is the concept of an adoption process. This is conceived as a set of five mental stages through which an individual passes from first hearing about an innovation until he finally adopts it. These are (1) awareness, (2) interest, (3) evaluation, (4) trial, and (5) adoption. Studies of each of these stages and the information and influence sources important at each stage have provided some significant generalizations about adoptions. It has been found that impersonal sources of information tend to be most influential at the awareness stage, and personal sources tend to be most influential at the evaluation stage. Commercial change agents, that is, advertising and selling, seem to be more important at the trial stage than at any other stage. In the earlier stages of the process nonlocal sources of information tend to be most important. But in the later stages local sources take the command position. These findings may be very significant for firms planning the introduction of products into new cultural environments.

Social-class identification by groups within a culture can also affect the diffusion of an innovation. A social class, however defined, is likely to exhibit some common variants of the overall national culture, particularly if its members are grouped in the same living environment. One landmark study suggests that the cultural norms of a social class at the particular time were a significant factor in the acceptance or rejection of a particular innovation.[34] The pattern of interaction and influence that leads to adoption or rejection may also be largely carried on within one social class.[35] Changes may thus not trickle down the social scale with each class striving to copy classes above it. The international businessman must be prepared, therefore, to observe what happens within social groups as well as across a society as a whole.

PROMOTING CULTURE CHANGE

In many situations, management will not passively adapt to the ever-changing patterns of cultural differences within which it operates but will endeavor to induce change in some aspect of a local culture. The most common targets for active attempts to induce change in this way are consumer buying patterns and employee work patterns. In most cases the attempt will be based on actual observation of the success of a culture change in another situation and will not stem merely from a management desire to "move ahead." Cultural transplants are more likely to be successful when an actual example of a similar culture change already exists.

---

[34] Graham Saxon, "Class and Conservatism in the Adoption of Innovations," *Human Relations* 9, no. 1 (1956), pp. 91–100.

[35] Charles W. King, "Fashion Adoption: A Rebuttal of the 'Trickle Down Theory,'" in *Toward Scientific Marketing*, ed. Stephen A. Greyser (Chicago: American Marketing Association, 1963), pp. 108–25.

The international enterprise may promote change, but it is the members of the foreign culture who have to accept change. The general strategy, therefore, must be to discover the ways and incentives characteristic of the culture that are likely to result in acceptance. The comparative business literature is replete with examples of unsuccessful attempts to induce cultural change. Yet the success stories are numerous also, and they provide considerable encouragement for the likely success of well-designed and well-informed efforts to promote cultural change. This section examines some of the elements that should be considered in deciding how the attempt to promote change is to be carried out.

Building on the old. Unless they produce dramatic benefits, the easiest way to have innovations accepted is to make sure they present no open conflict with traditional values and customs and to graft onto them. Medicine is one field in which problems have often occurred. In societies that have continued to rely on folk-medical practices, it has frequently been effective to relate new Western medical products to irrational traditional beliefs. Use of existing power and influence structures is also recommended, as Zaltman and Duncan have pointed out:

> Strategies that involve using existing power or influence structures such as midwives to disseminate birth-control pills or faith healers to distribute condoms do not cause a loss of pride or dignity among these often highly regarded individuals. To the contrary, their status, which is a source of their pride, is reinforced and enhanced.[36]

Identifying the rational. The straightforward approach of presenting information and rational argument assumes that individuals are guided by reason. Such a strategy, called a reeducative strategy,[37] is the most neutral of all strategies, and can be effective in many situations. Firms providing training and technical help to customers as part of their sales approach are adopting this sort of strategy. Nevertheless, education is a slow process, and what is rational to the protagonist of the change might not be what the change target believes is rational. Rationality, after all, does not exist independently of the objectives that are adopted. An individual's actions to protect an established status position against change may be very rational.

Avoiding the unknown. When the full nature of a change and its outcome are unknown, uncertainty and anxiety abound for those who perceive they may be affected. Resistance to the change then builds up as a protection against the unknown. The promoter of change should thus take great care to specify exactly what the change is and how it will

---

[36] Gerald Zaltman and Robert Duncan, *Strategies for Planned Change* (New York: John Wiley & Sons, 1977), p. 71.

[37] Ibid., p. 111.

work. Even prior to this stage, the development of awareness of the need for change may be desirable. Conceivably, an innovation may be brought about simply through providing the necessary tools with which to recognize the problem.

Recognizing the influence of others.   The attitudes of individuals toward change are influenced by those around them.[38] Individuals may change because of a desire for recognition by others, prestige, or to emulate others with more status than themselves. If an individual is asked to change behavior in a way that will not be supported by others of significance to that individual, then the change is unlikely to come about.[39] The introduction of a change may have more chance of success, therefore, if its promoter works through opinion leaders who will influence others.[40]

Providing support.   Anything new is likely to require further changes in using it. A change should not be introduced and dropped. It should be supported until it is thoroughly operational. Examples abound of modern equipment lying abandoned in fields, factories, homes, and offices because of lack of instruction on use or maintenance.

Compensating the losers.   It is often argued that when a net gain results through change, nobody loses. In more cases than not, however, there will be net costs to some party affected. Measures to protect those affected adversely, from economic loss or from decreases in personal status and dignity, can go a great way toward smoothing the adoption of innovations. Firms within single nations have developed policies of compensating workers for adopting changes in technology. So, too, in multinational corporations will there be increased demands to compensate employees hurt economically by innovations, even though the same innovations have already been adopted in other parts of the multinational organization.

INTERNATIONAL BUSINESS AS A CHANGE AGENT

A final topic related to the cultural components of the international business environment is the role of international business as a change agent. Here we are referring to the cultural fallout as well as the deliberately promoted cultural changes. The concept of international business as a change agent usually has a favorable connotation in business circles

---

[38] Daniel Katz and Robert I. Kahn, *The Social Psychology of Organizations* (New York: John Wiley & Sons, 1966).

[39] Chris Argyris, *Interpersonal Competence and Organizational Effectiveness* (Homewood, Ill.: Irwin-Dorsey, 1962).

[40] Rogers and Shoemaker, *Communication of Innovations*, pp. 243–44.

and refers to such benefits as the transfer of technology and management skills,[41] the training of workers, and the social and economic modernization effects in the host country. All of these features of international business are generally assumed to be positive and desirable contributions to the countries in which international business activity takes place. But as the social scientists have observed, cultural change can have both positive and negative aspects for the members of a given society.

Some cultural changes for which international enterprises can claim credit are consistent with the goals of national leaders who are anxious to modernize and industrialize their society. The nature or the pace of other changes can provoke negative reactions to the international enterprise by government leaders or groups in the society. Because it is an agent of change, whether or not the change is intentional, the international enterprise should attempt to anticipate the changes for which it might be held responsible and the full chain of results from changes it is promoting. Such anticipation requires the international executive to construct a model, or description, of the changing society. The classification of socioeconomic effects of industrialization shown in Figure 17–4 might be usefully adapted for this purpose.

Figure 17–4

Socioeconomic effects of industrialization

A. Effects on individuals:

Organization of production involves the movement of local inhabitants from self-contained village societies to an urban advanced economy. Personal adjustments include the transition from a rural to an urban existence, and from the timeless subsistence economy to an efficiency-oriented system geared to profit orientation.

Relationship to work changes from that of the rural village work situation to that of an industrialized society. Differences include moving from a leisurely pace of production to the programmed efficiency of the MNC industrial environment. The diversified range of living skills indigenous to the rural village setting contrasts with the narrow, more repetitive skills resulting from the division of labor.

Motivation and enterprise for the individual change with the move to an advanced society. The philosophy of cooperation inherent in the rural village setting fades into the competitive environment characteristic of modern industry. Responsibility for the acquisition of wealth and income now depends upon the individual's effort, not upon hereditary or seniority principles, as in the rural village.

B. Population effects:

The population shift from a rural to an urbanized economy is a key element in the westernization of an LDC's culture. First, there is an increase in the economically active population. Second, the population grows as a result of greater life expectancy and decreased infant mortality due to better health facilities.

---

[41] See Karl P. Sauvant, "The Potential of Multinational Enterprises as Vehicles for the Transmission of Business Culture," *Controlling Multinational Enterprises: Problems, Strategies, Counterstrategies,* ed. Karl P. Sauvant and Farid G. Lavipour (Boulder, Colo.: Westview Press, 1976).

Figure 17–4 (concluded)

C. Effects on economic institutions:

Occupational aspects. Changes in occupational structure occur as workers entering the monetarized economy broaden the occupational base and move gradually away from their unskilled status. Education and training contribute to the upward movement of the local inhabitant in the occupational hierarchy.

Savings and investments. The mobilization of savings and investments is an essential ingredient of industrialization. Investments by MNCs in manufacturing stimulate industrial growth and employment. MNCs in the financial sector help to mobilize savings for investment, and provide a stimulus for consumption through the hire-purchase mechanism.

Consumption and distribution. As monetarization of the economy proceeds, more money is available for consumption purchases that, in turn, require additional distributive outlets. MNCs provide the expertise and organization required for a complex wholesaling and retailing setup.

D. Effects on the social structure:

Kinship and family. Breakup of kinship and family patterns occurs as the geographically dispersed nuclear family supplants the extended family. The woman ceases to be the primary producer in the family unit, a role the man now assumes as he moves into industrial work. Arranged marriages give way to the Westernized free market courtship mechanism.

Community organization and problems. Voluntary associations take the place of blood and kinship ties. The transition to urban life causes adjustment problems and a loss of emotional security, as urban Western values clash with a traditional rural village outlook. Increases in vandalism, alcoholism, and drug addiction can result. The severity of poverty also increases as the low wages of unskilled laborers prove insufficient in an environment where the consumption of many Western products becomes increasingly obligatory.

Education and science. As industrialization progresses, institutions of higher learning in the LDC offer more vocationally oriented courses such as engineering, commerce, and agricultural sciences. These courses are aimed toward supplying manufacturing units with local skilled labor, thus reducing the propensity to import labor.

Communication and popular culture. Multinational corporations aid the development of a communications system occasionally through actual ownership of media, but more often through their commercial sponsorship of media. The media (a) provide vehicles through which the local population learns of Western lifestyles and consumption habits, (b) make accurate and permanent records more likely, (c) make timely reporting of major events possible, (d) extend man's empathetic comprehension beyond his personal experiences, (e) coordinate the groups that constitute the personal contact network.

Interest groups and organizations. Affiliations with trade unions expand as the population becomes both more educated and more active in the monetarized economy. During early stages of economic development, however, labor remains largely unorganized and in an unadvantageous bargaining position.

Religious groups and organizations. Transition from rural village to urban life often results in a mixture of organized religion and witchcraft as religious beliefs.

Social stratification. The static rural village system, which ranks by heredity and seniority, is replaced in the industrial society by rankings on the bases of wealth, education, income, and occupation. The structure of society becomes more flexible and social mobility increases.

Organization of the state. As the LDC industrializes, the state may orient its functional parts to redressing the inequalities produced by the system (income, wealth, location of industry, etc.). As the MNCs undertake much of the private investment, the LDC's government focuses upon establishing an economic infrastructure and broadening educational opportunities.

Source: Adapted from John S. Hill and Richard R. Still, "Cultural Effects of Technology Transfer by Multinational Corporations in Lesser Developed Countries," *Columbia Journal of World Business* 15 (Summer 1980), pp. 40–51.

Where the changes are perceived as beneficial by local interests, the bargaining position of the enterprise is strengthened. Where the expected changes are likely to appear dysfunctional and be negatively received, the international enterprise may want to modify its operational patterns or prepare to meet local antagonism, for a while at least.

SUMMARY

When the business firm crosses national boundaries and begins to operate in a number of countries, it is faced with a wide range of cultural differences that can significantly affect the achievement of business objectives. The problem of identifying cultural differences is· difficult because of the natural tendency for people to observe and evaluate behavior of others in terms of the cultural conditioning of their own country. Furthermore, cultural patterns are not static but constantly changing. The problems faced in the cultural field involve much more than an intellectual appreciation that differences exist. International managers must develop cultural sensitivity, frequently through living experience in different cultures. With cultural sensitivity, the enterprise will be aware of the need to identify cultural variables and to adjust its organization and its operations to cultural differences. In many situations, the enterprise will have to promote cultural change in order to achieve its business goals. In a broader sense, the international enterprise itself is a powerful change agent. It must anticipate the changes that it causes and the reception that such changes will receive in host countries.

EXERCISES AND DISCUSSION QUESTIONS

1. "Cultural anthropology has certainly spawned a lot of empirical research, but as far as theory is concerned it is barren. The few tested theories that are available, moreover, have to be stretched a long way to reach anything of value to inter-cultural business." Discuss.

2. Give your own definition of culture.

3. Some multinational firms issue a standard corporate manual for international use containing set organizational definitions and rules, personnel policies, and budget and accounting instructions. What limits on the types of standardized instructions would you recommend that a firm with operations in many countries adopt?

4. From whatever sources are available to you, build a comparison of the family decision-making process for a major consumer purchase in two different cultures. Specify the roles played by the different family members, the pattern over time of interaction among the family with respect to the purchase, the weighting placed upon different producc characteristics by each family member, and the rules by which a consensus is finally reached.

5. Select one of the aspects of a culture—(1) the status ranking of different occupations, (2) the roles of the sexes, (3) the times of life with which different

activities are associated, (4) the exercise of organizational authority, or (5) courtship patterns—in which you are aware of a change in the cultural norms and carry out the following activities:

a. Describe the nature of the change.
b. Give your opinion as to whether the culture regarded it formally, informally, or technically.
c. Identify some distinguishing characteristics of the innovators and early adopters.
d. Describe any role you think business played in stimulating the change.
e. Describe the business significance of the changes for any foreign firm operating within the culture.

6. "The prime function of most executive development courses is not knowledge transmissions but rather the transfer of a set of norms which conform with organizational objectives." Do you think it is acceptable for a U.S. top executive of a multinational firm to use executive-development courses to transfer to the management of foreign subsidiaries the norms that he has chosen?

Chapter 18

Multinational marketing management

Markets and marketing decisions play a crucial role in the development of a firm's global strategy, as discussed in Chapter 13. Marketing managers participate heavily in overall strategy formulation. They also have an operating responsibility for implementing the marketing dimension of the global strategy.

This chapter focuses on the marketing management function at both the strategy formulation and operational levels. It begins with the organizational issue of how marketing responsibility should be allocated between headquarters and country managers. It then considers the principal marketing functions of product strategies, marketing research, advertising, pricing, and channel management as these functions are affected when a firm extends its operations from its home market to a number of different national markets.

How does multinational marketing differ from domestic marketing? Both are similar in objectives, methods, and functions required. They differ in that the multinational firm operates simultaneously in a number of national markets that vary widely in economic, cultural, and competitive characteristics. Also, many governments with varied national interests—rather than a single government—are shaping the environment within which the marketers operate. As we shall see, the multinational setting expands manyfold the task of adjusting the marketing mix to the varied needs of the target markets.[1]

CENTRAL COORDINATION VERSUS LOCAL AUTHORITY

In multinational marketing, how should the function be divided between corporate headquarters and the foreign subsidiaries? A traditional view has been that most of the marketing responsibility should be handled at the local level because subsidiary managers are most familiar with the special characteristics of their markets. Where products and marketing approaches are extended from the center market to foreign areas with little or no adaptation, a contribution by headquarters was not needed. And where major adaptations were required, the managers closest to these markets were best able to make these adjustments.[2] As a result, marketing, more than any other function, was often conspicuous by its absence from the functions performed at corporate headquarters.

More recently, the trend has been toward an increased role by headquarters in the form of "interactive market planning."[3] One reason for this trend is that headquarters staff can better fulfill its role in strategic planning and controlling performance by participating in the marketing function. Another reason is that headquarters can perform certain operational functions more effectively than can be done at the subsidiary level. National markets have similarities as well as differences, and this creates opportunities for the enterprise to benefit from applying some common marketing policies in the different markets. The degree of headquarters participation will vary, of course, by marketing function, by industry, by company, and over time.[4]

At the operational level, headquarters staff normally plays a significant role in standardizing some parts of the marketing strategy while the

---

[1] See Robert Bartels, "Are Domestic and International Marketing Dissimilar?" *Journal of Marketing* 32 (July 1968), pp. 56–61.

[2] Warren J. Keegan, "Multinational Marketing: The Headquarters Role," *Columbia Journal of World Business*, January–February 1971.

[3] Robert D. Buzzell, "Can You Standardize Multinational Marketing?" *Harvard Business Review*, November–December 1968, pp. 102–13.

[4] R. J. Aylmer, "Who Makes Marketing Decisions in the Multinational Firm?" *Journal of Marketing*, October 1970, pp. 26–27.

subsidiaries have principal responsibility for handling the differences and unique factors. A sample study of major U.S. and European companies in four consumer industries illustrates this pattern.[5] By function, headquarters participation was greatest in decisions on product policies such as physical characteristics of the product, brand name, packaging, and product line. Headquarters participation was far less in decisions on pricing, distribution, and advertising and promotion.[6] By industry, centralized decision making was stronger for nonfood than for food products, the latter perceived to be more "culture bound."

To carry out its strategic planning responsibility, headquarters must be adequately informed concerning markets. Headquarters staff, therefore, should monitor market research. It should also standardize certain market measures so that the market potential and marketing performance of different national markets can be compared. The extent of headquarters involvement will depend, of course, on an assessment of the benefits from such involvement compared to the costs in terms of personnel, information flows, and standardization of the research formats.

An interactive process is two-way. Headquarters must also make affirmative marketing contributions to the local subsidiaries. It can make available experience that has succeeded in one country to other countries where comparable conditions prevail. It may discover opportunities that consist of a number of small market segments in different countries that country subsidiaries consider too small to warrant development. It can supervise marketing experiments in selected areas and make the results available to all units in the system. As an example, where there is uncertainty about the relative effectiveness of advertising versus personal selling, headquarters could experiment in country A with 75 percent of the communications budget for advertising and 25 percent for personal selling and reverse these proportions in country B, where both countries were preselected as reasonably comparable in other marketing dimensions.

Another contribution of headquarters staff can be to make certain that individual markets are developed in ways that fit the overall strategy of the firm, so that performance in those markets can fit without problems into later stages of the global plan. It may be necessary, for example, to choose outlets not initially the best for a small range of products selling in low volumes but that are preferred for later planned expansion. The brand image may also be important for carrying future lines and require special attention when products are first introduced.

[5] Ulrich Wiechmann, "Integrating Multinational Marketing Activities," *Columbia Journal of World Business* 9 (Winter 1974), pp. 7–16.

[6] Similar conclusions were reached in a study of Japanese, European, and American multinational subsidiaries in Brazil. See William K. Brandt and James M. Hulbert, "Marketing Strategy in the Multinational Subsidiary: The Role of Headquarters," in *Making Advertising Relevant*, Proceedings of the American Academy of Advertising, 1975.

One of the more common ways of placing responsibility at the level of those closest to the customer, yet still retaining central control over the marketing function, is through the use of a standard annual plan and review routine. Plans are requested in a standard format working from an assessment of the market environment toward specific action proposals and budgeted profit performance and resource requirements. These are then subjected to careful scrutiny and related to the overall plan for global performance. Any clashes or omissions discovered can then be raised before actions are taken.

This method of central control also acts as a major implement in educating the international organization in the use of marketing. A good grasp of marketing cannot be assumed to exist throughout any international organization. The ideas are alien to many cultures and frequently opposed to the message of the programs under which many international executives have been educated. Furthermore, foreign countries do not have a product management system as developed as that in the United States.[7]

The decisive question is not where ultimate control of strategic planning should lie, for this inevitably must rest with top management. The real question is the extent to which headquarters executives should be involved in the marketing-planning process. In the absence of headquarters involvement in the individual subsidiary planning processes, it is difficult, indeed impossible, for headquarters to impose global considerations effectively. On the other hand, in the absence of subsidiary involvement at a strategic level, the local adaptation requirements of a market may be overlooked.

As a general rule, headquarters should be involved in subsidiary planning processes to the extent necessary to keep informed of the nature of basic opportunities and threats globally. Also, headquarters involvement should be measured against the degree to which it stimulates or contributes to subsidiary planning efforts. Alternatively, a check should be kept on the extent to which it may detract from initiative and enterprise on the part of subsidiary managers. The organizational form must facilitate the task of multinational marketing, particularly where marketing skills are important as a key element in the competitive advantage of the international company. As Terpstra has pointed out, marketing skills and orientation were critical components of the competitive advantage on which many U.S. companies based their expansion into European markets.[8]

Of course, the relationship between headquarters and subsidiary on the marketing front seldom operates without some problems. Some are

---

[7] Alladi Venkatesh and David Wilemon, "American and European Product Managers: A Comparison," *Columbia Journal of World Business* 15 (Fall 1980), pp. 67–74.

[8] Vern Terpstra, *American Marketing in the Common Market* (New York: Praeger Publishers, 1967).

to be expected because of the obvious conflicts of interest built into matrix organizations and the differences in the cultural background and training of the marketers themselves. Wiechmann and Pringle identified 23 key problems as seen by headquarters executives of 40 European and United States multinationals and 22 key problems as seen by subsidiary executives.[9] These are reproduced in Figure 18–1. The multinational marketer, however, may find it more constructive to regard these issues less as problems and more as indicators of the ongoing need for management flexibility and involvement in a complex coordination task.

INTERNATIONAL PRODUCT STRATEGIES

The product strategy of an international firm generally falls somewhere between the extremes of central market focus and decentralized development, as discussed in Chapter 13, and between the extremes of marketing-mix standardization or mix adaptation. The choices available can be illustrated by the five alternative strategies for product features and communications approaches summarized in Table 18–1.[10]

Strategy one: One product, one message—worldwide

The easiest and most profitable strategy is that of product and communications extension. The same product is sold worldwide using the same sales message. International cosmetics firms sell the same products worldwide and use the same advertising and promotional appeals that are used in their central markets. They find little variation from country to country in target consumer groups, product usage patterns, and consumer attitudes. As one executive explained

> A woman is a woman is a woman,
> irrespective of where she lives. . . .
> Even in Japan we use the same copy,
> with American models and English words.[11]

The "product-communications extension" strategy has great appeal to most international companies because of the enormous cost savings associated with this approach. Important among these are the substantial

---

[9] Ulrich E. Wiechmann and Lewis G. Pringle, "Problems That Plague Multinational Marketers," *Harvard Business Review* 57 (July–August 1979), pp. 118–24. A similar set of problems emerged from research into the management of North American, European, and Japanese multinationals operating in Brazil. See James M. Hulbert, William K. Brandt, and Raimar Richers, "Marketing Planning in the Multinational Subsidiary: Practices and Problems," *Journal of Marketing* 44 (Summer 1980), pp. 7–15.

[10] This section is based largely on Warren J. Keegan, "Multinational Product Planning: Strategic Alternatives," *Journal of Marketing*, January 1969, pp. 58–62.

[11] Ulrich Wiechmann, "Integrating Multinational Marketing Activities," *Columbia Journal of World Business*, Winter 1974, p. 12.

Figure 18—1

Key problems identified by headquarters executives

Lack of qualified international personnel:

Getting qualified international personnel is difficult.

It is difficult to find qualified local managers for the subsidiaries.

The company can't find enough capable people who are willing to move to different countries.

There isn't enough manpower at headquarters to make the necessary visits to local operations.

Lack of strategic thinking and long-range planning at the subsidiary level:

Subsidiary managers are preoccupied with purely operational problems and don't think enough about long-range strategy.

Subsidiary managers don't do a good job of analyzing and forecasting their business.

There is too much emphasis in the subsidiary on short-term financial performance. This is an obstacle to the development of long-term marketing strategies.

Lack of marketing expertise at the subsidiary level:

The company lacks marketing competence at the subsidiary level.

The subsidiaries don't give their advertising agencies proper direction.

The company doesn't understand consumers in the countries where it operates.

Many subsidiaries don't gather enough marketing intelligence.

The subsidiary does a poor job of defining targets for its product marketing.

Too little relevant communication between headquarters and the subsidiaries:

The subsidiaries don't inform headquarters about their problems until the last minute.

The subsidiaries do not get enough consulting service from headquarters.

There is a communications gap between headquarters and the subsidiaries.

The subsidiaries provide headquarters with too little feedback.

Insufficient utilization of multinational marketing experience:

The company is a national company with international business; there is too much focus on domestic operations.

Subsidiary managers don't benefit from marketing experience available at headquarters and vice versa.

The company does not take advantage of its experience with product introductions in one country for use in other countries.

The company lacks central coordination of its marketing efforts.

Restricted headquarters control of the subsidiaries:

The headquarters staff is too small to exercise the proper control over the subsidiaries.

Subsidiary managers resist direction from headquarters.

Subsidiaries have profit responsibility and therefore resist any restraints on their decision-making authority.

Key problems identified by subsidiary executives

Insensitivity of headquarters to local market differences:

Headquarters management feels that what works in one market should also work in other markets.

Headquarters makes decisions without thorough knowledge of marketing conditions in the subsidiary's country.

Marketing strategies developed at headquarters don't reflect the fact that the subsidiary's position may be significantly different in its market.

The attempt to standardize marketing programs across borders neglects the fact that our company has different market shares and market acceptance in each country.

Shortage of useful information from headquarters:

The company doesn't have a good training program for its international managers.

New product information doesn't come from headquarters often enough.

The company has an inadequate procedure for sharing information among its subsidiaries.

There is very little cross-fertilization with respect to ideas and problem solving among functional groups within the company.

Lack of multinational orientation at headquarters:

Headquarters is too home-country oriented.

Headquarters managers are not truly multinational personnel.

Excessive headquarters control procedures:

Reaching a decision takes too long because we must get approval from headquarters.

There is too much bureaucracy in the organization.

Too much paperwork has to be sent to headquarters.

Headquarters staff and subsidiary management differ about which problems are important.

Headquarters tries to control its subsidiaries too tightly.

Excessive financial and marketing constraints:

The emphasis on short-term financial performance is an obstacle to the development of long-term marketing strategies for local markets.

The subsidiary must increase sales to meet corporate profit objectives even though it operates with many marketing constraints imposed by headquarters.

Headquarters expects a profit return each year without investing more money in the local company.

Insufficient participation of subsidiaries in product decisions:

The subsidiary is too dependent on headquarters for new product development.

Headquarters is unresponsive to the subsidiaries' requests for product modifications.

New products are developed centrally and are not geared to the specific needs of the local market.

Domestic operations have priority in product and resource allocation; subsidiaries rank second.

Source: Ulrich E. Wiechmann and Lewis G. Pringle, "Problems That Plague Multinational Marketers," *Harvard Business Review* 57 (July–August 1979). Copyright © 1979 by the President & Fellows of Harvard College; all rights reserved.

Table 18–1

Multinational product communications mix: Strategic alternatives

Strategy	Product function or need satisfied	Conditions of product use	Ability to buy product	Recommended product strategy	Recommended communications strategy	Relative cost of adjustments	Product examples
1	Same	Same	Yes	Extension	Extension	1	Soft drinks
2	Different	Same	Yes	Extension	Adaptation	2	Bicycles, motorscooters
3	Same	Different	Yes	Adaptation	Extension	3	Gasoline, detergents
4	Different	Different	Yes	Adaptation	Adaptation	4	Clothing, greeting cards
5	Same	—	No	Invention	Develop new communications	5	Motor vehicles

Source: Warren J. Keegan, "Multinational Product Planning, Strategic Alternatives," *Journal of Marketing*, January 1969, p. 59.

economies resulting from the standardization of marketing communications. For a company with worldwide operations, the cost of preparing separate print and TV-cinema films for each market would be extremely high.

This strategy is widely used in marketing advanced-technology producer goods. As Holton has noted, "The world of advanced technology is more nearly a single world than is the world of consumer goods."[12] A firm selling equipment to commercial television stations, for example, normally does not find specifications varying as much across markets as is likely to occur in the case of consumer goods. Even in the less developed countries, the technological specifications for producers' goods generally follow those developed in the advanced countries.

Unfortunately, the product communications extension strategy does not work for all products. When Campbell Soup tried to sell its U.S. tomato soup formulation to the British, it discovered after considerable losses that the English prefer a more bitter taste. Numerous other examples can be cited of cases where consumer preferences in new markets do not favor a product developed for the central market, and where an adjustment or innovation rather than an extension strategy is required. Differences in consumer behavior patterns between countries, however, may reflect different market and retailing conditions and the products available to date, rather than differences in underlying attitudes and preferences. Nevertheless, where there are differences, the multinational ignores them at its peril.[13]

Strategy two: Product extension— communications adaptation

When a product or service fills a different need or serves a different function under use conditions identical with or similar to those in the central market, the only adjustment required is in marketing communications. Bicycles, for example, satisfy needs mainly for recreation in the United States but provide basic transportation in countries like India. The appeal of the "product extension-communications adaptation" strategy is that savings in manufacturing, research and development, and inventory costs can still result. The only additional costs are in identifying the different functions the product will service in foreign markets and in reformulating advertising, sales promotion, and other dimensions of market communications around the newly identified functions.

---

[12] Richard H. Holton, "Marketing Policies in Multinational Corporations," *Journal of International Business Studies*, Summer 1970, p. 18.

[13] Robert T. Green, Bronislaw J. Verhage, and Isabella C. M. Cunningham, "Household Purchasing Decisions: How Do American and Dutch Consumers Differ?" in Lionel Mitchell et al., "Comparative Marketing in Action," *European Journal of Marketing* 15, no. 1 (1981), pp. 68–77.

Strategy three: Product adaptation—
communications extension

A third international product strategy is to extend without change the basic communications strategy developed for the central market but to adapt the product to different use conditions. The "product adaptation-communications extension" strategy assumes that the product will serve the same function in foreign markets under different use conditions. McDonald's followed this approach when it adapted the physical characteristics of its hamburgers to the different taste and user conditions of different countries while continuing to advertise on a standard basis the invitation to join Ronald McDonald under the golden arch. International companies in the soap and detergent fields have adjusted their product formulation to meet local water conditions and the characteristics of local washing machines, with no change in the companies' basic communications approach.

Strategy four: Dual adaptation

Strategy four is to adapt both the product and the communications approach when differences exist in environmental conditions of use and in the function that a product serves. In essence, this is a combination of strategies two and three. U.S. greeting-card companies have faced these circumstances in Europe, where the occasions for using greeting cards differ from those in the United States. Also, in Europe the function of a greeting card has been to provide a space for the sender to write his own message, in contrast to the U.S. situation where cards contain prepared messages. Dual adaptation, though, may not lose all the benefits of standardization. Many basic attributes may remain constant, bringing economies of scale in the functions concerned with those attributes.

Strategy five: Product invention

A final strategy is that of product invention. When potential customers cannot afford one of the firm's products, an opportunity may exist to invent or design an entirely new product that satisfies the identified need or function at a price that the consumer can afford. If product-development costs are not excessive, this may be a potentially rewarding product strategy for the mass markets in the less developed countries.

The choice among these five product and communications strategies in international marketing is a function of three key factors:

1.   The function or need the product is intended to serve in a particular market.

2. The market conditions under which the product is used, including customer preferences and their ability to buy the product in question.
3. The competitive position of a company and its relative costs of adaptation and manufacture.

Only through analysis of the product-market fit, and the company's capabilities and costs, will the most profitable international product strategy be identified.

INTERNATIONAL MARKETING RESEARCH

National forecasts of aggregate demand, the subject of Chapter 14, are a starting point for international marketing research. But, much more detailed market data are needed to determine the appropriate product strategy for a particular market. National aggregates can hide major sectoral differences. Potential demand, for example, can vary dramatically between agricultural and industrialized sectors and between urban and rural districts. There are also major regional disparities in the United States. California is not Appalachia. Italy divides into an industrialized north and a backward Messogiorno. Global strategy might thus be developed with greater precision and a changed emphasis if subnational data are available. In fact, for marketing decisions that have a locational element, such as advertising allocation or retail location, almost no unit of analysis is too small.

The smaller the size of the basic geographical unit for which statistics are published, the more precisely can market segments be targeted. But homogeneity within these basic units may be even more important than size.[14] In the United Kingdom, for example, few statistics are published for smaller areas than the 11 U.K. standard regions that themselves are not usably homogeneous units. They each contain a mixture of urban and rural areas and industry and agriculture.

Published statistics, however, will seldom fulfill all international marketing needs. Decisions to adjust elements of the marketing mix to suit individual markets ideally require factual information about customer motivation, attitudes, and usage of the product or service, and local market and distribution conditions. As Mayer has pointed out, "Most major multinational marketing failures result from neglecting to recognize that a specific product can be viewed completely differently in different cultures."[15]

---

[14] W. N. Barnes, "International Marketing Indicators," *European Journal of Marketing* 14, no. 2 (1980), p. 98.

[15] Charles S. Mayer, "The Lessons of Multinational Marketing Research," *Business Horizons*, December 1978, p. 8.

The research task

When undertaking the costly task of collecting detailed consumer data, the international market researcher must specify carefully and with discrimination the questions to be answered. The questions listed in Figure 18–2, although originally designed for decisions on international advertising, may also be used for decisions on the standardization of

Figure 18–2

Basic market research questions for determining international marketing standardization

Consumption patterns

Pattern of purchase:
1. Is the product or service purchased by relatively the same consumer income group?
2. Do the same family members motivate the purchase?
3. Do the same family members dictate brand choice?
4. Do most consumers expect a product to have the same appearance?
5. Is the purchase rate the same?
6. Are most purchases made at the same kind of retail outlet?
7. Do most consumers spend the same amount of time making the purchase?

Pattern of usage:
8. Do most consumers use the product or service for the same purpose or purposes?
9. Is the usage rate or quantity of usage the same?
10. Is the method of preparation the same?
11. Are the products or services used in conjunction, similar?

Psychosocial characteristics

Attitudes toward the product or service:
1. Are the basic psychological, social, and economic factors motivating purchase and use the same?
2. Are the advantages and disadvantages of the product or service in the minds of consumers basically the same?
3. Is the symbolic content of the product or service the same?
4. Is the psychic cost of purchasing or using the product or service the same?
5. Is the appeal of the product or service the same for a cosmopolitan sector?

Attitudes towards the brand:
6. Is the brand name equally known and accepted?
7. Are customer attitudes toward the package basically the same?
8. Are customer attitudes toward pricing basically the same?
9. Is brand loyalty the same?
10. Will images from past advertising conflict with a standardized approach?
11. Are the media suitable for a standardized advertising approach?

Cultural criteria

1. Does society restrict the purchase or use of the product or service to particular sex, age, religious, or educated groups?
2. Is there a stigma attached to the product or service, brand name, advertising content, or artwork?
3. Does usage of the product or service suggested by advertising interfere with tradition in any country?

Source: Adapted from Stewart Henderson Britt, "Standardizing Marketing for the International Market," *Columbia Journal of World Business* 9 (Winter 1974), pp. 39–45.

other marketing variables. The questions attempt to uncover national similarities. If sufficient similarity is discovered, then there is a case for standardized marketing; otherwise, local adjustment is required.

The aim of international market research should not be to identify general national stereotypes of persons or behavior in purchasing a particular product or service. National stereotyping not only tends to emphasize differences rather than similarities between countries but also tends to minimize the importance of differences in behavior patterns within a country.[16] National stereotypes are not very useful for international marketers who are looking for segment similarities that permit some standardization across national boundaries. Much cross-national market research, therefore, should be designed to identify customer subgroups in different countries that have similar behavior patterns.[17]

Deciding whether adequate customer similarity exists is a difficult problem in multinational market research. Representative cross-country samples of national and subnational populations are difficult to design. Careful design of research aimed at determining the similarity of potential buyers will include more nonusers in the samples for countries with low penetration. Nonusers, however, may find it very difficult to provide any reasonable assessment of their likelihood of purchasing a product that they may not even have considered. Opinions about product features might be equally suspect.

Sample sizes may also have to be limited by cost factors. Where sample sizes are limited, the researcher may be left with something that could only be validly titled "a comparison of a small sample of New York housewives with a small sample of Parisian housewives." To draw conclusions from such a limited study as to basic similarities or differences between U.S. and French consumers would be both presumptuous and dangerous.[18]

Linguistic and conceptual differences can create distortions, even with the use of the same questionnaire and with careful translation and back-translation. Differences can occur in the administration of the questionnaires. Thus, the reliability of findings may vary as between samples, and the power of the usual tests of statistical significance may be greatly reduced. Consequently, international marketers must be ever sensitive to reliability variations and the need to make appropriate adjustments before accepting cross-national sample readings as indicators of real simi-

---

[16] Susan P. Douglas, "Cross-National Comparisons and Consumer Stereotypes: A Case Study of Working and Non-Working Wives in the U.S. and France," *Journal of Consumer Research* 3 (June 1976), pp. 12–20.

[17] For an attempt to do just this see Helmut Becker, "Is There a Cosmopolitan Information Seeker," *Journal of International Business Studies* 7 (Spring 1976), pp. 77–89.

[18] Jean J. Boddewyn, "Comparative Marketing: The First Twenty-five Years," *Journal of International Business Studies*, Spring–Summer 1981, p. 67.

larities or differences.[19] Even where customer differences rather than similarities are identified, such differences may simply reflect country differences in product availability or in distribution channels rather than differences in underlying attitudes or preferences.

Not all international market research should be aimed at establishing similarity or differences between market or segment averages. For products or services at different stages of diffusion in different markets, the research should attempt to identify the characteristics and buying motivations of the next tranche of buyers within each market, whether they be innovators, opinion leaders, laggards, or whatever.[20] The marketing mix for a market where diffusion is almost complete and potential buyers have long been familiar with the product concept cannot be effectively transferred into a market in which no one is familiar with the product concept. Pricing, for example, would probably have to be higher in the new market to allow for adequate advertising expense to build demand and still leave adequate profit margins for the outlets during the low volume stages of market buildup. The special value of this type of research is that it recognizes that markets are not static and that researchers need to be aware of the dynamics of cultural change as discussed in Chapter 17.

Data collection

In many countries, market researchers may have to collect their own primary data because what they need is not available from existing sources. This task has many pitfalls in foreign countries.[21]

To begin with, large segments of many foreign populations are virtually unreachable for marketing research purposes. Culture patterns may proscribe the interviewing of women, even by women interviewers. Or women may be extremely reluctant to discuss details of family purchasing. Males, too, may be reticent in replying to questioners or questionnaires. They may fear that information they give may be turned against the giver, or they may feel that it is undignified to discuss details of personal preferences in such things as food, clothing, toiletries, or household goods.

Even where there is no such reticence, locating the potential con-

---

[19] Harry L. Davis, Susan P. Douglas, and Alvin J. Silk, "Measure Unreliability: A Hidden Threat to Cross-National Marketing Research?", *Journal of Marketing* 45 (Spring 1981), pp. 98–109.

[20] Stephen C. Cosmas and Jagdish N. Sheth, "Identification of Opinion Leaders Across Cultures: An Assessment for Use in the Diffusion of Innovations and Ideas," *Journal of International Business Studies* 11 (Spring–Summer 1980), pp. 66–73.

[21] For a fuller development, see Philip R. Cateora and John M. Hess, *International Marketing*, 4th ed. (Homewood, Ill.: Richard D. Irwin, 1979), chap. 9.

sumers may be difficult. Many areas have no telephone books, no address lists, few telephones, and inadequate postal systems. These limitations severely hamper the design and administration of a sample survey. Even where these media are available, comparative research that relied on telephone ownership might, for example, end up sampling the top 6 percent in one country against 60 percent in another country. Where the literacy rate is low or where dialects are spoken, written questionnaires can also eliminate many possible purchasers. Even where respondents are reached, the surveys may not be directed to the actual decision makers in the family. In countries where husbands make more decisions, a research design aimed at wives would automatically build in a bias.[22]

INTERNATIONAL ADVERTISING

Should advertising themes and advertisements be uniform internationally or developed specifically for individual national markets? Increasingly, advertising experts have been accepting the view that the advertising task is essentially the same in most markets—namely, to communicate information and persuasive appeals effectively. Therefore, the same approach to communication can be used in every country but the specific advertising messages and media strategy may have to vary from country to country.[23]

Any component making up an advertisement—the words used, the symbols, the illustrations, and so on—may have to be changed. While the nature and motives of people are more or less universal, the ways in which they satisfy their needs are not. Cultural and socioeconomic differences play an important part in shaping the demand for specific goods and services and in determining what promotional appeals are best. The age of a product user depicted in an illustration might appear just right in one culture yet young and immature in another. The overall message that an advertisement conveys might also be changed for different cultures (see Box 18–1). The product image that would most influence purchasing will differ in many ways from country to country. Finally, media characteristics vary from country to country.

Good advertising built specifically for a given culture will usually be superior to that imported from abroad. One comparison of the relative

---

[22] Robert T. Green and Isabella C. M. Cunningham, "Family Purchasing Roles in Two Countries," *Journal of International Business Studies* 11 (Spring–Summer 1980), pp. 92–97.

[23] See Gordon E. Miracle, "International Advertising Principles and Strategies," *MSU Business Topics*, Autumn 1968, pp. 29–36, and Jacob Hornik, "Comparative Evaluation of International vs. National Advertising Strategies," *Columbia Journal of World Business*, Spring 1980, pp. 36–45.

effectiveness of American and British television commercials in the British market concluded as follows:

> Current or fairly recent American commercials, even of the highest creative caliber, are less likely than current British commercials to be effective in the British market. The reasons may be either (a) that despite a common language, the social, cultural, and marketing differences between the two countries are so great that a commercial which is successful in one country is unlikely to be very successful in the other or (b) that in marketing and advertising terms, Britain is five years behind the United States, exemplified possibly by the fact that the successful British commercials for Coca-Cola and Excedrin were, perhaps, similar in style to American commercials for those same products of a few years ago. It may be that both of these factors apply in some measure.[24]

Box 18–1

Tokyo trauma or an American advertising man in Japan

The Japanese are different. Ambiguity floats like a fine mist around all but the most intimate relationships. Little wonder, then, that marketing and advertising men, "professional communicators," unravel sooner than most other foreigners in such an alien atmosphere.

The first copy review session can be a shattering experience. You struggle in vain to get your mind around the English translation of the headline for your new product launch: "Set your gaze toward the morning horizon with a refreshed heart." And the illustration: A cowboy, one foot in the stirrup, stares dreamily out across Marlboroland. You remonstrate.

"But we're selling electric shavers, for Godsakes. Where's the product?" (In the saddle bag.) "And why a cowboy?" (John Wayne, Clint Eastwood—big box office in Japan.) "And what's all this twaddle about horizons and what kind of hearts?" (Refreshed.) "Yeh, well, we're a long way from where we ought to be."

All you ever learned about product positioning, marketing strategy, and consumer psychology convinces you that inscrutability never moved any product off the shelf. You want to believe, to leave it up to them. But how do you explain it all to headquarters? Unless you have some notion yourself of how the Japanese communicate, you haven't a prayer.

Source: Adapted from *Advertising Age*, May 20, 1974.

For these reasons, there is an initial bias in favor of separate advertising in each country. Good advertising campaigns, however, are expensive to produce. When they have proven effective in one culture, it seems worthwhile testing them in others before starting at the beginning again to develop separate campaigns for each culture. As the head of a Swedish

---

[24] John Caffyn and Nigel Rogers, "British Reactions to T.V. Commercials," *Journal of Advertising Research* 10, no. 3 (June 1970), p. 27.

advertising agency has said, "Why should three artists in three different countries sit drawing the same electric iron and three copywriters write about what after all is largely the same copy for the same iron?"[25] The economic arguments for using a standard appeal in international media are great, particularly in new markets that do not warrant the cost involved in developing entirely new material.

In developing a standard appeal to fit different markets from the outset, the compromise sought is that which will maximize total sales across markets. The model used by Ford of Europe to decide on a common European campaign when launching the Ford Granada is a good example of how such an optimum might be identified.[26] A complex model was used that developed data by country on buyers' preferences, after different levels of exposure to advertising, for the attributes of Ford's product against those of its competitors. With this data it was possible to simulate buying preferences between competing products in each country and then estimate how total sales will be affected by heavy exposure advertising of selected attributes.

There have been numerous successful attempts to carry one message internationally. Esso was able to use its advertising theme "Put a tiger in your tank" with considerable success in most countries in the world. In French, however, the word tank is *reservoir*, which in the context of the phrase could be highly suggestive, so the word *moteur* was substituted. And in Thailand, where the tiger is not a symbol of strength, the campaign was not understood.[27] In England, an American-designed advertising campaign built on the slogan "Don't spend a penny until you've tried . . ." had to be modified because the phrase "spend a penny" in Britain is the equivalent of "got to see a man about a dog" in the United States.

Even where the basic advertising approach is feasible, the advertiser must choose with care the symbols used in advertisement for a market. Colors as one form of visual symbol may have a different significance in one culture as compared to another. In China, yellow has always been the imperial color and is not used extensively except for religious purposes. In many countries, to illustrate women in power roles working closely with men even incidentally may raise antagonism from both men and women. Illustrations for the same product may have to differ from country to country. In Germany, an advertisement for cheese might show a large, foaming glass of beer, but in France, the advertisement would substitute a glass of red wine.

---

[25] Eric Elinder, "International Advertisers Must Devise Universal Ads; Dump Separate National Ones, Swedish Adman Avers," *Advertising Age*, November 27, 1961, p. 91.

[26] Michael Colvin, Roger Heeler, and Jim Thorpe, "Developing International Advertising Strategy," *Journal of Marketing* 44 (Fall 1980), pp. 73–79.

[27] "Put a Tiger in Your Tank," *Marketing Insights*, November 28, 1966, p. v.

Another important consideration in international advertising is the national and supranational image of the product. Nations hold stereotyped impressions of the products of other nations, and the ratings by different nationalities of a nation's products, on a variety of attribute scales, will differ significantly.[28] These differences, moreover, show even when respondents have not purchased a nation's products. They are widely believed to influence purchasing,[29] can vary among purchasing agents of different nationalities employed in the same multinational purchasing unit,[30] and change over time. Many advertising campaigns directly or indirectly emphasize the "nationality" of products or services, so awareness of the implied stereotype is important. Japanese manufacturers in the United States have moved their advertising emphasis over time from themes that emphasized Japanese performance and origin to themes that emphasize the worldwide marketing performance.[31] A message such as "Number One Worldwide" is clearly contributing to a supranational image that may have a payoff superior to even a highly positive national image. It is possible, moreover, that both national and supranational images could be successfully combined in the one message.

In the area of media selection, considerable deviation from home-country patterns may be required, particularly for American companies. In many countries, ownership of radio and television media is in the hands of the government and no commercials are allowed. Radio is also barred to advertisers in much of Europe. Except for these media restrictions, the availability and capability of media in foreign countries are similar to those in the United States. But the coverage and relative economic cost of foreign media are different and require adaptation.

In summary, the principles underlying communication by advertising • are the same in all nations, but the specific methods, techniques, and symbols sometimes must be varied to take account of diverse environmental conditions. Uniform advertising for various market segments, whether national or international, has tremendous economic advantages for the firm. The critical questions for the multinational firm are *when* and *when not* to make adjustments. The best strategy is to try to take into account the international differences when preparing an advertising

[28] Akira Nagashima, "A Comparative 'Made in' Product Image Survey among Japanese Businessmen," *Journal of Marketing* 41 (July 1977), pp. 95–100; see also Chem L. Narayana, "Aggregate Images of American and Japanese Products: Implications on International Marketing," *Columbia Journal of World Business* 16 (Summer 1981), pp. 31–35.

[29] T. V. Greer, "British Purchasing Agents and the European Economic Community," *Journal of Purchasing* 7 (1971), pp. 56–63.

[30] Brian Toyne, "Procurement-Related Perceptions of Corporate-Based and Foreign-Based Purchasing Managers," *Journal of International Business Studies* 9 (Winter 1978), pp. 39–54.

[31] Norihiko Suzuki, "The Changing Pattern of Advertising Strategy by Japanese Business Firms in the U.S. Market: Content Analysis," *Journal of International Business Studies* 11 (Winter 1980), pp. 63–72.

campaign and to export the same advertising approach to as many different markets as possible. But final decisions on copy or media should be handled by personnel who have intimate knowledge of foreign markets.

INTERNATIONAL PRICING

Price is only one of many variables in the marketing mix requiring careful consideration and monitoring. Yet it is the variable that normally produces the most direct and most rapid change in customer value and competitive impact. Hence the selection of price relative to competition is important and justifiably highlighted.

Pricing decisions must take into account the interests of many factions within the multinational enterprise frequently with conflicting price objectives.[32] The director of international marketing and the managers of foreign subsidiaries seek prices that will be competitive in the marketplace. But the managers of the divisions that produce and supply products or components to other divisions for merchandising will be pressing for prices that maximize the profits of their own division. The tax manager is concerned with the implications of pricing decisions on the total tax liability of the corporation, tax deferral opportunities, and government regulations on transfer pricing. With these and other sectors of the enterprise crucially affected by pricing decisions, top management invariably assumes substantial responsibility for formulating pricing policies and strategies. The implementation of these policies, however, may be widely diffused throughout the organization.[33] Inevitably, transfer pricing will be a contentious issue and the rules adopted will shape market performance. This issue, however, will be left until Chapter 22, and the attention here will be on appropriate market prices.

The role of pricing differs considerably for different types of goods and from market to market. In the case of standardized or relatively undifferentiated products, the market sets the price and the seller has little control over the level of prices. The same will be true of situations where government price controls prevail or prices are fixed through patent-licensing agreements. But for differentiated products selling in nonregulated markets, the producer has genuine alternatives in setting prices. And much international business activity is based on differentiated products and oligopoly elements.

In setting its pricing policies, the company has two basic choices. It may use prices as an active instrument for accomplishing market objectives. Or it may consider prices as a static element in business decisions.

---

[32] *Solving International Pricing Problems* (New York: Business International, 1965).

[33] For an example of how the responsibility for pricing is distributed among the various units of an international company in the pharmaceuticals and chemicals field, see Enid Baird Lovell, *The Changing Role of the International Executive* (New York: National Industrial Conference Board, 1966), p. 52.

American companies generally regard price as an important variable in their marketing decisions. Japanese companies are probably even more aggressive in pricing and often use low pricing strategies. Their newly established foreign subsidiaries generally have sales growth as their prime target. And low-price strategies are used to achieve their sales goals, assuming that profits will come in due course.[34] Their strategy is similar to that advocated by some consulting firms that advise companies to set market share as the objective in the early stages of a product life cycle.[35] Profits are then expected to come from later market share leadership when the demand has grown and stabilized.

In using pricing as part of the strategic product mix, the international company will develop a pricing system and pricing policies that recognize the diversity of national markets in three basic dimensions—cost, competition, and demand. For any individual country market there is an optimum price, usually above the cost of sourcing the product, which is a function of the local demand curve for the product and its cost. Pricing, however, will have to be consistent with a number of international constraints such as dumping legislation, resale price-maintenance legislation, and governmental price controls where they exist. Another constraint may be multinational customers who demand equal price treatment regardless of location.

Firms must decide whether they are going to use marginal costs or full costs in calculating the payoff from alternative pricing decisions. In marginal cost pricing, the company is concerned only with the marginal or incremental cost of producing the goods sold in foreign markets. The logic for using marginal costs may be that foreign sales are incidental to a company's main operations and any returns over the marginal costs are a bonus contribution to net profit, or that the firm has to price more competitively to enter a foreign market or to meet local competition. But companies selling products in foreign markets at lower prices than in domestic markets are subject to charges of "dumping," which may subject the company to antidumping tariffs or penalties.

The firmly established global enterprise is more likely to think in terms of full-cost pricing targets for individual markets. Full costs, however, do not have to be covered in every market. In adopting a full-cost approach, the determination of full costs is again not a clear-cut matter. How much of general administrative, research and development costs, and other overhead items should be included in intracorporate transfer prices? What share of marketing, sales, and advertising costs incurred in the domestic market, but that generate marketing approaches that can be

[34] William K. Brandt and James M. Hulbert, "Marketing Strategies of American, European and Japanese Multinational Subsidiaries" (Paper presented at the Academy of International Business Meetings, Fontainebleau, France, July 7–9, 1975).

[35] Boston Consulting Group, *Perspectives on Experience* (Boston: Boston Consulting Group, 1968), chap. 13.

extended abroad, should be included in the cost to foreign subsidiaries? Where capital is tied up for longer periods because of the time lags inherent in international transactions, and where foreign exchange risks are involved, how should these financing and risk costs be incorporated into the pricing decisions? And innumerable other cost uncertainties exist depending on the market, the product, and the situation.

A cost-plus pricing strategy has the advantage of simplicity since information on competitive or market conditions is not required for its implementation. It is widely used for export pricing and can be designed with some flexibility for adjusting the markup over costs to fit different market conditions. But it has the serious disadvantage that it is not directed toward maximizing the company's sales and revenues or profits in each national market.

Without ignoring the realities of cost, a market-pricing strategy gives principal emphasis to the demand and supply conditions of each market and the state of competition. The example in the appendix to this chapter shows how different demand elasticities in different markets can result in advantages from different price policies for subsidiaries in each market. Through the separate adjustment of prices for each market, a greater profit can be achieved for the total system than by any choice of a common price for both markets. It should be noted, however, that in situations where national markets are not separated from each other, a common, final price policy may be necessary in order to minimize country-to-country arbitrage by intermediaries that are not controlled by the international firm.

A powerful argument that U.S. multinational firms have tended to restrict their worldwide performance through overpricing in less developed countries has been propounded by Leff.[36] He argues that marketing practices in less-developed countries have been adopted with the United States bias toward nonprice forms of competition. Faced with low levels of per capita income and small sales levels in less-developed countries, marketing executives have tried to enlarge their sales with advertising and promotion, unaware of the highly price-elastic nature of market demand at low prices. While individual families might not buy more at low prices—that is, household demand is inelastic—at a low enough price many more families become able to purchase. If firms planned from the outset for large production runs and low merchandising support they could adopt a penetration rather than a skimming strategy. They would make goods that are mass-consumption goods in developed countries also mass-consumption goods in less-developed areas. Too often they now position such goods in the luxury or semiluxury class in less-developed countries. Leff suggests that the entry of Japanese

---

[36] Nathaniel H. Leff, "Multinational Corporate Pricing Strategy in the Developing Countries," *Journal of International Business Studies* 6 (Fall 1975), pp. 55–64.

multinational firms into manufacturing in less-developed countries may provide the catalyst that will upset traditional market arrangements of this sort and precipitate a shift toward low price-high output strategies.

INTERNATIONAL CHANNEL MANAGEMENT

In the marketing literature dealing with the choice of distribution channels, the message is clear that the distribution product mix for reaching consumers must be carefully selected against an assessment of merchandising needs, the longer-term strategy for the product line and characteristics of the channels that are available or can be built.[37] Channels cannot be changed frequently and moves are usually not reversible. Alternatives foregone may not remain open and outlets that have been dropped in the past may not be again willing to carry the line.

International channel management is intimately related to many other dimensions of marketing management and global strategy. If the best strategy for entering a given market appears to be through licensing, the primary responsibility for developing and managing distribution channels becomes that of the licensee. Likewise, if the indicated strategy is to serve a market through exports, the channel decision may be a choice among exporting indirectly through export merchants or middlemen, exporting directly to an importer in the market area, or establishing overseas sales branches, subsidiaries, or foreign warehouse facilities.[38] If the entry strategy is through foreign production as a joint venture or wholly owned subsidiary, then the channel management problem is largely a domestic business question.

No matter what the initial entry strategy, the choice of channels must be evaluated against the longer-range as well as the immediate goals of the company in the specific market. Will the channels be sufficiently effective to develop the scale of sales in the country that will permit the company to move at a later stage to local production? Or will the channels be a barrier to the expansion of direct selling activities in the area when such a channel strategy becomes economic and desirable? Or will the channels be an efficient transmitter of information to the producer that will help it to match its product policies to changing consumer demands?

As a first step after identifying attractive markets and their potentials, the marketing manager should specify the functions that the channel system is expected to accomplish.[39] These functions will be determined

---

[37] For a good survey of literature on distribution channels, see L. W. Stern and A. I. El-Ansary, *Marketing Channels* (Englewood Cliffs, N.J.: Prentice-Hall, 1977).

[38] See Franklin R. Root, *Strategic Planning for Export Marketing* (Scranton, Pa.: International Textbook, 1964), pp. 72–88.

[39] For more detailed discussions of international channel management, see Vern Terpstra, *International Marketing*, 2d ed. (Hinsdale, Ill.: Dryden Press, 1978), pp. 357–87; and Warren J. Keegan, *Multinational Marketing Management*, Second edition (Englewood Cliffs, N.J.: Prentice-Hall, 1980), pp. 331–52.

both by the nature of the product mix and by the characteristics of the markets. As producers of automobiles exporting to the U.S. market or producers of construction machinery exporting to less-developed markets have discovered, a necessary function that must be performed by the channels of distribution is the provision of after-sales service and repairs. In other types of products, an essential function may be the carrying of an adequate inventory in order to stimulate sales, or the provision of consumer financing.

The next step is to understand the channel alternatives available and the characteristics of the institutions in their particular environment.[40] (See Box 18–2.) In most areas the distribution system is in process of change, and the selection of channels must take into account the process of change. Retailers and wholesalers are middlemen, not only in the flow of goods, but also in the whole process of satisfying the material needs and desires of a society. Consequently, their effectiveness will be largely determined by the changing environment in which they stand.[41]

The key elements in decisions as to a distribution system are (1) the availability of middlemen, (2) the ability and effectiveness of the alternatives in performing the necessary functions, (3) the cost of their services, and (4) the extent of control that the multinational enterprise can exert over the middlemen's activities. The multinational is searching for the system that will provide the optimum pattern of function, cost, and control. Variations among nations, however, may indicate different solutions to channel distribution needs for various market areas.

The broad alternatives available for exporting are the manufacturer's own sales and distribution network, agent middlemen, or merchant middlemen. In general, the manufacturer retains most control over subsequent marketing decisions the further it can justify extending its own distribution system down the international chain of distribution. The scale of operations, however, may not justify the firm extending its own system right up to the point at which final consumers buy, or even building a system to cover any stages at all. At some point in the international distribution chain it is, therefore, usual to turn to agents or merchant middlemen. Merchants purchase for their own account and bear the majority of the trading risks for the products handled. Agents do not take title to the merchandise but work on a commission basis. The firm therefore retains more control over prices and other aspects of the distribution function through agents. But this control does not extend more

---

[40] For studies in comparative marketing, see Jean Boddewyn, *Comparative Management and Marketing* (Glenview, Ill.: Scott, Foresman, 1969); David Carson, *International Marketing: A Comparative Systems Approach* (New York: John Wiley & Sons, 1967); and Montrose S. Sommers and Jerome B. Kernan, eds., *Comparative Marketing Systems* (New York: Appleton-Century-Crofts, 1968).

[41] Understanding of the forces leading to change in channel structure is still in its infancy. For a challenging survey see Louis W. Stern and Torger Reve, "Distribution Channels as Political Economies: A Framework for Comparative Analysis," *Journal of Marketing* 44 (Summer 1980), pp. 52–64.

Box 18–2

Japan: A nation of wholesalers

Japan has more shops and wholesalers per head of population than any other big industrial nation. Productivity per worker in Japanese distribution is very low, while in Japanese manufacturing it is very high. This has annoying consequences for foreign countries.

Japanese goods sometimes sell more cheaply in suburban London than in suburban Tokyo. This is not because of Japanese dumping. The goods leave efficient Japanese factories at the same price for abroad or for home. They then suffer a bigger markup while traveling a few miles down Japan's convoluted distribution system than they do while crossing half the world and reaching British shops through Britain's efficient distribution system. Meanwhile goods leaving less-efficient British factories can cost four times as much in Tokyo as in London because they have to pass through Japan's inefficient distribution system on the way.

There are almost as many retail outlets and wholesalers in Japan as in twice-as-populous America. Despite the explosion of supermarkets in the past decade, by 1979 60 percent of Japanese retail outlets still employed no more than two people and 45 percent of wholesalers employed four people or less. The Japanese are as sentimental about their tiny shops as the French are about their peasants and the British about their old industries. Small Japanese shops are the centers of village neighborhoods in big cities. The survival of small stores has kept the wholesalers who supply them in business.

New tastes and fads, and the ease with which wholesalers can start peddling goods on a small scale, have brought nearly 50,000 new wholesalers into business since 1975, 80 percent of them with a capital of less than $40,000. This suggests that Japan's multitude of wholesalers survive because people want their services, rather than as crusty remnants from the past.

How do foreign firms find a way in? Successes and failures of foreign products in weaving through the distribution system are repeated like parables in Japan. Traders who have given up hope of finding competitive inlets generally say the best policy is to secure a Japanese partner with a powerful, established place in the distribution system.

Source: Adapted from *The Economist*, September 19, 1981, pp. 88–89.

---

than one further stage in the chain as agents invariably sell to merchants at the next stage.

Middlemen tend to avoid expenditure on developing product brands and instead devote their resources to the sales of those brands or items that sell without merchandising effort. This tendency puts small firms with unestablished products in double jeopardy. To establish their product, they may have to opt for the more costly direct sales approach at the time they can least afford it. It is not uncommon for firms to move from a direct approach adopted at the beginning of international expansion to later use of outside middlemen once the demand has been established. A halfway approach that is less expensive initially is to reimburse or subsidize middlemen for promotion expenditure or the time of their sales force spent on selling the product.

A diagram in Figure 18–3 shows the potential stages in the international distribution chain to which the manufacturer may extend its own network in reaching toward the eventual foreign consumer. At the very

Figure 18–3

Potential stages of entry into the external international distribution chain

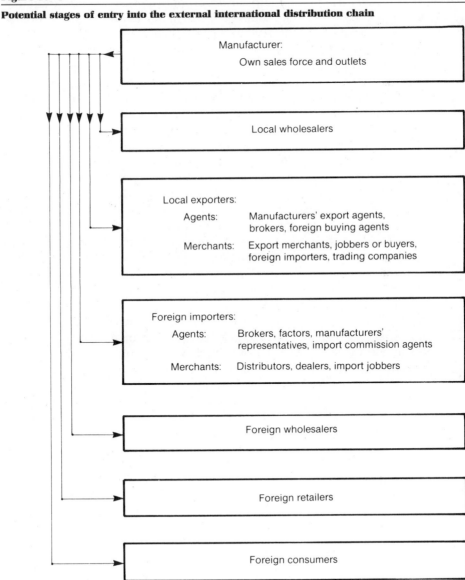

extreme, it might operate its own retail stores, mail order operation, or even door-to-door sales force as Avon Products has in Europe. It is possible, too, for the firm to use agents at intermediate stages and then enter back into the chain at a later stage. A firm whose sales depend heavily on consumer promotion might employ distributors as agents to export, to store, and to distribute goods while it operates its own sales force to foreign retailers.

The further down the distribution chain the manufacturer retains its own system, the more technical exporting expertise and international marketing knowledge is required. If the manufacturer turns to home-country middlemen, it is adopting indirect exporting. Foreign sales are handled in essentially the same way as domestic sales, and a minimum of international marketing know-how is required by the firm. For U.S. firms, the indirect approach generally means that the enterprise is small and that its international commitment and potential is limited. For a Japanese company, on the other hand, the use of the indirect approach may be explained by the availability of large and experienced international trading firms that have a significant comparative advantage in foreign selling even over direct operations by large enterprises.

In direct exporting, the firm retains the complete responsibility for identifying markets, physical distribution, export documentation, pricing, and so on. Where exporting is only part of the activities of a multinational firm, and sales are mainly to foreign subsidiaries as components or inputs to foreign production or to sales subsidiaries of the enterprise itself, many of the marketing functions such as market research, promotion, and pricing are assumed in whole or in part by the subsidiary. But where export sales are directed primarily to independent foreign buyers, export pricing in particular becomes a critical issue. Decisions have to be made as to whether exports should be at full-cost or marginal-cost pricing, whether prices should be quoted as f.o.b. (free on board) or c.i.f. (cost, insurance, freight) to foreign ports and in home-country currencies or in the currency of the market being served, and on how to use export credit. An extensive literature is available on the how-to-do-it of export promotion and most governments have incentive programs and facilities for offering technical assistance to exporters with which international managers need to become familiar. This assistance, however, may not confront the most difficult problems.[42]

Within the foreign country, the wholesale distribution function can be handled by foreign importers, by the companies own overseas facilities, or by independent wholesalers. A wholesaler is a middleman who sells to retailers or industrial users and whose chief functions are negotiating for the buyer, buying, selling, and storing. Wholesalers may also offer other

---

[42] See Michael R. Czinkota and David A. Ricks, "Export Assistance: Are We Supporting the Best Programs?" *Columbia Journal of World Business* 16 (Summer 1981), pp. 73–78.

services such as financing or servicing. The distribution system for industrial goods in advanced countries is generally quite similar.

In the less developed countries, because a large share of industrial goods is imported and the volume of any one item may be small, the distribution of industrial goods is generally handled by importers who deal in a wide range of products in order to generate enough sales to support their operations. The smaller the market, the wider the range of products the wholesaler must carry. This feature reduces the choice of alternatives and frequently means that a distributor handles goods of several competing firms in the same field.

The retail distribution systems vary greatly among countries in the size of distribution units, in the services they perform, and in the assortment of goods they handle (see Box 18–2). In many less-developed countries, for example, retail distribution is characterized by large numbers of little shops with small capital investments, much imitation, low turnovers, high margins, and high mortality.

Generally, as we go up the economic scale, the sizes of retail units increase, the amount of personal attention given to customers decreases—moving toward self-service—and the assortment of goods handled changes from a high degreee of specialization to a wide variety of goods in one retail unit. Again, many comparative studies of retailing patterns are available for the marketing manager to secure essential information for deciding on the channel choices for a specific country.

In summary, international channel management requires the design of a structure of distribution units that will perform the physical distribution task, provide service and other functions, and provide an effective transmission system for returning necessary market information to the company. The alternatives vary tremendously with the environment and are in a process of change around the world. Starting from its market targets and an understanding of the functions that the distribution system must perform for each product or group of products, the marketing manager must design a system that not only serves present needs but also has a flexibility to permit changes in the channel structure over time.

How is the international channel-management responsibility shared between headquarters and the subsidiaries in a multinational company? Obviously, in the case of foreign production, the responsibility must be highly decentralized. But headquarters has a need, under all circumstances, for keeping informed and for appraising the effectiveness of distribution channel experience. Some of the experience might be profitably transferred from one area to another. Some of the experience may indicate changes that should be made in the product mix in order to permit distribution channels to be more effective. Where distribution channels are having great difficulty in providing postsales service, for example, product redesigns that reduce or simplify the service requirement add to the effectiveness of the available channels.

The need to develop working relationships with outside channels in a different cultural background presents further problems in the international firm. The firm faces problems not only in seeking to transmit its past experience to these channels but also in communicating with them about current questions. Particular concepts will often not be directly translatable, and the approach to market assessment is likely to have many cultural biases.

One way of overcoming some of the problems is to develop representatives with preparation in both liaison with channels and the peculiarities of particular cultures. Caterpillar, for example, developed a range of international representatives with language and area courses and special training for aiding distributors in solving inventory, financial, and merchandising problems.

SUMMARY

The basic marketing functions involved are the same for both domestic and international markets, but the implementation can be quite different because of environmental differences. Consequently, the international firm faces many special problems in selecting its marketing mission and in adjusting its mix of marketing actions. Throughout most dimensions of the marketing function, there is a conflict between differentiation to meet the needs of market segments and international standardization to reduce costs. The conflict relates to product strategies, pricing, advertising, and the way in which the marketing activity is organized. Unfortunately, there are no general or fixed rules for resolving this conflict. The international marketing manager must therefore be constantly alert to the impact of decisions for any unit in the multinational system on the corporation as a whole.

APPENDIX

Table 18A–1 illustrates how different price elasticities will lead to different price policies for subsidiaries in different markets where each obtains its supplies at the same unit cost and acts to maximize its profit. At a transfer price of £50 from the supplying unit, country A would sell at £75 and country B at £90. An increased transfer price, however, would lead to increased prices in both countries.

Given that the selling subsidiaries are motivated to maximize their profits, they will price so that their marginal revenue just equals the marginal cost to them. The greatest system profit will then emerge if a unit is charged a transfer price equal to the cost of supplying a unit which in most cases can be taken to be the variable cost of production and distribution. The nearer the transfer price is to this variable cost, the

Table 18A–1

	Price (in £)							
	100	*95*	*90*	*85*	*80*	*75*	*70*	*65*
Sales volume that would result:								
Country A (units)	900	1,400	2,000	2,600	3,300	4,000	4,500	5,000
Country B (units)	1,200	1,400	1,600	1,800	2,000	2,200	2,400	2,600
Total revenue:								
Country A (£000s)	90	133	180	221	264	300	315	325
Country B (£000s)	120	133	144	153	160	165	168	169
Contribution when transfer price =								
£50								
Country A (£000s)	45	63	80	91	99	100*	90	75.
Country B (£000s)	60	63	64*	63	60	55	48	39
£60								
Country A (£000s)	36	49	'60	65	66*	60	45	25
Country B (£000s)	48	49*	48	45	40	33	24	13
£70								
Country A (£000s)	27	35	40*	39	33	20	—	—
Country B (£000s)	36*	35	32	27	20	11	—	—

* Indicates greatest contribution for a given transfer price.

closer a subsidiary's pricing policy will bring the firm to maximizing its contribution over and above this variable cost. Table 18A–2 illustrates how the system profits increase as the transfer price is brought down to variable cost in this way.

Suppose now that the firm were to fix the final market price in order to maintain uniform world prices. Inevitably this would lead to a decreased system contribution because, in this case, one subsidiary or both would be forced away from an optimal adjustment to the particular situation ruling in its market. Comparing Table 18A–3 with Table 18A–2, it can be seen that no choice of a common price level for the two markets would

Table 18A–2

	Sales volume to maximize contributions				System contribution when variable cost =		
Transfer price	*Country A (units)*	*Country B (units)*	*Total units*	*Total revenue (£000s)*	*£40 (£000s)*	*£50 (£000s)*	*£60 (£000s)*
£40	4,000	1,800	5,800	453	221*	—	—
£50	4,000	1,600	5,600	444	220	164*	—
£60	3,300	1,400	4,700	397	209	162	115*
£70	2,000	1,200	3,200	300	172	140	108

* Indicates transfer price bringing greatest contribution for a given variable cost.

Table 18A—3

Common market price (£S)	Combined volume country A + B (units)	Contribution when variable cost =		
		£40 (£000s)	£50 (£000s)	£60 (£000s)
100	2,100	126	105	84
95	2,800	154	126	98
90	3,600	180	144	108
85	4,400	198	154	110*
80	5,300	212	159*	106
75	6,200	217*	154	93
70	6,900	207	138	69
65	7,600	190	114	38

* Indicates price bringing greatest contribution for a given variable cost.

produce a contribution for any given variable cost that is as high as that possible when the prices are adjusted separately.

EXERCISES AND DISCUSSION QUESTIONS

1. "Until we achieve One World, there is no such thing as international marketing—only local marketing around the world." Do you agree or disagree and why?

2. The food division headquarters of a U.S. multinational with subsidiaries throughout OECD countries is considering the design of a standardized range of salad dressings worldwide. Until now, it has sold salad dressings in a range of flavors mainly in the United States with a few exports. What market research data do you think they should collect?

3. "There is a movement on the part of European companies for greater standardization and guidance of marketing policies in U.S. operations, particularly in relatively low-technology, high-market-saturation product areas such as petroleum, paper, and various sorts of consumer goods." In what ways do you think the type of product influences the degree of centralization and standardization?

4. Do products sold primarily on the basis of objective physical characteristics, such as razor blades and automobile tires, lend themselves to uniform international advertising strategies more than products such as foods or dress clothing? If so, why?

5. Examine tables 18A—2 and 18A—3 and explain why no choice of a common price level for the two markets will contribute as much to profits as is possible when prices are adjusted separately.

6. Why do national differences in distribution channels frequently result in gaps in market coverage?

7. In what ways does a strategy of joint ventures rather than wholly owned subsidiaries place constraints on the task of managing the international product mix?

Chapter 19

Managing international technology transfers

International technology transfers have become recognized in recent years as one of the most important—and controversial—components of international business activity. This represents a striking shift in values. For many years following World War II, the role of multinational enterprises as vehicles for international transfers of capital was given more attention. A global shortage of capital existed. Furthermore, both government officials and experts in development perceived increased capital inputs as the magic key to rapid economic growth. But as capital steadily became more easily available, and as many development efforts based almost solely on capital inputs produced disappointing results, the strategic importance of technology for stimulating economic expansion became ever more apparent. As a result, the technology transfer role of the international firm has moved to the forefront as an issue for international managers and for both host and home countries. While international firms account for a large share of the international technology transfers and most of the commercial transfers, many noncommercial organizations are also responsible for international technology transfers.

It is important to note also that the subject of international technology transfers has a broad setting that extends beyond the field of international business. And many national policies concerning technology that affect international business actually involve broader development issues. The importance of the broader setting can be illustrated by the controversy that has emerged over the cost of technology transfers to the developing countries. International firms encounter difficulties in some countries because local officials believe that their countries are paying "too much" for foreign technology imports. This may or may not be true, depending on what is the appropriate measuring stick. In any event, the international manager should be aware that such beliefs usually stem from focusing exclusively on commercial transfers and that the many technology transfers by governments and others that require little or no payment by the recipients are normally neglected.

This chapter will not attempt to cover the broad field. It will be limited to international technology transfers in international business activity. As necessary background, it will discuss the nature of technology, the international technology transfer process, and the various modes of transfer. It will then consider the international technology transfer issues facing the firm and the constraints and incentives of host and home governments as they affect the management of international technology transfers. The control issues have already been introduced in chapters 9 and 10.

THE NATURE OF TECHNOLOGY AND THE TRANSFER PROCESS

In controversial areas, it is vitally important to have a clear definition of terms. Unfortunately, much discussion and controversy over technology transfers occurs where the parties are using different definitions and are not aware that others have a different concept in mind.

Technology: A definition

A comprehensive definition of technology might be as follows:

> Technology is a perishable resource comprising knowledge, skills, and the means for using and controlling factors of production for the purpose of producing, delivering to users, and maintaining goods and services for which there is an economic and/or social demand.[1]

---

[1] Stefan H. Robock, *The International Technology Transfer Process* (Washington, D.C.: National Academy of Sciences, 1980), p. 2.

Technology is distinguished from science in that science "organizes and explains data and observations by means of theoretical relationships (while) technology translates scientific and empirical relationships into practical use."[2]

The proposed definition includes social as well as economic goods. "Development" has come to mean "improving the quality of life" rather than simply "increased economic output." Therefore, technology transfers in the social sector such as education, health, and public administration are encompassed.

The definition recognizes that distribution factors can constitute a barrier to development as easily as can lack of production expertise. The definition, therefore, includes the knowledge, skills, and other means for the distribution of goods and services, as well as their production. The capacity to create new technology and to maintain existing technology is also included. Technology transfers can contribute to the ability of a receiving country to develop new technology and to the capability for maintaining existing machinery, equipment, or tools.

Classification schemes

Some of the more useful classifications of technology distinguish between (1) hard and soft, (2) proprietary and nonproprietary, (3) front-end and obsolete, and (4) bundled and unbundled technology. Although such groupings are presented as dichotomous classes, they are often in fact simply divisions into two groups falling on the different sides of some point on a continuous scale. Moreover, the technologies are frequently interrelated. Thus, hard technology often requires accompanying soft technology.

Capital goods, blueprints, technical specifications, and knowledge and assistance necessary for the efficient utilization of such hardware are characterized as hard technology. Soft technology refers to management, marketing, financial organization, and administrative techniques. Proprietary technology is owned or controlled by particular individuals or organizations. It may be held as a trade secret or it may be published as a patent. Nonproprietary technology includes knowledge contained in technical literature, hardware, and services that can be imitated or reproduced by observation and through reverse engineering without infringement of the proprietary rights. "Reverse engineering" simply means to learn how to reproduce equipment by taking it apart.

Front-end technology is the latest available technology, while old technology in some cases is obsolete. Bundled technology refers to controlled technology that the owner is willing to transfer only as part of a package, generally including an ownership interest in the foreign affiliate using the

---

[2] G. R. Hall and R. E. Johnson, "Transfers of United States Aerospace Technology to Japan," in *The Technology Factor in International Trade*, ed. Raymond Vernon (New York: Columbia University Press, 1970), p. 306.

technology. Unbundled technology is made available independent of the technology supplier's total package of resources.

The transfer process

Technology is not a self-contained physical object that is stored on a warehouse shelf and shipped as a package from the supplier to the user. Technology is a body of knowledge transferred by a learning process. When the transfer is from one national environment to another, it can be complex, time consuming, and costly,[3] even when transfers are between units of the same multinational enterprise. Many transfer modes are available, and many parties may participate in the process.

The complexity of the actual transfer process between affiliated parties has been illustrated by recent studies.[4] Many distinct phases are involved, ranging from planning and product and facilities design to personnel training, engineering for quality control, and technical support to local suppliers. The transfers usually require documentation, instruction programs, personnel exchanges, and continued communication on whatever problems arise.

Transfers made to nonaffiliated parties through licensing agreements can also require that the licensor show the licensee how to use the knowledge or equipment.[5] In the case of cross-licensing, the principal objective of the parties may be to permit free exchanges of information under an umbrella agreement, rather than to simply permit the use of each other's existing patents.

The time required, the expense necessary, and the effectiveness of technology transfers will vary with such factors as (1) the nature of the technology being transferred, (2) the characteristics, capabilities, and objectives of the parties involved, and (3) the absorptive capability of specific economic and social sectors within the recipient country. A transfer of electronic technology from a U.S. firm to a Japanese company could occur rapidly, effectively, and relatively inexpensively, while a similar transfer to a developing country with a limited supply of trained and experienced personnel might not.

Modes of technology transfer

Technology may be transferred in many ways. The principal noncommercial modes are foreign study in regular university programs, govern-

---

[3] David Teece, *The Multinational Corporation and the Resource Cost of International Technology Transfer* (Cambridge, Mass.: Ballinger, 1978).

[4] See, for example, Jack Behrman and Harvey Wallender, *Transfer of Manufacturing Technology within Multinational Enterprises* (Cambridge, Mass.: Ballinger, 1976).

[5] See Jack Baranson and A. Harrington, *Industrial Transfers of Technology by U.S. Firms under Licensing Arrangements: Policies, Practices and Conditioning Factors* (Washington, D.C.: Developing World Industry and Technology, 1977).

ment-to-government agreements in such realms as nuclear energy and space research, and development assistance under bilateral and multilateral aid programs. In the commercial area, the principal modes are:

Foreign direct investment: establishing a foreign operation.

Turnkey projects: all the necessary elements for an operating plant are provided in one package for an inclusive price.

Trade in goods and services: sale of equipment, tools, end products, materials, and consulting services.

Contracts and agreements: licensing of patents, trademarks, trade-names, and know-how; management contracts for equipment maintenance and service facilities; franchising.

Research and development: location of R&D operations in foreign countries, research subcontracting; joint R&D projects.

Personnel: employment of nationals by foreign firms; employment of foreign technicians; migration of trained personnel; internal training programs of business firms; commercial training programs of professional associations, and educational institutions and research institutes.

Other: investment in or acquisition of foreign companies; transfers through international tender invitations; industrial espionage.

Much existing technology is nonproprietary and freely available. Whether a potential user is able to exploit that technology depends upon a number of factors. The user must be able to define the need for the technology. The user must also have qualified personnel available who have access to scientific and technical publications and an ability to apply that information. Also, the receiving country must have an infrastructure adequate to support the absorption, translation, and utilization of the technology.

The transfer of technology through international tender offers is an especially interesting mode. Thus, a middle eastern country invited tenders for a contract to install a national communications system. The potential value of the contract—hundreds of millions of dollars—prompted many multinational companies and consortia to invest millions of dollars in designing systems they hoped would win the contract. In the process of negotiating and awarding the contract, the responsible officials of the purchasing country received a massive amount of transferred technology.

Expediters and controllers of the transfer process

International transfers frequently involve participants other than the suppliers and users of technology. A range of government and private groups, for example, perform expediting and controlling functions. These expediters and controllers can have a major influence on the timing, kinds of transfers, and terms negotiated. National patent authorities assisted by national patent laws and international treaties and conventions, aid in expediting international technology transfers. International standards organizations also act as technology transfer expediters and controllers. Thus, the International Civil Aviation Organization (ICAO) promotes international standards and regulations in civil aviation. The International Telecommunications Union (ITU) has similar responsibilities in radio, telegraph, telephone, and space communications. The objectives of these agencies are primarily safety and uniformity.

The most extensive control activities are those of national governments. These have been discussed in previous chapters and will be examined further below.

INTERNATIONAL TECHNOLOGY ISSUES FOR THE FIRM

What special technology issues are encountered by the firm in international operations? Certain issues arise when the firm's motivation for "going international" is to acquire foreign technology. Other issues arise when the motivation for international expansion is to exploit technology advantages.

When the firm's competitive advantage abroad is based on technology, it faces such issues as how to maintain its technology advantage over time, which strategy to choose for profiting from the technology advantage, and how to price the technology. If the strategy chosen is to invest directly in foreign production, the firm must choose the technology alternative that best fits the foreign environment. And in all these managerial decisions the present and future control environment in both home and host countries must be considered. But let us first turn to the matter of foreign technology acquisitions.

Foreign technology acquisitions

Although technology is highly concentrated in the industrialized countries, these nations differ in the areas of technology in which they lead. The United States has been a leader in computer technology. Germany and Switzerland have a long tradition of advanced research in chemicals and pharmaceuticals. European and Japanese firms have been leaders in fuel-economy transportation vehicles, in large part because heavy government taxation in their countries kept gasoline prices much higher than in the United States. These national differences have been a motivation for many types of international business expansions, including foreign technology acquisitions through direct investment, joint ventures for research cooperation, and cross-licensing agreements.

An interesting example of technology acquisition through direct investment is the case of a leading Japanese computer company (Fujitsu) and a new computer company (Amdahl) started in the United States.[6] In 1970, a former chief scientist of IBM founded the Amdahl Corporation to produce large-scale, general purpose mainframes. The new firm had difficulty raising capital from U.S. sources. The U.S. stock market was depressed at the time. Also, American investors were not anxious to risk their capital in a new company that would have to compete with IBM to be successful. But a large Japanese computer company, Fujitsu, Limited, was willing to provide capital by taking a substantial equity position in the Amdahl Corporation.

Fujitsu was developing its own technology and having difficulty producing large computers. The investment in Amdahl gave Fujitsu access to large computer technology and resulted in arrangements for joint development, cross-licensing, coproduction, and joint-venture sales agreements. It has been estimated that this investment enabled Fujitsu to close a three- to five-year technological gap between it and the U.S. industry.[7]

Other examples include the acquisition by a Dutch company of a substantial equity interest in a U.S. company to gain access to pollution control technology, a joint French-U.S. venture established in the United States by the desire of the French firm to acquire process technology for making soft contact lenses,[8] and a large investment by Corning Glass of the United States in a small British company that invented a revolutionary biotechnology for producing antibodies. In the British case, the new technology was given television publicity in the United Kingdom, but only one British offer of finance was forthcoming—and that on onerous terms. So the new company turned to an American investor that now owns 49 percent of the venture.[9]

The acquisition of technology through foreign operations has been a frequent occurrence in international business. And such foreign expansions are not limited to the acquisition of product and process technology. A major European consumer-products firm established operations in the United States to gain firsthand knowledge and experience in marketing. Such technology was then made available to other units of the multinational enterprise in other foreign countries.

Maintaining the technology advantage

Where foreign operations are based on technology advantage, it is crucial for the international firm to maintain that advantage over time.

---

[6] Jack Baranson, *Technology and the Multinationals* (Lexington, Mass.: Lexington Books, 1978), pp. 75–84.

[7] Ibid., p. 84.

[8] U.S. Department of Commerce, *Foreign Direct Investment in the United States*, vol. 1 (Washington, D.C.: U.S. Government Printing Office, April 1976), pp. 201–206.

[9] *The Economist*, April 21, 1979, p. 124.

Technology is perishable and advantages can easily erode. Where the international firm is exporting, the need to maintain its foreign competitive advantage is similar to the need to stay ahead in its domestic market. Because it has transport costs and other disadvantages as compared to a local firm, however, the foreign firm must maintain a greater margin of technology advantage than against domestic competition.

Where the international firm has established foreign production facilities based on technology advantages, the need to maintain its advantage over time has an additional dimension. Not only must it maintain a large enough technology superiority over potential local producers to remain competitive but it also needs to maintain its advantage in order to retain bargaining power against national control policies. This latter need is particularly important for firms operating in developing countries. The ever present nationalism means that local enterprises are preferred and that foreign firms are almost always viewed by the host country as a second-best choice.

The need to maintain a technology advantage in the future applies to resource seekers as well as market seekers. Many international firms with foreign mining projects have been forced to divest or share ownership locally as their initial technology contribution has been absorbed locally and their technology advantage has eroded. The same need is present in foreign licensing arrangements. As will be discussed below, the licensor's ability to supply new technology can be a key factor in maintaining and profiting from arrangements with licensees.

How does the firm maintain its technology advantage over time? One way is to keep its unique know-how secret. Coca-Cola has done this with considerable success by safeguarding the mixture formula of its syrup. Another way is through reliance on trademarks. These are normally granted by law in perpetuity whereas patent monopolies expire after a fixed number of years. The most effective means, however, is to have a research capability to develop new technologies and technological improvements.

Locating R&D facilities abroad

In many situations, the true source of a company's technology advantage is not its current technology assets but its research and development capability. In international business operations, this reality raises the issue of where R&D facilities should be located. Multinational enterprises are frequently under pressure by host countries to locate R&D facilities abroad, along with production facilities. And a number of firms have deviated, with successful results, from the usual pattern of keeping R&D operations in the home country. As a recent study of the experience of several U.S. multinationals concluded, foreign R&D units made these firms more competitive in both foreign and U.S. markets than if they had performed R&D only in the United States.[10]

A more ambitious study, undertaken in 1978, of 31 American and 18 European multinationals revealed a surprising amount of foreign R&D activity. In total, the group had more than 200 active foreign R&D units, many of which had their origin in pressures from host countries.[11]

What are the motivations for establishing foreign R&D units? At a minimum, such units can assist in the process of technology transfer, make product and process adaptations to local conditions, and strengthen the subsidiary's competitive position by providing technical services to customers. A more ambitious mission for such units, and even more crucial for maintaining a technology advantage in the future, is to develop new and improved products and processes expressly for foreign markets, after identifying opportunities different from those perceived in the home country. Still another motivation is to take advantage of a concentration of knowledge and talent in a foreign area.

The adaptation function can be illustrated by the agricultural chemical firm that needs to test and adapt its product to the climatic, soil, and other conditions in the foreign markets it is serving. Similarly, U.S. pharmaceutical firms have European formulation laboratories to meet European drug administration practices that differ from those in the United States.

The motivation of better serving distinctive foreign markets through foreign R&D units has been explained by the following underlying philosophy:

> Scientists in one country are not good at answering the specific market needs of another country. . . .
>
> We believe that the best way to overcome this problem is to have subsidiaries in important markets away from the parent company develop their own complete R&D organizations to take full and direct advantage of the opportunities peculiar to their environment.[12]

The French subsidiary of the Otis Elevator Company, as an example, was missing out on a major market for small elevators to be installed in low-rise buildings. Otis had not entered this market in the United States and did not have technology to transfer abroad. A unit established in Europe was able to develop technology for the small-elevator market.[13]

---

[10] Robert C. Ronstadt, "International R&D: The Establishment and Evolution of Research and Development Abroad by Seven U.S. Multinationals," *Journal of International Business Studies*, Spring–Summer 1978, pp. 7–24.

[11] Jack N. Behrman and William A. Fischer, "Transnational Corporations: Market Orientation and R&D Abroad," *Columbia Journal of World Business*, Fall 1980, pp. 55–60.

[12] Rosemarie Van Rumker, "Multinational R&D in Practice: Chemagro Corporation," *Research Management*, January 1971, p. 52.

[13] Ronstadt, "International R&D," p. 12.

The motivation of benefiting from a highly favorable research environment is illustrated by the decision of many foreign firms to locate R&D facilities in the United States. R&D expenditures by U.S. affiliates of foreign firms totaled almost $1 billion in 1974. As explained by the foreign firms, the basis for their extensive R&D activity in the United States is the size and advanced nature of the U.S. market and the special attractiveness of the U.S. environment for R&D.[14]

The decision to locate R&D in a specific foreign country will depend, of course, on other practical considerations such as host government controls and incentives, whether an economic size research unit can be justified, the availability of adequate infrastructure and universities, and the foreign supply of needed technical skills.

Technology transfer strategies

Another important decision in managing international technology transfers is the strategy chosen by the firm for appropriating the potential returns from its technology advantage. As in the case of other sources of competitive advantage, the two broad strategy options are to internalize by extending its own operations, or to use external markets. The decision variables affecting this choice were discussed in Chapter 3.[15] But two specific forms of using external markets—licensing and selling "turnkey projects"—deserve special attention as they relate to technology transfers. These strategies have gained in importance as government policies in many countries have become increasingly restrictive against direct investment.

Turnkey projects. Numerous firms in the United States and elsewhere specialize in the design, construction, and startup of "turnkey plants." In such transactions, the contractor agrees to handle every detail of the project including the training of operating personnel. At the completion of the contract, the customer is handed the key to a completed plant that is fully ready for operations. In some cases, however, the contractor will take an equity interest in the project.

Japanese firms, in particular, have been using this strategy, and plant exports on a turnkey basis have been accounting for an increasingly large portion of Japan's trade. For example, in 1982, the giant trading company, Mitsubishi Corporation, was constructing four oil refineries and gas plants, in cooperation with several other Japanese firms, in a Mideast oil-producing country. The size of this export business is illustrated by the

---

[14] U.S. Department of Commerce, *Foreign Direct Investment in the United States*, Vol. 1, p. 197.

[15] See Chapter 3, pp. 44–45.

fact that an oil refinery with a daily capacity of 100,000 barrels would cost $450 million (in 1982 prices), and some Mideast countries were planning refineries with a daily capacity of as much as 250,000 barrels.[16]

The strategy of selling technology in the form of turnkey plant exports is used extensively in the chemical, petrochemical, and petroleum refining industries. A large number of U.S. and other international companies have as their main business the selling of newly developed technology for these industries, rather than the sale of end products from the use of the technology. These firms reinvest a share of their profits in developing new generations of technology and have little concern for the potential competition from technology purchasers.[17]

International companies that are in the business of selling end products normally derive their profit indirectly from their proprietary technology commercialized into end products. In such cases, the direct sale of technology has the disadvantage of creating competitors and reducing the seller's competitive advantage in the marketplace. Nevertheless, end-product companies can use the turnkey strategy with success in certain special circumstances, as shown in Box 19–1.

As another example, a major U.S. company in the consumer electronics industry signed a contract in late 1974 valued at more than $200 million with an Algerian enterprise to construct a turnkey consumer electronics plant in Algeria. The special circumstances were that the U.S. company had no export potential in this market because Algeria intended to close the domestic markets to foreign imports after the new plant was built. Also, several foreign competitors stood ready to make the sale if the U.S. company had not done so, and the project allowed the U.S. company to sell components to the new plant for a period of time. In addition, the new Algerian plant was not expected to become an important competitive factor in the world market. An interesting detail of the contract was that about $25 million of the contract price was earmarked for technical and managerial training in the United States.[18]

Licensing.   Although long considered an inferior strategy, the licensing alternative is uniquely significant for international technology transfers and appears to be gaining in importance. A recent study concluded, "Licensing in many selected situations is not only very profitable, but superior in a net risk-adjusted comparison with alternatives."[19] Licensing has special advantages for small companies that lack capital, manage-

---

[16] Mitsubishi Corporation, *Tokyo Newsletter,* January 1982.

[17] See Baranson, *Technology and the Multinationals,* pp. 115–42, for several case studies of international turnkey projects.

[18] Ibid., pp. 99–102.

[19] Farok J. Contractor, "The Role of Licensing in International Strategy," *Columbia Journal of World Business,* Winter 1981, p. 74.

Box 19–1

Exporting technology

Kawasaki Steel Corp., Japan's fourth largest steelmaker, is taking that nation's edge in steel-producing technology both to new heights and to non-Western foreign markets in an unusually aggressive fashion. The new approach at Kawasaki began in mid-1977 with the naming of a new president whose new corporate design seems to have two essential elements. First, he is pressing Kawasaki's 800 scientists and engineers in Japan to come up with new, more sophisticated methods of making its sheet, plate, and tubular steels used in everything from bridges to buses. At the same time, Kawasaki's 380 export specialists are stalking overseas markets and projects to export products and steelmaking expertise directly tied to R&D work in Japan.

Now that emerging countries increasingly want their own steelmaking facilities, rather than relying on imports, Kawasaki is placing much greater emphasis on exporting its technology. Today, technology exports contribute just 5 percent of the company's business. Within five years they are expected to account for at least 10 percent of sales.

If there is any drawback to Kawasaki's technology exporting drive, it would seem to be that one day the plants it helps build elsewhere will become competition for the company's own production. The potential threat, however, does not worry the president. He is confident that his company's engineers will keep coming up with new breakthroughs. "By the time the exported steel plant comes on stream, our technology will have advanced, so we will still be ahead."

Source: Adapted from *Business Week*, January 29, 1979, pp. 119–20.

---

ment, and the necessary experience for expanding internationally through direct investment.[20] Many large firms also make extensive use of licensing, both with their foreign affiliates and with unaffiliated parties.

A frequent argument against licensing unaffiliated parties is that the licensor may in time lose its competitive edge to the licensee and be barred in the future from direct expansion in overseas areas served by the licensee. This argument, usually assumes a simple and discrete relationship between the licensor and the licensee. But licensing can be a part of a multifaceted strategy that permits the licensor to take an ownership interest in the foreign venture. Also, trademarks are often a part of the licensing package, and trademarks remain the property of the licensor in perpetuity whereas licenses normally have a finite period. In many cases, the licensing firm retains considerable bargaining power because of the perishable nature of technology and the licensor's ability to supply new technology in the future to the licensee.

---

[20] Eugene M. Lang, "Venturing into the World: Prospects for Small Business," *Enterprise,* September 1978, pp. 12–13.

The circumstances under which licensing may be a preferred strategy can be summarized as follows:[21]

Where host countries restrict imports and/or direct investment.

Where a specific foreign market is small.

Where prospects of technology feedback are high.

Where licensing is a way of testing and developing a market that can later be exploited by direct investment.

Where the pace of technology change is sufficiently rapid that the seller can remain technologically superior.

Where opportunities exist for licensing auxiliary processes without having to license basic product technologies.

Where small companies have limited resources and expertise for direct foreign expansions.

In general, the advantages of the licensing strategy will depend upon the specific technology, size of firm, product maturity, extent of international experience of the firm, and environmental constraints in host countries. As shown in Box 19–2, licensing can be an attractive strategy for generating a flow of royalties, export sales, and valuable technology feedback.

Choice of technology

When a firm decides to internalize its competitive advantage through establishing foreign production, it must also make a choice as to the technology it intends to use. When the expansion is into an industrialized country by a firm from another industrialized country, the choice-of-technology decision has few special international elements. Normally, the same technology as that used in the home country will be transferred, but with minor adaptations for differences that may exist in foreign supply sources and markets.

In contrast, where foreign production is established in developing countries, the choice-of-technology decision must take into consideration the international controversy over "appropriate" technology. Many developing countries believe, as discussed in Chapter 11, that the technology imported by foreign firms should not be the same as that used in capital-rich countries with large markets, but should be appropriate to the factor endowments of the host country. This usually means that imported technology should be more labor intensive and smaller scale.

The appropriate technology controversy raises several key questions

---

[21] Contractor, "The Role of Licensing," Table 3, p. 76; see also P. Telesio, *Foreign Licensing Policy in Multinational Enterprises* (D.B.A. dissertation, Harvard University, 1977).

Box 19-2

> **An international technology licensing success story**
>
> "Heli-Coil" industrial fasteners (screw thread inserts) were developed during World War II to meet aircraft and military needs for stronger threaded connections in aluminum and light metal alloys. After the war, the company (now the Heli-Coil Division of MITE Corp., Danbury, Connecticut) developed civilian industry sales and began to expand abroad through licensing.
>
> Through an international program involving 10 licensees, the company achieved overseas sales of $15 million (in 1976) from a base of zero in 1950. Eighty percent of the royalty-paying sales involve product applications developed abroad, which account for less than 10 percent of U.S. sales. On top of royalties, an annual six-figure Heli-Coil export volume has grown up because foreign licensees find it more economical to import certain U.S.-made items.
>
> Another benefit has been technology feedback, now available to all licensees. The Japanese licensee conducted studies and succeeded in applying Heli-Coil fasteners on iron and steel. The English licensee developed power tools for automatically installing the fasteners. The French licensee adapted designs for applications in wood and developed production gauges used in the United States and by licensees in other countries.
>
> The German licensee devised compound fasteners—a new product for themselves and all members of the Heli-Coil enterprise. Finally, the Indian licensee designed equipment that could be efficiently employed for short-run production, making it economically feasible to set up operations in other developing countries.
>
> Source: Adapted from *Iron Age*, February 7, 1977, pp. 47–48.

for the international manager. To what extent are commercially feasible alternative technologies readily available? If not available, can the cost of developing more appropriate technology be justified? And, what mix of factors other than differences in the relative cost of labor and capital should influence the managerial decision?

Availability of technology alternatives. The availability of commercially feasible technology alternatives varies from industry to industry. In some fields, a considerable choice in production technologies exists. In other industries, significant technology alternatives may not be readily available.

A field study that examined the textile and pulp and paper industries in Colombia, Brazil, the Philippines, and Indonesia revealed a range of available technologies for most processing steps that required significantly different quantities of capital and labor.[22] But the number of alternatives were limited and the differences in the labor/capital mix were

---

[22] Michel A. Amsalem, *Technology Choice in Developing Countries* (Cambridge, Mass.: MIT Press, 1983).

small for some steps. Another field study of six light manufacturing industries also encountered a wide range of technologies in use. In cigarette manufacturing, as one example, the technologies ranged from automatic machines that rolled 2,000 cigarettes a minute to hand rolling with the aid of an inexpensive, simple tool. The capital-intensive technology with only three workers produced the same output as the labor-intensive method using 40 workers.[23]

In general, the nature of a process or product can determine the extent to which technology alternatives might be available.[24] In the textile industry, the manufacturing process is composed of a number of discrete processing steps, each performed by one or a group of machines. Consequently, the choice of technology and equipment on the basis of labor/capital trade-offs can be made for each of these processing steps independently from the choice for the other steps. In a chemical industry, the transformation of raw materials is achieved through the interaction of chemicals, heat, and pressure, and there is little room for manual intervention in the continuous transformation process. Trade-offs between capital and labor are available in the choice of manual or automatic controls but not in the choice of the basic processing equipment.

The nature of the industry or product also influences the cost and availability of technical information on alternative technologies needed by the firm to make its technology choices. In mechanical process industries, alternative technologies are embodied in standardized equipment that is available on an "off-the-shelf" basis. Thus alternatives and their characteristics can be known at little or no cost. In chemical process industries, equipment is normally custom made for each plant, and the decision maker may have to make a substantial investment in engineering and design work to secure the technical data needed to evaluate the technology alternatives. In general, information on capital-intensive equipment is more likely to be available to decision makers since information flows usually run from developed to developing countries rather than between developing countries.

Technology decision criteria. Contrary to the implicit assumption of many advocates of appropriate technology, the trade-off between capital and labor cannot be the sole criterion in the management decision on alternative technologies. As one writer suggests, management variables are often "the forgotten factor in technology choice."[25] Considerations that often tip the decision to more automated methods are quality

---

[23] Louis T. Wells, Jr., "Economic Man and Engineering Man: Choice and Technology in a Low-Wage Country," *Public Policy*, Summer 1973, pp. 319-42.

[24] See Amsalem, *Technology Choice.*

[25] Michel A. Amsalem, "Management: The Forgotten Factor in Technology Choice," in *Technology Assessment and Development,* ed. Magalain Srinivasan (New York: Praeger Publishers, 1982).

control maintenance, waste minimization, response time to market-demand fluctuations, labor training costs, labor relations problems, and the prestige of having the latest equipment.[26]

Host government policies can also push the decision toward the capital-intensive alternative. Such policies include making investment capital available at below-market rates, restricting the import of used machinery, and adopting worker-welfare and labor-relations legislation that is viewed by business firms as excessively burdensome. Where host countries protect local firms from competitive pressures through tariffs and import controls and by limiting the number of producers, the competitive incentive to reduce production costs by adapting technology to different capital/labor cost situations is also greatly weakened.

Pricing of international technology transfers

The pricing decision for technology transfers, whether domestic or international, can be complex. The market for technology is highly imperfect and relatively little pricing information is publicly available to guide the negotiating parties. Furthermore, the compensation package may include many types of payments. A simple agreement might provide for a lump-sum payment or specified royalties over a fixed period of time. Under a more comprehensive agreement, the licensor might also receive compensation in the form of fees for technical assistance and other services performed, dividends from an equity share granted by the licensee, profits on goods supplied or received by the licensor, valuable technology feedback, and tax savings arising out of the arrangement.[27]

As in the case of technology choice, special factors arise in pricing the technology for transfers to developing countries. Increasingly, host governments are intervening in the negotiation of agreements on technology payments. They are generally aware that payments to parent companies by controlled foreign affiliates are likely to be shaped by the various elements of transfer pricing strategies discussed in Chapter 22.[28] There is also a general presumption that the prices paid for technology are "too high."

Many host countries believe that the weak negotiating position of developing countries has resulted in higher technology prices than for similar transfers to industrial countries. They also argue that technology is generally protected by a patent monopoly that inherently permits the technology seller to extract an excessive monopoly price. Still another

---

[26] Farok J. Contractor and Taji Sagafi-Nejad, "International Technology Transfer: Major Issues and Policy Responses," *Journal of International Business Studies*, Fall 1981, p. 122.

[27] See United Nations Industrial Development Organization, *National Approaches to the Acquisition of Technology* (New York: UNIDO, 1977), pp. 70–74; Farok J. Contractor, *International Technology Licensing* (Lexington, Mass.: Lexington Books, 1981), p. 35.

[28] See G. Kopits, "Intrafirm Royalties Crossing Frontiers and Transfer-Pricing Behavior," *Economic Journal*, December 1976, pp. 791–803.

argument is that the technology development costs have previously been amortized over home market sales. Consequently, international transfers need not be compensated at much more than the incremental cost of the transfer.

Some indirect evidence exists to support the argument of higher prices to Colombia during the early 1970s in the pharmaceutical industry.[29] But broader empirical evidence on this issue is difficult to develop because of the combination of payments that might be involved. In any event, the expanding exchange of information among national agencies has better prepared host countries for preventing discriminatory pricing.

The monopoly pricing argument confuses the concept of a patent as a monopoly with monopoly power in the marketplace. Patented technology can face competition in the market where substitutable technology is available. In recent years, even in high-technology areas such as pharmaceuticals, computers, and petrochemicals, several sources of substitutable technology have typically become available.[30] Thus potential users in developing countries generally have several technology suppliers competing against each other.

The "sunk cost" argument is rejected by business firms on several grounds. They believe that the sale of present technology should not only cover sunk costs but also revenue to fund future research and development.[31] Furthermore, some governmental tax authorities such as the U.S. Internal Revenue Service, have policies requiring that R&D expenditures be shared by all users of the resulting technology. This policy attempts to protect home-country income tax revenues from being reduced by expensing all R&D expenditures in the home country.

In summary, the international firm has no standard model available for pricing international technology transfers. In practice, the pricing decision for nonaffiliated foreign buyers will be a negotiated price that reflects the bargaining power and skills of the parties. The lower price limit will be set by the costs of effecting the transfer. The upper limit will be either the value of the technology to the buyer or a limit imposed by host-government policies.

NATIONAL AND INTERNATIONAL CONTROL ENVIRONMENT

National controls over international technology transfers are certain to continue into the future. As is true for other control measures, they reflect the reality that the private interests of the buyers and sellers can

---

[29] See Constantine Vaitsos, *Intercountry Income Distribution and Transnational Corporations* (New York: Oxford University Press, 1974).

[30] Nathaniel H. Leff, "Technology Transfer and U.S. Foreign Policy: The Developing Countries," *Orbis*, Spring 1979, p. 146.

[31] Isaiah Frank, *Foreign Enterprise in Developing Countries* (Baltimore: Johns Hopkins University Press, 1980), p. 81.

diverge from the national interests of the countries. At the international level, the developing countries can be expected to continue their pressure for an international code to govern technology transfers. But universal agreement on such a code is not likely to be achieved in the near future. Each of the participating countries is a sovereign power and the national interests of the participants diverge sharply in a number of respects. Thus, the principal control environment of concern to the international manager will be at the national level.

Home countries will continue to control technology transfers for national security reasons and to protect tax revenues. The broader concern for losing international competitiveness through foreign technology transfers will persist as a government policy issue. But the problem of international competitiveness is only one element of a complex economic adjustment problem that many countries are facing as a result of a changing world economy. Also, there is not substantial agreement that the national costs of such international technology transfers exceed the benefits.[32] In any event, it is difficult to envision controls intended to protect a nation's international competitiveness that are feasible and effective.

On the host-country side, the developing countries can be expected to become even more active in the national monitoring of international technology transfers. And the competence of such agencies should steadily increase with experience and with more information becoming available. The specific instruments used to press for reduced payments, more appropriate technology, more local R&D, and so on, will change as countries appraise their past experience with controls and as new strategies are conceived. But the determination to increase national benefits from technology transfers is not likely to weaken.

What are the implications of the suggested future control scenario to the international manager? First, the manager must be constantly aware that the negotiation of international technology agreements is what has been called a "quadrilogue,"[33] meaning that it involves four parties: the seller, the buyer, the home country, and the host country. In managing international technology transfers, therefore, the manager must be informed, attempt to understand the motivation, and even forecast the national control policies that must be recognized in managerial decision making. It may also be incumbent on the manager to participate in national policymaking by making available relevant information and views.

---

[32] See John H. Dunning, "The Consequences of International Transfer of Technology by Multinational Enterprises: Some Home Country Implications," in *International Production and the Multinational Enterprise,* ed. J. H. Dunning (London: George Allen & Unwin, 1981), pp. 321–63; R. G. Hawkins and T. N. Gladwin, "Conflicts in the International Transfer of Technology: A U.S. Home-Country View," in *Technology Transfer Control Systems,* ed. T. Sagafi-Nejad, R. W. Moxon, and H. V. Perlmutter (Elmsford, N.Y.: Pergamon Press, 1981).

[33] Howard V. Perlmutter and Tagi Sagafi-nejad, *International Technology Transfer: Codes, Guidelines and a Muffled Quadrilogue* (New York: Pergamon Press, 1981).

A second implication is that the manager should remain open to the possibility that control pressures may not be a zero-sum game. The pressure of host governments to have local R&D facilities may benefit the firm with expanded opportunities for developing technology and for maintaining its technology advantage in local markets.

Still another implication is that the manager should be exploring the feasibility and benefits of alternative strategies for transferring technology. This may mean a shift by some firms to more arm's-length licensing. It may also mean technology sharing with host countries through cross-licensing agreements or cooperative projects for technological development.

SUMMARY

The management of international technology transfers has become a major aspect of international business activity and promises to become even more critical in the future. As a management function, technology transfers that cross national boundaries raise a series of special international issues. In particular, the international enterprise is likely to encounter substantial involvement by governments of developing countries that are technology recipients.

EXERCISES AND DISCUSSION QUESTIONS

1. You are seeking governmental approval in a Third-World country for a licensing agreement. The government officials want to reduce the agreed-upon royalty rate on the grounds that "technology is the common heritage of mankind." What logical counterargument would you make?

2. What criteria should the international firm use in selecting its strategy for overseas expansion to profit from a competitive technology advantage?

3. A Swedish firm has a central staff charged with developing processes specifically for use in Third-World countries. Under what circumstances would you recommend that your international company follow this same pattern?

4. "The export of U.S. technology, much of which has been financed by government funds, should be controlled so as to protect U.S. international competitiveness and protect U.S. jobs." Do you agree or disagree and why?

5. In negotiating an international licensing agreement, how would you try to protect your U.S. firm so that it would not be foreclosed in the future from expanding in the market area of the licensee? Take into account the U.S. antitrust law, which makes illegal licensing provisions that restrict the geographic area in which the licensee can compete.

Chapter 20

Multinational accounting

An accounting system for multinational enterprises must provide sufficient and satisfactory information to fulfill several requirements simultaneously.[1] First, it must provide financial data for information and decision purposes that is understandable and useful to the local management of the particular unit. At the enterprise level, the system must provide internal statements that can be used for comparison, and on which decisions involving more than one country can be based. The

---

[1] See Hanns-Martin W. Schoenfeld, "International Accounting: Development, Issues, and Future Directions," *Journal of International Business Studies*, Fall 1981, pp. 83–100; see also Jeffrey S. Arpan and Lee H. Radebaugh, *International Accounting and the Multinational Enterprise* (New York: Warren, Gorham, and Lamont, 1981).

system must also provide financial statements that can be consolidated on an enterprise-wide basis. Finally, the accounting for the total enterprise and the individual subunits of the firm must respond to external reporting requirements, particularly those of the different countries in which the firm operates. As no single set of accounts can fulfill all these needs, multinationals have little choice other than to maintain parallel sets of accounting records.

A more detailed examination of these multiple requirements of accounting systems follows, along with an outline of the various national and international accounting standards and practices that have evolved to guide and regulate the ways in which accounts are presented. Managers need to be familiar with these standards if they are to interpret successfully the messages contained in a multinational's accounts. They should also understand how accounts based on different accounting standards and expressed in different currencies are restated onto a consistent basis for consolidation and then translated into a common currency. The technical details of translation, which are discussed in the final section of the chapter, can make a considerable difference to a firm's annual profit performance—particularly under fluctuating exchange rates.

REQUIREMENTS OF MULTINATIONAL ACCOUNTING

Subsidiary reporting requirements

At the subsidiary level, understandability of financial reports must be guaranteed within the national environment. National accounting standards and procedures, prescribed either by law or by local professional organizations, must be followed in order that financial reports can be understood by tax and other government officials. For countries operating under the so-called civil code law system, firms domiciled within their jurisdiction are required to present financial statements in a form specified by law. The format of these legal accounts is far removed from the format expected for public financial reportings. In some countries, subsidiaries may also be subjected to unusually stringent demands because of the foreign nationality of the parent.

Adherence to national accounting standards permits each local manager to manage on the basis of familiar data and concepts, to compare performance with that of local competitors, and to evaluate results against local rather than parent-company standards. Furthermore, many managerial decisions are dependent on local conditions and have to be based on relevant local data. For example, local inflationary conditions may require price-level adjustments for company expenses or sales for different time periods, even though such accounting practices are not typical in the country of the parent.

Given the multiple purposes that must be served by financial reporting, the national operating units often find it necessary to prepare three or four different sets of financial statements. One set is prepared on the basis of nationally accepted accounting principles. A second set of financial statements is prepared that complies with the accounting principles and the translation methods that are accepted in the country of the home office. Still another set may be prepared to comply with the regulations of the various tax authorities involved. And, finally, separate financial statements may be prepared that present a picture of the enterprise for management. In the internal enterprise statement, for example, uniform valuation methods for assets of all subsidiaries might be used, regardless of the different legal regulations or locally accepted accounting practices.

Corporate reporting requirements

At the headquarters of the multinational, comparability between accounts of subsidiaries is likely to be an important requirement. Allocation of resources and management attention is not infrequently based on comparative performance. The central accounting staff must also produce parent company financial statements and consolidated financial statements that meet the requirements of the jurisdiction in which the parent is incorporated, the requirements of regulatory bodies such as the Securities and Exchange Commission, and their own external audit requirements. Statement No. 14 of the U.S. Financial Accounting Standards Board, in particular, requires separate disclosure of figures for the United States and for foreign operations by geographic area, including revenue, sales to unaffiliated customers, operating profit or loss, and identifiable assets.

The multinational enterprise may also have to report beyond its country of incorporation. External reporting requirements are particularly extensive for firms raising capital in the U.S. capital markets or having their shares listed on the U.S. stock exchanges. Many European firms have great difficulties with the U.S. requirements because they are unaccustomed by national tradition to making so much detailed information publicly available. An important force for greater disclosure is the growing practice of following the norms of the U.S. Securities Exchange Commission when raising capital in the Eurobond markets.

Where shareholdings are multinational, and a single set of financial statements could cause communications difficulties, the Accountants International Study Group (AISG) has recommended "secondary" financial statements.[2] Some Dutch and Japanese multinationals, for example,

---

[2] Accountants International Study Group, *International Financial Reporting*, Study no. 11 (Toronto: AISG, 1975).

report both according to their own home accounting principles and also on the basis of United States principles with statements in English.

The broadest pressures for external reporting have been from the movement for establishing guidelines for multinational enterprises already discussed in Chapter 10. The guidelines agreed to by the OECD countries are not substantially broader than U.S. requirements (Figure 20–1) but they carry the requirements to all OECD-based multinationals.

Figure 20–1

OECD Guidelines for Multinational enterprise

Disclosure of Information

Enterprises should, having due regard to their nature and relative size in the economic context of their operations and to requirements of business confidentiality and to cost, publish in a form suited to improve public understanding a sufficient body of factual information on the structure, activities, and policies of the enterprise as a whole, as a supplement, insofar as necessary for this purpose, to information to be disclosed under the national law of the individual countries in which they operate. To this end, they should publish within reasonable time limits, on a regular basis, but at least annually, financial statements and other pertinent information relating to the enterprise as a whole, comprising in particular:

1. The structure of the enterprise, showing the name and location of the parent company, its main affiliates, its percentage ownership, direct and indirect, in these affiliates, including shareholdings between them.
2. The geographic areas* where operations are carried out and the principal activities carried on therein by the parent company and the main affiliates.
3. The operating results and sales by geographical area and the sales in the major lines of business for the enterprise as a whole.
4. Significant new capital investment by geographical area and, as far as practicable, by major lines of business for the enterprise as a whole.
5. A statement of the sources and uses of funds by the enterprise as a whole.
6. The average number of employees in each geographic area.
7. Research and development expenditure for the enterprise as a whole.
8. The policies followed in respect of intragroup pricing.
9. The accounting policies, including those on consolidation, observed in compiling the published information.

* For the purposes of the guideline on disclosure of information the term *geographic area* means groups of countries or individual countries as each enterprise determines is appropriate in its particular circumstances. While no single method of grouping is appropriate for all enterprises or for all purposes, the factors to be considered by an enterprise would include the significance of operations carried out in individual countries or areas as well as the effects on its competitiveness, geographic proximity, economic affinity, similarities in business environments and the nature, scale, and degree of interrelationships of the enterprises' operations in the various countries. Source: Organization for Economic Cooperations and Development, *International Investment and Multinational Enterprises* (Paris, 1976), pp. 14–15.

The guidelines are voluntary and require implementing national legislation in the OECD countries to be compulsory. Yet the existence of the guidelines, even though "voluntary," exerts strong pressure on the multinationals to comply. The requirements to disclose intergroup pricing policies, and geographical information on operations, performance

and employment go one step further toward strengthening national controls over activities that span country boundaries.[3] The United Nations
Centre on Transnational Corporations has also been active in developing
international standards of accounting and reporting. Extensive recommendations in this area made by a UN Group of Experts in 1977 were still
under consideration in 1982.[4]

Another important trend has been the growing demand and expectations that business firms act in a socially responsible fashion.[5] It may be
further in the future, but there is a strong probability that multinational
firms may have to publish a social audit and report on their relationship
to the social environment and the effects of this relationship. As some
business leaders have predicted, "In addition to their independently
audited annual statements, firms will some day be legally obliged to
submit audited social utility accounts—even if the definitive form of such
accounts is not yet clear."[6]

Consolidation requirements

The accounting treatment for consolidated financial statements recommended by the International Accounting Standard No. 3 and adopted
in the United States and other countries is as follows:

Foreign subsidiaries: Financial statements must be consolidated line-
by-line with the parent company and other subsidiaries.

Foreign associates: Not consolidated but recorded under the *equity
method* in the parent company books. The equity method requires
that the value of the investment in the parent company's books be
increased or decreased to recognize the parent's share of profits or
losses after the acquisition. To calculate this profit or loss, though, a
foreign associate's financial statements must be translated into U.S.
currency, as described later, with the translation profit or loss specified.

Investments: Recorded under the *cost method*. They are retained at
cost on the parent company's books and income is recognized only
to the extent that dividends are paid from profits rising after the
date of acquisition.

---

[3] See Karl P. Sauvant and Farid G. Lavipour, eds., *Controlling Multinational Enterprises:
Problems, Strategies, Counterstrategies* (Boulder, Colo.: Westview Press, 1976).

[4] See United Nations, *International Standards of Accounting and Reporting for Transna-
tional Corporations* (New York, 1977) (E/C.10/33): N. T. Wang, "The Design of International
Standards of Accounting and Reporting for Transnational Corporations," *The Journal of
International Law and Economics* 2, No. 3 (1977), pp. 447–64.

[5] Isaiah A. Litvak and Christopher J. Maule, "Foreign Corporate Social Responsibility in
Less Developed Economies," *Journal of World Trade Law*, March–April 1975; and Melvin
Anshen, ed., *Managing the Socially Responsible Corporation* (New York: Macmillan, 1974).

[6] John Moore, "Social Accounts: France Sets the Pace," *World Accounting Report*, February 1978.

Subsidiaries are entities over which the parent exercises control. Control is indicated by ownership of a majority of the equity capital, or control of the board. But control may even occur below 51 percent ownership. Associates are companies in which the investment interest is substantial and over which the investor has the power to exercise significant influence. Power to exercise significant influence, however, is not presumed to exist below a holding of 20 percent voting power. Investments are all equity holdings not in subsidiaries or associates.

Another set of consolidation requirements of multinationals is in the process of being formed within the EEC. The proposals are contained in the "Proposal for a Seventh Directive" published by the EEC Commission in April 1976. Article 6 of the proposal requires preparation of consolidated EEC accounts for every "dominant undertaking," that is, a company controlling another, with its registered office in the EEC wherever its subsidiaries are located. There is no exemption if this undertaking is itself a subsidiary of a foreign multinational preparing consolidated accounts. Even further, there is a requirement to consolidate separate "dependent undertakings" within the EEC reporting to the same dominant undertaking outside the EEC. Thus a U.S. multinational with separate German, United Kingdom, and Greek subsidiaries would have to present consolidated EEC accounts for these three operations.

NATIONAL ACCOUNTING STANDARDS AND PRACTICES

Accounting standards have been issued in most countries. In the United States, the Financial Accounting Standards Board (FASB) is the principal rule-making body. FASB standards are recognized by the American Institute of Certified Public Accountants (AICPA), which in effect sets auditing standards, and by the Securities and Exchange Commission (SEC), which requires compliance with the standards for all corporations with public issues of securities in the United States. The FASB is independent of the AICPA and other accounting associations, although it seeks their comments on "exposure drafts" of all proposed standards before they are finally announced. In most other countries recommendations as to accounting standards are issued by the professional accounting associations. In some countries, though, there is more than the one association issuing such recommendations.

Members of national accounting associations will usually adhere to the local standards both in preparing and auditing financial statements, but within-country variations in practice are common for a variety of reasons. Few, if any, national standards are set out as a comprehensive code of rigid rules. The local standard may indicate preferred alternatives, but leave the choice to the discretion of the practitioner. There is also an overriding requirement to give a true and fair view that on occasions may justify departure from a standard. Normally, such departures would be indicated in notes accompanying the financial statements, making it important for the cross-national user to examine entire statements and not just the accounting figures. Nor are most standards supported by a statutory requirement. Most go well beyond the requirements of corporation law or other statutes. Consequently, there is little that can be done to enforce a standard, particularly if there are practicing accountants and auditors outside the discipline of the standard-setting accounting association.

There is a strong tendency for national accounting standards to have common elements because most national accounting associations are members of the International Federation of Accountants (IFAC). The national associations may also be members of regional accounting bodies such as the Inter-American Accounting Association (IAA) Union Européene des Expertes Comptables Economiques et Financiers (UEC), or Confederation of Asian and Pacific Accountants (CAPA).

International contacts, however, do not mean that national standards are identical—not by a long way. Local standards have developed over the years out of varying social, political, and economic influences interacting with the current accounting practices and theories.[7] For example, where there has been widespread public ownership of corporate securities and a felt need to offset insider advantage, as in the United States, there has been a strong move toward standardization, consistency, and much disclosure. On the other hand, Swiss accounting practices have grown up requiring minimum disclosure in an environment that favors conservatism and that has sought to shelter more closely held corporations and their owners from external political action. Accounting practice is not an end in itself. It is a service justified by the extent to which it reflects the needs of its environment and adapts as those needs change. A move toward international standards may thus run counter to maximum usefulness.[8]

The situation is not as bad as it seems, however, because national accounting practices cluster into about a dozen groups.[9] National differences in accounting standards have been quite minor where practices have evolved from a common base or a country has adopted the practices of a more advanced country.

The cross-national user of financial reports will on many occasions need to know specifically how national standards and practices differ in order to compare reports on a common basis. Two comprehensive reference works that provide such details are the American Institute of Certified Public Accountants, *Professional Accounting in 30 Countries*,[10] and

---

[7] Stephen A. Zeff, *Forging Accounting Principles in Five Countries: A History and an Analysis of Trends* (Champaign, Ill.: Stripes, Publishing, 1972).

[8] Irving L. Fantl, "The Case against International Uniformity," *Management Accounting*, May 1971.

[9] Frederick D. S. Choi and Gerhard G. Mueller, *An Introduction to Multinational Accounting* (Englewood Cliffs, N.J.: Prentice-Hall, 1978), pp. 28–34.

[10] New York: AICPA, 1975. (792 pp.)

Box 20–1

Last days for "creative" accounting

Italian companies face tighter controls

The headline in *La Repubblica* said that Montedison had made a profit. *Il Giornale* said the chemical company had exactly broken even. *La Stampa* said it had finished heavily in the red, but with reduced losses. That is how three Italian newspapers interpreted Montedison's 1979 results when they were announced last year.

Each newspaper was right. The first had taken the results of the whole group, the second those of the parent company—a common source of confusion with big Italian concerns. The third had disentangled from the parent company's profit and loss account a capital gain made on the sale of subsidiaries—an item which in Britain for example, normally would not have been there—and subtracted it from the final figure.

The accounts of those Italian companies which publish figures at all are all too often a source of confusion and mystification. Companies can present evidence of a striking transformation in their affairs simply by the deft transfer of an item from one category to another. The reason is that Italian companies, with a few honorable exceptions, do not follow international accounting principles and do not have their accounts signed by external auditors.

All this is changing rapidly. From next year, publicly quoted companies above a certain size must produce audited accounts to satisfy the Consob, the stock exchange regulatory authority. Smaller companies will follow suit up to 1985, by which time all publicly quoted companies will have to comply. That, however, will cover only about 150 concerns, so small is the stock exchange. Over the same period, state-owned companies must also conform, as well as publishing houses.

Meanwhile, Parliament is discussing a law which, when it comes into force, will require all Italian companies to produce certified accounts to a uniform set of principles within five years of the law being passed—which ought to be next year. This will bring Italy into line with the fourth directive of the EEC, which it is supposed to implement by next year.

These two developments should gradually revolutionize the whole presentation of the affairs of Italian companies. It will particularly affect the big state-owned groups which, because of the absence of consolidated balance sheets, have been able to claim impressively high levels of turnover thanks to the double-counting of transactions between subsidiaries.

Source: James Buxton, *Financial Times*, Friday, December 4, 1981.

Price Waterhouse & Co., *A Survey in 46 Countries: Accounting Principles and Reporting Practices.*[11] This second publication is in English, French, German, and Spanish. Four examples of differences in accounting prac-

---

[11] London: Price Waterhouse & Co., 1975. (264 pp.)

tices that serve to illustrate the lack of comparability are as follows:

Exchange losses

In countries as diverse as Argentina, India, and the Philippines, exchange losses may be treated as assets. Losses arising on foreign currency liabilities incurred for purchase of goods may be added to the cost of the goods in inventory when the losses are incurred instead of being written off as an expense for the period in which they arise. Valuation at the lower of cost or market value still applies, but with the cost including the exchange losses.

Valuation of liabilities

German and Swiss practice takes a conservative approach to contingent liabilities and permits them to be overestimated hence creating secret reserves. In other countries, hidden reserves are created by provision for taxes contingent on the distribution of funds when distribution is not intended. On the other hand, material rental commitments on long-term leases are not required to be disclosed in a wide range of countries—for example, Argentina, Australia, Brazil, France, Germany, and Japan.

Capital gains and losses

In the United Kingdom, Ireland, Australia, and New Zealand, as well as Peru, capital gains can be carried directly to capital reserve accounts without passing the credit through the income account as required in other countries. For the same countries, too, there is no requirement to amortize goodwill.

Price-level adjustments

In recent years, high inflation rates worldwide have focused a great deal of attention on accounting methods of adjusting for inflation. Debates have waged fiercely over different approaches. The resulting compromise patchwork of approved, recommended, and required approaches introduces many national differences into accounts.[12] Major variations in national inflation rates are likely to continue. When combined with variations in accounting treatment, inflation will be a prime

---

[12] R. W. Scapens, *The Treatment of Inflation in the Published Accounts of Companies in Overseas Countries* (London: Research Committee of the Institute of Chartered Accountants in England and Wales, 1973).

area for potential distortion in comparability of financial reports. Three main types of price-level adjustment may be encountered:

1. Appropriations of income or retained earnings. The least refined approach is to appropriate some current income, or retained earnings from past years, to a reserve for the increased replacement cost of the firm's assets. It is usually resorted to when the depreciation charges based on the historical cost of assets would be inadequate to finance the replacement of those assets. The idea is to reduce the funds viewed as available for dividend declaration and prevent the firm paying out its real capital. The appropriation, however, may be quite an arbitrary amount and is likely to be more influenced by available "profits" than by actual price changes. The user of financial statements, moreover, may be unable to tell on what basis the appropriation has been calculated. Appropriations out of retained earnings have been made quite frequently in the past, even in the United States. Charges direct to current earnings are less common but still arise in many countries.

2. Revaluations of assets. This approach, revalues assets to approximate current replacement costs, either directly against the market or through use of an appropriate price-level index. If depreciation is then deducted on the revalued assets, operating income will reflect inflation more accurately. In many countries, revaluation is allowed if noted. In other countries, maximum revaluation levels are established and, in yet others, such as Brazil, companies are required to revalue assets each year using a government price index.

3. Comprehensive adjustment for price-level changes. This method adjusts all items in the financial statements—assets, liabilities, costs, and revenues. Either a general price index can be used that retains historical cost as the basis or specific adjustments can be made to bring each item to its current market or replacement value. The United Kingdom has taken a lead in this field and in March 1980 finally adopted a comprehensive solution of Current Cost Accounting. The details are specified in the U.K. Statement of Standard Accounting Practice No. 16. SSAP 16 requires current cost statements with either historical cost statements in addition or adequate information to enable calculation of historical cost profit.

INTERNATIONAL ACCOUNTING STANDARDS

While differences in national accounting principles and practices can be justified in terms of the needs of the local environment, an opposing case can be made for uniform international standards. International standards reduce problems that arise from cross-national use of reports produced to different standards. Differences in accounting principles can affect performance comparisons and bias competitive decisions and allocations of resources. Choi and Mueller give examples of how the U.S. accounting rule requiring that goodwill on acquisition be written off over 10 years as a nondeductible pretax expense, gave German firms not governed by the rule an apparent, if not real, advantage over American bidders in making U.S. acquisitions.[13]

The most significant move toward a set of international standards was made with the establishment of the International Accounting Standards Committee (IASC) in June 1973. The committee is comprised of representatives from professional accountancy associations of some 40 countries and operates through a secretariat in London. The member associations have pledged to support the standards promulgated by the committee and to use their best endeavors to ensure that published financial statements and audit statements comply with the standards or that there is disclosure of the extent to which they do not. They also pledge action to persuade governments, authorities controlling securities, and the business community to comply with these standards. The World Federation of Stock Exchanges, for example, has adopted a resolution that its members will require conformance with IASC standards in their listing requirements.

The IASC moves toward its standards through committee study of accounting topics that leads to exposure drafts that are circulated for comments and then restudied before final issuance of International Accounting Standards. Figure 20–2 lists the standards published up until March 1982.

A variety of other bodies are concerned with recommending or legislating international standards of one sort or another.[14] In fact, there are so many interested parties, both politically as users and professionally as preparers, that pressures for change and arguments about how changes are to be specified are likely to proceed for generations.[15] Figure 20–3 shows the source of national and international reporting requirements for firms based in the United Kingdom alone. Add the requirements of all the countries in which a multinational operates and the complexity becomes a minefield.

RESTATEMENT OF ACCOUNTS

The restatement of accounts is the process of adjusting financial reports, as stated in foreign currencies, to meet home-country accounting

---

[13] Choi and Mueller, *Introduction to Multinational Accounting*, pp. 150–51.

[14] Joseph P. Cummings and William L. Rogers, "Developments in International Accountings," *CPA Journal*, May 1978.

[15] S. J. Gray, J. C. Shaw, and L. B. McSweeney, "Accounting Standards and Multinational Corporations," *Journal of International Business Studies* 10 (Spring–Summer 1981), pp. 121–36.

Figure 20–2

International accounting standards (as of March 1, 1982)

IAS 1	Disclosure of Accounting Policies.
IAS 2	Valuation and Presentation of Inventories in the Context of the Historical Cost System.
IAS 3	Consolidated Financial Statements.
IAS 4	Depreciation Accounting.
IAS 5	Information to Be Disclosed in Financial Statements.
IAS 6	Accounting Responses to Changing Prices.
IAS 7	Statements of Changes in Financial Position.
IAS 8	Unusual and Prior Period Items and Changes in Accounting Policies.
IAS 9	Accounting for Research and Development Activities.
IAS 10	Contingencies and Events Occurring after the Balance Sheet Date.
IAS 11	Accounting for Construction Contracts.
IAS 12	Accounting for Taxes on Income.
IAS 13	Presentation of Current Assets and Current Liabilities.
IAS 14	Reporting Financial Information by Segment.
IAS 15	Information Reflecting the Effects of Changes in Prices.
IAS 16	Accounting for Property, Plant, and Equipment.

standards. After such adjustments, local currencies are translated into home-country currency amounts.

The process of restatement brings accounts onto a basis deemed suitable for consolidation purposes. But it does not necessarily produce an ideal common comparison base—and can raise as many problems as it solves. The financial statements to be consolidated have a domicile in terms of an underlying set of accounting principles, and such domicile orientation cannot be easily changed through adjustments to the financial statements themselves. For example, financial statements prepared in Argentina according to local accounting practices and then restated to a Canadian basis would differ markedly from those resulting if the Argentine operation had taken place in Canada and been accounted for originally in terms of Canadian practices.

Consolidation raises such problems as the treatment of reserves for future taxes on repatriated profits. A conservative accounting approach that includes such reserves in a consolidation, even though it is unlikely that the taxes will be paid, can be misleading as to the profitability of a foreign operation. A similar problem can arise in the treatment of depreciation expenses. To secure comparability among subsidiaries, a uniform rate of depreciation may be used. But to reduce current taxes and increase cash flows, the most rapid rate of depreciation allowed for local tax purposes should be taken. Faster depreciation for a subsidiary in a country where tax laws permit will increase cash flows but decrease net income in the short run.

Figure 20–3

Financial reporting requirements for companies in the United Kingdom—sources, authority, scope

				U.K. Accounting Bodies		
1. Issuing agency	U.K. Parliament		U.K. Stock Exchange	Accounting Standards Committee (ASC)	Councils of accounting bodies	International Accounting Standards Committee (IASC)
2. Status of agency (i.e., government or private sector)	Government		Private	Private	Private	Private
3. Forms of instruments	Companies' bills	Companies' acts, statutory instruments	Listing; agreement	Exposure drafts (EDs)	Statements of Standard Accounting Practices (SSAPs)	Exposure drafts (E) / International Accounting Standards (IAS)
4. Status of instruments	Proposed statute	Statutes and secondary legislation	Legal contract	Consultative documents	Approved methods of accounting	Consultative documents / Approved methods of accounting
5. Scope of application	Companies	Companies	Listed companies	All financial accounts intended to give a true and fair view (any limitations are specified in individual statements)		Audited financial statements of any commercial, industrial or business enterprise
6. Authority	n.a.*	Legally binding	Contractual	None, but indicative of proposed best practice	Binding on members to observe them (or disclose and explain any departures); listed companies to explain departures	None, but indicative of proposed best practice / Members undertake to support them & to use their best endeavors to ensure compliance (or disclosure of noncompliance); listed companies to disclose departures
7. Enforcement	n.a.	British courts	Quotations department	n.a.	Monitoried by the Professional Standards Committees of the U.K. Accountancy Bodies; Incorporated in listing agreement for listed companies	n.a. / Members undertake to ensure that appropriate action is taken in respect of auditors whose reports do not refer to noncompliance not disclosed in the accounts

* n.a. = not applicable.

Source: Prepared by Michael Renshall, partner Peat Marwick Mitchell, first published in *The Investment Analyst*, Vol. 52, December 1978, p. 35.

The alignment of price-level adjustments also requires special attention. The aim of consolidation is to bring financial statements onto a common basis of valuation. If this is not achieved, consolidated financial statements become an amalgam of different price-level approaches without conceptual meaning. The asset values and revenue disclosed in the

EEC		Organization for Economic Co-operation and Development (OECD)	United Nations (UN)	Major Overseas National Agencies	
Commission	Council of Ministers			(e.g., for United States the SEC)	(e.g., for United States the FASB)
Government	Government	Government	Government	Government	Private
Draft Directives or draft regulations	Directives or regulations	Declaration on International Investment and Multinational Enterprises (1976)	Report of the Group of Experts on International Standards of Accounting and Reporting (1977)	Regulations	Financial accounting standards
Proposed legislation	Required to be incorporated in national legislation of member states within a specified time (directives) or directly applicable (regulations)	Recommended guidelines	Recommendations for discussion by the UN Commission on Transnational Corporations	Requirements on form and content of accounts	Statements of financial accounting standards
As specified (e.g., companies)	As specified (e.g., companies)	Multinational enterprises	Transnational corporations (specified size test)	Companies listed in United States and certain other companies	Accounts presented in conformity with generally accepted accounting principles
n.a.	Mandatory when incorporated in national law	Voluntary	n.a.	Mandatory on SEC registered companies	Mandatory on members of AICPA (or disclose and justify any departures)
n.a.	The Commission is responsible for ensuring that directives are implemented	n.a.	n.a.	SEC U.S. courts	Monitored by AICPA Division of Professional Ethics

consolidated statements cannot be said to reflect any standard concept of asset valuation.

When a change is made in the date at which an asset valuation is set, the date of the exchange rate used for translation should also be changed. After all, an exchange rate roughly equates the relative purchasing power of two currencies at a given date. When an asset is revalued to a new date, there will be a new exchange rate reflecting the relative change in the inflation rates of the two currencies between the two dates. Thus, historical cost valuations should be translated at the appropriate historical exchange rate. But historical costs that have been revalued to approximate current costs should be translated at the current exchange rate. Techniques of translation are dealt with in more detail in the next section. It is important to remember, though, that restatement and translation must be consistent in the exchange rates chosen.

It is also recommended that restatement for price-level differences be carried out before translation into the currency of consolidation. This permits some concept of valuation pertinent to the country of origin.

Figure 20–4

Restatement of a subsidiary's financial statements for consolidation purposes

	Before adjustment (000 guilders)	Adjustments (000 guilders)	Restatement (000 guilders)
Revenue account:			
Sales	3,600	—	3,600
Less cost of sales	2,400	−120	2,280
Gross margin....................	1,200	120	1,320
Less expenses...................	1,075	− 80	995
Profit before tax	125	200	325
Taxation provision..............	25	137	162
Net profit.......................	100	63	163
Assets and liabilities:			
Cash	50		50
Accounts receivables............	850		850
Inventories.....................	700		700
Current assets..................	1,600		1,600
Current liabilities	1,100	137	1,237
Working capital	500	−137	363
Fixed assets....................	600	80	680
	1,100	− 57	1,043
Long-term liabilities............	300	—	300
Net worth	800	− 57	743
Capital	600	—	600

Adjustments are required as follows:

1. Reduce cost of sales by 120,000 guilders representing parent-company margin eliminated from last year's consolidation.
2. Reduce depreciation by 80,000 guilders to express it at standard rates used by parent company.
3. Increase taxation provision from 20 percent to 50 percent to allow for tax on future profit remittances.

Above all, it would be quite unacceptable to translate first and then to restate in the new currency, using the inflation rate recorded for that new currency. The asset remains in the first country and the inflation rate there since the date at which the translation is set may have been quite different. An example of restatement of a subsidiary's accounts is shown in Figure 20–4. Three adjustments are made: to add back profit margin eliminated from last year's consolidation (this margin was originally taken as profit when goods were transferred within the multinational system, but as they were not sold outside by balance date had to be deducted from last year's profit and added to this year's); to reduce excessive local depreciation to the home-country standard; and to increase the tax allowance to the level required if profits were remitted.

CURRENCY TRANSLATION

Translation is the term applied to reexpressing, in any required currency, financial statements expressed in another. This process is sometimes loosely referred to as conversion, but conversion should be reserved for actual physical exchange of one currency for another. Conversion takes place at a specific market rate at a specific time. Translation is a notional reexpression and the exchange rate used should be chosen to produce the equivalent value in the new currency.

Alternative translation methods

Revenues and expenses, with the exception of depreciation and amortization charges, are usually translated at an average exchange rate for the period over which the revenue statement extends. For balance sheet items and depreciation on those items, however, four clearly distinguishable methods might be used. These are tabulated in Figure 20–5.

The *current-noncurrent* method translates current assets (for example, cash, receivables, and inventories) and current liabilities at the current rate of exchange—that is, the spot exchange rate on the balance sheet date. All other assets and liabilities are translated at the historical rate prevailing when assets were acquired and liabilities incurred. The only conceptual justification for favoring or disfavoring current assets and liabilities with the current rate of exchange is that their dating does not have to be recorded and the translation calculation is simplified. Significant fluctuations in current rates will produce translation profits or losses that distort the operating results even if the value of current assets and liabilities in the base currency remains constant. Also, the inherent advantages in the event of a devaluation of holding inventory in preference to cash or receivables, and in financing by local long-term borrowing, are not recognized. The method assumes that in the event of a devaluation assets held as inventory will suffer the same degree of

Figure 20–5

Four currency translation methods

	(1) *Current- noncurrent*	(2) *Monetary- nonmonetary*	(3) *Temporal*	(4) *Current rate*
Items translated at:				
Current rate	Current assets and current liabilities	Financial assets and all liabilities	Financial assets and all liabilities and physical assets valued at current prices	All assets and all liabilities and common stock
Historical rate	Fixed assets and long-term liabilities Common stock	Physical assets Common stock	Physical assets valued at historical cost Common stock	—

foreign exchange loss as the holding of cash and receivables, an assumption that is generally not valid.

The *monetary-nonmonetary* method applies the current exchange rate to all financial assets and all liabilities, both current and long term. Physical, or nonmonetary, assets are translated at historical rates. This method is more defensible if all physical items are stated at historical cost. But if physical items have already been revalued at current market prices, translation at historical exchange rates will produce questionable results. In comparison with the current-noncurrent method, this method rewards holding of physical assets under devaluation. The implication is that physical assets will appreciate in local currency to the extent that the exchange value of that currency depreciates.

The *temporal* method differs from the monetary-nonmonetary only in the treatment of physical assets that have been revalued. It is based on the temporal principle, which states: "Money, receivables, and payables measured at the amounts promised should be translated at the foreign exchange rate in effect at the balance sheet date. Assets and liabilities measured at money prices should be translated at the foreign exchange rate in effect at the dates to which the money prices pertain." Cash, receivables, and payables are translated at the current rate, along with physical assets carried at current values. Assets carried at historical cost are recorded at the historical rate. The method thus produces similar results to the monetary-nonmonetary method when physical assets are valued at historical cost. The advantage of this method, then, is that it gives the best indication of real performance in the translated currency when assets are valued on a mixed basis of historical cost and market price. As we shall see later, though, it does have drawbacks.

The fourth method is called the *current-rate* method, the *closing-rate* method, or sometimes the *net-assets* method. All of a foreign subsidiary's assets and liabilities are translated at the current rate of exchange. The use of the current rate throughout ignores the idea that there will be appreciation in assets to offset currency devaluation, or depreciation to offset revaluation. In fact, it seldom follows that appreciation is directly in step with devaluation. The method is simple and produces the same result as the temporal method when assets are carried at current prices. Moreover, there is no change in the balance sheet ratios on translation, as occurs when historical and current rates are mixed.

These four named methods are not the only approaches. Hybrid methods are also possible. Two variations of the monetary-nonmonetary approach, for example, are: (1) translate inventories at current rate, or (2) translate long-term debt at an historical rate. Translation of inventories at current rate would be an acceptable practice when the inventories have been revalued at current market values. The use of current rate would also make sense following a devaluation if the market value of inventories would not rise proportionately and use of an historical rate would postpone recognition of an unrealized loss. Translation of long-term debt at an historical rate would avoid recording translation gains or losses on an item that does not have to be repaid for many years, yet for which translation gains or losses under a fluctuating exchange rate might obscure what is really happening on operations.

The different translation methods can lead to major variations in translated balance sheet figures with significant differences in the translation gain or loss. These variations are illustrated in Figure 20–6, where a 16.7 percent devaluation in the peseta produces gains from $266,000 to losses of $200,000—a range equal to nearly 40 percent of the equity invested in the subsidiary concerned:

Current-noncurrent method. The net working capital position determines the accounting exposure to exchange fluctuation under this method because the current rate is applied only to current, or working capital, items. In the example, a positive net working capital of $800,000 existed before devaluation. Hence a 16.7 percent devaluation shows a translation loss of $134,000.

Monetary-nonmonetary method. The firm's accounting exposure is measured by its net monetary asset position. This is negative, that is, −$1,600,000. Consequently, the firm records a gain on devaluation of 16.7 percent or $266,000.

Temporal method. Inventories are valued at market rates so must be translated at the current rate and added into the exposure. The negative exposure is reduced to $800,000, and the gain on devaluation is halved to $133,000.

Current-rate method. Since all assets and liabilities are translated at the current rate, the firm's accounting exposure is equal to the net asset figure of $1,200,000. This gives a 16.7 percent devaluation loss of $200,000.

Required translation methods

Prior to 1976, U.S. corporations were permitted to choose among alternative translation procedures. From 1960, the American Institute of Certified Public Accountants (AICPA) advocated the monetary-nonmonetary approach, but corporations still widely used the current-noncurrent method, which had been advocated previously, and the two hybrid methods mentioned in the previous section. The latitude in selection of the translation method, however, was removed in 1975. From 1976, all U.S. public corporations and foreign corporations that issued securities in the United States were required to adopt the temporal method, as embodied in Statement No. 8 of the Financial Accounting Standards Board (FAS 8).

Figure 20–6

Translation gains and losses following a foreign currency devaluation: Four alternative methods

Foreign subsidiary's balance sheet	Local currency (pesetas millions)	Historical rate pts. 100 = $1 ($000s)	Translated U.S. $ equivalents New current rate pts. 120 = $1			
			Current-noncurrent ($000s)	Monetary-nonmonetary ($000s)	Temporal ($000s)	Current rate ($000s)
Assets:						
Cash	40	400	333c	333c	333c	333c
Accounts receivable	40	400	333c	333c	333c	333c
Inventories: (Cost 120 pts. millions)						
Market	80	800	667c	800	667c	667c
Fixed assets	200	2,000	2,000	2,000	2,000	1,667c
	360	3,600	3,333	3,466	3,333	3,000
Liabilities:						
Current liabilities	80	800	667c	667c	667c	667c
Long-term debt	160	1,600	1,600	1,333c	1,333c	1,333c
	240	2,400	2,267	2,000	2,000	2,000
Shareholder's equity	120	1,200	1,200	1,200	1,200	1,200
Translation gain (loss)			(134)	266	133	(200)
	360	3,600	3,332	3,466	3,333	3,000

Note: c indicates translation at current rate

FAS 8 required that translation gains and losses be carried directly into the revenue account. They could not, as was previously the case, be charged to a foreign exchange reserve account that made it possible to smooth the impact of foreign exchange fluctuations upon reported earnings. As a result, "accounting exposure," in the sense of the net amount of assets that were exposed to foreign exchange fluctuations, became an important consideration. All items translated at current prices are "exposed" to fluctuations in the spot exchange rate, and the greater the net exposure, the greater the exchange gain or loss that was required to be recorded against earnings.

There was widespread discontent with FAS 8 among U.S. multinationals. Two studies found 70 percent of financial executives preferring other methods.[16] The unhappiness mainly stemmed from the fluctuations that the system imposed upon earnings. Although apparently the effect on reported earnings was felt to be under 5 percent in 93 percent of cases,[17] over 40 percent of financial executives believed that even security analysts considered translation gains and losses as part of the normal earnings stream of the firm.[18] There was evidence that numbers of multinationals took active steps to hedge against short-term translation losses—at a cost. There are various methods for doing this. Exposed assets can be matched by exposed liabilities—but this means local borrowing when devaluation is expected, which is usually expensive. Payables and receivables can be led and lagged and money market operations and forward exchange hedging are also possible. Hedging or covering against accounting exposure, however, is uncovered. The firm in essence increases economic exposure to reduce its accounting exposure, which may be uneconomic.

By late 1981, after several exposure drafts, the FASB issued a new statement—FAS 52—to take effect from December 1982. FAS 52 adopts the *current-rate* method and removes the translation gain or loss from reported earnings by recording it in the balance sheet in a new subsection of shareholder's equity. Under FAS 52, all items on the foreign subsidiary's balance sheet are calculated at the current value of their historical cost in the "functional currency," in effect adjusting for inflation. The change in net worth calculated on this basis is then translated at the current exchange rate to provide the translation gain or loss. The functional currency for a self-contained subsidiary is that in which it transacts most of its business—in other words, its local currency. For foreign

[16] Frederick D. S. Choi, Howard D. Lowe, and Reginald Worthley, "Accountors, Accountants, and Standard No. 8," *Journal of International Business Studies* 9 (Fall 1978), p. 85; Marjorie T. Stanley and Stanley B. Block, "Response by United States Financial Managers to Financial Accounting Standard No. 8," *Journal of International Business Studies* 9 (Fall 1978), p. 92.

[17] Choi et al., "Accountors," p. 83.

[18] Stanley and Block, "Response," p. 96.

branches that are really an extension of a parent unit in some other country, the functional currency is that of the parent.

The retention of historical cost—although adjusted for inflation—produces a problem in hyperinflation currencies. FAS 52 has allowed for this with an arbitrary rule that any currency that inflates by more than 100 percent in three years is not stable enough to be accepted as a functional currency. Dollar reporting must be used instead.

Analysts point out that they must now work with two numbers in place of the earnings figure they analyzed under FAS 8. Now they have earnings per share and a fluctuating book value per share reflecting currency changes. Some firms, of course, object to the fact that translation gains can never be incorporated into earnings until a subsidiary is closed or sold.

Outside the United States, use of the temporal method was never widespread. In some countries, the monetary-nonmonetary method predominates, in others the current-noncurrent method, but in those with most overseas investment the current-rate method has been more common—for example, France, Japan, the Netherlands, and the United Kingdom.[19] Well-advanced exposure drafts that promise to produce standards very similar to FAS 52 are circulating in both the United Kingdom and Canada.

Selecting the translation exchange rates

The guiding principle in selection of exchange rates is to choose the rate that best reflects the business reality. Hence, if the firm has actually engaged in capital conversion from one currency to the other, it is the actual rate for the conversion that would be used—even if that rate is obtained at a high official rate level or a subsidized level. Most translations of financial statements, however, are purely notional calculations. In these cases, the preferred rate is the quoted spot buying rate on the free market. Such a rate will frequently differ from government official exchange rates, and it may be difficult because of exchange controls and regulations to transfer funds obtained at such a rate into and out of the country in question. But official rates may not reflect the underlying currency value and the firm may have no intention of converting its capital investment at those controlled rates.

Because many exchange rates fluctuate by the hour, some authorities recommend the use of a bookkeeping rate that approximates the current exchange rate and is changed only when there has been a significant move in the exchange rate. While simplifying both calculation and the recording of exchange rates, this approach introduces an arbitrary decision into translation practice.

---

[19] Thomas G. Evans, "Foreign Currency Translation Practices Abroad," *CPA Journal*, June 1974, pp. 47–50.

SUMMARY

The multinational faces a wide array of requirements for financial disclosure both at subsidiary and corporate level. Many of these requirements seek different information. Frequently, too, the accounting practices and standards under which the accounts of a multinational's unit are prepared will differ. The firm's accountants, therefore, may have to make many adjustments to restate basic figures before they can be consolidated. With fluctuating exchange rates, translation of restated financial statements into a single currency also requires a great deal of care. Throughout this process, the accountants will be faced with the need to meet a growing body of international and national accounting standards, each with detailed rules and guidelines.

EXERCISES AND DISCUSSION QUESTIONS

1. Choose a large U.S. multinational and from its last annual report identify adjustments that have been made in subsidiary statements to make them consistent with U.S. reporting standards. Are there any balance sheet notes that are included to meet special requirements of non-U.S. users?

2. What adjustments would be needed to a set of financial statements conforming to the U.K. *Statement of Standard Accounting Practice No. 16* on *Current Cost Accounting,* in order to enable its current cost figures to be consolidated with those of a U.S. parent corporation? (This question will require the detailed texts of SSAP 16 and FAS 52.)

3. Explain in your own words why historical cost valuation should be translated at historical exchange rates and current valuations at current exchange rates.

4. Translate the restated figures for the subsidiary shown in Figure 20–4 into U.S. dollars using the four alternative translation methods. Assume that the historical rate was $1 = 1.5 guilders, the rate at balance sheet date is $1 = 2 guilders, the average rate is $1 = 1.75 guilders, and inventories are valued at end-of-year market prices.

5. What in your opinion are the strengths and weaknesses of the four major translation methods?

6. Present an argued case against the requirement of FAS 52 to record translation gains and losses only in the balance sheet and never against earnings.

Chapter 21

Management information and control in the multinational

Most large firms operate a formal planning and control system. The need for such a system, therefore, is not uniquely related to international operations. Nevertheless, the planning and control systems frequently cited as examples of advanced practices are those of multinational firms. This reflects the special importance in multinational operations of an effective planning and control system as a tool for knitting the entity together across national boundaries.

This chapter describes the operation of the overall control process in the multinational and then goes on to examine the accounting rules adopted for internal budgeting and financial reports. Exchange fluctuations introduce special difficulties not faced in the control of domestic units. The firm's internal audit procedures must also be viewed as an integral part of the control system. Internal auditing holds the control system together by ensuring that the quality of data, reports and operating procedures are maintained at acceptable levels throughout the organization. The final section takes a brief look at the special problems of controlling joint ventures where, without 100 percent ownership, the legal power to exercise complete control over decisions is limited.

THE CONTROL PROCESS

Objectives of multinational control

A good multinational control system will fulfill three objectives. It will supply adequate data for top management to monitor, evaluate, and adjust as necessary the global strategy of the enterprise. It will provide the means for coordinating the units of the enterprise so that they work toward a common objective. It will also provide the basis for evaluating the performance of managers at each level of the organization.

For strategy evaluation, the information system should deliver data from the organizational units on the business environment, customer demand, and competitive developments that the units are facing. For coordination purposes, the control system should be structured to show where multinational economies can be realized and to discourage units from following independent suboptimization patterns. The firm that fails to achieve multinational economies by expanding competition to a global level is likely to be left behind in the global competitive race.[1] For performance evaluation, the system must measure the achievements of managers toward corporate objectives against those elements that each manager can control.

The annual planning cycle

The formal control process is usually constructed around an annual planning cycle, beginning with the submission to the subsidiaries of planning guidelines from the central office. These guidelines often emerge from the development of a global strategy, as discussed in Chapter 13. The guidelines will vary in amount of detail depending on the firm's managerial philosophy. Some companies believe that extensive corporate guidelines, even to the extent of specific sales targets, provide "better coordination between regions, better execution of plans after they have been approved, better allocation of capital spending, and the acceptance of more ambitious goals by units in the field."[2] Others take the

---

[1] See C. H. Prahalad and Yves L. Doz, "An Approach to Strategic Control in MNCs," *Sloan Management Review*, Summer 1981, pp. 5–13.

[2] Michael Duerr and John M. Roach, *Organization and Control of International Operations* (New York: Conference Board, 1973), p. 22.

view that "bottom-up" planning, which relies heavily on local initiative, encourages better performance from local units because they best understand their own capabilities. In the latter case, guidelines are minimal and the subsequent global strategy assessment process at the center is used to highlight those units whose plans seem to be out of line.

After receiving the guidelines, subsidiary managers prepare their own plans, usually in a format specified in a standard planning or budget manual. The trend has been to increase the central requirements for detailed information on markets and competitors and to move away from internal accounting figures as the sole focus of the planning.[3] The subsidiary management's plan, including an assessment of the competive situation and proposed actions, is then subjected to critical central review.

Some corporations have formal review meetings that pit the functional specialists at headquarters against the line managers who have submitted the plans. At such meetings, the chief executive may play the role of grand inquisitor cum adjudicator. In the case of ITT, somewhat of a legendary example in this respect, the review sessions have traditionally been attended by the top managers of other subsidiaries.[4] The purpose of such attendance is to facilitate coordination between the subsidiaries or divisions, avoid repetition of similar planning problems, and generally raise the standard of planning. The transfer of standards obtained in this way can be particularly valuable when subsidiaries are of comparable size and situation.

The formal acceptance of plans gives the line manager a license to implement the proposals in the plans and acknowledges the targets as reasonable expectations of achievement. Seldom are plans formally rejected. They may, however, be referred back for amendment or review. In this way, the planning cycle tries to avoid any implication of failure.[5]

Reporting and achievement reviews

Periodic reporting and review of progress during the year are standard requirements. Most firms require monthly reports on sales and certain financial items. Other types of reports may be required quarterly or semiannually.

Several channels are used for reporting within the multinational system. The prime channel is reporting by managers up the line ultimately to the chief executive officer. In addition, controllers or financial officers, production managers, chief engineers, and directors of research and

---

[3] Specification of the contents of Business Unit Plans can be found in David S. Hopkins, *The Marketing Plan* (New York: Conference Board, 1981); Derek F. Channon and Michael Jalland, *Multinational Strategic Planning* (London: Macmillan, 1979), pp. 70–74.

[4] *Business Week*, November 3, 1973, p. 46.

[5] Michael Z. Brooke and H. Lee Remmers, *The Strategy of Multinational Enterprise*, 2d ed. (London: Pitman, 1978), pp. 85–126.

development frequently report directly to their headquarters counterpart on certain aspects of performance without going through their own chief executive. As a headquarters official of ITT explained, "On every company we get four or five inputs and the problems can't fail to surface."[6]

In some companies, the various reports are an input for periodic or monthly management meetings where progress is evaluated and trouble spots identified. Where problems have been identified, plans may be revised or, when appropriate, a task force may be dispatched from headquarters or some other subsidiary to make repairs. Subsidiary managements hold more positive attitudes toward international reporting when the frequency, quantity, and quality of feedback are higher.[7] Low-quality feedback would include, for example, clarification on accounting definitions while high-quality feedback would include relevant questions on strategy and the changing competitive environment. When the chief executive asks specific questions, such as on inventory levels for a specific product, subsidiary managers tend to feel that top management is well informed and there is a strong impact on the subsidiary managers behavior.[8] Such questioning from headquarters, however, may have unwanted effects. As one executive vice president of a Swedish multinational stated:

> I am very careful in asking subsidiary presidents overly specific questions regarding their operating efficiency. If you repeat the same question too often, they start to believe it's the most important evaluation criterion. Instead, I try to stick to their budgets and some specific performance goals.[9]

Attitudes toward feedback appear to vary among cultures. A study of Brazilian subsidiaries of multinationals showed that most of the U.S. subsidiaries received monthly feedback whereas less than 10 percent of the European and Japanese subsidiaries received regular feedback.[10]

Control through communication

Formal control procedures are only one part of the overall control process. Formal control communications are supplemented by many more informal exchanges via telephone and telex, and at meetings. In many cases, the informal communications will even bypass the organizational hierarchy.

---

[6] *Business Week*, November 3, 1973, p. 46.

[7] Laurent Leksell, "The Design and Function of the Financial Reporting System in Multinational Companies," in *The Management of Headquarters—Subsidiary Relationships in Multinational Corporations*, ed. Lars Otterbeck (Aldershot, England: Gower, 1981), pp. 205–32.

[8] Ibid., p. 219.

[9] Ibid., p. 224.

[10] William K. Brandt and James M. Hulbert, "Patterns of Communications in the Multinational Corporation: An Empirical Study," *Journal of International Business Studies*, Spring 1976, pp. 17–30.

Where operations are in different countries and managers have different cultural and language backgrounds, control through programs of "corporate acculturation" and "people transfer" can be important and effective. *Corporate acculturation* is the process of training subsidiary managers extensively so that they understand and generally accept the company's way of doing business.[11] Part of this process is to have key subsidiary personnel spend part of their career at the head office. Likewise, headquarters personnel should have some experience working in the subsidiaries. A serious problem can arise, however, when short-term people transfers are viewed by the subsidiaries as a "half-spying" tactic.

Personnel contacts through either short-term or long-term people transfers or through periodic group meetings of headquarters and subsidiary personnel greatly increase the ability of managers with diverse backgrounds to understand each other's viewpoints. The importance of personal contact was underlined in the study of Brazilian subsidiaries of 63 European, Japanese, and U.S. multinational firms.[12] As reported by the subsidiary managers, two factors that strongly influenced the effectiveness of communications with headquarters were (1) whether a superior at headquarters had worked in the Brazilian subsidiary, and (2) the tenure with the company of the chief executive officer of the subsidiary.

Communications patterns differed, however, with the nationality of the parent firms. U.S. companies employed Brazilian nationals for managerial positions in the subsidiary more frequently than did either European or Japanese firms. This employment policy explains in, part the fact that most U.S. companies held annual meetings for the chief executive officer of their affiliates, whereas less than half of the European and Japanese firms held such meetings annually. Also, visits between the head of the Brazilian subsidiary and his or her home office superior averaged 4.8 times per year for the U.S. firms as compared to 3.4 and 2.9 for the European and Japanese companies, respectively.

ACCOUNTING ASPECTS OF THE MULTINATIONAL CONTROL SYSTEM

Most multinational enterprises are relatively sophisticated in obtaining the internal accounting information they use in planning and control. A uniform system for planning, budgeting, and performance reporting provides headquarters with comparable data from all parts of the enterprise. It ensures that all managers, regardless of background or nationality, speak a common "company language" when discussing business. In designing such a uniform system, however, many decisions have to be made as to exactly how the data are to be recorded. And, once recorded,

---

[11] Ulrich Wiechmann, "Integrating Multinational Marketing Activities," *Columbia Journal of World Business*, Winter 1974, pp. 13–14.

[12] Brandt and Hulbert, "Patterns of Communications."

there are many pitfalls in interpreting standard data from what will certainly be nonstandard situations.

Income measurement

The design problems begin with the measurement of net income. Headquarters frequently charges royalties, service fees, and allocations of headquarters and research expenses to the subsidiaries. Generally, the headquarters management reserves final authority in such matters and attempts to make them in terms of systemwide optimization. Financial performance of a subsidiary may thus be determined as much by headquarters decisions as by local management.

On occasion, the performance of the foreign subsidiary will have been determined when it was first set up in order to reinforce performance elsewhere in the system. A reserve production unit established with replaced equipment, or a unit deliberately saddled with very high debt to provide funds to be used elsewhere in the multinational system, would be examples. Taxation can add yet further complications. A low local tax rate may encourage the multinational to charge only low amounts of central overhead. Both before-tax income and after-tax income would be affected.

Such headquarters' decisions can complicate immeasurably the task of adjusting a subsidiary's net income so as to make a fair comparison of the intrinsic profitability of individual units. In fact, recorded profitability as a basis for performance evaluation might even have to be abandoned and replaced with realized profit before charges and tax. Alternatively, some measurement of notional profit might be developed to reflect profit taken elsewhere in the system. Efforts to evaluate managers' performance on what is within their control and indicative of their real impact on objectives set them are, however, generally worth the cost and complexity involved.

Investment measurement

Many multinationals wish to use more than income measurement and measure performance by relating income to the investment utilized. In such cases, care is again needed in specifying the investment base. The choice of what is to be included and how it is to be valued can have a major influence on the behavior of managers. If, for example, the firm does not incorporate inflation adjustments in its control measures, investment will be understated and favor managers in countries with the highest inflation rates. As a result, these managers may tend to underprice and to expand volume and investment beyond what would be considered optimal if performance were measured in real terms.

Standard return-on-investment measures used companywide are not uncommon. Because of the many difficulties in providing an equitable comparison, however, most managers prefer that return-on-investment measurements be replaced with performance measures designed to reflect the specific objectives and environmental conditions of each subsidiary. Full participation in the establishment of objectives by subsidiary management whose performance is to be measured, will contribute to a spirit of cooperation and responsibility for achievement.

The measurement currency

Many multinationals require that all data, from market-demand assessments to profit and balance-sheet items, be presented in one "corporate" currency. In such cases, the rules used for exchange translation can have a significant effect on reported results. For example, a subsidiary's performance in a high-inflation country will look better (or worse) than it should if the exchange value of the subsidiary's currency depreciates less (or more) in relation to the corporate currency than relative inflation rates would indicate.

A significant school of thought considers that subsidiary performance should be judged solely in terms of the subsidiary's local currency. The subsidiary manager's performance can then be evaluated on operating efficiency, uncomplicated by any gain or loss from fluctuating currency values. Nevertheless, many multinationals use the home-country currency as the basis for budgets and for monitoring performance against those budgets. The choice of currency exchange rates, therefore, will shape the performance shown in the corporate currency and influence managerial behavior.

There are three ways of handling the translation of a budget into the corporate currency:

1. The current spot rate at the time of the budget can be used. This is called the initial rate.
2. A spot rate can be forecast for the end of the budget period. This is called the projected rate, and of course raises considerable forecasting difficulties.
3. The budget itself is translated at the rate current whenever a comparison is made. This is called the ending rate method.

The same three alternatives can be used for translating the actual performance figures for comparison against the budget. As illustrated in Figure 21-1, the three alternatives imply nine possible combinations of exchange rates that might be used in the budgeting and control process. Of these nine, five seem reasonable. The remaining four, shaded in the figure, are illogical because actual performance is translated neither at the rate used in translating the budget nor at the exchange rate current when the comparison is made.

Under the three combinations, (II, PP, EE) in which the same exchange rate is used for translating both budget figures and actual performance, a

Figure 21–1

Possible combinations of exchange rates in the control process

Rate used to translate actual performance for comparison with budget

Rate used for translating budget	Initial (I)	Projected (P)	Ending (E)
Initial (I)	(II) Budget at initial Actual at initial	Budget at initial Actual at projected	(IE) Budget at initial Actual at ending
Projected (P)	Budget at projected Actual at initial	(PP) Budget at projected Actual at projected	(PE) Budget at projected Actual at ending
Ending (E)	Budget at ending Actual at initial	Budget at ending Actual at projected	(EE) Budget at ending Actual at ending

change in exchange rates creates no variance for the manager concerned. Thus, the responsibility for exchange-rate variations rests with the central corporate treasury. In only one of these three cases (PP) does the operating manager have to deal with an exchange-rate forecast. This is when a projected rate is used to translate both the budget and the actual performance. The projected rates under this combination are termed "internal forward rates" (IFRs). They produce the effect of the corporate treasurer acting as a banker to buy forward receipts in foreign currencies at a guaranteed rate. Besides its elimination of exchange-rate variation from measurement of management, the PP combination has the additional advantage of being able to incorporate the internal forward rate most appropriate to the corporation's position when the budget is being made. The manager assembling the budget will base the budget on the most profitable alternatives, bearing in mind the internal forward rate that is set. This rate may well be different from the best forecast of what the actual rate may be, if the firm wishes to bias its business in favor of or against the particular currency.[13]

The remaining two combinations (IE, PE) leave the exchange risk with the operating manager. This risk is somewhat reduced when the budget is based on a projected rate (PE) rather than on the rate ruling at the time of the budget. The manager to be measured on actual performance translated at the ending rate will under both combinations be tempted to take steps to cover against the risk. In a large multinational, numerous man-

---

[13] Donald Lessard and Peter Lorange, "Currency Changes and Management Control: Resolving the Centralization/Decentralization Dilemma," *Accounting Review*, July 1977, p. 634.

agers acting in this way could produce significant costs with very little gain to the multinational. While the best combination seems on balance to be (PP) "Budget at Projected—Actual at Projected," this is only a poor second in terms of general usage. A survey of 100 U.S. multinationals in 1977 reported the use of the various combinations as follows:[14]

Method	Approximate percent of firms
(PE) Budget at Projected —Actual at Ending	50
(PP) Budget at Projected —Actual at Projected	20
(II) Budget at Initial —Actual at Initial	12½
(IE) Budget at Initial —Actual at Ending	12½
(EE) Budget at Ending —Actual at Ending	5

The most common method does save some accounting costs, but it also makes the operating manager responsible for discrepancies between the projected and final exchange rate. If the projected rate were forecast by the corporate treasury, the manager's results would vary according to the quality of someone else's forecasts.

INTRACOMPANY TRANSFER PRICING

Intracompany transfer prices—that is, prices for goods and services exchanged within the corporate family—have an important effect upon performance and control. Not only are there difficulties in setting a fair price when there is not a free market, but when transactions between units of the same enterprise are subject to different customs duties, tax rates, and currency risks, adjustments in transfer prices can also be used to advance various enterprise goals and increase overall enterprise profits.[15]

Firms operating foreign units as profit centers, however, confront difficulties in manipulating transfer prices. If foreign units are made profit centers for purposes of monitoring their performance and financially rewarding their managers, goods must be transferred at competitive and relatively uniform prices between units in the system whose performance is being compared. On the other hand, there are techniques that can be used to maximize total system profits through manipulating transfer prices while still retaining the profit-center concept. One method is to share the total realized profits of the company between the parent and foreign subsidiary on the basis of assets used, costs incurred,

---

[14] Business International, "Evaluating Foreign Operations: The Appropriate Rates for Comparing Results with Budgets," *Business International Money Report*, May 20, 1977, pp. 153–54.

[15] See the discussion in Chapter 22.

or on a more subjective basis of equitable treatment.[16] Another way is to keep two sets of accounts—official accounts for tax and other local purposes and another set for management control purposes. Still another is to take account of transfer-price manipulations in the budget and measure performance against planned results, even if a loss were intended. But each of these techniques has drawbacks. The practices verge on the unethical, and it is doubtful whether the gains from manipulating transfer prices more than offset the resulting cost and complexity of judging performance.

INTERNAL AUDITING IN THE MULTINATIONAL

Internal auditing performs a number of important functions in the control system of the multinational corporation. First, the internal auditing system establishes monitoring procedures for safeguarding the firm's assets, whether physical, monetary, or intangible. Second, the internal audit staff has the function of controlling the control system itself. Someone in the multinational organization is required to ensure that procedures for planning, reporting, and financial accounting are carried out as they should be. The good internal audit staff, however, will not confine itself to financial procedures, but will also extend its monitoring across the range of the firm's operations. At its very best, the internal audit function becomes a feedback link in appraising operating performance.

The firsthand knowledge of the local situation acquired by internal auditors can add significantly to the understanding at corporate headquarters and lead to modifications in plans and procedures. Equally, the external perspective of the internal auditor exposed to a wider range of the multinational's operations can be of value to local management, who may tend to see problems solely in terms of the local environment. The internal audit staff can act in a management services capacity, transferring best practices throughout the multinational organization.

Feedback to both local and corporate management is important for the multinational internal auditor. Without a reporting requirement directly to the corporate level, the credibility and power of the auditor to influence local management would be lower. The internal auditor's reports could be conditioned by allegiance to the local management group. Above all, any local management inclined to misrepresent the situation in business reports might be more tempted to do so if audit reports came solely through them, and if they had power and time to question a report and cover their position. Where national management in a subsidiary has a strongly independent leaning with nationalistic bias, an internal audit

---

[16] James Greene and Michael G. Duerr, *Intercompany Transactions in the Multinational Company* (New York: National Industrial Conference Board, 1970), p. 10.

staff reporting directly to corporate headquarters can prevent the loss of control that can happen all too quickly when reports are biased, sketchy, and provided after the event.

Responsibility to report to local management as well as to corporate headquarters, however, goes some way toward avoiding the image of internal auditors as corporate spies. Where they can be viewed as a supportive part of the local management team, rather than as an external threat to be guarded against, the internal audit staff is likely to find out more, to find it our earlier, and to bring about change before potential troubles escalate.

Many multinationals find that to maintain headquarters-based internal audit staff as traveling auditors is too expensive, both monetarily and in the personal costs to the audit staff of continual foreign travel. There are also the language and communication problems. Thus, it is not uncommon to base internal audit staff within local subsidiaries and even to use local nationals in these posts. The local identity problems are greatly reduced in these cases, but, conversely, there is an increased need to keep the direct reporting channels to corporate headquarters wide open, and to rotate the internal audit staff regularly.

The Foreign Corrupt Practices Act of 1977 brought an added importance to internal auditing procedures of U.S. multinationals. The act focused on bribe payments to foreign governments, politicians, or political parties to obtain or retain business and provided for fines of up to $1 million on a corporation and fines of up to $10,000 and imprisonment of up to five years for individuals. The act, however, goes beyond the direct concern with bribery to specify requirements for record keeping and internal accounting control, presumably with the intent of limiting bribery. The result is that for the first time the internal control of U.S. corporations is made a question of law, and not simply one of technical proficiency.[17] The requirements of the act apply to every publicly held U.S. corporation and require that the company shall:

1. Make and keep books, records, and accounts, which accurately and fairly reflect the transactions and dispositions of the assets of the company.
2. Devise and maintain an adequate system of material accounting controls sufficient to provide reasonable assurances that—
    a. transactions are executed in accordance with management's general or specific authorization;
    b. transactions are recorded as necessary (1) to permit preparation of financial statements in conformity with generally accepted accounting principles or any other criteria applicable to such statements and (2) to maintain accountability for assets;

---

[17] See David N. Ricchiute, "Illegal Payments, Deception of Auditors, and Reports on Internal Control," *MSU Business Topics*, Spring 1980, 57–62.

  c. access to assets is permitted only in accordance with management's authorization; and

  d. the recorded accountability for assets is compared with the existing assets at reasonable intervals and appropriate action is
   taken with respect to any differences.

CONTROLLING JOINT VENTURES

Joint ventures present a special control problem in multinational business operations. By desire or by necessity, multinational firms commonly
have joint-venture affiliates as part of their multinational operations. And
if the firm tries to implement a global strategy and realize the special
advantages of multinational operations, it has to deal with conflicts that
may arise between the interests of the local partners and the global
objectives and opportunities for the enterprise. Frequently, joint ventures
are located in the less developed countries, where the governments enforce a joint-venture policy as a means of increasing local control over
business decisions to ensure that these decisions are compatible with
national objectives.[18]

The experience of Japanese multinationals with joint ventures is of
special interest because Japanese firms have had a much higher ratio of
joint ventures than have U.S., European, or Canadian firms. The extent to
which a joint-venture subsidiary can be controlled by the parent, according to one study, depends upon the control that the parent has over key
resources required by the subsidiary.[19] These key resources are informational (technology and management know-how), financial, and input-
output leverage. The informational resources are controlled through
technical assistance contracts and through placing parent-company personnel in subsidiary managerial positions. The so-called input-output
leverage exists when the subsidiary is dependent upon the parent for
securing components, equipment, and replacement parts or for marketing a significant share of the subsidiary's output.

For Japanese firms, the most important source of control has been the
technical assistance contract and information and know-how flows. The
second most important means has been the placing of home-country
personnel in the subsidiary. The production manager position was more
heavily relied upon than the financial manager position as a means of
control.

Control through home-country personnel frequently ran into difficulties because of the desire of foreign countries to have local nationals in

---

[18] Richard W. Wright and Colin S. Russel, "Joint Ventures in Developing Countries: Realities and Responses," *Columbia Journal of World Business*, Summer 1975, pp. 74–80.

[19] Kichiro Hayashi, "Japanese Management of Multinational Operations: Sources and
Means of Control" (Paper presented at the annual meetings of the Academy of International
Business in Dallas, Texas, December 1975).

managerial posts. Host governments in Malaysia, Singapore, Indonesia, and Thailand, for example, have at times been unwilling to issue visas or work permits to financial officers from Japan. The country motivation was not only to promote local financial talent, but also to try to make accounting information more accessible so that local demands for higher wages could be supported. At one time Malaysia and Singapore also attempted to control the assignment of home-country engineers and technical personnel, but they had to reverse this policy because qualified local personnel were not available.[20]

Control problems are less likely to arise when the joint venture has been clearly thought through and agreement has been reached from the outset on business strategy, degree of autonomy, financial and accounting policies, and so on.[21] There is also some evidence that these problems are only marginally less than for wholly owned affiliates.[22] But there is no easy solution to the joint-venture control problem. In some cases, multinational firms have had to resolve the difficulties and frustrations associated with control attempts by increasing their ownership position or by selling out to local interests.

SUMMARY

The complexity, scale, and diversity of multinational operations make the control function in multinational business both extremely important and unusually difficult. Because information systems cross national boundaries and varied cultures, special efforts are required to improve the effectiveness of communications. It is difficult to develop performance standards that are meaningful and that do not interfere significantly with operating objectives. The environments and the ground rules for operations change rapidly in both the home and host countries. Control systems, therefore, must be flexible and continuously adapted to new circumstances.

Great care should be taken to avoid leading subsidiaries to take inappropriate actions simply because of the rules of the internal accounting system by which they are measured. In particular, practices adopted for translating budgets and accounts into a common currency can distort performance and lead managers to cover themselves against exchange risk. Transfer pricing raises further problems. To ignore opportunities for increasing system performance through managerial transfer prices might be to place the multinational at a disadvantage against competition. Yet every changed transfer price will alter the recorded performance on either side of the transaction.

---

[20] Ibid., pp. 16–17.

[21] Richard H. Holton, "Making International Joint Ventures Work," in *The Management of Headquarters*, ed. Otterbeck, pp. 255–67.

[22] Lars Otterbeck, "The Management of Joint Ventures," ibid., p. 279.

Internal auditing is an integral part of the control system. Properly managed internal auditing ensures a well-functioning and accurate system. The Foreign Corrupt Practices Act, moreover, has now made proper internal audit a legal requirement for U.S. corporations.

Finally, the concept of control must be adapted to joint ventures and partly owned operations. The same principles of control apply but, where statutory obligation is absent, there will be a greater premium on personal contact and persuasion to meet the goals of the multionational.

EXERCISES AND DISCUSSION QUESTIONS

1. The principles, procedures, and general problems of planning, information systems, and control appear to be fundamentally the same for operating in one or many national environments. Discuss.

2. Enumerate and discuss the relative advantages and disadvantages of giving subsidiaries detailed indications of what they should include as planned achievements in their annual plans.

3. "The performance of subsidiary businesses should never be measured by one overall return-on-investment figure; therefore, such figures should not be calculated and certainly not circulated." Discuss.

4. In choosing performance criteria, what are examples of potential conflicts of interest among units of the enterprise that must be considered?

5. Different combinations of exchange rates for translating budget and actual performance either leave exchange risk with the subsidiary manager or transfer it to the corporate center. Explain why you think it is good or bad to leave the risk with a subsidiary manager.

6. A foreign subsidiary is considering an expansion that will require a 50 million francs investment and that is budgeted to perform over the next year as follows:

	(Million francs)
Sales	100
Cost of sales and operating expenses	85
Operating profit	15

The current exchange rate is 8 frs. = $1 but there is an equal chance that the exchange rate at the end of the first year will have remained at 8 frs. = $1 or will have dropped to 10 frs. = $1. As a consequency, the projected future exchange rate is 9 frs. = $1. Assuming that any change in exchange rate will not affect the local currency operating results, and that there will be no income taxes, show the comparisons of budget and operating performance in dollars under each of the five feasible methods in Figure 21–1. Where the rate at the end of the year is used, show alternatives for 8 frs. and 10 frs. = $1. Calculate the variance from budget performance and any exchange loss on the exposed investment of 50 million francs. Under which alternative would you be tempted to cover yourself against exchange loss if you were managing the subsidiary, and for how much?

7. Draw up a set of instructions for the reporting responsibility of an internal auditor based with a foreign subsidiary.

Chapter 22

Multinational financial management

Multinational, as compared to domestic, financial management involves new environmental considerations, new sources of risk, and new opportunities for economies and efficiencies. The new risks arise out of fluctuations in foreign currency values, changes in tax liabilities as funds move across national boundaries, and the impact of national controls on financial flows. New opportunities arise with the access to multiple capital markets and the possibilities for achieving financial benefits in one part of the system from activities in another part.

As essential background, the multinational financial manager must be thoroughly familiar with the institutional setting for international financial transactions. The main components of the international framework—the international monetary system, foreign exchange markets,

and international money markets—have already been introduced in Part
II. The financial manager also needs a continuing flow of meaningful
reports from units of the enterprise and on international financial markets. The development of an effective global intelligence system requires
an understanding of the special features of multinational accounting,
which have been discussed in chapters 20 and 21.

This chapter recasts the international environmental elements into a
managerial framework. It relates them to the functions of organizing the
financial management activity, managing foreign exchange risk, and making decisions on long-run investments, financing techniques, financial
structures, and management of working capital. The scope of this chapter, however, is limited to the multinational financial function in industrial and commercial firms. Financial intermediaries, such as banks and
insurance companies, have their own financial problems, which will not
be considered here.

ORGANIZING THE MULTINATIONAL FINANCIAL MANAGEMENT FUNCTION

Control over the financial function is a key element in achieving global
corporate goals. Thus pressure usually builds up for strong central guidance from corporate headquarters and systemwide optimization. Ideally,
the financial management function of a multinational enterprise would
have three goals:

1. To take advantage of the potentials in multinational operations for
   reducing financial costs and increasing efficiency.
2. To adapt to environmental constraints at the national and regional
   level.
3. To protect the value of assets and revenues so that the benefits of
   multinational operations are not eroded through financial risks.

The efficiency contribution can occur through the ability of the multinational enterprise to secure capital at a lower cost since it has access to
many different sources and can achieve economies of scale in financing.
The adaptation responsibility is one of meeting national constraints on
remittances of funds across national boundaries in both home and host
countries. The protective function is to avoid losses through foreign exchange devaluations or revaluations, or through differential rates of inflation.

A study of U.S. practices in organizing and managing the international
financial function illustrates organizational patterns and the allocation of
responsibility between headquarters and the subsidiaries. In the early
stages of foreign operations, the domestic financial staff at headquarters
generally copes with the new problems, ignoring at times some of the
more sophisticated approaches to foreign financing and planning. At

later stages, many companies decide to employ full-time specialists in international financial management or to designate one of their financial staff for handling foreign financial matters. A few companies try to have all senior financial executives develop equal expertise in both the international and domestic aspects of their particular function.

In broad terms, the principal U.S. international companies follow three basic patterns in organizing the management of the international financial function.[1] The international functions of both policy making and performance of financial services may be:

1. centralized at corporate headquarters.
2. centralized at the headquarters of the international management unit with only overall guidance from corporate headquarters.
3. split between corporate headquarters and some subordinate headquarters (that is, central international unit, regional headquarters, product division headquarters, and so forth).

The important determinants of organizational patterns and the resulting financial behavior have been the size of an international company and its degree of international involvement. Small firms, defined as having foreign sales of about $50 million, typically run a decentralized operation with an "every tub on its own bottom" policy. Headquarters provides little direction, few decision rules, and makes little effort to move toward optimum financing for the entire system. Medium-sized firms, with foreign sales of about $200 million, typically run a centralized operation with strong direction from headquarters and substantial concern for the net cost of an action to the total system. Large firms, with foreign sales of about $1 billion, often run a decentralized operation but with guidelines issued from the headquarters staff, which also performs a coordination function.[2]

Large multinational enterprises strongly favor systemwide optimization but are too large and too complex to attempt an overall system approach even with modern computer systems. As a result of this complexity, headquarters' management uses a variety of rules of thumb to assist them in decision making, for example, setting equity equal to fixed assets in forming a new subsidiary. Even if the large multinational enterprise were to calculate an overall systems optimum, it could not take actions that might jeopardize its position in a foreign country.

Medium-sized firms have a greater tendency than other enterprises to attempt an overall systems optimization, and more nearly approach the

[1] Irene W. Meister, *Managing the International Financial Function* (New York: National Industrial Conference Board, 1970), p. 5; Business International Corporation, *Organizing for International Finance* (New York: BIC, 1981).

[2] This section is a summary of Robert B. Stobaugh, Jr., "Financing Foreign Subsidiaries of U.S.-Controlled Multinational Enterprises," *Journal of International Business Studies*, Summer 1970, pp. 43–64.

economists' concept of one "economic man" running the enterprise from headquarters. Small firms, on the other hand, typically lack international experience and tend to have decentralized operations without close control from headquarters or coordination among subsidiaries. In fact, each subsidiary may be viewed as an independent operation, and little attempt is made to take the overall system into account in financing one subsidiary.

The different patterns of organization and of financial policy behavior that prevail among U.S. international firms undoubtedly represent different stages of evolution along the path toward following global strategies and integrated management policies. They also reflect the state of knowledge in optimizing complex systems and the likely constraints on such optimization because of potential conflicts between optimization on a world basis and the interests of nation-states. As increasingly sophisticated organization and management techniques emerge, organizational patterns for the international financial function will continue to change.

LONG-RUN INVESTMENT AND FINANCING STRATEGIES

Investment decisions represent ultimate control over the operating subsidiaries and a principal means of implementing global strategy. Investment decisions to establish new operations or expand existing ones are based on a mix of strategic, behavioral, and economic considerations. They are not exclusively financial decisions. Yet the financial manager plays a key role by being responsible for analyzing the financial implications and comparing the expected returns and other financial features of alternative proposals.

Capital budgeting

The financial manager's responsibility in decision making on long-term investments is normally performed within a capital-budgeting framework. *Capital budgeting* is a process of matching advantages from possible uses of funds against the cost of alternative ways to obtain the needed resources. In domestic business, capital budgeting has become highly developed with sophisticated analytical approaches available for investment decisions.[3] In the international field, the use of capital budgeting techniques has also developed despite a variety of complications and uncertainties that must be handled when national boundaries are crossed.[4]

---

[3] See Harold Bierman, Jr., and Jerome E. Hass, "Capital Budgeting Under Uncertainty: A Reformulation," *Journal of Finance*, March 1973, pp. 119–29.

[4] Alan C. Shapiro, "Capital Budgeting for the Multinational Corporation," *Financial Management*, Spring 1978, pp. 7–16.

Capital budgeting analysis for foreign as compared to domestic projects introduces the following complications:

1. Cash flows to a project and to the parent must be differentiated.
2. National differences in tax systems, financial institutions, and financial norms and in constraints on financial flows must be recognized.
3. Different inflation rates can affect profitability and the competitive position of an affiliate.
4. Foreign exchange-rate changes can alter the competitive position of a foreign affiliate and the value of cash flows between the affiliate and the parent.
5. Segmented capital markets create opportunities for financial gains or they may cause additional costs.
6. Political risk can significantly change the value of a foreign investment.

The additional international elements to be considered arise at each of three stages in investment appraisal of an international project. In the first stage, the estimated receipts and disbursements for the project are analyzed by including problems of exchange rates, financial costs, and risk measurement. In the second stage, the analysis moves from the subsidiary to the headquarters level. This requires estimating (1) what amounts will be transferred, at what time, and in what form from the subsidiary to the parent company, (2) what taxes and other expenses will be incurred due to these transfers, and (3) what incremental revenues and costs will result elsewhere in the system. In a third and last stage, the project is evaluated and compared with other investment projects on the basis of incremental net cash flow accruing to the system as a return on the investment.[5]

The projection of receipts and disbursements begins, of course, with the market forecasts, including export possibilities from the project. A unique aspect of projecting receipts and disbursements for a foreign project is the need to develop schedules of relevant, anticipated exchange rates for each type of transaction involved. This task goes beyond the general requirement for foreign exchange forecasting. Some countries have both an official and a free rate of exchange, each applying to different transactions. Many transactions involving foreign exchange are subject to duties, special taxes, and exemptions. Equipment imports, for example, may be exempted or receive exchange rate concessions. In some instances, foreign exchange rates are subject to negotiations between the government and the international enterprise. Consequently, the international financial manager may need separate projections over

---

[5] See David K. Eiteman and Arthur I. Stonehill, *Multinational Business Finance*, 2d ed. (Reading, Mass.: Addison-Wesley Publishing, 1979), pp. 265–302, for a detailed case example of capital budgeting for a foreign project.

time of exchange rates for equipment imports, raw material imports, and export sales, and the importance of such rates to the revenues and costs of the project will have to be evaluated.

A second international consideration may be the need to consider alternative financial structures for the proposed project, which in turn will affect projected receipts and disbursements. Local debt financing, for example, tends to reduce both foreign exchange and inflation risk. But the availability of local credit for international enterprises varies greatly among countries for national policy or other reasons. In certain countries, the international firm may be required to finance up to certain limits by local sales of equity. Or the country may offer special incentives if external rather than local financing is used for imported equipment, in order to encourage foreign investment inflows. Consequently, the firm may want to develop separate receipts and disbursement forecasts for several alternative financial plans that are feasible for a particular national situation.

Still another international consideration is the need to include risk elements of a political- or national-controls nature in the investment analysis. As an extreme example, high probabilities of expropriation or confiscation can markedly change the projections of receipts and disbursements. These risks have been discussed in chapters 13 and 15, where techniques for handling such risk elements have been suggested. In addition to their impact on projected receipts and disbursements for a project analyzed at a national level, these risk elements must be considered at the headquarters level from the standpoint of how they might affect income flows such as dividend remittances and royalty payments available to the parent and the rest of the system.

In the second stage, where the analysis moves to the headquarters level, the principal additional issues become the availability to headquarters of income flows from the project and the net incremental benefits, if any, to the system. Operations within the same country can reasonably assume that cash flows from one unit of an enterprise are freely available to another unit. In many countries, the repatriation of cash flows above a certain percentage return is not allowed or is heavily taxed and forecasts of remittance policies are required in such cases. Profits that are freely available to the parent concern have a different value than profits that must be reinvested. Forced reinvestment may, however, have desirable and beneficial results in cases where opportunities are growing or where the firm has initially set up a new venture on a narrow financial base to minimize its exposure. In any event, the firm will have to decide whether it should assign lower values to project flows that cannot be converted into home-country currency or transferred freely to other countries, or whether all earnings from the project should be considered as available inflows to the parent company. It will also have to take into account the tax and other costs of transferring income to the parent companies. The estimated inflows must also be translated into home-country currency units on the basis of foreign exchange forecasts over the planning period.

The incremental benefits to the rest of the system should be imputed as additional available income from the proposed project. These can be profits from increased export sales from the parent company; payments of license fees, royalties, or management services; or even transfers of technological or marketing know-how available to the rest of the system from the activities of the new venture.

At the third and last stage, the alternative investment projects are compared with each other and ranked on the basis of expected return on investment, in which order they will be accepted up to the limit of the investment sums considered available for the capital budgeting period. One of the issues at this stage may be the method used for comparing projects. Another will be the criterion used for the cost of capital.

The "net present value" method has become widely used for evaluating investments. The method takes into account earnings over the life of a project. It discounts the expected future net cash flows, using the cost of capital as the discount rate, and then deducts the original cost of capital to determine the present net value of the project.[6]

Policies on cost of capital may range from a *pool-of-funds concept* with a presumed single pool of corporate funds and a single target rate to the use of separate costs of capital for each country of operation or each project.[7] The pool-of-funds approach assumes that funds are raised on a worldwide basis with debt incurred where the terms are most favorable and transferred to the places where funds are most desired.

Where a philosophy of "every tub on its own bottom" is being followed and a subsidiary is responsible for its own financing after the initial phase, the cost of capital must be estimated separately for each project. Also, where special sources of financing are available for specific projects, such as through financial incentives uniquely available to projects located in the depressed region of southern Italy, such special costs would most likely be taken into account by using separate target rates for the cost of capital. Ordinarily, however, a single, company-wide cost of capital measure should be used as the discount factor in evaluating foreign investment projects.[8]

The principal international risk elements—foreign exchange, national controls, and political risk—have already been incorporated into the analysis. The recommended risk-adjustment procedures are to analyze

[6] See G. David Quirin, *The Capital Expenditure Decision* (Homewood, Ill.: Richard D. Irwin, 1967), pp. 27–58, for a discussion of alternative techniques such as the payback method and average-rate-of-return method, and for an explanation of the way to apply the alternative methods.

[7] See Rita M. Rodriguez and E. Eugene Carter, *International Financial Management*, 2d ed. (Englewoods Cliff, N.J.: Prentice-Hall, 1979), pp. 395–402.

[8] Ian H. Giddy, "The Cost of Capital in the International Firm," *Managerial and Decision Economics*, December 1981, p. 269.

the specific sources of risk and through the use of subjective probabilities to estimate the specific impact of the possible outcomes on the expected return from the investment. In making a final selection, the enterprise will have its estimates of the net present value of available inflows and a measure of risk for each alternative. The alternatives may consist of different projects or the same projects financed in different ways. The final choices from the financial point of view will then depend upon the firm's attitudes toward taking risks.[9]

Financial structures of foreign affiliates

The choice of financial structure and financing plan, as previously noted, can greatly influence the attractiveness of new projects and expansions. At the enterprise level, the overall exposure of the firm to foreign exchange and political risk can also be affected. The options will differ, of course, for a wholly owned subsidiary and a joint venture.

In choosing optimal financing plans for foreign affiliates, the financial manager will have to decide such questions as the appropriate mix of debt and equity and the extent to which debt should be local or imported. The alternatives will depend on the local and foreign sources of capital available for financing projects in specific countries, national governmental regulations regarding financing and ownership arrangements, relative costs of the various options, and other factors.

What constitutes an appropriate mix of debt and equity has long been debated by financial experts. Equity financing is the sale of ownership interests. The suppliers of equity assume the business and financial risks of the company and share in the profits (or losses) of the enterprise. Suppliers of equity have no guarantee of a return on their investment, nor is there a limit on the profit they can make.

Debt financing is a loan that does not carry with it any ownership interests. Debt is a fixed obligation to pay interest and repay principal regardless of business conditions. The lender has first claim on earnings in each period and priority claim to assets in case of bankruptcy or liquidation. Because the cost of debt is generally fixed and tax deductible, it gives the suppliers of equity leverage for maximizing their earnings. There are limits to the amount of debt that can be used, however, because as the proportion of debt increases, both lenders and purchasers of new equity may demand a higher return because of the risk that the firm may not meet its fixed obligations in periods of bad business conditions. But the tolerable limits of debt will vary from country to country.

---

[9] For an example of the large amount of literature on portfolio selection covering this point, see Alexander A. Robichek and Stewart C. Myers, *Optimal Financing Decisions* (Englewood Cliffs, N.J.: Prentice-Hall, 1965); Richard Brealey and Steward C. Myers, *Principles of Corporate Finance* (New York: McGraw-Hill, 1981).

In the United States, an extensive literature exists on optimal financial structures for different types of industries and for different levels of risk. But the international financial manager discovers very early that debt-ratio norms differ markedly from country to country. Firms in mature manufacturing industries in Japan, Norway, and Sweden typically have debt ratios (at book value) well over 70 percent. In contrast, firms in the same industries in the United States and the United Kingdom traditionally hold their debt ratios under 50 percent. Debt ratios in France, Germany, and the Netherlands lie between these extremes. The variations in debt-ratio patterns are explained by differences in national environmental characteristics.[10]

The so-called modern finance theory, with the Capital Asset Pricing Model (CAPM) as its centerpiece, presumes that stockholder wealth maximization should be the principal goal in financial decisions.[11] Modern finance theory, however, has been developed mainly by U.S. and U.K. scholars and is based on assumptions about capital markets and investor preferences found in those countries. The fact that capital markets and stockholders' attitudes in most foreign countries differ markedly from the situation in the United States and the United Kingdom limits severely the transferability of finance theory to other countries.

The gospel that a firm should be operated for the ultimate benefit of its stockholders is a value judgment. It is not a law of nature or an incontrovertible rational choice. If foreign affiliates operate with this goal, they will often conflict with host-country environmental characteristics. They may conflict with local business norms, value systems of local managers, and host-country economic, political, and cultural aspirations. This does not mean that multinational firms should forget about modern finance theory. But it does mean that they must recognize serious limitations on their ability to implement this goal in dealing with foreign affiliates.

To what extent should an international firm be guided by different country debt-ratio norms? Conforming to host-country debt norms has several advantages, particularly if it does not involve a cost penalty, but merely replacement of debt in one affiliate by debt in another. One advantage is that management can more easily evaluate its return on equity relative to local competitors in the same industry. There may be other worthwhile advantages in satisfying local authorities. As a general policy, however, a multinational firm should probably borrow at the lowest cost

---

[10] Arthur Stonehill, Theo Beekhuisen, Richard Wright, Lee Remmers, Norman Toy, Antonio Pares, Alan Shapiro, Douglas Egan, and Thomas Bates, "Financial Goals and Debt Ratio Determinants: A Survey of Practice in Five Countries," *Financial Management*, Autumn 1975, pp. 27–41; see also R. Aggarwal, "International Differences in Capital Structure Norms," *Management International Review* 21, nos. 1–81 (1981): 75–88.

[11] See Eiteman and Stonehill, *Multinational Business Finance*, pp. 157–84, for an excellent discussion of modern finance theory and financial patterns in foreign countries as they relate to the financial goals of a multinational corporation.

anywhere in the world, without regard to the cosmetic impact on the financial structure of any particular affiliate.[12]

The choice of financial structure for affiliates must, of course, consider the effect on the total enterprise, where the parent's and affiliates' financial statements will be consolidated. High debt ratios may be acceptable in the country of the subsidiary, but the consolidated balance sheet may show a higher debt ratio than is considered appropriate in the country of the parent. As a result, the cost of financing for the parent company is increased because the financing plan for the affiliate is suboptimal for the total enterprise.

Local debt financing in weak-currency countries tends to reduce both devaluation and inflation risks. When devaluations occur, the amount of local currency required to meet interest payments and retire principal is not affected by the devaluation. Local debt can reduce inflation risk in that repayment obligations may remain fixed in local currency while revenues and profits rise along with inflation. In other words, debt is being paid off with "cheaper" money. For these reasons, firms are frequently willing to borrow locally even though the cost is higher than imported funds, and the additional cost is considered an insurance payment against devaluation and inflation risk.

The inflation advantage of local debt, however, has been eliminated in some countries with traditionally high rates of inflation. Brazil, for example, has widely adopted the device of "monetary correction" in order to make long-term financing available in a country with continuing inflation. Under this system, called *indexing*, debts are readjusted upward on an annual basis by the amount of inflation as determined by an official index. The practice is followed in cases of mortgages and even government bonds.

Debt imported from strong-currency countries has the disadvantage that the amount of local currency required to meet interest and repayment obligations will increase in the case of devaluation. But even where devaluations are anticipated, nonlocal debt may have advantages from the standpoint of providing greater freedom for foreign remittances where exchange controls prevail. Most countries give preference in the allocation of foreign exchange to remittances of interest and debt repayment over the remittance of dividends on equity.

The enterprise should determine its financial structure preferences for affiliates, but it should also recognize that in some countries these preferences cannot be implemented. Companies prefer to use locally borrowed funds in areas that appear to be politically and economically unstable. Yet the risky areas chronically lack loan capital. Furthermore, certain countries restrict local borrowing by foreign companies on the

---

[12] Ibid., p. 371.

grounds that foreign firms should increase the total amount of local investment by bringing in capital. Another reason is that the growth of local enterprise should not be stunted by having to compete for scarce funds with large, profitable, and well-known international enterprises that have easier access to outside capital markets. Some less developed countries that are greatly concerned with their balance-of-payments situation object to high debt proportions when it appears that such a financial structure is intended to support high levels of foreign exchange remittances to the parent companies.

The preference for minimizing the amount of equity capital supplied to the affiliate by the parent company frequently leads to the subsidiaries being seriously undercapitalized. This problem has been met in many cases by open account inventory financing. The parent company sells merchandise to the subsidiary but does not require payment until much later even though the goods have been sold by the subsidiary. This method allows the parent company to increase and develop its foreign operations without actually sending either additional equity capital or formal cash loans. Furthermore, the length of the credit is flexible.

The desire to minimize equity is not characteristic of the large and internationally committed multinational enterprises. They typically use a guideline such as "let equity equal fixed assets" in order that host countries do not become concerned about excessive local borrowing or unduly high dividend remittances. This strong equity base facilitates local borrowing after the subsidiary has become established and gives it greater independence in the future from the parent's central source of funds.

The decision to enter into a joint-venture arrangement with a group of local partners or to sell equity shares in the subsidiary locally can also reduce the financial burden on the multinational enterprise and increase access to other local sources of capital. If the outside ownership groups have similar expectations, equity costs would be unaffected. But where expectations are dissimilar among the participants, equity costs of the financial plan can be increased. Outside shareholders, for example, may expect to receive larger dividends than are traditional for the international enterprise. If so, the larger (or smaller) return expectations should be included explicitly in the flow projections used to appraise the desirability of a project.

Financing sources and techniques

For many decades, the highly developed capital markets of the United States were the best source for both large quantities of capital and low cost of capital. U.S. firms, in particular, generally limited their source of funds alternatives to the United States, the local country in which a project was being established, or foreign funds generated by the company in other foreign projects.[13] But the international situation has changed rapidly as to availability and comparative cost of capital, and most international firms have become accustomed to considering an ever wider variety of capital sources and financing techniques in their decisions about financial structures for affiliates.[14]

The multiplicity of sources greatly enlarges the financial manager's task.[15] The manager must follow world financial markets and local markets in the countries in which the firm operates. The evaluation of alternatives must be a continuing activity. As a general principle, the manager should go to the markets for funds when the markets are attractive, and not necessarily when the funds are required by the company. Surplus funds can be managed so as to attain high yields and still be available when needed.

In using the various national capital markets, the multinational manager will encounter commercial banking patterns, securities market regulations, and government controls that vary greatly from country to country. The American firm when going international will have to learn about overdraft lending by commercial banks, which permits a customer to write checks in excess of amounts he has deposited, up to some previously agreed upon limit. The U.S. firm will have to become familiar with government financing institutions such as Nacional Financiera in Mexico and Kreditanstalt fur Wiederaufbau (KFW) in Germany, which are major sources for local financing and for which there is no American counterpart. Likewise, Shell, the Anglo-Dutch international oil enterprise, had to develop special skills for using the highly regulated U.S. securities markets in providing local financing for its U.S. subsidiary, Shell Oil Company. Foreign firms have been shocked, and sometimes disturbed, by the detailed disclosure requirements for issuing securities in the United States. Interestingly, these disclosure standards are generally being followed in the Eurobond markets, even though there are no legal disclosure requirements.

The Eurocurrency and Eurobond markets are the most important uniquely international sources of financing. These markets offer great attractions to both borrowers and investors, as discussed in Chapter 4. Eurobonds are always issued in such a way that interest is paid free of withholding tax. When they are issued in "bearer" form—that is, the

---

[13] Stefan H. Robock, "Overseas Financing For U.S. International Business," *Journal of Finance*, May 1966, pp. 297–307.

[14] For detailed current information on financing techniques, sources for cross-border financing, and the domestic financing situation in a large number of countries, see the monthly service, *Financing Foreign Operations* of Business International, or other similar services.

[15] See Gunter Dufey and Ian H. Giddy, "Innovation in the International Financial Markets," *Journal of International Business Studies*, Fall 1981, pp. 33–51.

bonds are not registered to a specific person but are considered to be the property of the bearer—the holder has additional means to defer or avoid income taxes.

The freedom from taxation, the diversification opportunities for both borrowers and currencies, and the absence of interference by national governments are features of the Eurobond market that appeal to investors. From the standpoint of the borrower, many of the attractive features are similar. In addition to offering a choice of currencies, interest rates in the Eurobond market have generally been at levels little different from the prevailing rates in the home country of the currency.

In summary, the financial structure of affiliates will depend first on the willingness of the parent company to assume equity risk. Although many companies prefer to minimize their equity commitments, for new foreign projects or expansions the hard-core financing will have to come from within the multinational enterprise. It must show a willingness to risk its own funds in order to tap external sources. A common pattern has been to finance fixed assets with company funds and long-term loan capital, and for working capital to use local borrowings to the maximum extent. The mix between local and imported debt depends on local availability, the relative costs of alternative sources, the degree of operating freedom associated with funds from different sources, and local government constraints on excessive debt ratios. Where local money costs exceed imported costs, a company will have to decide how much it wants to pay for risk avoidance. Tax factors and the effect of the financing plan on both the financial situation of the parent company and the total system will be additional considerations.

INTERNATIONAL MONEY MANAGEMENT

The multinational financial manager plays a major role in the management of a firm's cash and near-cash assets. This function, referred to as international money management or working capital management, has the potential for decreasing the overall cost of funds to the enterprise and the overall risk to company assets. It can also increase the availability of funds and the overall return on available funds. These potentials emerge when the enterprise works toward optimizing the financial function on a systemwide basis, rather than having each subsidiary operate independently.

International money management can be considered as comprising a series of interrelated subsystems that perform the following functions: (1) positioning of funds—choice of location and currency of denomination for all liquid funds; (2) pool funds internationally; (3) keep costs of intercompany funds transfers at a minimum; (4) increase the speed with which funds are transferred internationally between corporate units;

(5) manage foreign exchange exposure; and (6) improve returns on liquid funds.[16]

A systems approach

The more advanced approaches to international money management that have been emerging are all systems approaches. The system consists of units in different countries, each of which operates in a different environment and has an accounting system of its own. The units are connected to each other by a series of links through which assets and liabilities can be shuttled. Inter-unit flows are subject to policy control within certain limits, and the challenge is to make use of the policy tools to produce the best results for the system as a whole.[17]

The primary links between the different units are equity flows, generally from the parent to the subsidiary. Dividends flow in the opposite direction. Other links are the provision of services and technology by the parent to the subsidiary, which results in return flows in the form of management fees, royalty payments, and the sale of goods, which result in payments for merchandise received. Finally, the units have credit links in the form of intercompany short- and long-term loans, accounts payable, and interest flows.

Matching each of these links are financial policy tools that can be adjusted to set the level at which the link will operate. Dividend policy, for example, is the tool associated with the equity link and the amount and timing of dividends to be paid can be adjusted. The relationships between links, tools, and the variables they control can be seen in Figure 22–1.

Limitations on the use of these policy tools arise out of government regulations, different patterns and mores of different financial markets, and internal constraints such as a desire to avoid disrupting the system of performance evaluation. Other limitations are the cost of having complete information at the optimization center, the difficulties of securing accurate information, and the need to make forecasts that handle future uncertainties such as foreign exchange risks.

A complex strategy under a systems approach would synchronize all the policy tools available to the various units of the multinational enterprise to maximize after-tax profits for the system as a whole. Although the use of complex strategies through a systems approach has not yet become common, exploratory work in this field has demonstrated that significant gains might be achieved as compared to a situation where units function as a collection of unrelated enterprises dealing with each

---

[16] See David B. Zenoff, *Management Principles for Finance in the Multinational* (London: Euromoney Publications, 1980), pp. 171–75.

[17] This section summarizes a pioneering study of Sidney M. Robbins and Robert B. Stobaugh, *Money in the Multinational Enterprise* (New York: Basic Books, 1973).

Figure 22–1

Financial links, associated policy tools, and affected variables

Link	Policy tool	Variables controlled
1. Equity	Dividend policy	Amount of dividends accruing
2. Services		
Management	Management fee policy	Amount (or rate and specified base) of fees accruing
Know-how	Royalty policy	Amount (or rate and specified base) of royalties accruing
3. Merchandise	Transfer-pricing policy	Intrasystem's sales price or deviation of intrasystem price from arm's-length price
4. Credit		
a. Accounts payable		
b. Mgt. fees payable		
c. Royalties payable	Payables policy	Amount outstanding, terms, and interest charged
d. Dividends payable		
e. Interest payable		
f. Short-term lending	Short-term lending policy	Amount outstanding, terms, and interest charged
g. Long-term lending	Long-term lending policy	

Source: Sidney M. Robbins and Robert B. Stobaugh, *Money in the Multinational Enterprise* (New York: Basic Books, 1973).

other at arm's length. In a hypothetical case, for example, the systems approach has been demonstrated to produce consolidated profits after taxes of 15 percent higher than when the strict rules of arm's-length behavior are followed.

In applying a strategy in practice, modifications may be needed to reduce conflicts between the subgoals of the various units and also to allow for international factors difficult to introduce into a systems calculation. For example, a higher interest rate source of credit to one unit may be preferred because it gives more protection against devaluation and is better for the system as a whole.

Although the use of a full systems approach is in the future, a series of less comprehensive techniques that focus on certain subgoals in international money management are in wide use.

International cash management

Pooling. The control of liquidity—liquid assets and short-term debt or credit facilities—is based largely on the concept of pooling. *Pooling* is a system for making the best use of liquid assets available on a regional or global basis. It attempts to optimize the use of corporate resources by making the surplus funds of cash-rich affiliates available to cash-poor affiliates. Any net surplus or deficit for the pool as a whole can be directed into short-term investments or financed by drawing on central credit facilities. A well-managed pool account can permit somewhat higher credit interest and lower debit interest when subsidiaries borrow from each other. Without a pool, subsidiary A might receive a 9 percent yield on short-term deposits while subsidiary B borrows at 11 percent. An interunit loan from A to B at a 10 percent rate would be favorable to both subsidiaries.

A pooling arrangement normally requires some degree of centralized financial control. It also requires a flow of information so that the financial manager is appraised of all intercompany transactions as well as of each affiliate's liquidity position and its local money market conditions.[18] When pooling is attempted on a multicountry, multicurrency basis, tax considerations and exchange controls may preclude the actual pooling of funds in communal accounts. Indirect financing between affiliates can be achieved, however, through the leading and lagging of intercompany payments—usually trade, but sometimes dividends, royalties, fees, and loan repayments.

Funds transfers.   International transfers of funds can require considerable time during which funds in transit cannot be used and may be exposed to undesired currency risk. By accelerating payments, less working capital is required and sizable savings can be realized. Improvements in this area may require changes in transfer means—cable rather than mail transfers—and improving the efficiency of the banking system being used.

The cost of international transfers can be reduced by decreasing the number of payments transactions and by minimizing foreign exchange costs. By analyzing the transactions of every affiliate with other units in the system, a central controller can arrange for the affiliates to remit or receive only their net debit or credit positions. This process is called *netting* or multicurrency clearing, where transactions can be offset on either a bilateral or a multilateral basis. The volume of actual transfers is cut sharply, with a consequent reduction in working capital requirements and foreign exchange costs and commissions. The savings are commonly estimated at up to 0.5 percent of the amount of the transfers eliminated.

Protection against Inflation.   In managing working capital and controlling liquidity, the international manager will be particularly concerned with the problem of protecting assets in countries with high rates of inflation. Physical assets such as property, plant, and equipment generally maintain their value in real terms during inflation. But the value of

---

[18] See Business International, *New Techniques in International Exposure and Cash Management, Vol. 1: The State of the Art* (New York: Business International Corporation, 1977); Alan C. Shapiro, "Payments Netting in International Cash Management," *Journal of International Business Studies,* Fall 1978, pp. 51–8; David P. Rutenberg, *Multinational Management* (Boston: Little, Brown, 1982), pp. 81–106.

working capital, particularly cash and receivables, is highly vulnerable to erosion through inflation. And the international financial manager is concerned about profits and the value of assets as measured in the home-country currency or some other strong convertible currency.

The traditional local strategy for protecting working capital in an inflationary situation is to operate with a minimum amount of liquidity by minimizing cash balances, reducing receivables, lagging in the payment of local expenses, and maximizing local borrowing. Where the penalties for tax delinquency are low, some companies try to lag as much as possible in local tax payments. The value of inventories, particularly imported goods, is less likely to suffer from inflation. Where a local unit is part of a multinational system, it has additional possibilities for protecting assets by accelerating cash remittances to the parent company or elsewhere in the system where inflation rates are lower and by delaying the receipt of payments from low-inflation countries. Such policies of taking advantage of leads and lags are similar to the strategy for protection against devaluation to be discussed below.

Traditional anti-inflation strategy, however, has shortcomings that result from treating individual components of working capital in isolation although they are in fact interrelated. For example, when credit and receivables are treated in isolation, the usual policy is to restrict credit to reduce the holding of monetary assets that lose buying power. But an optimal policy under a systems approach that recognizes the interrelationships may be to increase rather than reduce credit. Inflation adds to the attraction of credit as part of the marketing mix and, by continuing to offer credit, the firm may generate a substantial increase in sales. The increase in profit margins that can result where large-scale economies can be exploited and where costs lag behind prices may more than offset the additional costs of increasing credit in an inflationary situation.[19]

Subsidiary remittance policies

Dividend remittances are probably the most common way that funds are transferred from affiliate to parent. The remittance decision should be made in relation to all the other facets of international money management. It should take into account the subsidiary's future financing requirements, the host country's concern about retaining an adequate equity base, tax considerations, foreign currency exposure management, alternative means of remitting funds, and international cash management objectives. Although many variables are involved in remittance strategy, companies can relatively quickly and inexpensively compute alternative remittance decisions. Through sensitivity analysis—that is,

---

[19] Lee A. Tavis, "The Management of Short-Term Funds under Conditions of Inflation: A Systems Approach" (D.B.A. diss., Graduate School of Business, Indiana University, 1969).

using a variety of scenarios—they can evaluate these alternatives under differing assumptions about the business performance and the external environment.[20]

In the interests of administrative simplicity, many companies overlook the opportunities in remittance policies and adopt general policies and administrative rules-of-thumb in this area. For example, dividend policy is frequently expressed in terms of a specific percentage of subsidiary earnings to be remitted to the parent. By remitting a fixed percentage of their earnings after foreign taxes, subsidiaries help the parent company meet its dividend payments to stockholders. A record of regular remittances in the operating country improves the company's chances for continuing to remit during difficult balance-of-payments periods for the country. Regular remittances also remind local managers that the parent company supplied the capital and that controlling objectives are set by headquarters.

When the local subsidiary is a joint venture with local shareholders, the problem of remittances becomes more complicated. When dividends are declared by local subsidiaries, local shareholders, as well as the parent company, share in the payments. While funds remitted to headquarters may still be available wholly or net of taxation to the multinational enterprise, dividends paid locally will generally leave the system and come back only through new financing. Also, it is not uncommon for local shareholders to expect high dividends, whereas the multinational enterprise may prefer to reinvest a large share of earnings and declare only modest dividends.

Transfer pricing

An exceptionally sensitive area of financial management for multinational enterprises is that of intracompany transfer pricing. A multinational firm normally has many transactions in goods and services between the parent and a foreign affiliate or between foreign affiliates. The prices established for these transactions within the corporate family are referred to as transfer prices. When transactions take place across national frontiers—and the units of the same enterprise are subject to different custom duties, tax rates, currency risks, and foreign exchange controls—transfer prices can be adjusted (or, as critics charge, "manipulated") to achieve a wide variety of results that will further the overall goals of the enterprise.

Transfer price setting can be used for positioning funds within an enterprise. A parent firm can move funds out of a particular country by

---

[20] David B. Zenoff and Jack Zwick, *International Financial Management* (Englewood Cliffs, N.J.: Prentice-Hall, 1969), p. 438.

charging high prices for goods sold to its affiliate in that country and by paying low prices for purchases from the affiliate. High transfer prices position funds in the selling country. Low transfer prices position funds in the buying country. As units in a multinational enterprise system may both buy and sell to each other, the positioning of funds can be reinforced by a combination of high selling and low buying prices or vice versa. The movements can be between affiliates as well as between the parent and a particular affiliate.

What might the firm gain by moving funds out of a particular country through transfer pricing policies? The enterprise may reduce its tax liabilities by shifting earnings from a high-tax to a low-tax country. It may reduce its exposure to currency devaluation by changing the currency in which enterprise assets are held. It may increase the flow of funds to the parent or another affiliate when financial transfers in the form of dividend remittances are restricted. The firm may want to show lower earnings in a particular country because high profits might encourage local authorities to ask for price reductions or labor unions to press for wage increases.

What might the firm gain by the reverse policy of positioning more funds in a country through transfer pricing? Low import prices can reduce customs duties where duties are ad valorem—that is, assessed as a percentage of value. Low import prices can reduce import deposit requirements where they exist, and allow the importer to bring in a greater quantity where import quotas are established in terms of value. Another objective might be to help a subsidiary show a profit during a startup period and thereby improve its ability to get local credit.

Given the opportunities to shift funds and profits by the transfer-pricing mechanism, how extensively is the instrument used by multinational companies? Pricing policies are inevitably a sensitive area where management seldom gives out factual information. If companies are using international transfer prices to achieve some particular end, they do not announce that fact. Several surveys undertaken in the early 1970s reported that transfer pricing was not widely used by U.S. companies for operations in Europe and North America and that few executives of British companies admitted that they used transfer pricing to shift profits between various units of the group.[21]

A more recent survey of many multinationals of different nationalities reported that "few transnationals admitted to the use of transfers at other than arm's-length prices." Also, many firms insisted that "the extent of manipulative practices has been exaggerated." Yet, at the same time, most companies claimed to "have no idea" how common non-arm's-

[21] Michael Z. Brooke and H. Lee Remmers, *The Strategy of Multinational Enterprise* (New York: American Elsevier, 1970), p. 176; Jeffrey S. Arpan, *International Intracorporate Pricing: Non-American Systems and Views* (New York: Praeger Publishers, 1972).

length transfer pricing is because of a lack of "firsthand knowledge."[22] Another survey attempt that was specifically focused on the use of transfer pricing in developing countries was not able to draw any conclusions as to the extent that transfer pricing was used.[23] But it was able to reach conclusions on company motivations, for using transfer pricing. Among a series of motivations, the desire to avoid profit repatriation and exchange controls restrictions received the highest ranking. Changing income tax liability was ranked as only a minor factor.

The developing countries, however, have been reluctant to accept these declarations of "innocence" and have made transfer pricing a major issue in their proposals for a code of conduct for the multinationals. They are aware that the controls prevailing in most developing countries make the rewards to the enterprise from manipulating transfer prices extremely attractive. And they fear that transfer-pricing policies will undercut the national objectives they are trying to achieve through controls. In support of their concerned view, the developing countries frequently cite a case study conducted in Colombia, which concluded that in 1968 the multinational pharmaceutical companies were "overpricing" sales to their Colombia affiliates by an average of 155 percent more than prices quoted in different markets around the world. Lesser rates of "overpricing" were documented for the rubber, chemical, and electronics industries.[24] As a result of this study, the international pharmaceutical industry claims that its pricing policies have been changed.[25]

Although conclusive evidence is not available, it is probably a fair conclusion that most multinational enterprises use transfer prices to switch funds at one time or another, depending on the particular investment involved and the particular host country. In any event, the tax authorities of the advanced countries continue to demonstrate a concern about the prevalence of transfer pricing, together with the use of tax havens, as a means of reducing tax liabilities. The developing countries also continue to list transfer pricing as a top priority conflict issue in their relations with multinational enterprises.

The use of transfer pricing is limited by both internal and external factors.[26] If foreign units are made profit centers for purposes of monitor-

---

[22] Isaiah Frank, *Foreign Enterprise in Developing Countries* (Baltimore: Johns Hopkins University Press, 1980), p. 97.

[23] Seung H. Kim and Stephen W. Miller, "Constituents of the International Transfer Pricing Decision," *Columbia Journal of World Business*, Spring 1979, pp. 69–77.

[24] Constantine V. Vaitsos, *Transfer of Resources and Preservation of Monopoly Rents*, Economic Development Report No. 168, Development Advisory Service (Cambridge, Mass.: Harvard University, June 1970); see also Constantine Vaitsos, *Intercountry Income Distribution and Transnational Enterprises* (London: Oxford University Press, 1974).

[25] See C. Fred Bergsten, Thomas Horst, and Theodore H. Moran, *American Multinationals and American Interests* (Washington, D.C.: Brookings Institution, 1978), p. 379.

[26] See, for example, M. Edgar Barrett, "Case of the Tangled Transfer Price," *Harvard Business Review*, May–June 1977, pp. 20–36, 176–78.

ing their performance and financially rewarding their managers, goods must be transferred at competitive and relatively uniform prices between units whose performance is being compared. Several techniques, however, can be used to maximize total system profits through manipulating transfer prices while retaining the profit center concept.

Another major constraint on transfer-pricing policies has been the rapidly expanding surveillance of tax and custom authorities. The transfer-price review program of the U.S. Treasury is perhaps the most advanced in the world today. It includes not only the sale of tangible property but also the pricing of money, services, the use of tangible property, and the transfer of intangible property such as patents and trademarks. From the viewpoint of the U.S. Treasury, Section 482 of the Internal Revenue Code (1954) and the regulations promulgated by the Treasury in 1968 to govern international pricing practices are intended to insure that the U.S. government gets its fair share of the taxes on income earned by the multinational corporate system.[27] The general rule of the Treasury governing the pricing of controlled intracompany transactions is that transfer prices should be set at a level comparable to prices where the two parties are relatively independent and "bargaining at arm's length."

Although more and more limits are being imposed on transfer-pricing policies by governmental tax and customs regulations in home and host countries,[28] within these limits there is frequently latitude for pricing to meet market and competitive factors. Even the U.S. regulations appear to leave an opening for a company to lower its transfer price for the purposes of entering a new market or meeting competition in an existing market. Consequently, for most companies the opportunity to support marketing goals and to increase systemwide profits by alternative transfer-pricing strategies should not be disregarded.

With all of these counterbalancing and conflicting forces to be considered, how does a multinational enterprise establish its international pricing policies? The international complications, added to those that always arise, whether or not national boundaries are crossed, clearly point to the impossibility of having fixed rules for pricing in the multinational corporation. They equally point to the need for central monitoring of price strategy and an open-minded approach to the possibility of significant gains from central action to alter patterns that otherwise emerge. Naive calculations of the profit in individual units should not be accepted without measurement of the ultimate effect on the system, and the effects on the enterprise as a whole can be complex. Nor should pricing decisions be imposed without a realization of offsetting costs. In sum, getting the most out of pricing decisions within a multinational corpora-

[27] See Warren J. Keegan, "Multinational Pricing: How Far is Arm's Length?", *Columbia Journal of World Business*, May–June 1969, pp. 57–66.

[28] OECD Committee on Fiscal Affairs, *Transfer Pricing and Multinational Enterprises* (Paris: Organization for Economic Cooperation and Development, 1979).

tion requires a mapping of the entire system and a calculation for any potential change of the net effects across all units.[29]

MANAGING FOREIGN EXCHANGE RISK

For many multinationals, managing foreign exchange exposures—that is, responding to anticipated changes in exchange rates—is the most important international financial challenge. Changes in the value of currencies, both devaluations and revaluations, have been frequent and significant in amount. Even more frequent have been the number of false alarms, which must be considered and dealt with.

Foreign exchange risk is not limited to companies with foreign operations. Any company with a receivable or payable to be collected or paid in a foreign currency is exposed to foreign exchange risk. As a dramatic example, let us assume that an American firm's only foreign business is exporting to Mexico. Let us also assume that the company sold $10,000 in merchandise in early February 1982 to a Mexican buyer and agreed to accept payment in Mexican pesos within 30 days. At the time, the exchange rate was fixed at 26.80 pesos to the U.S. dollar, so the sale price was 268,000 pesos. On February 18, 1982, Mexico devalued the peso to 38.50 pesos to the U.S. dollar and allowed the peso to float. By March 5, the peso had declined further to 45.20 to the dollar. Thus the 268,000 pesos received by the U.S. company had to be exchanged for only $5,929 at the March 5 rate, or an exchange loss of about 40 percent. If the sale had been denominated in U.S. dollars, the Mexican importer would have had to pay 452,000 pesos instead of 268,000 pesos, or almost 70 percent more.

The exposure of the multinational enterprise is far more complex. Changes in relative foreign exchange values affect the value of transactions, cash flows, assets, liabilities, and current and future earnings as measured by the yardstick or reference currency of the company. As examined in Chapter 21, the U.S. dollar has normally been the headquarters measurement currency for U.S. companies because it is in U.S. dollars that the company's results are recorded and published. A truly multinational company, however, might logically consider the strongest world currency, such as the Swiss franc, as its yardstick and try to manage foreign exchange risk so as to protect values in that currency.

Changes in currency values also affect a company's competitive position in its home market and abroad. Another major effect can be a change in the national control environment as governments adopt new policies to moderate or adapt to changes in currency rates. The various adjust-

---

[29] See Thomas Horst, "The Theory of the Multinational Firm: Optimal Behavior Under Different Tariff and Tax Rates," *Journal of Political Economy*, September-October 1971, pp. 1059–72.

ments that governments can take to correct payments imbalances were discussed in Chapter 6.

There are five components to managing foreign exchange risk. First, the enterprise must specify and analyze through an exposure audit all aspects of its operations that have foreign exchange implications. Second, it must identify and measure the types of exposure it has to changes in currency values. Third, it must have a strategy for exposure management. Fourth, it must develop a procedure for forecasting the amount, timing, pattern, and probability of changes in foreign exchange rates. Finally, it must develop a system to implement its exposure strategy.[30]

The audit

The importance of having a comprehensive understanding of the implications of foreign currency changes on a company's operations cannot be overstressed. The audit should include an analysis of:

1. The types of transactions that are affected.
2. How each unit in the system both at home and abroad is affected.
3. How elements of corporate strategy are affected.
4. How each function of management is affected, that is, marketing, production, personnel, and so on.

The implications of currency changes can be extensive.[31] Companies are generally aware that their methods of financing and their composition of assets and liabilities can be affected. They may be less aware that currency changes can have major implications for personnel and compensation policies. A compensation policy for company personnel of different nationalities and located in different countries can be equitable at one exchange rate and inequitable when currency values change. Or even more fundamentally, the best strategy for serving a foreign market can change from exporting to foreign production, or vice versa, as a result of major changes in exchange rates.

Foreign exchange exposure

The formulation of an appropriate strategy depends on how management defines and measures its exposure to changes in currency values. The types of exposure are generally defined as transactions, economic, translation, and tax exposure.

---

[30] For general background see Laurent L. Jacque, "Management of Foreign Exchange Risk: A Review Article," *Journal of International Business Studies*, Spring–Summer 1981, pp. 81–101.

[31] See Zenoff, *Management Principles for Finance in the Multinational*, pp. 106–8; and Richard M. Levich and Clas G. Wihlborg, *Exchange Risk and Exposure* (Lexington, Mass.: Lexington Books, 1980).

Transactions exposure.   Transactions exposure is the extent to which immediate or near-term cash flows of current business operations are affected by fluctuations in foreign exchange values. This type of exposure refers to outstanding obligations that are to be settled in the near future when changes in exchange rates may have taken place. Such exposure includes obligations for purchase or sale of goods and services, as well as the borrowing or lending of funds in foreign currencies. Transactions exposure is the uncertain value to the firm of its open position in cross-currency commitments. Transactions exposure can result in real, as contrasted to bookkeeping, gains and losses.

Economic exposure.   Economic exposure measures the extent to which a company's *future* international business earning power is affected by changes in currency values. It is concerned with the impact of currency changes on future sales, prices, and costs. In technical terms, it reflects the extent to which the net present value of expected after-tax flows will be affected as exchange rates change. From the standpoint of the long-run health of an enterprise, economic exposure is far more important than changes caused by either transactions or translation exposure.

Translation exposure.   Translation exposure, also referred to as accounting exposure, measures the impact of currency changes on the reported consolidated results and balance sheet of a company. Translation exposure is essentially concerned with present measures of past events, and the accounting gains or losses in translation are said to be unrealized. Translation exposure results from the need to report consolidated worldwide operations. To meet this need, the financial statements must be translated from the local currencies in which they are recorded to the measurement currency used by headquarters. This translation, as explained in Chapter 20, follows rules set by the government of the parent firm, an accounting association, or the firm itself.

The amount of exposure a company has due to translation will depend upon which of the alternative translation methods discussed in Chapter 20 are used. The significance of translation exposure depends upon how the company's reported results are evaluated by the investment community, shareholders, financial institutions, and so on.

Tax exposure.   Changes in foreign exchange values generally have income tax implications. As a rule, only realized gains or losses affect the income tax liability of a company. Translation losses or gains are normally not realized and are not taken into account in tax liability. Some steps that can be taken to reduce exposure, such as entering into forward exchange contracts, can create losses or gains that enter into tax liability. Other steps that can be taken have no income tax implications.

To summarize, transactions exposure refers to the immediate or near-term effects on cash flows. Economic exposure refers to the same types of effect on cash flows over the long term. Translation exposure is the accounting reflection of a change in position that has not yet been realized.[32]

Exposure reports

A financial manager should have enough information available to evaluate and analyze the foreign exchange position of the firm's overseas operations. In particular, the manager requires monthly foreign exchange exposure and flow-of-funds reports from each subsidiary. These reports, plus balance sheet and income statements, provide the necessary information on which to base currency decisions related to short-term transactions and translation exposure. They are not oriented, however, to economic exposure.

A foreign exchange exposure report is similar to a balance sheet, but it differs in three respects. It omits balance sheet items that are not considered exposed in an accounting sense. Which specific items are omitted will depend on the translation method being used. It includes off-balance sheet items such as foreign exchange contracts and future commitments such as lease payments or purchase and sales contracts. And, most important, the exposure report states all assets and liabilities in the currencies in which they are denominated. The currency distinction is crucial because a receivable in Mexican pesos, for example, is unlikely to have the same future value as a receivable in German marks, even though they had the same value at the time of sale

The flow-of-funds report shows on a monthly or quarterly basis the expected cash flows over a future period—say, a year—for each of the various currencies in which the subsidiary does business. The expected flows for each currency are based on such factors as estimated sales during the forthcoming year, and assumptions about receivables collection. Such a report is really a cash budget subdivided by type of currency. It provides the necessary dynamic elements for incorporating cash-flow considerations into exposure management decisions.

The funds-flow report may reveal that exposures in the different currencies vary dramatically over time. It may also show that the static balance sheet exposure is often insignificant as compared to the exposure generated by the flows of an ongoing business. With the added information from the funds-flow report, the international financial manager can evaluate how various means of protection against foreign exchange risk affect exposure to accounting and cash-flow losses over time.

---

[32] See Eiteman and Stonehill, *Multinational Business Finance*, 2d ed., pp. 75–96.

Without this added information, decisions will be based on incomplete knowledge.[33]

Exposure management strategy

As a third component for exposure management, each enterprise must formulate its objectives and strategy for exposure management. These are needed to provide guidance to managers responsible for making correct and timely decisions in a complex business environment.[34] And senior management must be involved in the formulation and approval process.

In most situations it is impossible to insure against all foreign exchange risk and anyway prohibitively expensive to insure against some risks. How much risk is the enterprise willing to accept? If management's goal is to maximize long-run stockholder wealth, protection against economic exposure is a first priority. If management feels that its performance is judged mainly on short-term results, it will give priority to protection against transactions and translation exposure.

It is important that senior management develop an appropriate approach for what might be termed speculation. There is always a temptation to seek speculative profits in foreign currency transactions. If successful, such profits can provide a competitive advantage. In fact, most companies avoid practices of outright speculation on the grounds that foreign exchange speculation is not consistent with the basic mission of multinational financial management. Their view is that the main focus of foreign exchange management should be directed to protecting corporate earnings at a minimum cost. Furthermore, governments and commercial banks are likely to disapprove of outright speculative activity not legitimately related to the firm's principal business activity.

Reacting to economic exposure

Reacting to economic exposure can require strategic changes that transcend the financial manager's function and encompass virtually every decision area, including marketing, production, sourcing, and plant location. The experience of Volkswagen of West Germany during the 1970s illustrates the potential impact of economic exposure and the variety of responses that a firm can make.[35]

---

[33] See *Corporate Foreign Exposure Management* (New York: Citibank, 1976).

[34] An excellent example of corporate guidelines is Robert S. Einzig, "Foreign Currency Exposure Management in Transamerica," in *International Finance and Trade*, vol. 2, eds. Marshall Sarnat and Giorgio P. Szego (Cambridge, Mass.: Ballinger, 1979), pp. 117–34; see also Michel Ghertman, "The Behaviour of French Firms toward Foreign Exchange Risk," in *Recent Research in the Internationalization of Business*, eds. L. G. Mattsson and F. Wiedersheim-Paul (Stockholm: Almqvist & Wiksell International, 1979), pp. 278–93.

[35] The Volkswagen example is summarized from S. L. Srinivasulu, "Strategic Response to Foreign Exchange Risks," *Columbia Journal of World Business*, Spring 1981, pp. 13–23.

In the late 1960s, VW was the largest automobile exporter in the world and its primary export market was the United States. In October 1969, and again in 1971 and 1972, the German mark (DM) was revalued against the U.S. dollar and other major currencies. Over the three-year period, the DM gained in value relative to the U.S. dollar by more than 40 percent. In absolute terms, the exchange rate was 4.00 DM = U.S. $1 in 1969 and 2.7 DM = U.S. $1 at the end of 1972.

The revaluation made VW noncompetitive in the U.S. market where its sales declined from 570,000 vehicles in 1968 to 200,000 in 1976. The revaluation made it increasingly difficult to compete in the United Kingdom, France, and Italy. At the same time, VW had to face increased competition within the West German market from Renault of France and Fiat of Italy, due to the weakening of the franc and the lira vis-à-vis the DM. The net earnings of VW's overall operations dropped from a profit of DM 330 million in 1969 to a loss of DM 807 million in 1973.

How could VW cope with the economic exposure? VW had little price flexibility because of competition and price sensitivity of the market segment to which it was catering. Tactical responses such as hedging, leads and lags (discussed below), and swaps provided no solution to the basic problem. The company needed to match cash inflows in a specific currency with cash outflows in that (or a similar) currency in order to insulate itself from the economic exposure. VW had dollar revenues from its business in the United States but DM costs. When the DM was revalued, VW's revenues in DM declined but its costs in DM remained the same.

Through a series of strategic responses, VW was able to reduce its economic exposure in the U.S. market. It shifted from a policy of having all of its loans in DMs to a diversification policy where a portion of its loans were in U.S. dollars. Thus if VW's revenues in DM went down because of revaluations against the U.S. dollar, its cost of debt servicing went down and partially offset the revenue lost. VW converted other costs to U.S. dollars by setting up a production facility in the United States and by buying parts and components in the United States. As a general strategy, VW stepped up intersubsidiary linkages that required subsidiaries in revaluing countries to buy from subsidiaries in devaluing countries. This diversification in financing, changed production siting, and sourcing— activated in large part by the major economic exposure the firm had encountered—transformed VW's strategic profile.

Reacting to transactions and translation exposure

Techniques to minimize transactions and translation exposure center around the concepts of hedging. A *hedge* is a contract or arrangement that provides defense against the risk of loss from a change in foreign exchange rates. Several forms of hedging have already been discussed in Chapter 4.

Leads and lags. Firms can reduce their foreign exchange exposure by leading and lagging payables and receivables—that is, paying early or late. Many types of periodic payments are generally made between units of a multinational enterprise, either as payments for goods and services or as financial transfers such as dividends. Leading and lagging can be used most easily between units of the same enterprise, but the technique can also be used with independent firms.

The guiding principle for leads and lags is to position liquid funds where they will best serve the overall interests of a multinational firm. This goal can be achieved by accelerating payments from soft-currency to hard-currency countries and by delaying inflows from hard-currency to soft-currency countries. As an example, suppose a multinational enterprise had anticipated the February 1982 Mexican peso devaluation. In January, the parent had the subsidiary make early payment to the parent for goods, services, interest, loan amortization, and dividends, even though such payments were initially scheduled for later in the year. At the same time, the parent firm delayed a dollar loan to the subsidiary intended for expansion until after the devaluation. The early peso payments were converted into more U.S. dollars and the delayed dollar loan into more pesos than if payments had been made as originally scheduled.

When the firm makes use of leads and lags, it must adjust its performance measures of the units and managers that are cooperating in the maneuver. The leads and lags can distort the profitability of individual units. Also, because the use of leads and lags is a well-known technique for minimizing foreign exchange exposure and because it has the effect of putting pressures on a weak currency, most governments impose some limits on leads and lags. For example, certain countries set 180 days as a limit for receiving payments for exports or making payments for imports.

Forward exchange market hedge. The use of forward markets and foreign exchange futures as protection against foreign exchange risk was already discussed at some length in Chapter 4. But the subject warrants repetition. A foreign exchange market hedge is a present agreement on an exchange rate for a foreign exchange transaction to take place at a specified future date. The rate agreed upon may turn out to be lower or higher than the spot rate at the future date. But the advantage of the hedge is that the firm can be certain of the value in its yardstick, or reference currency, of foreign currencies it is scheduled to receive or to pay in the future. The hedge may be used for amounts receivable in foreign currencies (selling forward), or for amounts payable in foreign currencies in the future (buying forward). The forward purchase or sale of foreign exchange for a future date is the easiest method of hedging to put in place or to remove. The method can be used, however, only when forward markets exist for the specific currency of interest to the firm.

Money market hedge. A money market hedge also involves a contract and a source of funds to fulfill the contract. The contract is a loan agreement. The firm using a money market hedge borrows in one currency and converts the proceeds into another currency. Funds to repay the loan may be generated from business operations, in which event the hedge is covered. Or funds to repay the loan may be purchased in the foreign exchange market at the spot rate when the loan matures. The latter is an "uncovered" or open hedge.

The cost of the money market hedge is determined by differential interest rates. The cost of the forward market hedge is a function of the forward exchange quotations, called the forward premium.[36]

Balance sheet hedge. A balance sheet hedge is carried out by bringing exposed assets equal to exposed liabilities. If the objective is to minimize translation exposure, the usual procedure is to have monetary assets in a specific currency equal monetary liabilities in that currency. If the objective is protection against economic exposure or transactions exposure, the procedure is to denominate debt in a currency whose change in value will offset the change in value of future cash receipts.

Foreign exchange forecasting

A fourth dimension to exposure management is foreign exchange forecasting.[37] Ideally such forecasts should produce estimates of the amount, timing, pattern, and probability of changes in exchange rates. The forecasts should suggest the magnitude of possible gains or losses from given levels of exposure. Thus, they provide an indispensable ingredient in calculating whether it pays to buy protection against given exposures. Given the multitude of circumstances that require a currency outlook, the development of forecasts should be guided by the specific needs of the enterprise. These include the time period for which the forecast is required, the degree of precision needed by managers using the forecasts, the company's criteria for a correct/useful forecast, and the cost of an incorrect forecast.

The current state of currency forecasting, as discussed in Chapter 4, is relatively modest. The international economy is extremely complex and the best of currency forecasts will be on target only part of the time. Yet with all their shortcomings, foreign currency forecasts are still an essential component of foreign exchange management. Implicitly, if not explicitly, forecasts underlie many decisions ranging from basic strategy formu-

---

[36] See Boris Antl and A. C. Henry, "The Cost and Implications of Two Hedging Techniques," *Euromoney*, June 1979.

[37] See Stephen H. Goodman, "Foreign Exchange Rate Forecasting Techniques: Implications for Business and Policy," *Journal of Finance*, May 1979.

lation and investment decisions to managing existing operations and setting policies for dividend remittances.

Implementation

A final exposure component is the implementation system. Given the analysis of the firm's exposure and the forecast of foreign exchange rates, the financial manager can work out a protection strategy, making use of the growing body of quantitative and model-building work available on managing foreign exchange risk.[38]

After calculating the types and amount of exposure, the financial manager will work out the reduction of exposure through financing alternatives and leads and lags. The rest of the exposure can be covered by the forward exchange market, providing the cost of such cover compares favorably with the prospective loss.

In some cases the cost of insurance will be too high or nonfinancial considerations such as local goodwill are involved so that the company itself will absorb the foreign exchange loss. To use a simple example, suppose that the forecaster gives an estimated devaluation size of 20 percent and a probability of occurrence of 75 percent, and suppose the forecaster has been wrong 10 percent of the time.[39] These three factors multiplied together $(0.20 \times 0.75 \times 1.10)$ equal 16.5 percent. This result is multiplied by the company treasurer's safety factor which reflects the company's willingness to accept risk, say, a 15 percent safety factor. Then, 16.5 percent multiplied by 1.15 equals 18.98 percent. This number can be compared with the market cost of cover to reach a decision. Suppose the annual market discount rate on forward contracts is 15 percent. The treasurer would spin off the risk because the cover cost is less than the expected loss indicated by the analysis. If the market price of cover is 22 percent, the company would self-insure because the cost of the cover would be more expensive than the probable loss.

IMPORT AND EXPORT FINANCING

In the traditional field of importing and exporting, an extensive range of financial services has been developed for financing international trans-

---

[38] For example, see Bernard A. Lietaer, *Financial Management of Foreign Exchange* (Cambridge, Mass.: MIT Press, 1971); Alan C. Shapiro and David P. Rutenberg, "Managing Exchange Risks in a Floating World," *Financial Management*, Summer 1976; William R. Folks, Jr., "The Analysis of Short-Term Cross-Border Financing Decisions," *Financial Management*, Autumn 1976, pp. 19–27; Raj Aggarwal, *The Management of Foreign Exchange: Optimal Policies for the Multinational Corporation* (New York: Praeger Publishers, 1976); Robert Z. Aliber, *Exchange Risk and Corporate International Finance* (New York: John Wiley & Sons, 1978).

[39] R. B. Shulman, "Are Foreign Exchange Risks Measurable?", *Columbia Journal of World Business*, May–June 1970, pp. 59–60.

actions. Whether for transactions within an international firm or with suppliers or customers, these offer the international manager important opportunities for extending the funds available to him.

There are two broad categories of credits. "Supplier" credit is extended by the exporter to the foreign importer and the exporter in turn is refinanced with credit from external sources. "Buyer" credit is granted directly to the foreign buyer to be used for stipulated imports. Supplier credit generally covers short-term credits and some medium-term transactions. Buyer credit is usually available only for medium- and long-term credits of large amounts, normally for purchasing capital goods.

In extending supplier credit, the seller is primarily concerned with credit risk, the protection of export proceeds against currency fluctuations, and political risk. In recent years, many countries have developed export credit insurance-guarantee programs to expand the country's export earnings by reducing these risks. Export-guaranteed paper may then be financed more easily and at a lower financing cost.

Financing may be with or without recourse. If the importer fails to pay the note or the bill when due, the financing institution may or may not have recourse to the exporter for the amount due. Most export credit is granted with recourse to the exporter. However, an insurance policy or guarantee issued by a government export credit insurance agency limits the financing without recourse to the extent that risks and losses are covered by the insurance.

Normally, the terms of sale in an export transaction are a matter of prior arrangement between the buyer and the seller. Usually, the actual collection of payment for goods sold abroad is accomplished through the international facilities of a commercial bank. The choice of payment method, or financial instrument, depends on such factors as the credit standing of the buyer (importer), the exchange restrictions, if any, that exist in the buyer's country, and the competition that the seller faces.[40]

Except for cash in advance, the export *letter of credit* affords the seller the highest degree of protection among all the commonly used methods of receiving payment for exports. A letter of credit is essentially a declaration by a bank that it will make certain payments on behalf of a specified party under specified conditions. It is called a "letter" because it takes the form of a notification to the party or parties likely to be the recipients of the payments. The letter of credit usually authorizes the exporter to receive funds upon presentation to the bank of the prescribed shipping documents.

The principal types of documents involved in export transactions are the commercial invoice, bills of lading, and insurance certification. The invoice shows the price of the sale. The bill of lading is evidence of the

---

[40] See Morgan Guaranty Trust Company, *The Financing of Exports and Imports* (New York, January 1980).

merchandise being shipped. The insurance certificate is evidence of insurance coverage for the goods shipped.

Some export letters of credit provide that drawings will be by time drafts. This means that payment is not to be made until some specified period after presentation—such as 30, 60, 90, or even 180 days. When accepted by the bank issuing the letter of credit, these drafts can be discounted readily at the prevailing rate for prime bankers' acceptances. Thus exporters can get their money immediately.

Commercial banks are the principal source of short-term export financing. Private commercial finance firms are also important in export financing but the growth of export guarantees has encouraged the use of commercial banks because private finance houses usually charge more than banks. Traditionally, commercial banks have been reluctant to grant medium-term financing, but as a result of government export promotion programs, sponsorship of new institutions, and guarantee programs, commercial banks and other private sources for medium-term financing have been increasing rapidly.

International trade is highly competitive and an important element in the competition is the terms of financing that the seller of goods or services can offer to foreign buyers. Most industrialized countries have government programs to assist their exporters in providing attractive terms. The Export-Import Bank of the United States (Eximbank) is the agency of the United States that is authorized to provide loans, guarantees, and insurance in order to facilitate U.S. exports on deferred credit terms. In these activities, it is meant to supplement but not to compete with private financing sources. It is particularly important for long-and medium-term financing.

The Foreign Credit Insurance Association (FCIA) is a joint enterprise of some 50 insurance companies in the United States that is affiliated with Eximbank. FCIA provides insurance, mainly for exporters but in some case for banks, against risks involved in extending credit on foreign sales. On the basis of FCIA insurance, the exporter normally is able to obtain sales financing from a bank or other lender.

As might be expected, in periods of intensive export competition, governments have been prone to make credit available at lower interest rates and for longer terms for national exporters. This tendency has started export credit wars that have led to periodic efforts by the industrial countries to negotiate international agreements on minimum credit terms.

A special form of payment increasingly used in trade with communist and some developing countries is the use of clearing currencies within the framework of currency-clearing arrangements between two countries. In the case of an export switch, the importer in a communist or developing market pays the exporter from a clearing balance held against a third country. The exporter then has the possibility, with the assistance of specialized agents (mainly in Austria, Germany, the Netherlands, and Switzerland), to use the clearing funds in the country holding the balance or to sell the bilateral funds at a discount.

THE TAX VARIABLE

In a world of independent taxing authorities, the multinational enterprise encounters an almost infinite variety of types of taxes, levels of tax burdens, tax incentives, patterns of tax administration, and possible overlaps in tax systems. As the tax variable is important in virtually all financial decisions, the enterprise needs the services of tax experts to anticipate tax burdens with accuracy and to minimize tax obligations within legal limits.

At the subsidiary level, the tax issue is to become informed on national differences and their impact on the profitability of operations in that country. At the multinational level, the firm must cope with overlapping tax jurisdictions, possible double taxation, and differential treatment of cross-border money flows. At the global level, another major issue is the use of tax havens.

National tax environments

National differences in taxation can change greatly the profitability of similar operations in different foreign subsidiaries.[41] Nations vary in the relative importance given to direct versus indirect taxes, in corporate income tax rates, and in the treatment of depreciation and many other expense items. The United States relies heavily at the federal level on direct taxes, mainly personal and corporate income taxes. In contrast, European countries rely heavily on indirect or turnover taxes, such as the value-added tax. The value-added tax has been adopted as the main source of revenue from indirect taxation by the European Community.

In the less developed countries, indirect taxes are generally more important than personal or corporate income taxes. Indirect taxes are relatively easy to administer. In contrast, income taxes are difficult to administer efficiently. Extensive record-keeping is required of individuals and companies, and an effective system of penalties is needed to secure reasonable compliance.

Among the industrial countries, nominal corporate income tax rates do not differ too widely. They more or less cluster around the level of 50 percent of net income. Some countries differentiate between retained and distributed earnings, charging a lower rate on distributed profits. In

---

[41] Various tax guides are published periodically by some international accounting firms such as Price Waterhouse Co. and Arthur Andersen Co. These give detailed information on the tax treatment of foreign income and related matters and are available for most countries where international business is a significant activity.

Germany, for example, undistributed profits are taxed at 56 percent but profits distributed to shareholders are taxed at only 36 percent.[42] Japan also taxes distributed earnings at a lower rate. Under such a system, corporations are under pressure to meet their needs for additional capital through new financing rather than through retained earnings.

The less developed countries fall into three tax categories. The first category consists of countries like Mexico and Singapore that have become established as attractive areas for foreign investment. These countries have been able to raise their income tax rates to the 40 percent level. A second group of countries use moderate income tax rates and tax incentives to encourage private investment. Tax rates in such countries as the Philippines and Taiwan are in the 30 to 40 percent range. But special tax incentives are offered that may temporarily spare the multinational enterprise from paying part or all of certain taxes.

The third category includes the so-called tax haven countries that assess low (or no) corporate taxes to affiliates of foreign companies. Some countries that impose no income tax are the Bahamas, Cayman Islands, and Bermuda. Countries like Panama and Liberia have special tax exemptions for foreign companies. In the case of Panama, only income earned there is subject to Panama income tax. In the case of Liberia, companies owned and controlled at least 75 percent by nonresident shareholders that do not derive any income from Liberia are outside the scope of local taxation.

The multinational tax environment

The tax variable becomes increasingly complex when profits are transferred from the subsidiary to the parent or to other units of the multinational enterprise. Countries differ in their treatment of foreign-source income earned by their own multinationals. The policies of the major industrial countries range from complete exemption of repatriated foreign income to full taxation at domestic rates. French parent companies, for example, can exclude from their corporate income taxes 95 percent of the gross dividends received from foreign subsidiaries. The United States taxes the worldwide income of its citizens, residents, and domestic corporations.

In the case of the United States, double taxation is mitigated by allowing a direct credit against U.S. taxes for foreign taxes paid. Also, an American firm is liable only for taxes on foreign earnings when it pays itself a dividend from a foreign subsidiary. The rest of the foreign earnings are deferred. As one study concluded, "In theory, the U.S. taxes foreign-source income, but in practice most U.S. manufacturing investors pay

---

[42] See Price Waterhouse & Co., *Corporate Taxes: A Worldwide Summary* (New York, January 1982).

little or no U.S. taxes on income earned abroad. The foreign tax credit is usually sufficient to offset U.S. taxes tentatively due on foreign-source income."[43]

In the tax field, as previously discussed in Chapter 8, governments have taken steps to avoid double taxation through bilateral treaties. Under such treaties, a country agrees to share with another on a prearranged basis the taxes imposed on business operations in the territory of one country by nationals of another country. Tax treaties may also provide for information exchanges between the governments that will aid each other in tax collection. The negotiation of a network of tax treaties has resulted in more tax uniformity among countries.

The topic of "tax sparing" was also discussed in Chapter 8. The special tax incentives provided by some countries to attract foreign investment offer little advantage to the business enterprise if the income is taxable at the same or higher rate in the home country of the parent company. Some countries permit a tax credit for taxes that have been spared in a foreign country. But others, particularly the United States, do not. The effect of policies such as that of the United States is to reduce or cancel the attractiveness of foreign tax incentives in influencing the investment decisions of multinational enterprises.

The matter of "tax havens" continues to be an extremely sensitive tax issue, although the use of tax havens is not limited to multinational enterprises. Income "sourced" in tax-haven countries, through transfer pricing or other means, could until 1962 avoid U.S. taxes by not being paid out as dividends to owners in the United States. The Revenue Act of 1962 was intended to reduce sharply the importance of tax havens. But a special study of the U.S. Internal Revenue Service completed in 1981 concluded that the use of tax havens by U.S. persons was increasing rapidly in both absolute and relative terms.[44] The report also made suggestions for changes that would correct the "tax-haven abuse."

As a general rule, the tax policy of an investor nation should be neutral. It should not favor or penalize foreign as against domestic investment. Whether the U.S. tax system is neutral or favors foreign investment has been periodically debated in the United States with inconclusive results. The labor unions, in particular, have argued that the tax system favors foreign investment and that such measures as the foreign tax credit, which is a direct reduction against tax liabilities, should be replaced by allowing foreign taxes as an expense. Other parties have concluded that U.S. tax policy provides a "surprising close approximation to neutrality."[45] The debate is likely to continue.

---

[43] Bergsten, Horst, and Moran, *American Multinationals*, p. 210.

[44] See Price Waterhouse & Co., *International Tax News*, June 1981.

[45] Bergsten, Horst, and Moran, *American Multinationals*, p. 461; see also Thomas Horst, "American Taxation of Multinational Firms," *American Economic Review*, June 1977, pp. 376–89.

Box 22–1

New tune for corporate tax fiddlers

Multinational companies fiddle their accounts and evade taxes. Right? Well, yes—and quite a few of them are getting better at it. Through the 1970s, the world's tax authorities tried to stop multinationals laundering profits through low-tax, and no-tax, countries. The new powers they sought (and got) were aimed at curbing legal, but costly, tax avoidance—mostly on the assumption that multinational companies were playing it straight and not stooping to illegal evasion. At the same time, most multinationals developed worthy policies—some real, some not—which ruled out tax fiddling. The baddies carried on as before, and some of the goodies lost their haloes. When the inevitable crackdown on transfer pricing manipulation arrives, many of the world's most respectable companies will be caught cheating.

In a windowless Paris conference room in February this year, 60 tax inspectors from industrial countries met for three days to talk about ways of plugging international tax leakage. This was the fourth in a series of confidential meetings (with more to come), under the wing of the OECD committee on fiscal affairs, to discuss the detection of tax avoidance and evasion. The 60 are all actively involved in auditing multinationals' accounts. They discussed, according to a terse statement, "questions related to the selection of cases for in-depth audit, transfer prices for exchanges of goods, research and development, capital and services, and the different opportunities available to tax administrations to cooperate with other countries through exchanging information, simultaneous audits and joint audits."

Source: *The Economist*, June 20, 1981, p. 108.

In summary, tax planning is a complex and highly technical subject that requires the input of tax experts. The financial manager must have familiarity with national tax environments in which the enterprise operates as well as understand the tax philosophy and policies of the parent country.[46] Important considerations are how the home country views tax neutrality, tax deferral, foreign tax credits, tax havens, and intercompany transactions.

SUMMARY

International financial management is primarily concerned with the maximization of profits after taxes for the multinational system as a whole, within the framework of a wider pursuit of corporate objectives.

---

[46] See Michael Adler, "U.S. Taxation of U.S. Multinational Corporations: A Manual of Computation Techniques and Managerial Decision Rules," in *International Finance and Trade*, vol. 2, eds. M. Sarnat and G. P. Szego (Cambridge, Mass.: Ballinger, 1979), pp. 157–210.

International operations add many complexities to the financial management function, ranging from the difficulties of developing an adequate financial information system, where the initial data input into the system must necessarily be shaped by varying patterns in national accounting systems, to the problems of dealing in multiple currencies and managing foreign exchange risks. At the same time, a multinational system affords opportunities to minimize interest costs, tax liabilities, and the effects of differential inflation rates among countries, and to reduce working capital needs through pooling liquidity among affiliates.

Thus, the major challenge and opportunity in international financial management is to optimize on a systemwide basis. Toward this end, major progress has been achieved in the development of concepts and tools for complex strategies that reveal profit-taking opportunities that normally do not become apparent under simple strategies focused on subgoals of financial management. But the use of complex and sophisticated techniques can be expensive in terms of required data, personnel, and experience. Given these cost and other limitations, many international firms deal with each subsidiary as an independent operation and make little or no effort to optimize the financial function on a systemwide basis.

Under most circumstances, however, the investment and capital-budgeting decisions above certain financial limits are a centralized responsibility for the multinational firm. The international financial manager has also become increasingly involved in decisions on financial structures of affiliates, financing techniques, and management of foreign exchange risk. The management of cash flows and liquidity on an international basis has been growing rapidly as an international financial management function.

APPENDIX: A SYSTEMS APPROACH TO FINANCIAL OPTIMIZATION: AN EXAMPLE

The possibilities for gains through a systems approach are illustrated in Figure 22A–1. If each company in the system raised capital from the cheapest source (country B) and paid local taxes, the net cost after taxes would be 4.0 percent for A (i.e., 8 percent less 50 percent taxes), 6.4 percent for B, and 4.8 percent for C. The average cost for the system would be 5.06 percent. But if the subsidiary with the highest tax rate (A) raised all the capital needed by the system from the cheapest source (B) and advanced the funds interest-free to the other units, the cost to the system would be only 4.0 percent.

The advantages of the system for altering transfer prices for materials, services, and components from one unit of the system to the others are also illustrated. For every $100 that A lowers its transfer prices to B, there

Figure 22A-1

A systems approach to financial optimization (an example)

Characteristics of the multinational system (by country):

	Three fully owned systems companies		
	A	*B*	*C*
Local corporation tax rates	50%	20%	40%
Import duty rates for system transfers	10	30	80
Local interest rates (After adjustment for forecast exchange rate change)	12	8	10

Each company transfers some production to the other two.
Each company has local profits and incurs corporation tax.

Possibilities for system savings over independent operation:
1. *Alter source of capital.*
    Independent decision: Raise capital from cheapest source (B) and pay local taxes. Net cost = (A) 4.0 percent; (B) 6.4 percent; (C) 4.8 percent.
    System decision: Company with highest tax rate (A) to raise capital from cheapest source and advance interest free to others. Net cost = (A,B,C,) 4.0 percent.
2. *Alter transfer prices.*
    Independent decision: Price somewhere between supplier company cost and receiving company revenue.
    System decision: Adjust prices as indicated on the table below. Gains would continue until lowered prices reached zero and increased prices eliminated all the profits of the receiving company, but there will be practical limitations in the real world.

		Gains from $100 change			
Goods transferred from:	*Direction of price change*	*Source country tax ($)*	*Destination country tax ($)*	*Import duty ($)*	*Net system gain ($)*
A to B	Lower	+50	−20	+30	+60
B to C	Lower	+20	−40	+80	+60
C to A	Adjust to give desired company profits				0
A to C	Lower	+50	−40	+80	+90
C to B	Lower	+40	−20	+30	+50
B to A	Raise	−20	+50	−10	+20

3. *Alter royalty charges and transfer prices:*
    Independent decision: Combined total to fall between supplier company cost and receiving company revenue.
    System decision: Lower *all* transfer prices to minimize import duties, and charge royalties from lowest taxed company to minimize corporation tax.

will be a net gain of $60 to the system. Half of this gain, $30, will be in taxes because profits are taxed at only a 20 percent rate in B as against a 50 percent rate in A. There will be another $30 gained in import duties because the price on which the 30 percent duty is charged has been lowered.

EXERCISES AND DISCUSSION QUESTIONS

1. Why might a multinational firm decide to invest in a project that shows a low expected rate of return on the basis of the first-level analysis at the local country level?

2. Which source of funds would be the cheapest—a loan in the United Kingdom at 11 percent annually on an overdraft basis or a loan from a U.S. bank at 9 percent annually but with the requirement of a 20 percent compensating balance?

3. A U.S. multinational enterprise has three subsidiaries, each located in a different European country. The British subsidiary imports semifinished products from its Dutch affiliate for further processing and distribution. Part of the British subsidiary's output is exported to its German affiliate, and the rest is sold in the British home market. Normal trade credit terms on all transactions are 60 days. In anticipation of British sterling depreciation during 1975, the British subsidiary was directed to give its German affiliate 110 days to pay and to reduce its liabilities to the Dutch affiliate to zero, that is, to pay for its imports C.O.D. How can such tactics provide a hedge against one-time exchange losses?

4. The chief financial officer of a U.S. multinational company says, "Our foreign exchange strategy is to avoid risk. We pursue the practice of offsetting all balance sheet exposures with foreign exchange hedges, thus neutralizing the exposures." Comment on the wisdom of such a strategy.

5. Why do modern finance theory and the Capital Asset Pricing Model have limitations as a guide for the multinational financial manager?

6. How does the tax variable enter into decisions on transfer pricing, capital budgeting, remittance policies, and the financial structure of affiliates?

Chapter 23

Multinational human resource management

The quality of a firm's executives is usually the single most important determinant of its success in international business. An aggressive global strategy implies managerial resources of a caliber to think out and implement such policies. In the words of one international executive, "Virtually any type of international problem, in the final analysis, is either created by people or must be solved by people. Hence, having the right people in the right place at the right time emerges as the key to a company's international growth. If we are successful in solving that problem, I am confident we can cope with all others."[1]

---

[1] Michael G. Duerr, "International Business Management: Its Four Tasks," *Conference Board Record,* October 1968, p. 43.

Multinational business brings with it many unique problems in the management of human resources, the most fundamental of which is the necessity for managers raised and experienced in one culture to play bicultural or multicultural roles. The managers of foreign subsidiaries play a boundary or middleman role between two sets of cultural patterns.[2] To their subordinates and customers, they are "the company" and represent headquarters. To headquarters, they are the "local manager" who belongs to the subsidiary. They must know the local culture and language and they must understand the foreign cultural assumptions underlying the technology and business practices being introduced into the local environment. Whether a national or an expatriate, the local manager is sandwiched between his or her own culture and the foreign cultures.[3]

At headquarters or the regional level, managers play a multicultural role. They must integrate and coordinate activities taking place in many cultural environments that are being directed by managers with diverse cultural orientations. Furthermore, they must deal with the natural tendency of local managers to identify with the national interests of their unit.

Another set of management problems arises when employees are transferred across cultural and national boundaries. The selection of those who are to be transferred involves a choice among the various nationalities involved; raises questions concerning desirable characteristics, education, and remuneration; and requires procedures to facilitate the adjustment of those who switch cultures and residences.

Finally, the international extension of a firm involves wide variances in the skills and supply of workers, different patterns of labor-management relations, and the possibility that the firm may have to face international union collaboration for multinational bargaining.

EXECUTIVE NATIONALITY POLICIES

What nationality policy should the multinational firm adopt for the recruitment and development of international executives? Essentially, the firm can choose from three policies for staffing management positions, or else adopt no standard policy and build a patchwork approach.[4] It can fill key positions everywhere in the world with personnel from the home country of the parent company—an ethnocentric policy. It can use local nationals to manage foreign subsidiaries and home-country nationals as headquarters managers—a polycentric policy. Or it can recruit and

---

[2] See Chapter 17.

[3] Chul Koo Yun, "Role Conflicts of Expatriate Managers: A Construct," *Management International Review* 13 (1973–76): 106.

[4] David A. Heenan and Howard V. Perlmutter, *Multinational Organizational Development* (Reading, Mass.: Addison-Wesley Publishing, 1979), chap. 2.

develop the best persons without regard to nationality for key positions anywhere in the multinational system—a geocentric policy. Each of the alternatives has advantages and disadvantages.

An international executive cadre

At first glance, the most effective policy would appear to be a geocentric one, where the best person is sought for a job, regardless of the person's nationality and the location of the job. Such a policy would be consistent with the unique strength of multinational business, namely, its ability to rationalize on an international basis the use of natural resources, financial resources, and technology. Why shouldn't it also rationalize on an international basis the use of managerial resources? To some degree and for a period of time, expatriate managers might be handicapped by not being fully immersed in the national cultural, political, and economic situation. But these disadvantages would be more than offset by their superior ability and experience. Even more important, the tendency of national identification of managers with units of the system would be reduced so that the firm would be better able to realize its multinational potential.

Yet there have been only modest beginnings by a relatively few international firms toward developing a truly international executive force. Several factors combine to limit the popularity of a geocentric policy. First, host countries want foreign subsidiaries to be staffed by their local nationals and frequently they adopt national controls to achieve this goal. Second, an international executive policy can be expensive. It requires widespread recruitment, a substantial investment in language training and cultural orientation programs for managers and their families, substantial costs in transferring executives and their families into and away from foreign posts, and salary levels that are significantly higher than national levels in many countries. Third, such a pattern requires a high degree of centralization in the control of personnel and their career patterns, and undercuts the cherished prerogative of local managers to choose their own personnel. A fourth reason is that the policy would take a long time to implement.

For firms wishing to build an international management cadre, promotion policies and practice must make it very clear that cross-national service is important to the firm. And in order to recruit promising executives to work with the subsidiaries, the firm must also have a policy of open career opportunities for top-management positions. The view of many ambitious and able young foreign nationals was expressed as follows by an international manager:

> He must feel that if he has the ability he can aspire to any job in the company, apart perhaps from the presidency. It may be that when he is faced with the prospect of going on the main board, and so spending the

rest of his working life outside his home country he will decide to reject the opportunity. If so, that will be his decision. But he must feel that his nationality does not, of itself, disqualify him from aiming for the stars.[5]

National executives within each unit

Hiring nationals has many obvious advantages, which are mainly the obverse of the disadvantages of an international executive cadre. Hiring nationals largely eliminates the language barriers, expensive training periods, and cross-cultural adjustment problems of managers and their families. It lowers the profile of a foreign firm in sensitive political situations. It permits the firm to take advantage of lower national salary levels, while still paying a premium over local norms to attract high-quality personnel. And since the career of nationals will be in their home country, they will give continuity to the management of foreign subsidiaries.

Nevertheless, there is a price to be paid in following a policy of hiring nationals. Nationals are likely to have difficulties in bridging the gap between the subsidiary and the rest of the system. The education, business experience, and cultural environment to which they have been exposed all their lives may not have prepared them to work as part of a multinational enterprise. They may experience cross-cultural problems because of different concepts as to business practices, differences in personal values such as a reluctance to "dirty one's hands," and many other cultural variables. They may identify with their country as against the spirit and advantages of multinationalism. They are not likely to be fully knowledgeable about the management techniques, products, and technology developed in the parent firm's home country on which the firm's international expansion is based. There is an inbuilt immobility. Once a foreign manager reaches the top position in the overseas subsidiary, he has nowhere to go. The narrow focus of his career can affect his own morale and block the promotion of those underneath him.[6] In turn, some of the most promising foreign nationals may be difficult to recruit and to retain because of limited promotion possibilities within the total enterprise. Also, many nationals are interested in only a limited tour of duty with foreign firms in order to get training and experience.

Japanese multinationals, because their international business language is generally Japanese, have unusual difficulties in finding nationals with the necessary language ability. Even if the language gap is bridged by hiring nationals of Japanese ancestry, the culture gap may still remain. As a Japanese executive complained about his company's experience in

[5] Christopher Tugendhat, *The Multinationals* (London: Eyre & Spottiswoode, 1971), p. 197; see also John D. Daniels, "The Non-American Manager, Especially as Third Country National in U.S. Multinationals: A Separate but Equal Doctrine?", *Journal of International Business Studies*, Fall 1974, pp. 25–40.

[6] See Yoram Zeira, "Overlooked Personnel Problems of Multinational Corporations," *Columbia Journal of World Business*, Summer 1975, pp. 96–103.

Brazil, where there is a large nisei population, "They look Japanese, they speak Japanese, but they think Brazilian."

A policy of employing nationals makes it difficult for young executives from headquarters or from foreign subsidiaries to get experience working outside of their home country and to develop their capacity to communicate, coordinate, and supervise effectively in a multicultural setting. Such a policy is unlikely to create a body of international executives able to switch between units of the multinational firm as the need arises. It also reinforces the dominance of home-country executives, frequently with little actual foreign working experience, in the higher corporate posts dealing with strategy and capital allocation decisions between subsidiary units dominated by local nationals.[7]

Retention of top corporate management at headquarters in the hands of nationals of the parent country has a number of advantages. The executives come from a reasonably similar cultural background and have little trouble in communicating with each other. They are likely to have experienced the buildup of the parent unit and to have developed skills and evolved a working pattern in the management of an international operation. In the longer run, however, a firm with this sort of management pattern can become a grouping of virtually independent national units with the prime responsibility for transfer of ideas and for general cohesion falling on executives of the parent unit who are not sufficiently prepared for this task.

Parent company executives everywhere

An ethnocentric policy of placing home-country nationals in key executive posts everywhere seems directly contradictory to current trends toward nationalism and equality of opportunity. Yet it is surprisingly widespread. Some companies still feel that they must have a home-country "presence" in each foreign subsidiary. For U.S. firms that follow such a policy, this presence is usually the local general manager or chief finance officer. Some companies go even further in insisting on home-country personnel as essential for transferring technological strength from the parent company and feedback from the subsidiaries. As one manager of a European company claimed, "There should be a European at the head of the U.S. operation. I have a rapport with our parent that dates back over 33 years. This rapport is terribly useful for communication back and forth. How could an American develop such a rapport . . . particularly with a French mother company."[8]

---

[7] Kenneth Simmonds, "Multinational? Well, Not Quite," *Columbia Journal of World Business,* Fall 1966, pp. 115–22; Kenneth Simmonds and Richard Connell, "Breaking the Boardroom Barrier: The Importance of Being British," *Journal of Management Studies,* May 1974, pp. 85–95.

[8] *European Strategies in the United States* (Geneva, Switzerland: Business International, S.A., 1971), p. 42.

In the early stages of internationalization, the use of home-country nationals may be the best approach. After all, most firms at this stage are involved in transplanting some part of the business that has worked in the home country, and detailed knowledge of that part is the critical factor. But disadvantages can quickly appear. The policy must mean blocked promotion for local executives. If there are many subsidiaries, the home-country nationals filling the many foreign posts will have to accept that their foreign service may not lead on to higher corporate positions.[9] In addition, there are the high cost disadvantages that also arise for geocentric policies and a much greater tendency to import into subsidiaries the management style of the parent company and its home-country cultural biases.

Mixed policies

Clearly, none of the three "pure" policies provides a complete answer to the complexities of managing multinational enterprises. Most multinational firms favor hiring local nationals for foreign subsidiaries, home-country nationals at headquarters, and, where a regional organization exists, a mix of foreign and home-country managers for regional positions. Within this general approach, however, the nationality mix will vary with the nature of a firm's business and its product strategy. Where area expertise plays a major role, as in the case of consumer goods and/or a limited product line, the use of home-country personnel for overseas assignments will be minimal. Where product expertise is highly important and/or industrial markets are being served, home-country personnel will be used more extensively for foreign assignments because they generally have quick access to the home-country sources of supply and technical information. Service industries also tend to have more home-country personnel in foreign posts, particularly where the firm is serving home-country multinationals in foreign areas, as has been the case in banking.

MULTINATIONAL MANAGEMENT RECRUITMENT

If a firm is to develop a management team with truly international capability, the best place to start is with recruitment policies. When a firm takes its first steps toward becoming international, it normally does not have the opportunity to develop a cadre of international managers. Its middle- and top-level managers would have been recruited in earlier periods when selection criteria were based on domestic business needs. Its recruitment would almost certainly have been limited to persons living in the home country. Prior to going international, the firm could

---

[9] Yoram Zeira and Ehud Harari, "Structural Sources of Personnel Problems in Multinational Corporations: Third-Country Nationals," *Omega*, no. 2, 1977.

not offer internal opportunities for managers to gain international experience except in the exporting field. Thus at such an early stage, managers for international operations have been mainly recruited from within the organization without having had any previous experience in foreign operations.[10] Where international expansion occurred through acquisitions, some firms were able to add key executives of the acquired companies to their international management staff. A third source may have been "buy-ins," or experienced international managers hired from outside the company.

Such makeshift methods, however, inevitably lead to surpluses and shortages that can be minimized with a planned approach to international recruitment. Such an approach begins with a forecast of future management manpower needs on an annual basis for at least a five-year forward period. Given the long lead time necessary to develop top and middle management within an enterprise, even 15-year forecasts are not too short.

With recruitment targets specified as to positions to be filled, their location, and the type of personnel required, the international firm can follow conventional recruitment practices, except for several additional international complications. It must decide:

1.   In what countries the company should recruit.
2.   What new techniques and sources will have to be used, when recruitment is planned outside the home country.
3.   Whether recruitment activities and decisions should be centralized in the parent company or decentralized in foreign subsidiaries.

A fruitful source of future subsidiary executives who are both highly selected and already sensitized to the parent company culture are foreign students graduating from business schools in the home country.[11] But recruitment for international managers should extend beyond the universities or business schools of the developed countries and include universities where the firm operates. Outside the United States, management training is a relatively new educational field, but the amount and quality of such academic training has expanded rapidly in most developed countries and in many less developed countries. In many countries, universities have not yet developed adequate facilities for assisting firms in their recruitment. In such cases, recruitment techniques may have to rely heavily on newspaper advertising, executive recruitment companies, or special efforts to contact young people when they finish their military service.

An enterprise-wide executive recruitment program will necessarily be a cooperative effort between the foreign subsidiaries and regional and

[10] Enid Baird Lovell, *The Changing Role of the International Executive* (New York: National Industrial Conference Board, 1966), p. 26.

[11] G. G. Alpander, "Foreign MBA: Potential Managers for American International Corporations," *Journal of International Business Studies*, Spring 1973.

global headquarters. This will mean the surrender of some power to make independent appointments on the part of individual units of the organization. Actual recruitment activities, however, can be decentralized and the managers of foreign subsidiaries should have a voice in the final decision on the hiring of personnel who will work under their direction. A company like Procter & Gamble has its subsidiaries establish their recruitment needs, which are then consolidated at the division level—for example, the European Division, which has responsibility for recruitment. Foreign nationals studying in the United States are recruited by the parent company for the foreign subsidiaries, but only up to a preselection phase. Such candidates are then interviewed by the manager of the division or the subsidiary, which makes the final offer. In some cases, the prospective candidate may even be flown back to his or her home country at company expense so that the local manager can interview the person and make the final decision.

MANAGEMENT DEVELOPMENT AND TRAINING

Whatever policy or combination of management recruitment policies is adopted, the international firm must also have a long-range and continuing program of management development that is integrated with its global strategy and business planning.[12] It needs to work constantly toward internationalizing the experience and outlook of all executive personnel including the higher echelons of corporate power. The most compelling argument for developing multinational executives is that it will avoid inbreeding and narrowness at the top. For the firm of the future, truly international management will have greater sensitivity to changes in the world environment and flexibility in adapting to them.

Promising managerial talent must be discovered early so that young managers can secure cross-national experience and be available in the middle of their careers for general management posts where this experience is needed. For the larger corporation, a central inventory of international executives will be needed to assure that promising executives do not become lost in a foreign posting. A central inventory will lead to further surrender of power to make appointments on the part of individual units of the organization. Unless there is a central voice in appointments, continued career development of the international executive might be sacrificed to the interests of individual units or jeopardized by preferred promotion of those known locally.

Such a management development program is usually supported by a range of training programs with a cross-national focus. There is no substitute for training in a multinational company. It transfers knowledge; it improves communications and it helps impart the parent company's

---

[12] Lawrence G. Franko, "Who Manages Multinational Enterprises?", *Columbia Journal of World Business*, Summer 1973, pp. 30–42.

way of operating. For all employees, whether at headquarters or working in foreign subsidiaries, training is also a means of increasing their sensitivity to cultural patterns that are foreign to their own experience and values. Some multinationals, therefore, try to extend the opportunity for foreign experience as widely as possible. Cummins Engine Co., for example, offers evening language courses that any employee may take and seeks to arrange foreign business trips for more than the "privileged management elite" so that large numbers of employees build a foreign awareness.[13]

Training for culture sensitivity should have at least two dimensions. It should develop in the individual an awareness of his or her own cultural assumptions and the nature of his or her cultural conditioning. It should also develop a special kind of intellectual and emotional radar that alerts the manager to situations where cultural assumptions other than his or her own are present. If culture sensitivity could be achieved simply through intellectual awareness that cultural patterns differ, the task of developing cultural sensitivity might be accomplished through readings and lectures. But the problem is more difficult. Human reactions are likely to be emotional, visceral, or psychological motor responses. One can be fully aware in an intellectual sense that time has a different meaning and value in Latin America, and yet have unkind and unfriendly reactions when forced to wait hours rather than minutes beyond the previously fixed time for an appointment.

The most lasting means of achieving culture sensitivity comes through a sustained experience of living and working in one or more foreign environments. Why then should the firm bother with training programs for those employees who are to be moved between countries? The answer is, of course, the high failure rate associated with cross-national transfers. However imperfect training may be as a substitute for actual foreign living experience, it is valuable if it can reduce the often painful and agonizing experience of transferring into another culture and avoid the great damage that culture shock and cultural misunderstanding can do to a firm's operating relationships.

Training to meet the specific needs of multinational management can be carried out through external programs, internal programs, or on-the-job internal training. Each approach has characteristic advantages.[14]

> External programs are those not tailored to a specific organization, and are used to broaden managers' horizons beyond the immediate concerns of their individual organizations. Programs covering for-

---

[13] Jeffrey L. Blue and Ulrich Haynes, Jr., "Preparation for the Overseas Assignment," *Business Horizons*, June 1977, pp. 61–67.

[14] See, for example, Yoram Zeira, "Management Development in Ethnocentric Multinational Corporations," *California Management Review*, Summer 1976, pp. 34–42.

eign language and culture, for example, may be extremely valuable for developing cultural sensitivity, yet may never touch on the terminology or customs specific to the particular business. It is possible, however, to find external programs that are designed for those in similar situations so that rather specific learning can take place from the experience of others. A course on transfer pricing in multinationals would be a good example. External programs such as this can expose managers to the most recent developments and to leading thinkers in an area. Some business schools have specific international management programs as well. On the other hand, general management programs are much more numerous and many multinational firms prefer to send managers to such programs run in a country to which a manager may be moving. Local programs can provide the manager with a more focused training in the business culture of a particular country.

Internal programs can be tailored to the specific needs of the individual multinational. They can also be easily changed as the organization learns and is confronted by different problems. Generally speaking, the impact of such training is more identifiable and more immediate. Participants from the one organization with different national and cultural backgrounds can be led together in the building of a common language to describe common problems. As the result of skillfully designed internal programs, persistent problems are often quickly surmounted—as much because of the stronger and common perception of the problem as because of the solutions discussed during the program. Internal participants also get to know each other and their individual points of view and it is quite possible to focus directly on problems of subunit identification that hold back overall performance of the multinational organization. With internal programs, the participants usually become more involved and more committed because topics have a closer relationship to their own work and the current problems of the organization.

Internal on-the-job training is usually tailored to requirements of individual managers and their specific job assignments, although some large multinationals do have general training schemes involving international job rotation experience. On-the-job training has the advantage that actual performance in the real situation is monitored, usually by a more experienced superior. Moreover, the learning is real and not just an intellectual experience. For cultural conditioning, on-the-job training is unsurpassed. It also has the advantage of time. Programs, whether internal or external, are generally time-constrained—yet real sensitivity training takes a long time.

CROSS-NATIONAL TRANSFERS

All multinationals, whatever their policy on executive nationality, transfer employees across national and cultural boundaries to some extent. Some transfers may be permanent postings, some are designed to meet temporary needs, and others are part of an international career-development program. Managers assigned to foreign posts for extended periods are likely to encounter special problems of working in a foreign environment, living in a different culture, and maintaining satisfactory relations with the parent company. Selection for such postings should not be taken lightly.

Adapting at work

Transferred executives have to establish new working relationships within a cultural environment vastly different from the one to which they are accustomed. The executives will have to be aware of cultural variations as they affect local patterns of decision making, issuing and accepting instructions, and conducting many other day-to-day aspects of management and business operations. They must deal with local foreign personnel with different backgrounds, languages, attitudes, values, and points of view;[15] adapt technical and managerial know-how to an unfamiliar environment; and cope with economic and political conditions that are unfamiliar and often more complicated than those encountered at home. Anecdotes and case examples abound of the problems encountered in cross-national assignments.[16] But the emphasis on problems, as Skinner cautions, "should in no sense imply that all men sent abroad fail to perform well, that most assignments abroad are unhappy ones, or that expatriate managers always present difficult and absorbing problems for executives in the home office. This is not so."[17]

Nevertheless, studies have disclosed patterns of suboptimal performance from expatriates at the beginning of foreign postings, followed by a gradual improvement as they adapt to their new situations.[18] Managers posted from a parent company to head established subsidiaries, for example, often adopt an individualistic management style at the outset,

---

[15] See, for example, Richard B. Peterson and Hermann F. Schwind, "A Comparative Study of Personnel Problems in International Companies and Joint Ventures in Japan," *Journal of International Business Studies*, Spring–Summer 1977, pp. 45–55.

[16] See Wickham Skinner, *American Industry in Developing Economies* (New York: John Wiley & Sons, 1968), pp. 222–48; John Fayerweather, *The Executive Overseas* (Syracuse, N.Y.: Syracuse University Press, 1969; Richard F. Gonzales and Anant R. Negandhi, *The United States Overseas Executive: His Orientations and Career Patterns* (East Lansing: Michigan State University, 1967).

[17] Skinner, *American Industry in Developing Economies*, p. 222.

[18] Zeira, "Management Development in Ethnocentric Multinational Corporations," p. 35.

shielding their decision making from their immediate subordinates. Furthermore, the new manager is likely to impose management patterns on the subsidiary that worked well in other environments but that do not suit the local situation. Such behavior may stem from a temptation to demonstrate a managerial superiority in the new post and to justify being chosen ahead of the local nationals who are the immediate subordinates. The behavior may also reflect a wish to prevent these subordinates from seeing the manager's limited comprehension of the new situation. Predictably, the relations between the manager and the local team will be strained, producing mutual mistrust and morale problems. Over time, the exposure of the manager to the new culture and interaction with its members will usually temper such an initial insensitivity to the differences. It has been observed, for example, that managers' perceptions of the differences in capabilities between themselves and their subordinates are reduced with the length of time they work overseas.[19]

Social adaptation

Outside the work situation, foreign executives and their families encounter environmental differences that are even more marked than the on-the-job differences. Social contacts may be severely curtailed, for example, if an expatriate's spouse cannot speak the local language. Wives of local business and social acquaintances are unlikely to speak anything other than the local language, and significant relationships are not likely to be built up across a language barrier. Wives in some countries will have several servants and with some relief from household duties have considerable free time. Boredom, excessive drinking, and high spending are not uncommon results. A broad study of almost 2,000 employees of a multinational firm on cross-national assignments, of whom about 20 percent were of American nationality, concluded that a male employee's satisfaction with his foreign assignment depended mainly on his wife's adjustment to the assignment. The wife's satisfaction ranked as the most important element among the American group, and only slightly lower than job-related elements in the total group.[20]

The stress of cross-national transfers on executives and their families may produce behavior patterns that prejudice the manager's job performance. Rejection of the new culture and glorification of the old is not uncommon. Frequently referred to as "culture shock," this can result in the establishment of tight groups of home-country personnel who devote

---

[19] Edwin L. Miller, "Managerial Qualifications of Personnel Occupying Overseas Management Positions as Perceived by American Expatriate Managers," *Journal of International Business Studies*, Spring–Summer 1977, pp. 57–69.

[20] Gillian Purcer-Smith, *Studies of International Mobility (in IBM World Trade Corp.)*, mimeographed (New York: National Foreign Trade Council, 1971), NFTC ref. no. M-9936.

themselves to re-creating the home culture and dwelling on the "weaker" points of that in which they reside. This is what a Shell executive calls "those bloody people" syndrome.

> The expatriate goes young and fresh to his first "new" country and he makes a big effort to integrate. He learns about local culture, he travels the country, and he tries to learn the language. Then he is moved. The next country is a little more difficult. Those people in his first overseas assignment were pretty unreliable anyway. The new lot are worse. He makes some kind of effort, but it's not such a big effort. By the fourth or fifth country, he may have given up. He locks himself up with expatriate colleagues and he doesn't want to see anything of the local scene except when he is actually working. That man, I submit, is a major liability in any multinational operation . . . for him, they are only "those bloody people."[21]

Selection for transfer

Few firms have large numbers of executives competent and available for cross-national postings. Thus a highly complex selection system is likely to be unnecessary. Moreover, so little is known about measuring characteristics that make for success in cross-cultural management and foreign postings that the accuracy of such systems is questionable. Listings of the qualities needed in a foreign posting seem very like those needed anywhere for success as an executive. The requirements, anyway, vary from situation to situation and country to country so that no single set of standards would be adequate.[22] It should be noted, though, that studies have found correlations between cross-national managerial success and personal values, attributes, and experience.[23]

Because of the difficulties in predicting success in foreign environments, the failure rate can be high and the costs so great that care is warranted in searching for factors that are likely to lead to failures. Thus, selection becomes more a check for weakness than an absolute testing. In this sense most selection methods are in effect rejection schemes. Inflexibility and insensitivity to others' views and to new political situations have been cited as frequent characteristics of failures. But failures can be equally caused by strong attachments to a family grouping left

---

[21] Donald N. Leich, *Transnational Executive Development in the Royal Dutch Shell Group of Companies*, mimeographed (New York: National Foreign Trade Council, February 1970), NFTC ref. no. M-9293.

[22] Richard D. Hays, "Expatriate Selection: Insuring Success and Avoiding Failure," *Journal of International Business Studies*, Spring 1974, pp. 25–37; and Edwin L. Miller, "The Selection Decision for an International Assignment: A Study of the Decision Maker's Behavior," *Journal of International Business Studies*, Fall 1972, pp. 49–65.

[23] See Brian Toyne, "Host Country Managers of Multinational Firms: An Evaluation of Variables Affecting Their Managerial Thinking Patterns," *Journal of International Business Studies*, Spring 1976, pp. 39–55; George W. England, "Managers and Their Value Systems: A Five-Country Comparative Study," *Columbia Journal of World Business* 13, no. 2 (Summer 1978): 35–44.

behind in the home country, health problems, or basic marital instability. Long interviews with executives being considered for foreign appointments are perhaps the best means of drawing out potential problems.[24] Of course, the most difficult time will be the first overseas posting. But then many executives will be younger, with their pattern of life less rigidly established.

Repatriation

Unless international assignments are part of a planned cross-pollination program—that is, the process of moving high-potential professionals between foreign affiliates for management-development purposes—the executives who undertake a foreign assignment may experience amplified feelings of insecurity and concern over their future career. As the distance and time away from headquarters increase, an "exile complex" may develop and the manager will begin to ask such questions as: "Will I be forgotten at the home office?" and "Where is my next assignment going to be?" Concern about reentry may arise even if the manager is scheduled to return to the parent company or the home subsidiary.

To reduce the potential dissatisfaction of executives being transferred, the international firm should have a policy for repatriation. Some firms make it clear that those going overseas do so on a career basis and will be returned only if they are asked to take another position in the firm. Other firms argue that even the more successful and experienced managers within the firm will have failures in foreign posts due to factors outside their control, and that these managers are worth retaining despite the cost of repatriation. If the firm always repatriates executives when they wish to return and finds them a post with equally high status in their home company, the cost can be high. Not only are transfer costs large, but the foreign unit they leave must find a replacement with additional transfer costs and lack of continuity in the job. Nor is it always easy to find a job for a returning expatriate at the precise time that the person is ready to return.

The return can produce another collection of problems.[25] The disappearance of the high compensation and benefits that often accompany a foreign assignment can leave executives a long way below their overseas level of living. House prices may have risen so much that they cannot afford to buy a level of housing equal to their peers who stayed at home.

---

[24] See William Alexander, Jr., "Mobil's Four Hour Environmental Interview," *Worldwide P & I Planning*, January–February 1970, pp. 18–27. Alexander reported that Mobil had "only 5 complete failures out of 750 employees placed abroad"; E. J. Karras, Roy F. McMillan, and Thomas R. Williamson, "Interviewing for Cultural Match," *Personnel Journal*, April 1971, pp. 276–79.

[25] William F. Cagney, "Executive Reentry: The Problem of Repatriation," *Personnel Journal*, September 1975, pp. 487–88.

Worse still, they may have been passed in promotion by executives of the same age who stayed home. And if their new job is a corporate post, it is also likely to give them less personal autonomy than they have had in a foreign subsidiary. All these experiences, together with schooling and adjustment problems for a family, can lead to reverse culture shock and the loss of experienced international talent as the executive turns to the job market to solve the problems. Careful counseling and repatriation services such as housing search and financial aid, however, can go a long way toward diluting the shock of reentry and avoiding the costly loss of executive talent it can bring.

INTERNATIONAL COMPENSATION POLICIES

Executive compensation

Compensation policies can produce some of the sharpest international conflicts within an international firm. They can also influence promotion patterns that executives seek within the corporation. Overpaid posts in peripheral foreign activity, for example, might attract good executives away from more important but lower-paid posts in the mainstream of the firm's development or, worse still, discourage them from returning to mainstream jobs later on. International compensation policies, thus, deserve the careful attention of top management.[26]

Why is it difficult to develop a satisfactory international compensation policy? The problem stems from the fact that salary levels and reward expectations differ among countries. Not only do reward patterns differ, but management is also motivated to behave differently. In the average British firm, for example, job performance is rewarded more than potential, and a high level of managerial effort is consequently directed toward job performance. In France, on the other hand, the reward arises more from the educational achievement before joining the firm and more managerial work effort is directed toward recognition outside the firm.[27] It would be a very foolish multinational that attempted to impose reward policies that did not fit national culture and managerial expectations.

A firm that attempts to maintain the same salary levels in all countries will cost itself out of markets where lower salary levels prevail and will not be able to attract managers in high-salary countries. Thus salary rates for roughly comparable jobs will differ between nations. But what policy should be followed when executives are transferred? Executives on the

---

[26] For surveys of the practices and problems of international companies in the compensation field, see *Setting Up an Overseas Compensation Package* (New York: Business International, 1970); Burton W. Teague, *Extra Pay for Service Abroad* (New York: Conference Board, 1975); Marion R. Foote, "Controlling the Cost of International Compensation," *Harvard Business Review*, November–December 1977, pp. 123–32.

[27] David Granick, "International Differences in Executive Reward Systems: Extent, Explanation and Significance," *Columbia Journal of World Business*, Summer 1978, pp. 45–55.

higher rates will not want any reduction when transferred. If they continue to receive their national salary level (plus allowances), they will be higher paid in the new post than local nationals with comparable responsibilities. If executives going to higher-wage areas are remunerated at the high-level rates, problems arise when they return to their home country. Do they revert to their old salary scales?

These fundamental questions of compensation policy have no one answer. The compensation policy is not an end in itself but a means of achieving company objectives. A top executive wanting to achieve an important company goal may be little concerned with the long-term implications of a salary decision required to relocate the managers who can achieve that goal. An effective compensation policy for expatriates, however, should strive to meet the following objectives:

1. Attract and retain employees qualified for overseas service.
2. Facilitate transfers between foreign affiliates and between home-country and foreign affiliates.
3. Establish and maintain a consistent and reasonable relationship between the compensation of all employees of any affiliate, whether posted at home or abroad, and between affiliates.
4. Arrange reasonable compensation, in the various locations, in relation to the practices of leading competitors.

Components of expatriate compensation

Most U.S. companies construct their international compensation policies for expatriates with three components: base salary, premiums to work overseas, and overseas allowances.

Base salaries. Most expatriates are originally hired in their home countries at salaries paid for domestic assignments. When expatriates are transferred cross-nationally, the base salary continues to be that of their home country. The basic underlying philosophy is that, in order to facilitate reassimilation into the home-base company, all personnel are tied to their respective home-country payrolls no matter where they are working.

Problems arise with retention of base salaries, however, when managers are transferred to countries where the going rate for their position is higher than the base salary. Most firms will raise the salary, although some will retain the base salary as a notional reference for repatriation. Few firms, though, will lower salaries to a local level. As a result, expatriates of different nationalities may find themselves working side by side for different compensation, and each of them on a higher rate than local nationals.

Fluctuating exchange rates can also cause problems when base salaries are retained. Expatriates can find themselves with lower incomes if their home currency falls against the currency of the country in which they are posted. The problem becomes more complex if part of the expatriate's salary is paid in the home currency. The home-currency payment is often arranged to minimize tax or exchange control difficulties for an employee who naturally wants savings to be available in the home currency.

Premiums.   Two types of premiums or inducements are commonly used: those to encourage mobility and those to compensate for the hardship of living in an undesirable location. Generally, the places where hardship premiums must be paid are not numerous and have few nonlocal employees. More important is the premium paid to encourage overseas mobility. This premium is usually a fixed percentage of base salary (10 to 20 percent) and is paid for the duration of a foreign assignment.

The disadvantage of continuing the mobility premium payment as long as the employee is assigned abroad is that the employee has no financial incentive to move from one foreign country to another, and that moves back to the parent country usually mean a substantial reduction in income. Several approaches have been adopted by companies to resolve these problems and to increase the mobility of international personnel. One approach is the "premium phase-out," whereby after x years (usually, three to five) the premium is phased out in increments. Another approach is the single payment "mobility premium," which ties the premium to the move instead of to the assignment. In both cases, the premium is paid each time a move is made. If the company's objective is to keep employees abroad for long assignments, it makes sense to pay a continuous premium. On the other hand, if the company is aiming at mobility and rapid movement, it will prefer the single-payment of phase-out premium.

Allowances.   Allowances are intended to assist personnel assigned to foreign posts to continue their normal pattern of living. The most common allowances are for cost of living, housing, education, and tax protection. The two largest items are usually taxes and housing.

With taxes, many international firms follow a policy of deducting taxes at the rate for residents in the employee's home country and then paying the actual tax assessment. Exemptions for income earned while overseas, however, can give a very low home-country tax—or none at all for nationals of some countries who are absentees longer than a specified period. Equalization to the home tax level can thus give a substantial bonus—unless the calculation is made as though the employee were still based at home. Generally speaking, it is only worth equalizing taxes if the differences are more than marginal and the differences in benefits, such as lower medical costs in the United Kingdom, fail to account for most of the variation. If double taxation problems arise for which the firm is responsible through the timing of its transfer, the firm should reduce an employee's tax obligation to that of residence in one country or the other.

In the case of other allowances, most U.S. companies adopt in varying degrees the allowance program of the U.S. Department of State. There are many problems, however, in developing international comparisons of the cost of living on which allowances are based, including changing exchange rates.[28] Also, as companies increase their mix of third-country nationals in foreign posts, the allowance schedules of the parent country become less relevant. The latter problem is handled in some companies by using the United Nations allowance system, which has been designed for professionals of many nationalities stationed throughout the world.

International wage and benefit policies

As they do for managerial salaries, multinationals usually pay the going wage rates for each country in which they operate. To raise all employees to the level of the highest wage country would raise the firm's cost above those of the competition. Furthermore, wage differentials for different jobs and skills differ markedly among countries, and within each country there are major pressures to maintain these differentials.[29] The same arguments apply to employment benefits. The types and levels of benefits that are customary can differ dramatically from country to country. Not only do individual benefits differ for such things as travel, holidays, insurance, and housing, but also the sum total of benefits can range from a small percent of the monetary wage to as much as 200 percent. Many benefits, too, are statutorily imposed. In West Germany a fired worker may get up to 18 months' salary. It would be an economically naive personnel function, therefore, that attempted to standardize wages or all benefits internationally.

This does not mean that a multinational should make no attempt to standardize wages and benefits. First, the firm may adopt the view that certain minimum standards are required for all its employees and that it must be able to meet the cost involved. For example, company liability for work-related injury, or for maintaining retired workers, may be viewed as a supranational responsibility. Second, there may be instances where international standardization may provide the same benefits at lower cost and save problems when employees are transferred between countries. Insurance cover is a case in point, as multinational insurance firms begin to offer worldwide programs.

---

[28] See Henri-J. Ruff and Graham I. Jackson, "Methodological Problems in International Comparisons of the Cost of Living," *Journal of International Business Studies*, Fall 1974, pp. 57–67.

[29] See Christopher Saunders and David Marsden, *Pay Inequalities in the European Communities* (London: Butterworths, 1981).

LABOR RELATIONS AND THE MULTINATIONAL FIRM

Centralized versus decentralized policies

Labor relations patterns differ markedly among countries. The varying patterns reflect the unique cultural, legal, and institutional settings in different nations that affect labor relations through varying social values, psychic needs of workers, the peculiar industrial relations lore, pertinent legal intricacies, and so forth. In recognition of these realities, multinational firms have generally delegated the task of work-force management to the managers of foreign subsidiaries. In the negotiation of agreements, local managers know the local situation in more detail, and as they will have to manage under the terms of the agreement, they should be responsible for its final arrangements. For international management to hold the final authority in negotiations would, moreover, tend to lower the status, authority, and efficiency of the local management.

In the view of one experienced multinational company, the affiliated companies must have continuing responsibility and authority for handling industrial relations. "Without this responsibility it would be extremely difficult, if not impossible, for the affiliates to develop and maintain the kinds of relationships with their employees and employee representatives that are a key factor to the success of their operations."[30] Such a policy assumes, of course, that local managers have been competently trained for administering labor affairs.

There are strong arguments, though, for international management exercising some central coordination.[31] In new units acquired as going concerns, local management experience in labor management may not be extensive nor up to the standard expected of a multinational corporation. Also, agreements made in one country may affect the international plans of the corporation or create precedents for negotiations in other countries. The more unions cooperate across country boundaries, the more need there will be for the firm to present a consistent front. The case for central labor relations coordination is thus strong, but such coordination should involve full participation by local management and infringe as little as possible on local autonomy.

Coordination does not necessarily mean that the international firm should have common policies in all countries. A whole range of elements may differ from environment to environment, leading to different arrangements in each. Any attempt to impose parent-company policies on new situations where they do not fit would be wrong. To have a world-

---

[30] Malcolm L. Denise, "Industrial Relations and the Multinational Corporation: The Ford Experience," in *Bargaining Without Boundaries*, eds. Robert J. Flanagan and Arnold R. Weber (Chicago: University of Chicago Press, 1974), p. 140.

[31] See Duane Kujawa, *International Labor Relations Management in the Automotive Industry* (New York: Praeger Publishers, 1971).

wide policy to avoid unionization simply because this had worked in the parent company would be one example. Many companies that are not unionized in the parent unit have successfully followed unionization in subsidiaries and vice versa.

To fulfill its coordination role and manage its own responsibilities, headquarters staff needs a considerable understanding of national labor-management patterns and a continuing flow of information. Assessments and forecasts of national labor relations conditions are crucial to decisions on the location and expansion of facilities. They are also necessary for evaluating the performance of subsidiaries and local managers. Where transnational sourcing patterns have been developed and a subsidiary in one country relies on a subsidiary in another country as a source of components or as a user of its output, labor relations throughout the system become of direct importance to central management for maintaining its global production strategy.

The union view of the multinationals' power

Perhaps the most pressing reason for headquarters involvement in labor-management affairs has been the move toward internationalization of the labor movement, in itself a direct reaction to the growth of the multinational corporation. Unions around the world have felt increasingly threatened by powerful multinational employers.[32] In essence, their situation parallels that of national governments. They are national institutions facing an international challenge.

Although many multinationals claim that authority in labor relations rests entirely with the local management of the subsidiary, union leaders point out that on all important matters the power rests with central headquarters. Furthermore, central headquarters may be working toward global goals or perhaps home-country goals that override local considerations. The very detailed central regulations issued by Citicorp that repeated for employee relations worldwide Citicorp's U.S. policy of avoiding unions were a case in point.[33]

Bargaining is inevitably more difficult when a union cannot deal directly with final decision makers. Some union leaders complain because the headquarters management is beyond the reach of a local trade union dealing with a subsidiary. Others feel seriously handicapped because of what they describe as a floating and invisible decision center for labor relations matters. Subsidiary companies, so the complaint goes, claim that decisions are made at central headquarters, and central headquarters responds that decisions are made by their subsidiaries.

---

[32] See International Labor Office, *Multinational Enterprises and Social Policy* (Geneva: I.L.O., 1973), pp. 90–91.

[33] See R. Blanpain, *The Badger Case* (Deventer, Netherlands: Kluwer, 1977), Annex VI, Anti-Union Policy by Citibank-Citicorp.

Many multinationals have multiple production sites and in the event of a strike may be able to continue to supply customers from the plants in other countries.[34] Some union leaders believe that many multinationals have adopted dual sourcing policies as a deliberate strategy for reducing the impact of national strikes and for weakening the bargaining position of a national union.[35]

Instead of transferring existing operations to another site, a multinational can also operate an "investment strike" by refusing to invest anything further in a site. Before long, the plant would become obsolete and uneconomic and labor might be forced to lower its demands in order to retain any employment at all.

Finally, unions argue that multinationals have a size advantage not matched by national unions. Their worldwide financial resources enable them to weather strikes and continue to make a profit even though a union may shut down operations completely in one country.

Multinational union organization

Membership of unions is limited to the employees within a particular country. Despite the use of "International" in the title of many unions, no union has the authority to bargain internationally for all the workers of a multinational corporation. Many unions, however, have affiliated themselves with International Trade Secretariats (ITSs), most of which are headquartered in Geneva and structured along trade and industry lines. There are about 20 of these ITSs, examples are the International Federation of Chemical and General Workers' Unions (ICF) and the International Metalworkers' Federation (IMF).

The ITSs are loose federations, leaving their national affiliates with complete autonomy. They generally have limited finances and small staffs. Nevertheless, the ITSs can play a role in helping member unions to deal with multinational corporations. They have developed an array of approaches, including research and dissemination of information about individual multinationals; advice and counseling services in handling particular disputes; international seminars for union leaders on how to deal with multinationals; publicity; organization of support messages and coordination of international action such as refusal to perform "struck work" elsewhere, sympathy strikes, and boycotts.[36]

The collection and dissemination of information on the activities and finances of multinationals and on their wages, benefits, and working

---

[34] Duane Kujawa, ed., *International Labor and Multinational Enterprise* (New York: Praeger Publishers, 1975).

[35] D. C. Hershfield, *The Multinational Union Challenges the Multinational Company* (New York: Conference Board, 1975), p. 3.

[36] David H. Blake, "International Labor and the Regulation of Multinational Corporations: Proposals and Prospects," *San Diego Law Review*, November 1973, pp. 179–205.

conditions has become highly developed. Both the IMF and ICF set up computer banks some years ago. The IMF established data banks at the United Automobile Workers' Union headquarters in Detroit and at I.G. Metall headquarters in Frankfurt, while the ICF built banks at the United Chemical Workers' Union in Akron, Ohio, and at I.G. Chemie-Papier-Keramik in West Germany.[37]

Unions have also joined into international federations outside their industry groupings. The most important are the International Confederation of Free Trade Unions (ICFTU) and the European Trade Union Confederation (ETUC). Both of these organizations have as members national confederations of trade unions. The British Trades Union Congress (TUC), for example, is a member, although the American AFL-CIO withdrew from the ICFTU in 1969. These international organizations serve as forums for discussion of union policies and as pressure groups within the International Labor Organization (ILO), the Organization for Economic Cooperation and Development (OECD), the United Nations, and the European Economic Community (EEC).

In 1975, the ICFTU at its congress in Mexico adopted a "multinational charter" calling for the establishment of a tripartite international agency of government, unions, and business to regulate multinational corporations.[38] Two years later the International Labor Organization, under great pressure from trades unions in Western Europe, approved a draft code regarding multinationals. It is a voluntary code but would require multinationals to engage in collective bargaining, establish grievance procedures, and adopt employment practices that assure job security. Within the EEC, labor representations have resulted in some legally binding requirements. To date, the requirements have not changed the power structure within firms to a major degree although proposals continue to be discussed concerning compulsory bargaining, workers' councils, prohibition on transfer of struck work, and so on.

OECD employment and industrial relations guidelines

The guidelines for multinational corporations issued in 1976 by the Organization of Economic Cooperation and Development included some guidelines on "Employment and Industrial Relations." Although these guidelines are not legally enforceable and were criticized by labor for not going far enough, they have been publicly accepted by leading multinationals. Furthermore, a quasi-legal practice has emerged of governments referring disagreements to the OECD Committee on International Investments and Multinational Enterprises (CIME). The most notable referral was the Badger case. The CIME ruling influenced the parent multina-

---

[37] Norris Willatt, *Multinational Unions* (London: Financial Times, 1974), p. 23.

[38] International Confederation of Free Trade Unions, *Multinational Charter of Trade Union Demands for Legislative Control of Multinational Companies* (Brussels: ICFTU, 1975).

tional, Raytheon, to meet the cost of termination payments to employees in its Badger subsidiary, for which Raytheon claimed it had no liability.[39]

Of the nine guidelines, six seem to strengthen the power of local unions in dealing with changes that have international ramifications. Guidelines 1 and 9 provide for recognition of unions and acceptance of collective bargaining. Guidelines 2 and 3 provide for extending assistance and information to employee representatives including, where appropriate, information on the enterprise as a whole. Guideline 6 requires reasonable notice of layoffs. Guideline 8 specifically provides that, during employment negotiations or employee efforts to organize, the multinational will "not threaten to utilize a capacity to transfer the whole or part of an operating unit from the country concerned." Against this, guidelines 4 and 5 seem to reinforce national differences between employees. Guideline 4 provides that the multinational "observe standards of employment not less favorable than those observed by comparable employers in the host country." And guideline 5 asks that, to the greatest extent practicable, the multinational use, train, and upgrade members of the local labor force.

Prospects for transnational bargaining

Those associated with international labor movements have as an ultimate objective the achievement of transnational bargaining. Unions, however, are basically nationalistic, and strong political and ideological cleavages exist between different national labor movements.[40] If the issue involved concerns the relocation of production activity, there will be a built-in conflict between the interests of the national union losing jobs and the interests of the national union gaining jobs. Furthermore, national governments will not always identify with their own national union.[41] Governments realize that there may come a time when certain jobs should migrate, with their place taken by other trades more appropriate to the changed economic environment. For all these reasons, the achievements from international collaboration by unions are not likely to be very great in the foreseeable future.

When International Trade Secretariats have attempted to introduce multinational bargaining into individual multinationals, they have had only minor successes. The standard procedure is to hold a worldwide "company conference" of national unions representing the company's

---

[39] R. Blanpain, *The Badger Case* (Deventer, Netherlands: Kluwer, 1977).

[40] See Gerard B. J. Bomers and Richard B. Peterson, "Multinational Corporations and Industrial Relations: The Case of West Germany and the Netherlands," *British Journal of Industrial Relations*, March 1977, pp. 45–62.

[41] Franklin R. Root and Bernard Mennis, "How U.S. Multinational Corporations, Unions and Government View Each Other and the Direction of U.S. Policies," *Journal of International Business Studies*, Spring 1976, pp. 17–30.

employees and to establish a company council, after discussing what might be gained through collaboration. The next step is to request a meeting with the central management of the multinational to discuss problems of mutual interest. Most multinationals have turned down such requests, claiming that labor matters are delegated to national management. Those multinationals that have cooperated at this stage, however, have been reluctant to agree to future meetings, and ITS efforts have tended to dissolve after a while.[42]

INDUSTRIAL DEMOCRACY AND THE MULTINATIONAL

The industrial democracy movement is essentially a European development and has focused largely on worker participation in management through representation on boards and compulsory negotiation with works councils. There have also been some attempts to promote legislation requiring employee profit sharing and even employee ownership. But these attempts have not been very successful to date.[43] Worker participation, or codetermination, poses a particular threat for multinationals because it has emerged as a series of national movements that give national workers a voice on local subsidiary boards—as well as on parent boards of multinationals based locally.

The country with the most experience of employee representation on boards is Germany. The representation takes place under three laws. A 1951 law applies to the coal, iron, and steel sector and provides for employee representatives equal in number and power to owner representatives. The following year the concept was extended to all other sectors, requiring firms with over 500 employees to appoint one third of the board as employee representatives. For companies with over 2,000 employees, these provisions were expanded in 1976 to give the employees one half of the board appointments. The chairman, however, who is an owner representative, has two votes in the event of a tie. The unions sponsoring the 1976 act had hoped for absolute parity in voting, for the union to be given the right to appoint all the employee directors, and for employee directors to be given a veto right in approving the company's labor director. Except for power to appoint a minority of the employee directors, these aims were not met. It is unlikely, too, that this process of codetermination will go much farther for some time, given the opposition that resulted from this attempt.

The board of directors, or Aufsichtsrat, has reporting to it a managing board or Vorstand responsible for the operations. No member of the

---

[42] See Herbert R. Northrup and Richard L. Rowan, "Multinational Union-Management Consultation: The European Experience," *International Labor Review*, September–October 1977.

[43] Thomas N. Gladwin and Ingo Walter, *Multinationals under Fire* (New York: John Wiley & Sons, 1980), pp. 391–2.

Vorstand may sit on the Aufsichtsrat, which may specify what matters are reserved for its own decision. West German companies report that employee membership on the Aufsichtsrat does not prevent management from working effectively. In fact, the efforts taken to communicate with employee representatives and through them to the workforce have tended to improve workforce relationships and to loosen union control somewhat (see Box 23–1).

Box 23–1

The Rosenthal experience

"We found that the major argument against codetermination—that it would lessen management's decision-making capability—was wrong. The fact that I had to explain to employee board members why we were doing something actually sometimes improved decisions. And sometimes decisions were carried through much more easily from the workers' side than they otherwise might have been."

These were the words of Philip Rosenthal, head of Rosenthal AG of Selb West Germany. Rosenthal was one of the first in Germany to put workers on its board, even before the legal requirement to do so. The firm also led in encouraging worker ownership by distributing shares instead of cash bonuses. Currently 90 percent of Rosenthal's 2,000-plus German employees own shares. With average individual holdings worth $1,700, workers as a group control 10 percent of the stock, compared with 4.5 percent held by the Rosenthal family.

Rosenthal reported: "We have less illness, fewer strikes, less trouble, and more contribution from our workers than the average."

Rosenthal's market share increased from 12.9 percent to 19.6 percent in fine china and from zero to 7 percent in glassware. At the same time it had become the largest producer in Europe of industrial ceramics and an important producer of furniture. Best of all, in Rosenthal's view, were the company's continuing productivity gains. From 1974 to 1979, productivity gains averaged 12 percent a year. In the past two years they averaged 7 percent a year.

Rosenthal admitted that much of the gain was due to an extensive plant modernization, but added: "Without employee cooperation, the modernization program could not have been so successful."

Source: Excerpted from Jean A. Briggs, "Is This an Answer?", *Forbes*, June 7, 1982, pp. 52–55.

For multinationals, the dangers come from several directions. First, the appointments to be filled by the unions provide a method for those believing in international bargaining to obtain appointments actually within the multinationals. Several large multinationals have had international trade unionists selected for board posts in this way. Charles Levinson, secretary general of the ICF and a vociferous critic of multinationals, was nominated for the Aufsichtsrat of the German Du Pont affiliate.[44]

---

[44] "The Trade Union Jet Set," *The Economist*, February 15, 1977, p. 89.

Second, the Aufsichtsrat interposes a group with strongly national interests between the subsidiary operating management and the parent company. It is possible that this subsidiary board could oppose head-office wishes on the remittance of funds for investment elsewhere. Since the Aufsichtsrat usually determines management appointments and salaries, Vorstand members may be less inclined to upset the employee directors by taking obvious sides—hence limiting the power of the parent management. The parent management may also find it difficult to remove intransigent executives from the subsidiary.[45] Third, for multinationals with employee directors on the parent-company board it is likely that the pattern of transferring production to foreign, lower-cost sites as the product matures will be more severely questioned. The decision of Volkswagen to build its American plant was delayed several years by just this problem.[46]

Other European countries have followed Germany. Legislation on employee directors exists in Austria, Sweden, Denmark, and Norway, and in the Netherlands works councils have the right to nominate and to veto candidates for the board. At the EEC level, a proposed directive requiring employee board representation has been circulated but it appears to have lost momentum with the addition of Britain and Greece to the Community. Britain itself rejected the suggestions of the 1977 Bullock report, which proposed employee directors, and the country generally seems to be moving away from union power.

In some ways, the legislation in various European countries concerning the powers of works councils poses a stronger threat to multinational flexibility than the legislation on employee board membership. In no case have the employees been given absolute voting power on boards, but in several countries not only has consultation with works councils been made compulsory, but it has also been required that agreement be reached. In the Netherlands, for instance, legislation came into force in 1979 requiring employee works council agreement on wages and remuneration, hiring and dismissal, promotion, training, personnel rating, welfare services, and grievance procedures.[47] Debate over the future role of works councils continues throughout Europe and a creeping expansion of their powers seems likely to continue. There is some indication, however, that national union power is not expanding at this level and that nonunion membership of works councils could expand. Whether or not unions dominate, the concerns of works councils will continue to be focused on detailed and immediate issues and will take a great deal of

---

[45] George S. McIsaac and Hubert Henzler, "Codetermination: A Hidden Noose for MNC's," *Columbia Journal of World Business*, Winter 1974, p. 70.

[46] Ibid., p. 70.

[47] Thomas Kennedy, *European Labor Relations* (Lexington, Mass.: D. C. Heath, 1980), pp. 380–84.

managerial time. Standard multinational policies are likely to be honored by their breach when local works councils enter the picture.

TREATMENT OF DISADVANTAGED GROUPS

Generally speaking, pressure to change policies to help disadvantaged groups is limited to a concern for those within the confines of a single nation. Concern for inequality tends to be limited by a more dominant principle of national identity. Hence those activating for positive discrimination in favor of women in the United States would not usually concern themselves with positive discrimination in favor of Korean women workers over more highly paid U.S. women workers. See the example in Box 23–2.

In a few cases, general concern for disadvantaged groups crosses national boundaries. In these cases, the multinational is the obvious target for pressure from those concerned with the plight of the disadvantaged in some other country. The most outstanding case to date has been pressure on multinationals to mitigate the effects of apartheid in South Africa. U.S. activist groups, however, have also raised questions about labor practices followed by such multinationals as Gulf & Western in the Dominican Republic, Del Monte in the Philippines, United Brands and Castle & Cook in Central America, Coca-Cola in Guatemala, and Motorola in South Korea.[48]

The policy of separate and unequal treatment for the black South African is openly fostered by the South African government. Pressure brought to bear on foreign multinationals is thus aimed at breaking the intent of the local government, if not the actual law. Multinationals often welcome such pressure as it reinforces their case against the local situation. On the other hand, if the pressure forces them to withdraw and changes the local situation little, it may be the disadvantaged workers themselves who suffer most.

The approach most widely adopted by activists has been to ask as shareholders for disclosure of the multinational's employment and labor relations practices. Several considerations lie behind this approach. First, motions for disclosure are more readily passed than shareholder directives. Second, the process of collecting information focuses management attention on the practices. Third, the threat of disclosure provides a powerful incentive to change practices that the firm would not be proud to publicize. And, last, the information itself can provide the basis for specific pressures.

Partly as a result of a disclosure campaign mounted by a coalition of Protestant denominations in the United States (the Church Project on U.S. Investments in South Africa) between 1972 and 1976, leading U.S. mul-

---

[48] Gladwin and Walter, *Multinationals under Fire*, pp. 414–16.

Box 23–2

Women scorned

A dozen women employees of Sumitomo's New York subsidiary, Sumitomo Shoji America Inc, have been trying to get the courts to rule that the Japanese trading company has been discriminating illegally against women and non-Japanese. Sumitomo claims that it is guaranteed freedom to hire whom it likes by the 1952 Japan-American trade treaty. At American insistence, the treaty allowed American and Japanese companies to hire "technical experts, executive personnel and other specialists of their choice" in the other country's territory. On April 26, the Supreme Court will hear arguments on Sumitomo's claim; if the Japanese firm loses, the case will go back to the lower courts for a full trial.

The 12 women include 11 American citizens and 1 Japanese. They argue:

Sumitomo hires only men—and Japanese men at that—to fill important jobs in the company.

Sumitomo's Japanese parent is covered by the treaty, but its American subsidiary is not.

Even if Sumitomo Shoji America Inc. is covered by the 1952 treaty, it is still not entitled to break American law in its hiring practices. The treaty was meant to protect foreign firms against restrictive hiring rules which might discriminate against them, not to exempt them from laws which apply to local companies.

Sumitomo cannot claim that familiarity with Japanese language and culture, or the ability to deal with Japanese male executives, is an occupational qualification, and thus legitimate grounds for breaking the civil rights acts. Japanese nationals, say Sumitomo's critics, are not the only people familiar with Japanese culture, and cultural bias is no excuse for discrimination.

Such discrimination, however, lies at the heart of Japanese hiring practices. Women are rarely appointed to executive jobs in Japan, on the assumption that they will leave as soon as they marry. And Japan's trading houses, which are expanding rapidly overseas, rely heavily on the homogeneity of outlook of the Japanese men they place in top jobs abroad. Japanese manufacturing firms, by contrast, often hire foreigners for senior jobs in their overseas plants.

Next twist: Japanese women working for American firms in Japan claim that their employers, adapting to local habits, have drifted back into the sex-discrimination now outlawed at home.

Source: Extracted from *The Economist*, April 24, 1982.

---

tinationals grouped together in 1977 to affirm a set of six operating principles for South Africa. The "Sullivan Principles" are shown in Figure 23–1. They were named after the Reverend Leon Sullivan, an American black minister, who as a board member of General Motors led the campaign. The movement attracted considerable criticism as avoiding the basic political issue of discrimination and failing to include recognition of

Figure 23–1

The Sullivan principles for multinationals' operations in South Africa

1. Nonsegregation of the races in all eating, comfort, and work facilities.
2. Equal and fair employment practices for all employees.
3. Equal pay for all employees doing equal or comparable work for the same period of time.
4. Initiation and development of training programs that will prepare, in substantial numbers, blacks and other nonwhites for supervisory, administrative, clerical, and technical jobs.
5. Increasing the number of blacks and other nonwhites in management and supervisory positions.
6. Improving the quality of employees' lives outside the work environment in such areas as housing, transportation, schooling, recreation, and health facilities.

We agree to further implement these principles. Where implementation requires a modification of existing South African working conditions, we will seek such modification through appropriate channels.

We believe that the implementation of the foregoing principles is consistent with respect for human dignity and will contribute greatly to the general economic welfare of all the people of South Africa.

black trade unions with full collective bargaining.[49] Later that year a voluntary code adopted by the EEC countries did include recognition of black unions and provided for collective bargaining.[50] For both the U.S. principles and the EEC code, however, conformance by the relevant multinationals has not been high.[51]

SUMMARY

In international business, as in most other activities, human resources are the critical elements. The peculiar problem that international firms face is that people are usually raised, educated, and rewarded in one culture, whereas international business management requires cross-cultural communication, coordination, and supervision. The challenge is to develop managers who can think globally or at least biculturally.

The multinational firm has various options in choosing a policy that will develop international managers with this ability. It can follow a policy of hiring local nationals to manage its subsidiaries, but it will then have to rely on training programs to internationalize its personnel. It will have to invest in training programs to prepare executives and their fami-

[49] Timothy Smith, "Whitewash for Apartheid from Twelve U.S. Firms," *Business and Society Review*, Summer 1977, pp. 59–60.

[50] "The European Community and South Africa," *Commission of the European Communities: Information*, November 1977, pp. 16–17.

[51] "Why Pretoria Is Giving Black Workers a Break," *Business Week*, June 18, 1979, p. 130; and "Black Wages," *The Economist*, February 17, 1979, p. 92.

lies for cross-national transfers. One of the most perplexing problems faced by multinational companies has been the matter of compensation policies, but with increasing experience most companies have been able to work out reasonably satisfactory solutions even for handling cross-national transfers.

The management of labor relations must necessarily be delegated largely to local management because of innumerable local variations in worker attitudes, labor union roles, and the degree of governmental participation in labor-management affairs. However, the growing internationalization of the labor movement, in response to a perceived threat from the multinational enterprise, has tended to bring headquarters management increasingly into the formulation and implementation of labor strategies, and is likely to continue to do so in the future.

EXERCISES AND DISCUSSION QUESTIONS

1. What are the advantages and limitations of a policy that favors hiring nationals as managers of subsidiaries?

2. Many international companies recruit potential managers for their home-country domestic operations and later look to this staff for their international managers, particularly at headquarters. Under what conditions, if any, would you advise a company to do specialized outside recruiting for its international management personnel?

3. Interview an American executive who has recently returned from a foreign posting. Record and analyze the executive's generalizations about the foreign employees with whom he or she worked. Or interview the wife of such an executive and record and analyze her experience in adjusting to life in the foreign country.

4. You have been asked to design an orientation program for personnel being transferred on a two-year assignment to a less developed country (you select the country). The program must be completed by the participants in three weeks of full-time study. What are the several most important subjects that should be included in the program and why?

5. How would the local labor situation affect your location decision for a new foreign plant that produced a product whose characteristics or technology would have to change rapidly to meet competitive conditions?

6. How would you answer the fear of labor unions that the multinational corporation can easily transfer its operations to a different country if it feels that the demands of labor unions in a specific area of operations are "unreasonable"?

7. The OECD guidelines for multinational enterprises with regard to employment and industrial relations state:

   Enterprises should, within the framework of law, regulations and prevailing labor relations and employment practices, in each of the countries in which they operate,

    1)   respect the right of their employees, to be represented by trade unions
. . . and engage in constructive negotiations . . . with a view to reaching agreements on employment conditions.

What would you advise an American corporation that has to date actively opposed unions in the United States? Would your advice differ for (a) multiple unions in the United Kingdom, or (b) fully representative black unions in South Africa?

8. "In the United States, the industrial democracy idea has been considered both by management and organized labor to be fundamentally inferior to hard-nosed profit-maximizing behavior of management coupled with equally hard-nosed and adversary collective bargaining by labor." Do you agree with this statement? Why or why not? How would you advise an American multinational in the consumer electrical goods field to organize the appointments to the Aufsichtsrat and Vorstand of its German manufacturing subsidiary?

PART SIX

Emerging issues

All of our decisions are about the future.
All of our knowledge is about the past.

Chapter 24

Looking into the future

Astrologers, mystics, chiromancers (palmists), prophets, psychics, haruspices (diviners from the entrails of animals), and other kinds of seers traditionally have had a corner on forecasting the future. Even today these "professionals" without a solid grounding in the field they forecast are by far the most numerous of all those who divine the future. The situation is not likely to change, and the international manager should be very careful to recognize the role of astrology that is so prevalent in business and government decision making in many societies.

In recent decades, however, new competition has emerged in the futures field. It comes from the "Futures Movement," which has been directed toward making forecasting less of an art and more of a science.[1]

---

[1] See Wayne I. Boucher, *The Study of the Future: An Agenda for Research* (Washington, D.C.: National Science Foundation, July 1977).

Futures forecasting has become a growth industry in which many progressive business and consulting firms have become well established.

Forecasting the future is a brave—and hazardous—undertaking, unless the forecast is sufficiently in the future so that its accuracy cannot be verified during the lifetime of the forecaster. A plethora of erroneous forecasts can be cited in the areas of economics, business, and technology. To mention just one example in the international business field, in a famous book published in 1968 the distinguished French journalist-politician, J. J. Servan-Schreiber, made the following forecast:

> Fifteen years from now it is quite possible that the world's third greatest industrial power, just after the United States and Russia, will not be Europe, but *American industry in Europe.*[2]

Contrast this forecast with the situation in 1983 when Japan had become the second largest industrial power, the output of the European Community had matched that of the United States, and many Americans were concerned about the rapidly expanding size of the foreign-owned industry sector in the United States.

The numerous forecasting failures may have discredited the forecasters but not the value of "futures studies." It should be accepted that none of us can foresee the future. Yet business firms, governments, and others have discovered great value in systematically formulating "alternative future scenarios" and doing advance thinking on actions to be undertaken as any of the alternatives become future realities.

As an introduction to futures studies, this chapter will discuss the principal methodologies being used and make reference to several major futures studies recently published. Some of the forecasts of direct relevance to international business will be summarized and their implications to the international manager will be noted.

FUTURES METHODOLOGIES

Familiarity with the principal forecasting techniques helps to evaluate the many forecasts being made. The four most widely used techniques are as follows:[3]

1. Extrapolation: projecting historical trends.
2. Econometric models: such as input-output.
3. Delphi: using informed judgment.
4. Alternative futures scenarios.

---

[2] J. J. Servan-Schreiber, *The American Challenge* (New York: Atheneum Publishers, 1968), p. 3.

[3] See S. Encel, P. K. Marstrand, and W. Page, eds., *The Art of Anticipation: Values and Methods in Forecasting* (London: Martin Robinson, 1975), chap. 8, pp. 63–91, C. W. J. Granger, *Forecasting in Business and Economics* (New York: Academic Press, 1979).

The extrapolation method consists essentially of extending historical trends into the future. Extrapolation can be based on simple or complex mathematical relationships, such as regression analysis and envelope curves. The core assumption of extrapolation is that a mathematical relationship existing between two parameters in the past will hold for the period of the forecast. The method can be useful for short time periods and for relatively stable situations. It can be seriously defective for situations where significant structural changes are occurring. Many electric power utilities, for example, have relied on extrapolation methods to forecast future power demand and the need for expansion of facilities. With the dramatic escalation of energy prices in the 1970s and the widespread adoption of energy conservation that followed, most of the firms in the United States found themselves in the 1980s with substantial and expensive excess capacity.

The econometric models are of various types. They are more complex and can handle changing relationships between parameters. They can be regarded as an analytic tool as well as a forecasting technique. Econometric models are systems of simultaneous regression equations used primarily for forecasting macroseries such as gross national product, consumption, investment, and so on. An interesting and significant example of the use of an econometric model for futures study is the United Nations report prepared under the direction of Wassily Leontief, who received the Nobel prize for his work on input-output techniques.[4] The objective of the study was to investigate the interrelationships between future economic growth and prospective economic issues, including the availability of natural resources and measures needed to close the income gap between the advanced and the developing countries.

The Delphi Approach is commonly used in forecasting future technological developments. It involves a panel of experts in a given field who answer a series of questionnaires about situations to be forecasted. The individual assessments are combined and returned to the participants, who are asked to respond once more with the benefit of the feedback. The process continues until a consensus is reached or the dispersion of predictions no longer narrows. The basic assumption of the method is that useful forecasts lie hidden away in the collective subjectivity of a group of people knowledgeable in the area of interest.

The Rand Corporation pioneered with the Delphi method in a 1964 forecast of important scientific breakthroughs expected in the next 30 years or so.[5] About two thirds of the events forecasted to occur by 1970 had actually occurred by then. But more important, perhaps, many sci-

---

[4] Wassily Leontief et al., *The Future of the World Economy* (New York: Oxford University Press, 1977).

[5] See H. Sackman, *Delphi Assessment: Expert Opinion, Forecasting and Group Process* (Santa Monica, Calif.: Rand Corporation, April 1974).

entific breakthroughs had occurred that were not included in the original forecast.

The technique of alternative scenarios has become the most popular methodology. It attempts to identify possible rather than predicted paths into the future. It asks the question of how might the hypothetical situations come about, and it attempts to identify the alternatives for various actors to prevent, divert, or facilitate the process. Herman Kahn and the Hudson Institute have been practitioners of the alternative scenario methodology. In a recent world forecast, Kahn works with three major scenarios: world A or a "surprise-free" scenario, world B—a high-growth scenario, and world C—a low-growth scenario.[6]

The key issue in scenario methodologies is the plausibility of the intuitively selected scenarios. To the extent that scenarios open up new horizons to decision makers and provide a broader framework within which to make decisions, they are a valuable futures methodology. Scenarios may also have an advantage over many other techniques, particularly those involving mathematical methods, in their ability to communicate ideas about the future.

SOME MAJOR FUTURES STUDIES

A landmark study in the futures field was the *Limits to Growth* report sponsored by the Club of Rome and published in 1972.[7] The club is a private association of about 100 individuals in different countries. The *Limits to Growth* study made forecasts, based on a computer model of the world, which concluded that the future growth of the world would be severely constrained by shortages of raw materials. The study has been criticized on several accounts. The Club of Rome took several of these criticisms into account and has subsequently sponsored reports that reach different and less apocalyptic conclusions.

The government of Sweden established a Secretariat for Future Studies in 1973 that has been working on a specific project basis and making its studies available to the government and the public. Such projects include futures studies on energy, resources and raw materials, working life in the future, and agricultural production and food supply.

Probably the most comprehensive and relevant studies for international business are the *Interfutures* study of the OECD[8] and the *Global 2000 Report*, published by the U.S. government in 1980.[9] The OECD study

---

[6] Herman Kahn, *World Economic Development: 1979 and Beyond* (Boulder, Colo.: Westview Press, 1979).

[7] D. Meadows et al., *The Limits to Growth* (New York: Universe Books, 1972).

[8] Organization for Economic Cooperation and Development, *Interfutures*, (Paris, 1979).

[9] Council on Environmental Quality and the Department of State, *The Global 2000 Report to the President: Entering the Twenty-First Century*, in three volumes (Washington, D.C.: U.S. Government Printing Office, 1980).

has a special focus on the future development relationships of the advanced industrial societies and the developing countries. It is an intergovernmental study and it uses the alternative scenario methodology. It analyzes the physical limits to growth, trade patterns, industrialization trends, and technological possibilities, and makes alternative forecasts in each of these fields.

The Global 2000 Report places a heavy emphasis on environmental problems and attempts to discover the long-term implications of world trends in population, natural resources, and economic growth within this context.

SOME FORECASTS OF THE INTERNATIONAL ENVIRONMENT

The various futures studies deal mainly with economic trends and all are concerned with population, resources, and food. Somewhat surprisingly, the various forecasts in these areas do not differ markedly.

Population

The human population of the earth probably passed the 4.3 billion mark in 1979. The "probably" is used because good population estimates are still not available for some countries. For the year 2000, current medium projections range from 5.9 to 6.4 billion. At present and projected growth rates, the world's population would reach 10 billion by 2030. The rate of growth to the year 2000 is expected to slow only marginally, from 1.8 percent a year to 1.7 percent. In terms of sheer numbers, the world will be adding 100 million people annually in the year 2000 as compared to 75 million annually in 1975.

The striking feature of the forecasts is that 90 percent of the growth will occur in the poorest countries. By the year 2000, an estimated 79 percent of the world population will be living in the less developed regions.

Urbanization is projected to continue apace with over 50 percent of the world's population living in towns and cities by the year 2000, up from 39 percent in 1975. The concentration expected in the larger cities is dramatic. In 1950, only one city (Greater Buenos Aires) in the less developed countries had a population of over 5 million. By the year 2000, the developing world will have about 40 cities of this size and the developed world only 12. Eighteen cities in developing countries are expected to have more than 10 million inhabitants. One at least—Mexico City—may have three times that number. Calcutta will approach 20 million. Greater Bombay, Greater Cairo, Jakarta, and Seoul are all expected to be in the 15 to 20 million range.

Natural resources

The future adequacy of natural resources has been a controversial issue in futures forecasting. Will physical limits on the availability of resources cause nations to halt or slow down their growth? This likelihood was forecast by the Club of Rome study previously mentioned.

The general response to the question in the United Nations' *Future of the World Economy* study is "that mineral resource endowment is generally adequate to support world economic development at relatively high rates but that these resources will most probably become more expensive to extract as the century moves towards its conclusion."[10] The *Global 2000* study reaches a somewhat more pessimistic conclusion. It notes that the world's finite fuel resources are theoretically sufficient but that they are not evenly distributed. Nonfuel mineral resources appear sufficient, but further discoveries and investments will be required to maintain reserves. The study also notes that regional water resource shortages will become severe and that significant losses of world forests will continue over the next several decades.

All of the natural resources studies, of course, recognize that important factors are the extent to which recycling occurs, technological developments in minerals exploration and production, and market prices as they affect the economics of utilizing low-quality reserves. In addition, a great unknown is the future availability of resources from the oceans.

Food

The future adequacy of food production has persisted as a matter of great global concern, particularly for the developing countries. This concern is supported by forecasts such as those of the World Bank that the number of malnourished people in the LDCs could rise from 400 to 600 million in the mid-1970s to 1.3 billion in 2000.[11]

At the same time, the various future studies are in general agreement that the physical and economic potential for eliminating hunger and malnutrition over the next several decades exists.[12] With improved policies and considerable investment, food production could be substantially increased, possibly from an annual rate of growth of 2.7 up to 3.7 percent a year. The Food and Agriculture Organization of the United Nations has concluded that improvement is possible even for Africa, where food production has been increasing at only 2 percent a year while population is rising at 3 percent a year. In a global sense, the world will

---

[10] Ibid., p. 6.

[11] See *Global 2000*, chap. 13, for original citation

[12] See Selwyn Enzer, Richard Drobnick, and Steven Alter, *Neither Feast nor Famine* (Lexington, Mass.: Lexington Books, 1978); see also United Nations World Food Council, *Toward a World without Hunger*, vol. 3 (Rome, March 23, 1979).

not "run out" of potentially arable land or other agricultural resources by the year 2000.

Whether there will be a food crisis will depend, according to the futures studies, on how specific scientific, environmental, and socioeconomic threats and opportunities are met. In particular, the developing countries will have to give higher priority in their development programs to the food sector. Furthermore, the distribution of income in many of the poor countries will have to change in order to give sectors of the population access to available food supplies.

Technology

All these facets of the future are intertwined, and technology especially so. It is generally agreed that the decades since the end of World War II have been an unusually prolific period of technological development. The main futures question is whether the world has moved into a new cycle in which the rate of technological innovation will slow down. Most of the forecasters are saying "No." The OECD *Interfutures* study, for example, concludes that "up to the end of the century, a substantial slowdown of growth due to lack of technological innovation seems unlikely. Nor does it seem that in the longer term the capacity for scientific discovery or even technological potential as such will set limits to growth. The obstacles, if any, will be due to the interaction between science, technology and society."[13]

What are the major technological developments that might be expected? The OECD study emphasizes four major areas of future technological innovation: (1) electronics, including the revolution in microprocessing, lasers, computers, robotics, and telecommunications, (2) ocean resources, (3) new energy forms, and (4) bioindustry technology.

Technological innovations in electronics, microprocessing, and communications are almost certain to make a major leap forward. These developments are revolutionizing the conditions for automating many industries, especially by removing many technical obstacles to the decentralized management of the production process. Patterns of consumption are being transformed through the spread of many kinds of computerized products and services. The economic organization of the service industries is being changed through the emergence of teleprocessing, a combination of telecommunications and data processing.[14]

The area of bioindustry technology has begun to receive major attention. According to some experts, biology will have as much impact on industry in the next century as chemistry and physics did in the present

---

[13] Organization for Economic Cooperation and Development, *Interfutures* (Paris, 1979), p. 113.

[14] See, for example, *Communications and the Future* (Bethesda, Md.: World Future Society, 1982).

century. The activity of living microorganisms might partly or wholly replace some physical-chemical processes. New products may emerge connected with the utilization of certain properties of microorganisms. Developments in bioindustry technology will affect such fields as energy, animal feed, agriculture, chemistry, and pharmacy.

SOME FORECASTS OF ECONOMIC TRENDS

The growing interdependence of the world economy is the most fundamental feature of future economic patterns. Any forecast of economic trends for the advanced industrialized nations depends on what happens in the low- and middle-income countries, and vice versa. In recognition of this interdependence, the various global economic forecasts present several scenarios that differ in their assumptions as to the relations between the advanced industrialized countries and the so-called Third World. The OECD forecast, for example, has four scenarios where the assumptions range from collegial relationships to north-south confrontation.

All the OECD scenarios, and those of Herman Kahn, project a slower future growth rate for the advanced countries than for the middle- and low-income countries. In 1975, the OECD countries accounted for 62 percent of world GNP. This share is projected to decline to between 47 and 53 percent by the year 2000. The counterpart to this trend is that the less developed countries are projected to increase their share of world GNP from 22 percent in 1975 to between 31 and 33 percent in the year 2000. The Eastern European socialist countries are projected to expand economically at a rate slightly above the world average and to increase their share of GNP from 16 to a maximum of 20 percent over the period from 1975 to 2000.[15] As Kahn observes, the period of slower growth for the advanced industrialized countries seems likely to persist for many years and to have important implications for social change.[16]

The various economic forecasts have profound importance for international business because they suggest the likely geographical patterns for future business activity. The forecasts present considerable detailed analysis by specific countries as well as by broad regions and merit the detailed attention of international managers.

Future trade patterns

What are the likely scenarios for world trade? The big markets of the world will continue to be the industrialized countries, even though growth rates are expected to slow down in these markets. But even in the

---

[15] Organization for Economic Cooperation and Development, *Interfutures*, Table 21, p. 29.

[16] Kahn, *World Economic Development*, p. 182.

various slow-growth scenarios, the exports of manufactured goods from developing countries to these markets are projected to continue increasing. The big uncertainty is the issue of protectionism. This, in turn, depends on the ability and willingness of the industrialized countries to adjust their economic structure to permit the more efficient production from the developing countries to enter their markets.

A deterrent to growing protectionism may be the matter of economic interdependence. More than one third of the exports of such nations as the United States and Japan have been going to the nonsocialist "middle-income" countries, other than the big oil-producing countries. And this market has been growing rapidly. Protectionist measures that reduce the export possibilities for the middle-income countries will also reduce their potential for importing. Under all of the scenarios, trade among the developing countries (south-south trade) is projected to increase significantly.

Future direct investment patterns

International direct investment and the multinationals are an important aspect of growing interdependency and future growth patterns. The extent to which the rapid growth rates of foreign investment will continue into the future is uncertain. A number of factors can support continued rapid expansion by the multinationals. Large expansion possibilities exist in the developing countries, and many of the LDCs have become more receptive to foreign investment. Also, a number of companies have developed momentum by learning how to operate worldwide, and they are looking for new opportunities to do so. Still another factor may be the increasing importance of technology, marketing skills, and management know-how—areas in which the multinationals have considerable competence.

The nationality mix of the multinationals will continue to change. The dominant position long held by the American multinationals will most likely continue to erode with the more rapid expansion of European and Japanese multinationals. The Eastern European socialist countries may become more significant in foreign production, and third-world multinationals are almost certain to grow in importance.

The target areas, or host countries, for foreign direct investment can also be expected to change. The United States will probably continue to receive massive foreign investments. In general, however, the middle- and low-income countries are likely to attract an increased share of direct investment. Growth trends in the industrialized countries are projected to taper off. Furthermore, foreign investment has reached a stage of saturation in most industrialized nations. As the multinationals have an inner drive to expand, the developing countries as well as mainland China and Eastern Europe become important expansion frontier areas.

An important center of dynamism for trade and investment is likely to be the Pacific Basin countries.

The industries in which foreign investment may expand most rapidly are manufacturing and agriculture, with raw material investments decreasing in importance. The manufacturing sectors in which the multinationals from the industrialized countries are projected to expand are the high-technology areas such as communications, photography, computers, and large electrical and other machinery. The third-world multinationals are likely to concentrate on products that have become standardized, such as textiles, and on areas where they have developed technology advantages such as tropical agriculture and construction.

THE INTERNATIONAL ENVIRONMENT FOR BUSINESS

Institutional and policy trends at the international and national levels, as well as economic forces, shape the future international environment for business. Although alternative future scenarios are difficult to postulate, a number of key areas can be identified where changes of major significance to international business are evolving.

The international level

As of the early 1980s, an institutional gap still existed for dealing with issues related to international direct investment and multinational enterprises. Pressures to fill this gap are most likely to continue, with the outcome quite uncertain. At the same time, many existing international institutions are extending their programs to handle problems that impact on international business. In particular, the demands for a New International Economic Order have major implications for international business patterns.[17]

A few examples can be cited of actions by existing international institutions that affect international business. In the health field, the World Health Organization has proved to be an effective forum for establishing a worldwide code to restrict the marketing of infant formula in third-world nations. In the area of international transfers of technology, UNCTAD continues its efforts to get agreement on a comprehensive code of conduct that is directed mainly to the activities of multinational enterprises. Although created to deal with international trade issues, GATT has been forced to move cautiously into the area of international direct investment because of complaints by member countries that other parties to the agreement have established restrictions on investment through the so-called performance requirements. These requirements, such as requiring

---

[17] See Nathaniel H. Leff, "Multinationals in a Hostile World," *Wharton Magazine,* Spring 1978, pp. 21–29.

certain degrees of local content in products manufactured by foreign firms, are alleged to be a trade restriction.

The issues exist. So too does the need for an international institutional mechanism for handling the problems related to international business. In the absence of an appropriate forum for dealing comprehensively with international business issues, other institutions will be called upon to resolve conflicts. The difficulties inherent in reaching international agreement on a new institution, however, are dramatized by the complex and extended negotiations that have taken place in the area of the ocean's resources.

The importance for international business of the development gap and the demands for a New International Economic Order cannot be overstressed. Almost 80 percent of the world's population by the year 2000 will be located in the developing countries. Business performance in these countries will depend upon the success achieved in raising the incomes (and purchasing power) of this vast population. Whatever contribution international business firms can make directly, or through their influence on the development assistance programs of their home countries, toward improving economic levels in these areas can be both good international citizenship and good international business.

Another issue at the international level that should not be overlooked is the possibility of accelerated moves toward military disarmament. As of the early 1980s, global pressures for disarmament have become extremely strong. To the extent that the "peace movement" is successful, patterns of international trade and production will change. International trade in arms, as noted in an earlier chapter, has been large and growing. As arms producers, many multinationals will be affected. Military goods have become high-technology products and many multinationals in aircraft, electronics, communications, chemicals, and so on have a significant share of their production in military goods.

The national level

At the national level, the general environment for multinational firms is certain to be one of increased and more sophisticated national controls. The developing countries in particular have become better informed on international business and more experienced in developing controls to increase national benefits. The LDCs will give great emphasis to employment benefits and the transfer of technology. There will also be continued pressure for joint ventures that share ownership with nationals and for licensing and turnkey projects in lieu of foreign-owned production facilities.

The concern for appropriate technology and for location of R&D facilities in host countries will continue unabated. Given the future importance of the developing countries, more multinationals are likely to respond to these pressures and will benefit accordingly. New products or adaptations of present products that can serve the vast markets of the Third World could open up valuable business opportunities.

A good possibility exists that the control environments in many countries may shift from a regulatory to an incentive approach—to use of a carrot rather than a stick. In this respect, the trend may follow the example of several developing countries that have been successful in attracting foreign direct investment and in influencing foreign firms to make major contributions toward national development goals. Such efforts have often succeeded because the host countries recognize that business firms can only undertake in the longer term what is profitable, and have accordingly offered profit incentives to influence business patterns.

The importance of government-owned enterprises is likely to continue and even to expand. The trend is mixed, however, with the United Kingdom moving toward denationalization and France moving toward nationalization. In the case of France and other countries, government enterprises have expanded internationally and become successful multinational enterprises.

INTERNATIONAL MANAGEMENT IN THE FUTURE

What does the future hold for the multinational enterprise and the international manager? The general consensus is that some form of the multinational enterprise will successfully survive for several more decades. But countervailing forces from governments, unions, and the wider public will undoubtedly cause major transformations in the forms of multinational enterprises.[18]

The ideological debate as to whether multinationals are good or evil continues in intellectual and academic circles, but is somewhat muted as compared to recent years. At the operational level, however, government officials and political leaders have evolved toward a pragmatic and receptive attitude, as they have become increasingly aware that host countries have great potential power for shaping the conditions under which foreign firms operate. In fact, the following observation by J. Kenneth Galbraith might be widely accepted in host-country circles:

> Like so many children, the multinational industrial corporation was unwise in the choice of parents and is visited with their sins . . . but the multinational corporation is the nearly inescapable accommodation to international trade in modern capital and consumer goods.[19]

---

[18] See Howard V. Perlmutter, "A View of the Future," in *The New Sovereigns: Multinational Corporations as World Powers*, eds., Abdul Said and Luiz Simmons (Englewood Cliffs, N.J.: Prentice-Hall, 1975), pp. 167–86; see also G. Hedlund and L. Otterbeck, *The Multinational Corporation, The Nation State and the Trade Unions: An European Perspective* (Kent, Ohio: Kent State University, 1977).

[19] J. Kenneth Galbraith, *Annals of an Abiding Liberal* (Boston: Houghton-Mifflin, 1979).

How will the role of the international manager change? It will change with the emergence of new organizational forms for the enterprise, with growing external demands, and with the increasing complexity of internal management.

The organizational patterns for multinational enterprises are increasingly having to respond to a more active role by governments and labor unions. Perlmutter foresees more enterprises becoming geocentric and less ethnocentric and less polycentric. He also sees the number of organizational forms increasing from the wholly owned and joint-venture types. The joint venture is a two-party agreement. Evolving forms in which a larger number of parties participate are referred to as "industrial systems constellations" that can have multinational ownership participation, including that of governments. A related forecast of changing organization forms is that of Peter Drucker, who foresees the multinational enterprise becoming a "transnational federation."[20]

With more complex organization forms and more constituencies within and outside of the enterprise involved, new and greater demands will be made on the managers who are heading foreign affiliates and the parent companies. One of the most apparent demands will be in the area of external relations. As one writer suggests, "The major challenge to the continued success of the multinational corporation is not lack of technical skills, but rather, the need to establish and develop procedures and practices which enable the corporation to operate effectively in an uncertain, challenging and concerned host country environment."[21] The same might be said about the need for managing external affairs in the home-country environment.

The growing external affairs responsibility is related to the almost universal pressures on business firms for greater social responsibility—except that in the international field the concerns and reactions of many groups in many national environments must be recognized. The management of external affairs requires that the firm should be measuring its social and economic impact on the country and make such information available. The firm should also take advantage of, and assume responsibility for, legitimately shaping the environment. External affairs will place demands on the manager for developing skills for political, diplomatic, and technical negotiations. They will also require great expertise in adapting to many varied cultures and understanding diverse national aspirations.

For the future, the manager will need much more information, particularly about the environment and possible future trends.[22] The "futures" planning of one major multinational is briefly described in Box 24–1.

---

[20] Peter Drucker, *Managing in Turbulent Times* (New York: Harper & Row, 1980).

[21] David H. Blake, *Managing the External Relations of Multinational Corporations* (New York: Fund for Multinational Management Education, 1977), p. 2.

[22] See Roy C. Amara and Andrew J. Lipinski, *Business Planning for an Uncertain Future: Scenarios and Strategies* (New York: Pergamon Press, 1982).

Box 24–1

The future according to Philips

Unless Philips NV, the giant Dutch electronics group, develops new markets and products by 1991, nearly a quarter of its 87,500 jobs in Holland will disappear. This startling piece of information is contained in a survey prepared by the group on likely social developments up to the year 1991.

How do companies like Philips, which has 391,500 employees worldwide and is the largest private sector employer outside the United States, go about looking into the future? And why the need to add its own crystal gazing to that carried out by many private and government forecasting institutes?

The aim is to see "if the forecasting was sufficiently tangible to make a real contribution to decisions on the company's social policies," the forecast group says. Philips, like many other companies, usually restricts itself to a four-year review. This survey was completed in May 1978 and looks 13 years ahead to 1991—not too close and not too far into the future.

The survey begins with a list of assumptions about the future, drawn from the written sources and based on Philips' own experience in social matters. These assumptions are then worked out in more detail in several areas, including income, personnel, and company structures. In the final section of the 65-page report, a number of points raised are checked to see if they could form the basis for policy decisions.

Source: Adapted from *World Business Weekly*, February 12, 1979, p. 25.

The internal management issues for the future are many. Some of these have been identified in a joint project undertaken by American and European business schools to examine the changing expectations of society as they relate to management training for the 21st century.[23] Some of the trends identified have special relevance for international business. Among these is the growing influence of worker participation in the decision-making function of management. With continued pressure for the hiring of nationals in overseas subsidiaries, international managers will have to deal with potential conflicts in cultural and moral systems.

SUMMARY

The changing economic, social, and political environment around the world has had a profound impact on international business and will continue to do so. The future of multinational enterprises depends heavily on their ability to anticipate rather than react to significant future

---

[23] See *Management in the XXI Century* (Washington, D.C.: American Assembly of Collegiate Schools of Business, 1980).

events, analyze their impact on the enterprise, and incorporate that analysis directly into corporate planning and decision making.

The field of forecasting "alternative futures" has become a growth industry and international firms are increasingly making use of such internal and external forecasting to guide their operations. These forecasts indicate that international managers and multinational enterprises will need new frames of reference, changing values, and revised skills. International managers can rely on present practices and hope to get by. Or they can treat the new trends and pressures as challenges and devise ways to harness them.

EXERCISES AND DISCUSSION QUESTIONS

1. What are the advantages and limitations of alternative futures methodologies? Give examples of international business issues that might most appropriately be analyzed by each of the principal methodologies.

2. What future developments are likely to cause a major growth in the expansion of multinational enterprises into the Third World with its vast population and market potential?

3. How do you evaluate the forecast that multinational enterprises are likely to involve more ownership participants and become "industrial systems constellations"?

4. What are the principal new demands on international managers for the 21st century that may be most difficult to meet?

PART SEVEN

Cases and problems in international business

The nature and scope of international business

Which company is truly multinational?*

Four senior executives of the world's largest firms with extensive holdings outside the home country speak:

Company A. "We are a multinational firm. We distribute our products in about 100 countries. We manufacture in over 17 countries and do research and development in three countries. We look at all new investment projects—both domestic and overseas—using exactly the same criteria."

The executive from company A continues, "Of course most of the key posts in our subsidiaries are held by home-country nationals. Whenever replacements for these men are sought, it is the practice, if not the policy, to look next to you at the head office and pick someone (usually a home-country national) you know and trust."

Company B. "We are a multinational firm. Only 1 percent of the personnel in our affiliate companies are nonnationals. Most of these are U.S. executives on temporary assignments. In all major markets, the affiliate's managing director is of the local nationality."

He continues, "Of course there are very few non-Americans in the key posts at headquarters. The few we have are so Americanized that we usually don't notice their nationality. Unfortunately, you can't find good foreigners who are willing to live in the United States, where our headquarters is located. American executives are more mobile. In addition, Americans have the drive and initiative we like. In fact, the European nations would prefer to report to an American rather than to some other European."

Company C. "We are a multinational firm. Our product division executives have worldwide profit responsibility. As our organizational chart shows, the United States is just one region on a par with Europe, Latin America, Africa, etc., in each division."

The executive from Company C goes on to explain, "The worldwide product division concept is rather difficult to implement. The senior

* Copyright 1971 by Professor Warren J. Keegan. This case is adapted with permission from Howard V. Perlmutter, "The Tortuous Evolution of the Multinational Corporation," *Columbia Journal of World Business*, January–February 1969.

executives in charge of these divisions have little overseas experience. They have been promoted from domestic posts and tend to view foreign consumer needs as really basically the same as ours. Also, product division executives tend to focus on the domestic market because the domestic market is larger and generates more revenue than the fragmented foreign markets. The rewards are for global performance, but the strategy is to focus on domestic. Most of our senior executives simply do not understand what happens overseas and really do not trust foreign executives, even those in key positions."

Company D (nonAmerican). "We are a multinational firm. We have at least 18 nationalities represented at our headquarters. Most senior executives speak at least two languages. About 30 percent of our staff at headquarters are foreigners."

He continues by explaining that "since the voting shareholders must by law come from the home country, the home country's interest must be given careful consideration. But we are proud of our nationality; we shouldn't be ashamed of it. In fact, many times we have been reluctant to use home-country ideas overseas, to our detriment, especially in our U.S. subsidiary. Our country produces good executives, who tend to stay with us a long time. It is harder to keep executives from the United States."

1. Which company is truly multinational?
2. What are the attributes of a truly multinational company?
3. Why quibble about how multinational a firm is?

Igloos versus Fastbacks

1. Assume that in each of two economies, the United States and Greenland, there are a total of five productive units. A productive unit can be used in the production of either Fastback cars or Igloos. The "cost" to an economy of producing a Fastback or an Igloo is measured in terms of opportunity cost, that is, the number of one good that must be given up in order to produce the other.

2. The table below summarizes the production possibilities in each of the two countries. *Assume that the countries decided on the respective production functions indicated by the asterisks.*

Productive units utilized		Goods produced United States		Goods produced Greenland	
For Igloos	For Fastbacks	Fastbacks	Igloos	Fastbacks	Igloos
5	0	0	30	0	10
4	1	4	24	.5	8
3	2	8	18	1.0	6
2	3	12	12	1.5	4
1	4	16*	6	2.0*	2
0	5	20	0	2.5	0

3. Analyze the data and work through the following questions:

   a. What country is best able to produce Fastbacks? Igloos?
   b. In which good is the United States advantage greatest? Why?
   c. Will it pay for either country to trade with the other? Why?
   d. If yes, which way should the goods flow? Why?
   e. In order for there to be an exchange of goods, a *price* is required. What is the minimum acceptable price to each country?

Anglo-American seeds

Before leaving to visit his firm's U.S. subsidiaries, Alan Normanby spent the first weekend in May 1981 preparing the summer flower beds around his home in London's stockbroker belt. A Saturday visit to the garden center provided him with seedlings and seed packets that he carefully planted in the spring rain on Sunday morning. Now, two days later, he stood in a Boston discount store facing a large container of reduced-price seed packets. He picked up a packet of Giant African Marigold seeds selling at 67 cents, reduced from 89 cents, that seemed much larger than the packet he had just paid 25p for in England. Instead of holding 50 or so loose seeds, Alan saw that it contained 150 prespaced seeds affixed to 15 feet of decomposable seed planting tape. The package bore the name of the Fredonia Seed Co. of Fredonia, New York, and a note, "Seed of U.S. origin. Assembled into strip in England."

At £1 = $2.30, which must have been about the exchange rate when the seeds were processed in the United Kingdom, the U.S. seeds were costing under one half what Alan had paid in London. Of course, the dollar had risen to £1 = $1.80 over the past few months, because oil prices had fallen while the United States had retained its tight monetary policy and high interest rates, but even at this exchange rate the U.S. seeds were still far cheaper. Furthermore, to bring prices back to purchasing power parity, the rate would have to fall again before too long.

One up for comparative advantage, thought Alan. If British manufacturing could fix U.S. seeds onto strips for the U.S. market more cheaply than similar seeds could be supplied loose for the U.K. market, then British firms could do the same in textiles too. Alan's international production director in London had, for the past six months, been pressing to shift more production to the United States, where productivity was higher in their household cotton textile mill. The marigold seeds would provide Alan with a good illustration for arguing that the best way might simply be to make sure that his U.K. factory increased its productivity ahead of the United States.

What could cause such a disparity in prices?

Does comparative advantage have any relevance for this example?

Is there any validity in the comparison between seeds and textiles?

What do you think of the productivity argument?

How does the change in exchange rate affect the textile situation?

What is the relationship between exchange rate, interest rate, and futures rate?

If exchange rates are affected by different interest rates, is it reasonable to expect purchasing power parity?

The framework for international transactions

Freelandia

Freelandia's main exports came from its primary industries and included wool, meat, butter, timber, fruit, and a variety of less advanced manufactures. For 1982 the total exported was $3,360 million.

Imports totaled $3,309 million, made up mainly of heavy manufactured goods, such as machinery and transport equipment, while an additional $36 million was spent on foreign transport and travel and $15 million on other services.

The country had recently begun to encourage foreign industry to invest in new factories and plants, provided that the output either substituted for imports or had export potential and included at least 40 percent of Freelandian content. This campaign had proven quite successful and during 1982 a total of $348 million was remitted for direct investment in Freelandia. The policy was beginning to meet resistance from the opposition political parties, however, because the considerable income these companies were earning was payable to them in overseas funds and placed a strain on the balance of payments. In 1982 a total of $198 million was repatriated by overseas companies, out of their net earnings of $294 million.

The Freelandian government had also been encouraging its major domestic producers to establish processing plants overseas to increase the country's income from primary exports. A total of $126 million was invested in this way in 1982 and was expected to add significantly to the future inflow from overseas business investments, which totaled only $54 million in 1982.

There was an additional reinvested income of $66 million from these direct investments overseas during 1982, but it was still true, as the opposition argued, that foreign firms' ownership in Freelandia far outweighed Freelandia's overseas business activities—in cumulative figures at the end of 1981, a comparison of $2,889 million to $726 million. This comparison, moreover, was similar for holdings of investment securities. Foreign investment in Freelandian securities totaled $1,080 million at the end of 1981 and increased in value by $132 million during 1982, while Freelandian holdings of overseas stocks and bonds were only valued at $366 million in 1981, increasing in value by $39 million over the year. Heavy restrictions permitted only $15 million to be remitted by Freelandia for further purchases during 1982, but foreigners purchased a further $126 million in Freelandia.

The government's policies had also led them to borrow $84 million from overseas investors during the year in order to finance new container facilities at the major ports, but their indebtedness to the IMF was reduced to $963 million with a repayment of $75 million. Interest payments of $168 million were made to service government debentures floated overseas that totaled $1,209 million at the end of 1981. The central bank's holdings of convertible currencies overseas increased during the year by $57 million to $378 million.

Shorter-term commercial finances were less important to the Freelandian situation but local holdings of foreigners again more than offset Freelandian holdings overseas. Short-term overseas holdings by Freelandian companies were $240 million at the end of 1981 and liquid holdings $18 million, while overseas companies held $168 million short-term claims and $144 million in liquid funds within Freelandia. By the end of 1982, the net change on short-term nonliquid funds was $42 million. Overseas companies had increased their claims by $18 million, and Freelandian companies had increased their claims by $60 million. There was no change over the year in Freelandian liquid claims, but foreign banks increased their holdings by $54 million.

1. From the above particulars, prepare balance-of-payments accounts for Freelandia for 1982 and show the country's international investment position at the end of 1981 and 1982.

2. What do you think might happen if Freelandia's currency were to be devalued against other currencies by 20 percent? Do you think this devaluation is likely?

The Korean won (A): A swap proposal[*]

In mid-December 1979, John Bergsma, general manager of the Seoul branch of a large U.S. multinational bank, was trying to decide whether or not his bank should contract a $5 million "swap transaction" with the Bank of Korea, the central bank of that troubled but dynamic country. If he wanted to contract the transaction he had to submit an application to the Bank of Korea before the end of the week. But Bergsma was pensive and reluctant to make his decision because of widespread rumors of an imminent devaluation of the Korean won.

Banking in Korea is attractive and very profitable for large multinational banks. Although there are some restrictions on foreign bank operations in Korea, almost unlimited domestic demand for credit and limited capability of local banks to meet domestic demand provide excellent opportunities for large multinational banks. But the key to the attractiveness of the Korean market is the very high interest rates at which banks can lend funds. Foreign banks have a special advantage because they can acquire lendable funds relatively cheaply from their home-country headquarters or from sister branches in various countries around the world and lend these less expensive funds at very high rates in Korea.

However, this foreign lending in Korea has attracted the attention and regulation of the Bank of Korea for two reasons: (1) the unfair advantage which foreign banks enjoy may lead to a long-term weakening of domestic Korean banks, and (2) the inflow of credit from abroad via foreign banks might undermine the effectiveness of the central bank's monetary policies. For these reasons, the Bank of Korea regulates the supply of foreign banks' loanable funds on a quarterly basis with swap transactions.

These swap transactions work as follows. Under the Korean Banking Law and the conditions of banking operation permits, loans denominated in foreign currencies are not allowed; that is, if an American bank wants to lend to a Korean client, that loan must be denominated in local currency, the Korean won. Foreign banks wishing to lend in Korea must sell foreign currencies to the Bank of Korea (i.e., buy won with dollars or yen or francs, etc.) and contract a swap transaction with the central bank in order to acquire won to make loans to local customers. In a swap transaction, foreign banks agree to repurchase the foreign currency at the

---

* Prepared by J. Frederick Truitt, Associate Professor of International Business, Kang-Rae Cho and Chong-S. Lee, research assistants, Graduate School of Business Administration, University of Washington, as a basis for classroom discussion. Copyright 1980 by the authors.

end of the transaction period at the market (official exchange rate) price prevailing then.

Although the last devaluation of the won had occurred in 1974, concern over the possibility of another devaluation has existed for years. This concern intensified after the assassination of President Park on October 26, 1979, but most observers had not expected a devaluation until at least after the election of the new government under the new constitution sometime late 1980. They thought the current "caretaker" interim government would not make such a tough and sensitive decision. But some observers expressed the possibility of devaluation by the interim government, pointing out the appointment of Mr. Shim and Mr. Lee as prime minister and head of the Economic Planning Board, respectively. The new prime minister was a career businessman and the head of EPB was a former professor of business and public administration. Both were believed to have no political background or ambitions, hence no reluctance to take a painful course of action if such action were necessary and correct for the health and prosperity of the Korean economy.

Bergsma had just returned from a meeting with several good, long-standing customers who urgently needed credits before year end. But if Bergsma's bank was to provide credit to these customers, he would have to make his decision by tomorrow morning so paper work on the swap application could begin.

Exhibit 1

Outlook for Korea's Won: Devaluation hinges on other policies' success

Despite Korea's current export slowdown and evidence of chronic inflation, discount rumors that a devaluation of the won is imminent. Devaluation will not come before year-end, and then only if other measures which the government has been vigorously promoting fail. These measures include:

Acceleration of industrial restructuring, with the emphasis on promotion of heavy and chemical industries and the development of higher value-added products more appropriate to Korea's increasingly expensive workforce.

Expansion of export credits and reduction of tariffs on key raw materials used by export industries in an attempt to ease cash flow traumas and boost exports.

Imposition of severe fiscal and monetary restraints aimed at reducing inflation but selectively relaxing these in order to promote high-priority industries.

Whether this combination of traditional belt tightening and industrial restructuring succeeds, remains to be seen. But devaluation for the moment clearly is viewed as a cure worse than the disease. Inflation is already running at 21–22 percent, and the Bank of Korea estimates that a 10 percent devaluation against the U.S. dollar would add 4.34 percentage points.

Three yardsticks will be used to measure the success or failure of this attempt to stave off devaluation and should be closely monitored by firms concerned: balance of payments, company profits, and unemployment.

Balance of payments

Although officials expect a trade deficit of nearly U.S. $4 billion in 1979, this poses no immediate problems. Invisibles—especially earnings from overseas construction services—will lower the current account deficit to about U.S. $3 billion. Seoul will borrow U.S. $3.9 billion to cover the balance and boost foreign exchange holdings to U.S. $5.9 billion by year-end. Korea has succeeded in lowering its debt service ratio in recent years and its excellent credit rating ensures that it will have no difficulty borrowing on favorable terms.

Pressure to devalue will intensify, however, if exports begin to fall appreciably. So far the government's remedial measures—expanding export credits and reducing tariffs—have succeeded in averting a serious downturn. Exports were poor in July but rebounded in August, posting a 26.8 percent increase over the same month last year. In the first eight months, exports totaled U.S. $9.2 billion, nearly 60 percent of the U.S. $15.5 billion goal. But if exports drop in the final quarter, it will have important repercussions—not only on balance of payments but also on the solvency of Korean companies and unemployment.

Corporate profits

Pressure to devalue has come primarily from exporters that have succeeded in increasing sales in recent years only by cutting profits. The central bank's analysis of the combined income statements of some 1,437 enterprises shows that exporters operated at a net loss in 1978. Even the large general trading companies (GTCs) have registered dangerously low profitability (*BA* '79, p. 286).

The difficulties Korean exporters face are clear from a comparison of inflation rates and foreign exchange fluctuations since 1975. The table shows that Korea's inflation rate since end 1975 has been 74.3 percent—much higher than that of major competitors like Taiwan, 26.1 percent; Hong Kong, 29.2 percent; or Singapore, 8.4 percent. At the same time, the won has only depreciated marginally against these currencies. The final column indicates the cost disadvantages based on inflation and currency fluctuations that Korean exporters have in each market. The cost disadvantages have been particularly serious in the U.S., which accounted for 31.9 percent of Korea's exports in 1978 and where the exchange rate has been fixed. In Korea's second largest market, Japan, which accounted for 20.7 percent of its exports in 1978, Korea's high rate of inflation has been offset by a 27 percent effective depreciation since 1975. But Korea's success in increasing exports to Japan this year is more a credit to Japan's expanding economy, since Korea's major competitors have enjoyed both depreciation of their currencies against the yen and lower rates of inflation than Korea.

The figures tend to support the exporters' contention that the won is overvalued. The government hopes that declining profitability will force exporters into more competitive product lines. But unless government efforts to restrain inflation begin to take effect, companies will be forced to cut back exports and sustain greater losses than they will be able to bear.

Exhibit 1 (*concluded*)

Unemployment

Given the labor shortage that has existed in Korea in recent years, the slight increase forecast in unemployment will not pose serious problems and, in fact, should help relieve inflation. But recent labor incidents, increased pressure from opposition groups (*BA* '79, p. 266), and the general threat of disorder ensure that the government will not let unemployment pass the 6 percent mark—the level at which it chose to devalue in 1974. Presently, the government is seeking to reduce the impact of layoffs by stepping up vocational education and retraining efforts, consistent with its goal of restructuring the economy.

The government will approach the triple threat of a widening trade gap, declining profits, and rising unemployment with selective measures. By year-end it will be clear whether selective action will have to be replaced by devaluation. At the moment, *BA* believes chances are good that the selective policies will head off an exchange-rate adjustment.

Long-term threat

The longer-term issue affecting the won's future is inflation. Boosting the value added of Korean exports, reducing the labor content, and increasing productivity will, in the long term, overcome the competitive disadvantages inflation has imposed on firms since the 1974 devaluation. Continued chronic cost spirals, however, would threaten Korea's industrialization plans and hence the value of the currency.

The crunch will not come this year or next. The sharp jump in inflation this year has been largely induced by the government, and *BA* believes prices will come under control by year-end. The government's decision to release many products from price control early this year and the decision to pass on immediately the full effect of oil price hikes—plus a comfortable margin to allow for future increases—forced up inflation rates in July, but should in the long run stabilize prices. Similarly, the sharp increase in imports has been caused largely by the liberalization of import restrictions. Together with the decontrol of domestic prices, however, this step should increase domestic supply and dampen inflation. Finally, the total money supply (M2) will be held to a 25–28 percent rate of increase this year, down from the 34.7 percent increase of last year.

Unless the government can maintain monetary and fiscal discipline and prevent both national and corporate expansion plans from overheating the economy, however, the won may again come under pressure.

Source: *Business Asia,* September 21, 1979, pp. 298–300. Reprinted with permission of the publisher.

Profile of Korea's won (relates to Exhibit 1)

	Inflation rate (%) 1975–June 1979*	Price parity ratio†	Equivalent exchange rate (won per unit of foreign currency)	Won's effective depreciation since 1975 (%)	Actual exchange rate (Sept. 19, 1979)	Korea's cost disadvantage in overseas markets (%)
Korea	74.3	—	—	—	—	—
Taiwan	26.1	1.38	17.58	6	13.56	22.9
Hong Kong	29.2	1.35	129.64	0	95.60	26.3
Singapore	8.4	1.61	313.01	13	224.59	28.2
United States	34.4	1.30	629.20	—	484	23.1
Japan	27.1	1.37	2.17	27	2.17	0.0
West Germany	16.3	1.50	276.86	31	268.59	3.0

* Measured by consumer price indexes reported by IMF; for Hong Kong based on *Hong Kong Monthly Digest of Statistics*.
† Korea's price index divided by the price index of the country to which it is compared yields the price parity ratio—the factor by which the won would have to be devalued to make the price of its exports competitive with those of the country to which it is compared.

Exhibit 2

Prospects for profits; South Korea
The next five years—political liberalization,
continued fast expansion, shift to heavy industry

Social dynamics. South Korea's reaction to the sudden death last month of its long-standing strong man, President Park Chung-hee, exemplifies the social cohesiveness that helps see the country through rapid growth that could otherwise cause major upheaval. Despite a succession problem still largely unresolved, normalcy has returned. Several factors account for the relative calm.

One is a single-mindedness concerning economic development. Ko-

reans are willing to accept virtually anything for the sake of this goal, which helps explain the acceptance of the Park regime for 18 years. The removal of Park from the scene has provoked a call for a political liberalization with initial support from the government and the military. However, the national consensus is to keep political confusion to a minimum so as not to endanger the economic development drive.

The other key factor is the pres-

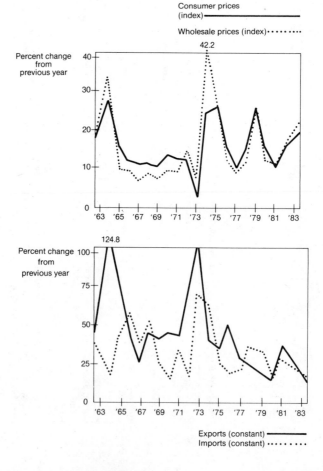

ence of a common enemy—North Korea. A strong anticommunist sentiment in South Korean society results in moderation and mutual cooperation among the different interest groups.

Labor and the middle class will emerge as the new power groups in the next five years. Labor, tightly controlled under Park's regime, will strongly assert its rights in a more liberal environment. Restrictions that have virtually prohibited strikes are likely to be lifted and labor unrest will intensify during difficult economic periods. Unionization will grow. The government will retain an important role in labor-management mediation, but officials will pay greater attention to labor's needs.

The growing middle class will become an important political force. Rising personal income has sparked an explosive demand for consumer goods, and has already prompted the government to reverse its previous policy of suppressing the consumer market.

Politics. Constitutional reforms that will allow for a more democratic election framework and a bigger role for the opposition parties have been pledged by the interim government. However, elections are not expected before 1981. Moreover, the ruling Democratic Republican Party (DRP) holds a clear advantage over the opposition in terms of party organization, financing, and control over the government's censorship apparatus. It can also use the transitional period to boost its candidate's image.

Ultimately, continued dominance by the DRP hinges on its ability to nominate a popular successor to Park. At present, the strongest contender from the DRP is new party boss Kim Jong-pil (a former prime minister and nephew-in-law of Park), who has both popular appeal and army support. By installing the politically weak Choi Kyu-hah as president of the interim government, the DRP may be able to allay opposition fears that the constitutional reform will be postponed indefinitely. It also allows Kim to further disassociate himself from Park's authoritarian system.

Major opposition candidates are Kim Young-sam, current leader of the New Democratic Party (NDP), and Kim Daejung, a formidable contestant in the last general, presidential election in 1972. However, the NDP, with its long history of factional disputes, may find it difficult to agree on a candidate or formulate a platform.

No matter who will lead South Korea in the 1980s, no significant change in economic policy is expected. Several adjustments will be made, however, to channel resources to the domestic consumer market and improve social welfare through better housing, infrastructure, and transportation. Close cooperation between the government and the private sector will continue to assure that growth, industrialization, and export targets are met, but government intervention is expected to be reduced.

The external political threat may assume less importance. The U.S. decision to delay troop withdrawal plans allows time for South Korea's economic growth to fund buildup of its own defensive forces. Meanwhile, North Korea is likely to be influenced by China's modernization and concentrate in the future on economic development and expanding trade relations rather than on armed conquest of the South.

Economy. South Korea is undergoing an anti-inflationary stabiliza-

Exhibit 2 (*continued*)

tion program that will slow the economy to 8.5 percent real annual growth for 1979 and 1980. However, over the following five years, a 10 percent yearly growth can be expected as the world economy picks up again and with it, the demand for the kinds of goods and services South Korea offers. Companies should watch out for a shift to heavy and high-technology industries as major growth sectors.

Exports will remain the lifeblood of the economy. Merchandise exports will exceed $17.5 billion in 1980 and reach nearly $40 billion by 1983. Imports will increase steadily as the government lifts restrictions and lowers tariffs to head off protectionism abroad, meet local demand, and fight inflation. Nevertheless, the $4 billion trade deficit anticipated in 1979 and 1980 will be significantly reduced in subsequent years, as exports increase and Korea becomes less dependent on imported machinery equipment and intermediate goods.

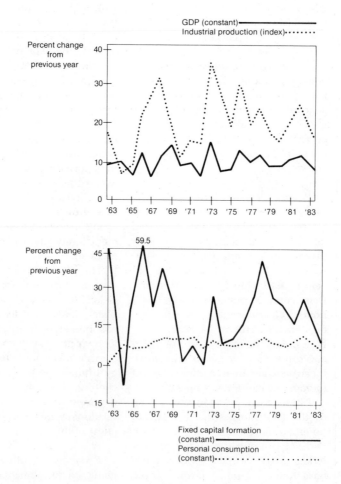

In the face of an increasingly costly labor force, the government will try to maintain the country's competitiveness by promoting high-technology, capital-intensive industries such as machinery, electronics, electrical power, and chemicals. MNCs that can provide technology and know-how that will improve the quality and reduce the price of light industrial or consumer products for either the domestic or overseas markets will also be welcome.

Given Korea's rapid growth and expanding domestic market, the profitability of foreign firms will remain high. However, despite efforts to contain inflation, the upward price spiral will remain a problem.

Investment. Foreign investment will be pursued, especially in advanced technological fields. While most foreign participation will be limited to a minority joint-venture position, projects involving a high level of technology that local companies cannot match may be able to bypass local equity requirement rules.

Recent foreign investments in Korea include: a $3.5 million investment by Continental Group Inc. of the United States for a 49 percent interest in the production of cans with Hanyang Food; a 50-50 joint venture between ITT and Daewoo Industrial Co. for the production of prefabricated pipes for nuclear plants; and a $4.2 million 50-50 undertaking by CPC International (U.S.) in food processing. Also, IBM is investing $4 million in an expansion of its electronic leasing/servicing operations. Foreign investment approvals will exceed $100 million in 1979.

While Korea will increase its national savings and significantly reduce its savings-investment gap, heavy dependence on foreign borrowing will continue, because of the large investment required to build up heavy industry.

Currency. In spite of a large current-account deficit—expected to reach $3 billion in 1979 and 1980—and high inflation, devaluation will be resisted. Instead, the government will employ tight monetary policy and channel resources to meet supply shortages in the domestic consumer market.

In the latter half of 1980, recovery of export demand and a possible weakening of the U.S. dollar [to which the Korean won is pegged] will head off pressure for devaluation. In the long run, rapid industrial restructuring, with emphasis on heavy and chemical industries and higher value-added products, will improve the trade picture, and will eventually eliminate the current-account deficit, possibly forcing a revaluation.

Source: *Business International*, November 23, 1979, pp. 374–75. Reprinted with permission of the publisher.

Exhibit 3

Exchange rates of won to U.S. dollar

Date	Official rate (won/$)
May 1, 1951	2.5
November 10, 1951	6.0
December 15, 1953	18.0
January 20, 1960	50.0
August 15, 1960	65.0
January 1, 1961	100.0
February 2, 1961	130.0
May 3, 1964	255.0
December 31, 1965	272.0
December 31, 1967	274.6
December 31, 1968	281.5
November 3, 1969	304.35
June 28, 1971	370.80
December 30, 1972	398.90
December 31, 1973	397.50
December 7, 1974	484.00

Source: Bank of Korea, *Monthly Economic Statistics.*

Exhibit 4a

Korea's balance of payments (U.S. $ millions, 1960–1972)

	1960	1961	1962	1963	1964	1965	1966	1967	1968	1969	1970	1971	1972
Goods and services (70)	-262	-198	-292	-403	-221	-194	-323	-417	-665	-793	-801	-1017	-540
Trade balance f.o.b. (70a)	-273	-242	-336	-410	-245	-240	-429	-574	-836	-992	-922	-1046	-574
Central government, n.i.e. (70b)	48	67	80	55	62	75	123	190	235	276	248	212	202
Other (70c)	-37	-23	-36	-48	-38	-29	-17	-33	-64	-77	-127	-183	-167
Transfers:													
Private (71a)	19	25	37	52	54	69	98	91	105	142	95	106	119
Central government (71b)	256	207	200	208	141	134	122	134	119	102	83	63	50
Capital, n.i.e.:													
Private (72a)	3	-2	-4	61	7	17	184	279	396	428	414	429	248
Central government (72b)	-13	17	11	34	16	-19	33	13	26	203	174	231	228
Net errors and omissions (76)	-2	-2	-2	-1	—	-2	4	10	5	-6	-15	12	39

Note: Minus sign indicates debit.
n.i.e.: Not included elsewhere.
Source: *International Financial Statistics*.

Exhibit 4b

Korea's balance of payments (U.S. $ millions, 1973–1979 III)

	1973	1974	1975	1976	1977	1978	1979 I	1979 II	1979 III
Merchandise: Exports f.o.b. (77aad)	3,284	4,516	5,003	7,814	10,046	12,712	3,025	3,590	3,991
Merchandise: Imports f.o.b. (77abd)	-3,849	-6,454	-6,674	-8,404	-10,526	-14,496	-4,054	-5,087	-4,942
Other goods, serv., & income: Cred. (77acd)	852	837	877	1,646	3,063	4,456	1,065	1,273	1,177
Other goods, serv., & income: Deb. (77add)	-783	-1,147	-1,322	-1,712	-2,754	-4,228	-1,093	-1,209	-1,168
Private unrequited transfers (77aed)	155	154	158	194	172	433	92	102	104
Official unrequited transfers (77agd)	36	67	71	156	53	39	5	17	3
Direct investment (77bad)	93	105	53	75	73	61	24	27	-52
Portfolio investment, n.i.e. (77bdd)	—	—	—	74	70	42	43	—	-10
Other long-term capital, n.i.e. (77bed)	520	939	1,291	1,176	1,256	2,009	770	455	878
Other short-term capital, n.i.e. (77ccd)	3	696	1,123	534	-9	19	222	1,153	492
Net errors & omissions (77d.d)	41	116	-213	-240	-71	-318	-240	47	-138
Counterpart to mon/demon of gold (78c.d)	—	—	—	—	—	—	—	—	—
Counterpart to SDR allocation (78b.d)	—	—	—	—	—	—	21	—	—
Counterpart to valuation change (78d.d)	4	-1	9	986	330	-1,350	2	1	-1
Liab. const. fgn. author reserves (79x.d)	—	—	—	—	—	—	—	—	—
Total change in reserves (79k.d)	-354	172	-374	-2,299	-1,703	622	119	-367	-334

Note: Minus sign indicates debit.

n.i.e.: Not included elsewhere.

Source: *International Financial Statistics.*

Exhibit 5

Korea's international reserves, 1973–1979 III (U.S. $ millions, except line D)

	1973	1974	1975	1976	1977	1978	1979 I	1979 II	1979 III
A. SDRs	31.5	1.7	3.9	7.9	12.2	14.9	42.8	29.7	27.5
B. Reserve position in the fund	24.1	—	—	—	—	13.6	13.4	25.1	25.6
C. Foreign exchange (held by Bank of Korea)	829.2	275.5	777.4	1,962.1	2,954.9	2,735.5	2,675.1	2,459.1	2,741.6
D. Gold (million fine troy ounces)	.110	.110	.111	.112	.147	.275	.276	.276	.277
E. Gold (national valuation)	4.6	4.7	4.7	4.7	6.2	29.7	29.7	29.8	29.8
F. Total (including all Korean banks' holdings of foreign exchange and gold at national valuation)	1,094.3	1,055.8	1,550.1	2,960.5	4,306.8	4,920.2	2,726.1	5,041.4	5,377.9

Source: IMF, *International Financial Statistics.*

Exhibit 6

Selected economic indicators

Year	Money supply M_2 billion won	Industrial production index (1975 = 100)		Economic growth rate	Unemployed as percent economically active population
		All items	Manfacturing		
1962	51.6	10.5	9.2	2.2%	—
1965	97.1	13.7	11.9	5.8	—
1970	897.8	37.4	35.3	7.6	—
1971	1,084.9	43.1	41.1	9.4	—
1972	1,451.8	49.4	47.8	5.8	4.5
1973	1,980.5	65.9	64.8	14.9	4.0
1974	2,456.5	84.0	83.7	8.0	4.1
1975	3,150.0	100.0	100.0	7.1	4.1
1976	4,204.8	129.8	131.8	15.1	4.0
1977	5,874.8	155.6	158.7	10.3	3.8
1978	7,928.7	191.2	196.4	11.6	3.2
1979:					
1	8,092.2	197.9	203.5	⎫	—
2	8,197.3	200.2	206.6	⎬ 13.2	—
3	8,190.3	223.0	229.8	⎭	4.0
4	8,211.0	218.3	225.2	⎫	—
5	8,084.7	229.9	237.5	⎬ 9.5	—
6	8,311.0	220.5	227.9	⎭	3.5
7	8.466.8	213.4	219.9	⎫	—
8	8,641.3	207.8	214.0	⎬ 4.8	—
9	8,992.4	217.1	223.9	⎭	*
10	9,061.1	206.0	212.2	—	—

* In late 1979 the Korean newspaper, *Hankuk-ilbo,* reported that unemployment was 4.1 percent and increasing.
Source: Bank of Korea, *Monthly Economic Statistics.*

Exhibit 7a

Commercial bank deposit rates (at or near end of month)

	1976	1977	1978	June	July	August	1979 September	October	November	December (projected)
United States	4.70	6.80	10.90	9.90	10.30	11.35	12.10	14.50	13.20	13.55
Canada	8.00	7.25	10.45	11.05	11.55	11.80	11.90	14.50	13.40	14.05
Japan	4.50	3.25	2.50	3.25	3.25	4.00	4.00	4.00	4.00	4.00
Switzerland	1.50	1.12	0.12	0.75	0.75	1.25	1.00	2.25	3.75	4.75
Brazil	45.60	39.60	46.80	41.04	40.92	40.80	40.68	42.12	43.20	45.00
Hong Kong	3.25	1.75	4.50	7.75	7.75	9.25	9.25	9.25	9.25	9.25
Korea	15.00	13.20	15.00	15.00	15.00	15.00	15.00	15.00	15.00	15.00
Mexico	9.50	9.50	12.00	12.00	12.00	12.34	13.68	15.13	16.80	16.75
Philippines	8.50	8.50	8.50	8.50	8.50	8.50	8.50	8.50	8.50	10.50
Singapore	3.75	5.31	7.31	7.00	7.44	8.12	8.44	8.31	8.12	10.31
Eurodollars	5.00	7.19	11.69	10.50	11.31	12.12	12.75	15.69	14.00	14.44

Source: Morgan Guaranty Trust Company, *World Financial Markets*.

Exhibit 7b

Commercial bank lending rates to prime borrowers (at or near end of month)

	1976	1977	1978	June	July	August	1979 September	October	November	December (projected)
United States	6.00	7.75	11.75	11.50	11.75	12.75	13.50	15.00	15.50	15.25
Canada	9.25	8.25	11.50	12.00	12.50	12.50	13.00	14.75	15.00	15.00
Japan	7.42	5.47	4.50	4.87	5.06	5.38	5.68	5.86	6.16	6.40
Switzerland	7.50	6.45	5.00	5.00	5.00	5.00	5.00	5.00	5.00	5.00
Brazil	30.00	52.05	61.70	61.82	63.00	63.00	57.00	57.00	57.00	57.00
Hong Kong	6.00	4.75	8.75	13.00	13.00	14.50	14.50	14.50	14.50	14.50
Korea	17.00	15.00	18.50	18.50	18.50	18.50	18.50	18.50	18.50	18.50
Mexico	15.50	17.00	17.50	17.50	17.50	17.50	17.50	19.00	19.00	19.00
Philippines	14.00	14.00	14.00	14.00	14.00	14.00	14.00	14.00	14.00	14.00
Singapore	6.78	7.02	7.65	8.12	8.35	8.78	8.92	9.10	9.18	9.50
Eurodollars	5.50	7.56	12.06	10.87	11.68	12.49	13.12	16.06	14.37	14.81

Source: Morgan Guaranty Trust Company, *World Financial Markets*.

Exhibit 8

Price index: Korea and selected countries

	Korea	China, Rep.	Japan	Philippines	Thailand	United States
Wholesale price indexes during:						
1974	79.0	105.3	97.1	94.9	96.4	91.5
1975	100.0	100.0	100.0	100.0	100.0	100.0
1976	112.1	102.8	105.1	109.2	103.9	104.6
1977	122.2	105.6	107.0	120.0	109.5	111.0
1978	136.5	109.3	104.3	128.2	114.7	119.7
1979:						
1	143.4	114.8	103.9	137.5	117.6	126.2
2	145.6	115.8	104.8	136.3	121.1	133.8
3	149.0	118.2	105.7	140.6	123.1	129.6
4	153.1	121.3	107.5	145.3	124.8	131.5
5	157.4	122.7	109.2	147.1	126.0	132.6
6	158.3	123.6	110.6	149.1	127.3	133.3
7	166.4	127.3	112.7	151.0	131.1	135.4
8	171.5	128.6	114.5	160.2	132.6	136.2
9	173.8	128.9	116.1	162.3	135.3	138.4
10	175.0	129.4	117.4	163.0	137.3	104.2
11	174.7	129.5	119.2	163.7	138.1	141.2
Consumer price indexes during:						
1974	79.8	95.0	84.4	92.4	96.1	91.6
1975	100.0	100.0	100.0	100.0	100.0	100.0
1976	115.3	102.5	109.3	106.1	105.0	105.8
1977	127.0	109.7	118.1	114.5	112.1	112.7
1978	145.3	116.0	122.6	123.2	121.0	121.2
1979:						
1	154.6	119.2	123.4	130.8	124.1	127.0
2	160.0	119.8	123.0	130.3	125.0	128.5
3	162.8	121.4	124.0	133.2	126.1	129.7
4	166.9	123.8	125.7	139.8	127.4	131.2
5	172.1	124.8	127.0	144.1	129.2	132.8
6	173.7	126.1	127.1	145.8	130.2	134.4
7	174.5	127.2	128.2	148.8	133.8	135.8
8	175.1	130.6	126.9	153.9	135.8	137.2
9	177.5	134.8	128.5	155.7	138.7	138.6
10	178.7	134.4	130.1	157.1	141.3	139.8
11	181.4	132.6	129.6	157.7	141.6	141.1
12	181.4	132.6	129.6	157.7	141.6	141.1
1980	192.1	138.8	131.6	—	—	144.7

Source: Bank of Korea, *Monthly Economic Statistics.*

Exhibit 9

Repayments of foreign debt (U.S. $ millions)

1974	338.4
1975	284.1
1976	406.6
1977	536.0
1978	825.1
1979	
I	209.3
II	290.8
III	349.0

Source: Bank of Korea,
*Monthly Economic
Statistics.*

The Korean won (B): Devaluation*

JAL flight 007 from Tokyo to Chicago leveled out at cruising speed after an uneventful takeoff on a crisp, unusually clear Tokyo morning. Kimono-clad hostesses were already scurrying about the first-class cabin bearing the first round of that endless flow of *saké, sushi,* and *sashimi* which made JAL first class so enjoyable.

David Louis didn't usually travel first class, but the tourist section was full when he made his reservation and he had just finished 10 rough days in Seoul negotiating with Korean government officials. Ten days in Korea in early January can be hard on even an experienced businessman, and Louis was still a bit under the weather from a bad case of the flu he came down with over Christmas and New Year's, which he had spent in Bangkok.

Louis enjoyed his new job as manager of the International Division at Willingford Electronics. He was home based in Chicago but spent one month out of three traveling in the Far East and Latin America. He had been with Willingford since leaving his position as assistant international treasurer at Fibrex Corporation in 1977. Recently most of his time was taken up with Willingford's plans to establish a subsidiary in Korea. Willingford had proposed a $2,000 million won semiconductor manufacturing operation, KOAM Electronics Company, in Korea. Negotiations with Korean government officials had been proceeding well, and Louis was looking forward to a meeting with Willingford's board of directors at 9:00 A.M. the day after he arrived home.

Louis settled back in the snug luxury of his wide first-class seat and opened his January 13, 1980, *Japan Times* to the front page. He could hardly believe what he saw. The headline, KOREAN WON DEVALUED 17 percent (from 484 to 580), rudely blasted away his anticipation of first-class creature comforts. He must have let out an audible gasp because when he looked up an attractive young woman seated next to him was staring intently at him.

"Anything wrong?" she inquired.

"Only this," he replied as he held up the headline, completely unprepared for the long low whistle the headline elicited from the young woman.

"Will this have some impact on you too?" Louis asked.

---

* Prepared by J. Frederick Truitt, Associate Professor of International Business, and Chong S. Lee, research assistant, Graduate School of Business Administration, University of Washington, as a basis for classroom discussion. Copyright 1981 by the authors.

Exhibit 1

Memo to Willingford Board

CONFIDENTIAL: Circulation Restricted

To: Willingford Board of Directors
From: Management Committee
Re: KOAM Electronics Company, *Prospectus*

I. After evaluating several potential sites in the Far East and Latin America, we have decided that Korea is the most promising location for our new semiconductor manufacturing operation.

   A. Under current Foreign Investment Promotion Regulations of Korea, our proposed investment is classified as a "recommendable investment project."

   B. As a recommendable investment project, it is entitled to favorable treatment including:
      1. Favorable tax treatment.
      2. Government financial assistance.
      3. Duty-free import of raw materials.
      4. Protection in the domestic (Korean) market.

   C. But the quid pro quo for this favorable treatment means that Willingford must:
      1. Train workers and managers.
      2. Surrender all equity in our project to the Korean government after five years at full compensation in won at value of initial equity contribution.

II. Willingford's proposed equity contribution to KOAM is 1,000 million won. Another 1,000 million won provide the other half of the investment and will be borrowed locally in Korea at favorable rates.

III. Pro forma income statement for KOAM for each of five years of Willingford ownership is given below:

Pro Forma Income Statement

	Won (millions)
Sales (1,000,000 @ 5,000 won/set[a]	5,000
Costs.	(4,000)
Labor—skilled[b] . . . . (1,700)	
Raw materials:	
Imported (duty-free) . . . . (1,000)	
Local . . . . (500)	
Overhead . . . . (300)	
Interest[c] . . . . (500)	
Profit (before tax)[d][e]	1,000

[a] The present market price of imported semiconductors is 4,500 won/set. This price includes 500 won/set of import duties.

[b] The prevailing market price of skilled labor is about the same as the price used in KOAM's income statement. The location where KOAM plans to build its plant is a booming region with very little unemployment.

[c] KOAM has access to a special low interest loan from local banks. It plans to borrow necessary capital at the interest rate of 10 percent per year, while the average lending rate in Korea is 20 percent for this kind of project.

[d] Tax incentives offered by the Korean government to encourage foreign investment will lower the profit tax rate on KOAM from the normal 30 percent to the "full incentive" rate of only 10 percent.

[e] KOAM plans to repatriate all net profits to Willingford, Chicago. These profits will play a crucial role in Willingford's modernization and expansion program.

"You'd better believe it! I'm the buyer for Midwest Sportswear, Inc., and it will certainly impact my operation and plans for this year's purchases. How is it going to affect you?"

"Well . . ." said Louis, as he opened his briefcase and pulled out his Texas Instruments MBA calculator, "that's what I'm going to have to figure out before this plane lands in Chicago. What say we pool resources and compare notes. I think we both have some work to do. By the way, maybe I could buy you a drink?" inquired Louis.

"The drinks are free and I'm having Perrier," she replied as she unzipped her programmable HP. "By the way, I'm Annika-Karin Vilms. I didn't catch your name."

The material that Louis and Vilms had in their briefcases is summarized in Exhibits 1 to 9 of the Korean won (A) case. Exhibits 1 and 2 of the Korean won (B) case show the reports that Louis and Vilms had recently composed concerning operations of their respective firms in Korea.

Exhibit 2

Summary of Midwest Sportswear position in Korea (December 31, 1979)

CONFIDENTIAL

To: Mr. F. X. O'Malley, President

From: Annika-Karin Vilms, Buyer

   Korea continues to be one of our principal offshore sources of high-quality merchandise. Along with Hong Kong and Taiwan, Korea provides more than half of the total value of our merchandise.

   We are currently buying from four major producers and expect to do $20 million (f.o.b. Korea) worth of purchases in Korea in 1980. The peak shipping period this year will be in May and June.

   We continue to finance our Korean imports with 90- or 120-day U.S. $ f.o.b.* letters of credit. The value of the letters of credit we have drawn will vary over the year, but at this time we project the following:

1980, 1st quarter	$4 million
1980, 2d quarter	$8 million
1980, 3d quarter	$6 million
1980, 4th quarter	$2 million

* The letter of credit authorizes the beneficiary (Korean exporter) to draw payment from a bank once the conditions stipulated (putting a specified shipment on a vessel in Korea) are met. The letter of credit is denominated in U.S. $ and is open for a period of from 90 to 120 days, i.e., the Korean exporter has from 90 to 120 days from the date the L/C is opened to do what is specified in the document.

Sun health foods*

In May 1980, Philip Aspinwall was contemplating the advice he would give Ernesto Sun, who had consulted him regarding the terms of his proposed business contract with the Chinese Republic. Ernesto imported into New York a wide range of specialist foods from Mediterranean and oriental countries. He had recently been approached by agricultural officials of the Chinese Republic to undertake the U.S. sale of their entire supply of pumpkin and melon seeds. These were generally high-quality seeds and had a ready market in the health food sector. Ernesto planned to sell to distributors and store chains that would package and brand the seeds and distribute them to retail stores.

The Chinese supply could amount to $3 million in a single year, and Ernesto would be given exclusive rights to these supplies. He would, however, be required to quote firm prices for shipments as they became available and to pay on shipment. When Ernesto had raised the issue of a formal agreement, the Chinese officials had expressed willingness to sign such a document and suggested that Ernesto submit a draft to them. it was about the specific terms he should include that Ernesto had approached Philip Aspinwall.

* This case was prepared by Professor Kenneth Simmonds of the London Graduate School of Business Studies. Copyright © 1981 Professor Kenneth Simmonds.

The nation-state and international business

Technology transfer: The Cyber 76*

Across the country, defenders of America rushed to their mail boxes and television stations in June 1977 to demand that the government deny Control Data Corporation a license to export a Cyber 76 computer to Russia. Jack Anderson wielded his mighty pen, congressmen petitioned the President, and Jimmy Carter and Zbigniew Brzezinski requested Juanita Kreps, Commerce Secretary, to deny the license even before the Commerce Department had completed examination of the proposed sale. Opposing the shipment one congressman commented, "I don't know what it is called today, but in earlier times it would have been called treason."

The Cyber 76 was intended for Hydromet (the Soviet Hydrometeorological Research Center in Moscow). Both the United States and the USSR were members of the World Meteorological Organization, a UN agency, and members had agreed to share information, analyses, forecasts, and research on weather. The U.S. National Oceanographic and Atmospheric Agency (NOAA) claimed that there were major gaps in the data available to the Worldwide Weather Watch (WWW) because inadequate Soviet computer capability prevented important weather data from Siberia being processed on time. With a third-generation computer such as Cyber 76, data would flow from the Soviets as well as to them. At the time, U.S. weather agencies had three such machines and Britain, Canada, West Germany, and Union of South Africa each had one. Furthermore, the United States and USSR had signed a series of agreements in 1972–73 to expand mutual technological cooperation and trade.

Representative Robert Dornan, a Republican congressman from California serving on the House Science and Technology Committee, argued, however, that the Cyber 76 could be used for "navigation and weapons guidance in modern missile, aircraft, tanks, high performance satellite-based surveillance systems, ABM [antiballistic missile] defense systems,

* This case was prepared by Professor Kenneth Simmonds, London Business School, from published data. Copyright © 1981 Professor Kenneth Simmonds.

and submarines. Soviet assurances that this computer will be used for peaceful purposes are unreliable at best and there is no practical method of monitoring the uses to which the computer is put."

At a press luncheon hastily pulled together by the American Security Council, Dornan called the sale "the top strategic issue in the country today—and selling to the country that wants to do us in.

"We've bailed out their agriculture; bailed out their aerospace industry.

"We risk making Lenin's prophecy come true" [i.e., capitalism will sell us the rope to hang them].

Dornan claimed that Control Data was pushing the sale because they had saturated the market for Cyber 76 and it was a survival instinct to keep on selling more—rationalizing that it was not a military threat.

Control Data grosses $2 billion in annual sales and had sold a total of 54 Cyber 76s, 30 within the United States. Depending on what the customer required in software, the selling price varied from $5 to $10 million per computer and about half a dozen were shipped per year. The Cyber 76 contained about 3 million transistors, with some so difficult to make and with so small a market that Control Data had had to make them itself and was the world's only supplier.

It would be possible, of course, to reprogram the Cyber 76. For a weapon systems tracking analysis something over 1,000 man-years of software development would be needed. Moreover, as the meteorological needs would use all of its capacity, it would be immediately obvious if the machine were not in use for meteorological purposes. It could not do both tasks at the same time—and supply of spare parts could be easily stopped. Some estimates of Cyber life without replacement parts placed it as low as 30 days but three months was more likely. To produce replacement transistors through "reverse engineering" would take the Soviets many years. Yet it was true that the Pentagon used Cyber 76s for a wide range of military purposes.

A strong Control Data argument for supplying the computer was that failure to supply could speed up USSR development of their own large main frames. This would totally remove an estimated annual $1 billion communist-bloc market from U.S. firms over the following eight years and build a further competitor for third-world sales of about the same amount. If the Soviets did not make their own main frame, they would anyway get something similar from Germany or Japan and strengthen these foreign competitors. Every $20,000 sales lost would represent one U.S. job lost.

Control Data claimed that the USSR had the basic technology to become completely self-sufficient in computers by 1980. Largely due to U.S. export restriction in the past, the Soviets had already developed a Ryad series of small and medium computers, several times faster than the IBM 360-145 for scientific calculations. For some time, the Soviets had been making the largest investments in basic research of any nation in the world and computer technology formed a large part of these amounts.

The Department of Defense policy on the Export Control of U.S. technology was being developed following the "Bucy Report" of the Defense Science Board Task Force the previous year. The following extracts are taken from the DOD Interim Policy Statement:

Background

U.S. policy on international trade consists of two elements that are not always reconcilable: (1) to promote trade and commerce with other nations and (2) to control exports of goods and technology which could make a significant contribution to the military potential of any other nation or nations when this would prove detrimental to the national security of the United States. While the Defense Department's chief concern is with the second of these goals, it must discharge its concern without restricting U.S. trade and exports any more than necessary.

Defense's primary objective in the control of exports of U.S. technology is to protect the United States' lead time relative to its principal adversaries in the application of technology to military capabilities. This lead time is to be protected and maintained as long as is practical, in order to provide time for the replenishment of technology through new research and development. In addition, it is in the national interest not to make it easy for any country to advance its technology in ways that could be detrimental to U.S. interests. These controls, however, are to be applied so as to result in the minimum interference in the normal conduct of commercial trade. This policy statement provides interim internal guidance to the Defense Department to maximize the above objectives to the maximum practical extent.

Definitions

The term *critical technology* as used herein refers to the classified and unclassified nuclear and non-nuclear unpublished technical data, whose acquisition by a potential adversary could make a significant contribution, which would prove detrimental to the national security of the United States, to the military potential of such country—irrespective of whether such technology is acquired directly from the United States or indirectly through another recipient, or whether the declared intended end-use by the recipient is a military or nonmilitary use.

"Technical data" means information of any kind that can be used, or adapted for use, in the design, production, manufacture, utilization, testing, maintenance, or reconstruction of articles or materials. The data may take a tangible form, such as a model, prototype, blueprint, or an operating manual, or they may take an intangible form such as technical service.

Control of such critical technology also requires the control of certain associated critical end products defined as "keystone" that can contribute significantly in and of themselves to the transfer of critical technology because they (1) embody extractable critical technology and/or (2) are equipment that completes a process line and allows it to be fully utilized.

Defense Department policy in export control of U.S. technology

In assessing and making recommendations upon those export applications referred to it by the State and Commerce departments, Defense will place primary emphasis on controlling exports to any country of arrays of design and manufacturing know-how; of keystone manufacturing, inspection, and test equipment; and of sophisticated operation, application, or maintenance know-how.

In order to protect key strategic U.S. lead times, export control of defense-related critical technology to all foreign countries is required. To this end, Defense will:

1. Request the Department of Commerce to alter existing regulations so as to require a validated license for proposed exports of critical technology to all destinations.

*   *   *   *   *

Defense will support the transfer of critical technology to countries with which the United States has a major security interest where such transfers can (1) strengthen collective security, (2) contribute to the goals of weapons standardization and interoperability, and (3) maximize the effective return on the collective NATO Alliance or other Allied investment in R&D.

*   *   *   *   *

Defense will normally recommend approval of sales of end products to potential adversaries in those instances where (1) the product's technology content is either difficult, impractical, or economically unfeasible to extract, (2) the end product in question will not of itself significantly enhance the recipient's military or warmaking capability, either by virtue of its technology content or because of the quantity to be sold, and (3) the product cannot be so analyzed as to reveal U.S. system characteristics and thereby contribute to the development of countermeasures to equivalent U.S. equipment.

There shall be a presumption for recommending disapproval of any transaction involving a revolutionary advance in defense-related technology to the proposed recipient country (if the resultant military capability threatens U.S. interests). Defense will assess a proposed export of technology not on the basis of whether the item is obsolete by U.S. standards, but on whether the proposed export would significantly advance the receiving country's potential and prove detrimental to the national security of the United States.

End-use statements and safeguards are not to be considered a factor in approving exports to potential adversaries of critical technologies and products except as may be otherwise provided in presidential directives. . . .

Defense recommendations to approve the export of end products to potential adversaries are to be made primarily on the basis of an assessment that the products' inherent performance capabilites, or the quantity sold, do not constitute a significant addition to the recipients' military capability which would prove detrimental to the national security of the United States.

Conference on International Trade*

Memo to:

From: Your Boss

Date: May 20, 1981

Subject: Conference on International Trade

I have been invited to participate in a conference on international trade which will culminate with policy recommendations to selected congressmen and Bill Brock, the special trade representative. Before attending the conference, however, I need clarification of an issue which I find confusing.

Following the Soviet invasion of Afganistan President Carter issued the wheat embargo, prohibiting the export of U.S. grain to the Soviet Union. This action was intended to damage the Soviet Union and express U.S. dissatisfaction with their aggression, without declaring war.

Recently, a similar trade policy was adopted by Japan. They have imposed quotas limiting exports of Japanese-made autos to the United States. This policy has been viewed by the United States as an act of friendship or alliance.

My confusion over trade policy is this: in both cases exports are restricted, yet, in one case the policy is intended to be harmful and in the other intended to be beneficial. Could it be that the Japanese secretly intend to damage the United States, or that President Carter was secretly supporting the Afghan invasion?

Obviously, the United States will damage the Soviet economy by not allowing them to consume our wheat or feed it to their livestock. And, obviously, the United States will benefit from protection against competition with Japanese automakers who face cheaper labor costs.

Please prepare a memo clarifying the issues and criteria for trade restrictions, with special attention to the two instances mentioned above and the continued deficit position in the U.S. balance of trade. If

---

* This case was prepared by Arthur B. Laffer and James C. Turney at the School of Business, University of Southern California. Reprinted by permission from Arthur B. Laffer.

appropriate, discuss differing points of view and theoretical constructs. The conference will be attended by businessmen and academics of all backgrounds. Use any information you can acquire by whatever means. The memo should be no more than ten pages double-spaced (regular margins please). I must have your clarification of trade policy no later than May 27, 1981.

    Thank you.

Russell Karagosian*

Winging south to Latin America aboard Pan American, Russell Karago-
sian had five hours flying time and an evening in his hotel room to prepare a presentation to the Minister for Industry outlining the basic characteristics of a scheme for evaluating new foreign investments.

Russell was a principal consultant for a Boston firm of business con-
sultants. He had worked with this firm since completing his degree at a
leading business school and had been mainly engaged in international
market surveys and feasibility studies for multinational corporations.

The current assignment stemmed from a Christmas party at which
Russell was introduced to Senor da Silva, a prominent lawyer from one of
the smaller Latin American countries. On learning that Russell was an
international business consultant, this gentleman had inferred that
perhaps Russell's specialty was inventing ways to get higher profits out of
Latin America and referred to the topical editorial shown in Appendix 1.
Defending himself, Russell argued that any problems stemmed from the
countries themselves. They had not made up their minds precisely what
 as in their best interests and then given a clear indication of what they
 nted and how they would measure it. It was not too difficult, Russell
  rted, to develop a standard set of questionnaire forms that would
   re potential investors to show clearly the benefits and disadvantages
    proposal from the viewpoint of the recipient country.

   e months later, after a change of government, Senor da Silva was
    d Minister for Industry of his country. Shortly thereafter, Russell
     n received a telephone call inviting him to meet the minister
     ig day to discuss his ideas further with a view to a more formal
      to develop them into operative plans. There was no time to
      ıl presentation but Russell was able to put his hands on a set
      ents introduced in the Philippines some years previously as
       ofit remittance, shown as Appendix 2.

AMERICAN

ter of Finance in South America, I'd get me a good
 oung guys trained in Uncle Sugar Able. Then I'd

eth Simmonds.
g, November–December 1969.

comb the books of the bigger *Yanqui* subs in my country . . . and I'd sock it to 'em, sock it to 'em, sock it to 'em."

With this malediction my international controller buddy, Chuck Mc-Gregor, slid into place next to me at Charlie Brown's in the Pan Am Building. He certainly was more than slightly steamed (and oiled) as he flipped open a copy of *Fortune* to the article "Threatening Weather in Latin America."

"Here's someone who says U.S. subsidiaries in Latin America contribute 20 percent of that area's tax revenues. If I had the job, I could get that up to at least 35 to 40 percent, without half trying. Hell, in some subs, my company is taking out its original investment every year or more and there are others like us."

I chastised him for being un-American, unpatriotic, and warned him, with loose talk like that he could be drummed out of the National Foreign Trade Council as well as the Council for Latin America and the International Executives Association. And, if he kept on blithering that he wanted to repatriate less money from South of the Border, he would soon talk his way out of the cushiest controller job in mid-Manhattan.

Didn't he know, I emphasized, that U.S. subs "down there" accounted for 12 percent of all Latin production? And 20 percent of that area's exports? Or didn't he care?

"Sure I know these things and I care," he sniffed. "But I'm running scared. What with the anti-*norteamericano* climate in Peru and Bolivia—and rumblings elsewhere—I don't want our five Latin plants to be expropriated. So we damn well better come up with some more loot for the locals—and fast. I hate to say it, but as *Fortune* hinted, they're beginning to wise up."

But hadn't his firm done a lot for local Latin economies? I mentioned a double-page ad spread in *Time*, which dramatically showed what his company's sub had done for a small Latin town "before" and "after." Money was pumped in with no promise of return. And look what happened. New schools, new roads, with illiteracy down, disease down, and employment up.

"I remember that ad," he chuckled. "Our local guys had a helluva time rounding up enough good-looking Indians for the photo. Sure we did something for them. But we're doing a lot more for us. Do you remember what the copy said? 'We are again proving our faith in_____by reinvesting profits for our workers' future.'

"But," Chuck went on, "do you want to know the real score? After our 'allowable' repatriation and after we took our several hundred thou' more in pre-tax 'expenses,' then we're glad to invest the little that's left. Because in weak-currency countries, we've been taking out 50 to 100 percent ROI every year."

Was he intimating U.S. subsidiaries in Latin America kept two sets of books?

"Well, it isn't two sets of books in the classic Tuscan sense. We only have one, but we make it do the work of two. Any local tax man can see we carry 'expenses' on the books. But they're just a neat device to siphon off as much pretax income as we can."

I cautioned him not to give away company secrets as I looked around to see if any of his competitors or Latin tax authorities were tuning in. Chuck tends to get boisterous after his third Tanqueray.

"The only trouble is," he said, ignoring my blunt warning, "that we're weakening, not shoring up, the economies of these countries by scarfing off all the foreign exchange the traffic will bear. Let's take a hypothetical case. I'll exaggerate somewhat but I'll show you how to play the Latin American repatriation game.

"Let's say our investment is $500,000 . . . and local authorities fix our repatriation ratio at 10 percent of investment. Then we quick pump in a $2 million loan from our Mexican sub at 20 percent interest for fixed asset expansion. We 'convince' Exchange Control that our fixed assets are now $2.5 million—and 10 percent of *that* begins to look pretty good. With our true return of $1 million on $6 million sales, then I can 'legitimately' get out $250,000—50 percent of our original investment—as our allowable dollar repatriation.

"But," Chuck grinned slyly, "I'm still way ahead of the game because I'm getting 400 thou' as interest on our $2 million Mexican loan. Then I work up some nifty Home Office charges such as technical management advice, special research, packaging design, etc. We figure these at 4 percent of sales, so this is a cool $240,000."

Are the charges real I wanted to know.

"Of course not," he said spiritedly. "You sure are green. But who's to prove me wrong? And aren't our trademark and name worth something? Of course, they are," he said, answering his own question. "And I value these at 3 percent of sales, which is another $180,000.

"When I have loaded on all the hard currency pretax expenses, I have one final fillip left. I make the local sub pay $500 a month toward the salary of our regional Latin vice president in Coral Gables. It's a real check, but he never sees it.

"Let's total up," Chuck said briskly, writing on the bar with his Cross ballpoint.

Home office charges	$ 240,000
Trademark value	180,000
Share of "salary"	6,000
Interest on loan	400,000
Repatriation	250,000
Total	$1,076,000

"So here I am repatriating just over twice our original $500,000 investment! Not bad for a country boy from Indiana. By the way, we never go through with expansion. We'll cancel the loan quietly, but it's served its real purpose—to really jump our investment base. The authorities won't catch on for some time—if ever—as we'll finance expansion out of local accounts."

As I reached for the check, he made one final point. "But we just have to cut back. Most Latin countries are training some sharp MBA types up here. And, remember, they have a legitimate bitch. A lot of us haven't left *that* much behind in the local economy—and I'm afraid we'll have to pay the piper and dance to the Finance Minister's tune."

How much would he pay and how fast would he dance I asked.

"A lot more. On our Baton Rouge tank farm, we went for 10 percent ROI over 10 years. I'd settle for 20 percent in five in Latin America. This should keep the wolves at bay for awhile. It's less for us, but it's better than losing everything. The good old carpetbagging days are done."

APPENDIX 2: CENTRAL BANK OF THE PHILIPPINES, MANILA—MEMORANDUM TO ALL AUTHORIZED AGENTS

As a result of continuing analytical studies, the system of measurements has been amended to improve the method of implementing the Central Bank's policy on investment remittance. Under this policy, which applies equally to precontrol investments as well as to approved post-control investment, Philippine companies and branches of foreign companies are allowed to remit profits and dividends due to their nonresident stockholders or head offices on the basis of the net contributions of the companies to (a) national income and employment or "the national income effect," (b) strengthening the balance-of-payments position of the country or "the balance-of-payments effect," and (c) supply of goods and services to serve the basic needs of the economy or "the product essentiality." The system of measurements, as amended, is indicated below.

I. NATIONAL INCOME EFFECT
   A. The national income effect is the ratio of the net domestic value added by the firm to the amount of scarce resources utilized in production and is expressed by the equation:

$$Y = (V_g/I_t) \times 100\%$$

where

Y = national income effect, percent
V_g = net domestic value added by the firm, pesos
I_t = amount of scarce resources utilized in production, pesos

   B. Net domestic value added consists of the sum of the shares of the four factors of production in the income of the firm. This is obtained by adding the shares of:

1. Labor—consisting of salaries and wages, bonuses, and commissions received by the employees and wage earners of the firm.
2. Land—rent of land and buildings used by the firm in production.
3. Entrepreneur—profits before income tax.
4. Capital—interest payments on loans.

C. Scarce resources consist of:

1. Replacement of fixed assets—current amortization (depreciation) of fixed assets of both domestic and imported origin.
2. Maintenance of fixed assets—cost of spare parts, labor, supplies, and other costs incurred in maintenance. (If maintenance is done by an outside firm, the total charges of the outside firm plus the cost of spare parts and supplies provided by the firm will be deducted.)
3. Foreign exchange utilized—the foreign exchange cost of raw materials and supplies (including fuel) directly imported and indirectly (domestically purchased) imported, salaries of foreign personnel remitted abroad, and all other foreign exchange costs (royalties, service charges, expenses of business trips abroad, and so forth.)

D. Automatic rating for firms producing intermediate products. Firms producing intermediate products necessary for the production processes of other essential industries are credited a minimum 3-point rating in the national income effect. Necessity is established if the intermediate product possesses either or both of the following characteristics:

1. It forms an integral part, physically or chemically, of the product of the other essential industry.
2. It is a necessary accessory for handling or merchandising, that is, containers, of the final product.

E. The rating accruing from contribution to national income effect is obtained by the following schedule:

Schedule 1

National income effect (percent)	Accrued rating* (points)
Above 300	5
251–300	4
201–250	3
151–200	2
101–150	1
100 and below	0

*Except for firms producing intermediate products which are credited a minimum 3-point rating.

II. BALANCE-OF-PAYMENT EFFECT
   A. The balance-of-payments effect is measured by the ratio of the net foreign exchange earned and saved to the amount of scarce resources utilized during the period and is expressed by the following equation:

$$B = (F_n/I_t) \times 100\%$$

where

B = balance-of-payments effect, percent
F_n = net foreign exchange earned and saved, pesos
I_t = amount of scarce resources utilized in production, pesos

   B. The net foreign exchange earned and saved is determined by subtracting the foreign exchange costs of production from the foreign exchange value of the product.
   C. The foreign exchange costs consist of the foreign exchange utilized in production (I [C][3] above) plus the current amortization of imported fixed assets. Generally, land, furniture, and building are considered domestic fixed assets; and all the rest, imported fixed assets.
   D. The foreign exchange value is determined by:
      1. Earnings—foreign exchange received for payment of exports.
      2. Savings—in the case of import substitute, the foreign exchange cost of the product if it were imported (c.i.f. value of the product shall be used). A product shall be considered as an import substitute if it is an essential commodity or its manufacture began subsequent to the imposition of exchange control (December, 9, 1949) and it displaces products imported prior to the import control.
   E. The rating accruing from the strengthening of the balance-of-payments position of the country is given by the following schedule:

Schedule 2

Balance-of-payments effect (percent)	Accrued rating (points)
Above 200	5
166–200	4
131–165	3
96–130	2
61– 95	1
60 and below	0

III. PRODUCT ESSENTIALITY
   A. Products are first classified according to (1) export products and (2) products for domestic consumption.

B. Export products are further classified according to the degree of processing they have undergone as:
1. Manufactured products.
2. Semimanufactured products.
3. Raw materials.
C. Products for domestic consumption are further classified into:
1. Highly essential products.
2. Essential producer products.
3. Essential consumer products.
4. Nonessential producer products.
5. Nonessential consumer products.

The Central Bank Commodity Classification shall be used as the primary basis of classifying products for domestic consumption. For this purpose, the unclassified items in the Central Bank Commodity Classification shall be reclassified. The criteria to be used in the reclassification shall be "utility" of the product.
D. The corresponding rating accruing from the essentiality of the product is determined by the following schedule:

Schedule 3

Products for domestic use	Export products	Category	Accrued rating (points)
Highly essential	Manufactured	I	5
Essential producer		II	4
Essential consumer	Semimanufactured	III	3
Nonessential producer		IV	2
Nonessential consumer	Raw materials	V	1

IV. SCHEDULE OF ALLOWABLE REMITTANCES
A. A straight 40 percent of the nonresident's share in the net profits shall be allowed to be remitted by the following firms:
1. Firms operating under a government franchise wherein the output is of the character of a public service.
2. Banks and insurance companies.
B. Beginning with profits realized for financial years ending in 1958, all other companies are allowed to remit dividends or profits to their nonresident stockholders or head offices abroad according to the following schedule of allowable annual remittances:

Schedule 4

Social productivity rating (SPR)	Allowable remittances (whichever is lower)	
	Percent of the nonresident's share in current net profit	Percent of foreign capital invested*
13–15	100	60
10–12	80	50
7– 9	60	40
4– 6	40	30
1– 3	25	20

* As of the beginning of the period for which the profit is realized.

The Social Productivity Rating of a firm is the sum of the ratings accruing from the national income effect, balance-of-payments effect, and product essentiality. For non-Philippine companies, the depreciated or net book value of capital assets as at the beginning of the fiscal year for which the profit is realized will be used instead of capital invested.

C. Withholding taxes on dividends are to be deducted from the remittable amounts as determined.

Flexoid Carribia*

The Flexoid Corporation wished to invest in a new plant in Carribia to manufacture Myoprene, a speciality chemical. The company held the patents for the process and had several plants on stream in Europe. Myoprene imports had been prohibited from Carribia for some years as they were not included within the local government's category of "essential imports," but Flexoid management had come to the conclusion that a plant solely to serve the Carribian market could be jusified.

The company analysts had worked out a pro forma income statement for a typical year of expected operations as shown in Exhibit 1, and were preparing a note for management as a basis for negotiations with the Carribian government's Foreign Investment Review Board. Management had asked for an evaluation of the advantages of alternative financing plans and an outline of the arguments that might be used to justify the project to the Review Board.

Carribia was still basically an agricultural country, reliant for foreign exchange earnings on the export of agricultural commodities. Mechanization in agriculture and a high birth rate, however, had combined to produce widespread underemployment, and the creation of new jobs in manufacturing had been given high priority on the government's list of objectives.

To spur the development of import-replacing investments, many "infant-industry" tariffs had been introduced. Normally only one investor was permitted to manufacture a given product, and the tariffs were set sufficiently high to give the manufacturer at least a temporary monopoly. Myoprene from a Carribian plant would be priced at 20 percent above the prevailing world supply price, but preliminary discussions with Carribian trade officials had indicated that a tariff of 30 percent ad valorem would be imposed on Myoprene and substitutes in the event of the plant being authorized.

As yet there was no important chemical investment in Carribia. The recent government five-year development plan, however, called for such investment. The establishment of a Myoprene facility would provide local demand for several base chemicals and would certainly add to the interest of major international chemical companies in further Carribian investment.

* This case was prepared by Professor John Stopford and Professor Kenneth Simmonds of the London Graduate School of Business Studies. Copyright © 1976 John Stopford.

Carribia had numerous development options, and it was known that the government planners had been using a rate of 20 percent per annum as a gauge of the "opportunity cost" of capital in determining priorities among competing projects.

The total capital cost for the new Myoprene operation was estimated at 900,000 pesos and would be financed by 400,000 pesos of equity from Flexoid and 500,000 pesos of long-term debt. Flexoid's founder, just recently retired as president, had viewed minority partners as "getting a free ride on profits" and had shaped Flexoid's financial policy to retain full ownership of all subsidiaries with maximum use of fixed interest debt. If Flexoid raised the debt finance outside Carribia and secured it against its home-base assets the interest rate would be 10 percent per annum. Money raised in Carribia solely against the security of the proposed plant, however, would cost 15 percent per annum. The peso was valued on a par with the U.S. dollar and the Carribian government had followed a policy, which seemed unlikely to change, of maintaining this parity.

Exhibit 1

Pro forma income statement for a typical year's operations in Carribia

		Pesos (000s)
Sales		1,000
Cost of goods sold		
Labor—local	200	
Raw materials—imported	400	
local	100	700
Gross margin		300
Indirect expenses—maintenance, depreciation, selling, administration, etc.		100
Profit before interest and 50 percent local taxation		200

Global business strategy

Alfa-Laval Thermal*

In November 1975, senior members of Alfa-Laval's Thermal Subdivision, based in Lund, Sweden, had come together to review the subdivision's strategy. The subdivision was a major international force in the manufacturing and marketing of thermal products. It still held—as it had done over the last two decades—the position of dominant market leader in its chosen product area; but small cracks appearing in its structure and strategy were causing some managerial concern.

ALFA-LAVAL'S INTERNATIONAL ORGANIZATION

Alfa-Laval was in 1975 one of the largest Swedish companies. The original establishment had been founded in 1883 and over the years the company had diversified into a wide range of businesses. A fundamental Alfa-Laval philosophy, however, was its intention to remain in the manufacture and marketing of industrial products.

The company's activities could by 1975 be divided into three broad categories:

Industrial Equipment—centrifuges, pumps, thermal equipment and installations for the food industry, power production, mechanical engineering industries, shipbuilding, the chemical, pulp and paper industries, as well as for environmental control.

Dairy Processing Equipment—special processes and complete plants for dairies and certain beverage industries.

Farm Equipment—equipment and systems for milking, feeding, manure removal, hygiene, and cooling.

In 1975 there were four major company divisions: Farm, Separation, Thermal and Dairy, and Rosenblads. Activities which could not be easily incorporated into one of the four divisions were referred to as "Other Companies and Units." The divisions were profit centers, each responsible for a defined range of products and applications, producing for sale

---

* This case was prepared by Professor Kenneth Simmonds and Mr. Shiv Mathur, Senior Research Officer, of the London Business School. It was written with the cooperation of Alfa-Laval management. Facts and figures have been disguised to preserve corporate confidentiality. Copyright © 1980 Professor Kenneth Simmonds.

to the Group's worldwide marketing network and monitoring and influencing worldwide performance within the scope of their business mission.

Alfa-Laval market companies, as listed in Exhibit 1, provided outlets for the Group's products in many countries of the world. In countries with less demand, Alfa-Laval had distributors and commission agents. Senior management felt the coverage more than adequate for the Group's current needs.

Over the years, many market companies had drifted away from their original role as outlets for Alfa-Laval products. Some had set up manufacturing operations, enabling them to cut down freight costs and reap the advantage of a better local presence. It was, however, neither technologically nor economically justified to move all stages of production to local sites and the more highly capital-intensive production tasks remained in Sweden for almost all products. As a consequence, the overseas manufacturing establishment needed for any one product was not large and the local market companies had generally combined local manufacturing for various products and divisions under one roof. These manufacturing activities had often expanded to such an extent that the term "market company" had become a misnomer.

In a few instances, the manufacturing activities of market companies had expanded to include production for export to other group companies. For items that were manufactured by market companies for export within the Group, "Product Centers" at Divisional Headquarters in Sweden attempted to coordinate the manufacturing activities of the various units. Production for local markets, however, was considered the sole responsibility of the domestic market company. Exhibit 2 shows the breakdown of manufacturing activities for the Group.

Though some market companies manufactured both for the local market and the Group, there was a significant difference between the manufacturing activities of market companies and divisions. Production within divisions was in higher volumes, involved larger capital investments and greater R&D, and produced a much more comprehensive range of products. For example, the basic plates for heat exchangers were pressed only in Lund, Sweden, while frames and other components were made in Germany, Spain, the United States, and some other countries.

LIAISON BETWEEN CUSTOMER, MARKET COMPANY, AND DIVISIONS

The primary contact for either a Scandinavian or overseas customer was the local market company. In some instances, the customer could have a choice of two or more market companies but such instances were rare and Alfa-Laval attempted to ensure that in any one market there was only one representative for a particular product or service. In many in-

Exhibit 1 Geographical distribution of market companies

NORTH AND
CENTRAL AMERICA

De Laval Co. Ltd., Peterborough, Ont., Canada

De Laval Separator Co., Poughkeepsie, N.Y., USA

American Heat Reclaiming Corp., New York, N.Y. and Lykens, Pa.

G. & H. Products Inc., Kenosha, Wisc.

Contherm Corp., Newburyport, Mass.

Alfa-Laval S.A. de C.V., Mexico City, Mexico

LATIN AMERICA

Alfa-Laval S.A.I., Buenos Aires, Argentina

Separadoras Alfa-Laval S.A., Sao Paulo, Brazil

Alfa-Laval S.A.C.I., Santiago, Chile

Alfa-Laval S.A., Lima, Peru

Alfa-Laval Venezolana S.A., Caracas Venezuela

Alfa-Laval Caribbean Ltd., Kingston, Jamaica

AFRICA

Alfa-Laval (South Africa) Ltd., Isando, Tvl, South Africa

EUROPE

AG. Alfa-Laval, Vienna, Austria

S.A. Alfa-Laval N.V., Brussel, Belgium

Alfa-Laval S.A., Paris and Nevers, France

Diabolo Menus S.A., Meurpos, France

Alfa-Laval Industrie-technik GmbH, Glinde, West Germany

Alfa-Laval Luftkuhler GmbH, Ludwigshafen, West Germany

Alfa-Laval Agar GmbH, Glinde, West Germany

Alfa-Laval (Ireland) Ltd., Dublin, Ireland

Societa Alfa-Laval S.p.A., Monza, Italy

Alfa-Laval N.V., Amersfoorten and Groningen, The Netherlands

Alfa-Laval S.A., Madrid, Spain

Equipos Agricoles Alfa-Laval S.A., Barcelona, Spain

Desco S.A., Bilbao, Spain

Alfa-Laval Landburg AS, Vale, Denmark

Alfa-Laval Wenger AG. (Industry) Zurich, Switzerland

Alfa-Laval AG. (Farm), Sursee, Switzerland

Alfa-Laval Co. Ltd., Brentford and Cwmbran, UK

Menus (Great Britain) Ltd., Moreton-in-Marsh, UK

Alfa-Laval Lantbruk Norden AB, Sodertalje, Sweden

Norsk AS Alfa-Laval, Ski, Norway

Finska Alfa-Laval AB, Helsinki, Finland

ASIA

Alfa-Laval Far East Sdn. Bhd. Kuala Lumpur, Malaysia

Alfa-Laval Iran Co Ltd. Teheran, Iran

Alfa-Laval Engineering K.K., Tokyo, Japan

AUSTRALIA AND
NEW ZEALAND

Alfa-Laval Pty. Ltd., Sydney, Australia

Alfa-Laval Hamilton Ltd., Melbourne, Australia

Alfa-Laval (N Z) Ltd., Hamilton, New Zealand

Manufacturing

Exhibit 2

Geographical distribution of manufacturing units

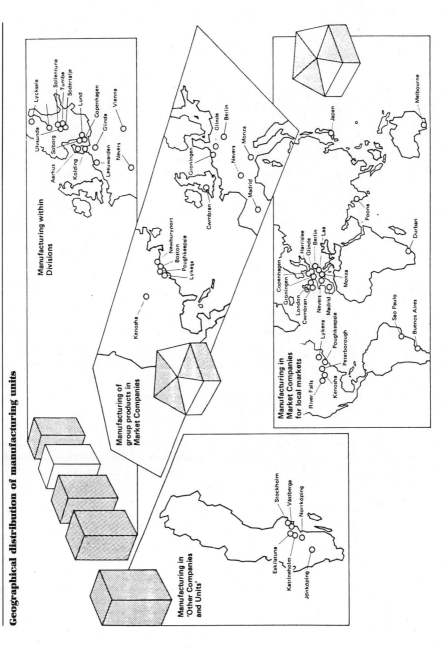

stances, the local market company was competent to deal with all aspects of customers' requirements. In others, especially in cases of small market companies and complicated inquiries, there was a need to refer the inquiry to the concerned division.

Just as Product Centers within divisions coordinated manufacturing, so "Application Centers" coordinated and assisted market companies with marketing. A market company requiring assistance would get in touch with the appropriate Application Center and the Application Center would answer the query or arrange for further assistance.

For the less sophisticated products, the local market company was usually competent to deal with the customers. For products like Farm and Dairy Equipment, where a complete system had often to be designed and tendered for, the liaison between the market companies and the concerned division had been developed through frequent contact. Over the last few years, the company had consciously promoted the sale of complete systems and often tendered bids on a turnkey basis, even to the extent of taking on the civil engineering work.

THE THERMAL SUBDIVISION

The Thermal and Dairy Division of Alfa-Laval had a total 1974 sales figure of Swedish kronor 312 million,[1] representing a tenth of the Group's total turnover. The division was in turn divided into four subdivisions. The Thermal Subdivision was responsible for the worldwide sale of thermal products and prided itself on being able to sell anything in its product area from small individual components to complete processes required for large and complex operations.

The key product in the thermal engineering field was the "heat exchanger." Heat exchangers were used whenever it was necessary to heat or cool any fluid. The conventional tubular heat exchanger, still used most frequently, consisted of a tube pack inside an outer casing with one fluid flowing through the tubes and the other fluid flowing around them at a different temperature and thus exchanging heat. The Afla-Laval product strategy had been to concentrate on specially compact heat exchangers, based on more sophisticated engineering designs. There were four basic types of heat exchangers in the Alfa-Laval range, of which the plate heat exchanger (PHE) was the most versatile and represented the bulk of the sales. The others were spiral, lamella, and closed tube heat exchangers.

The principle of the plate heat exchanger is fairly simple. As shown in Exhibit 3, it consists essentially of a pile of metallic plates clamped together. Each adjacent pair of plates forms a "flow channel" with the two fluids at different temperatures flowing in alternate channels. Gaskets

---

[1] In December 1975, 1 Swedish krona = £0.12 Stg. or $0.22 U.S.

separate each plate from the others thus preventing the mixing of the two fluids. Though the basic concept is comparatively straightforward, it is essential that the material used for the plates, the corrugations on them, and the material for the gaskets be chosen to fit the particular task in hand. Thus a corrosive fluid of high viscosity at a high temperature and pressure necessitates an entirely different solution from another at different operating conditions.

Alfa-Laval prided itself on its lead in the design of the most efficient engineering solutions for various operating conditions. The choices of plates, material, size, corrugations, and gaskets were carefully examined to provide a tailor-made match for a customer's thermal requirements. Often it would be necessary to include other types of heat exchangers and ancillary equipment such as cooling towers and air coolers to meet the complete requirements of a client. The Thermal Subdivision had gradually expanded and diversified its activities in these fields to meet the market. In fact, this emphasis on technical competence and coverage had been explicitly recognized by the Subdivision in 1968 in its "Business Mission and Policy" statements:

> We are in the "heat transfer market" and should act and become known as "thermal engineering specialists." Our goal is to develop, produce, and market on a worldwide level, thermal engineering equipment and processes of a high technical standard and to get a growing share of the world market.
>
> It is our aim to obtain a reputation among engineering customers as the most reliable supplier in our range and also to maintain our reputation as the biggest and most advanced supplier of heat exchangers including software services.

With the growing software needs, the Application Centers at Lund expanded to take on a number of qualified thermal engineers capable of designing complicated systems and of consultation on a wide variety of design problems. There was also a gradual shift in the development section at Lund toward the development of large PHEs and those made of special materials for difficult operating conditions. Emphasis on the manufacture of large units and complete systems gave Alfa-Laval a competitive edge in the more advanced uses. Quality of Alfa-Laval products had always been good but with steady attention to quality, it had become difficult by 1975 for company officials and customers to recall an example of outright failure of an Alfa-Laval component. After-sale service was mainly limited to replacing plates and gaskets which had succumbed to wear and tear:

By 1975, the Thermal Subdivision had five Application Centers in its Marketing Department at Lund (Exhibit 4). Market companies requiring assistance on an inquiry were free to get in touch with the relevant Application Center but were under no compulsion to do so. Market

Exhibit 3

Plate heat exchangers

Alfa-Laval Plate heat exchangers are assembled on the construction kit principle from individual standard channel plates that can be arranged according to the needs of the specific duty.

The plates are assembled in packs and clamped in a frame, each adjacent pair of plates forming a flow channel with the two media flowing in alternate channels. Different channel groupings can be chosen to give the desired pressure-drop characteristics and flow pattern. Two or more independent sections, separated by special connection plates, can be housed in the same frame. The gaskets separating the plates—which may be made of different materials according to the nature of the medium—prevent any mixing of the two media in the unit.

Flexible construction system

The construction system used for Alfa-Laval plate heat exchangers makes it possible to tailor them exactly to the requirements of varying working conditions throughout their wide range of applications. A plate unit is easily opened for inspection and cleaning of the plates and gaskets, but it can also be cleaned in place by detergent circulation, in which case it need not be dismantled at all.

The special corrugations of the channel plates generate an intensely turbulent thin-layer flow. They also stiffen the plates so that extremely thin-gauge material can be used. This improves the heat transfer coefficient and at the same time makes it economically feasible to use such expensive materials as titanium.

Typical applications

Plate heat exchangers are maids of all work. Their handiness, high thermal efficiency, and flexibility make them far and away the most economical choice in a host of applications, subject only to the pressure and temperature limits of the type.

This is true above all in the food industry with special reference to pasteurization and sterilization of cheap food and beverage products, where heating costs must be kept to a minimum and regular cleaning of the equipment is an essential feature of the high standard of hygiene demanded today.

Other suitable fields are general heating and cooling duties. Dissipating the heat from engine and machinery coolants—for example, on shipboard and in stationary power plants—is a field in which plate heat exchangers have proved their worth many times over. Another natural application for the plate type of unit is heat recovery in cases where a small difference in temperature between the media means that only a really efficient heat exchanger can do the job economically.

Flow pattern in a plate heat exchanger

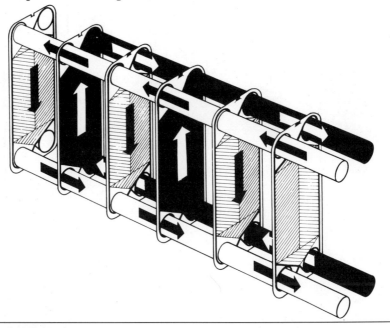

Plate heat exchanger type A 20

Exhibit 4

Subdivision U.2—organization 1975

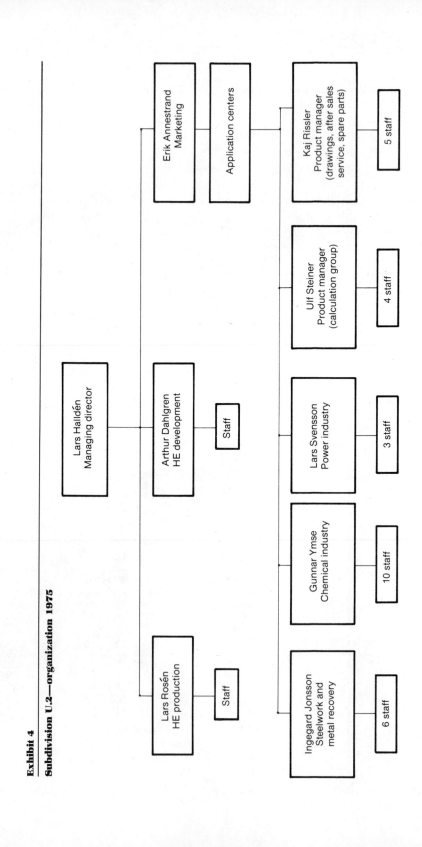

companies were given direct access to the comprehensive computer programs that had been written to calculate specific heat exchanger requirements, and a backup service assisted with technical drawings and after-sale service. The Marketing Department also offered training for marketing personnel in the technical aspects of the heat exchanger business. For all these services there was little or no direct charge, as Lund believed that these services more than paid for themselves through increased sales and better customer liaison and gave the company the very advantage that it was eager to retain in a market that was becoming increasingly competitive.

Thermal know-how was particularly important in the chemical, steel, power, and mining industries. These market segments were distinguished by large orders and large HE units often involving international contracting. Thermal management saw a great opportunity here for expansion in sales. While few products from other Alfa-Laval divisions were sold along with HEs to these industries, Thermal could draw on its strength of a complete thermal line and use its extensive application know-how to effect. In 1975, the subdivision's "Business Mission" was amended to read:

> We shall also promote marketing of complete functions for the large and fast growing central cooling market. That can be done by selling complete installations for seawater or cooling towers or by selling installation software with our heat exchangers.
>
> We shall have the largest resources, the best know-how with superior products and a reliable delivery capacity.

On large bids, or on business that might involve international contracting or that might be of continuing importance to the Group, market companies could if they wished approach the Application Center for an advantageous transfer price on centrally produced components to enable them to make a more competitive quote. Frequently, a market company would ask for assistance to get Alfa-Laval products specified at the design stage for a major contract; but in keeping with the company's policy of autonomy for its market units, the rule was quite clear—assistance was given by invitation rather than any Head Office imposition.

COMPETITIVE POSITION

The greater part of Alfa-Laval's heat exchanger orders—about 75 percent—was accounted for by plate heat exchangers, which competed with conventional tubular heat exchangers and PHEs of other makes. The tubular HE was, by far, the most widely used HE for industrial application and had a surprisingly strong hold on the American market. Acceptance of the PHE as a suitable replacement, however, was growing. For application in the marine, dairy, and other fields where compactness, hygienic, or environmental effects of heat exchangers were major considerations, the competition was all between different makes of PHEs. In marine and dairy industries, moreover, Alfa-Laval's other subdivisions had strong process know-how. Exhibit 5 shows a breakdown of Thermal PHE sales by industry of application.

Exhibit 5

Plate heat exchangers: Sales by industry of application

	1970 percent	1972 percent	1974 percent
Power	2	3	2
Factory	5	4	4
Mining	1	1	1
Steel	12	15	18
Chemical, organic	14	13	12
Chemical, inorganic	18	15	15
Marine	18	20	21
Brewing, fermentation	7	7	7
Dairy plant	12	12	10
Other	11	10	10
Total	100	100	100
Index of invoice value adjusted to 1974 prices	83	78	100

Through conscious choice, Alfa-Laval had not involved itself in the market for conventional tubular HEs, which were fabricated in a large number of countries by many small, highly competitive but technically less advanced companies. In the view of Alfa-Laval management, this market, though many times larger than that for PHEs, was generally more suited to small local manufacture and was not one where a company like Alfa-Laval could compete effectively.

The mix of small, medium, and large PHEs sold from Lund had altered over the years as shown in Exhibit 6. Exhibit 7 also indicates the increase in size of orders serviced from Lund. Thermal Subdivision sales were

Exhibit 6

Plate heat exchangers: Sales and profitability by size

	Percent of total thermal subdivision sales		Percent of total thermal profit contribution
	1974	(1975 est.)	1974
Small PHE	13	(10)	4
Medium PHE	51	(48)	40
Large PHE	12	(19)	35

Exhibit 7

Plate heat exchangers: Alfa-Laval Thermal sales by size of order and model

	Percent of total number of orders	
Size of order in Sw. Kr.	1972	1975
Below 50,000	92	80
50,000–500,000	7	18
Above 500,000	1	2
Total	100	100

	Percent of total unit sales	
	1972	1975
Small	48	34
Medium	52	56
Large	—	10
Total	100	100

shifting toward larger units and larger customers. This shift was not altogether an unwelcome change. The percentage of profit contribution from small PHEs for 1974 was not very significant and the segment was coming under increasing fire from small national competitors. They had cut prices in order to break into a stronghold where Alfa-Laval had earlier had great market and technical superiority.

In 1975, there were about 20 PHE manufacturers in the world. Of these, about seven were of any significance. The more important competitors were:

1. APV—United Kingdom.
2. Schmidt—West Germany.
3. Hisaka—Japan.
4. Vicarb—France.
5. Ahlborn—West Germany.
6. DDMM—Denmark.

There were very significant variations in the market share of these main competitors. Alfa-Laval now held perhaps 50 percent of the world market for PHEs as against 60 percent in 1970. APV was the leading contender with Schmidt and Hisaka following to take much of the remaining volume. Even more noticeable, however, was the different level of technical services provided. Competition was largely confined to small and medium PHE segments. The bigger specialized products and systems that

Lund was putting on the market faced little or no competition. Alfa-Laval's advanced designs, protected by patents, had given the company substantial cost advantages which the smaller companies found difficult to match. For applications in which the competition for plant construction was international, then, Alfa-Laval held a very high percentage of the market share.

The international distribution outlets for the leading competitors as estimated by Alfa-Laval staff are listed in Exhibit 8. Not all could be

Exhibit 8

Alfa-Laval and competitors' distribution systems

	Affiliated or associated companies	Licensees	Agents
APV	15 in principal industrialized countries	—	Numerous globally
Schmidt	Austria	—	10–15
Hisaka	—	1—United Kingdom 1—United States	Australia, India, Korea, Taiwan, Netherlands
Vicarb	—	—	10
Ahlborn	—	—	10–15; several agents in same country
DDMM	—	—	5–10

thought of as competitors in the international PHE market. Some could more adequately be described as national companies with export activities.

Of the really international competitors, APV of the United Kingdom was the closest with a broad range of activities in thermal engineering and a wide distribution and marketing system. APV had fifteen affiliated companies in the principal industrialized countries and numerous agents across the globe. In a manner similar to Alfa-Laval, APV had developed a wide variety of technical information and computer programs to promote its products. APV was particularly strong in the chemical, food, and dairy industries.

Competition from the remaining companies had been largely confined to domestic markets and, even then, often in specialized segments of the market. But the competition when faced could be very real indeed and there were increasing instances of prices and quotations undercutting Alfa-Laval by as much as 15 percent or 20 percent, and these companies seemed to be gradually looking further afield for business.

In spite of its great strength and momentum, Alfa-Laval was receiving small bits of information from various market companies that were causing concern. The Japanese company, Hisaka, for instance, had captured about 85 percent of the Japanese market and was looking enviously at the European and North American markets. There were rumors that Hisaka, DDMM, and the French company Vicarb were about to expand plate pressing capacity and might extend the size range of PHEs they manufactured. DDMM and the French had been having some success in getting into the coveted marine market. Exhibits 9 and 10 summarize Alfa-Laval's information about competition in various industrial sectors and indicate the changes taking place.

PRODUCT DEVELOPMENT PHILOSOPHY

Product Development in the Alfa-Laval group of companies continued to build on the very impressive technological lead that the company had established. There had been a steady expansion of the range of thermal equipment offered and the company had most recently ventured into central cooling systems. Instead of providing individual HEs for the many local requirements in various parts of a factory, these developments made it possible to provide a single central cooling system. Such systems meant a substantial change in not only the hardware sold by the company but also in the software service provided. Some Thermal managers believed that the emphasis should be to educate the market on the economic and technical benefits of single large PHEs and associated complete systems, and to explain that these benefits far outweighed the disadvantages. Smaller but parallel systems could provide a built-in backup facility in the event of technical failure of single large units. Alfa-Laval management pointed to the absence of technical failure to emphasize the very low probability of such an event.

The philosophy of the Development Department at Lund, as shown in the following extract, was to retain Alfa-Laval leadership through creative new products:

> A brief historical sketch of the 50s and 60s shows clearly that the key concepts for successful companies have been production and marketing. The company that realized the importance of building up an efficient, rational production apparatus in the 50s and learned to do so, was able to compete most successfully. In the 60s, which can be characterized as the decade of marketing, it was the companies who concentrated on developing their marketing capability that laid the best foundation for favorable development.
>
> In the future, production engineering and marketing are unlikely to have the same decisive importance as in the past. They are, of course, still two important components of a company's operations, but their importance from the point of view of competition is declining. Most companies know how to run their production and marketing operations, so standards in these respects have now become more uniform.
>
> It is research and development that will be the big thing in the future. Although product development has always played an important part in corporate strategic planning, the constantly changing external demands

Exhibit 9

Penetration of market segments

Company	Industrial sector									
	Dairy		Brewery		Food		Marine		Industrial	
	1973	1975	1973	1975	1973	1975	1973	1975	1973	1975
APV	Good	Strong	Strong	Strong	Strong	Strong	—	Weak	Good	Strong
Schmidt	Fair	Good	Good	Good	Strong	Strong	—	Good	Good	Good
Hisaka	Weak	Fair	?	?	Weak	Fair	—	Good	Good	Good
Vicarb	—	—	?	?	—	Weak	—	?	Fair	Good
Ahlborn	Good	Strong	?	?	Good	Good	—	Weak	Weak	Weak
DDMM	Good	Strong	?	?	Good	Good	—	Strong	Weak	Fair

Exhibit 10

Plate heat exchangers: New models introduced 1965–1975

Company	Number of PHEs introduced 1965–73	Number of PHEs introduced 1973–75	Expected introduction
Alfa-Laval	8	1	—
APV	3	—	1
Schmidt	12	—	1
Hisaka	—	3	1
Vicarb	4	—	1
Ahlborn	3 (2 withdrawn)	1	—
DDMM	—	4	—

on both our company and our products means that in the future it will not be enough to concentrate only on the traditional engineering aspects. We shall have to broaden the base of product development in the future and integrate it into the corporate strategic planning process in a more concrete manner.

An ambition to lead the market, demands products of a very high standard and by the same token, product development of a very high standard. It is not enough for our products to satisfy the demand of the market, they must also be technically superior to those of our competitors.

The Thermal marketing group, however, believed that the development of new products and systems should follow an increase in the application of know-how within the company, including:

1. The search, within known and established processes, for areas of application:
   a. Where heat exchangers have not previously been used.
   b. Where compact heat exchangers have not previously been used but where other types such as tubular heat exchangers are already used.
   c. Where it is possible to deliver a high degree of process know-how.
2. The search for applications of the company's product mix in new processes.

Only a small part of the company's application resources had been directed in the past toward these objectives. The division's application centers had been more occupied in providing technical and commercial support to the field organization within established markets. This past orientation was partly an outcome of the technical superiority of Alfa-Laval's products, which had created their own markets in areas where the competition was not troublesome. There had been, however, a gradual change in the attitude of Lund's marketing personnel, who now felt that with the increase in competitive activity and pressure on Alfa-Laval's profits and margins, the application departments should adopt a more aggressive stance. Marketing personnel felt that they should be informed as a matter of course of all important activity and specially large projects in their respective industrial sectors and not have to sit and hope that the marketing companies would have the goodness to get in touch with them. To face the growing competition, the Marketing Department saw the remedy in aggressive central marketing activity.

There was another school of thought, however, that argued for decentralization of product development rather than centralization of marketing. Frequent discussions had taken place as to whether it would be preferable to retain the relatively large development group working internationally with the national market companies or build small engineering groups in each of the major national companies. Until now the primary responsibility for product development had rested with the division, but it had been found practical to keep some development activities close to production and sales in market companies. Thus most of the development work for cooling towers had been done in Spain where the relevant production unit was located.

PRICING POLICY

The Thermal Subdivision administered a complicated pricing policy. Despite a general acceptance that this policy was unsatisfactory, it had not been changed because the various alternative suggestions were either too cumbersome to implement or did not accomplish what the subdivision considered to be the central purpose of its pricing strategy—that is, to maintain divisional autonomy and, at the same time, provide the required incentive to maximize total company performance. Management's attitude had been to accept the "devil you know."

A company catalog laid down the Internal Sales Prices for products calculated as follows; note that these are disguised percentages but should be taken as actual for the purpose of this case:

Standard variable production costs, stock holding charges, etc.		*Production cost*
Work's overheads, specially installed equipment.		
Product Division's charge for development and coordination.	Approximately 30% on MP	*Manufacturing price* (MP)
Product Division's profit charge.	Approximately 20% on MP	
Market company cost charge.	Av. 40% on MP	*Internal sales price*
Market company profit.	Av. 10% on MP	
		Customer sales price (CSP)

Interdivision sales took place at the manufacturing price, and in about 80 percent of the cases the market companies paid the catalog price less a discount varying according to the country of destination. The size of the discount was determined through negotiation between the management of the Thermal Subdivision and the respective market company, though occasionally Group Management was involved. The discount for a particular market company, however, remained constant unless there were very special reasons. The aim of this market discount was to allow for the different competition, and hence price levels, that had grown up in the different country markets. In Germany, for example, Alfa-Laval held a leading market share but Germany was a large, price-conscious market and under continual competitive pressure.

Where it was felt that a particular order was of such importance to the Group that a particularly low price be quoted, it was possible to request a special discount. This happened for under 10 percent of the business but the assessment of whether an order justified a specially preferential price had become one of the major concerns of the application centers at Lund.

A number of dysfunctions of the pricing system had been recognized. These statements are taken from internal subdivision papers:

—It appears that the subsidiary is treated as an external customer. Since the easiest way for a subsidiary to improve its profitability is to obtain extra discounts from the product division, attention is drawn to the wrong quarter. But, on the other hand, the price system does not guarantee that the subsidiary gets enough freedom of action, e.g., in external pricing. The information transferred to the subsidiaries via the price system does not correspond to the actual position for the current decision.

—A subsidiary company can show good profits at the expense of a product division in Sweden.

—Each fixed internal pricing system has effects on resource allocation. To use a price system with a resource allocating purpose without either informing the units involved or drawing out the consequences must be condemned. The relation between different product divisions (e.g., competition for the favors of the subsidiary) or between different subsidiaries (e.g., competition for the same international buyer) can be serious.

—The structure of the internal pricing system provides the subsidiary with little incentive to increase its volume. There is a tendency to "skim" the market.

—The Internal Sales Price is determined by a precalculated standard catalog price. A preliminary calculation such as this is always based on a number of assumptions about volume, distribution of joint costs, depreciation, and interest on fixed assets. Each estimation of these costs is more or less arbitrary and, in turn, is based on a number of more or less unspoken assumptions. With the present system for internal sales price calculation, it is hard to relate the cost calculation to the actual decisions.

As the Thermal Subdivision found itself dealing more and more with large international customers, problems were becoming evident on large bids with regard to division of profits, differences of price levels, and differences in technical solutions suggested by various market companies. For the Thermal Conference of 1975, a partially fictitious case had been written to open the discussion as to how the marketing approach, particularly pricing, should be amended.

THE CASE OF A MAJOR OPPORTUNITY

Alfa-Laval has market companies (MkA, MkB, etc.) in six countries: A, B, C, D, E, and F. There are three contractors competing to obtain the main contract:

> Contractor 1B has its head office in country B and subsidiaries in countries C and D.
>
> Contractor 2E has its head office in E.
>
> Contractor 3F has its head office in F and a subsidiary in B.

The ultimate customer, an end user, is located in Country A and local regulations require 20 percent of the equipment to be manufactured in A. Alfa-Laval's MkA in A has local assembly facilities for some types in the product range, but not the types specified in the quotations.

Step 1. MkA informs Thermal about the project, stating which contractors are bidding.

Step 2. Thermal forwards information to MkB, MkE, and MkF where the three contractors have their head offices. Since the project is at a very early state, none can obtain material for a quotation but must wait.

Step 3. Contractors start work in project design, and MkC, which has previously collaborated with Contractor 1B's subsidiary in C on other projects, receives an inquiry without knowing which project it refers to.

Step 4. MkB, MkD, MkE, and MkF now also receive inquiries from Contractor 3F's subsidiary in B. All inquiries except the one to MkF are forwarded to Thermal for coordination. MkA receives an inquiry direct from the end user.

Step 5. MkC, which has its own manufacturing facilities for some products, makes its own technical solution and its own price quote to Contractor 1B's subsidiary in C, still unaware of which project is involved.

Step 6.   Thermal makes its calculations and prepares quotations with a recommended technical solution and bid price, which are then forwarded to our MkA, MkB, MkD, MkE, and MkF.

Step 7.   The reactions to Thermal's proposal from the various Mks are:

MkA.   Our MkA accepts and quotes the price proposed by Thermal direct to the end user and persuades him to specify plate heat exchangers.

MkB.   Relations with Contractor 1B have previously been good, and MkB has virtually a fixed price level for this customer. Contractor 1B is committed to a particular technical solution for this kind of application and MkB will, therefore, not accept the Thermal proposal.

MkD.   MkD has generally been able to maintain a very high price level and, therefore, does not approve the level recommended by Thermal. The technical solution is acceptable.

MkE.   The quotation is accepted and passed on to Contractor 2E.

MkF.   It is discovered that MkF has already submitted its own quotation to Contractor 3F with almost the same technical solution but at a higher price than the one recommended by Thermal.

Step 8.   Thermal advises that its technical solution and price level should be used regardless.

Step 9.   Contractor 1B gets the order.

Step 10.   What happens now to relations between Alfa-Laval and the contractors?

Contractor 1B is irritated because Alfa-Laval has also quoted direct to the end user and takes the line that Alfa-Laval is competing with its own customer. Discovers that Alfa-Laval has different price levels in different countries and will in future ask for quotations from several Alfa-Laval offices.

Contractor 1B is annoyed that we argue for different technical solutions for the same application depending on the country in which the discussion takes place. We can, however, counter this by pointing to a different operational experience in different countries.

Contractor 2E has no problem.

Contractor 3F has also discovered that Alfa-Laval has different price levels in different countries, and having previously done business with MkF on other projects, now suspects that he has been overcharged on previous occasions. Will not give Alfa-Laval another chance.

Step 11.   Contractor 1B places the order with MkB.

Step 12.   What efforts have the Alfa-Laval market companies made and what permanent changes have resulted?

MkA.   Has persuaded the end user to specify PHEs.
Has passed on Thermal's quotation.
Gets the after-sales service.

MkB.   Has passed on Thermal's quotation.
Has carried on technical and economic discussions with the customer to explain away the differences in price and technical solution.
Has secured the order.
Has lost some of its goodwill in its relations with Contractor 1B.
Has lost a customer: Contractor 3F's subsidiary in B.

MkC.   Has worked out its own technical solution.
Has written its own quotation.

MkD.   Has passed on Thermal's quotation.
Has had its price level cut.

MkE.   Has passed on Thermal's quotation.

MkF.   Has lost a customer: Contractor 3F.

Subjects for discussion

How should we modify our organization and methods to ensure:

Closer contacts and coordination with main contractors?

Involvement at an earlier stage?

A correct price policy?

Optimum technical solutions?

How can we keep the question of division of profits out of the quotation work and ensure that a fair division is made *after* the order has been secured?

Who should be responsible for the technical solution?

The price level?

Who should make the quotation?

THE WAY AHEAD

Though "The Case of a Major Opportunity" was fictitious, it was sufficiently accurate to characterize the sort of problems that the Thermal Subdivison was facing in the international marketplace. The discussion brought home to all participants that fairly fundamental changes were called for, both in terms of distribution strategy and cross-country sales.

Management was keen to decide what a future Thermal Subdivision should be like, what it should do, how it should control, and how such an organization should be reached, given the constraints of a hundred years of organizational tradition. Some managers felt that the well-established organizational culture was going to be a major stumbling block, that changes should be moderate and gradual. Others disagreed.

Blue Ribbon Sports*

Blue Ribbon Sports, BRS, was the developer, manufacturer, and distributor of Nike athletic shoes. Based in Oregon, BRS management was currently considering the strategic impact of expanding manufacturing via a company-owned factory in Malaysia.

The BRS story

Jogging first gained widespread attention in the United States in 1964 through the efforts of Bill Bowerman who was the University of Oregon track and field coach. Recently returned from New Zealand where recreational jogging was being made popular by the famous New Zealand coach, Arthur Lydiard, Bowerman published a book titled *Jogging* which sold over 2 million copies. Then in the summer Olympic Games (1972) in Munich, Frank Shorter, an American, won the marathon. At the same time, a series of articles published by American doctors endorsed the physical benefits of jogging. What followed was a surge of interest in road races covering a range of distances from 10,000 meters to the 26-mile 385-yard marathon. Until 1972, a marathon was considered a quirk event, which kept many good athletes from competing.

These events and the resultant public interest highlighted the need for better designed, more comfortable racing flats. With insight, Phillip Knight formed BRS, Inc. and launched a new line of shoes designed by and for American athletes. This new line was named "Nike" after the Greek goddess of Victory. The first Nikes were manufactured in Japan based on designs developed by Bill Bowerman who was by now the head track and field coach for the 1972 U.S. Olympic team. The famous Nike "wing" design made its debut across the cover of sporting magazines as John Anderson, wearing a pair of Nikes, won the prestigious Boston Marathon in 1973.

During 1973, BRS established four "Athletic Department" retail stores in key areas across the nation to bring Nike shoes to the public. Three more stores were added later, with a goal of bringing product information to consumers as well as feedback to the expanding research and development team. Contract assembly for new shoes was expanded into

* This case was prepared by L. N. Goslin. It is based on research by J. E. Isbell. The case provides a basis for class discussion and does not illustrate either effective or ineffective handling of administrative situations. Names and data are disguised. Copyright © 1981 by Lewis N. Goslin.

Taiwan and later into Korea. Up until the 1980s, all foreign manufacturing of Nike shoes was based on supply agreements with non-company-owned factories.

These factories produced shoes to the exact specifications and requirements of BRS. To ensure a superior product quality standard, BRS maintained branch offices in Taiwan and Korea, which were staffed by American BRS employees. Branch staff visited each factory on a weekly basis spot checking the manufacturing process and finished goods inventory. Exhibit 1 shows BRS production totals by country.

Also in 1973, Nike shoes were distributed to non-company-owned retail stores by independent salesmen. In 1973, the Nike court shoe and wrestling shoe were introduced to the marketplace.

In 1974 BRS brought its innovative shoe-making technology to the United States with the opening of the first BRS factory in Exeter, New Hampshire. Before the year was out, 250 employees were cranking out 50,000 pairs of shoes a month. Research and development operations were transferred from Eugene, Oregon, to the Exeter facility.

The patented waffle sole, which was introduced in 1975, moved the Nike shoe line to the forefront of popularity in a nation suddenly obsessed with a need to revitalize itself through physical fitness.

To meet growing sales demand (see Exhibit 2) BRS expanded domestic production by acquiring a bankrupt shoe factory in Saco, Maine, during 1978.

BRS currently produced over 100 different style shoes for the athletic and the recreational market. The running market continued to dominate Nike sales (see Exhibit 3). Nike shoes had a dominant market share position in the United States for running flats and tennis/racquet sports (see Exhibit 4). The company expected soon to become the number one seller of premium basketball shoes. Premium athletic shoes excluded those brands sold in discount stores or under a private brand label for Sears, Penney's, or Kinney's.

By 1981, BRS distributed Nike athletic shoes throughout the United States and in 25 foreign countries. For all practical purposes, the sales shown in Exhibit 2 consisted entirely of shoes. Approximately 89 percent of all Nike shoes were manufactured in contract assembly factories in the Orient, with the remaining 11 percent manufactured in its two company-owned domestic factories. Contract assembly factories refer to non-company-owned factories that contracted with BRS to produce Nike shoes for a specified f.o.b. price.

Marketing strategy

The goal of Nike's marketing strategy was to achieve a generic brand identification, thereby making the name Nike synonymous with high-quality athletic shoes. Initial marketing was based on the idea that if you

Exhibit 1

BRS, Inc. annual production (by country)

	Calendar year 1978			Calendar year 1979			Calendar year 1980		
	Number of factories	Pairs (000)	Percent of total	Number of factories	Pairs (000)	Percent of total	Number of factories	Pairs (000)	Percent of total
United States	2	1,208	11	2	1,915	11	2	2,750	11
Republic of Korea	2	3,804	34	3	9,172	52	4	13,700	53
Taiwan	4	4,377	40	5	6,159	35	5	8,000	31
Japan	1	1,705	15	1	332	2	1	180	1
Malaysia	—	—	—	—	—	—	1	540	2
Thailand	—	—	—	—	—	—	1	400	1
Philippines	—	—	—	—	—	—	1	230	1
Total production	9	11,094	100	11	17,578	100	15	25,800	100

Exhibit 2

Nike sales history*

	Fiscal year-end sales ($ millions)	Percent increase
1972	2.0	—
1973	3.2	60
1974	4.8	50
1975	8.3	73
1976	14.1	70
1977	28.7	104
1978	72.4	152
1979	149.8	107
1980	270.0	80
1981	430.0 (est.)	59

* Data estimated.

Exhibit 3

Nike sales by sport (percent of total sales)

	FY 1977	FY 1978	FY 1979	FY 1980
Running	45	49	52	43
Basketball	25	23	19	24
Tennis/Racquet	16	15	17	18
Children's	—	2	4	9
Other	14	11	8	6
Total	100	100	100	100

Exhibit 4

Estimated market share (percent)

	Running flats		Basketball		Tennis/Racquet	
	10/77	10/79	10/77	10/79	10/77	10/79
Nike	42	50	11	36	6	30
Adidas	33	18	9	18	35	26
Brooks	1	12	—	—	—	—
Converse	2	—	61	37	3	1
Etonic	—	5	—	—	—	—
New Balance	3	5	—	—	—	—
Tiger	10	2	—	—	—	—
Puma	6	—	13	4	5	3
Pro Keds	—	—	—	3	—	—
Tretorn	—	—	—	—	15	7
All other	3	8	6	2	36	33
Total	100	100	100	100	100	100

could develop a shoe to satisfy the serious athlete, then the market would follow. Excluding its leisure, children's, and "athletic look" shoes, this philosophy continued to be the focus of Nike's development efforts.

Nike achieved its dominant market position in sales of running, basketball, and tennis shoes sold in the United States by: (1) being an innovator in new shoe design, (2) demonstrating commitment to stand behind its product, (3) establishing a strong sales and distribution network throughout the United States, and (4) instituting a program which guaranteed price and delivery for up to six months from date of order. These points continued to guide the marketing efforts as the company developed its foreign market sales.

The concept of guaranteed price and delivery was first introduced to the shoe industry by Nike. The "futures" program was available to qualifying accounts (based on a minimum number of pairs ordered per year) under one of two programs. Futures I was available to large accounts, which placed their orders five months in advance of delivery. Smaller specialty stores could order under the Futures II program. These accounts placed their orders six months in advance of delivery. Accounts accepting 90 percent of its futures order qualified for a discount of 6 percent under Futures I and 3 percent under Futures II.

The futures programs accounted for approximately 60 percent of Nike unit sales. Besides bringing some stability to production scheduling, valuable market feedback for ordering the balance of the inventory was obtained from the futures programs.

Advertising was based on a soft sell approach, relying mainly on word-of-mouth and through the wearing of Nike shoes by top professional and amateur athletes, although printed advertisements appeared regularly in selected running and specialty sports magazines. Financial support was also available to retailers who placed Nike advertisements in local newspapers. Top professional athletes in basketball, tennis, and, more recently, football, baseball, and soccer were on financial contracts to wear Nike shoes. The company also worked with amateur athletes and schools in promoting the use of Nike shoes. Regarding the latter, Nike offered athletic teams shoes which were often color coordinated to match the individual school's colors.

Nike's attitude toward marketing was best summed up by a phrase appearing in one of its more popular jogging posters: "Beating the competition is easy, but beating yourself is a never ending commitment."

Competition

Converse and Keds were the predominant manufacturers of branded athletic footwear in the United States during the fifties and sixties. Their product was primarily canvas upper court shoes. Adidas and Puma were the two major foreign manufacturers. From the late 1970s, however, the athletic shoe market in the United States had become extremely competitive, reflecting a continuing high-growth demand and apparent ease of entry for new competition. Many shoe companies throughout the United States and the world had excess manufacturing capability and were willing to manufacture shoes under someone else's brand. Distribution and quality control, however, were crucial barriers for new shoe companies to surmount. Quality control was especially difficult where foreign manufacturing was involved. In some cases quality inspection at the factory by American personnel was done by U.S. firms.

Company	Market area penetration	Type of shoes representing majority of product line
Nike	Nationwide	Running/basketball/tennis
Adidas	Nationwide	Running/basketball/cleated*/soccer
Converse	Nationwide	Basketball
Keds	East Coast	Basketball/children's shoes
Puma	East Coast	Basketball/cleated/soccer
Brooks	Nationwide	Running/baseball
Pony	East Coast	Basketball/cleated
New Balance	Nationwide	Running

* Cleated shoes refer to both football and baseball shoes.

The future demand for Nike shoes appeared strong. Current projections showed Nike's domestic shoe sales growing at an annual rate of 40 percent to 60 percent. These projections took account of the current state of the United States and world economy, production capacity, and BRS's ability to warehouse and distribute shoes.

Production

BRS was currently focusing their attention on high-quality athletic shoes, either running or court shoes, sold within the United States. Characteristics of construction and material used for each of these two shoe categories are shown:

	Running shoes	Court shoes
Construction method*	Heat activated cement	Autoclave
Material used in upper	Nylon, suede, canvas leather, PVC	Canvas, leather, PVC
Tongue material	Polyester, polyether, foam	Polyether, foam
Midsole	Sponge, EVA	———
Outsole	Natural and synthetic rubber combination	Natural and synthetic rubber combination
Foxing tape/toe cap	———	Natural and synthetic rubber combination

* See Exhibits 5 and 6 for definitions of terms.

Exhibit 5

Heat-activated cement shoe

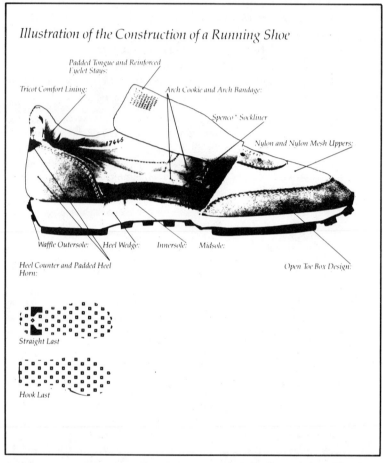

Illustration of the Construction of a Running Shoe

For shoe construction, cement is defined as chemical fasteners to make objects adhere to each other. Athletic shoes use a latex cement which is applied to the surfaces to be combined, air dried, and then heat activated prior to assembly. It is this process in which the sole (midsole and outsole unit) is attached to the upper.

Malaysian alternatives

Investigation of possible Malaysian manufacturing sources was begun in late 1978. A supply agreement was signed with a Malaysian shoe company, Malay Shoe Company, in 1980. Monthly production, 20,000 pair of autoclave-style shoes, commenced in April 1980, to reach 130,000 pairs by December 1980.

Exhibit 6

Autoclave shoe

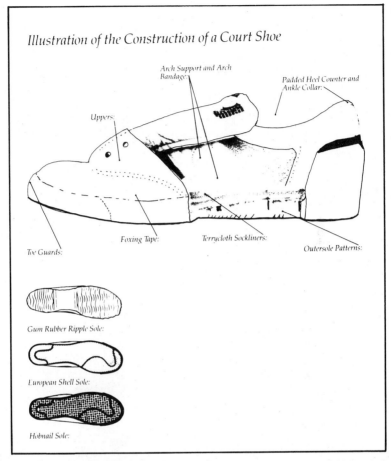

Illustration of the Construction of a Court Shoe

Arch Support and Arch Bandage:

Padded Heel Counter and Ankle Collar:

Uppers:

Foxing Tape:

Terrycloth Sockliners:

Toe Guards:

Outersole Patterns:

Gum Rubber Ripple Sole:

European Shell Sole:

Hobnail Sole:

Autoclave is a steam-filled chamber used for curing or vulcanizing rubber-soled canvas upper footwear. Vulcanization involves cross-linking the linear chain molecules of rubber to produce a stronger, less plastic material more resistant to temperature changes. The shoes are "cooked" within the oven at a temperature around 230°F. for 70 minutes. The oven is a pressurized chamber to prevent the rubber from sagging during vulcanization.

Exhibit 7

Nike production by style of construction

	Percent of total	
Style of construction	*FY 1979*	*FY 1980*
Cement	53	51
Autoclave	46	48
Other	1	1
Total	100	100

Two additional shoe companies—one ceased operations in August 1979—had also been evaluated. Both companies had the potential to manufacture Nike court shoes. Since each company manufactured very inexpensive canvas court shoes, a major capital investment would be required. The one factory still operating faced continuing financial losses ($1.9 million current accumulated losses). These losses were attributable to poor management and a product with too low a gross margin.

In order to utilize either factory to manufacture Nike shoes, BRS felt it would need to make an acquisition and insert its own American personnel to manage the operation. Since this would be the first company-owned, foreign manufacturing operation, BRS was giving this decision careful consideration.

Malaysia offered several attributes for an equity position.

Malaysia was the largest producer of natural rubber. BRS's chemist, in working with Malay Shoe Co., had developed a natural rubber compound which when compared to the regular synthetic rubber outsole demonstrated a higher wear resistance.

Malaysia's political stability was excellent.

English, besides being the business language, was spoken by the majority of Malaysians.

Malaysia had a good source of labor with a prevailing daily wage rate for semiskilled workers ranging between $2.38 and $4.76.

Malaysia offered substantial financial and tax incentives to investors, especially to investments generating 100 percent export sales (see Exhibit 8).

Two firms were available for acquisition, NoMal and SoMal.

NoMal Shoe Company

NoMal was located in the city of Ipoh (E-poe) which is in the inland, central portion of peninsular Malaysia. NoMal commenced shoe production in 1976. Due to poor management and an insufficient market for its product, the company ceased operations in August 1979. The asking price for the land, building, and equipment was $1.4 million. The total six-year capital investment would be $3,420,000 (see Exhibit 9).

A pro forma cash-flow statement for the NoMal investment is available in Exhibit 10. The calculations assume that one half of the capital investment, excluding replacement of worn equipment, would be financed by a Malaysian governmental agency (MIDF) at 9 percent with equal semiannual payments over six years. Principal payments would not commence until 15 months after project startup. Short-term financing would be obtained at 4½ percent under the government's preexport shipment scheme. (These assumptions regarding financing would also apply to the other investment opportunity, SoMal.)

Exhibit 8

Malaysia investment incentives

Pioneer status:
1. BRS would receive six-year grant (five years for investment and one year for local content).
2. No taxes paid during pioneer period.

Postpioneer period:
1. Capital investments during pioneer period are redepreciated at their original cost.
2. Cumulative net losses during pioneer period can offset profits earned in postpioneer period.
3. Dividends withheld during pioneer period can be paid without being taxed.

Basic tax structure:
1. 40 percent basic corporate income tax.
2. 5 percent development tax.
3. 5 percent excess profits tax levied on chargeable income in excess of 25 percent of shareholders' funds or M$200,000, whichever is higher.

Tax incentives:
1. Export allowance: 2 percent of total export sales plus 10 percent applied to export sales in excess of previous period's export sales.
2. Foreign content: 5 percent if foreign investment is less than 30 percent of total paid-in capital and Bumiputra participation is 30 percent or more. If BRS were to manage the operation, MIDA requested an investment above 30 percent.

Financing available:
1. Short-term loans at 1 percent over prime, which was 7½ percent.
2. Malaysia Industrial Development Financing (MIDF) would finance 50 percent of total fixed assets for a period of six years with a 12-month grace period during which only interest would be payable.
3. Preshipment financing was available up to a maximum of 90 days at 4½ percent. Amount was based on export sales.

Exhibit 9

NoMal Shoe Company capital investment

Timing of investment	Description	Amount ($000)
Initial	Land, building, equipment	$1,400
Initial	New equipment	950
2d year	Replacement of worn equipment	50
	New rubber mixer	200
3d year	Equipment to extend capacity	670
4th year	Replacement of worn equipment	50
5th year	Replacement of worn equipment	50
6th year	Replacement of worn equipment	50
Total capital investment		$3,420

The major uncertainty surrounding NoMal was how much of the previous labor force would be rehired. The former personnel manager felt he could recall approximately 200 of the previous 400 employees. Employment needs would reach 750 employees by the third year after plant startup.

Exhibit 10

NOMAL SHOE COMPANY
Cash-Flow Statement
($000)

	Initial investment	First year	Second year	Third year	Fourth year	Fifth year	Sixth year
Raw material purchases	$ 325	$3,418	$7,290	$ 9,880	$10,859	$10,849	$10,849
L/C and exchange costs		39	71	98	112	112	112
Nonmaterial portion of cost of sales		600	1,436	1,912	2,174	2,190	2,190
Operating expenses:							
Administration payroll		230	230	213	191	191	191
Administration expenses		180	180	166	152	152	152
Freight expenses		81	198	265	302	307	307
Interest on MIDF loan		99	79	119	115	93	69
Startup expenses		100					
Training expense		335	110				
Total operating expense		1,025	797	763	760	743	719
Capital investment	2,350		250	670	50	50	50
Portion financed by MIDF	(1,175)		(100)	(335)			
Principal payments			76	198	239	261	285
Total expenditures	1,500	5,082	9,820	13,186	14,184	14,205	14,205
Revenue received		4,084	9,926	13,318	15,179	15,400	15,400
Positive/(negative) cash flow		(998)	106	132	995	1,195	1,195
Accumulated S.T. borrowing		1,804	1,877	835	0		
S.T. interest expense		32	43	41	17		
Pairs shipped (000s)		952	2,206	2,760	3,373	3,422	3,422

Two major problems existed with NoMal's location which could negatively impact the proposal. One problem concerned transporting the completed shoes to the nearest seaport at Penang. The shoes would be loaded into containers at the factory for ocean vessel shipping. Normally, BRS would use 40-foot containers on inland highways. This meant NoMal's freight costs would be almost double SoMal's annual freight costs.

The second problem involved living conditions in Ipoh for BRS's three American employees. Ipoh was largely a Chinese community, population about 500,000. The nearest international airport in Penang was a three-hour drive away. Although the international community was small, a British school was available. These aspects, together with Ipoh's inland, isolated location, could have a negative impact on the wives and families who would live there. See Exhibit 11 for other pros and cons associated with NoMal Shoe Company.

Exhibit 11

Evaluation of NoMal

Location: North Central Malaysia

Pros:
1. Purchase would include fixed assets only, assume no liabilities of previous company.
2. Labor market appears strong, located in Malaysia's third largest city (500,000).

Cons:
1. Transportation limited to 20-foot containers from factory to ocean ports. Round trip cost to nearest port plus port fees is $336 per container.
2. The two autoclave ovens need to be modified to minimize labor involved in opening and closing door. Changing pressurized vessels in Malaysia involves a lot of red tape and time (five to eight months).
3. Labor force unknown quality.
4. Future expansion of the stitching operation will have to be off-site.

SoMal Shoe Company

SoMal was located in Johore Bahru (Joe-hoe Ba-rue), which is situated across from the island of Singapore in the southernmost tip of peninsular Malaysia.

SoMal currently produced a low-quality canvas court shoe for a Japanese company. Although their contract expired six months earlier, they still had four months of production to process. Because of the shoe company involved, BRS could not begin manufacturing Nike shoes until SoMal discontinued manufacturing for the Japanese company. See Exhibit 12 for SoMal's most recent balance sheet.

The present owners were willing to sell SoMal for $2,187,000 or $.63 per share. For conservative purposes, the cash-flow projections, Exhibit 13, incorporate this price.

Exhibit 12

SOMAL SHOE COMPANY
Balance Sheet
9/30/79
(U.S. $000)

Assets

Current assets:

Accounts receivable:	trade	$ 37
	L/C	80
Inventory:	Raw material	253
	Fuel and parts	80
	Work in process	82
	Finish goods—first quality	197
	Finish goods—second quality	132
Prepayments and deposits		44
Total current assets		$ 905

Fixed assets:

Land (current market value with building $1,500)	319	
Building	680	
Equipment	1,270	
Total fixed assets		2,269
Intangible assets		101
Total assets		$3,275

Liabilities and Stockholders' Equity

Current liabilities:

Current portion L/T debt	$ 176	
Accounts payable	501	
Interest payable	253	
Other	36	
Total current liabilities		$ 966

Long-term debt:

MIDF loan*	633	
Bank of Bumiputra†	234	
Private loan‡	100	
Total liabilities		967

Stockholders' equity§

Initial paid-in capital	$1,248	
Additional paid-in capital	1,465	
Premium on stock	2	
Asset reevaluation reserve (current market value $1,017)	516	
Retained earnings	(1,889)	
Total equity		1,342
Total liabilities and equity		$3,275

---

* MIDF loan:

Outstanding loan as of October 31, 1979	$663
Interest payments in arrears	253
Total balance due	$916

This would be restructured over six-year term at 9½ percent with 12- to 15-month grace period during which only interest would be paid.

† Bank of Bumiputra restructured at 8 percent over four years with semiannual payments.

‡ This loan has to be paid off immediately.

§ Equity:

Number shares outstanding: 3,471,000

Goodwill estimated by current owners: $.10/share:

	Without goodwill	With goodwill
Without reevaluation	$.39	$.49
With reevaluation	$.53	$.63

Owners' proposed purchase price: 3,471,000 × $.63 = $2,187,000

Exhibit 13

SoMal Shoe Company Cash-flow statement ($000)

	Investment	First year	Second year	Third year	Fourth year	Fifth year	Sixth year
Raw material purchases	$ 325	$ 4,519	$ 7,332	$ 9,880	$10,849	$10,849	$10,849
L/C and exchange costs		47	73	98	112	112	112
Nonmaterial portion of cost of sales		801	1,512	1,912	2,174	2,190	2,190
Operating expenses:							
Admin. payroll		230	230	213	191	191	191
Admin. expenses		180	180	166	152	152	152
Freight expenses		50	99	123	151	153	153
Interest on MIDF loan		100	200	190	168	134	98
Interest on Bumiputra loan		11	17	13	7	2	
Startup expenses		100					
Training expense		297					
Total operating expense		$ 968	$ 726	$ 705	$ 669	$ 632	$ 594
Private loan payment		100					
Capital investment	2,600		50	400	50	50	50
Portion financed by MIDF	(1,300)			(200)			
Principal payments		25	196	376	426	430	432
Total expenditures	1,625	$ 6,460	$ 9,889	$13,171	$14,280	$14,263	$14,227
Revenue received		5,108	9,936	12,420	15,179	15,400	15,400
Pos./(neg.) cash flow		$(1,352)	$ 47	$ (751)	$ 899	$ 1,137	$ 1,173
Accum. S.T. borrowing		2,490	2,696	2,157	1,337	279	
S.T. interest expense		41	60	79	79	36	
Pairs shipped (000s)		1,135	2,208	2,760	3,373	3,422	3,422

Comparing NoMal's and SoMal's individual cash-flow statements, there were the following differences:

1. SoMal had an existing loan with MIDF and the Bank of Bumiputra (Malaysian State Bank) which would be restructured and paid off over a term of six years and four years, respectively.
2. Assuming you could retain most of SoMal labor force, the training time would be less and output would be higher in the first 18 months.
3. A private loan to the Japanese shoe company would be paid off immediately.
4. Less future capital investment, Exhibit 14, would be required at SoMal due to the existing equipment configuration.

Exhibit 14

SoMal Shoe Company capital investment

Timing of investment	Description	Amount ($000)
Initial	Land, building, equipment	2,600
2d year	Replacement of worn equipment	50
3d year	Equipment to expand capacity	400
4th year	Replacement of worn equipment	50
5th year	Replacement of worn equipment	50
6th year	Replacement of worn equipment	50
Total capital investment		3,200

Exhibit 15

Evaluation of SoMal

Location: Southern tip of Malaysia, across the channel from Singapore

Pros:
1. Acquiring an existing labor force, although requiring extensive retraining, should result in faster achievement of desired production goals.
2. Location to Singapore will facilitate shipping. Forty-foot containers can be shipped directly from factory to ocean port. Round trip cost plus port fees is $357.
3. Autoclave ovens employ hydraulic-lift door mechanisms allowing fast loading and unloading.
4. Includes purchase of five acres adjacent to the plant for future expansion.

Cons:
1. Acquiring working capital and debts of an existing company.
2. Competition with electronic firms and Singapore regarding future labor source. At one time, plant employed 700 people; although current employment is 400 people.
3. Currently committed to manufacturing shoes for Japanese company through April 1980, based on a contract which expired in September 1979.

Although SoMal's labor force would have to be completely retrained to manufacture the Nike athletic shoe, BRS felt the training would be less extensive because of the employees' present knowledge and understanding of shoe construction. Retraining was required because Nike shoes were machine lasted as opposed to hand lasted. BRS quality control demands were much higher due to major changes in the assembly process. One problem regarding labor involved the availability of additional labor in the area to staff future growth. The Johore Bahru area competed with Singapore (higher pay) and electronic firms which offered higher pay and better working conditions. Since SoMal's employment reached a high of 700 people one year ago, the present management felt BRS could attract an additional 350 people to reach the necessary 750 people required for the third year expansion plans. See Exhibit 15 for a further assessment on SoMal.

Observations

If BRS decided to acquire either NoMal or SoMal, they would relocate three of their U.S. employees to run the operation. A personal sketch of each individual is shown below:

Art Evans—Selected for general manager position
> Age: 50
> Years of employment with BRS: 2 years
> Years of shoe mfg. experience: 20 years
> Current position: Assistant general manager at Saco factory (Maine)

Sam Pickett—Selected for production control manager position
> Age: 30
> Years of employment with BRS: 5 years
> Years of shoe mfg. experience: 2 years
> Current position: Production control manager at Saco factory

Jim Anderson—Selected for controller position
> Age: 29
> Years of employment with BRS: 2 years
> Years of shoe mfg. experience: 2 years
> Current position: Assistant controller at Saco plant

The production control and controller functions would be eventually handled by Malaysian nationals. Sam and Jim would probably be reassigned after the second and third years, respectively.

BRS, in conjunction with the Malaysian government's desire, would keep their foreign equity in the new corporation at 49 percent. The remaining equity would be contributed by Malaysian partner(s) whom BRS

Exhibit 16

Organization chart

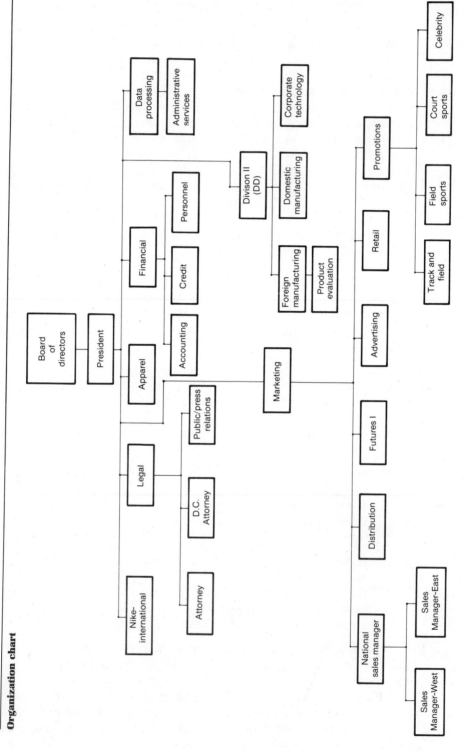

NIKE, INC.
Consolidated Statement of Income
Nine Months Ended February 28 ($000)

	1981	1980
Revenues	$322,958	$177,149
Costs and expenses:		
Cost of sales	231,279	130,074
Selling and administrative	43,673	26,365
Interest expense..	11,569	5,610
Other (income) expense	(57)	(94)
	286,464	161,955
Income before taxes	36,494	15,194
Income taxes...	17,874	7,444
Net income	$ 18,620	$ 7,750
Net income per common share	$ 1.11	$ .48
Average number of common and common equivalent shares outstanding	16,740	16,140

NIKE, INC.
Consolidated Balance Sheet
February 28 ($000)

	1981	1980
Assets		
Current assets:		
Cash	$ 2,261	$ 18
Accounts receivable......................................	90,845	53,629
Inventories..	126,556	53,659
Deferred income taxes	1,150	—
Prepaid expenses..	3,030	1,405
	223,842	108,711
Property, plant, and equipment	21,476	12,513
Less: Accumulated depreciation	6,507	3,069
	14,969	9,444
Other assets	672	432
Total assets	$239,483	$118,587
Liabilities and Shareholders' Equity		
Current liabilities:		
Current portion of long-term debt	$ 6,411	$ 467
Notes payable to bank	64,065	36,000
Accounts payable..	61,111	31,586
Accrued liabilities	13,332	17,378
Income taxes payable	8,874	3,696
Deferred income taxes	—	531
	153,793	89,658
Long-term debt...	9,697	4,621
Redeemable preferred stock	300	300
Shareholders' equity	75,693	24,008
Total liabilities and shareholders' equity	$239,483	$118,587

had already invited to participate. Depending on which company, if any, was acquired, the equity picture would be:

	NoMal	*SoMal*
BRS, Inc.	49%	49%
Malaysian partners in rubber	51	30
SoMal's president and largest shareholder	—	21

BRS felt Malaysia could become a valuable production source country. A supply agreement had been signed with the Malay Shoe Company (MSC), which would be producing 130,000 pairs of Nike athletic shoes per month by December 1980. MSC, however, wanted to limit Nike shoe capacity to 175,000 per month.

If BRS decided to purchase either NoMal or SoMal, this would be the first equity position in a foreign factory. BRS was estimating that an additional monthly production of 285,000 pairs could come from Malaysia.

Strong Trends in the 80s

Nike would surpass Adidas in domestic shoe sales.

Converse would remain a solid number three, having stabilized their previous years of sales decline. They should continue to lose market share to Nike in basketball sales.

Keds, having been purchased from Uniroyal by Stride-Rite, should have renewed momentum; although not significant, it should keep them at number four.

Brooks would continue its fast growth if they had another good year of ratings in the Runners World survey. Nike had publicly withdrawn from the shoe survey which could have a negative impact on its sales of running shoes. Brooks was also introducing a line of court shoes in 1980.

New Balance also showed strong growth in running shoes.

Dorcas International Corporation*

Dorcas International manufactured a line of electric razors and over the years had built a significant market position in most of the more developed countries. There had been recent signs, however, that the electric razor market had matured to a point where competition on price, and therefore cost, would be the outstanding characteristic of the industry over the next half-dozen years. Recognizing the changed situation, Jorg Moroney, the Dorcas president, had established a central management services group to look into the question of concentrating further expansion of production into a smaller number of sites in order to gain greater scale economies.

In setting up this group, however, Moroney indicated that he did not intend to dispense with a policy of holding operating units to profit achievement. While profit achievement had always been applied quite loosely, each manufacturing unit had been free to set its own price for its local markets and for supply to other marketing units.

The task of proposing a plan for future plant expansion fell to Stephan Morse as head of the new management services group. He decided that the first essential in preparing his recommendations was to collect basic cost and revenue data for the Dorcas International system. This he did, and as he considered the current situation irrelevant to the problem, he projected market growth, alternative price-sales figures, and cost estimates for four years ahead in current dollars. These are summarized in Exhibit 1. All this involved many simplifications, but Morse felt they would not materially affect a decision. For example:

1. Export duties and rebates were ignored as immaterial.
2. Any new capacity would take about two years to build and cost variations among alternative sites were unpredictable.
3. About 30 percent of fixed production cost was represented by depreciation in the first year (15 percent of plant cost). As depreciation reduced, it would be more or less offset by increased repair cost. The three existing plants could continue production at the indicated figures indefinitely. Plants would have little scrap value.

* This case was prepared by Kenneth Simmonds, professor, London Graduate School of Business Studies. Copyright 1972 by Kenneth Simmonds.

4. Tax rates applied to nonremitted funds only, but as Dorcas had large
    borrowings in each country no profit remittances were envisaged in
    the foreseeable future.

The next task seemed to be to calculate some sort of approximation to
an optimum and then to mold this into reasonable management recommendations.

Exhibit 1

Summary of cost and revenue data for Dorcas International System

	Unit	General	A	B	C	D	E	F
					Country			
Annual sales volume in four years' time for alternative average prices to wholesale	000 units							
$9.00			50	150	250	80	250	50
8.50			55	160	320	120	300	60
8.00			60	180	340	160	350	70
7.50			65	210	370	190	500	80
7.00			75	250	400	200	600	100
Variable cost of local marketing, selling, and distribution per average unit	$		0.50	0.60	0.40	0.40	0.20	0.50
Corporation tax rate	%		30	50	40	20	50	40
Customs tariff on imports based on transfer price	%		40	60	25	25	10	25
Transport costs per unit of transfers:								
Among A, B, C, F	$	0.10						
Between D and others	$	0.20						
Between E and others	$	0.20						
Existing production capacity:								
Volume limit	000 units			400	300		400	
Fixed production cost per annum (including interest and depreciation)	$000			800	1,100		1,200	
Variable production cost per average unit	$			3.00	2.00		2.00	
Additional production capacity:								
Fixed production cost for plant with annual volume:								
200,000 units	$000	800						
300,000 units	$000	1,100						
400,000 units	$000	1,350						
500,000 units	$000	1,500						
Variable production cost per average unit from new plant	$		1.50	2.00	1.80	1.80	1.50	1.80

Dexion Overseas Ltd.*

In November 1975, Mr. John Foster, recently appointed Managing Director, and Mr. Keith Galpin, Marketing Manager, of Dexion Overseas Limited (DOS), were attempting to give new direction to Dexion's overseas activities. Dexion had, over the years, grown substantially but somewhat haphazardly in its export markets and it seemed to the two managers that it was time for a full review of the company's present position and future overseas activities. They were particularly concerned with DOS's operations in Africa and the Middle East as these regions characterized the changing political and economic conditions in most of Dexion's overseas markets.

DEXION-COMINO INTERNATIONAL LTD.

Dexion-Comino International Ltd. was founded before World War II to manufacture slotted angles invented by Demetrius Comino as a solution to the recurring need for easily erectable and demountable industrial structures. What was initially jokingly referred to as "industrial meccano" soon acquired wide acceptance. Mr. Comino's initial investment of £14,000 in a 4,000-square-foot factory in north London had by 1968 grown into a 200,000 square-foot site at Hemel Hempstead producing well over 50 million feet of slotted angles. By 1973 Dexion was well established as a worldwide name with wholly owned subsidiaries in North America, Europe, and Australia, with exports accounting for over 60 percent of the U.K. factory's total turnover.

Product range

As the group's turnover and geographic coverage had increased, so had the company's range of products. What had started as ordinary slotted angles (known as DCP—Dexion Catalogue Products) that could be erected by almost anybody, had gradually grown in sophistication. By 1975 Dexion was a world leader in manufacturing and installing complete materials handling systems.

In the developed countries the continuing search for more efficient techniques of storage and materials handling resulted in a rapid growth

* This case was prepared by Shiv Mathur, of the London Business School. It was written with the cooperation of Dexion management. Facts and figures have been disguised to preserve confidentiality. Financial support was provided by The British Overseas Trade Board. © London Business School, 1976. Revised 1981.

of the "unit load concept" (various small parts being containerized for efficient storage)—and in particular the use of pallets. Dexion systems like "Speedlock" adjustable pallet racking were developed to meet this need. The Speedlock range permitted vertical storage to a height limited only by the height of the building itself. When fitted with wheels the racks, then known as "Powerpacks," could be mounted on steel rails permitting the closing down of an aisle and opening up of a new one at the touch of a switch.

By 1975 Dexion manufactured a whole family of products that served particular applications. "Apton" square tube framing had been designed for the smarter display of goods; "Clearspan" and "Impex" shelving for better storage of hand-loaded goods; and "Maxi" for storing small items. The basic DCP range was also modified and extended to meet entirely new applications. For example, DCP products that were usually used for storage had been modified to facilitate the construction of prefabricated housing units in developing countries. The growth of new products in many instances had also produced growth for DCP products as they constituted basic ingredients of the more advanced designs.

Overseas activities

Until 1970 overseas growth of Dexion's activities had been largely organic. As Dexion products had gained popularity, the company had set up subsidiaries in North America, Europe, and Australia. In other countries of the world Dexion had appointed distributors to stock and retail the products. Where local demand was fairly substantial but import restrictions prevented direct export and circumstances did not justify a subsidiary, local manufacturers had been licensed to produce and sell some products in the Dexion range. By the early 1970s Dexion had licensing arrangements with manufacturers in various parts of the world (Exhibit 1), although few were in Africa and the Middle East.

The actual agreement varied from licensee to licensee and reflected the company's attitude at the time the agreement was actually signed. Agreements usually specified a royalty income based on a percentage of turnover, often with a minimum annual payment. Dexion had little control over the pricing and marketing policies of its licensees, though sometimes restrictions were placed on their export activities. As the majority of licensees were mainly concerned with building up strong positions in their home markets, pressure to export to third countries in competition with Dexion's own direct export activities was not a major factor. The problems as seen at Dexion headquarters were not so much of licensee exports to third-country markets, but of ensuring that they developed their home markets and that licensee income due was in fact repatriated. Since many of the licensee markets had recurring balance-of-payment problems the actual collection of royalties was of continuing concern.

Exhibit 1

Licensed product sales, royalty income, and products licensed

Country (year of agreement)	Licensee 1974 sales (£)	Royalty rates*	Products licensed
Spain (1957)	650,000	£13,000 per annum (fixed sum)	DCP, pallet racking
Portugal (1957)	620,000	2%	DCP, Apton, Speedlock
New Zealand (1959)	210,000	2%	DCP
India (1960)	420,000	Profit participation agreement	DCP, Apton
El Salvador (1961)	50,000	4%	DCP
Canada (1964)	1,950,000	£25,000 per annum (fixed sum)	DCP and accessories
Mexico (1964)	1,170,000	2%	DCP, Apton, Speedlock
Brazil (1966)	490,000	4%	DCP, Apton Speedlock
Argentina (1966)	160,000	4%	DCP, Speedlock
Peru (1967)	230,000	£4,000 per annum (fixed sum)	DCP
Jamaica (1968)	87,000	4%	DCP
Nigeria (1970)	490,000	4%	DCP and accessories
S. Africa (1971)	325,000	4%	DCP, Apton Speedlock
Hungary (1971)	650,000	£65,000 (lump sum royalty)	DCP

* Expressed as percentage of turnover unless otherwise indicated.

Competition with Dexion products, both in the United Kingdom and overseas, had multiplied. Dexion, however, had maintained its market leadership in the United Kingdom. Overseas, in addition to budding indigenous manufacturers, Dexion was facing growing competition from Italian and continental exporters and lately the Japanese and Indians. But Dexion products were well established and the company prided itself on having a much more comprehensive product range and better design and other backup services than the non-European competition. Cheaper British steel gave Dexion exports a very real advantage, but it seemed that the position was gradually changing. Mr. Foster was getting increasingly concerned about Japanese and subsidized Indian competition in the Middle East and the gradual erosion of the cost advantage of using steel made in Britain.

DEXION OVERSEAS LIMITED

In 1970 Dexion-Comino International Ltd. had set up Dexion Overseas Limited (DOS) as a separate company within the organization to look after and coordinate its entire overseas export and licensing activities. Markets where Dexion had established subsidiaries or associates were excluded. In order to supervise distribution closely, DOS had divided the overseas market into five regions and appointed regional sales managers (RSMs) located in London to oversee Dexion's interests in each of these areas. The five regions were: (1) the Middle East and North Africa, (2) Europe, (3) the rest of Africa, (4) the far East and Southeast Asia, (5) the Caribbean and South America. Exhibit 2 gives DOS results for 1973 to 1975 and Exhibit 3 gives a breakdown of 1975 results by region.

Exhibit 2

DOS operating results (£000s)

	1973	1974	1975
Invoiced sales	5,672	6,444	6,914
Gross profits*	1,076	1,770	2,088
Variable distribution costs	156	221	290
Gross profit (after distribution costs)	920	1,549	1,798
Home office and regional expenditure	565	560	703
Operating profit	355	989	1,095
Miscellaneous income (including royalties)	94	122	136
Interest	(13)	(75)	(75)
Profit before tax	436	1,036	1,156

* After deducting transfer prices payable to Dexion-Comino International Ltd.

Exhibit 3

Allocation of 1975 DOS results by region (£000s)

	Invoiced sales	Gross profit	Regional expenses
Middle East and North Africa	3,016	1,006	96
Europe	1,829	378	33
Africa	1,090	408	42
Far East	257	61	26
Caribbean and South America	426	142	49
Miscellaneous	296	93	13
Total	6,914	2,088	259
Variable distribution expenses		290	
Gross profit (after distribution)		1,798	

Less:

Regional expenses	259
Central expenses	133
Marketing and promotion	104
Administration and rent	130
Technical	77
Total	703

Operating profit	1,095

Direct exports and involvement in the Far East and Central and South Europe were comparatively small. Dexion's operations in Europe were mature in nature and the increasing similarity between the United Kingdom and continental Europe in terms of competition, products, and customers had gradually resulted in most of Western Europe being treated as an extension of the home market, at least so far as the existing product range was concerned. With U.K. entry into the EEC in 1973, this similarity between the home market and continental Europe was becoming even more obvious, although differences in channels of distribution remained.

Keith Galpin had carried out a detailed analysis of the various international markets that could provide it with substantial business in the future. This analysis had incorporated not only informed views within the company but also interpreted demographic and economic data. The attempt was to highlight not only those markets which would continue to grow, but also select those which could become major profit generators in future. This exercise had brought to light some Southeast Asian and Middle Eastern countries which could be the target for more concentrated attacks.

DOS was of the opinion that during the next five years the company's business in the oil-rich countries of the Middle East and North Africa would expand much more rapidly than elsewhere. This called for a strategy that took into account the prominent position of the region. But the company felt that such a strategy would be applicable in principle to most overseas activities of the company, and Africa generally might follow the developments in the north.

DOS'S INTERNATIONAL POLICY

Markets and organization

Galpin divided the Dexion market in Africa and the Middle East roughly into three kinds of buyers. *Bazaar buyers* were customers who bought mostly DCP-type products to erect small and fairly crude storage and other structural units. Though DOS had no hard data on the buying behavior of these customers, it was generally believed that they designed their requirements themselves or with some help from local Dexion dealers. Their main criteria for buying Dexion products in preference to those of other suppliers were price and availability. The demand was more for the less sophisticated Dexion products and an important characteristic of the buyer was his lack of awareness and perhaps need for more sophisticated storage and material handling systems.

The second group were *installation buyers*. Installations could vary from small simple racking units (similar to those put up by the bazaar buyer himself) to complete warehouse units made up of products such as Speedlock pallet racking and Impex hand-loaded shelving. This type of business was invariably handled by local distributors, sometimes with the help of Dexion staff, and often required detailed designs and site construction. This design and construction service was increasingly being provided by the local distributor, although Dexion's U.K.-based units assisted with jobs which were outside the resources and capability of a particular distributor.

There was occasional demand for relatively large and sophisticated systems requiring special resources such as system analysis, structural design, subcontracting, contract negotiation, financing, project management, and so on, outside the scope of any distributor. DOS referred to this third type of business as *project business* and it invariably involved sales and implementation resources not available locally from a distributor even when supported by a local Dexion salesman. Support of the local distributor for this type of work was by the payment of a negotiated commission.

In order to serve the growth in both installation and project business, DOS had established in London a technical services cell (see Exhibit 4 for organization chart). The regional sales managers could refer their design problems to this unit and the cell itself undertook some marketing activities. It stayed in touch with U.K.-based architects, specifiers, and designers to influence them to use Dexion equipment in projects they were associated with. The cell had developed over the years the expertise to quote for and supervise a wide variety of overseas projects. Its links with the regional sales managers were close.

As part of its central marketing function the DOS staff at headquarters attempted to coordinate the advertising and sales promotion campaign for Dexion products in national markets. Films, pamphlets and information material in various languages had been prepared. The marketing department together with regional staff undertook to arrange seminars in various overseas capitals aimed at specific audiences. The marketing department also looked after the promotion of individual products and retained staff product managers who coordinated the activities for a particular product in the regions.

Pricing

DOS was supplied by the plant at Hemel Hempstead at a transfer price that reflected the direct costs of production and an allocation of works and general overheads. DOS, in turn, set prices for its distributors by adding a percentage markup to cover the cost of its own operations and provide a satisfactory profit.

Exhibit 4

DOS organization chart

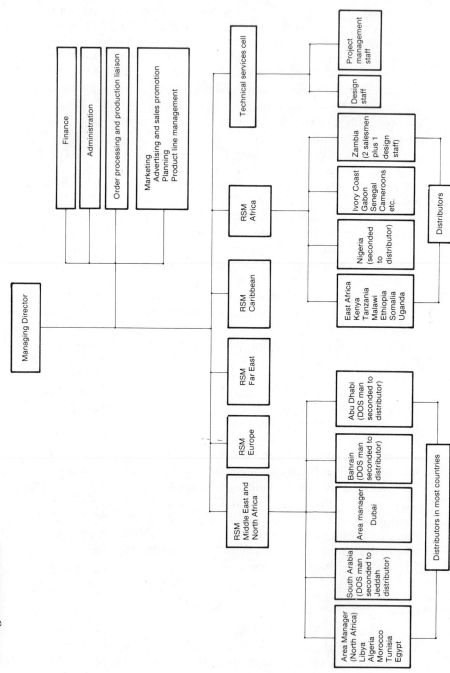

Note: Full-time distributor staff looking after DOS sales and design in Kuwait, Oman, and Lebanon.

In Mr. Foster's view, the essence of DOS's policy on distributor pricing was

> A question of competitive activity—we should evaluate what price competitive products are selling at and adjust our margins to account for the comparative advantages and disadvantages of Dexion goods.

Distributors in national markets were quoted different prices to take into account expected local distributor markup, the prices of competitive products, and the local customers' ability to pay. For example, during 1974, when transfer prices charged to DOS rose by 15 percent (Exhibit 5a), there was no corresponding across-the-board increase in prices

Exhibit 5a

Increase in transfer price to DOS, 1974

	Cost increase		Percentage costs	Increase
Steel	− 5%	on	40%	− 2.0%
Auxiliary material	20	on	35	7.0
Accessories	10	on	10	1.0
Other costs	0	on	15	0
Volume down				
30 percent on budget				9.0
Total increase in transfer price				15.0%

charged to customers. European customers were charged only an extra 5 percent, while Middle East prices went up the full 15 percent in sterling prices. When the devaluation of sterling had been accounted for, however, the local prices ended up lower.

As a result of the value pricing policy, the markups charged to distributors on various Dexion products differed considerably. Exhibit 5b gives an indication of gross margins by product category. Though DOS informally indicated to its distributors in various national markets the price at

Exhibit 5b

DOS product margins (excluding project sales) (£000s)

	1973			1974		
	Sales	Gross profits	Percent	Sales	Gross profits	Percent
DCP	2,079	610	29.3	2,530	874	34.5
Apton	305	120	39.3	481	164	34.1
Speedlock	1,120	238	21.3	1,347	393	29.2
Others	590	108	18.3	570	107	18.8
Total	4,094	1,076	26.3	4,928	1,538	31.2

which they should retail their products, it did not, and in management's view could not, lay down firm directives. This policy had both its advantages and disadvantages. The company did not retain any firm control on its prices and occasionally found distributors in well-protected or prosperous markets charging exorbitant markups. But with its flexible pricing policy, DOS had built for itself an extensive distributor network. Distributors, it was hoped, would in turn set retail prices to maximize their own and consequently DOS's profits. That this did not always happen was seen as a largely unavoidable consequence of using independent companies as part of the distributor system.

AFRICA

The regional sales manager (Africa) had for administrative convenience divided the countries south of the area of Arab influence into four areas: East Africa, Zambia, Nigeria, and the erstwhile French West Africa. The four areas were roughly equal in terms of market potential and four area managers were based in convenient local capitals. Though Dexion had a distributor in virtually every African capital, choice had been limited and determined more by the distributor's general business standing and connections with the local government than by previous experience of selling products related to storage and materials handling.

Apart from South Africa and Nigeria, the region was comprised largely of developing countries with foreign exchange problems and complicated systems of tariff and exchange controls. Often there was no dearth of demand for Dexion products but a noticeable lack of buying power for foreign products. This was in the regional sales manager's view the single most important impediment in exporting to the African market. There were few areas where concentrated marketing effort could be justified. Not only was the entire region plagued by controls but it was also in a state of constant economic and political flux.

Many suppliers besides those in the developed countries had found it possible to meet the less sophisticated level of African demand. Continental, Japanese, and Indian exports abounded, but Dexion with its wide and well-established network of distribution had a firm grip and in some countries like Tanzania had almost wiped out the use of competitive products. In virtually all markets, small local manufacturers making a restricted range of generally low-quality products were a continuing threat. In the regional sales manager's opinion, what Dexion had and the competition did not, were the local contacts and a name for quality and service that was well established.

It was not the overseas exporters who provided the major threat in African markets but the growing desire in most developing countries to set up their own production units. As the outlay for such a project would

Exhibit 6

Africa: Orders received (£000s)

	1973			1974			1975		
	DCP	Other	Total	DCP	Other	Total	DCP	Other	Total
Ethiopia	32	—	32	25	2	27	16	—	16
Ivory Coast	12	—	12	5	3	8	38	7	45
Kenya	26	—	26	18	5	23	55	8	63
Nigeria	44	61	105	60	79	139	103	109	212
South Africa	3	8	11	11	9	20	16	56	72
Sudan	44*	—	44	—	—	—	—	—	—
Tanzania	—	—	—	5	—	5	18	—	18
Zambia	74*	35*	109	61*	71*	132	140*	279*	419
Zaire	5	13	18	1	2	3	—	—	—
Others: Cameroons Gabon Ghana Gibraltar Senegal Niger Etc.	85	26	111	72	29	101	49	8	57
Total	325	143	468	258	200	458	435	467	902

* Project activity.

be about £500,000 it was well within the reach of most governments, if not individual entrepreneurs. It was possible that the small African markets would not support economic production units. But there was always the possibility of some countries getting together to come to tariff arrangements to form a quasi-common market or to look actively for regional exports. Some countries in East Africa and French West Africa had shown just this sort of inclination and this was seen as the thin end of the wedge at DOS headquarters.

The richer countries of Africa—Nigeria, Zambia, and South Africa—were different in their purchasing behavior. Areas of industrial concentration had resulted in a demand for a host of Dexion products and services. To South Africa and specially Nigeria, in spite of the presence of local licensees, Dexion directly exported the more modern systems, which were not manufactured locally. In Zambia, the company had obtained a large contract to design, supply, and erect a complete materials handling and storage system. The Zambian case characterized an obvious trend in buying behavior. Developing country governments keen to put up large industrial complexes, often with the help of overseas funds, increasingly contracted for the complete supply, design, and erection of turnkey projects.

MIDDLE EAST AND NORTH AFRICA

The regional sales manager (Middle East) described his region:

> In spite of popular beliefs it's not all gold. For us there are three to four countries that contribute most of the sales. And it would be fair to say that in most countries the results are directly proportional to the effort we put in. When I say "we," I mean "we"—the local distributors have far too much on their plates and are often so badly organized that they need all the assistance we can give. The real selling force is frequent visits and resident expatriate staff—people who are willing to live in Arab countries and promote the Dexion name. And they are harder to find than you would imagine.

In spite of the massive oil revenues there was a growing inclination in some Arab countries to ban foreigners from setting up purely trading companies. The United Arab Emirates, Iraq, Iran, and Algeria had formulated, or were in the process of formulating, controls for limiting the activities of foreigners. Others like Libya, who were at that moment big customers of DCP products, had already outlined their intention to set up their own slotted angle plants to reduce the economy's dependence on imports.

Everywhere there was an explosive industrialization underway. All over the Middle East new plants were being constructed and the host countries, while embarrassingly rich financially, lacked human skills and infrastructure to cope with the growth. Even Iraq and Algeria, while attempting to lower their reliance on foreign companies, recognized the necessity to permit foreigners to bid for and undertake large projects. In fact, almost all Dexion's business in Iraq, Algeria, Iran, and a substantial portion of that in Saudi Arabia had been obtained by negotiating large contracts (see Exhibit 7).

Though the growth in project activity was generally welcomed by Dexion management, it had created some organizational problems. Contract negotiation took a comparatively long time and resulted more often than not in "next year's sales and this year's expenses." The regional sales managers were always under considerable pressure to maintain expenditure within agreed budgets and treated project activity with mixed emotions. However, when the organizational problems, both within DOS and with the local distributors, had been overcome, the profits were very welcome. Gross profits on successful tenders in the Middle East were broadly similar to those obtained on the sale of hardware alone.

Competition in the Middle East was strongest from the Japanese, Italians, and Indians in the supply of DCP-type hardware and from Japan and Germany in the project market. The Japanese and Germans often had a slight edge on Dexion as they had been able to quote for complete turnkey projects. In Libya, DOS's distributor had established very good

Exhibit 7

Middle East and North Africa—orders received (£000s)

	1973			1974			1975		
	DCP	*Other*	*Total*	*DCP*	*Other*	*Total*	*DCP*	*Other*	*Total*
Abu Dhabi	73	7	80	155	25	180	285	33	318
Dubai	32	11	43	78	3	81	85	27	112
Iraq	147*	—	147	478*	2	480	209*	4*	213
Libya	377*	21*	398	356*	17*	373	252*	60*	312
Oman	18	15	33	58	80	138	130	104*	234
Saudi Arabia	65	48	113	134	247	381	257	369†	626
Bahrain	18	9	27	35	34	69	25	21	46
Qatar	9	—	9	17	3	20	25	—	25
Algeria	—	1,235†	1,235		47*	47	—	—	—
Others: Cyprus Egypt Iran Jordan Kuwait Lebanon Malta Pakistan Syria Tunisia Yemen	94	14	108	294	29	323	91	9	100
Total	833	1,360	2,193	1,605	487	2,092	1,359	627	1,986

* Project activity.

† Projects not broken up by product groups.

links with the local government and Dexion products had reached a large market share, but only by pricing below DOS's normal markup to offset the price advantage of Italian products. In Saudi Arabia and the UAE, which still constituted the bulk of the hardware business, DOS's response to competition had been first to pare margins and second to promote slightly more advanced systems like Speedlock. In spite of overseas and local manufacturers crowding these markets, there was still ample opportunity for all. Saudi Arabia and the UAE had five-year plans that budgeted a threefold increase in public expenditure—justification enough for the most forceful of selling efforts.

Alternative possibilities

With its target of achieving a 15 percent annual increase in sales and profits, DOS management was aware that a series of long-term strategic decisions had to be made. These decisions would have to encompass almost all the activities of the company and would have to bear in mind

that 100 percent owned subsidiaries would be difficult to establish overseas. They included:

1. Should the company continue to license overseas manufacturers to
    produce the DCP range in areas of high tariffs and foreign exchange
    problems, or should the licensing policy be extended to cover more
    products and markets? In particular, should DOS agree to permit the
    manufacture of the Speedlock and Apton range in Nigeria?
2. If licensing was not a viable option, in view of local government
    hostility to royalties, should DOS look to joint ventures?
3. Another possibility could be to discontinue all overseas manufacture
    and cancel where possible the existing licensing arrangements and
    manufacture and export from the United Kingdom, or another suit-
    able European base.
4. Which markets should be focused on and with what products?
5. Should the existing policy be changed?
6. Was there any need to restructure the distribution strategy?

The list of issues which needed to be questioned and sorted out
seemed endless. DOS management was also aware of the fact that it
would be impossible to put hard figures on many of these options but
Mr. John Foster felt that the data he had were reliable, in the sense that
they were indicative of the situation. He was particularly aware that the
issues were interrelated (e.g. the company could not have a production
policy that required licensing arrangements and a marketing strategy
that required distributors) and the direction that DOS's total strategy took
should at least be compatible within itself.

Hamesin International*

*This case was prepared by Mr. Yoav Eizenberg under the direction of Dr. Igal Ayal of the Leon Recanati Graduate School of Business Administration, Tel-Aviv University. Reprinted with permission of the authors.

THE ISRAELI PERIOD (1960–1969)

Hamesin, Ltd. was founded in 1960, as a joint venture of Geha chemicals company (70 percent) and Rimon, Inc. (30 percent). Hamesin, Ltd. was intended to penetrate the Israeli veterinary products market in the area of special food additives. As a main entry into that market, the company would use a license obtained a short time before by Rimon from a French company named Solar, producing a chicken-feed enriching compound.

Nine years later, at a board meeting held in October 1969, the company's situation was reviewed by the chairman of the board and general manager, Mr. Eli Yahalomi. The balance sheet for September 30, 1969 was presented, and future prospects for the company were discussed. The following are highlights from Mr. Yahalomi's presentation.

Areas of activity

The company markets two types of products in Israel: (1) a chicken-feed enriching compound, and (2) special additives for poultry and cattle feed.

Chicken-feed enriching compound. The enrichment compound is produced by Hamesin under license. The product is used for the feeding of broilers. It is also used to increase the yield of egg-laying hens. Hamesin holds 60 percent of this market and has only one competitor.

Special feed additives. The product is produced through a rather simple process. It is a small ingredient in the feed produced by kibbutzim and by regional feed-processing plants for feeding poultry and livestock. The market includes two other firms, the leader being Tiv-Tov, with a 70 percent market share. The trend in recent years has been away from small processing plants and toward concentration of feed processing in large regional plants. This trend, if continued, could severely cut down the size of the existing market due to backward integration by the large plants producing their own premixes.

Financial and sales data

Annual sales volume (in tons)

Product	1966	1967	1968	1969
Feed enrichment compound	1,921.3	2,245.9	2,597.9	2,857.7
Special additives	199.4	300.4	321.1	324.5

Distribution of sales revenues in 1969:

Feed enrichment compound: 73.3%

Special additives: 26.7%

Income statements

	1966	1967	1968	1969
Gross margin (000 Israeli £s.)	3,570	4,760	5,950	6,970
Expenses	3,060	3,400	5,780	6,885
Income before taxes	510	1,360	170	85

Reviewing the company's financial situation, Mr. Yahalomi pointed out the gap between the rates of growth for expenses and for the gross margin. The outlook for sales growth in both areas of activity was not encouraging, since the market was well established and in fact may have reached a saturation level for Israel. There also did not appear to be much chance of increasing Hamesin's share of the market.

The best alternative, unanimously adopted by the board, was to develop export markets for the company.

Export potential—existing capabilities

Existing export licenses—feed enriching compound. The license agreement signed in 1960 with Solar, Inc. gave Rimon the right to produce and market the feed enriching compound in several foreign markets, including Turkey, Greece, Iran, and all of South America. The use of such compounds was not common in any of these markets in 1969. The main provisions of the agreement were:

1. Raw materials would be purchased from Solar.
2. Royalties would be paid on all sales in all markets, according to a specified formula.
3. The product should never fall below Solar's quality standards and would be marketed everywhere, except in Israel, under the Solar brand.

Existing marketing channels. The Geha Corp. had branches in several South American countries, including Argentina, Brazil, Chile, and Uruguay. The branches marketed pesticides in these countries. None of the branches amounted to much in the way of marketing power, and in fact they were company representatives, marketing the pesticides through local channels in each country. The main point, though, was that there existed a highly experienced export administration system within the Geha home office. This system could be utilized to organize planned exports by Hamesin.

Professional know-how. Professional personnel developed and employed by Hamesin for marketing its products in Israel were divided into two main groups:

The field group. This included seven agronomists who operated as the company's main selling force. Each agronomist, who really served as a combination extension agent and salesman, had a separate territory. Each one of these agronomists was highly experienced in animal feeding, with some of them specializing in livestock feed and the others in poultry feed. Special skills acquired during eight years of work for Geha were:

1. Experience in "selling" the benefits of using feed enriching compound to farmers using regular feed.
2. The capability of explaining professionally the advantages of the Solar compound over a rival compound.
3. The ability to handle all the economic and nutritional elements involved in selecting feed for poultry and for livestock.

The development group. This was an ad hoc working group of well-known experts on animal feeding. The group gathered technical information on building and operating feed processing plants, and particularly on new developments in this area. Through this group, Hamesin hoped to be able to sell to the large plants complete feed formulations designed to achieve stated nutritional objectives at a minimum cost.

Productive capacity. Forty percent of Hamesin's productive capacity for feed enrichment compound was not utilized during 1969. It was clear that production could be substantially increased without any capital investment, and with only a very small increase in workforce.

The situation was somewhat different for special additives, but even there export operations could be started without additional investments since the company could use subcontractors' plants.

Operational alternatives

The immediate problems before the board of directors were what to export, to what markets, and how. It was decided to conduct a basic market research study and decide according to the findings.

Ideal market conditions for introducing the feed enriching compound, as presented to the market researchers, were:

1.   A well-developed egg industry. Production by economic units which produce a maximum for the market and a bare minimum for local consumption.
2.   Egg production in large, intensive chicken farms, utilizing relatively advanced technology.
3.   A well-developed market for meat, so that a broiler industry either exists already or has good chances of developing.
4.   Feed prices should be above a certain minimum, so that the use of enriching compound to increase the broiler food conversion index will be worthwhile for the farmer, while leaving a reasonable profit for the compound manufacturer.

Target markets surveyed were Turkey, Iran, and the South American markets. Market potentials for special additives were also examined. The survey concluded:

> *Argentina:* Right from the beginning it was clear to the market researchers that this market holds the best promise for their products. Argentina has a highly developed farm industry and is one of the largest livestock producers. Agricultural production is concentrated in large farms managed according to economic criteria. While production in Argentina is mainly in large chicken farms, the yield of eggs per hen is much lower than in Israel. In general, agricultural technology in Israel is substantially more developed than in Argentina. This means that Israel can professionally contribute to Argentinian chicken farming, and on the other hand Argentina has farm personnel capable of assimilating new knowledge.
>
> The chicken farms in Argentina are organized in cooperatives, which buy raw materials for the members and market their output. The market potential for feed enrichment compound amounts to 6,800 tons per year, or almost twice the Israeli market size.

ESTABLISHING AN INTERNATIONAL MARKETING SYSTEM

Strategy formulation

On the basis of the market survey, an export strategy for Hamesin was formulated during late 1969 and early 1970, as follows:

Target markets.   In the first phase, the company would build a marketing system based on exporting to a single market—Argentina. While operating in this market for several years, the company would develop personnel and a management system capable of conducting business in faraway markets. At the same time, the company would learn to deal with the problems of operating as a foreign company in a market and competing with local companies, and would develop appropriate control and information systems. These capabilities would be utilized in the second phase for extension in other markets.

Products.   It was decided that international operations would not be limited to a single product. On the other hand, the initial thrust would concentrate on the feed enriching compound as a base for building export activities.

Economic objectives.   It was agreed between the partners that all of Hamesin's operations abroad would be based on exports from Israel. In this manner, the company hoped to circumvent currency exchange and capital transfer problems, and to solve the Hamesin profitability problems.

Organizational structure.   It was decided that the organizational structure for operations abroad would be tailored to each market. It was clear that the Geha branch in Argentina would not be usable for Hamesin because of its limited nature. On the other hand, it was agreed that the administration of export activities would be handled by the Geha export department, which was well versed in dealing with the banks and government agencies, as required.

Application to Argentina

In March 1970, Mr. Avraham Eshed, formerly sales manager for Hamesin, was sent to Argentina to examine the possible methods for marketing feed enrichment compound in Argentina. The following are the main conclusions reached by him during the first two months of his stay:

1.   There was no possibility to market the product through local channels, since such channels did not exist for a product of this nature and the product requires development of basic awareness of its value throughout the farming community.

2.   An independent distribution system fully controlled by Hamesin had to be established. It should be based on regional warehouses, holding sufficient inventories and serving farms up to 300 kilometers distant from the warehouse.

3.   Distribution should be based on selling to the farm cooperatives. These would buy for their members and handle payments. Thus, the firm would only have to ship the product from the regional warehouse to the cooperative warehouse rather than to individual farms. The procedure would also simplify collections and reduce the risk of bad debts.

4.   Following the Israeli format, two fieldmen should be assigned to each regional distribution center. Their function would be to establish product awareness among farmers and to conduct business with merchants. Regarding the cooperatives, the fieldmen would seek to increase "pull" from below. Actual transactions with cooperatives would be concluded at the enterprise management level.

5.   The product was marketed in Israel in three versions: (a) high-energy feed enrichment compound for rapid fattening of special high-grade broilers, (b) high-protein feed enrichment compound for raising reasonable quality broilers on farms where the care and maintenance level was mediocre, and (c) low-protein feed enrichment compound for enriching egg-laying hens on farms with good maintenance and care levels. Mr. Eshed concluded that there was no need in Argentina for the first version of the compound, since the existence of a well-developed beef industry limited the potential for high-grade broilers. He also concluded that there was no need to differentiate between the other two versions. The general care and maintenance level in Argentina was quite low, due to availability of cheap labor. Under these conditions, only the second high-protein version was capable of producing good results.

6.   Language problems convinced Mr. Eshed that the company should look for local, Spanish-speaking agricultural experts.

7.   His conclusions regarding the appropriate distribution system pointed to the need for a sizable level of focal expenditures. It became clear to Mr. Eshed that substantial bank financing would be necessary. Since Argentinian law drastically limited credit availability for foreign-owned firms, Mr. Eshed recommended the establishment of a joint venture with a local company. The local partner would hold 75 percent of the stock, giving the firm maximal access to local bank financing.

These recommendations led Hamesin's board of directors to adopt the following operational decisions:

1.   A new company, named Hamesin Argentina, would be set up. Twenty-five percent of the stock would be owned by Hamesin (Israel) and 75 percent by local investors.

2.   The company manager would always be an Israeli, appointed by Hamesin. The firm would issue voting stock, giving Hamesin the lion's share of voting power.

3.   A founding team would be sent to Argentina. The team would be comprised of Mr. Eshed as general manager, two Israeli fieldmen with substantial experience, and one new agronomist hired for this purpose. The Israeli fieldmen would be assigned for the first six months to different chicken-farming areas in Argentina. Each one of the field men would do missionary selling in his area, convincing the local farmers of the benefits attendant to the use of feed enrichment compounds. At the same time, the general manager would recruit six local agronomists, and these would be trained by the Israeli fieldmen.

4. Twenty tons of feed enrichment compound, worth $8,700, would be allocated for demonstrations, samples, and experiments in the initial periods.

5. All policy-level decisions (including pricing, recruitment, and unusual contracts) by the local general manager would require authorization from the management in Israel. A monthly reporting system was established, covering the financial situation, sales, and inventory levels.

6. A three-year plan and budget were drawn up as follows:

a. Start-up period: January 1, 1970–September 30, 1970.
   Revenues from sales: None.

Expenses:	Samples (20 tons)	$ 8,700
	Salaries and wages	60,000
	Other expenses	11,300
	Total investment	$80,000

b. Sales were budgeted after the six-month startup period as follows:

	Sales per month (tons)	Sales for period (tons)
Next six months of operation	110	660
Second year of operation	200	2,400
Third year of operation	270	3,240

c. Expected monthly expenditure levels were:

	Second half of first year	Second year	Third year
Fieldmen wages	$ 4,400	$ 7,000	$ 9,000
Office salaries and wages	4,500	5,000	5,500
Transportation	6,380	9,800	10,500
Financing and miscellaneous	2,500	5,000	6,000
Total monthly expenditure	$17,780	$26,800	$31,000

d. The feed enrichment compound price to the final consumer could not exceed $650 per ton, considering feed prices in the local market. Price after a 10 percent discount to various distributors, including the cooperatives and independent merchants, was $585 per ton, net to the company.

e. Cost-accounting data in Israel showed that production and shipping costs (to Buenos Aires) would amount to $383 per ton.

f. In accordance with these data, the following sales and profit plan was developed (all in 1970 prices):

Item	First six months of sales ($)	Second year of operation ($)	Third year of operation ($)
Net selling price in Argentina/ton	585	585	585
Net selling price to Hamesin Argentina/ton	435	435	435
Cost to Hamesin Israel/ton	383	383	383
Profit/ton, Hamesin Israel	52	52	52
Contribution/ton, Hamesin Argentina	150	150	150
Total sales for period, in tons	660	2,400	3,240
Profit for period, Hamesin Israel	34,320	124,800	168,480
Total contribution for period, Hamesin/Argentina	99,000	360,000	486,000
Forecasted expenses for period, Hamesin/Argentina	106,680	321,600	372,000
Profit (loss) for period, Hamesin/Argentina	(7,680)	38,400	114,000

From these data, it appeared that Hamesin would recover its initial investment of $80,000 in the middle of the second year of operations. Hamesin Argentina was planned to show an accumulated profit of $145,000 by the end of the third year. This budgeted profit should provide sufficient reserve against unforeseen developments and present a reasonably attractive image to banks and to the local government.

THREE YEARS LATER

Early in 1973 Mr. Eshed was summond to Israel to participate in a series of discussions regarding the situation of Hamesin Argentina, and plans for the continuation of Hamesin operations in Argentina, and possible expansion to other markets. Some serious charges were made against Mr. Eshed during these discussions.

Mr. Yahalomi, Hamesin's chief executive officer, urged that sales in Argentina were far below expectations. Average sales in the second year were only 185 tons per month, and only 230 tons per month in the third year. According to him, most of Mr. Eshed's time was spent in trying to develop local business in partnership with some operators in the animal feed market, which prevented him from reaching budgeted sales levels. Mr. Yahalomi insisted that the Argentinian venture was established in order to promote Hamesin's exports—not to develop the Argentinian economy.

Mr. Shamir, Hamesin's export manager, states that throughout the period he had to fight with Mr. Eshed in order to receive updated inventory reports and other reports that were included in the planned information system. Finally, personal relations between himself and Mr. Eshed had deteriorated to the point where they could no longer work together.

Mr. Tidhar, Geha general manager, stated that he was severely disappointed with Hamesin Argentina's inability to utilize its distribution system to market Geha pesticides in Argentina. He charged Mr. Eshed with attempting to increase Hamesin Argentina's sales volume through local business deals, thereby increasing his bonus (which was based on total sales volume). Mr. Tidhar suggested that Mr. Eshed's contract should be changed, to give him a bonus on sales from Israeli imports only.

Mr. Yahalomi summarized the charges by stating that while the Argentinian operation exceeded budgeted profit levels, the company was no longer directed by the shareholders' aims and objectives, and its operations were being extended too far afield by its general manager.

Responding to the charges, Mr. Eshed reviewed the first three years of operations, and presented the following arguments:

1.   Management in Israel does not understand the complications involved in operating in a foreign country so far from headquarters. The initial definition of his responsibilities and authority was wrong, leaving too many policy decisions to the Israeli management. Hamesin management should have decided on central policy guidelines and then let him manage the company, rather than trying to manage Hamesin Argentina from Israel.

2.   The far-reaching market development activities conducted during the startup period attracted two other firms with foreign technical know-how to enter the market. These firms offered lower-quality products at lower prices. Since the product offered by Hamesin had not had a chance to prove its superior quality in the field prior to the outset of competition, price became a critical variable. Using painstaking comparative feed conversion experiments, Hamesin Argentina personnel succeeded in proving the superiority of the Israeli feed enrichment compound. This success, however, did not prevent the competitors from selling, and Hamesin Argentina was obliged to reduce its price to the final consumer to $629 per ton. Mr. Eshed argued that the three-month delay between the time he reached his conclusion regarding the necessary price change and the time of obtaining concurrence from the Israeli management was crucial, enabling the competitors to establish a strong market position.

3.   Another major problem was personnel. As it turned out, "job-hopping" is the accepted custom among young Argentinian university graduates. Labor turnover was high throughout the period, and even now there are only two satisfactory fieldmen out of a crew of six. Mr. Eshed explained that the phenomenon results from a wealth of job opportunities facing educated young people in Argentina, and an absence of "patriotic" feelings toward an employer (such as exists in Israel).

4.   Midway through the second year of operations it became clear to Mr. Eshed that he could not meet planned profit levels. Sales of 185 tons per month at a net price of $566 would cause the firm losses of over $2,500 per month, since expenses ran at about the forecasted level. His repeated requests to reduce his purchase price for enrichment com-

pound were denied. Thus, he felt he had to search urgently for additional local sources of revenue for the company. Early in 1971 he reached separate agreements with three large feed processors. It was agreed that his fieldmen, who had to meet chicken farmers in any case while selling the compound, would promote feed sales for the processing plants. Within six months, sales commissions on feed were providing 25 percent of the total contribution, and total profits exceeded budgeted levels by 30 percent.

5.   Mr. Eshed tried to impress upon the listeners that a management information system between parent company and subsidiary should be designed to promote the common interests—not to hinder operations. According to him, informational demands placed upon him were never ending, including subjects that were totally irrelevant to the solution of his pressing problems and even Hamesin problems. On the other hand, all of his requests for sending experts on nutrition and feed technology (experts that were available among Hamesin personnel) went unanswered. Even his requests for special products that could easily be marketed in Argentina (but had to be developed in Israel) did not receive proper treatment. On the other hand, he was always asked to use his fieldmen to market pesticides, an area that was completely out of their sphere of operations.

6.   Summing up his arguments, Mr. Eshed stated that there is a certain internal logic in the evolution of a business venture. In the long run, a business must retain flexibility and adaptability in order to survive. It cannot operate in a very rigid and unyielding framework, and the farther away from the center it is, the more it needs independence.

Adjourning the meeting, Mr. Yahalomi announced the agenda for the next board meeting:

1.   What form should future operations in Argentina take, and under what guidelines?
2.   What actions have to be taken to prepare for entrance to another market?
3.   Should Mr. Eshed be kept on as Hamesin Argentina's general manager?

Multinational operations management

British Airborne*

Dr. Amar Singh, an Indian national who had been in Canada for four weeks at the invitation of the government to lecture on some obscure aspects of neurosurgery—a subject on which he was a leading expert— was going back to Delhi. He had, in fact, been on his way to Montreal's airport at Dorval, when he decided that he would like to stop in London for a day or two on his way home to meet his old friend and teacher, Sir Michael Shannon.

On arrival at Dorval Airport, the 5'4" disheveled and untidy doctor made his way to the counter of British Airborne. There was a well-groomed and charming lady in attendance with "Jane Smith" boldly splashed on her name tag.

"Yes, sir?"

"I want a booking on your evening flight—to London and on to Dehli," said Dr. Singh.

Miss Smith punched a few keys. "Yes, we can manage that, sir."

Dr. Singh handed over his ticket. "I would like to stop in London for about 12 hours."

Miss Smith looked at the ticket, her brows furrowed, and she consulted a manual on her desk. "You have an excursion ticket, sir, and there's no way we can permit you to break your journey in London."

"But when I came to Montreal, Trans Am permitted me to stop over in London. Perhaps I can speak to someone in your organization who could assist me."

"I can't speak for Trans Am, sir. It may have been an oversight on their part, but we don't do it. The airline's rules are very specific and the answer is no. There's nobody else who could help you," said Miss Smith firmly but suavely, adding with a smile, "Should I make a reservation straight to Delhi?"

Dr. Singh was slightly taken aback. "Perhaps I could pay the difference."

* This case was prepared by Mr. Shiv Mathur, Research Fellow, and Professor Kenneth Simmonds of the London Graduate School of Business Studies. It is not intended to illustrate the policies or practice of any particular firm. Financial support was provided by the British Overseas Trade Board. Copyright 1976 by London Business School.

"We can't accept that ticket in part exchange. You will have to buy an entirely new ticket and perhaps you wouldn't want to do that, sir."

Dr. Singh looked at her.

"I am afraid the answer remains definitely no." With these words Miss Smith looked over Dr. Singh's head at the tall American hippie next in the queue.

Dr. Singh looked around, seemed upset, then picked up his bags and walked over to the Mediterranean Airways counter.

Later that evening when Miss Smith was having a cup of tea with John Parry-Green, British Airborne's marketing manager for eastern Canada, she recounted the incident with Dr. Singh.

"Quite right, too," agreed Mr. Parry-Green when he heard the stand she had taken. But when Miss Smith had returned to her counter, Mr. Parry-Green continued to think about the matter.

Since his appointment to the region six months previously, Mr. Parry-Green had been trying to drum up business for British Airborne in the eastern provinces of Canada. He had had talks with travel agents and some of the larger business houses in the province of Quebec and he felt that negotiations had, by and large, been satisfactory. However, he had been unable to come to terms with the two Indian travel agents who made the majority of bookings for the large population of Indians and other Asians resident in eastern Canada. Mr. Parry-Green had invited them to his office and quite specifically laid down his attractive terms on discounts and commission, but they had, in his opinion, taken an extreme bargaining position and it all seemed of little use. The two travel agents had telephoned him on several occasions to ask him if he would contact British Airborne's London office to explain their position, but Mr. Parry-Green had assured them that though he could not alter his terms he quite understood the nature of their demands and would advise them if his airline was ever in a position to change its policy. As he felt quite competent to deal with the situation, he did not think it necessary to refer the question to London and negotiations had now been deadlocked for a few weeks.

Asians and Arabs with their extended families were frequent travelers and British Airborne could certainly do with their business. But Mr. Parry-Green felt that they wanted him to bend not only British Airborne, but also IATA (International Air Transport Association) rules. He suspected other airlines, and especially Mediterranean Airways, of making illegal concessions to passengers. These concessions could take many forms, such as overlooking excess baggage and giving unallowed stop-overs and large discounts.

Of course, local managers of other airlines denied this, and Jean Cohen of Mediterranean Airways was most vociferous in his denials. But could one trust that lot? Mr. Parry-Green had, on his own initiative, once or twice tried to check on Mediterranean Airways' activities, but had been unable to document any irregularity. However, such concessions were almost impossible to detect on a cursory check and would require a much more thorough investigation. Mr. Parry-Green had himself been tempted to make some concessions to his passengers that would technically infringe IATA rules and had, in fact, noted this as a point of serious discussion at the forthcoming marketing managers' conference in London. If London did not permit him to try some concessions, he had almost decided that he would register a complaint anonymously with the IATA authorities regarding Mediterranean Airways' activities. IATA would surely uncover many irregularities and although the substantial fines that would be imposed following the detection of such offenses might not worry an airline of Mediterranean Airways' standing, it would at least give Jean Cohen something to account for to his head office and customers. The International Air Transport Association had not been lenient in recent years about infringement of rules.

Over the last three months, British Airborne's comparative load factor from Dorval had fallen at an increasing rate, in spite of the additional facilities and staff that Mr. Parry-Green had employed to serve customers. Mr. Parry-Green felt that this was partly due to the growing recession and consequent excess capacity on flights and competition for customers. Still, it did not look good in the first year of his appointment, and the incident with Dr. Singh made him wonder again whether he should not suggest that counter staff fail to notice excursion rates when passengers held British Airborne's own tickets and wanted to stop over.

John Marshall*

Following the sudden death of the chief accountant of General Engineers Proprietary, John Marshall was promoted to fill the vacancy. The position reported directly to the firm's vice president of finance and entailed responsibility for the commercial side of the firm's operations, including invoicing, costing, accounts payments, and financial accounting, and full control of an office staff of over 100. John, who was only 29, was a chartered accountant and for two years previously had been an assistant accountant responsible for the development and installation of a new cost-control system.

General Engineers Proprietary carried out a range of engineering activities in Australia, operating from headquarters in Brisbane. In a section of its works on the Brisbane waterfront, some 300 men were regularly engaged in ship repair and maintenance work. This work was largely undertaken at cost plus a fixed percentage to cover overheads and profit. The fixed percentage was usually 8 to 10 percent and usually negotiated with the Australian offices or agents of the shipping companies owning the vessels.

Two days after taking up his new post, John was brought an invoice for signature by Bill Brady, the chief shipping clerk. It amounted to A$59,587 and was for repair work just being completed on the *M. V. Hull.* Bill explained to John that the invoice must be signed in quintuplicate by the chief accountant and then taken for countersigning by the captain and chief engineer before the ship sailed.

John immediately requested to see the cost sheets backing up the cost-plus invoice. Bill, who was an older man of over 60 and had always seemed to John to be reliable and helpful, if perhaps a little fatherly, was reluctant to bring the cost sheets. He first argued that Mr. Knox, the previous chief accountant, had never bothered to check the cost sheets. Then he explained that the last two days' costs were not yet posted and had been taken from time records and material requisitions and purchase orders. Nevertheless, John insisted and Bill brought him the records and rapidly demonstrated the transfer of cost sheet totals onto the summary sheet shown in Exhibit 1. When these were checked, Bill left John with the summary sheet, suggesting he add it and compare the totals with the invoice.

Exhibit 1

Cost summary sheet

Job number and particulars		Hours	Wages	Material and supplies	Machinery and transport cost	Total cost
8064	M. V. *Hull*—engine room	5,444	$10,009.64	$ 2,964.13	$1,167.79	$14,141.56
8065	M. V. *Hull*—engine room	2,939	5,123.15	822.65	756.29	6,702.09
8066	M. V. *Hull*—deck repairs	1,497	2,896.15	964.21	326.11	4,186.47
8073	M. V. *Hull*—pump and winch overhaul	2,329	5,093.60	1,064.22	3,421.61	9,579.43
8074A	M. V. *Hull*—shipwrights	1,261	2,939.20	1,745.50	491.27	5,175.97
8074B				405.00		405.00
8076	Electricians	2,413	4,762.79	980.73	1,731.32	7,474.84
		15,883	30,824.53	8,946.44	7,894.39	47,665.36
Above jobs			515.00	2,175.25	165.00	2,855.25
	Unposted		2,625.00			2,625.00
			$33,964.53	$11,121.69	$8,059.39	$53,145.61

As John added the summary sheet, the last entry for unposted wages caught his eye. He could not understand why the activity had jumped on the last day. He called the time office to check the figure and was told that the unposted cost was A$515, including an estimate for work still being completed.

When Bill came back to pick up the signed invoice copies John raised this point:

John: That's fine, Bill, but where do the unposted wages of $2,625 come from?

Bill: Well, those are for ship's crew that helped us with the work instead of taking shore leave.

John: How do we pay them?

Bill: Well, I draw up a list of names and amounts, have it countersigned by the shipping manager, draw cash, and then make the payment when I take the invoice.

John: Does anybody audit these payments?

Bill: No. There is no need.

John: Well, I would like to come down today.

Bill: It's not really practical. You see, I usually give it to the chief engineer for distribution.

John: But how do we know the right men get it?

Bill: We don't—and it might be best for you not to worry further. What you have no cause to pursue can never hurt you.

It finally dawned on John that this was probably a payoff to ship's officers. He sat thinking for a while. Should he sign the invoice or should he push for more accurate particulars?

If he was not going to sign, he would have to take immediate action before the ship sailed—find out exactly to whom the amounts were paid, insist on an amended invoice, and take whatever consequences the likely loss on the job would bring. With a rueful smile he signed the five copies and handed them to Bill, thinking as he did that it would be best to take a few days to look into things and think it through.

That evening and the following day John considered the alternatives. He could do nothing and continue to sign invoices as the chief accountant had done in the past. Taking this approach he could always argue that he knew nothing of any payoffs, but then it was his responsibility to know what he was signing and to ensure adequate internal checking. Moreover, referring to the code of ethics of his accountancy institute he read quite clearly: "No member shall make, prepare, or certify as correct any statement which he knows to be false, incorrect or misleading. . . ." And John reasoned he would be no less unethical because no one could prove he knew what was going on. As a second alternative he considered the possibility of delegating responsibility for signing invoices to one of the accountants reporting to him. He felt they might have less ethical qualms than he, and everything work out much better. Third, he could acknowledge the practice and set up an occasional audit check to make sure the cash was actually reaching the ship's officers. And finally he might make an ethical stand on the issue and insist that the practice either be discontinued or he be formally exonerated in writing. He suspected, however, that neither would be done and he would have to leave or live with the situation. At the very least there would be considerable annoyance and embarrassment at what many would consider a youngster's Sunday school idealism.

The evening after this discussion with Bill Brady, John happened to enter the elevator with George Mitchell, the assistant shipping manager, so he suggested they call in for a drink on the way home. During the conversation John asked George what percentage of an invoice was usually paid ship's officers and how it was distributed, endeavoring to convey at the same time that he knew all about the practice. George explained that it varied with the officers, but rarely as high as 10 percent, and that it might be distributed between as many as 10 engineers on a large vessel. The arrangements as to percentage were part custom, part bantering negotiation over drinks, and part intuition by General Engineers' executives. George claimed that payoffs existed all around the world, although some firms operated their own ship repair yards where they insisted on major overhauls being done. However, the ship's officers frequently had plenty of latitude for repairs and could always have storm damage, corroded pipes, winches, and refrigeration equipment repaired wherever it suited them. George also pointed out that most of the superintendents of the shipping companies knew all about the practice—having been ships' captains or chief engineers themselves at one time.

John could see that any action might affect the livelihood of the 300 men in the ship repair section. This was the biggest ship repair unit in Brisbane, and in all likelihood the work would go to another port, possibly outside Australia, if officers were not remunerated. The men employed could of course be absorbed over time in other work but many were specially trained and had spent their working lifetime in ship repair. Before he made his final decision, John decided to have a look at the figures for ship repair activity to see what profits, volume, and payoffs were involved. The day after his conversation with George Mitchell, John had the tabulation shown in Exhibit 2 prepared for him.

Exhibit 2

Ship repair section, 1964–1969

Year	Average number of men employed	Ships repaired	Total invoiced ($000s)	Markup on total cost (percent)	Payments to ship's crews ($000s)
1964	351	108	2,419	12.1	162
1965	337	101	2,386	11.8	157
1966	341	93	2,435	11.4	143
1967	331	99	2,264	11.3	127
1968	309	94	2,161	11.1	110
1969	305	85	2,216	11.0	102

Amtexco venture in Asiana (Case A)*

Amtexco has just received the preliminary approval of its plans to set up a textile mill in Asiana from the Foreign Investment Board of that country. The company is now proceeding with the detailed planning of the investment. At this stage the Asiana Project Committee, which is responsible for this planning work, is choosing the equipment to be installed in the new mill. Since the choice of equipment will be the main determinant of the size of the investment to be made in Asiana and of the size of the labor force to be hired and trained there, this issue promised to be a very controversial one. The Project Committee therefore decided to give it a lot of attention and to be ready for a full justification of the choices made.

As a member of the staff of the Project Committee, you have been put in charge of writing a short issues paper proposing a methodology to compare alternative types of equipment and making recommendations about the guidelines that should be followed in choosing equipment for the Asiana Project. You have been instructed to make these as simple and precise as possible since, after consideration by the Project Committee, your method of analysis and guidelines will be used for the actual choice of equipment. Furthermore, you are to apply your proposed methodology and make specific recommendations as to the choice of looms for the Asiana project.

Company background

Amtexco is one of the largest textile producers in the United States. Its textile sales were nearly half a billion dollars in 1975. Twenty plants manufacture a wide range of products including sheets, pillow cases, towels, draperies, quilted bedspreads, and various woven, nonwoven, and knitted fabrics for apparel, decorative furnishings, and home sewing.

Amtexco has gained recognition in the American textile industry for its capacity for technical innovation. A pioneer of the one level flow-through design of textile plants, it found low-cost, efficient ways to modernize its old multilevel plants rather than write them off. In the same fashion, old modernized machinery and equipment of the latest technology are often combined in its plants in such a way as to minimize both investment and production costs.

* This case was prepared by Professor Michel Amsalem of the Graduate School of Business, Columbia University. Copyright © 1982 Professor Michel Amsalem.

However, like most of the textile industry in the United States, Amtexco has been suffering for several years from depressed sales resulting from a general recession as well as increased competition from low-cost textile producers in Asia and Latin America. In fact, Amtexco net sales have been stagnant in real terms and its net income has been declining for several years.

The decision to go abroad

As a part of a strategy aimed at restoring the company's market position and profitability, Amtexco's management has decided to start textile manufacturing ventures abroad, particularly in the low-wage countries which are the source of the competition. Amtexco's international exposure has been very limited up to now. Its International Division's main activity is the export of high-quality items, mostly to other developed countries, and its foreign investment is limited to marketing ventures for the distribution of export products in a few European countries.

As a first step in the expansion of its international activities, it was decided that Amtexco should make an investment in a developing country from which it would learn more of the problems and opportunities of this kind of venture. The first choice to be made was whether this facility should produce for export and sale on the American market or whether it should produce for the local market of the country in which it was to be established. Given Amtexco's general level of inexperience with overseas manufacturing ventures, it was decided that a safer strategy would be to produce for the local market first. Production for the American market would only be considered at a later stage, in the framework of either an extension of this facility or of a new one to be set up specifically for this purpose.

To minimize financial exposure and to have a facility of a relatively easy size to manage, it was decided that the project would be of the minimum size compatible with economies of scale in the industry. In the words of one of the managers responsible for planning the project, although the plant should be profitable and self-sufficient, "this investment is not made for profit as the volume is too small to pay for the effort and staff time involved. This investment is made as a learning experience in going abroad. This is why we are ready to spend so much time on each of its details."

Characteristics of Asiana

Following the screening of a number of possible host countries and preliminary contact with their foreign investment authorities, it was decided that Asiana offered the best prospects. An investment proposal describing the main features of Amtexco's proposed venture was presented to and approved by Asiana's Foreign Investment Board. Amtexco is now proceeding with the detailed definition of the proposed production facilities prior to final negotiations with the government of Asiana as to investment incentives.

Asiana is one of the largest countries of Asia, both in terms of area and in terms of population. Although its level of per capita income is extremely low, it offers a very large market for a basic product such as woven polyester/cotton cloth. Its textile sector is mostly composed of artisan spinning and weaving firms, and the modern sector is extremely small for a country of its size, owing to the economic and political difficulties the country went through during the last decade. Although it is estimated that about 100,000 handlooms are in operation in the artisan sector, the textile sector of Asiana cannot satisfy local demand, and large quantities of cloth and yarn are imported. The quality of cloth available on Asiana's market is relatively inferior. However, the low income levels of the population put a definite limit on the price premium that better quality cloth can command.

As can be expected, the availability and cost of the factors of production in Asiana are very different from the United States. Due to large unemployment, unskilled workers can be hired at a cost to the firm, including social charges, of about $1.50 a day, a twentieth of their salary plus social benefits in the United States. However, these workers generally come from the agricultural sector and have never been employed in an industrial firm. They have to receive some basic training even to perform simple production tasks. Semiskilled, skilled, and supervisory workers, on the other hand, are in extremely short supply in Asiana.

This means that all semiskilled workers have to be hired as unskilled and trained on the job by skilled and supervisory workers who themselves have been hired at the semiskilled level and trained at headquarters and during the firm's construction and startup. Through discussions with other firms operating in Asiana, it was estimated that at the beginning, Asiana workers' efficiency can be expected to be 50 percent of the U.S. workers' efficiency and to climb to about two thirds of U.S. workers' efficiency after two years on the job.

Electric power in the quantity needed to operate a textile plant is unavailable outside of Asiana's main cities. Even in the main cities power supply is unreliable. All modern industrial ventures therefore have to generate their own power, and this at a cost per kilowatt hour generated roughly two and a half times the U.S. cost. Building costs, including air conditioning and humidity control equipment, are comparable to U.S. costs although their breakdown is very different. Construction costs are low in Asiana due to the low cost of labor, while air conditioning, humidifying, and even some metallic structures have to be imported and the installation of such equipment requires expatriate labor.

On the raw materials side, cotton and polyester fiber as well as the chemicals required for finishing are not produced in Asiana and will be imported. Amtexco has received assurances that no import duties will be levied on them.

Main characteristics of the project

In light of a study of Asiana's market, the following main features of the project have been decided upon and approved by the Foreign Investment Board:

1. The production facility would be an integrated, balanced facility composed of a spinning department, a weaving department, and finishing facilities.

2. The output of the mill would be a 65 percent polyester/35 percent cotton suiting fabric of medium weight. The production of such fabric requires a higher degree of expertise than the production of shirting material, for example, but the production process is still simple enough not to require the use of any specialized equipment. In selecting this product, Amtexco hoped to emphasize its technical expertise without becoming heavily dependent upon the skills of untrained manpower or sacrificing flexibility in its manufacturing facilities.

3. The production facilities should be able to produce, at full capacity, 12 million linear yards of dyed and finished 58-inch-width suiting fabric.

4. The facility would be operating 8,400 hours per year, which means 350 days a year, 7 days a week, 24 hours a day. Given that the legal number of working hours per week per worker in Asiana is 42, the factory would function on a three-shifts basis with four gangs, the fourth gang filling in on a rotation basis for weekly rest days and holidays.

5. The investment would be made in the form of a joint venture in which Amtexco would hold a majority position and a local partner a minority position. Following contacts with development banks and businessmen in Asiana, a capital structure where Amtexco would hold about 60 percent of the equity, a local partner between 15 and 20 percent, and development banks 20 to 25 percent was thought to be feasible. A potential local partner was found in a leading local businessman who up to now had been involved in the import-export business and the wholesale distribution of textiles. Such an association was thought to bring better relations with the government, which favors joint ventures rather than wholly owned subsidiaries by foreign investors and extends better investment conditions to them. It should also facilitate relations with local authorities, marketing channels, and workers of which the local partner will be in charge. Furthermore, it should help Amtexco in its learning process of how to manage ventures in developing countries.

The choice of equipment

The next major issue to be dealt with was the choice of equipment for the Asiana production facility. In preliminary discussions held by the Project Committee on this issue, a large amount of controversy emerged, most of which had centered around two points.

The first was the extent to which alternative technologies were available. Most members of the committee were of the opinion that equipment embodying alternative technologies or different levels of automation of the same technology were available in most steps of the textile production process. Some, however, argued that a number of these alternatives were outdated and inefficient, not leaving much scope for a real choice. The second controversial issue was the criteria to be used to make choices if and when alternatives were available.

Nevertheless it was agreed that:

1. The magnitude of the differences in availability and cost of the factors of production between the United States and Asiana justified a reexamination of the alternative equipment available and of the criteria used by Amtexco to proceed to a choice.
2. The Project Committee should reach an agreement on this question and issue guidelines to be used by the staff in selecting equipment for the Asiana venture.

The Asiana Project staff was therefore asked to prepare an issues paper dealing with these questions. In a first meeting on this assignment, the Asiana Project staff discussed the format and content of the paper, and reached several conclusions. First, it was agreed that the textile manufacturing process is composed of a number of discrete processing steps and that the choice of technology and equipment in each of these processing steps can be made independently from the choices in the other steps. The study could therefore concentrate on the evaluation of alternatives at the processing step level without having to replace this step in the framework of the whole plant. Second, it was decided that, rather than try to prepare an all-encompassing general document, it would be more effective to concentrate on one step in the production process for which a choice of equipment had to be made. General principles that could be used as guidelines for other cases would then be derived from the analysis of this particular step.

Weaving was selected as the processing step on which to base this document. Looms traditionally represent a large percentage of the total investment in equipment in a textile mill. Weaving is also considered by engineers to offer a wide range of alternative production technologies of varying degrees of sophistication and cost.

In further discussions about the way in which this issue should be tackled it was agreed that the analysis should proceed in three steps.

First, engineers should study equipment available and determine which could be considered as alternatives for the production of the output desired. Second, a financial analysis should be performed on each of the alternatives identified in the first step in order to estimate the processing cost of each alternative. The third step should be a qualitative evaluation of the factors not quantified in the financial analysis but to be taken into account in the choice of technology decision.

The engineering unit was asked to perform the first step. They came up with a list of eleven technologies (see Exhibit 1) that "technically"

Exhibit 1

Classification of the different looms available (by type of technology)

Technology level			Characteristics		
1	Hand				
2	Power	Shuttle	Nonautomatic		
3	Power	Shuttle	Shuttle change		
4	Power	Shuttle	Cop change	Side picking	Mechanical control
5	Power	Shuttle	Cop change	Parallel picking	Mechanical control
6	Power	Shuttle	Cop change	Parallel picking	Electronic control
7	Power	Rigid rapier			
8	Power	Flexible rapier			
9	Power	Projectile			
10	Power	Air jet			
11	Power	Multiphase			

could produce the type of suiting material contemplated for the Asiana venture. However, they voiced such strong reservations about the use of hand looms and multiphase looms that these two alternatives were dropped. They also provided the project staff with a list of the main equipment manufacturers producing looms embodying these different technologies (see Exhibit 2). They insisted that, from their point of view, the choice of a manufacturer was as important as the choice of a technology. Following discussions between the project staff and the engineering unit, the range of shuttleless loom technologies was further reduced in order to simplify the analysis. Only projectile looms were kept to represent this group of technologies.

To evaluate the processing cost using each alternative technology, project staff requested from the engineering unit an estimate of the factor requirements of each technology. The engineering unit chose, in each of the six technologies retained, the models of looms it considered most suited to the task, computed the number of such looms necessary to obtain the volume of production desired, and listed the factor usage of

Exhibit 2

Manufacturers of looms and types produced by them

Company*	Country	Loom types	Technology level
Draper Division, Rockwell	United States	Automatic cop change	4, 5, and 6
		Shuttleless flexible rapier	8
		Shuttleless projectile	9
Machinenfabrick Rüti A. G.	Switzerland	Automatic cop change	5 and 6
		Shuttleless flexible rapier	8
		Shuttleless air jet	10
		Shuttleless multiphase	11
Adolph Saurer, Ltd.	Switzerland	Automatic cop change	5 and 6
		Shuttleless rigid rapier	7
Sulzer Brothers, Ltd.	Switzerland	Shuttleless projectile	9
N. V. Weefautomaten Picanol	Belgium	Automatic cop change	4, 5, and 6
		Shuttleless flexible rapier	8
SACM	France	Shuttleless rigid rapier	7
Howa Machinery, Ltd.	Japan	Automatic cop change	4, 5, and 6
Toyoda Automatic Loom Works, Ltd.	Japan	Automatic cop change	5 and 6
Enshu, Ltd.	Japan	Automatic cop change	4, 5, and 6
		Shuttleless projectile	9
	India†	Nonautomatic	2
		Automatic shuttle change	3
		Automatic cop change‡	4 and 5
	Korea†	Nonautomatic	2
		Automatic shuttle change	3
		Automatic cop change	4

Note: Manual looms—technology level 1—are not included in this list.
* Named companies are major manufacturers of looms, accounting for 80 percent of loom sales worldwide.
† Various manufacturers.
‡ Manufactured under license from Ruti A. G.

these models (see Exhibit 3). The business economist assigned to the project staff then prepared a document showing the cost of the different factors of production in Asiana (see Exhibit 4) as well as a description of a few modern textile mills in Asiana and of the weaving technology they chose (see Exhibit 5).

Exhibit 3

Characteristics of looms by type of technology used[a]

Technology level	Shuttle looms[b]					Shuttleless looms
	Power nonautomatic (02)	Shuttle change (03)	Cop change simple (04)	Cop change (05)	Cop change electronic (06)	Projectile (09)
Number of looms needed[c]	380	303	260	228	190	88
Cost of a loom[d] (U.S. $)	1,200	1,700	4,000	7,000	12,000	33,000
Power consumption (kwh per loom)	0.49	0.74	0.74	1.10	1.10	2.58
Floor space requirement[e] (m² per loom)	9.00	9.50	10.36	10.36	10.36	35.00
Spare parts requirement per loom[f]	0.02	0.025	0.025	0.02	0.02	0.01
Labor requirements:[g]						
Supervisory	6	6	3.5	3.5	3.5	3.5
Skilled	19	14.5	12	12	9.5	7
Semiskilled	344	99	51	48	46	22
Unskilled	21	21	16	15	14	10

Notes:

[a] The loom types in this table correspond to the different technologies described in Exhibit 1.

[b] In shuttle looms the weft (filling) yarn is supplied from small bobbins (cops or pirns) which are placed in the shuttle while in shuttleless looms it is supplied from large bobbins attached to the side of the loom. For this reason, shuttle looms require one processing step more than shuttleless looms before weaving. In the pirn winding step the large spools produced by the winding machines are rewound on pirns before being supplied to shuttle looms while these large spools are directly supplied to shuttleless looms. Therefore the cost of pirn winding has to be added to the shuttle looms alternatives (technologies 1 to 6) to make them comparable. The capital cost of pirn winding would be $60,000, the power consumption would be 31.35 kw per hour of operation, the floor space required for this processing step would be 103 square meters, and the spare parts requirement .02 of the capital cost of the equipment. Pirn

winding labor requirements have been included into the shuttle looms labor requirements.

[c] Number of looms of a given technology required to obtain a plant output of the level sought for the factory in Asiana (12 million linear yards per year on the basis of 8,400 working hours per year).

[d] The estimated cost of a loom is a total cost, "ready to operate." It includes the loom itself, its driving motor, its auxiliary parts (harness, belts, etc.), as well as packing for sea shipment and transport. Equipment will be depreciated over 10 years on a straight-line basis. Looms of good construction, if well maintained, normally operate more than 10 years. Because of hard working conditions expected to result from the low skill level of the workers it should be considered that looms have no salvage value at the end of the 10 years.

[e] The "floor space requirement per loom" figures include not only the area covered by the loom but also the working space needed around it for service. The total area of the weaving shed required can be obtained by multiplying this figure by the number of looms to be installed. Buildings should be depreciated over 20 years and be considered to have a zero residual value at the end of that time.

[f] The "spare parts requirement per loom" is expressed in terms of the proportion of the price of the loom to be spent in spare parts each year. It includes all "consumables," parts that wear out during normal operation and have to be regularly replaced. It does not include spare parts necessary for exceptional breakdown and assumes that the loom is operated and maintained properly.

[g] The "labor requirement" figures are for a weaving shed with the number of looms of that technology recommended for this plant. These estimates have been made on the manufacturers' manning specifications and should therefore be adjusted to reflect the expected productivity of Asiana's workers in comparison with the hypothetical workers' productivity used by equipment manufacturers.

Exhibit 4

Cost of the factors of production in Asiana versus in the United States

	Unit	United States	Asiana
Labor:[a]			
Supervisory	U.S. $ per 8-hour day	63.08	4.50
Skilled	U.S. $ per 8-hour day	43.24	2.79
Semiskilled	U.S. $ per 8-hour day	32.75	2.00
Unskilled	U.S. $ per 8-hour day	27.92	1.55
Power[b]	U.S. $ per kw/h	0.013	0.03
Capital[c]		9%	12%
Construction cost[d]	U.S. $ per sq. meter	210	207
Labor efficiency[e]		0.9	0.6

Notes:

[a] Labor costs include all fringe benefits, whether paid to the worker directly (transportation allowance), given in kind (work clothes), or paid by the firm to a fund (accident insurance) or to the government on the basis of salaries paid; they, therefore, represent the total cost to the firm of employing a worker of a given category. Furthermore, the eight-hour day cost has been adjusted to reflect payments for sick leave, weekly holidays, and annual leave as well as premiums paid for night work to reach a 24-hours-a-day, 7-day-a-week operation. These costs have been estimated on the basis of the salaries paid by similar foreign-owned companies; they are some 15 percent above the ones paid by modern local firms of a comparable size.

[b] In the locations being considered for the plant, power will have to be self-generated. These cost estimates have been based on the cost of diesel fuel in Asiana and include depreciation cost of the generating equipment as well as direct and indirect costs.

[c] This cost of capital is to be used in constant terms computations. It takes into account business and political risks but does not reflect inflation. It reflects the debt equity ratio of the company and the cost of equity capital and borrowed funds.

[d] The estimated cost of construction is an all-inclusive cost in the sense that it includes building cost, electrical wiring, air conditioning, and humidity control installations. It does not include the cost of the land. However, as constructed area only represents a small portion of the land to be acquired for this project, the latter should not be influenced by the choice of technology decisions.

[e] Factor by which manning requirements proposed by equipment suppliers should be divided to obtain a likely figure for manning needs in a country, given the worker's productivity in this country.

As the coordinator of the project staff on this issue, you must now prepare a draft report to the Asiana Project Committee. In your report you want to provide management with a complete analysis of and recommendation on the choice of looms. You want this analysis to provide a methodology to be applied to other steps in the production process and you want to propose guidelines as to what these other choices should be.

Upon inquiring about the choice of looms made for the U.S. production facilities of Amtexco, you have found that the main criterion has been savings in manpower even when, in some cases, it did not seem to minimize production cost at today's wage rates. The oldest looms to be found in Amtexco U.S. plants are Draper automatic cop change looms, dating from the 1950s. At one time electronic features were added to a number of these looms. During the last few years, Draper flexible rapier

Exhibit 5

Choice of loom technology by some other textile producers in Asiana

Characteristics	Companies			
	A	B	C	D
Volume of production (million yards)	10.2	24.0	4.1	9.5
Number looms	400	912	200	520
Technology level*	4	4	5	4
Ownership	Japanese— weak local partner	Japanese— strong local partner	Local cooperative— government	Government
Start of operations†	September 1972	July 1972	February 1972	1973

* Technology level of most recent looms acquired; levels as defined in Exhibit 1.
† Date at which the plant started commercial production.

looms were purchased. Recently, however, several Sulzer projectile looms were purchased and following satisfactory testing of these looms, it has been decided that these will be adopted in further replacements or expansions.

Bancil Corporation (A)*

Struggling to clear his mind, Remy Gentile, marketing manager in France for the toiletry division of Bancil, stumbled to answer the ringing telephone.

"Allo?"

"Remy, Tom Wilson here. Sorry to bother you at this hour. Can you hear me?"

"Sacrebleu! Do you know what time it is?"

"About 5:20 in Sunnyvale. I've been looking over the past quarter's results for our Peau Doux . . ."

"Tom, it's after 2:00 A.M. in Paris; hold the phone for a moment."

Remy was vexed with Tom Wilson, marketing vice president for the toiletry division and acting division marketing director for Europe, since they had discussed the Peau Doux situation via telex no more than a month ago. When he returned to the phone, Remy spoke in a more controlled manner.

"You mentioned the Peau Doux line, Tom."

"Yes, Remy, the last quarter's results were very disappointing. Though we've increased advertising by 30 percent, sales were less than 1 percent higher. What is even more distressing, Remy, is that our competitors' sales have been growing at nearly 20 percent per year. Furthermore, our percent cost of goods sold has not decreased. Has Pierre Chevalier bought the new equipment to streamline the factory's operation?"

"No, Pierre has not yet authorized the purchase of the machines, and there is little that can be done to rationalize operations in the antiquated Peau Doux plant. Also, we have not yet succeeded in securing another distributor for the line."

"What! But that was part of the strategy with our increased advertising. I thought we agreed to . . ."

Tom Wilson hesitated for a moment. His mind was racing as he attempted to recall the specifics of the proposed toiletry division strategy for France. That strategy had guided his earlier recommendation to Gentile and Pierre Chevalier, the Bancil general manager in France, to in-

733

crease advertising and to obtain a new distributor. Tom wanted to be forceful but tactful to ensure Gentile's commitment to the strategy.

"Remy, let's think about what we discussed on my last trip to Paris. Do you recall we agreed to propose to Chevalier a plan to revitalize Peau Doux's growth? If my memory serves me well, it was to increase advertising by 25 percent, groom a new national distributor, reduce manufacturing costs with new equipment, increase prices, and purchase the 'L'aube' product line to spread our marketing overhead."

"Oui, oui. We explored some ideas and I thought they needed more study."

"Remy, as you recall, Peau Doux has a low margin. Cutting costs is imperative. We expected to decrease costs by 5 percent by investing $45,000 in new equipment. Our test for the new strategy next year was to increase advertising this quarter and next quarter while contracting for a new distributor. The advertising was for naught. What happened?"

"I really don't know. I guess Pierre has some second thoughts."

Tom spoke faster as he grew more impatient. Gentile's asking Tom to repeat what he had said made him angrier. Tom realized that he must visit Paris to salvage what he could from the current test program on Peau Doux. He knew that the recent results would not support the proposed toiletry division strategy.

"Remy, I need to see what's going on and then decide how I can best assist you and Chevalier. I should visit Paris soon. How about early next week, say Monday and Tuesday?"

"Oui, that is fine."

"I'll fly in on Sunday morning. Do you think you can join me for dinner that evening at the Vietnamese restaurant we dined at last time?"

"Oui."

"Please make reservations only for two. I'm coming alone. Good night, Remy."

"Oui. Bon soir."

COMPANY BACKGROUND

Bancil Corporation of Sunnyvale, California, was founded in 1908 by pharmacist Dominic Bancil. During its first half century, its products consisted primarily of analgesics (branded pain relievers like aspirin), an antiseptic mouthwash, and a first-aid cream. By 1974, some of the top-management positions were still held by members of the Bancil family, who typically had backgrounds as pharmacists or physicians. This tradition notwithstanding, John Stoopes, the present chief executive officer, was committed to developing a broad-based professional management team.

Bancil sales, amounting to $61 million in 1955, had grown to $380 million in 1970 and to $600 million in 1974. This sales growth had been aided by diversification and acquisition of allied businesses as well as by international expansion. Bancil's product line by 1970 included four major groups:

	Sales ($ millions)	
	1970	1974
Agricultural and animal health products (weedkillers, fertilizers, feed additives)	52	141
Consumer products (Bancil original line plus hand creams, shampoos, and baby accessories)	205	276
Pharmaceutical products (tranquilizers, oral contraceptives, hormonal drugs)	62	107
Professional products (diagnostic reagents, automated chemical analyzers, and surgical gloves and instruments)	60	76

In 1974, Bancil's corporate organization was structured around these four product groups which, in turn, were divided into two or three divisions. Thus, in 1973 the consumer products group had been divided into the Dominic division, which handled Bancil's original product line, and the toiletry division, which was in charge of the newer product acquisitions. The objective of this separation was to direct greater attention to the toiletry products.

INTERNATIONAL OPERATIONS

International expansion had begun in the mid-1950s when Bancil exported through agents and distributors. Subsequently, marketing subsidiaries, called National Units (NUs), were created in Europe, Africa, Latin America, and Japan. All manufacturing took place in the United States. Virtually the entire export activity consisted of Bancil's analgesic Domicil. An innovative packaging concept, large amounts of creative advertising, and considerable sales push made Domicil a common word in most of the free world, reaching even the most remote areas of Africa, Asia, and South America. A vice president of international operations exercised control at this time through letters and occasional overseas trips. By the mid-1960s, overseas marketing of pharmaceutical and professional products began, frequently through a joint venture with a local company. Increasing sales led to the construction of production facilities for many of Bancil's products in England, Kenya, Mexico, Brazil, and Japan.

Bancil's international expansion received a strong commitment from top management. John Stoopes was not only a successful business executive but also a widely read intellectual with an avid interest in South American and African cultures. This interest generated an extraordinary sense of responsibility to the developing nations and a conviction that the mature industrial societies had an obligation to help in their development. He did not want Bancil to be viewed as a firm that drained resources and money from the developing world; rather, he desired to apply Bancil's resources to worldwide health and malnutrition problems. His personal commitment as an ardent humanist was a guideline for Bancil's international operations.

While Bancil had been successful during the 1960s in terms of both domestic diversification and international expansion, its efforts to achieve worldwide diversification had given rise to frustration. Even though the international division's specific purpose was to promote all Bancil products most advantageously throughout the world, the NUs had concentrated mainly on analgesics. As a result, the growth of the remaining products had been generally confined to the United States and thus these products were not realizing their fullest worldwide potential.

According to Bancil executives, these problems had their roots in the fact that the various product lines, though generically related, required different management strategies. For consumer products, advertising consumed 28 percent to 35 percent of sales; since production facilities did not require a large capital investment, considerable spare capacity was available to absorb impulses in demand created by advertising campaigns. For agricultural and animal health products, promotion was less than 1 percent of sales, but the capital-intensive production (a facility of minimum economic scale cost $18 million) required a marketing effort to stimulate demand consistently near full production capacity. Furthermore, the nature of the marketing activity for the professional and pharmaceutical products placed the burden on personal selling rather than on a mass-promotion effort.

In response to this situation, a reorganization in 1969 gave each product division worldwide responsibility for marketing its products. Regional marketing managers, reporting to the division's vice president of marketing, were given direct authority for most marketing decisions (e.g., advertising, pricing, distribution channels) of their division's products in their area. The manufacturing division, with headquarters in Sunnyvale, had worldwide responsibility for production and quality control. (See Exhibit 1 for the 1969 organization chart.)

Corporate management also identified a need in key countries for a single local executive to represent Bancil Corporation's interests in local banking and political circles. There was no single criterion for selecting, from the divisions' representatives in each country, the Bancil delegate, the title given to this position. A corporate officer remarked: "We chose whom we thought was the best business executive in each country. There was no emphasis on functional specialty or on selecting an individual from the division with the greatest volume. In one country, the major candidates were opinionated and strong-willed, and we therefore chose the individual who was the least controversial. The Bancil delegate gener-

Exhibit 1

Bancil Corporation 1969 organization chart

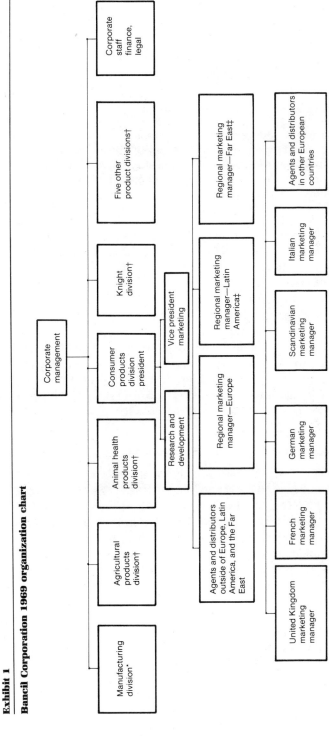

*The manufacturing division manufactured products for all the product divisions. Overseas manufacturing (not shown) reported to the manufacturing division in Sunnyvale.

†Organization similar to that of the consumer products division.

‡Organization similar to that for Europe.

Source: Company records.

ally had a marketing background if marketing was the primary Bancil activity in the country or a production background if Bancil had several manufacturing facilities in the country."

While international sales had grown from $99 million in 1970 to $147 million in 1972, profit performance from 1971 to 1972 had been disappointing. A consultant's report stated:

> There are excessive communications between the NUs and Sunnyvale. The marketing managers and all the agents are calling for product-line information from the divisional headquarters. Five individuals are calling three times per week on an average, and many more are calling only slightly less often.

It appeared that a great deal of management time was spent on telex, long-distance communications, and travel. In response to these concerns, the divisions' staffs increased in each country. Overhead nearly tripled, affecting the growth rate of profits from international operations.

With the exception of financial decisions which were dictated by corporate headquarters, most decisions on inventories, pricing, new product offerings, and facility development were made by corporate headquarters in conjunction with the local people. Local people, however, felt that the key decisions were being postponed. Conflicting demands also were a problem as every division drew on the local resources for manpower, inventories, receivables, and capital investment. These demands had been manageable, however, because even though profits were below target no cash shortages had developed.

Current organization of international operations

To improve the performance of its international operations, Bancil instituted a reorganization in mid-1973. The new organization was a matrix of NU general managers and area vice presidents, who were responsible for total resource allocation in their geographic area, and division presidents, who were responsible for their product lines worldwide. (See Exhibit 2 for a description of the matrix in 1975.)

The general manager was the chief executive in his country in charge of all Bancil products. He also was Bancil's representative on the board and executive committee of local joint ventures. The Bancil delegate usually had been chosen as the general manager. He was responsible for making the best use of financial, material, and personnel resources; pursuing approved strategies; searching for and identifying new business opportunities for Bancil in his NU; and developing Bancil's reputation as a responsible corporate citizen. The general manager was assisted by a financial manager, one or more plant managers, product-line marketing managers, and other functional managers as required.

Exhibit 2 Bancil Corporation shared responsibility matrix

Vice president international operations
Clark B. Tucker

Product group vice presidents / Division presidents	Europe — Andre Dufour			Latin America — Juan Vilas			Far East	Area vice presidents / General managers
	France P. Chevalier	Germany D. Rogge	Four other national units	Argentina and Uruguay S. Portillo	Brazil E. Covelli	Two other national units	Four national units	
Agricultural and animal health (3 divisions) Rodgers division								
Division B								
Division C								
Consumer products (2 divisions) Dominic division								
Toiletry division (Robert Vincent)								
Pharmaceuticals (2 divisions) Division A								
Division B								
Professional (3 divisions) Knight division								
Division B								
Division C								

Source: Company records.

The divisions were responsible for operations in the United States and Canada and for worldwide expertise on their product lines. Divisions discharged the latter responsibility through local product-line marketing managers who reported on a line basis to the NU general manager and on a functional basis to a division area marketing director. The latter, in turn, reported to the divisional marketing vice president. Where divisions were involved in other functional activities, the organizational structure was similar to that for marketing. The flow of product-line expertise from the divisions to the NUs consisted of (1) operational inputs such as hiring/ termination policies and the structure of merit programs, and (2) technical/professional inputs to the NU marketing, production, and other staff functions on the conduct of the division's business within the NU.

Only the Dominic division was represented in every NU. Some divisions lacked representation in several NUs, and in some cases a division did not have a marketing director in an area. For example, the Rodgers division had area marketing directors in Europe, the Far East, and Latin America, all reporting to the divisional vice president of marketing to whom the division's U.S. marketing personnel also reported. However, the Knight division, which had a structure similar to that of the Rodgers division, could justify area marketing directors only in Europe and Latin America.

The new matrix organization established for each country a National Unit Review Committee (NURC) with its membership consisting of the general manager (chairman), a financial manager, and a representative from each division with activities in the NU. Corporate executives viewed the NURC as the major mechanism for exercising shared profit responsibility. NURC met quarterly, or more frequently at the general manager's direction, to (1) review and approve divisional profit commitments generated by the general manager's staff; (2) ensure that these profit commitments, viewed as a whole, were compatible with and representative of the best use of the NU's resources; (3) monitor the NU's progress against the agreed plans; and (4) review and approve salary ranges for key NU personnel. When the division's representatives acted as members of the NURC, they were expected to view themselves as responsible executives of the NU.

Strategic planning and control

NURC was also the framework within which general managers and division representatives established the NU's annual strategic plan and profit commitment. Strategy meetings commenced in May, at which time the general manager presented a forecast of Bancil's business in his NU for the next five years and the strategies he would pursue to exploit environmental opportunities. The general manager and the divisional representatives worked together between May and September to develop a mutually acceptable strategy and profit commitment. If genuine disagreement on principle arose during these deliberations, the issue could be resolved at the next level of responsibility. The profit commitment was reviewed at higher levels, both within the area and within the product divisions, with the final approval coming from the Corporate Executive Committee (CEC), which required compatible figures from the vice president of international operations and the product group executives. CEC, the major policy-making forum at Bancil, consisting of the chief executive officer, the group vice presidents, the vice president of international operations, and the corporate secretary, met monthly to resolve policy issues and to review operating performance.

For each country, results were reported separately for the various divisions represented, which, in turn, were consolidated into a combined NU statement. The NU as well as the divisions were held accountable, though at different levels, according to their responsibilities. The division profit flow (DPF) and NU net income are shown in the following example for the Argentine National Unit in 1974:

	Rodgers division	Dominic division	Toiletry division	National unit
Division sales	$250,000	$800,000	$1,250,000	$2,300,000
Division expenses	160,000	650,000	970,000	1,780,000
Division profit flow (DPF)	$ 90,000	$150,000	$ 280,000	$ 520,000
NU other expenses (general administrative, interest on loans, etc.)				350,000
NU income before taxes				170,000
Less: Taxes				80,000
NU net income				$ 90,000
Working capital	$100,000	$300,000	$ 700,000	

The product divisions were responsible for worldwide division profit flow (DPF), defined as net sales less all direct expenses related to divisional activity, including marketing managers' salaries, sales force, and sales office expenses. The NU was responsible for net income after charging all local divisional expenses and all NU operating expenses such as general administration, taxes, and interest on borrowed funds. Because both the general managers and the divisions shared responsibility for profit in the international operations, the new structure was called a shared responsibility matrix (SRM). The vice president of international operations and the division presidents continually monitored various performance ratios and figures (see Exhibit 3). In 1975 international operations emphasized return on resources, cash generation, and cash remittance, while the division presidents emphasized product-line return on resources, competitive market share, share of advertising, and dates of new product introductions.

Exhibit 3

Bancil Corporation control figures and ratios

Vice president of international operations for national unit		Division president for product line
X	Sales	X
X	Operating income: percent sales	X
X	General manager expense: percent sales	
X	Selling expense: percent sales	X
X	Nonproduction expense: percent operating income	
X	Operating income per staff employee	
X	Percent staff turnover	
X	Accounts receivable (days)	X
X	Inventories (days)	X
X	Fixed assets	X
X	Resources employed	X
X	Return on resources	X
X	Cash generation	
X	Cash remittances	
X	Share of market and share of advertising	X
X	Rate of new product introduction	X

Note: X indicates figure or ratio on organization's (national unit or division) performance of interest to the vice president of international operations and the division presidents.
Source: Company records.

The impact of the 1973 organizational shift to the SRM had been greatest for the general managers. Previously, as Bancil delegates, they had not been measured on the basis of the NU's total performance for which they were now held responsible. Also, they now determined salary adjustments, hiring, dismissals, and appointments after consultations with the divisions. In addition, general managers continued to keep abreast of important political developments in their areas, such as the appointment of a new finance minister, a general work strike, imposition of punitive taxes, and the outbreak of political strife, a not-infrequent occurrence in some countries.

Under the new organizational structure, the area marketing directors felt that their influence was waning. While they were responsible for DPF, they were not sure that they had "enough muscle" to effect appropriate allocation of resources for their products in each of the countries they served. This view was shared by Nicholas Rosati, Knight division marketing manager in Italy, who commented on his job:

> The European marketing director for the Knight division keeps telling me to make more calls on hospitals and laboratories. But it is useless to make calls to solicit more orders. The general manager for Italy came from the consumer products division. He will neither allocate additional manpower to service new accounts for the Knight division nor will he purchase sufficient inventory of our products so I can promise reasonable delivery times for new accounts.

Divisions, nevertheless, were anxious to increase their market penetration outside the United States and Canada, seeing such a strategy as their best avenue of growth. The recent increase in international sales and profits, which had by far exceeded that of domestic operations (see Exhibit 4), seemed to confirm the soundness of this view. Not all NU general

Exhibit 4

Sales and profits for Bancil Corporation, domestic and international ($ millions)

	Domestic		International		Total	
Year	Sales	Profit	Sales	Profit	Sales	Profit
1955	61	5.5	—	—	61	5.5
1960	83	8.3	6	0.2	89	8.5
1965	121	13.5	23	1.3	144	14.8
1969	269	26.7	76	9.2	345	35.9
1970	280	27.1	99	12.3	379	39.4
1971	288	28.7	110	14.2	398	42.9
1972	313	32.5	147	15.8	460	48.3
1973	333	35.3	188	21.4	521	56.7
1974	358	36.7	242	30.9	600	67.6

Source: Company records.

managers shared this approach, as exemplified by a statement from Edmundo Covelli, the general manager of Brazil:

> The divisions are continually seeking to boost their sales and increase their DPF. They are not concerned with the working capital requirements to support the sales. With the inflation rate in Brazil, my interest rate of 40 percent on short-term loans has a significant effect on my profits.

The Peau Doux issue

The telephone conversation described at the beginning of the case involved a disagreement between Tom Wilson, who was both marketing vice president for the toiletry division and acting division marketing director for Europe, and Pierre Chevalier, Bancil's general manager for France. It also involved Remy Gentile, who reported on a line basis to Chevalier and on a functional basis to Wilson.

Pierre Chevalier had been a general manager of France for 18 months after having been hired from a competitor in the consumer products business. Upon assuming the position, he identified several organizational and operational problems in France:

> When I took this job, I had five marketing managers, a financial manager, a production manager, and a medical specialist reporting to me. After the consumer products division split, the new toiletry division wanted its own marketing manager. Nine people reporting to me was too many. I hired

Remy for his administrative talents and had him assume responsibility for the toiletry division in addition to having the other marketing managers report to him. That gave me more time to work with our production people to get the cost of goods down.

In less than two years as general manager, Chevalier had reduced the cost of goods sold by more than 3 percent by investing in new equipment and had improved the net income for the French NU by discontinuing products which had little profit potential.

Remy Gentile had been the marketing manager for the toiletry division in France for the past year. In addition, five other marketing managers (one for each Bancil Corporation division operating in France) reported to him. During the previous six years Gentile had progressed from salesman to sales supervisor to marketing manager within the Knight division in France. Although he had received mixed reviews from the toiletry division, particularly on his lack of mass-marketing experience, Chevalier had hired him because of his track record, his ability to learn fast, and his outstanding judgment.

The disagreement involved the Peau Doux line of hand creams which Bancil Corporation had purchased five years earlier to spread the general manager's overhead, especially in terms of marketing, over a broader product offering. Wilson's frustration resulted from Chevalier's ambivalence toward the division's strategy of increasing the marketing effort and cutting manufacturing costs on the Peau Doux line.

The total market in France for the Peau Doux product line was growing at an annual rate of 15–20 percent, according to both Wilson and Gentile. However, Peau Doux, an old, highly regarded hand cream, had been traditionally distributed through pharmacies, whereas recently introduced hand creams had been successfully sold through supermarkets. The original Peau Doux sales force was not equipped to distribute the product through other outlets. To support a second sales force for supermarket distribution, the toiletry division sought to acquire the L'aube shampoo and face cream line. When Gentile had informed Chevalier of this strategy, the latter had questioned the wisdom of the move. The current volume of the Peau Doux line was $800,000. Though less than 10 percent of Chevalier's total volume, it comprised the entire toiletry division volume in France.

Tom Wilson viewed the Peau Doux problems primarily in terms of an inadequate marketing effort. On three occasions within the past year, he or his media experts from Sunnyvale had gone to Paris to trouble-shoot the Peau Doux problems. On the last trip, Robert Vincent, the toiletry division president, had joined them. On the return flight to Sunnyvale, Wilson remarked to Vincent:

> I have the suspicion that Chevalier, in disregarding our expertise, is challenging our authority. It is apparent from his indifference to our concerns

and his neglect in allocating capital for new machinery that he doesn't care about the Peau Doux line. Maybe he should be told what to do directly.

Vincent responded:

> Those are very strong words, Tom. I suggest we hold tight and do a very thorough job of preparing for the budget session on our strategy in France. If Chevalier does not accept or fundamentally revises our budget, we may take appropriate measures to make corporate management aware of the existing insensitivity to the toiletry division in France. This seems to be a critical issue. If we lose now, we may never get back in the French market in the future.

After Wilson and Vincent had departed for Sunnyvale, Chevalier commented to Dufour, his area vice president:

> I have the feeling that nothing we say will alter the thinking of Wilson and Vincent. They seem to be impervious to our arguments that mass advertising and merchandising in France do not fit the Peau Doux product concept.

Andre Dufour had been a practicing pharmacist for six years prior to joining Bancil Corporation as a sales supervisor in Paris in 1962. He had progressed to sales manager and marketing manager of the consumer products division in France. After the untimely death of the existing Bancil delegate for France in 1970, he had been selected to fill that position. With the advent of SRM he had become the general manager and had been promoted to vice president for Europe a year later. Dufour had a talent for identifying market needs and for thoroughly planning and deliberately executing strategies. He was also admired for his perseverance and dedication to established objectives. Clark B. Tucker, vice president of international operations and Dufour's immediate supervisor, commented:

> When he was a pharmacist he developed an avocational interest in chess and desired to become proficient at the game. Within five years he successfully competed in several international tournaments and achieved the rank of International Grand Master.

In the fall of 1974, Dufour had become the acting vice president of international operations while his superior, Clark Tucker, was attending the 13-week Advanced Management Program at the Harvard Business School. Though Dufour had considerable difficulty with the English language, he favorably impressed the corporate management at Sunnyvale with his ability of getting to the heart of business problems.

The toiletry division had only limited international activities. In addition to the Peau Doux line in France, it marketed Cascada shampoos and Tempestad fragrances in Argentina. The Cascada and Tempestad lines had been acquired in 1971.

Tom Wilson and Manual Ramirez, toiletry division marketing director for Latin America, were ecstatic over the consumer acceptance and division performance of Cascada and Tempestad in Argentina. Revenue and DPF had quintupled since the acquisition. In his dealings with Gentile, Wilson frequently referred to the toiletry division's success in Argentina. Given this sales performance and the division's clearly stated responsibility for worldwide marketing of toiletry products, Wilson felt that his position in proposing the new strategy for France was strong.

On the other hand, Sergio Portillo, general manager of Argentina and Uruguay, and Juan Vilas, vice president for Latin American operations, had become alarmed by the cash drain from marketing the toiletry division products in Argentina. The high interest charges on funds for inventories and receivables seemed to negate the margins touted by the division executives. In describing the Cascada and Tempestad operation to Vilas, Portillo commented:

> I have roughly calculated our inventory turnover for the toiletry division products marketed in Argentina. Though my calculations are crude, the ratio based on gross sales is about four, which is less than one half the inventory turnover of the remainder of our products.

Neither Portillo nor Vilas shared the toiletry division's enthusiasm and they suspected that Cascada and Tempestad were only slightly above breakeven profitability. Chevalier and Dufour were aware of this concern with the toiletry products in Argentina.

As Chevalier contemplated the toiletry division strategy, he became convinced that more substantive arguments rather than just economic ones would support his position. In discussing his concerns with Dufour, Chevalier asked:

> Are the toiletry division product lines really part of what John Stoopes and we want to be Bancil's business? Hand creams, shampoos, and fragrances belong to firms like Colgate-Palmolive, Proctor & Gamble, and Revlon. What is Bancil contributing to the local people's welfare by producing and marketing toiletries? We have several potentially lucrative alternatives for our resources. The Rodgers division's revenues have been increasing at 18 percent. We recently completed construction of a processing plant for Rodgers and we must get sales up to our new capacity. The Knight division is introducing an electronic blood analyzer that represents a technological breakthrough. We must expand and educate our sales force to take advantage of this opportunity.

Chevalier sensed that Gentile was becoming increasingly uneasy on this issue, and the feeling was contagious. They had never faced such a situation before. Under the previous organization, NUs had been required to comply, although sometimes reluctantly, with the decisions from Sunnyvale. However, SRM was not supposed to work this way. Chevalier and Gentile stood firmly behind their position, though they recognized the pressure on Tom Wilson and to a lesser degree on Vincent. They wondered what should be the next step and who should take it. Due to the strained relationship with Wilson, they did not rule out the possibility of Wilson and Vincent's taking the Peau Doux issue to the consumer products group vice president and having it resolved within the corporate executive committee.

Peters Brass Company*

Peters Brass Company, a rapidly growing Pittsburgh casting company, invested $2,350,000 in 1966 to establish a local unit in Argentina. The investment represented a 65 percent share in a new Argentinian company established in partnership with Sr. Pedro Gomez y Silvo of Buenos Aires. At the time of the initial investment, the Argentinian peso was worth 1.2 U.S. cents, but periodic devaluations of the Argentinian currency brought the exchange rate to a point in mid-April 1971 when it fell from 180 pesos to 205 pesos to the U.S. dollar.

Exhibit 1a

PETERS BRASS COMPANY OF ARGENTINA
Cuadro Demostrativo de Ganancias y Perdidas al 31 de marzo de 1971
(Profit and Loss—Year Ending March 31, 1971)

	Pesos	
Entrada (Revenues):		
Ventas menos costo de la mercaderia vendida		
(Sales less cost of goods sold)	220,500,000	
Comision		
(Commissions)	40,000,000	
Renta		
(Rental income)	50,000,000	
Varias entrada		
(Miscellaneous income)	30,000,000	
Total entrada (total revenue)		340,500,000
Gastos (Expenses):		
Remuneraciones al personal		
(Wages and salaries)	130,500,000	
Gastos de operacion		
(Fuel, heat, and light)	40,000,000	
Amortizaciones		
(Depreciation)	15,500,000	
Gastos de comision y regalias		
(Commission expenses and royalties)	35,000,000	
Impuestos		
(Taxes)	50,500,000	
Total gastos (Total expenses)		271,500,000
Utilidad del Ejercicio (Net profit)		69,000,000

---

*Adapted from a case written by Professor Richard N. Farmer, Graduate School of Business, Indiana University.

Exhibit 1b

PETERS BRASS COMPANY OF ARGENTINA
Balance General al 31 marzo de 1971
(Balance Sheet, March 31, 1971)

Pesos

Activos (Assets)

Caja y bancos	
(Cash on hand)	8,100,000
Deudores en cuenta	
(Accounts receivable)	32,700,000
Bienes de cambio	
(Inventories)	90,700,000
Maquinarias y accesorios	
(Machinery and equipment)	142,400,000
Immuebles (menos amortizacion)	
(Buildings, less depreciation)	253,400,000
Terreno	
(Land)	129,800,000
Total	657,100,000

Pasivos (Liabilities)

Deudas (Debts):	
Comerciales	
(Accounts payable)	40,000,000
Bancarias	
(Bank overdraft)	25,000,000
Equipo hipotecarios	
(Equipment notes payable)	55,000,000
Capital, reserves y resultados	
(Shareholders' equity):	
Suscripto	
(Common stock)	300,000,000
Reservas y utilidades	
(Capital surplus)	237,100,000
Total	657,100,000

For four years the parent company had shown the Argentinian operation in its books at the original investment cost, recording the profits (which were all paid out as dividends) as investment income. At the time of the April 1971 devaluation, the new president had been thinking about consolidating the subsidiary accounts for 1971 (see Exhibit 1). He asked Bill Adams, the controller, to calculate for him what the effect of consolidation would be and what the recent devaluation would mean.

American Level Corporation

On graduation from business school, James Bennett joined American Level Corporation in June 1981 as assistant to the corporate treasurer in the New Jersey headquarters.

American Level had two wholly owned manufacturing subsidiaries, one in Australia and a second in Brazil, but apart from a quarterly review of the foreign exchange situation by the corporate finance committee, there had been no regular procedure for avoiding the foreign exchange risks arising from the international operations. The treasurer was aware of the gaps in the American Level procedures and asked Bennett as his first major assignment to outline a methodology for forecasting exchange-rate changes as well as a set of decision rules to be followed for minimizing foreign exchange costs. The treasurer thought it would be wise to prepare the way for the procedure recommendations with a clear statement of the foreign exchange exposure of the two subsidiaries, based on their accounts to May 31. This was to be ready for the finance committee meeting on July 25, along with the usual estimate of the previous month's foreign exchange gains or losses.

The spot rate on May 31 for the Australian dollar was .878 = U.S. $1, and for the Brazilian cruzeiro 84.5 = U.S. $1. During June, however, the high levels of foreign investment into Australia were maintained, pushing the Australian dollar to .871 = U.S. $1. The Federal Reserve authorities continued their tight money policies and the rate of inflation decreased. With the conventionally higher inflation levels in Brazil, the exchange rate for the cruzeiro moved to 91.0 = U.S. $1.

The balance sheets of the two subsidiaries on May 31, 1981, are shown in Exhibit 1. In the case of Amel S.A. about 50 percent of the raw material and packaging material was imported from the United States, mainly from the parent company.

Exhibit 1

AMERICAN LEVEL CORPORATION
Subsidiary Balance Sheets
As of May 31, 1981

	Amel Ltd. (Aust. $000)	Amel S.A. (cruzeiro millions)
Assets		
Current assets:		
Cash	4,419	8.3
Accounts receivable: trade other	25,134	261.6
Inventories:		
Raw materials	9,807	319.4
Packaging material	744	64.4
Work in process	10,323	106.4
Finished goods	3,525	39.4
Total current assets	53,952	799.5
Fixed assets	11,246	62.1
Less: Depreciation	1,479	18.3
Net fixed assets	9,767	43.8
Deferred expenses	—	22.4
Total assets	63,719	865.7
Liabilities		
Current liabilities:		
Notes payable	3,418	177.5
Accounts payable: trade and intercompany	18,259	276.1
Accrued expenses	1,369	9.5
Accrued taxes, miscellaneous	7,803	87.3
Total current liabilities	30,849	550.4
Reserve for patent infringement	186	—
Capital	16,508	130.5
Retained earnings	11,075	163.8
Current profit	5,101	21.0
Total net worth	32,684	315.3
Total liabilities	63,719	865.7

Stability, Inc.

Stability, Inc. was founded in the mythical republic of Bellerivia on January 1, 1977. On December 31, 1980, its condensed balance sheet was as shown in Exhibit 1. All figures are stated in Bellerivian doubloons, a decimal currency represented by the dollar symbol($).

Exhibit 1

STABILITY, INC.
Condensed Balance Sheet
December 31, 1980
($000)

Assets

Current assets:

Cash	$ 400	
Accounts and notes receivable	1,500	
Inventories	2,500	
Total current assets		$4,400
Fixed assets:		
Plant and equipment	$2,000	
Deduct accumulated depreciation	400	
Total fixed assets		1,600
Total assets		$6,000

Liabilities

Current liabilities:		
Accounts and notes payable	$1,300	
Total current liabilities		$1,300
Stockholders' equity:		
Capital stock	$2,000	
Retained earnings	2,700	
Total stockholders' equity		4,700
Total liabilities		$6,000

Stability, Inc. does only wholesale business, with no manufacturing operations. All wages and salaries are charged to expense as earned. Inventory is valued on the first in, first out (FIFO) basis.

Prices were stable during the first four years of the company's life. The general price index on December 31, 1980 was 100—the same as it had been on January 1, 1977. Early in 1981, however, the government of Bellerivia launched large-scale rearmament and social-welfare programs.

These activities were financed mainly by government borrowing from the Bellerivian central bank, which was allowed to treat the government's promissory note as part of its required legal reserves. Taking prices at January 1, 1977, as 100, the general price index changed as follows during the year:

Date	General Price Index
January 1, 1981	100
First quarter average	110
Second quarter average	130
June 30	140
Third quarter average	150
Fourth quarter average	170
December 31	180
1981 average	140

The company's trial balance, on an original cost basis, was as follows on December 31, 1981 (in thousands of doubloons):

	Debits	Credits
Cash	190	
Accounts and notes receivable	1,400	
Inventories	4,250	
Plant and equipment	2,210	
Accumulated depreciation		521
Accounts and notes payable		1,550
Capital stock		2,000
Retained earnings, December 31, 1980		2,700
Sales		15,400
Cost of goods sold	12,250	
Salaries and other current expenses	1,750	
Depreciation expense	121	
Total	22,171	22,171

Purchases during 1981 were as follows (in thousands of doubloons):

Quarter	Historical cost
1	2,750
2	3,250
3	3,750
4	4,250
Total	14,000

Under the FIFO inventory method, the goods in the December 31, 1981, inventory were those purchased at various times during the final quarter of 1981. The ending inventory represented the same physical quantity as the January 1, 1981, figure. During the year, purchases and sales of physical units of goods were the same in each quarter.

The major part of the plant and equipment, costing $2 million, was acquired on January 1, 1977, when the business was founded. Depreciation had been recorded on this part of the asset account at the rate of 5 percent per year. On June 30, 1981, additional equipment costing $210,000 was acquired. It was expected to have a useful life of five years, but depreciation was recorded for only one-half year in 1981.

At a meeting early in 1982, the board of directors was considering the question of how large a cash dividend to pay.

1.   Prepare an income statement, balance sheet, and a source and application of funds statement for 1981 on the basis of historical cost.
2.   Prepare the same statements for 1981 on a price-level adjustment basis.
3.   Compute the gain or loss from holding monetary assets in 1981.
4.   Compute the gain or loss from holding inventories and fixed assets during 1981. What is the meaning of your answer?
5.   How do the procedures used for adjusting account balances for general price-level changes resemble the procedures for translating the accounts of a foreign business subdivision into the domestic currency? In what major ways do the two types of procedures differ?
6.   What policy should Stability, Inc. follow if it wishes to minimize the gain or loss on monetary accounts?
7.   How can the management of Stability, Inc. use the adjusted financial information? What are its shortcomings?

Standard Electronics International*

On December 29, 1978, Charles Duvalier, the Treasurer of Standard Electronics International (SEI), began to review a loan request just received from the firm's German affiliate (Exhibit 1). The loan was for DM 2,500,000 and intended to be used for financing working capital needs.

SEI was a medium-size manufacturer of computer peripheral equipment based in Sunnyvale, California (40 miles south of San Francisco). It had grown rapidly during the past 10 years and sales were forecasted to reach $250 million in 1979. About 40 percent of its revenues were earned outside of the United States, mostly in Europe. Manufacturing affiliates were located in Sunnyvale, Munich, and Singapore. Eleven sales affiliates were located throughout Europe, Japan, and the United States.

SEI maintained excellent relations with its banks and had been able to obtain financing on favorable terms in the countries where it operated as well as on the Eurocurrency markets. The affiliates commonly borrowed or temporarily placed on deposit funds in a number of major currencies including U.S. dollars, U.K. sterling, Swiss francs, deutsche marks, French francs, and yen. It had been SEI practice, until recently, to allow the foreign affiliate management considerable discretion to negotiate the terms and currency of these arrangements providing that the overall amounts had been included in the budget and approved at corporate headquarters.

However, the continuing volatility of the foreign exchange markets had convinced Duvalier that the effective cost (return) of many loans (time deposits) was turning out to be substantially different from that originally thought when the terms were agreed upon and the decision taken. He strongly believed that the cost of borrowing (or return from a time deposit) had to be measured in terms of the effect on after-tax parent consolidated profits; he was concerned that these could be seriously affected by movements in the exchange rates, by the tax treatment of certain costs and earnings at both the level of the affiliate and the parent company, and by the accounting rules used to translate the financial statements of foreign affiliates in preparing the consolidated accounts of the corporation (see Exhibit 2).

For these various reasons, Duvalier had instructed the affiliates to begin to submit to his office for approval all requests to borrow or place funds on deposit. He realized, however, that to make a detailed analysis

---

Exhibit 1

Working capital loan request

To: Charles Duvalier, Corporate Treasurer, SEI, Sunnyvale
From: Fritz Schmidt, Director of Finance, SEI, Munich
Subject: Request for approval of working capital loan

As you have instructed, we have set out below the required information concerning our request for a loan to finance working capital needs over the next three months.

1. *Amount of Loan:* DM 2,500,000 (or foreign currency equivalent)
2. *Period for which loan is required:* 3 months

	Nominal interest rate 12-month basis

3. *Loan Options:*

a.	Deutsche marks	6.200%
b.	Eurodollar	11.75
c.	EuroSterling	14.125
d.	EuroSwiss francs	0.8125
e.	Intracompany (as indicated in your telex of 22/12/78)	12.00

4. *Exchange Rates*

   Please note that foreign currency loans can be covered for the period of the loan by a forward contract to buy the foreign currency forward in the amount of the loan principal and interest.

	DM per $	*SFR per $*	*$ per £*
Spot rate (28/12/78)	1.90500	1.69175	1.97160
Forward rate (contract maturity 28/3/79)	1.87055	1.64625	1.96325

5. *Tax Rates*

   We assume that the present policy of remitting all earnings after tax will continue. On this basis, corporation and municipal taxes will be 43.70 percent. To this, another 15 percent withholding tax on dividends should be added. Total taxes will therefore be 52.145 percent on these assumptions. We also expect that foreign exchange gains will be added to, and losses can be deducted from, taxable income. This applies equally to gains and losses on interest, principal, and forward contracts. All interest expense, including that on intracompany loans, can be deducted from taxable income.

6. *Earnings*

   Earnings *before* interest on the above loan and before taxes are expected to be DM 4,000,000 during the next three months.

7. We would be grateful if you would telex your reply as soon as possible.

of each request would add considerably to the administrative burden of his office as well as perhaps create some resentment in the affiliates by reducing their autonomy.

Therefore, in reviewing the request just submitted by the German affiliate, he hoped also to be able to come up with a simple approach that would allow such decisions to be taken from the point of view of maxi-

---

Exhibit 2

Standard Electronics International selected financial data

SEI GERMANY
Pro Forma Balance Sheet
December 31, 1978

	Deutschemarks (000)	Dollars† (000)
1. *Assets*		
Plant and equipment	8,500	4,461.94
Inventories	5,000	2,624.67
Accounts receivable	4,000	2,099.74
Cash.	3,000	1,574.80
	20,500	10,761.15
Capital and liabilities		
Owners equity	12,000	6,299.21
Loans*	6,000	3,149.61
Accounts payable	2,500	1,312.34
	20,500	10,761.15

2. As one of the loan options, SEI Sunnyvale would lend dollars to SEI Germany at a 12 percent rate of interest. This would be financed by borrowing dollars in the U.S. domestic money market at 11.25 percent.
3. Earnings of SEI as a whole before taxes and exclusive of any foreign income received from SEI Germany or expenses connected with financing the DM 2,500,000 loan were expected to be $6 million during the first three months of 1979.
4. The tax rate applicable to U.S. domestic earnings is 48 percent. A maximum of 48 percent on foreign source income (dividends, interest, royalties, etc.) could be charged, but this may be changed if excess foreign tax credits are available.

* Includes the DM 2,500,000 loan requested.
† DM amounts translated into dollars at DM 1.905 per $.

---

mizing parent consolidated after-tax earnings, and yet be easily delegated to the affiliate management. To be effective, Duvalier believed that any such approach would have to be simple and easily understood, and require a minimum amount of data and computation.

Imperial Power Corporation (B)*

In 1971, Imperial Power Corporation, a U.S.-based multinational firm, completed a new plant in Spain to manufacture fractional horsepower electric motors. These motors were sold to IPC subsidiaries in France and Germany, which assembled them into various end products which were then sold throughout Europe. Penetration of the Spanish market was, however, negligible. The site of the plant, near Madrid, had been chosen as a result of inducements from the Spanish government, availability of a stable, suitably skilled labor force, and the expectation that presence in Spain would aid the marketing effort. To provide the required capital for the new Imperial Power of Spain (IPS) subsidiary, IPC provided U.S. $800,000 as a long-term loan in addition to equity capital. Chase Manhattan Bank in New York provided U.S. $300,000 as an equipment mortgage guaranteed by IPC. In early 1975, the Madrid plant was operating at 70 percent of design capacity. The French and German subsidiaries were operating near full design capacity.

In late 1974, top management at IPC had become concerned about the possibility of a devaluation of the Spanish peseta. Strong political unrest and a strike-weakened economy led management to conclude that a devaluation of up to 20 percent was likely by the end of September 1975. Although the peseta/dollar exchange rate was technically floating, it was known that Spanish monetary authorities intervened often to keep the exchange rate within a narrow band. Therefore the devaluation, if it happened, would occur suddenly rather than gradually. The current exchange rates (local currency per U.S. $) were:

DM	2.434	S. peseta	56.000
FF	4.307	£	0.4275

In addition to the debt incurred at the time of startup, IPS had borrowed P. 7.5 million each from Banco Espanol de Credito and Chase Manhattan Bank (Madrid). The equipment mortgage, however, had been 50 percent repaid. Monthly reports received by IPC indicated that IPS had an average gross margin of 50 percent, and manufacturing costs varied directly with volume. Direct and indirect imported material accounted for 25 percent of the variable manufacturing cost, Spanish domestic material 15 percent, and the remainder (60 percent) was labor and overhead.

In an effort to reduce cash balances in anticipation of the devaluation, IPS had purchased a $250,000 CD from Credit Lyonnais and Spanish

* By David Binder with Ian Giddy; March 1975. © 1975, Ian Giddy, Graduate School of Business, Columbia University.

treasury notes for P. 14 million. Payments due from the French and German subsidiaries totaled FF 250,000 and DM 200,000, respectively. IPS owed £32,000 to Essex Wire (U.K.) Ltd., and DM 125,000 to Ruhr Steel. The remainder of accounts payable was owed to local suppliers.

Exhibit 1 is the balance sheet for IPS as of March 31, 1975. Budgeted sales for the year ending March 31, 1976, were P. 280 million.

Exhibit 1

IMPERIAL POWER OF SPAIN
Balance Sheet as of March 31, 1975

P. (000s)*

Assets:	
Cash..............................	P. 6,300
Receivables and securities............	35,850
Inventories	41,000
Net plant and equipment	55,100
Total assets..........................	P. 138,250
Liabilities:	
Accounts payable	P. 28,067
Accrued wages and taxes	2,300
Long-term debt	68,200
	98,567
Equity	39,683
Total liabilities and equity..............	P. 138,250

* Foreign currency assets and liabilities translated at current exchange rates.

1. As Vice president, Finance, for IPC, prepare an analysis of the effects and risks of the possible devaluation and recommend a plan to prevent or minimize any losses. It is IPC policy to adjust transfer prices so that buyer and seller share equally in the price effect of exchange-rate changes. State clearly any assumptions you make.

2. How would your analysis change if the Spanish plant were a 50 percent joint venture with a Spanish company? With a German company?

3. What effect does the company's transfer-pricing policy have on the gains or losses from exchange-rate changes?

The personnel manager's viewpoint*

Mr. Aziz Ahmed, a personnel executive of a large British company, had settled back after lunch to talk to a university study group about the problems and practices of managing a minority group in a multiracial workforce. Mr. Ahmed was, in the view of many of the listeners, singularly well qualified to talk about these issues. Coming from an aristocratic Pakistani family, he had graduated from Cambridge, worked both in his own country and in the United Kingdom in senior management positions, and was obviously at home in the relatively rarefied atmosphere of a British university.

"I want to start by talking about policies. Some of the race agencies have had a lot to say about policies: about the need for a policy and about what it should say. In fact, the old Race Relations Board even produced a model policy based on the United Nations four freedoms," Mr. Ahmed said as he settled back in his chair. "Very little work has been done, on the other hand, on the strategy of applying such a policy. After all, the key question is: How do you bring about a change in the situation? Where do you begin? How do you arouse concern and not hostility? What level of management do you start with? What is the end result you are aiming at? Perhaps, most important of all, who is to be responsible, and how do you build this into the everyday processes of managing people? In fact, the last question is of the greatest importance. It seems to be commonly believed that an equal opportunity policy requires continuing commitment, not only from senior management, but from the chairman himself."

"Well, I don't agree: involvement, yes—commitment, no. Of course, the chairman's role in initiating such a policy is critical but, having done so, he should *definitely* retreat into the background and give this new plant the space and the time to grow, rather than kill it by overattention. For, if the chairman is seen to have a bee in his bonnet about this, it is not an equal opportunity policy any longer, it is a 'management opportunity.' Management opportunity: let me explain what I mean by this. It means that managers will respond to this pressure by overreacting. They will see an opportunity to impress the chairman by overrecruiting, by overpromoting, in such a way that they demonstrate that they themselves are

* This case study was written by Shiv Mathur as part of the Minority Groups' Case Study Project at the London Business School, which was funded throughout by the Department of Employment. Copyright © 1977 London Business School.

performing well. But, indiscriminate recruitment and promotion can sound the death knell of an equal opportunity policy.

"But, if the chairman is not going to be involved on a day-to-day basis, who should look after the progress of such a policy?" Mr. Ahmed answered the question himself. "In my view it is best looked after by a well-respected and senior executive who has a few years to go and has reached a plateau in his career. It is he who should concern himself with the day-to-day running of this policy—who should decide what objectives are set and how it is to be monitored. The chairman's role should be limited to an occasional reaffirmation of the company's commitment to equal opportunity, and initially to keep it in the forefront of people's minds."

"Speaking of monitoring, the question arises: Who should monitor? Leaving it to any one department leaves it open to the accusation and danger that the facts are being distorted. If it is viable, it is best that one department should monitor another. Marketing should report on Production, Production on Finance, and so on. In one large local authority that I know of, it was left to the Transport Department to assess the progress of such a policy, and it proved to be a satisfactory arrangement.

"About objectives," said Mr. Ahmed, changing the topic. "This is a very sensitive area, you have to take it step by step. Perhaps equal opportunity will start in the Production Department at the lower levels, where most minority groups in the country are congregated, and work its way up through other levels and departments. I find myself disagreeing with the American 'across-the-board' approach: it can lead to confrontation, and this is not so much because of blatant prejudice of other races, as of inbred expectation, which takes time to erode. And, anyway, our position is different—we don't have the American quota system and we can do things differently. The tactics of an equal opportunity policy must be 'a little carrot and a little stick.' And it is not only in the major things like the determination of strategy and tactics that corporations can go wrong. It's the little things that need attention."

"I remember talking to the M.D. of a small company, who called one of his employees 'Tarzan' Singh, because he found his first name unpronounceable. 'He doesn't mind being called Tarzan,' the M.D. assured me. When I called his company by a different name, assuring him at the same time that it shouldn't matter as he knew what I was referring to, he took great exception. And that is the point—we must give people an *opportunity to mind*, and to object."

"Another company had a bonus system which was totally incomprehensible to the workers—black or white. The Asians felt that they were being fiddled, and being perhaps more concerned about money than others, were causing trouble. The management, on the other hand, was not willing to disclose the exact basis of bonus payment—perhaps because it would give away the very wide differentials between management and workers; what would have been equally inflammatory, it would have revealed the gap between middle and senior management. So, a not infrequent management-worker problem of British management was fast taking on racial overtones, and the employment of a minority group was exposing a very poor system."

"But, there are other problems which are explicitly cultural—sometimes white women are reluctant to work on production lines where there are Pakistani or Asian men—not West Indian, mind you. Perhaps it is the lack of social chitchat that causes this hesitation, but we are going to have problems like this while different colors almost invariably mean different cultures. But in twenty years' time this is not likely to be so—you could then be a vastly different color and still have a fairly similar cultural background as far as the work situation is concerned.

"Before I finish and you all start cutting me to pieces," said Mr. Ahmed, "let me return to cultural differences and how they compound the problems which result when 'management opportunity' takes over what was meant to be an equal opportunity policy, and middle managers, anxious to please, overrecruit and overpromote minority groups. The promoted worker is often moved to another department or shift. If he doesn't perform adequately, his new manager blames him because he is black, and the worker, in turn, blames 'white management.' I feel that if a black worker is promoted, he should initially be promoted within his own group or shift, where he is accepted as an individual and not so easily stereotyped and, further, the manager concerned has to live with his decision."

"In the company I was with, we promoted three minority chargehands and recruited two Asian managers, and all the five decisions were dangerously wrong. One of the managers was exceptional. He was, I think, from the Punjab, had been to university here, and was taken on by the company during an initial surge of equal opportunity enthusiasm. One would think that one of the ways to advance the aspirations of an Asian workforce would be to have Asian managers. So he was given a predominantly Asian workforce and soon this was indistinguishable from a Punjabi factory. The workers started calling him 'Sir,' the tea breaks became longer, first for the Asians, and then for the whites, who followed suit. But the Asians worked very hard for him."

"The crunch came when a West Indian woman who was not a very good worker started taking longer tea breaks. The manager wouldn't have it: he reprimanded her. She complained to senior management. This led to him picking on her. The senior management defused the situation by promoting him out of the department. But his reputation had preceded him and trouble followed him. The last I heard of it, an Asian woman of dubious morals, who works for the company in a different department, had asked her solicitor to write to him, asking him to stop bothering her. The company knows of this, but since the so-called incidents had not taken place on company premises or time, feels that it could not meddle. I know the company would like to fire him but he threatens them with all sorts of race relations legislation and machinery, and a company so publicly committed to equal opportunity is a bit worried with threats of that nature.

"And this incident," continued Mr. Ahmed, "brings me to the last point. Even though you have, and believe in, equal opportunity, you still need to select the right people: qualifications are not enough. The person must be culturally suitable. The most dangerous person, culturally, is one who has been here for a few years and spent those in a British university. Universities have nothing to do with ordinary, everyday life. They have an environment of their own. It is important to determine whether the candidate for a job understands democracy and especially industrial democracy, and if employed, whether the company would be able to meet his expectations? Most overseas graduates would probably return to senior management positions in their own country but, here, it's likely to be a different story. So, cultural compatibility becomes crucial, and the question remains: How is it to be determined? What battery of tests must be instituted, if any? What sort of inferences should be drawn from what types of behavior? In all probability, the need for such tests will die out as the cultures intermingle, but until then they are important.

"I've covered a fair amount of territory," Mr. Ahmed concluded. "I've argued that the crucial decision is about the strategy and tactics of an equal opportunity policy, rather than its need. I've mentioned the role of the chief executive; the problems of objectives and those of cultural compatibility and the need for tests to determine this; how I feel the policy should be monitored and who should do it. I've pointed out the difficulties that arise with overcommitment and the management opportunity that this gives rise to, because, in my experience, this is crucial. But, tell me, what do you feel about these issues?"

Dahl Systems Incorporated*

"Salary policy has got to be the main item on the board agenda. What I want the board to agree on is the principle of local salary levels for all those on the payroll of any subsidiary, and a shift of the international headquarters staff in London out of the United Kingdom division and into a separate company for pay purposes." Ronald Cunningham was speaking by telephone in October 1976 to Brent Wojciekowski, Vice President International of Dahl Systems Incorporated. As managing director of Dahl's German subsidiary, Ronald Cunningham sat on the international board which met bimonthly in London at Brent's headquarters for all of Dahl's operations outside the Americas. Cunningham went on, "We have lost two English team heads to our competitors in the last month. With the deutsche mark revaluation of 6 percent this week and more to come, and the fall in sterling with more to come too, we will probably need a 30 percent increase in salary level to keep any nonGermans. An increase in housing subsidies and education allowances may be needed as well."

Himself an Englishman, Ronald Cunningham had nearly 20 expatriate Englishmen and Americans in his managerial team in Frankfurt. This had come about because Dahl had expanded to London from its Chicago base very early in the development of the specialist computer and systems services industry. It was only four years ago, however, that the company had moved into Germany in any strength. To establish the unit Dahl had moved a senior team to Frankfurt, including many who had already been handling some German business from the London office. While the proportion of expatriates in Germany was especially large, the international movement of management and systems specialists would remain at a high rate throughout Dahl. Dahl was in a fast-moving business and the transfer of state-of-the-art knowledge of systems and applications was best achieved through transferring individuals who had built up the appropriate expertise and proved they could sell it.

Dahl's salary policy for those transferred internationally was to set the salary in the currency of the executive's home country at a level that would be appropriate in the home country and to translate this base salary at the current exchange rate. With fluctuating exchange rates, the sum received could change dramatically from month to month. On top of this base salary, though, a local sum was established yearly for each executive to cover increased cost of living. This sum covered actual in-

* This case was prepared by Professor Kenneth Simmonds of the London Graduate School of Business Studies. Copyright 1976 by Kenneth Simmonds.

creases in the cost of housing, including local taxes, heating, telephones, and so on, plus costs of children's schooling and a further percentage of base salary set annually for the country of residence. The percentages allowed for each country were reviewed at the main board each year and tended to reflect both differences in relative price levels and subjective assessments of the costs felt by the various executives who were affected. Currently the percentage allowed for expatriates in Germany was 30 percent and for expatriates in the United Kingdom it was 20 percent.

Differential movement in price levels and exchange rates during 1976, as shown in Exhibit 1, indicated that some trenchant memoranda would

Exhibit 1

	United Kingdom	West Germany	United States
Consumer price index (1970 = 100):			
1973	127	119	114
1974	147	127	127
1975	182	135	138
1976 (second quarter)	208	141	145
Exchange rate:	£1 =	1DM =	
March 1973	$2.48	$0.354	
March 1974	2.39	0.387	
March 1975	2.41	0.426	
March 1976	1.91	0.392	
October 1976	1.57	0.415	
Representative local salary of a Dahl senior systems specialist in 1976	£9,500	DM 130,000	$36,000
Marginal tax rate (on last $1,000 of an income of $40,000 after deductions)	83%*	45%	58%

* Ninety-eight percent on interest and dividends over $1,600.

be arriving at the head office over the next few months arguing for increases in these rates. To date, no foreign executives had been transferred to the U.S. parent company for other than short visiting periods, so there was as yet no U.S. residence percentage.

Dahl's policy was quite new. It had been reshaped under considerable pressure from expatriate U.S. executives in London barely three years previously. The U.S. executives had also pressed for taxation equalization to reduce the impact of U.K. taxes down to the U.S. levels, and Brent Wojciekowski had himself been a prime mover in making these demands. The taxation equalization privilege had not been extended beyond U.S. expatriates, however, as others had not presented a specific case for it. Moreover, Dahl's treasurer in Chicago said that he was not prepared to have corporate staff diverted from their main function into a morass of calculations concerning taxation differences between third countries.

Following his telephone conversation with Cunningham, Brent Wojciekowski had a long luncheon discussion with John Jones, the managing director of the United Kingdom division. "I think Ronnie is really thinking about himself," said John. "He already receives 50 percent more than I do, for instance. And that's before tax. If we followed Ronnie's suggestion we would have an even greater outflow of U.K. staff to cope with. Before we do anything on salaries we should first change the policy of internal advertisement of all job openings internationally. We really promote transfers by selecting the best-qualified applicants and paying relocation costs. It is a ridiculous situation when overqualified Englishmen apply in large numbers for any continental job opening at all. Our bread and butter still comes from the U.K. division and if we are going to continue to perform against our competition here, we just have to hang on to the key people we still have. What's more, we should bring some back on salaries that bear some relationship to British levels. We really need David Symes back here. But I can never forgive him bragging to everyone before he went off to join Ronnie last year that his children would now get a good English public school education."

Author index

A

Abdalla, Ismail-Sabri, 106
Adams, F. Gerard, 56
Adler, F. Michael, 198, 242, 550
Aggarwal, Raj, 44, 523
Aharoni, Yair, 7, 41
Ajami, Riad A., 351
Alexander, W., 567
Aliber, Robert, 2, 44, 78, 544
Alpander, G. G., 560
Alter, Stevan, 592
Alves, John, 116
Alymer, R. J., 430
Amara, R. C., 599
Amsalem, M. A., 249, 472, 473
Anestos, Dennis, 414
Anshen, M. H., 4, 253
Antl, Boris, 563
Apter, David E., 49, 232
Arensberg, C. M., 218, 405, 415, 419
Argyris, Chris, 429
Armstrong, J. Scott, 334
Arpan, J. S., 478, 533
Ayal, Igal, 281, 285, 286
Aylmer, R. J., 430

B

Baerresen, Donald W., 217
Balassa, Bela, 148
Ballou, Ronald H., 288
Bame, Jack J., 121

Baranson, J., 462, 465
Barnes, W. N., 439
Barrett, Edgar M., 534
Bartels, Robert, 430
Bartlett, C. A., 367, 394, 396
Basche, James R., 385
Bass, Bernard M., 408
Bass, Frank M., 409
Bates, Thomas, 523
Becker, Helmut, 441
Bedos, Alexsis, 414
Beekhuisen, Theo, 523
Behrman, Jack N., 145, 178, 234, 241, 244, 267, 277, 462, 467
Bergsten, C. Fred, 227, 231, 237, 549
Bhattacharya, A., 84
Bierman, Harold, 518
Blake, D. H., 574, 599
Blank, Stephen, 178, 341, 353, 365
Blanpain, R., 573, 576
Blitzer, Charles P., 320
Block, Stephen B., 263
Blue, J. L., 563
Boddewyn, Jean, 5, 24, 217, 267, 367, 441, 451
Bomers, G. B. J., 576
Boucher, W. I., 587
Brandt, William K., 279, 430, 433, 448, 504
Brearley, R., 522
Brislin, R., 410
Britt, S. H., 440

Brooke, Michael Z., 296, 298, 393, 503, 533
Buckley, Peter J., 44–45
Bunn, D. W., 365
Buzzell, Robert D., 276, 430

C

Caffyn, John, 444
Cagney, W. F., 567
Calvet, A. L., 41
Cannon, Warren M., 279
Cardoso, F. H., 325, 349
Carlson, Sune, 28
Carson, David, 451
Carter, Eugene E., 521
Cassel, Gustav, 81
Casson, Mark, 44, 45
Cateora, Philip R., 165, 442
Caves, Richard E., 43
Chandavarkar, Anand, 322
Chenery, Hollis B., 309, 311
Choi, F. D. S., 484, 488, 498
Chopra, Jasbir, 24
Chrisholm, R. K., 335
Clark, Peter B., 320
Clee, Gilbert H., 374
Clutterback, David, 404
Colvin, M., 445
Conley, Patrick, 280
Connell, R., 558
Contractor, F. J., 469, 471, 474
Corden, W. M., 40
Cosmas, Stephen C., 442
Cox, Keith, 409

Subject index

This book has been set VIP in 10 and 9 point Zapf Book Light, leaded 2 points. Part numbers and titles are 18 and 24 point Zapf Book Medium. Chapter numbers and titles are 18 and 20 point Zapf Book Light. The size of type page is 30 by 47½ picas.